济南统计年鉴

JINAN STATISTICAL YEARBOOK

2020

（总第38期　NO.38）

济南市统计局
国家统计局济南调查队 编

Jinan Municipal Bureau of Statistics
NBS Survey Office In Jinan

图书在版编目（CIP）数据

济南统计年鉴. 2020 = Jinan Statistical Yearbook 2020 : 汉英对照 / 济南市统计局，国家统计局济南调查队编. -- 北京 : 中国统计出版社，2020.9
ISBN 978-7-5037-9233-5

Ⅰ. ①济… Ⅱ. ①济… ②国… Ⅲ. ①统计资料－济南－2020－年鉴－汉、英 Ⅳ. ①C832.521-54

中国版本图书馆CIP数据核字(2020)第153574号

济南统计年鉴-2020

作　　者／济南市统计局　国家统计局济南调查队
责任编辑／李冲
装帧设计／山东麦德森文化传媒有限公司
出版发行／中国统计出版社有限公司
地　　址／北京市丰台区西三环南路甲6号
邮政编码／100073
电　　话／邮购（010）63376909　书店（010）68783171
网　　址／http://www.zgtjcbs.com
印　　刷／山东麦德森文化传媒有限公司
经　　销／新华书店
开　　本／890mm×1240mm　1/16
字　　数／284千字
印　　张／27.75
版　　别／2020年9月第1版
版　　次／2020年9月第1次印刷
定　　价／396.00元　Price:396.00yuan(RMB)

如有印装差错，由本社发行部调换。

《济南统计年鉴－2020》
编辑委员会及编辑工作人员

编辑委员会

主　　任：苑子建

副 主 任：崔　刚　唐　军

委　　员：（以姓氏笔画为序）

卜繁钢　吕历源　乔　森　刘传云　孙夕良　孙昭信　李士营
李中亮　李　亮　李　勇　李登杰　沈桂欣　张兴利　张秀玲
张谨国　陈　鹏　范坤文　周光萍　谈友军

编辑工作人员

总 编 辑：张谨国

执行编辑：朱立峰　吴培利

编　　辑：（以姓氏笔画为序）

王　亮　王殿嵩　刘　媛　齐志为　牟　刚　纪　强　杜肇鹏
李云龙　李　咏　李咏梅　杨　冰　宋　磊　张衍新　陈　更
邵元振　周　倩　郑海燕　赵　刚　赵学强　姜晓燕　徐明习
唐　丽　梁　浩　董扬震　韩　冰　缪爱斌

资料整理：（以姓氏笔画为序）

于　涛　王胜雷　王　颖　王源华　石　紫　田泽宪　吕　萍
朱立峰　刘　璞　许明智　李　丽　李　艳　李　涛　李海波
李　靖　李　静　杨光玉　肖春晓　吴培利　何宇晖　汪　浩
张　文　张晓璟　张媛媛　范　玲　林　清　周长顺　赵文君
赵丽涵　柳　青　修代红　秦法忠　顾文娇　高少松　高　雷
郭　林　黄　伟　蒋　波　韩庆锐　温秀芬　蓝　东　谭　欣
潘正浩　薛立娣　糜长山

英文翻译：邢林静

英文校对：王　颖　吕　萍　朱立峰　郭　林

Jinan Statistical Yearbook–2020
Editorial Board and Editorial Staff

编辑说明

一、《济南统计年鉴－2020》是一部全面反映济南市国民经济和社会发展情况的资料性统计年刊。本书收录了济南市及所辖县、区2019年经济和社会发展各方面大量的统计数据，以及历史重要年份的主要统计数据，是认识和研究济南市情、经济和社会发展，制定宏观政策、指导工作的重要工具书。

二、本年鉴以丰富、翔实的统计资料为主，辅以直观的统计图、特载，全面反映了济南市国民经济和社会发展状况。全书统计资料共分为二十二个部分，即：1．行政区划；2．人口；3．综合；4．国民经济核算；5．劳动就业；6．固定资产投资；7．城市公用事业和环境保护；8．财政和金融保险；9．物价；10．人民生活；11．农业；12．工业；13．建筑业；14．运输与邮电；15．国内贸易；16．对外贸易与国际旅游；17．科技；18．教育与文化；19．体育与卫生；20．民政、司法和其他；特载和附录。各篇末附有《主要统计指标解释》，对主要统计指标的含义、统计范围、统计方法以及历史变动情况作了简要说明。

三、本年鉴中使用的度量衡均采用国际统一标准计量单位，统计口径除特别注明外，均包括济南市区、平阴县、商河县。资料取自济南市统计局、国家统计局济南调查队及有关部门的统计报表。

四、本年鉴中部分数据合计数或相对数由于计量单位取舍不同而产生的计算误差，均未做机械调整。

五、本年鉴表中的符号使用说明：

“空格”表示该项统计指标数据不足本表最小单位数、数据不详或无该项数据；

“-”表示无此项事实；

“#”表示其中的主要项；

“*”或“①”表示本表下有注解。

《济南统计年鉴》自出版以来，受到了社会各界的关心和支持，对此我们深表感谢。同时，欢迎使用《济南统计年鉴－2020》，敬请广大读者提出宝贵意见。帮助我们进一步提高统计年鉴编辑工作，更好的为社会各界服务，谢谢！（网址：http://jntj.jinan.gov.cn/）

编　者

2020年9月

EDITOR'S NOTES

Ⅰ. *Jinan Statistical Yearbook-2020* is a statistical reference book published yearly that comprehensively reflects the development of Jinan's national economy and society. With a vast amount of statistical data on various aspects of economic and social development in Jinan and the counties and districts under its jurisdiction in 2019, as well as the main statistical data of important historical years, the yearbook is an important reference book for people to understand and study Jinan and its economic and social development, for government to formulate macro policies and guidance work.

Ⅱ. The yearbook is centered on rich and detailed statistical data with intuitive statistical charts and special articles added, comprehensively reflecting Jinan's economic and social development. Statistical data of the yearbook contains 22 parts, namely:1. Division of Administrative Areas;2. Population;3. General Survey;4. National Accounts;5. Labor and Employment;6. Investment in Fixed Assets;7. Urban Public Utilities and Environmental Protection;8. Government Finance and Financial Insurance;9. Prices;10. People's Livelihood;11.Agriculture;12. Industry;13. Construction;14. Transportation, Post and Telecommunications;15. Domestic Trade;16. Foreign trade and International Tourism;17. Science and Technology;18. Education and Culture;19. Sports and Public Health;20. Social Welfare Civil Administration and Justice; Special Published and Appendices. We edit *Exploratory Notes on Main statistical Indicators* at the end of every article, briefly explaining the meaning, statistical scope, methods and historical changes of the main statistical indicators.

Ⅲ. The units of measurement used in this yearbook are internationally unified and standard measurement units. The statistical caliber includes Jinan City, Pingyin County and Shanghe County unless otherwise noted. The data in this yearbook are from the statistical reports of Jinan Municipal Bureau of Statistics, Jinan Investigation Team of National Bureau of Statistics and relevant departments.

Ⅳ. The statistical discrepancies caused by the unit of measurement in the total or relative numbers of some data in this yearbook are not adjusted.

Ⅴ. Notations used in this yearbook:

"Blank Space" indicates that the statistical index data is not large enough to be measured with the smallest unit in this table, or data are unknown or not available;

"–" means that there is no such fact;

"#" indicates the main item;

"*" or "①" means there are annotations in this table.

Since its publication, *Jinan Statistical Yearbook* has received the concern and support of all sectors of society, for which we are deeply grateful. At the same time, welcome to use *Jinan Statistical Yearbook-2020* and offer valuable suggestions, so as to help us further improve the editing of statistical yearbooks and better serve all sectors of society, thank you! (Website: http://jntj.jinan.gov.cn/)

Editor

September 2020

目　录

特载　Special Report

特载 -1　济南概况

Introduction of Jinan ······ 3

特载 -2　2019 年济南市国民经济和社会发展统计公报

Statistical Communique of the Jinan Municipal on the 2019 National Economic and Social Development ······ 5

特载 -3　统计制图

Statistical Chart ······ 19

一　行政区划　Divisions of Administrative Areas

1-1　行政区划

Divisions of Administrative Areas ······ 41

1-2　县区所辖镇、街道办事处（2019 年末）

Town and Street Communities Under the Jurisdiction(End of 2019) ······ 42

二　人　口　Population

2-1　主要年份总户数、总人口（户籍人口）

Total Household and Population in Major Years(registered population) ······ 45

2-2　主要年份市区总户数、总人口（户籍人口）

Total Household and Population of Urban in Major Years(registered population) ······ 47

2-3　主要年份人口自然变动情况

Natural Changes of Population in Major Years ······ 49

2-4　分地区户数、人口数（2019 年）（户籍人口）

Household and Population by Region(2019)(registered population) ······ 51

2-5　计划生育情况（2019）

Basic Statistics of Family Planning (2019) ······ 52

2-6　分地区人口机械变动情况（2019 年）

Un-Natural Changes of Population by Region (2019) ······ 53

2-7　分地区人口自然变动情况（2019 年）

Natural Changes of Population by Region (2019) ······ 53

2-8　结婚情况

Number of Marriages ······ 54

2-9　离婚情况

Number of Divorces ······ 54

主要统计指标解释

Explanatory Notes on Main Statistical Indicators ······ 55

三 综 合 General Survey

3-1 国民经济和社会发展总量指标
Principal Aggregate Indicators on National Economic and Social Development …… 58

3-2 国民经济和社会发展比例和效益指标
Indicators on Proportions and Efficiency in National Economic and Social Development …… 66

3-3 平均每天主要社会经济活动
Selected Indicators on Average Daily Social and Economic Activities …… 70

3-4 国民经济人均指标
Per Indicators of National Economic …… 74

3-5 国民经济主要指标及占全国、全省比重（2019）
Main Indicators of National Economy and Their Proportion in China and Shandong Province(2019) …… 76

主要统计指标解释
Explanatory Notes on Main Statistical Indicators …… 78

四 国民经济核算 National Accounts

4-1 各时期生产总值（按当年价格计算）
Gross Domestic Product in Each Period(Calculated at Current Prices) …… 84

4-2 各时期生产总值环比指数（以上年为 100）
Circle Indices of Gross Domestic Product (Preceding Last Year=100) …… 86

4-3 资本形成总额（按当年价格计算）
Gross Capital Formation(Calculated at Current Prices) …… 88

4-4 最终消费支出（按当年价格计算）
Final Consumption Expenditure(Calculated at Current Prices) …… 89

4-5 实际最终消费（按当年价格计算）
Final Real Consumption(Calculated at Current Prices) …… 90

4-6 生产总值分布
Distribution of Gross Domestic Product …… 91

4-7 生产总值（2009 年—2013 年）（分行业、按当年价格计算）
Value of Gross Domestic Product(2009—2013)(Sub Industry, Calculated at Current Prices) …… 92

4-8 生产总值（2013 年—2017 年）（分行业、按当年价格计算）
Value of Gross Domestic Product(2013—2017)(Sub Industry, Calculated at Current Prices) …… 95

4-9 生产总值贡献率（2009 年—2013 年）（分行业、按不变价格计算）
Distribution Rate of Gross Domestic Product(Calculated at Fixed Prices)(2009—2013)(Sub Industry, Calculated at Constant Prices) …… 98

4-10 生产总值贡献率（2013 年—2017 年）（分行业、按不变价格计算）
Contribution Rate of Gross Domestic Product(2013—2017)(Sub Industry, Calculated at Constant Prices) …… 101

4-11 生产总值行业比重（2009 年—2013 年）（按当年价格计算）
Ratio of Gross Domestic Product by Sector(2009—2013)(Calculated at Current Prices) …… 104

4-12 生产总值行业比重（2013 年—2017 年）(按当年价格计算)
Ratio of Gross Domestic Product by Sector(2013—2017)(Calculated at Current Prices) …… 107
4-13 分地区生产总值（2019 年）
Value of Gross Domestic Product by Region(2019) …… 110
4-14 生产总值（2019 年）(分行业、按当年价格计算)
Value of Gross Domestic Product(2019)(Sub Industry，Calculated at Current Prices) …… 111
4-15 规模以上服务业企业分行业主要经济指标（2019 年）
Main Economic Indicators of Service Enterpriese Above Designated Size by Sector(2019) …… 112
主要统计指标解释
Explanatory Notes on Main Statistical Indicators …… 114

五 劳动就业 Labor and Employment

5-1 按三次产业分从业人员及构成
Number of Employed Persons and Structure by Type of Industry …… 123
5-2 主要年份职工工资
Wage of Staff and Workers in Major Years …… 124
5-3 城镇非私营单位从业人员人数（2019 年）
Number of Employed Persons in Urban Non Private Entities(2019) …… 125
5-4 城镇非私营单位从业人员工资总额（2019 年）
Total Wage of Employed Persons in Urban Non Private Entities(2019) …… 129
5-5 城镇非私营单位从业人员平均工资（2019 年）
Average Wage of Employed Persons in Urban Non Private Entities(2019) …… 133
5-6 国有单位从业人员和工资（2019 年）
Number and Wage of Employed Persons in State-owned Units(2019) …… 137
5-7 城镇集体单位从业人员和工资（2019 年）
Number and Wage of Employed Persons in Urban Collective-owned Units (2019) …… 138
5-8 城镇其他单位从业人员和工资（2019 年）
Number and Wage of Employed Persons in Other Urban Collective-owned Units(2019) …… 139
5-9 社会保障基本情况
Basic Conditions of Social Sewrity …… 140
主要统计指标解释
Explanatory Notes on Main Statistical Indicators …… 140

六 固定资产投资 Investment in Fixed Assets

6-1 固定资产投资
Total Investment in Fixed Assets …… 143
6-2 固定资产投资分类（2019 年）
Classification of Fixed Assets Investment(2019) …… 144
6-3 房地产开发投资分类（2019 年）

Classification of Estate Development Investment(2019) ······ 146
6-4 固定资产投资资金来源（2019 年）
Investment by Source of Funds (2019) ······ 147
6-5 新增主要生产能力和效益（2019 年）
Newly Increased Production Capacity and Administrative(2019) ······ 147
6-6 历年房地产开发建设情况
Basic Situations of Real Estate Development in Major Years ······ 148
6-7 历年房地产开发公司经营情况
Real Estate Development and Managment in Major Years ······ 149
6-8 房地产开发公司经营情况（2019 年）
Real Estate Development and Management(2019) ······ 150
主要统计指标解释
Explanatory Notes on Main Statistical Indicators ······ 151

七 城市公用事业和环境保护 Urban Public Utilities and Environmental Protection

7-1 城市道路与公共交通
Basic Statistics on Muncipal Engineering and Public Transportation ······ 159
7-2 水、电、气、热供应情况
Basic Statistics on Water、Electricity、Gas and Heating in Cities ······ 160
7-3 环境状况及污染治理情况
Basic Statistics on Environment and Treatment of Pollution ······ 161
7-4 城市园林绿化、环境卫生及其他
Basic Statistics on Parks、Gardens、Green Areas and Urban Sanitation in Cities ······ 162
主要统计指标解释
Explanatory Notes on Main Statistical Indicators ······ 163

八 财政和金融保险 Government Finance and Financial Insurance

8-1 各时期地方财政收支及指数
Expenditures and Indices of Major Years ······ 166
8-2 地方财政收入（2019 年）
Local Financial Revenue(2019) ······ 167
8-3 各区财政收入（2019 年）
Financial Revenue by District(2019) ······ 168
8-4 各县财政收入（2019 年）
Financial Revenue by County(2019) ······ 170
8-5 地方财政支出（2019 年）
Local Financial Expenditures(2019) ······ 171
8-6 各区地方财政支出（2019 年）

Local Financial Expenditures by District(2019) …… 172

8-7 各县地方财政支出（2019 年）

Local Financial Expenditures by County(2019) …… 174

8-8 金融机构本外币各项存、贷款期末余额

The Ending Balance of all Deposits and Loans in RMB and Foreign Currencies of Financial Institutions …… 175

8-9 金融机构人民币各项存、贷款期末余额

The Ending Balance of all Deposits and Loans in RMB of Financial Institutions …… 176

8-10 保险业务情况

Insurance Business …… 177

8-11 证券机构及证券交易情况

Institution and Trading Summary for Stocks …… 178

主要统计指标解释

Explanatory Notes on Main Statistical Indicators …… 178

九 物 价 Price

9-1 主要年份物价指数（以上年价格为 100）

Price Indices of Major Years(Preceding Last Year=100) …… 183

9-2 主要年份物价指数（以 1950 年价格为 100）

Price Indices of Major Years(Preceding 1950=100) …… 184

9-3 分月居民消费价格指数（2019 年，以上年同期价格为 100）

Consumer Price Indices by Month(2019，Preceding Last Year=100) …… 186

9-4 分月商品零售价格指数（2019 年，以上年同期价格为 100）

Retail Price Indices by Month(2019，Preceding Last Year=100) …… 192

9-5 主要年份零售商品和服务项目年平均价格

Per Retail and Services Price of Major Years …… 194

9-6 工业生产者出厂价格总指数（2019 年，以上月价格为 100）

Producer Price Index for Manufactured Goods (2019,Preceding Last Month=100) …… 196

9-7 工业生产者出厂价格总指数（2019 年，以上年同期价格为 100）

Producer Price Index for Manufactured Goods(2019,Preceding Last Year=100) …… 198

9-8 工业生产者购进价格指数（2019 年，以上月价格为 100）

Purchasing Price Index for Industrial Producers(2019，Preceding Last Month=100) …… 200

9-9 工业生产者购进价格指数（2019 年，以上年同期价格为 100）

Purchasing Pri ce Index for Industrial Producers(2019,Preceding Last Year=100) …… 202

9-10 住宅销售价格指数（2019 年，以上月价格为 100）

Sales Price of Residential Buildings(2019,Preceding Last Month=100) …… 204

9-11 住宅销售价格指数（2019 年，以上年同期价格为 100）

Sales Price of Residential Buildings (2019,Preceding Last Year=100) …… 205

9-12 主要年份工业生产者出厂、购进价格指数（以上年价格为 100）

Purchasing Price Index for Industrial Producers and Producer Price Index for Manufactured Goods in Main Years (Preceding Last Year=100) …… 206

主要统计指标解释
Explanatory Notes on Main Statistical Indicators …… 207

十　人民生活　People's Livelihood

10-1　人民物质文化生活提高情况
Improvement in People's Material and Cultural Life …… 210
10-2　各时期城镇居民生活情况
Basic Conditions of Urban Households in Each Period …… 212
10-3　主要年份农村居民生活情况
Basic Conditions of Rural Households in Major Years …… 214
10-4　每百户城镇居民家庭主要耐用消费品拥有量
Number of Durable Consumer Goods Owned Per 100 Urban Households in Major Years …… 215
10-5　农村每百户居民家庭主要耐用消费品拥有量
Number of Major Durable Consumer Goods Owend Per 100 Rural Households …… 216
10-6　居民人均可支配收入和消费性支出（2019 年）
Per Capital Annual Income and Per Capital Annual Expenditure(2019) …… 216
主要统计指标解释
Explanatory Notes on Main Statistical Indicators …… 217

十一　农　业　Agriculture

11-1　各时期农业主要经济指标
Major Economic Indicators of Agriculture in Each Period …… 221
11-2　农村基层组织和农业基本情况
Basic Conditions of Rural Grassroots Units and Agriculture …… 223
11-3　分地区农村基层组织和农业基本情况（2019 年）
Basic Conditions of Rural Grassroots Units and Agriculture by Region(2019) …… 224
11-4　各时期农林牧渔业增加值（按当年价格计算）
Added Value of Agriculture, Forestry, Animal Husbandry and Fishery in Each Period(Calculated at Current Prices) …… 226
11-5　各时期农林牧渔业总产值（按当年价格计算）
Gross Output Value of Agriculture, Forestry, Animal Husbandry and Fishery in Each Period
(Calculated at Current Prices) …… 228
11-6　各时期农林牧渔业总产值定基指数（以 1952 年为 100）
Gross Output Value and Indices of Farming，Forestry，Animal Husbandry in Each Period(1952=100) …… 230
11-7　主要农作物播种面积及产量
Sown Areas and Output of Main Farm Crops …… 232
11-8　林、牧、渔业生产情况
Basic Statistics on Forestry，Animal Husbandry and Fishery …… 234
11-9　分地区主要农作物播种面积及产量（2019 年）
Sown Areas and Output of Main Farm Crops by Region(2019) …… 236

11-10 分地区林、牧、渔业生产情况（2019 年）
Basic Statistics on Forestry，Animal Husbandry and Fishery by Region(2019) …… 240
11-11 农业“四化”情况（2019 年）
Basic Statistics on Four Modernization of Agriculture(2019) …… 242
11-12 主要农副产品产量与上年和历史最高年份比较
Output of Major Agricultral Products in Comparision with Last Year and Maximum Year …… 242
主要统计指标解释
Explanatory Notes on Main Statistical Indicators …… 243

十二　工　业　Industry

12-1 各时期全部工业基本情况
Basic Statistics on Total Industry in Each Period …… 249
12-2 各时期规模以上工业基本情况
Basic Statistics of Industrial Enterprises Above Designated Size in Each Period …… 251
12-3 各时期主要工业产品产量
Output of Major Industrial Products in Each Period …… 253
12-4 规模以上工业主要经济指标（2019 年）
Main Economic Indicators of Industrial Enterprises Above Designated Size(2019) …… 255
12-5 规模以上国有及国有控股工业主要经济指标（2019 年）
Main Economic Indicators of State-Owned and State-Controlled Industrial Enterprises Above Designated Size(2019) …… 258
12-6 规模以上私营工业企业主要经济指标（2019 年）
Main Economic Indicators of Private Industrial Enterprises Above Designated Size(2019) …… 261
12-7 规模以上工业资产实力（2019 年）
Capital Power of Industrial Enterprises Above Designated Size(2019) …… 264
12-8 规模以上国有及国有控股工业资产实力（2019 年）
Capital Power of State-Owned and State-Controlled Industrial Enterprises Above Designated Size(2019) …… 268
12-9 规模以上工业损益及分配（2019 年）
Profit，Loss and Distribution of Industrial Enterprises Above Designated Size(2019) …… 272
12-10 规模以上国有及国有控股工业损益及分配（2019 年）
Profit，Loss and Distribution of State-Owned and State-Controlled Industrial Enterprises Above Designated Size(2019) …… 276
12-11 分地区规模以上工业主要经济指标（2019 年）
Main Economic Indicators of Industrial Enterprises Above Designated Size by Region(2019) …… 280
12-12 规模以上大中型工业企业经营情况（2019 年）
Main Indicators of Large and Medium-Sized Enterprises(2019) …… 282
12-13 规模以上大中型工业企业一览表（2019 年）
Summary of Large and Medium-Sized Enterprises(2019) …… 286
12-14 主要工业产品生产量（2019 年）
Output of Major Industrial Products(2019) …… 291
12-15 工业企业能源购进、消费及库存（2019 年）
Purchases，Consumption and Invetory of Main Energy Source in Industrial Enterprises(2019) …… 297

12-16 工业分行业主要能源消费量（2019 年）
Consumption of Main Energy Source in Industrial Enterprises by Sector(2019) …… 298
主要统计指标解释
Explanatory Notes on Main Statistical Indicators …… 300

十三 建筑业 Construction

13-1 建筑业主要指标
Main Indicators of Construction Enterprises …… 306
13-2 建筑业增加值构成（2019 年）
Value Added of Construction by Structure(2019) …… 307
13-3 建筑企业资产实力（2019 年）
Assets of Construction Enterprises (2019) …… 308
13-4 建筑业施工产值构成（2019 年）
Output Value of Construction by Structure(2019) …… 310
13-5 建筑企业损益及分配（2019 年）
Output Value of Construction by Structure(2019) …… 311
13-6 施工工程施工面积（2019 年）
Number of Floor Space Under Construction(2019) …… 312
13-7 济南市建筑业特级、一级资质企业一览表（2019 年）
Summary of Construction Enterprises with Grade Ⅰ Qualification(2019) …… 313
主要统计指标解释
Explanatory Notes on Main Statistical Indicators …… 317

十四 运输与邮电 Transportation Post and Telecommunication

14-1 邮电业务量
Postal and Telecommunications Services …… 321
14-2 交通运输业基本情况
Basic Conditions of Transportation …… 322
14-3 规模以上交通运输、仓储和邮政业企业财务指标（2019 年）
Main Financial Indicators of Transport,Storage and Postal Services above Designated Size(2019) …… 323
14-4 分地区公路交通（2019 年）
Road Transportation by Region(2019) …… 324
主要统计指标解释
Explanatory Notes on Main Statistical Indicators …… 324

十五 国内贸易 Domestic Trade

15-1 各时期分行业社会消费品零售
Total Retail Sales of Consumer Goods by Section in Each Period …… 328

15-2 限额以上批发零售业法人企业商品销售情况（2019 年）
Total Purchase Sales and Inventory by Sector Above Designated Size(2019) …… 330
15-3 限额以上批发零售贸易企业资产实力（2019 年）
Capital Power of Wholesales and Retail Sales Trade Above Designated Size(2019) …… 332
15-4 限额以上批发零售贸易企业损益及分配（2019 年）
Profit Loss and Distribution of Wholesales and Retail Sales Trade Above Designated Size (2019) …… 336
15-5 限额以上餐饮业主要经济指标（2019 年）
Main Economic Indicators of Enterprises in Cataring Trades Above Designated Size (2019) …… 340
15-6 限额以上住宿业主要经济指标（2019 年）
Main Economic Indicators of Enterprises in Quartering Trades Above Designated Size(2019) …… 342
15-7 限额以上住宿业和餐饮业法人企业经营情况（2019 年）
Main Economic Indicators of Enterprises in Quartering Trades and Cataring Trades Above Designated Size(2019) …… 344
15-8 商品交易市场分类情况（2019 年）
Free Markets in Urban and Rural Areas(2019) …… 346
15-9 销售过亿元的商品交易市场一览表（2019 年）
Summary of Consumer Goods Markets with Annual Transaction Value Above 100 Million Rmb Yuan(2019) …… 347
主要统计指标解释
Explanatory Notes on Main Statistical Indicators …… 348

十六 对外贸易与国际旅游 Foreign Trade and International Tourism

16-1 海关进出口商品总额
Total Value of Imports and Exports by Category of Commodities …… 352
16 2 主要国别（地区）海关进出口商品总额
Total Value of Imports and Exports of Main Countries or Territories by Categoty of Commodities …… 353
16-3 海关进出口商品分类金额
Value of Imports and Exports by Category of Commodities …… 355
16-4 按企业性质分海关进出口商品总额（2019 年）
Import and Export Value of Commodities by Ownership(2019) …… 359
16-5 历年海关进出口总额
Total Imports and Exports by Category(Customs Statistics) …… 360
16-6 利用外资情况
Utilization of Foreign Capital …… 361
16-7 对外经济技术合作
Technological Cooperation with Foreign Countries or Territories …… 361
16-8 出口 1000 万美元以上企业一览（2019 年）
Summary of Enterprises with Annual Exports Value Above 10 Million Dollar(2019) …… 362
16-9 旅游住宿单位接待入境游客
Received Inbound Tourists by Hotels …… 364
16-10 济南与国外结成友好城市一览表（2019 年末）
Foreign Friendly Cities of Jinan(End of 2019) …… 365

16-11 济南市与各友好城市交流

Basic Statistics of Transmission Between Foreign Friendly Cities and Jinan ··· 365

主要统计指标解释

Explanatory Notes on Main Statistical Indicators ··· 366

十七 科 技 Science and Technology

17-1 科技综合情况

Basic Statistics on Science and Technology ··· 370

17-2 科技投入情况（2018 年）

Basic Statistics on Scientific and Technological Funds(2018) ··· 371

17-3 规模以上工业企业科技活动情况（2018 年）

Main Indicators of Industrial Enterprises Above Designated Size(2018) ··· 372

17-4 规模以上工业企业技术改造及引进吸收（2018 年）

Innovation and Resorb of Industrial Enterprises Above Designated Size（2018）··· 374

17-5 规模以上工业企业技术资源（2018 年）

Technical Resources of Industrial Enterprises Above Desitnated Size（2018）··· 376

17-6 规模以上工业企业科技活动项目（2018 年）

Technology Projict Activities of Industrial Enterprises Above Designated Size(2018) ··· 378

17-7 规模以上工业企业 R&D 经费情况（2018 年）

R&D Funds of Industrial Enterprises Above Designated Size(2018) ··· 380

17-8 规模以上工业企业办科技机构情况（2018 年）

Science and Technology Institutions of Industrial Enterprises Above Designated Size (2018) ··· 384

17-9 规模以上工业企业自主知识产权及相关情况（2018 年）

Independent Intellectual Property Rights of Industrial Enterprises Above Designated Size(2018) ··· 386

17-10 行政区划调整前原莱芜市规模以上工业企业主要指标情况（2018 年）

Science and Technology Activities Main Indicators of Industrial Enterprises Above Designated Size of Laiwu Before the Administrative Division Adjustment(2018) ··· 390

主要统计指标解释

Explanatory Notes on Main Statistical Indicators ··· 391

十八 教育与文化 Education and Culture

18-1 教育事业基本情况

Basic Statistics on Education ··· 394

18-2 普通高等院校一览（2019 年）

Basic Statistics on Institutions of Higher Education(2019) ··· 396

18-3 中等专业学校一览（2019 年）

Basic Statistics on Specialized Secondary Schools(2019) ··· 397

18-4 分县区儿童学前教育基本情况（2019 年）

Student Enrollment in Pre-school Education(2019) …… 397
18-5 文化事业机构和人员
Number of Institutions and Persons in Culture …… 398
主要统计指标解释
Explanatory Notes on Main Statistical Indicators …… 398

十九 体育与卫生 Sports and Public Health

19-1 体育事业
Statistics of Sports Instituons …… 401
19-2 各时期卫生事业情况
Statistics of Health Institutions in Major Years …… 402
19-3 卫生事业机构及床位
Number of Health Institutions and Beds …… 404
19-4 分地区卫生事业机构及床位（2019 年）
Number of Health Institutions and Beds by District(2019) …… 405
19-5 医疗机构年收入与支出 （2019 年）
Revenue and Expenditure in Health Insititutions(2019) …… 406
19-6 医院、卫生院工作情况
Basic Statistics on Hospitals and Health Institutions in Rural Areas …… 407
19-7 分地区卫生技术人员分类情况（2019 年）
Medical Technical Personnel by Region(2019) …… 408
主要统计指标解释
Explanatory Notes on Main Statistical Indicators …… 408

二十 民政、司法和其他 Social Welfare Civil Administration and Others

20-1 社会治安主要指标
Main Indicators of Social Offense …… 411
20-2 分地区社会治安主要指标（2019 年）
Main Indicators of Social Offense by District(2019) …… 412
20-3 社会保障和救济
Basic Statistics on Social Security and Receiving Relief Flinds …… 413
20-4 分地区社会保障和救济（2019 年）
Basic Statistics on Social Security and Receiving Relief Flinds by Region(2019) …… 414
20-5 律师、公证、司法基本情况（2019 年）
Basic Statistics on Law， Notarizations and Mendiation(2019) …… 416
主要统计指标解释
Explanatory Notes on Main Statistical Indicators …… 417

附 录 Appendix

附录一　山东省十六城市主要经济指标（2019 年）

Main Statistical Indicators of 16 Cities in Shandong(2019) ······ 420

附录二　十五副省市主要经济指标（2019 年）

Main Statistical Indicators of 15 Vice-provincial Cities(2019) ······ 422

附录三　二十六省会城市主要经济指标（2019 年）

Main Statistical Indicators of 26 Provincial Capitals (2019) ······ 424

附录四　中华人民共和国统计法

Statistical Law of The People's Republic of China ······ 426

附录五　中华人民共和国统计法实施条例

Regulations for the Implementation of the Statistics Law of the People's Republic of China ······ 430

附录六　统计违法违规行为处分规定

Statistics Regulation Violations of Law ······ 434

附录七　济南市统计局二〇一九年统计工作大事记

Chronicle of Events of Jinan Statistical Undertaking ······ 436

特载

SPECIAL REPORT

特载 -1

济 南 概 况

济南市位于山东省中部，地理位置介于北纬 36° 01′ 至 37° 32′、东经 116° 11′ 至 117° 44′ 之间，面积 10244 平方公里。南依泰山，北跨黄河，地处鲁中南低山丘陵与鲁西北冲积平原的交接带上，地势南高北低，依次为低山丘陵、山前倾斜平原和黄河冲积平原。境内河流较多，河流分属黄河、小清河、海河三大水系。湖泊有大明湖、白云湖等。济南属于暖温带大陆性季风气候区，四季分明，日照充分，年平均气温 13.6℃，年平均降水量 614.0 毫米。

济南矿产资源丰富，主要有铁、煤、花岗石、耐火粘土以及 铜、钾、铂、钴等多种有色金属、稀有金属和非金属。特别是石灰岩品位高、储量大。花岗石中的黑色花岗石，质地纯正，为国内独有。有植物 149 科，1175 种和变种。陆栖野生动物 211 种。南部山区盛产苹果、黄梨、柿子、核桃、山楂、板栗等，并产有远志、丹参、野菊、香附等多种药材。北部沿黄河的平原地带，大枣也有很高的产量。济南种植和养殖资源也相当丰富，有多种粮食作物、经济作物以及家禽、家畜、水产品等。这些资源为济南城乡建设和经济发展储备了一定的物质基础。

济南自然景色秀丽，名胜古迹众多，是中国历史文化名城之一。尤以泉水遍布、清冽甘美而闻名于世，有“济南泉水甲天下”和“泉城”之美誉。主要风景名胜有趵突泉、黑虎泉、珍珠泉、五龙潭、百脉泉五大泉群，大明湖、千佛山、龙洞、灵岩寺、五峰山、华山、城子崖龙山文化遗址、孝堂山汉代郭氏祠、隋代四门塔、唐代龙虎塔、九顶塔以及抢救挖掘的洛庄汉墓、野生动物世界、红叶谷生态旅游区等供人们观赏游览。

济南辖历下、市中、槐荫、天桥、历城、长清、章丘、济阳、莱芜、钢城十区和平阴、商河二县。2019 年，全市地区生产总值 9443.4 亿元，比上年增长 7.0%。年末全市常住人口 890.87 万人，户籍总人口 796.74 万人。济南又是一个多民族聚居的城市，除汉族外，主要有回、满、苗、蒙古、壮、朝鲜等 55 个少数民族。

济南是国务院公布的历史文化名城。因地处古四渎之一“济水”（故道为今黄河所据）之南而得名。据史学家考证，早在公元前 45 世纪之前，已有人类在此繁衍、生息。传说东夷族的首领舜，曾躬耕于济南历山（今千佛山）之下。2600 多年前，就建有城郭，最早出现史册上的名称为“泺”（《春秋左传》），系因济南诸泉汇为泺水，故名。春秋战国时代，济南属齐国，称“泺”“鞍”“历下”等邑，为齐国西南边陲重镇。西汉始置济南郡，公元前 164 年设立济南国。公元前 154 年又废国改郡。东汉建武十七年（公元 41 年），济南郡复称济南国。宋代至道三年(公元 997 年)，分全国为 15 路，济南属京东路，为齐州（《宋史》）。徽宗政和六年（公元 1116 年），齐州升为济南府，辖历城等五县，治所设历城，为府治之始。自明代以来，一直是山东省的省会。 1929 年 7 月设济南市至今。1928 年 4 月至 1937 年底，日本帝国主义先后二次侵占了济南，济南人民深受暴虐的民族压迫和经济掠夺，致使大部分工厂倒闭，无辜同胞惨遭杀戮。1945 年 8 月，日寇投降后，国民党反动派又进行强盗式的劫收，城市又遭到了摧残蹂躏，民生凋敝，物价飞涨，古城一片萧条。1948 年 9 月 24 日，济南获得解放，这座古城终于回到了人民的怀抱，开始了她新的历史时期。

新中国建立后，济南市始终是中国东部沿海经济大省——山东省省会。是全国副省级城市之一，环渤海地区南翼的中心城市，是全省的政治、经济、文化、教育、交通和科技中心，是山东半岛城市群和济南都市圈核心城市。2017 年，荣膺“全国文明城市”称号，跨入全国文明城市行列。2018 年 12 月 26 日，国务院批复同意山东省调整济南市莱芜市行政区划，撤销莱芜市，将其所辖区域划归济南市管辖。济南是全国区域性金融中心，2019 年年末金融机构本外币各项存款余额达 18646.1 亿元，各项贷款余额 18768.7 亿元。

济南是山东省铁路、公路、航空的交通枢纽，京沪、胶济铁路在市区交汇，北连北京、天津，南接南京、上海、福州，东达港口城市青岛、烟台。济南为京沪高铁沿线 5 个始发终到站之一。济南机场是经国家批准的国际空港，有通往北京、上海、香港、澳门、广州、深圳、福州、厦门、西安、武汉、哈尔滨、珠海、海口等城市的 198 条空中航线，通航城市 120 个。“济青高速”“济聊高速”与“京福高速”在济南交汇，从而形成了辐射全省、连接全国的高速公路系统省内中心、全国区域性枢纽的格局。济南基本形成了铁路、航空、公路立体构造，联结全省、全国和海外的现代交通网络。

Introduction of Jinan

Jinan is located in the middle of Shandong Province with an area of 10,244 km2. The geographic position is between 36° 01′ N ~ 37° 32′ N and 116° 11′ E ~ 117° 44′ E with the Mount Tai land in the south and Yellow River plain in the north. Jinan City is located at the junction of low mountains and hills in the middle and south of Shandong Province and alluvial plain in the northwest of Shandong Province. The terrain in the south is higher than that in the north, featuring low mountains and hills, sloping plain in front of mountains and Yellow River alluvial plain. Jinan mainly enjoys many rivers under the Yellow River, Xiaoqinghe River and Haihe River systems. The lakes here are Daming Lake, Baiyun Lake, etc. Jinan City is in the temperate continental monsoon climate zone. Jinan City has four distinctive seasons with sufficient sunlight hours. The annual average temperature is 13.6℃, the annual amount of precipitation is 614.0 mm.

Jinan has abundant mineral resources, mainly including various non-ferrous metals, rare metals and non-metals, such as the iron, coal, granite, fire clay and copper, kalium, platinum and cobalt, etc. In particular, the limestone has large reserves with high grade. The texture of black granite is pure and unique in China. There are 149 families of plants, 1175 species and varieties. There are 211 species of terrestrial wild animals. The apple, yellow pear, persimmon, walnut, hawthorn and Chinese chestnut, etc. are rich and the polygala tenuifolia, Salvia, chrysanthemum indicum and rhizoma cyperi, etc. medicinal materials are produced in the southern mountain area. The output of Chinese-date is very high in the flat-bottomed land along the Yellow River in the north. Jinan has rather abundant planting and breeding resources with various grain crops, economic crops and poultry, livestock and aquatic products, etc. These resources reserve a certain of material basis for the urban and rural development and economic development of Jinan.

As one of China's famous historical and cultural cities, Jinan has beautiful natural scenery and many scenic spots and historical sites. It is especially famous for clear and luscious springs and enjoys good reputations of "Jinan Springs Are the Best in the World" and "Spring City". The main scenic spots are Baotu Spring, Heihu Spring, Pearl Spring, Five Dragon Pool, Five Groups of Baimai Spring, Daming Lake, Qianfo Mountain, Dragon Cave, Lingyan Temple, Five Mountain, Mount Hua, Chengziya Longshan Cultural Site, Stone Memorial Hall at Guos' Temple on Xiaotang Mountain, Sui Dynasty Pagoda of Four Gates, Tang Dynasty Dragon Tiger Tower, Jiuding Tower and Luozhuang Han Tombs through rescue and excavation, newly-built Wildlife World and Red Leaves Canyon, etc. for viewing and sightseeing.

Now, Jinan City has jurisdiction over ten districts of Lixia, Shizhong, Huaiyin, Tianqiao, Licheng, Changqing, Zhangqiu, Jiyang, Laiwu and Gangcheng and two counties of Pingyin and Shanghe. In 2019, local GDP of Jinan city reached RMB 944.34 billion, with an increase of 7.0 % over that of the previous year; The permanent resident population of the whole city at the end of the year was 8.9087 million and the total registered population was 7.9674 million. Jinan is a city inhabited by multiple nationalities which mainly include 55 ethnic minorities, such as Hui, Man, Miao, Mongol, Zhuang and Korean, etc., in addition to Han.

Jinan is a famous historic and cultural city listed by the State Council. It is named after its location at the south of "Jishui River" (now occupied by the Yellow River), one of four ancient channels. According to the historians textual research, human beings had lived here long before 45th Century B.C. Legend has it that Shun, the leader of Dongyi Tribal Groups, farmed at the foot of Mount Li once(Qianfo Mountain today). More than 2600 years ago, the city walls had been built. It was named as "Luo" first appeared in history annals (Zuo's Commentary). Because Jinan springs converge to the Luoshui River, hence the name is gained. Jinan was the State of Qi in the warring state period, named "Luo", "An" and "Lixia" counties. It was in a key position in the southwest of the State of Qi. In the Western Han Dynasty, Jinan was changed Jinan Prefecture. The State of Jinan was set up in 164 B.C. Then it was changed into the County of Jinan in 154 B.C. In the 17th year of Jianwu Period of the Eastern Han Dynasty (41 A.D.), Jinan was renamed the State of Jinan. The whole state was divided into 15 regions in Emperor Taizong Zhidao 3th year (997 A.D.), Jinan belonged to Jingdong Region, named Qizhou (History of the Song Dynasty). Qizhou was promoted to Jinan Palace in Emperor Huizong Zhenghe 6th year (1116 A.D.), governing five countries of Licheng, etc. with the seat in Licheng. It is the provincial capital of Shandong Province all the time since the Ming Dynasty. Jinan City was set up in Jul. 1929 to this day. The Japanese imperialist successively occupied Jinan for two times at the end of Apr. 1928 to 1937. Jinan people are deeply influenced by tyrannical national oppression economic plundering. Most of the factories closed down and innocent compatriots are massacred in cold blood. In Aug. 1945, KMT reactionaries took over the city like bandits upon surrender of Japanese aggressors. The city was destroyed and devastated again. The people live in destitution, the prices are soaring and the city was in the great depression. On Sep. 24, 1948, Jinan was liberated and finally returned to the people's arms, starting her new historical period.

Jinan is always the provincial capital of Shandong Province which is the coastal economic big province of East China after the founding of new China. It is one of sub-provincial cities around the country, central city of Circum-Bohai Sea Region South Wing, the center of the whole Province in politics, economics, culture, education, transportation and science and technology and the core city of Shandong Peninsula Urban Agglomerations and Jinan Metropolitan Circle. In 2017, it was awarded as the title of "National Civilized City" and stepped into the national civilized city list. The State Council approved Shandong Province adjusted the administrative division of Laiwu city in Jinan, cancelled Laiwu City and incorporated its jurisdiction under the jurisdiction of Jinan. Jinan is the regional financial center around the country. The outstanding of deposits of local and foreign currencies for the financial institutions at the end of 2019 was RMB 1.86461 trillion and the loan balance was RMB 1.87687 trillion.

It is the transportation junction of Shandong railway, highway and aviation. Beijing-Shanghai Railway and Jiaozhou-Jinan Railway converge at the city, connecting Beijing and Tianjin in the north, Nanjing, Shanghai and Fuzhou in the South and port cities of Qingdao and Yantai in the east. Jinan is one of 5 starting-terminating stations along Beijing-Shanghai High-Speed Railway. Jinan Airport is an international airport with 198 airways approach to Beijing, Shanghai, Hong Kong, Macao, Guangzhou, Shenzhen, Fuzhou, Xiamen, Xi'an, Wuhan, Harbin, Zhuhai and Haikou, etc. and 120 destinations. "Jinan-Qingdao Expressway", "Jinan-Liaocheng Expressway" and "Beijing-Taibei Expressway" converge at Jinan, thus forming the provincial central and national regional hub pattern of expressway system which radiates the whole province and connects the whole nation. Jinan basically forms the stereometric structure of railway, aviation and highway and modern traffic network that connects the whole province, the whole nation and foreign countries.

2019 年济南市
国民经济和社会发展统计公报[1]

济　南　市　统　计　局
国家统计局济南调查队

2019 年，在市委市政府坚强领导下，全市上下坚持以习近平新时代中国特色社会主义思想为指导，坚决贯彻落实习近平总书记视察山东重要讲话、重要指示批示精神，牢牢把握“走在前列、全面开创”的目标定位，坚持稳中求进工作总基调，坚持新发展理念和推动高质量发展，扎实做好稳就业、稳金融、稳外贸、稳外资、稳投资、稳预期工作，聚焦推进“1+474”工作体系，奋力拼搏，顶住下行压力，经济运行呈现总体平稳、量质齐升、再上新台阶的良好态势，高质量发展取得明显成效，人民生活福祉进一步提高，各项社会事业健康发展，“大强美富通”现代化国际大都市建设迈出坚实步伐。

一、综合

初步核算，全年全市地区生产总值[2]9443.37 亿元，比上年增长 7.0%。其中，第一产业增加值 343.06 亿元，增长 1.3%；第二产业增加值 3265.22 亿元，增长 7.8%；第三产业增加值 5835.09 亿元，增长 7.0%。三次产业构成为 3.6：34.6：61.8。人均地区生产总值[3]106416 元，增长 5.7%，按年均汇率折算为 15430 美元。

年末常住人口 890.87 万人，比上年末增长 0.78%。户籍人口 796.74 万人，增长 1.46%。申报出生率 12.86‰，申报死亡率 6.62‰，人口自然增长率 6.24‰。常住人口城镇化率为 71.21%，比上年末提高 0.42 个百分点。

全年新增城镇就业 19.39 万人，年末城镇登记失业率 2.01%。

全年居民消费价格上涨 3.3%。工业生产者出厂价格上涨 0.3%。工业生产者购进价格回落 1.4%。新建商品住宅销售价格指数环比涨幅基本保持稳定。

2019 年居民消费价格比上年涨跌幅度（%）

指　标	全市
居民消费价格指数	3.3
# 食品烟酒	9.1
衣着	1.3
居住	1.3
生活用品及服务	0.3
交通和通信	-2.7
教育文化和娱乐	2.7
医疗保健	1.7
其他用品和服务	4.5

2019年新建商品住宅销售价格指数（%）

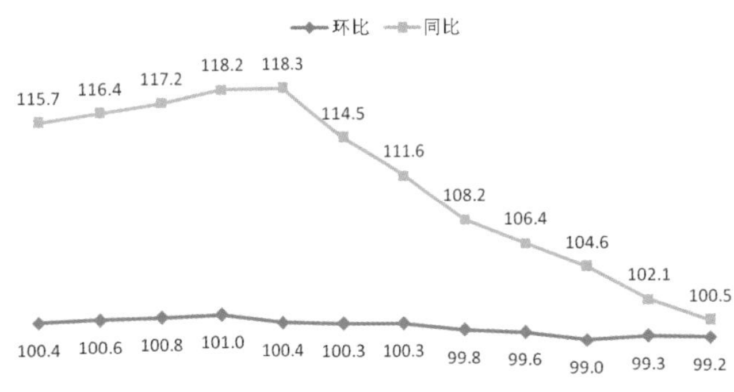

二、重点工作

四个中心建设全面提升。经济中心建设实现新突破。全年全市地区生产总值占全省比重达到 13.3%，居全省第 2 位；一般公共预算收入占全省比重达到 13.4%，居第 2 位；固定资产投资增速居第 2 位；社会消费品零售总额居第 2 位；第三产业增加值占 GDP 比重 61.8%，居第 1 位。加快央企总部城、省企总部城建设，26 个世界 500 强、47 个内资总部项目成功落地。金融中心服务功能明显提升。金融业增加值增长 7.4%。年末金融机构本外币各项存贷款余额均居全省第 1 位。新增新三板挂牌公司 11 家，总数达到 184 家，占全省比重 23.8%。物流中心承载能力拓展增强。开行欧亚班列 158 列，新开通国际（地区）航线 10 条。国家 5A 级物流企业达到 14 家，居副省级城市第 1 位。重点物流园区 16 个，重点物流企业 325 家，营业收入 369.6 亿元，增长 10.8%。科创中心集聚效应显著提高。高新技术企业达到 2231 家，规模以上工业高新技术企业 955 家，实现产值占规模以上工业总产值比重为 51.2%。R&D 经费投入[4]235.58 亿元，占 GDP 比重为 2.66%，比上年提高 0.07 个百分点。国家级企业技术中心 28 家，省级工程实验室（工程研究中心）140 家。

重点改革成效显著。重点领域有序推进。持续深化国资国企改革，市属国有企业资产总额突破万亿元。创新实施“五位一体”融资服务体系。深入推进服务民营经济发展机制创新，组织 3.8 万名干部开展“遍访民企”服务活动，民营企业实现税收 812.4 亿元。营商环境优化提升。大力深化“一次办成”改革，“在泉城　全办成”服务品牌全国打响，市场主体总量突破 115 万户，我市营商环境指数位列全国第 7 位。“双招双引”推深走实。签约项目 892 个，计划总投资 1.06 万亿元，20 个境外世界500强项目入驻济南。新增泰山产业领军人才27人，引进院士及诺奖团队30余个、高层次外国专家团队50余个。建成全国首家人力资本产业园，发布全国首个“人才有价”评估平台。对外开放打造新高地。中国（山东）自由贸易试验区济南片区建设高点起步，162项试点任务进展顺利，推出一批制度创新措施，诞生全省首张区块链存储和传递的数字营业执照。济南综合保税区提前半年封关验收，济南章锦综合保税区启动申建，跨境电子商务综合试验区获批设立。全国首个泛北方区域性签证中心正式启用，实现32个国家就地签证。

动能转换提质增速。工业新动能加速发展。规模以上工业高技术产业实现增加值比上年增长11.9%，占规模以上工业增加值比重达到21.6%。大数据与新一代信息技术、生物医药产业营业收入分别增长12.1%、9.1%。新兴消费潜力释放。限额以上可穿戴智能设备、新能源汽车零售额分别增长117.3%和199.3%，限额以上餐饮配送和外卖送餐服务营业额增长28.7%，限额以上企业网上零售额增长15.6%。现代服务业[5]增势强劲。现代服务业实现增加值3508.04亿元，增长10.5%，占服务业比重为60.1%。互联网和相关服务、软件和信息技术服务业、商务服务业营业收入分别增长77.3%、22.5%和22.9%。平台建设支撑有力。新旧动能转换先行区建设全面铺开，跨黄河“三桥一隧”建设加快，绿地国际博览城、中科新经济科创园等项目顺利推进。国际医学科学中心加快建设，国家健康医疗大数据北方中心、质子临床治疗中心主体封顶，山东第一医科大学首批师生入驻。国家超算中心科技园建成启用，我市成为全国第二个人工智能创新应用先导区，入选全国首批5G商用城市。省会高质量发展动能更加强劲。

乡村振兴扎实推进。深化农村集体产权制度改革，深入实施十大特色产业振兴工程，北方国际种业之都建设坚实起步，大力开展农村人居环境整治三年行动，成功创建3个省级乡村振兴齐鲁样板示范区。脱贫攻坚取得丰硕成果，全市建档立卡贫困户10.5万户、21.6万人全部脱贫，1006个贫困村全部摘帽退出，脱贫攻坚目标任务基本完成。建档立卡贫困户人均纯收入增加到10826元，贫困群众“两不愁”质量水平明显提升，“三保障”及饮水安全突出问题总体上得到解决。

三、农业

全年农林牧渔业总产值637.3亿元，比上年增长0.9%；农林牧渔业增加值360.5亿元，增长1.7%。全市现代高效农业增加值47.87亿元，占农林牧渔业增加值的13.3%，提高0.8个百分点；现代高效农业增加值增长率9.6%，提高3.8个百分点。

全年粮食种植面积719.0万亩，减少1.0%；蔬菜种植面积150.5万亩，减少2.2%。粮食总产量285.5万吨，增产3.1%；蔬菜产量671.2万吨，增产1.9%。

2019年主要农产品种植面积和产量

指　　标	单位	面积／产量	比上年增长（%）
粮食种植面积	万亩	719.0	-1.0
棉花种植面积	万亩	5.8	-6.8
油料种植面积	万亩	28.8	-9.5
蔬菜种植面积	万亩	150.5	-2.2
实有果园面积	万亩	58.4	-1.9
粮食总产量	万吨	285.5	3.1
棉花产量	万吨	0.5	23.4
油料产量	万吨	6.6	-6.0
蔬菜产量	万吨	671.2	1.9
水果产量	万吨	62.9	-0.5

全年完成造林面积10758公顷，增长38.7%；经济林种植面积89959公顷，增长6.2%；植树造林1576万株，增长8.1%。

全年肉类总产量35.9万吨，下降5.0%；禽蛋产量36.6万吨，下降3.8%；奶类产量32.1万吨，下降3.2%。水产品产量1.6万吨，下降54.4%。

市级以上农业龙头企业发展到470家，农民合作社、家庭农场注册数量达到9002家、4965家。全年新增有效灌溉面积和节水灌溉面积分别为15.7万亩和13.1万亩。农业机械总动力达543.5万千瓦，主要农作物综合机械化率达87.9%。

四、工业和建筑业

全年全部工业增加值比上年增长4.1%。规模以上工业增加值增长4.2%，分经济类型看，公有制经济增长6.8%，非公有制经济增长2.1%；分轻重工业看，轻工业增长2.7%，重工业增长4.5%。

全年规模以上工业营业收入增长3.1%。41个大类行业中，营业收入超百亿的行业达到13个，总量占比86.0%。其中，黑色金属冶炼和压延加工业、汽车制造业超过千亿规模。

2019年规模以上工业重点行业营业收入增长速度

行业名称	比上年增长（%）
黑色金属冶炼和压延加工业	3.3
汽车制造业	3.1
计算机、通信和其他电子设备制造业	9.9
非金属矿物制品业	11.1
电气机械和器材制造业	7.2
通用设备制造业	2.1
石油、煤炭及其他燃料加工业	12.1
金属制品业	-6.2
化学原料和化学制品制造业	-12.0
医药制造业	13.1
专用设备制造业	9.7
电力、热力生产和供应业	-6.1
食品制造业	2.8

全年规模以上工业产品产销率为96.8%。所生产的160种大类产品中，有83种产品产量实现增长，增长面为51.9%。其中，增幅超过30%的产品有22种，占比为13.8%，比上年提高0.2个百分点。

2019年规模以上工业企业[6]主要产品产量及增长速度

产品名称	单位	产量	比上年增长（%）
鲜、冷藏肉	万吨	14.9	-0.3
乳制品	万吨	47.7	-7.3
饮料酒	万千升	31.0	12.7
合成氨（无水氨）	万吨	69.3	14.5
聚丙烯树脂	万吨	11.5	20.7
初级形态塑料	万吨	29.3	7.8

产品名称	单位	产量	比上年增长(%)
中成药	吨	3263.1	9.0
水泥	万吨	1232.8	32.0
石墨及碳素制品	万吨	181.0	-6.8
钢材	万吨	2255.5	-0.2
锻件	万吨	93.6	0.9
粉末冶金零件	万吨	2.9	33.0
发动机	万千瓦	3583.6	25.6
数控金属切削机床	台	1027	-1.2
气动元件	万件	1675.6	473.7
矿山专用设备	万吨	6.2	-7.2
工业机器人	套	1074	7.0
载货汽车	万辆	17.4	-1.1
铁路货车	辆	5311	6.3
变 压器	万千伏安	15448.4	-5.3
太阳能电池（光伏电池）	万千瓦	55.7	37.7
电子计算机整机	万台	118.4	16.4
服务器	万台	116.5	16.6
集成电路	万块	1561.1	9.4
原油加工量	万吨	521.1	17.9
发电量	亿千瓦时	295.1	-5.8

全年建筑业增加值1107.98亿元，增长18.7%，占GDP比重11.7%。在建工程总施工面积达到14955.4万平方米。具有资质等级的建筑业企业895家，增加243家。实现建筑业总产值3514.0亿元，增长20.3%。其中，国有及国有控股企业产值2577.5亿元，增长16.2%。签订合同额8403.3亿元，增长21.0%。其中，本年新签合同额4543.8亿元，增长21.6%。

五、固定资产投资

全年固定资产投资比上年增长12.6%。分产业看，第一产业投资下降49.6%，第二产业投资下降23.5%，第三产业投资增长22.6%。年末亿元以上固定资产投资项目1108个，增加9个。其中，五十亿元以上项目32个，增加13个，完成投资增长70.3%。济南轨道交通R1、R2、R3线项目投资进度77.2%，山东第一医科大学项目投资进度65.8%，济南市东客站综合交通枢纽项目投资进度75%，济南市济泺路穿黄隧道工程项目投资进度30.7%，济南超算中心科技园项目一期完工。

全年民间投资下降10.9%，基础设施投资增长23.3%。服务业投资增长22.6%，其中，物流业投资增长28.4%。

全年房地产开发完成投资1576.9亿元，增长9.7%。其中，住宅完成投资1135.7亿元，增长15.8%。房屋施工面积9980.0万平方米，增长3.2%。其中，住宅施工面积6524.8万平方米，增长2.7%。房屋竣工面积1070.0万平方米，下降17.9%。其中，住宅竣工面积770.7万平方米，下降20.9%。商品房销售面积1246.5万平方米，下降7.5%。其中，住宅销售面积1020.7万平方米，下降4.5%。商品房销售额1380.8亿元，下降10.7%。其中，住宅销售额1173.9亿元，下降5.3%。

六、国内贸易

全年社会消费品零售总额5162.2亿元，比上年增长8.1%。其中，商品零售4393.1亿元，增长8.0%；餐饮收入769.2亿元，增长8.5%。分城乡看，城镇社会消费品零售额4656.0亿元，增长8.1%；乡村社会消费品零售额506.2亿元，增长7.7%。限额以上单位[7]实现零售额1349.1亿元，增长1.1%。

限额以上单位商品零售额中，粮油、食品类128.7亿元，增长11.4%；金银珠宝类35.9亿元，增长18.1%；家用电器和音像器材类77.4亿元，增长5.3%；汽车类373.2亿元，增长2.6%。

2019年限额以上批发和零售业单位商品零售额及增长速度

商品类别	零售额（亿元）	比上年增长（%）
粮油、食品类	128.7	11.4
饮料类	11.1	3.4
烟酒类	20.9	13.4
服装、鞋帽、针纺织品类	103.0	-0.3
化妆品类	15.9	-4.4
金银珠宝类	35.9	18.1
日用品类	35.6	0.8
家用电器和音像器材类	77.4	5.3
中西药品类	44.6	-12.9
文化办公用品类	30.8	0.9
通讯器材类	54.7	-16.5
石油及制品类	222.3	-3.1
汽车类	373.2	2.6

七、开放型经济

全年货物进出口总额1103.3亿元，比上年增长17.9%。其中，出口622.5亿元，增长5.2%；进口480.8亿元，增长39.6%。出口市场中，对欧洲国家和地区出口增长7.5%，对韩国、日本出口分别增长9.3%和3.0%，对美国出口下降28.3%。主要出口商品中，机电产品出口387.3亿元，其中，运输工具出口133.9亿元，增长19.3%；高新技术产品出口91.2亿元，下降7.8%；农产品出口52.6亿元，增长46.0%。

全年实际使用外资22.4亿美元，增长23.8%。其中，制造业使用外资2.9亿美元，服务业使用外资14.5亿美元。新批外商投资项目228个。总投资过亿美元的项目26个，合同外资53.1亿美元，增长5.0%。

全年对外承包工程营业额40.9亿美元，备案设立境外企业（机构）79家，派出各类劳务人员8047人。

全年经济外向度11.7%，比上年提高1.1个百分点。

八、交通、邮电和旅游

年末公路通车里程17770.9公里，比上年增长2.3%。其中，境内高速公路653.6公里，增长3.9%。公路客运量3244.0万人，下降1.6%；旅客周转量54.1亿人公里，下降1.4%。公路货运量3.4亿吨，增长2.8%；货运周转量585.5亿吨公里，增长1.8%。年末拥有民用机动车285.5万辆，其中，民用汽车258.4万辆。年末公交线路596条，增加60条；线路总长度10807.2公里，增加1188.1公里；旅客运输量8.5亿人次，增加2304.6万人次。济南机场累计保障起降13.0万架次，增长2.5%；旅客吞吐量1756.0万人次，增长5.7%；货邮吞吐量13.5万吨，增长19.1%。

全年邮政行业业务收入（不包括邮政储蓄银行直接营业收入）69.5亿元，增长12.9%；业务总量114.0亿元，增长27.0%。快递服务企业业务收入56.0亿元，增长15.7%；业务量51605.9万件，增长19.5%。年末移动电话用户1122.9万户，其中，4G电话用户888.8万户、增长10.1%。

全年接待国内外游客10026.0万人次，增长8.5%。其中，接待国内游客9980.3万人次，增长8.5%；接待入境游客45.7万人次，增长12.2%。实现旅游总收入1285.9亿元，增长12.7%。其中，国内旅游收入1266.9亿元，增长12.6%；入境旅游收入27493.5万美元，增长19.8%。A级旅游景区80家。其中，5A级景区1家，4A级景区17家。省级以上旅游度假区2家。

九、财政和金融

全年一般公共预算收入874.2亿元，比上年增长7.2%。其中，税收收入700.1亿元，增长4.5%，占一般公共预算收入比重为80.1%。一般公共预算支出1197.3亿元，增长7.0%。其中，教育支出185.8亿元，增长5.7%；社会保障和就业支出163.9亿元，增长13.3%；城乡社区支出253.2亿元，增长0.5%。

年末金融机构单位数800家。其中，银行52家，保险公司93家，证券公司及营业部147家，期货公司及营业部64家，财务公司11家，其他各类机构433家。

年末金融机构本外币各项存款余额18646.1亿元，增长3.1%。金融机构本外币各项贷款余额18768.7亿元，增长11.2%。

全年完成证券交易额3.6万亿元，增长24.8%；期货营业部交易额7.9万亿元，增长0.1%；新增直接融资2023.1亿元。年末全市区域内上市公司37家，股票39只；在证券投资基金协会登记的私募基金管理机构总数达到180家，管理基金352只，管理规模797.9亿元。

全年保费收入532.3亿元，增长19.3%。其中，财产险公司保费收入131.5亿元，增长34.2%；人身险公司保费收入400.8亿元，增长15.1%。各项赔款与给付121.9亿元，增长7.5%。

十、科技、教育、文化、卫生和体育事业

全年万人有效发明专利拥有量29.25件，比上年增长13.4%。技术合同实现交易额278.4亿元，增长113.0%。规模以上工业企业研发人员数量6.3万人。规模以上工业企业办研发机构333个。全市获国家科技进步一等奖2项、二等奖9项，省科技进步一等奖9项、二等奖34项。专利申请量46563件，其中，发明专利申请量16117件。专利授权量25158件，其中，发明专利授权量4843件。

加快中心城基础教育设施三年建设规划任务落实，全市开工新建、改扩建中小学校（幼儿园）140所。创新幼儿园网格化触点式管理，推行“互联网+”家园共育。巩固“双零择”成果，全市义务教育阶段集团化建设率达到70%，484所被帮扶学校实现特色发展。坚持职业教育现代融合发展，11所院校44个项目进入教育部首批1+X证书制度试点项目，新设24个专业服务新旧动能转换工程。

2019年教育事业基本情况

学校类别	学校所数（所）	在校生（万人）	专任教师（人）
驻济高等学校	52	76.2	40627
中等职业学校	40	5.7	4058
普通中学	312	39.4	34177
小学	683	54.1	36067
特殊教育学校	13	0.1	536

年末（国有）艺术表演团体15个，文化馆（站）及群众艺术馆169个，博物馆13个，档案馆17个，公共图书馆14个。市级以上文物保护单位435处，其中，国家级30处。城市可统计票房数字影院65家，放映81.7万场次，观众1306.7万人次，票房收入4.9亿元。年末广播人口混合覆盖率99.7%，电视人口混合覆盖率99.3%。建成“泉城书房”12个，基层综合性文化服务中心覆盖率100%。

年末拥有卫生机构7487个，增加144家，增长2.0%，其中，医院、卫生院351家（三甲医院24家、民营医院180家）。卫生机构床位6.7万张，增长2.8%。各类卫生技术人员9.8万人，增长6.4%；执业（助理）医师3.8万人，增长7.4%。按常住人口计算，每千人拥有病床7.5张，增长2.1%；每千人拥有执业（助理）医师4.3人，增长6.7%。

全年新成立体育社会组织8个，培训社会体育指导员2187人。组织各类全民健身活动（赛事）220次，参与人数200万人次。获省级及以上金牌565枚，银牌357枚，铜牌431枚。成功举办了济南市冬季畅游泉水国际邀请赛、马拉松游泳冠军赛暨世界杯选拔赛、国际泳联游泳世界杯、泉城（济南）马拉松等多项高端国际赛事。

十一、城市建设[8]、环境和安全生产

年末城市建成区面积760.6平方公里，比上年增加79.6平方公里。建成区绿化覆盖率41.2%，人均公园绿地面积13.3平方米。全年天然气供气量14.36亿立方米，增长10.4%；液化石油气供气量4.55万吨，减少10.4%。集中供热面积26073万平方米，增长15.8%。自来水供水量4.45亿吨，增长4.4%。垃圾无害化处理率100%。

全年城区环境空气中可吸入颗粒物（PM10）年均浓度103微克/立方米，细颗粒物（PM2.5）53微克/立方米，二氧化硫15微克/立方米，二氧化氮41微克/立方米。小清河出境断面辛丰庄化学需氧量浓度18毫克/升，小清河出境断面辛丰庄氨氮浓度1.46毫克/升。区域环境噪声昼间平均等效声级54.9分贝，市区道路交通噪声平均等效声级69.6分贝。初步核算，万元GDP能耗下降8.87%，完成当年节能降耗目标任务。

全年新能源装机容量130.4万千瓦，占全市装机容量的15.4%。其中，太阳能装机容量65.2万千瓦，风电装机容量49.1万千瓦，生物质发电装机容量15.9万千瓦。

全年刑事案件立案25382件。破获当年刑事案件10345件。受理社会治安案件79355件。

全年发生各类生产安全死亡事故240起，下降14.9%；死

亡 262 人，下降 14.7%。

十二、居民生活和社会保障

全年城镇居民人均可支配收入 51913 元，比上年增长 7.3%；城镇居民人均生活消费支出 33439 元，增长 6.7%。农村居民人均可支配收入 19454 元，增长 9.1%；农村居民人均生活消费支出 12300 元，增长 8.0%。城乡居民收入比由上年的 2.71：1 缩小为 2.67：1。城镇居民恩格尔系数[9]23.8%，农村居民恩格尔系数 30.1%。

2019年城镇、农村居民人均可支配收入及其构成

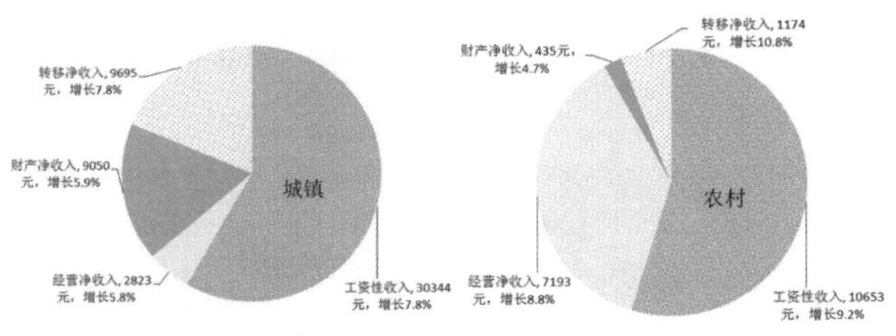

2019年末每百户居民家庭主要耐用消费品拥有量[10]

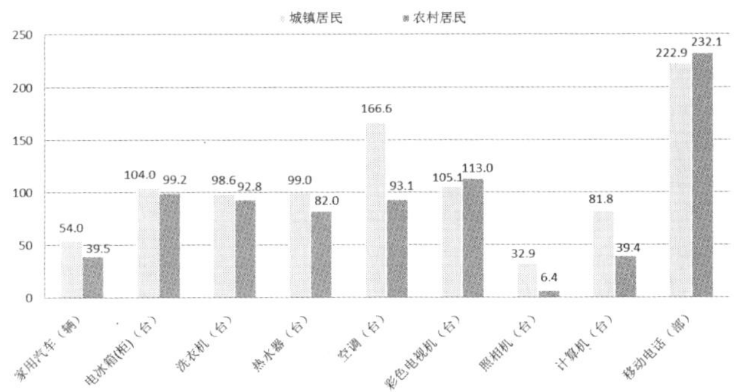

年末城镇职工基本养老保险参保人数 408.33 万，增加 30.82 万；职工医疗保险参保人数 288.04 万，增加 18.57 万；失业保险参保人数 189.70 万，增加 9.55 万；工伤保险参保人数 262.56 万，增加 15.18 万；生育保险参保人数 201.24 万，增加 17.98 万。居民养老保险和医疗保险参保人数分别达到 293.91 万和 502.38 万。

城市最低生活保障标准由上年人均每月 616 元提高到 685 元，享受城镇最低生活保障的城镇居民 1.01 万户、1.55 万人，发放最低生活保障金及各类补贴 1.14 亿元。农村最低生活保障标准由年人均不低于 4928 元提高到 5480 元，享受农村最低生活保障的农村居民 5.23 万户、7.33 万人，发放最低生活保障金及各类补贴 3.13 亿元。农村特困人员基本生活标准每人每年 7124 元；照料护理标准按照自理、半自理和完全不能自理人员分三种档次，每人每年分别为 2292 元、3820 元、7640 元。

全市共有救助管理站 3 处，流浪未成年人保护中心 1 处。培训残疾人 6922 人次，安置残疾人员就业 2563 人，帮扶救助残疾人投入资金 1.4 亿元。

注释：

[1] 2019 年统计数据为统计快报数或初步核算数，正式数据以出版的《济南统计年鉴－2020》为准。

[2] 全市地区生产总值、各产业增加值绝对数按现价计算，增长速度按不变价格计算。根据第四次全国经济普查结果，对国内生产总值、各产业增加值等相关指标的历史数据进行了修订。

[3] 人均地区生产总值按年均常住人口计算。

[4] R&D 经费投入相关指标错年使用 2018 年数据。

[5] 现代服务业包括：信息传输、软件和信息技术服务业，金融业，房地产业，租赁和商务服务业，科学研究和技术服务业，水利、环境和公共设施管理业，居民服务、修理和其他服务业，教育，卫生和社会工作，文化、体育和娱乐业。

[6] 规模以上工业企业指年主营业务收入 2000 万元及以上的工业法人单位。

[7] 限额以上单位是指年主营业务收入 2000 万元及以上的批发业单位、500 万元及以上的零售业单位、200 万元及以上的住宿和餐饮业单位。单位包括法人企业、产业活动单位和个体户。

[8] 城市建设指标口径为包含两县的整个济南地区。

[9] 恩格尔系数是指食品支出在消费支出中的比重。

[10] 数据来自于住户收支与生活状况调查。

资料来源：本公报中全面深化改革数据来自市委全面深化改革领导小组办公室、发展改革委；扶贫数据来自市扶贫开发领导小组办公室；国家级企业技术中心数据、省级工程实验室（工程研究中心）数据来自发展改革部门；教育数据来自教育部门；科技数据来自科技部门；电信相关数据来自工业和信息化部门；户籍、社会治安数据来自公安部门；城乡最低生活保障、农村特困人员救助供养相关数据来自民政部门；财政数据来自财政部门；城镇新增就业、登记失业率、城镇职工保险参保数据、人才数据来自人力资源社会保障部门；环境保护相关数据来自生态环境部门；城市建设相关数据来自城乡建设部门；公路里程、公交数据、公路运输、航空运输数据来自交通运输部门；邮政、快递数据来自邮政管理部门；水产品产量、农业数据来自农业农村部门；林业数据来自园林和林业部门；进出口、新设境外企业、外派劳务人员数据来自商务部门；旅游、文化数据来自文化和旅游部门；卫生数据来自卫生健康部门；安全生产数据来自应急管理部门；外事数据来自外事部门；市场主体、知识产权数据来自市场监管部门；体育数据来自体育部门；医疗保险类数据来自医疗保障部门；金融数据来自地方金融管理部门；招商引资、外资数据来自投资促进部门；物流数据来自口岸物流部门；民营经济数据来自民营经济部门；档案馆数据来自档案部门；残疾人保障数据来自残联；装机容量数据来自供电部门；居民收入与支出数据、恩格尔系数、价格指数、粮食数据来自国家统计局济南调查队；新旧动能转换先行区建设数据来自新旧动能转换先行区管委会；国际医学科学中心建设情况来自国际医学科学中心管委会；自由贸易试验区济南片区建设数据来自中国（山东）自由贸易试验区济南片区管委会；其他数据均来自市统计局。

STATISTICAL COMMUNIQUÉ OF THE JINAN MUNICIPAL ON THE 2019 NATIONAL ECONOMIC AND SOCIAL DEVELOPMENT [1]

Jinan Municipal Bureau of Statistics
NBS Survey Office In Jinan

In 2019, Jinan City fully adhered to the guidance of Xi Jinping Thought on Socialism with Chinese Characteristics for a New Era, under the firm leadership of the Jinan Municipal Party Committee and the Jinan Municipal People' s Government, and stoutly implemented the principles of General Secretary Xi Jinping' s important speeches and instructions during his inspection tour to Shandong Province. We firmly grasped the goal orientation of "walking in the forefront of times, creating in all aspects", followed the general work guideline of making progress while ensuring stability, performed the new development concept and promoted high–quality development, realized and kept stable employment, stable finance, stable foreign trade, stable foreign capital, stable investment and stable expectations, and focused on promoting the "1+474" work system. We worked hard and withstood downward pressure to ensure the economic operation in a good momentum of overall stability, increased quantity and quality, and advanced growth, achieved significant results in high–quality development, further improved people' s lives and well-being, sustained the sound development of social undertakings, and took solid steps towards the construction of a "big, strong, beautiful, wealthy and unblocked" modern international metropolis.

I. General

According to preliminary calculations, the city' s regional GDP [2] for the whole year was RMB 944.337 billion, increased by 7.0% over the previous year. Of those, the value added of the primary industry was RMB 34.306 billion, increased by 1.3%; the value added of the secondary industry was RMB 326.522 billion, increased by 7.8%; the value added of the tertiary industry was RMB 583.509 billion, increased by 7.0%. The proportion of these three industries is 3.6: 34.6: 61.8. The regional GDP per capita [3] was RMB 106,416, increased by 5.7%, equivalent to USD15,430 on the average annual exchange rate.

The permanent resident population at the end of the year was 8.9087 million, increased by 0.78% over the end of the previous year. The registered population was 7.9674 million, increased by1.46%. The birth rate declared was 12.86‰, the death rate declared was 6.62‰, and the natural population growth rate was 6.24‰. The urbanization rate of the resident population was 71.21%, increased by 0.42% over the end of the previous year.

The newly increased urban employed population all year round was 193,900, and the urban unemployment rate registered at the end of the year was 2.01%.

The annual consumer prices rose by 3.3%. The ex–factory prices for industrial producers went up by 0.3%. The purchasing prices of industrial producers fell by 1.4%. The month–on–month increase in the sales price index of newly–built commercial residential buildings remained basically stable.

Consumer Price Index of 2019 (over the previous year, %)

Indicator	The whole city
CPI	3.3
Food, tobacco and wine	9.1
Clothes	1.3
Residence	1.3
Daily necessities and services	0.3
Transportation and communication	–2.7
Education, culture and entertainment	2.7
Health care	1.7
Other goods and services	4.5

Sales Price Index of New Houses In2019（%）

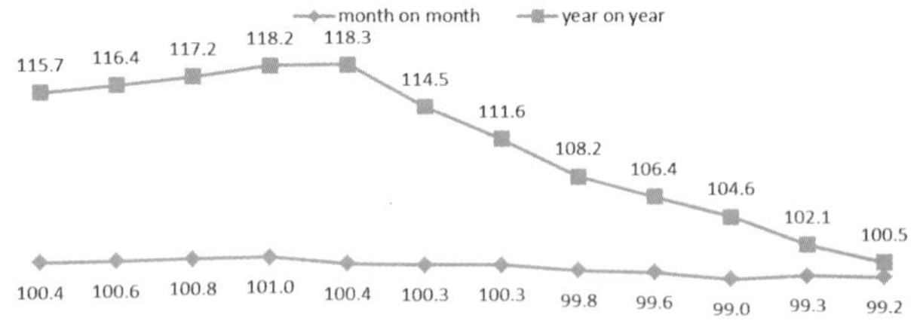

II. Key Work

The construction of Four Centers was comprehensively improved. New breakthroughs have been achieved in the construction of the economic center. The annually regional GDP of the whole city accounted for 13.3% of that of the province, ranking second in the whole province; the general public budget revenue accounted for 13.4% of that of the whole province, ranking second; the growth rate of fixed asset investment ranked second; the total retail sales of social consumer goods ranked second; the values added of the tertiary industry accounted for 61.8% of GDP, ranking first. We have accelerated the construction of the city of central enterprise headquarters and the city of provincial enterprise headquarters, and have put 26 projects of global top 500 enterprises and 47 projects of domestic-funded headquarters into practice. **The service functions of the financial center have been significantly improved.** The values added of the financial industry increased by 7.4%. The balance of deposits and loans of financial institutions in local and foreign currencies at the end of the year ranked first in the whole province. Eleven (11) newly listed companies were added on the New OTC Market, with the total number up to 184, accounting for 23.8% of the whole province. **The carrying capacity of the logistics center has been expanded and strengthened.** A total of 158 Euro-Asia trains were opened, and 10 international (regional) routes were newly launched. There were 14 national 5A-level logistics enterprises, ranking first among sub-provincial cities. There were 16 key logistics parks and 325 key logistics enterprises in the city. The operating income reached up to RMB 36.96 billion, increased by 10.8%. **The combined effect of research centers of technological creation has been significantly improved.** There were 2,231 high-tech enterprises and 955 above-designated-scale industrial high-tech enterprises in the city, and the output value accounted for 51.2% of the total industrial output value above the designated scale. R&D fund [4] investment reached up to RMB 23.558 billion, accounting for 2.66% of GDP, increased by 0.07% over the previous year. There were 28 national-level enterprise technology centers and 140 provincial-level engineering laboratories (engineering research centers) in the city.

The results of key reforms were remarkable. Great progress has been orderly made in key fields. We continued to deepen the reform of state-owned assets and enterprises, and the total assets of state-owned enterprises directly under Jinan Municipality exceeded RMB one trillion. We creatively implemented the "five-in-one" financing service system. We deeply promoted the new mechanism of serving the development of the private economy, organized 38,000 leaders to carry out the service activities of "visiting private enterprises", and the private enterprises completed the tax revenue of RMB 81.24 billion. **The business environment has been optimized and improved.** We vigorously deepened the reform of "One-time Completion", and pushed the service brand "In the City of Spring All Affairs Well Done" nationwide. The total number of market entities broke through 1.15 million, and the business environment index of the city ranked 7th throughout the country. **"Attracting business and investment, attracting experts and intelligence" has been further promoted and put into practice.** Specifically, 892 projects have been executed with a total planned investment of RMB 1.06 trillion, and 20 overseas projects of global top 500 enterprises have settled in Jinan. Besides, 27 Taishan Industrial Experts were newly-added, and more than 30 academicians and Nobel prize winner teams as well as more than 50 high-level foreign expert teams were introduced. We have built the first human capital industrial park in China, and released the first "Value of Experts" evaluation platform all over the country. **Opening up to the outside world marches on new heights.** The construction of the Jinan Area of the China (Shandong) Pilot Free Trade Zone started on a higher level, and 162 trial tasks have progressed successfully. A number of new institutional measures have been launched, and the first digital business license for blockchain storage and delivery came into being in the whole province. The Jinan Comprehensive Free Trade Zone half a year ahead of the closing acceptance, the Jinan Zhangjin Comprehensive Free Trade Zone started its application for construction, and the comprehensive pilot zones for cross-border E-commerce was approved for its establishment. The first Pan-northern Regional Visa Center was officially put into operation in China, providing on-site visa service for 32 countries.

Transformation from old growth drivers to new ones has been improved and accelerated. New industrial growth drivers have achieved the accelerated development. The values added of industrial high-tech industries above the designated scale increased by 11.9% over the previous year, accounting for 21.6% of the values added of industries above the designated scale. The operating income of big data and new-generation information technology industry and biomedical industry increased by 12.1% and 9.1%, respectively. **Emerging consumption potential is have been released.** The retail sales of above-norm wearable smart devices and new energy vehicles increased by 117.3% and 199.3%, respectively, the turnover of above-norm catering delivery and takeout services increased by 28.7%, and the online retail sales of above-norm enterprises rose by 15.6%. **The modern service industry [5] has been increasingly growing.** The modern service industry has achieved an added value of RMB 350.804 billion, increased by 10.5%, accounting for 60.1% of that of the service industry. The operating income of Internet and related services, software and information technology services, and business services increased by 77.3%, 22.5% and 22.9%, respectively. **The construction of platform was supported.** The construction of the Pioneer Area -Driving the Transition from Old to New has been fully extended, the construction of the "three bridges and one tunnel" across the Yellow River has been accelerated, and the Greenland International Expo City, the Zhongke New Economy Science and Technology Park and other projects have progressed successfully. The construction of the Jinan International Center for Medical Sciences has been accelerated, main buildings of the National Health and Medical Big Data Northern Center and the Proton Clinical Treatment Center have been completed, and the first batch of teachers and students from Shandong First Medical University settled in. The National Supercomputing Center Science and Technology Park was completed and put into use, and Jinan city became the second pilot area for creative applications of artificial intelligence in China, and was included into the first batch of 5G commercial cities throughout the country. The high-quality development drivers of the provincial capital have been strengthened.

The revitalization of the rural areas has been progressed steadily. The reform of the rural collective property rights system has been deepened, ten characteristic industry revitalization projects have been further implemented, the construction of the capital of northern international seed industry started in a solid manner, and the three-year action of renovating the rural settlement environment was vigorously carried out. Three provincial-level Qilu model demonstration areas of rural revitalization were successfully established. The results of poverty alleviation were remarkable. In the whole city,105,000 impoverished households and 216,000 people have all been lifted out of poverty, and1,006 poor villages have been relieved from poverty. The goal and task of poverty alleviation have been basically completed. The per capita net income of poverty-stricken households registered increased to RMB 10,826, and the quality of "no worries of foods and clothes" in the poor population was significantly improved, and the outstanding problems of "three guarantees" and drinking water safety were generally resolved.

III. Agriculture

The total output value of agriculture, forestry, animal husbandry and fishery in the whole year was RMB 63.73 billion, increased by 0.9% over the previous year; the values added of agriculture, forestry, animal husbandry and fishery were RMB 36.05 billion, increased by 1.7%. The values added of modern high-efficiency agriculture in the city reached RMB 4.787 billion, accounting for 13.3% of those of agriculture, forestry, animal husbandry and fishery, increased by 0.8%; the growth rate of the values added of modern high-efficiency agriculture was 9.6%, increased by 3.8%.

The annual planting area of grain was 7.190 million mu, decreased by 1.0%; the planting area of vegetables was 1.505 million mu, decreased by 2.2%. The total output of grain was 2.855 million tons, increased by 3.1%; the output of vegetables was 6.712 million tons, increased by 1.9%.

Planting Area and Output of Main Agricultural Products in 2019

Indicator	Unit	Area/output	Increment over the previous year (%)
Planting area of grain	10000 mu	719.0	-1.0
Planting area of cotton	10000 mu	5.8	-6.8
Planting area of oil plants	10000 mu	28.8	-9.5
Planting area of vegetables	10000 mu	150.5	-2.2
Planting area of orchard	10000 mu	58.4	-1.9
Total output of grain	10000 tons	285.5	3.1
Output of cotton	10000 tons	0.5	23.4
Output of oil-bearing crops	10000 tons	6.6	-6.0
Output of vegetables	10000 tons	671.2	1.9
Output of fruits	10000 tons	62.9	-0.5

The annual afforestation area completed was 10,758 hectares, increased by 38.7%; the planting area of economic forest was 89,959 hectares, increased by 6.2%; 15.76 million trees were planted, an increased by 8.1%.

The total output of meat in the whole year was 359,000 tons, decreased by 5.0%; the output of poultry eggs was 366,000 tons, decreased by 3.8%; the output of dairy products was 321,000 tons, decreased by 3.2%. The output of aquatic products was 16,000 tons, decreased by 54.4%.

The number of leading agricultural enterprises above the municipal level has grown to 470, and the number of registered farmer cooperatives and family farms has reached 9,002 and 4,965, respectively. The newly-increased effective irrigation area and water-saving irrigation area were 157,000 mu and 131,000 mu, respectively. The total power of agricultural machinery reached 5.435 million kilowatts, and the comprehensive mechanization rate of main crops reached up to 87.9%.

IV. Industry and Construction Industry

The total value added of industrial enterprises in the whole year increased by 4.1% over the previous year. The value added of the industrial enterprises above designated scale increased by 4.2%, from the view of economic types, presenting the public economy increased by 6.8% and the non-public economy increased by 2.1%; in terms of light and heavy industries, the light industry increased by 2.7% and the heavy industry increased by 4.5%.

The operating income of industrial enterprises above designated scale increased by 3.1% throughout the year. Among 41 sectors of industries, 13 industries achieved an operating income of more than RMB 10 billion, accounting for 86.0% of the total. Of those, the ferrous metal smelting and rolling processing industry and the automobile manufacturing industry exceeded RMB 100 billion.

Growth Speed of Operating Income for Key Sectors of Industries above Designated Scale in 2019

Name of sector	Increment over the previous year (%)
Ferrous metal smelting and rolling processing industry	3.3
Automobile manufacturing industry	3.1
Computer, communication and other electronic equipment manufacturing industry	9.9
Non-metallic mineral products industry	11.1
Electrical machinery and equipment manufacturing industry	7.2
General equipment manufacturing industry	2.1
Petroleum, coal and other fuel processing industry	12.1
Metal products industry	-6.2
Chemical raw materials and chemicals manufacturing industry	-12.0
Pharmaceutical manufacturing industry	13.1
Special equipment manufacturing industry	9.7
Electricity and heat production and supply industry	-6.1
Food manufacturing industry	2.8

The output-sales ratio of industrial products above designated scale was 96.8%. Among 160 kinds of products, the output of 83 kinds of products has been grown, and the growth surface reached 51.9%. Of those, there were 22 products with an growth rate of more than 30%, accounting for 13.8%, increase by 0.2% over the previous year.

Output and Growth Speed of Main Products of Industrial Enterprises above designated scale[6] in 2019

Name	Unit	Output	Increment over the previous year (%)
Fresh and chilled meat	10000 tons	14.9	-0.3
Dairy products	10000 tons	47.7	-7.3
Food alcohol	10000 kl	31.0	12.7
Synthetic ammonia (anhydrous ammonia)	10000 tons	69.3	14.5
Polypropylene resin	10000 tons	11.5	20.7
Primary form plastics	10000 tons	29.3	7.8
Chinese patent medicine	Ton	3263.1	9.0
Cement	10000 tons	1232.8	32.0
Graphite and carbon products	10000 tons	181.0	-6.8
Steel	10000 tons	2255.5	-0.2
Forging	10000 tons	93.6	0.9
Powder-metal part	10000 tons	2.9	33.0
Engine	10000 KW	3583.6	25.6
CNC metal-cutting machine tools	Pcs	1027	-1.2
Pneumatic component	10000 pcs	1675.6	473.7
Mine-specific equipment	10000 tons	6.2	-7.2
Industrial robot	Pcs	1074	7.0
Goods vehicle	10000 pcs	17.4	-1.1
Railway wagon	Pcs	5311	6.3
Transformer	10000 KVA	15448.4	-5.3
Solar battery (photovoltaic cell)	10000 KW	55.7	37.7
Electronic computer machine	10000 pcs	118.4	16.4
Server	10000 pcs	116.5	16.6
Integrated circuit	10000 pcs	1561.1	9.4
Crude oil processing volume	10000 tons	521.1	17.9
Generated energy	100 million KWH	295.1	-5.8

The value added of the construction industry throughout the year reached RMB110.798 billion, with an increase of 18.7%, accounting for 11.7% of GDP. The total construction area of projects in process reached 149.554 million square meters. There were 895 qualified construction enterprises, increased by 243. The total output value of the construction industry reached RMB 351.4 billion, with an increase of 20.3%. Of those, the output value of state-owned and state-controlled enterprises reached RMB 257.75 billion, increased by 16.2%. The value of signed contracts was RMB 840.33 billion, with an increase of 21.0%. Among them, the value of newly-signed contracts this year reached RMB 454.38 billion, increased by 21.6%.

V. Fixed Asset Investment

The annual fixed asset investment increased by 12.6% over the previous year. In terms of different industries, investment in the primary industry fell by 49.6%, investment in the secondary industry fell by 23.5%, and investment in the tertiary industry increased by 22.6%. At the end of the year, there were 1,108 fixed asset investment projects in the amount of over RMB 100 million, with an increase of 9 projects. Among them, there were 32 projects in the amount of more than RMB 5 billion, with an increase of 13 and completed investment growth of 70.3%. The investment progress of Jinan Rail Transit R1, R2 and R3 project reached 77.2%, that of Shandong First Medical University was 65.8%, the investment progress of Jinan East Passenger Station Comprehensive Transportation Hub was 75%, and the investment progress of Jiluo Road Crossing Yellow Tunnel Project in Jinan City reached 30.7%. The first phase project of the Jinan Supercomputing Center Science and Technology Park was completed.

Non-government investment for the year fell by 10.9%, and investment in infrastructures increased by 23.3%. The investment in the service industry rose by 22.6%, among which investment in the logistics industry increased by 28.4%.

The completed investment in the real estate development reached RMB 157.69 billion in the whole year, with an increase of 9.7%. Of those, the completed residential investment was RMB 113.57 billion, increased by 15.8%. The construction area of buildings reached 99.8 million square meters, increased by 3.2%. Among them, the residential construction area was 65.248 million square meters, with an increase of 2.7%. The area of as-built buildings was 10.7 million square meters, decreased by 17.9%. Of those, the completed residential area was 7.707 million square meters, with a decrease of 20.9%. The sales area of commercial residential buildings was 12.465 million square meters, with a decrease of 7.5%. Among them, the residential sales area was 10.207 million square meters, decreased by 4.5%. The sales volume of commercial residential buildings was RMB 138.08 billion, decreased by 10.7%. Among them, residential sales were RMB 117.39 billion, with a decrease of 5.3%.

VI. Domestic Trade

The total annual retail sales of social consumer goods were RMB 516.22 billion, increased by 8.1% over the previous year. The retail sales of commodity were RMB 439.31 billion, with a growth rate of 8.0%; the revenue of catering was RMB 76.92 billion, with an increase of 8.5%. In terms of urban and rural areas, the retail sales of social consumer goods in urban areas were RMB 465.60 billion, increased by 8.1%; while the retail sales of social consumer goods in rural areas was RMB 50.62 billion, with an increase of 7.7%. Units above designated scale[7] have achieved the retail sales of RMB 134.91 billion, with an increase of 1.1%.

For units above designated scale, the retail sales of grain, oil and food products were RMB 12.87 billion, with an increase of 11.4%; those of gold, silver and jewelry were RMB 3.59 billion, with a growth rate of

18.1%; those of household appliances and audio and video equipment were RMB 7.74 billion, with an increase of 5.3%; and those of automobiles were RMB 37.32 billion, increased by 2.6%.

Retail Sales and Growth Rate of Commodities for Wholesale and Retail Units Above Designated Scale in 2019

Category	Retail sales (100 million yuan)	Increment over the previous year (%)
Grain and oil and food	128.7	11.4
Beverage	11.1	3.4
Tobacco and wine	20.9	13.4
Clothes, shoes and hats, knitwear and textile	103.0	-0.3
Cosmetics	15.9	-4.4
Gold, silver and jewelry	35.9	18.1
Daily necessities	35.6	0.8
Household appliances, audio and video equipment	77.4	5.3
Traditional Chinese and western medicine	44.6	-12.9
Stationery and office supplies	30.8	0.9
Communication equipment	54.7	-16.5
Petroleum and products	222.3	-3.1
Automobile	373.2	2.6

VII. Open Economy

The total imports and exports of goods for the year reached RMB 110.33 billion, increased by 17.9% over the previous year. Among them, the export amount was RMB 62.25 billion, increased 5.2%; the import amount was RMB 48.08 billion, increase by 39.6%. In the export market, exports to countries and regions in Europe increased by 7.5%, exports to South Korea and Japan increased by 9.3% and 3.0% respectively, while exports to the United States decreased by 28.3%. Among the main commodities for exports, the export amount of mechanical and electrical products was RMB 38.73 billion, of which the export volume of transportation vehicles was RMB 13.39 billion, with an increase of 19.3%; the export volume of high-tech products was RMB 9.12 billion, decreased by 7.8%; the export volume of agricultural products was RMB 5.26 billion, with an increase of 46.0%

The actual use of foreign capital in the whole year reached USD 2.24 billion, with an increase of 23.8%. The manufacturing industry used USD 290 million in foreign investment and the service industry used USD 1.45 billion in foreign investment. In the year 228 foreign investment projects were newly approved. There were 26 projects with a total investment of over USD 100 million and contractual foreign investment of USD 5.31 billion, with an increase of 5.0%

The annual turnover of contracted foreign projects was USD 4.09 billion, 79 overseas enterprises (institutions) were incorporated on record, and 8,047 laborers were dispatched abroad.

The annual economic export orientation was 11.7%, increased by 1.1% over the previous year.

VIII. Traffic, Post and Communications and Tourism

The mileage of highways opened to traffic reached 17,770.9 kilometers at the end of the year, increased by 2.3% over the previous year. The length of domestic expressways reached 653.6 kilometers, with an increase of 3.9%. The passenger capacity of highways was 32.440 million, decreased by 1.6%; passenger turnover was 5.41 billion person-kilometers, decreased by 1.4%. The freight volume of highways was 340 million tons, with an increase of 2.8%; freight turnover was 58.55 billion ton-km, with an increase of 1.8%. There were 2.855 million of civilian motor vehicles at the end of the year, including 2.584 million of civilian cars. There were 596 bus lines at the end of the year, with an increase of 60; the total length of the lines was 10,807.2 kilometers, with an increase of 1,188.1 kilometers; the passenger transport volume was 850 million persons, with an increase of 23.046 million persons. Jinan Airport has completed a total of 130 thousand sorties, with an increase of 2.5%; passenger throughput of 17.56 million persons, increased by 5.7%; cargo and mail throughput of 135,000 tons, with an increase of 19.1%

The business income of the postal industry (excluding the direct operating income of the Postal Savings Bank of China) in the year totaled RMB 6.95 billion, with an increase of 12.9%; the total business volume achieved RMB 11.4 billion, increased by 27.0%. The business income of express service enterprises reached RMB 5.60 billion, with an increase of 15.7%; the business volume was 516.059 million pieces, increased by 19.5%. There were 11.229 million of mobile phone users at the end of the year, including 8.888 million of 4G phone users, increased by 10.1%.

The number of domestic and foreign tourists was 100.26 million persons over the year, with an increase of 8.5%. A total of 99.803 million of domestic tourists were received, with an increase of 8.5%; while 457 thousand of inbound tourists were received, increased by 12.2%. The total tourism revenue reached RMB 128.59 billion, with an increase of 12.7%. Domestic tourism revenue totaled RMB 126.69 billion, with a growth rate of 12.6%; inbound tourism revenue was USD 274.935 million, with an increase of 19.8%. There were 80 A-level tourist attractions, including 1 5A-level scenic spot and 17 4A-level scenic spots as well as 2 tourist resorts above the provincial level.

IX. Finance and Banking

The annual general public budget revenue reached RMB 87.42 billion, increased by 7.2% over the previous year. The tax revenue totaled RMB 70.01 billion, with an increase of 4.5%, accounting for 80.1% of general public budget revenue. The general public budget expenditure was RMB 119.73 billion, with an increase of 7.0%. Of those, education expenditure reached RMB 18.58 billion, with an increase of 5.7%; social security and employment expenditures were RMB 16.39 billion, with an increase of 13.3%; expenditures of urban and rural communities reached RMB 25.32 billion, increased by 0.5%.

The number of financial institutions reached 800 at the end of the year, including 52 banks, 93 insurance companies, 147 security companies and business departments, 64 futures companies and business departments, 11 financial companies, and 433 other institutions.

At the end of the year, the balance of deposits of financial institutions in domestic and foreign currencies reached RMB 1864.61 billion, with an increase of 3.1%. The balance of loans of financial institutions in domestic and foreign currencies was RMB 1,876.87 billion, with a growth rate of 11.2%.

The turnover of security transactions over the year was RMB 3.6 trillion, with an increase of 24.8%; the turnover of the futures business department was RMB 7.9 trillion yuan, increased by 0.1%; and the amount of new direct financing was RMB 202.31 billion. At the end of the year, there were 37 listed companies and 39 stocks in the city; the total number of private equity fund management institutions registered with the Asset Management Association of China reached 180, with 352 funds under management in a scale of RMB 79.79 billion.

The annual premium income was RMB 53.23 billion, with an increase of 19.3%. The premium income of property insurance companies reached RMB 13.15 billion, increased by 34.2%; the premium income of life insurance companies totaled RMB 40.08 billion, with an increase of 15.1%. Various indemnities and payments were RMB 12.19 billion, with a growth rate of 7.5%.

X. Science and Technology, Education, Culture, Health and Sports

The number of valid invention patents per 10,000 people throughout the year was 29.25, increased by 13.4% over the previous year. The transaction value of technology contracts was RMB 27.84 billion, with an increase of 113.0%. The number of R&D personnel in industrial enterprises above designated scale was up to 63,000. There were 333 R&D institutions established by industrial enterprises above designated scale. The city has won 2 first prizes and 9 second prizes for national scientific and technological progress, and 9 first prizes and 34 second prizes for provincial scientific and technological progress. The number of patent applications was 46,563, including 16,117 invention patent applications. The number of authorized patents was 25,158, of which the number of authorized invention patents was 4,843.

We have accelerated the implementation of the three-year construction plan for basic education facilities in the central city, and have started to build, renovate and expand 140 primary and secondary schools (kindergartens). We created the kindergarten grid-based contact management, and promoted the "Internet +" homeland co-education. We strengthened the achievements of the "double zero choice", the group construction rate in the compulsory education stage reached 70%, and 484 aided schools have achieved characteristic development. We persisted in the modern integrated development of vocational education, 44 projects from 11 colleges and universities were included into the first batch of 1+X certificate system pilot projects by the Ministry of Education, and 24 new majors were added to serve the transformation from old growth drivers to new ones.

Basic Statistics of Education Business in 2019

Category	Number	Students (10000 persons)	Full-time teachers (person)
Colleges and universities in Jinan	52	76.2	40627
Secondary vocational schools	40	5.7	4058
Ordinary secondary school	312	39.4	34177
Primary school	683	54.1	36067
Special education schools	13	0.1	536

At the end of the year, there were 15 (state-owned) art performance groups, 169 cultural centers (stations) and mass art centers, 13 museums, 17 archives, and 14 public libraries. There were 435 cultural relics protection units above the city level, including 30 ones at the national level. The city had 65 box office digital cinemas, showing 817,000 times and containing 13.067,000 viewers, and with box office revenue of RMB 490 million. At the end of the year, the mixed coverage rate of radio population was 99.7%, and the mixed coverage rate of TV population was 99.3%. Besides, 12 " Study Rooms of Spring City " have been built, and the coverage rate of the primary-level comprehensive cultural service centers reached 100%.

At the end of the year, there were 7,487 health institutions, with an increase of 144 and growth rate of 2.0%. There were 351 hospitals and health centers (24 Class-A hospitals and 180 non-governmental hospitals). There were 67,000 beds in health institutions, with an increase of 2.8%. There were 98,000 health professionals, with an increase of 6.4%; and 38,000 licensed (assistant) physicians, with an increase of 7.4%. Calculated based on the permanent population, there were 7.5 beds per 1,000 people, with an increase of 2.1%; there were 4.3 licensed (assistant) physicians per 1,000 people, with an increase of 6.7%.

Statistically, 8 new social sports organizations were established throughout the year, and 2,187 social sports instructors were trained. We have organized 220 national fitness activities (events), with 2 million of participants. We won 565 provincial and above gold medals, 357 silver medals, and 431 bronze medals. We successfully held a number of high-end international events, such as the Jinan Winter Spring Swimming International Gymnastics Tournament, Marathon Swimming Championship and World Cup Trial, FINA Swimming World Cup, Spring City (Jinan) Marathon, etc.

XI. City Construction[8], Environment and Safety Production

At the end of the year, the urban built-up area reached 760.6 square kilometers, increased by 79.6 square kilometers over the previous year. The green coverage rate of the built-up area is 41.2%, and the per capita green area of parks was 13.3 square meters. The annual supply of natural gas was 1.436 billion cubic meters, with an increase of 10.4%; the supply of liquefied petroleum gas was 45,500 tons, decreased by 10.4%. The area of central heating was 260.73 million square meters, with an increase of 15.8%. The tap water supply counted 445 million tons, with an increase of 4.4%. The harmless treatment rate of garbage reached 100%.

The annual average concentration of inhalable particulate matter (PM10) in urban ambient air throughout the year was 103 micrograms/cubic meter, fine particulate matter (PM2.5) was 53 micrograms/cubic meter, sulfur dioxide was 15 micrograms/cubic meter, and nitrogen dioxide was 41 micrograms/cubic meter. The chemical oxygen demand concentration of Xinfengzhuang at the exit section of Xiaoqinghe River was 18 mg/liter, and the ammonia nitrogen concentration was 1.46 mg/liter. The average equivalent sound level of regional environmental noise in the day was measured at 54.9 decibels, and the average equivalent sound level of urban road traffic noise was 69.6 decibels. Preliminary calculations show that energy consumption per RMB 10,000 GDP has declined by 8.87%, and the goal of energy saving and consumption reduction of the year has been achieved.

The annual installed capacity of new energy was 1.304 million kilowatts, accounting for 15.4% of that of the whole city. Among them, the installed capacity of solar energy was 652,000 kilowatts, that of wind power was 491,000 kilowatts, and that of biomass power generation was 159,000 kilowatts.

In the whole year, 25,382 criminal cases were filed. A total of 10,345 criminal cases were handled that year and 79,355 social security cases were accepted.

There were 240 production safety fatalities throughout the year, dropped by 14.9%; the number of deaths reached 262, decreased by 14.7%.

XII. Living and Social Security of Residents

The annual per capita disposable income of urban residents was RMB 51,913, increased by 7.3% over the previous year; and the per capita living consumption expenditure of urban residents was RMB 33,439, with an increase of 6.7%. The per capita disposable income of rural residents was RMB 19,454, with an increase of 9.1%; the per capita living consumption expenditure of rural residents was RMB 12,300, with a growth rate of 8.0%. The income ratio of urban and rural residents decreased from 2.71:1 in the previous year to 2.67:1. Engel coefficient of urban residents[9] was 23.8%, while that of rural residents was 30.1%.

Per Capita Disposable Income of Urban and rural inhabitant and composition in 2019

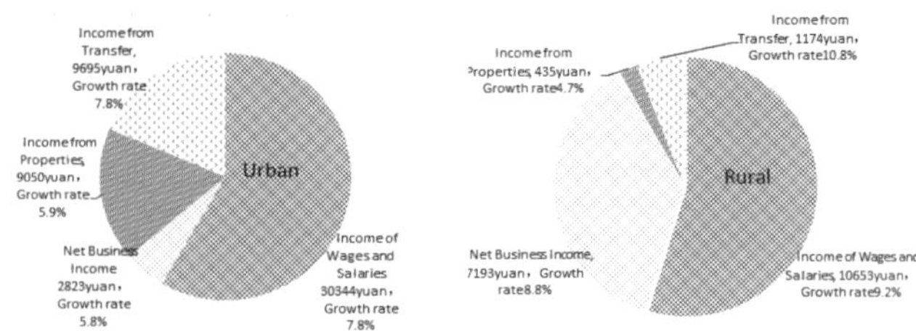

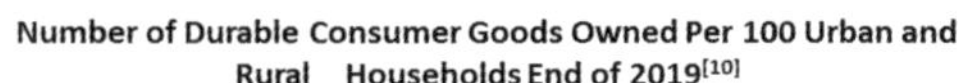

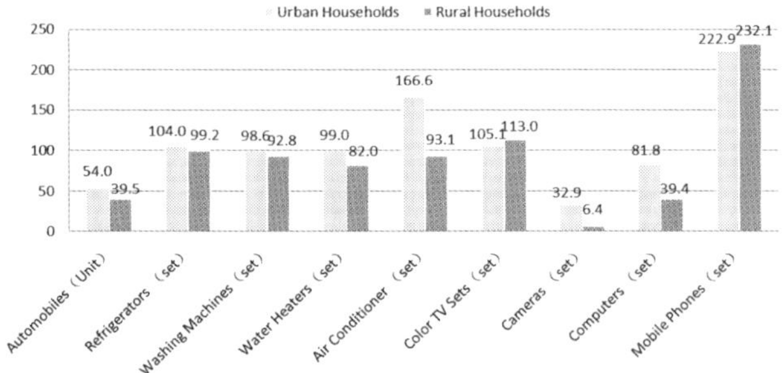

At the end of the year, the number of urban employees participating in basic endowment insurance was 4.0833 million, with an increase of 308,200; the number of employees participating in medical insurance was 2.884 million, increased by 185,700 persons; the number of participants in unemployment insurance was 1,897,700, with an increase of 95,500 persons; the number of employees participating in work injury insurance was 2,625,600, increased by 151,800 persons; the number of people participating in maternity insurance was 2.0124 million, with an increase of 179,800 persons. The number of residents participating in pension insurance and medical insurance reached 2,939,100 and 5,023,800, respectively.

The minimum living allowance standard of urban residents was raised from RMB 616 per capita per month to RMB 685 in the previous year. There were 10,100 urban residents and 15,500 persons entitled to the urban minimum living allowance and subsidies totaling RMB 114 million. The minimum living standard in rural areas has been raised from no less than RMB 4,928 per person per year to RMB 5,480, and 52,300 rural households and 73,300 rural residents under the rural minimum living security, with a minimum living allowance and various subsidies of RMB 313 million. The basic living standard of the extremely poor persons in rural areas was RMB 7,124 per person per year; the care and nursing standards were divided into three levels according to self-care, semi-self-care and completely unable to self-care: RMB 2,292, RMB 3,820 and RMB 7,640.

There were 3 rescue management stations and 1 protection center for vagrant minors in the city. We have trained 6,922 persons with disabilities, placed 2,563 disabled persons in employment, and invested RMB 140 million in helping and assisting persons with disabilities.

Notes:

[1]Statistics 2019 are statistical bulletin or preliminary accounting

data, and the official data are subject to the published Jinan Statistical Yearbook–2020.

[2] The city gross regional product and the absolute amount of the value added of various industries are calculated on current price, while the growth rate is calculated at a constant price. Based on the results of the fourth national economic census, historical data on relevant indicators, such as GDP and the added value of industries have been revised.

[3] Per capita gross regional product is calculated by the average annual permanent resident population.

[4] The related indexes of R&D expenditure input uses the data of 2018.

[5] Modern service industry includes: Information transmission, software and IT, financial industry, real estate, leasing and business services, scientific research and technology services, water conservancy, environment and management of public facility, residential service, repair and other services, education, health and social work, culture, sports and entertainment.

[6] Industrial enterprises above designated size refer to industrial legal entities with annual prime business revenue of RMB 20.000.000 and above.

[7] Units above quota refer to wholesale enterprises with annual prime business revenue of RMB 20,000,000 and above, retail enterprises with annual prime business revenue of RMB 5,000,000 and above, and accommodation and catering enterprises with annual prime business revenue of RMB 2.000.000 and above. Unit includes corporate enterprises, industrial activity units and self–employed business.

[8] The index caliber of urban construction is the entire Jinan area including two counties.

[9] Engel's Coefficient refers to the proportion of food expenditure in consumption expenditure.

[10] The data is from the survey of household income and expenditure and living conditions.

Source of data: The data on the comprehensive deepening of reform in this communique come from the Municipal Committee's Comprehensive Deepening Reform Leading Group Office and the National Development and Reform Commission; the poverty alleviation data come from the Municipal Poverty Alleviation and Development Leading Group Office; the national enterprise technology center data and the provincial engineering laboratory (engineering research center) data come from the development reform departments; education data come from the education department; science and technology data come from the science and technology department; telecommunications–related data comes from the industry and information department; household registration and social security data come from the public security department; data on urban and rural minimum living guarantees, and the assistance and support of rural people in extreme poverty come from the civil affairs department; Fiscal data come from the financial department; urban new jobs, registered unemployment rate, urban employee insurance participation data, and talent data come from the human resources and social security department; environmental protection data come from the ecological environment department; urban construction data come from the urban and rural construction department; highways mileage, bus data, road transportation, and air transportation data come from the transportation department; post and express data come from the postal administration department; aquatic product output and agricultural data come from the agricultural and rural departments; forestry data come from the garden and forestry department; Data on import and export, newly established overseas enterprises and expatriates come from the business sector; tourism and cultural data come from the culture and tourism sector; health data come from the health and health sector; safety production data come from the emergency management department; foreign affairs data come from the foreign affairs department; market entities and intellectual property data come from the market Regulatory departments; sports data come from sports departments; medical insurance data from medical security departments; financial data come from local financial management departments; investment and foreign investment data come from investment promotion departments; logistics data come from port logistics departments; private economic data come from private economic departments ; Data on the archives come from the archives department; data on the protection of the disabled come from the Disabled Persons' Federation; data on installed capacity come from the power supply department; data on residents' income and expenditure, Engel coefficient, price index, and grain data come from the NBS Survey Office in Jinan of the National Bureau of Statistics; data on the construction of pilot area of transformation from old growth drivers to new ones come from the management committee of pilot area of transformation from old growth drivers to new ones; the construction of the international medical science center comes from the management committee of the international medical science center; the construction data of the Jinan area of the free trade pilot zone comes from Jinan Area of the China (Shandong) Pilot Free Trade Zone; Other data come from the Municipal Bureau of Statistics.

2019 年的济南
Jinan in 2019

9443.4
地区生产总值（亿元）
Gross Domestic Product
(100 million yuan)

61.8
第三产业比重 (%)
Proportion of Tertiary
Industry(%)

890.87
常住人口（万人）
Permanent Population
(10 000 persons)

874.2
一般公共预算收入（亿元）
General Pubilic Budget
Revenue(100 million yuan)

12.6
全社会固定资产投资增长幅度 (%)
Growth Rate Total Investment in
Fixed Assets(%)

163.0
海关进出口总额（亿美元）
Total Value of Imports and
Exports(100 million USD)

106416
人均地区生产总值（元）
Per Capita Gross Domestic
Product(yuan)

51913
城镇居民人均可支配收入（元）
Per Capita Disposable Income of
Urban Inhabitant(yuan)

4420.4
社会消费品零售总额（亿元）
Total Retail Sale of Consumer
Goods(100 million yuan)

19454
农村居民人均可支配收入（元）
Per Capita Disposable Income of
Rural Inhabitant(yuan)

103.3
居民消费价格指数 (%)
Consumer Price Index(%)

济南一日

A Day in Jinan

每日创造
Daily Production

23950.4
一般公共预算收入
（万元 / 天）
General Pubilic Budget Revenue
(10 000 yuan/day)

32803.2
一般公共预算支出
（万元 / 天）
General Public Budget Expenditure
(10 000 yuan/day)

4466.1
海关进出口总额
（万美元 / 天）
Total Value of Imports and Exports
(10 000 USD/day)

1251
入境游客人数
（人次 / 天）
Number of Inbound Tourists
(person-time/day)

75.3
旅游外汇收入
（万美元 / 天）
Foreign Exchange Income of Tourism
(10 000 USD/day)

9398.9
第一产业（万元 / 天）
Primary Industry(10 000 yuan/day)

258722.5
地区生产总值（万元 / 天）
Gross Domestic Product (10 000 yuan/day)

88877
公路客运量
（人 / 天）
Highways Passenger Traffic
(person/day)

89458.1
第二产业（万元 / 天）
Secondary Industry(10 000 yuan/day)

25647
民航客运量
（人 / 天）
Civil Aviation Passenger Traffic
(person/day)

159865.5
第三产业（万元 / 天）
Tertiary Industry(10 000 yuan/day)

481
生产汽车
（辆 / 天）
Automobile Manufacturing
(unit/day)

8086
发电量
（万千瓦时 / 天）
Power Generating Capacity
(10 000 kwh/day)

18390
蔬菜产量
（吨 / 天）
Output of Vegetables
(tons/day)

7820
粮食产量
（吨 / 天）
Output of Grain Crops
(tons/day)

14277
原油加工量
（吨 / 天）
Crude Processing Volume
(tons/day)

3192
生产服务器
（台 / 天）
Server Manufacturing
(unit/day)

每日生活
Daily Life

279
出生人口
（人 / 天）
Population of Birth
(person/day)

144
死亡人口
（人 / 天）
Population of Death
(person/day)

2126.5
城乡居民生活用电量
（万千瓦时 / 天）
Household Electricity Consumption of Urban and Rural Residents
(10 000 kwh/day)

143
登记结婚
（对 / 天）
Registered Marriages
(couple/day)

276
城镇非私营单位在岗职工平均工资
（元 / 天）
Average Wages of On-post Staff in Urban Non Private Entities(yuan/day)

98
离婚
（对 / 天）
Divorces
(couple/day)

142
城镇居民人均可支配收入
（元 / 天）
Per Capita Disposable Income of Urban Inhabitant(yuan/day)

121.8
自来水供水量
（万吨 / 天）
Volume of Water Supply
(10 000 tons/day)

103026.6
批发零售业零售额
（万元 / 天）
Total Retail Sale of Wholesale and Retail Trades (10 000 yuan/day)

755.3
住宿业零售额（万元 / 天）
Total Retail Sale of Wholesale and Retail Trades (10 000 yuan/day)

17325.2
餐饮业零售额（万元 / 天）
Total Retail Sale of Catering Industry
(10 000 yuan/day)

121107.1
社会消费品零售总额（万元/天）
Total Retail Sale of Consumer Goods
(10 000 yuan/day)

393.4
天然气供气量
（万立方米 / 天）
Total Natural Gas Supply
(10 000 cu.m/day)

7637
生活垃圾清运量
（吨 / 天）
Domestic Waste Removed and Transported(tons/day)

34
农村居民人均生活消费支出
（元 / 天）
Per Capita Consumer Expenditure of Rural Inhabitant(yuan/day)

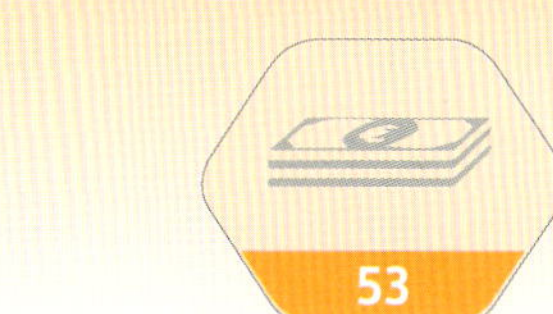

92
城镇居民人均生活消费支出
（元 / 天）
Per Capita Consumer Expenditure of Urban Inhabitant(yuan/day)

53
农村居民人均可支配收入
（元 / 天）
Per Capita Disposable Income of Rural Inhabitant(yuan/day)

综 合
General Survey

地区生产总值（亿元）
Gross Domestic Product (100 million yuan)

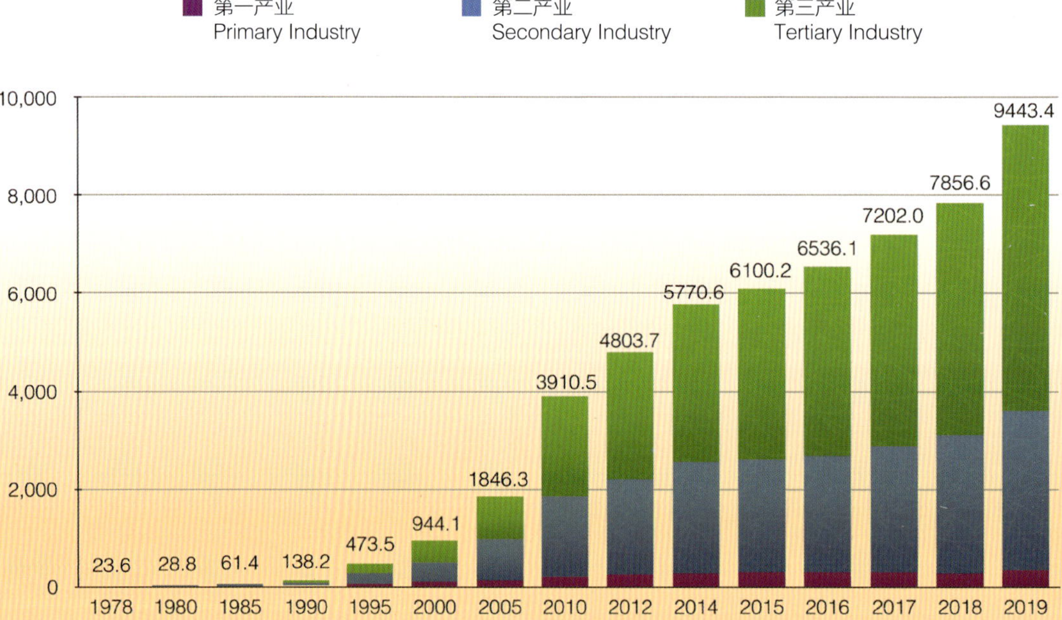

人均地区生产总值（元）
Per Capita Gross Domestic Product (yuan)

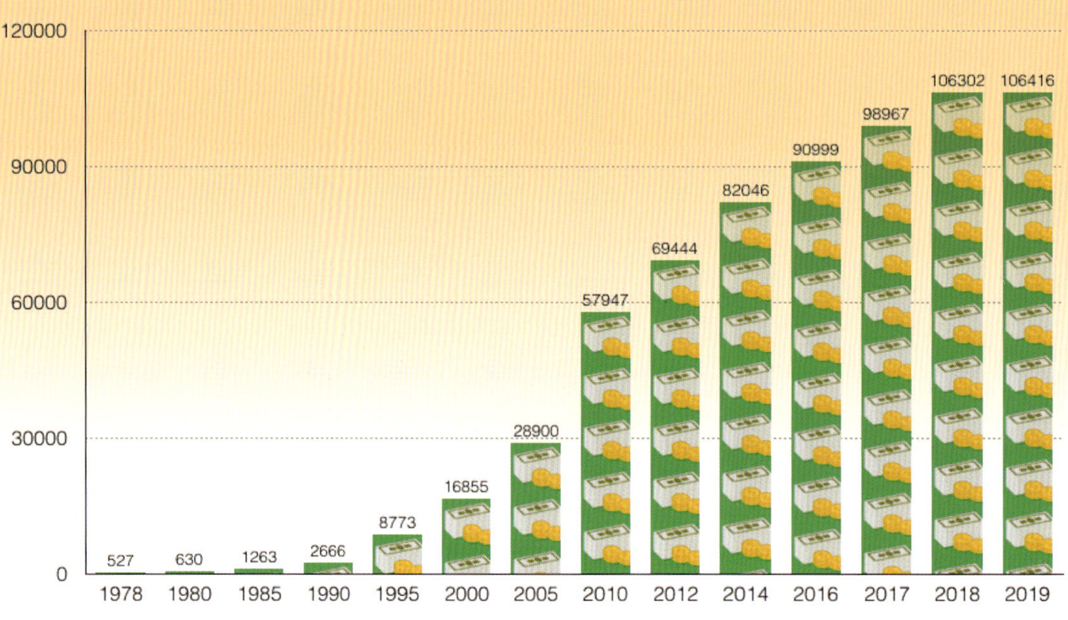

人口
Population

年末户籍总人口（万人）
Registered Population Year-end (10 000 persons)

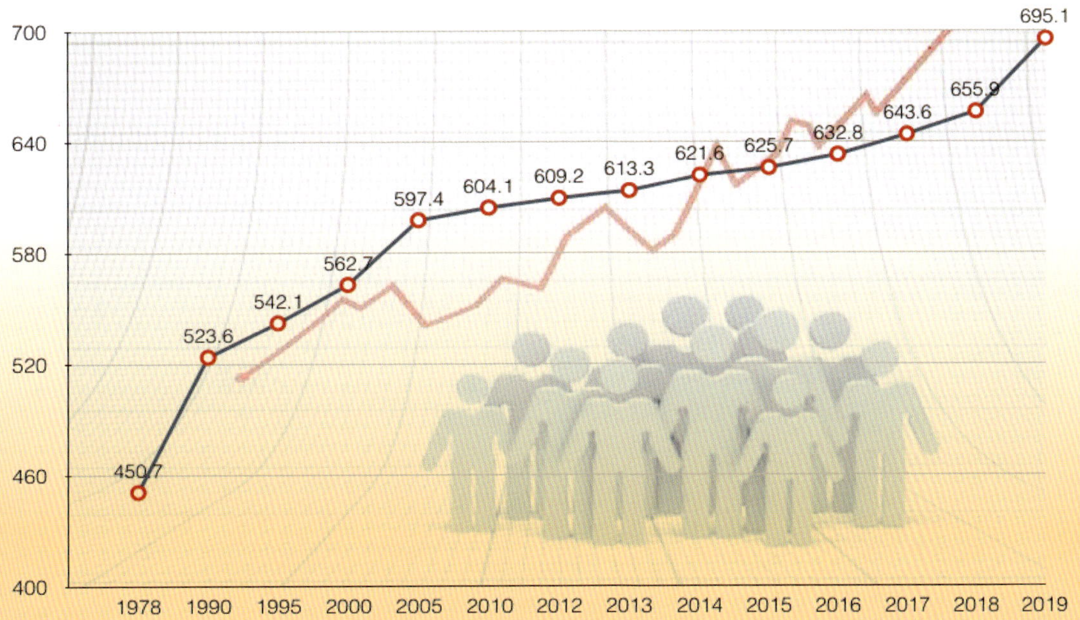

人口自然变动情况（‰）
Natural Changes of Population (‰)

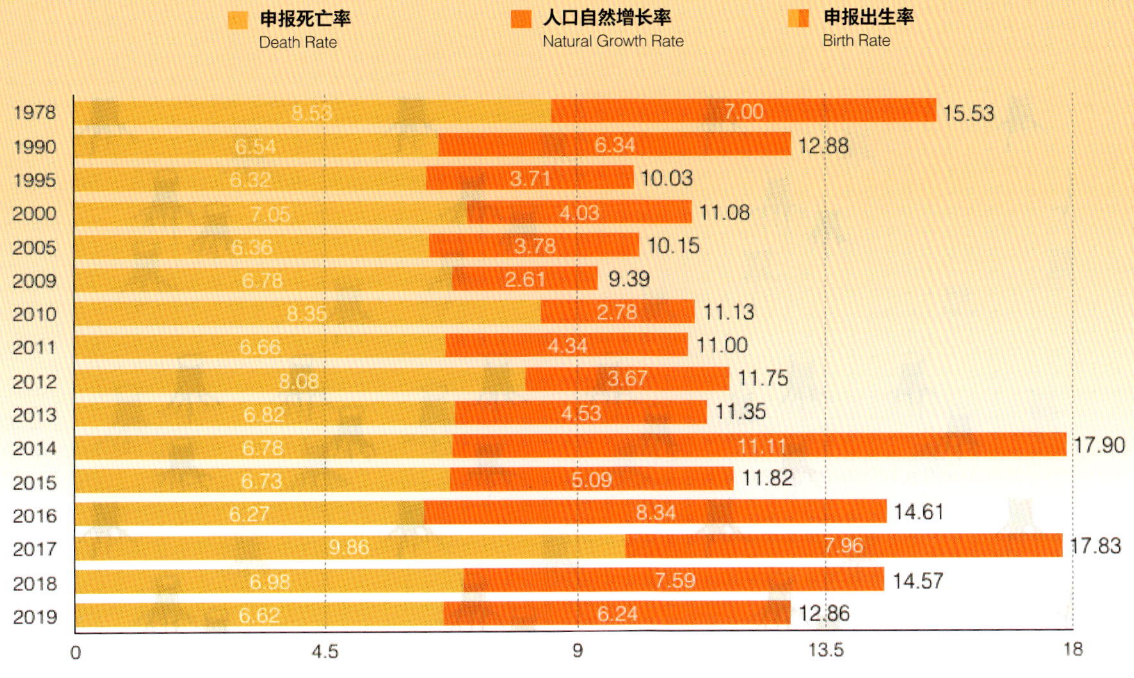

就 业
Employment

全社会从业人员（万人）
Total Employed Persons (10 000 persons)

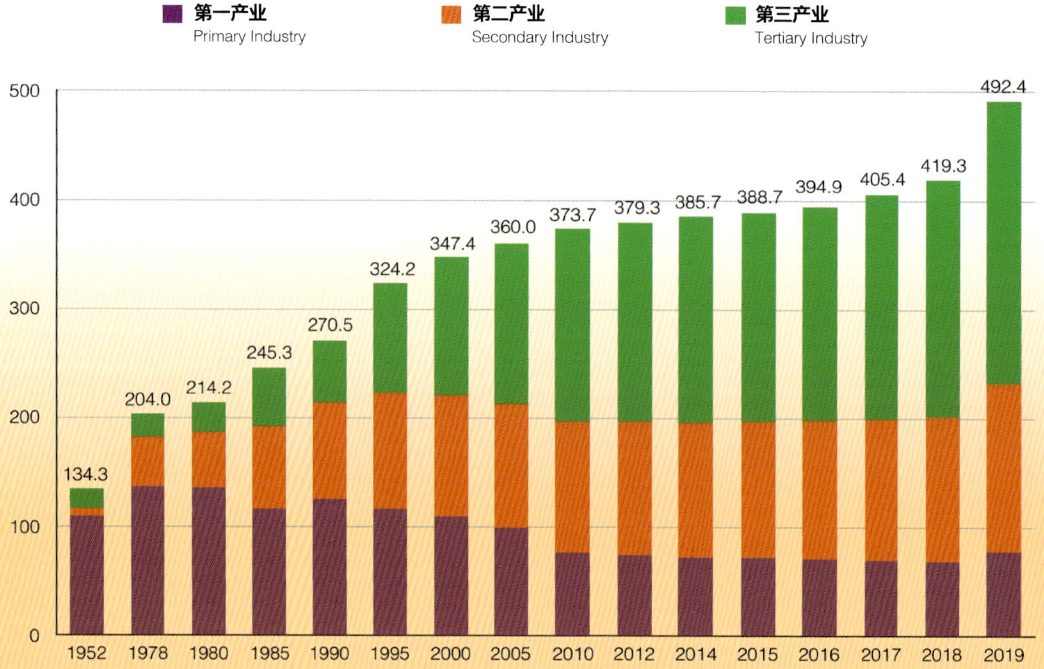

在岗职工平均工资（元）
Average Wage of Staff and Workers (yuan)

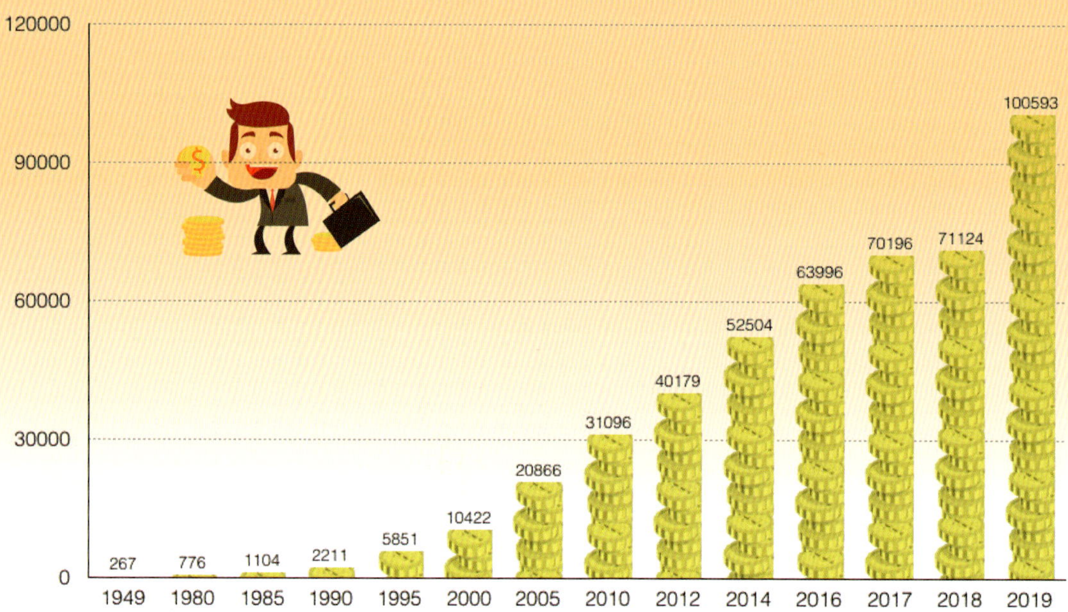

注：1、2006 年以后为法人单位在岗职工口径；2、2019 年以后为城镇非私营单位在岗职工口径。

Notes: 1.The data after 2006 are based on the caliber of on-the-job employees of legal entities.
2.The data after 2019 are based on the caliber of on-post staff in urban non private entities.

财政 金融
Government Finance Financial

一般公共预算收入支出（亿元）
General Public Budget Revenue and Expenditure (100 million yuan)

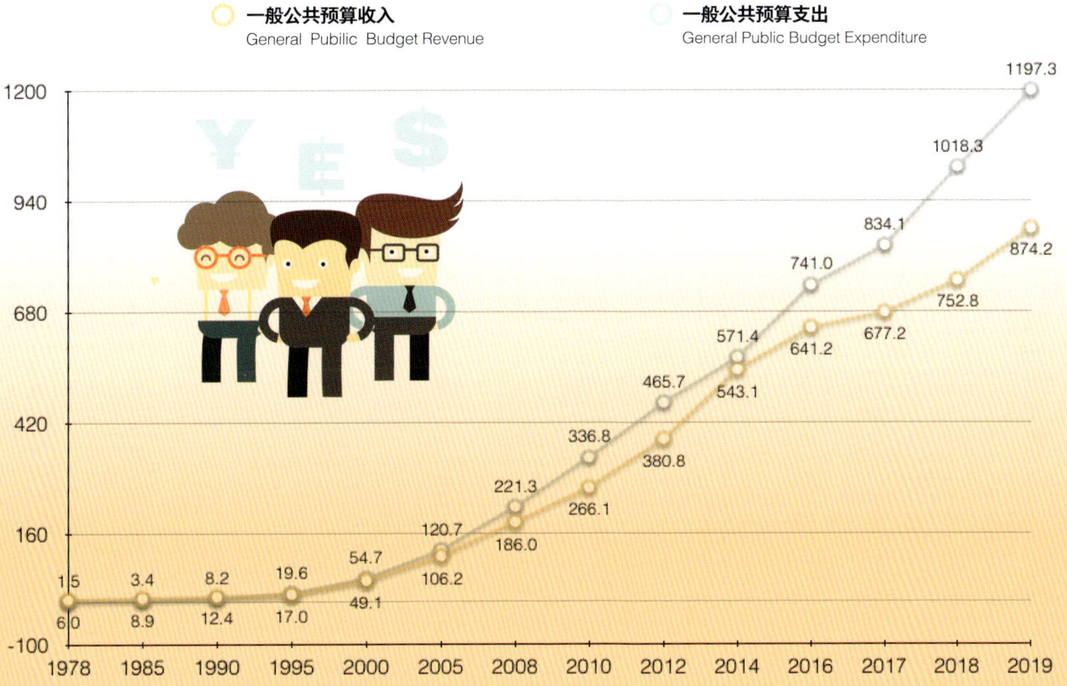

金融机构人民币存、贷款余额（亿元）
The Ending Balance of all Deposits and Loans in RMB of Financial Institutions (100 million yuan)

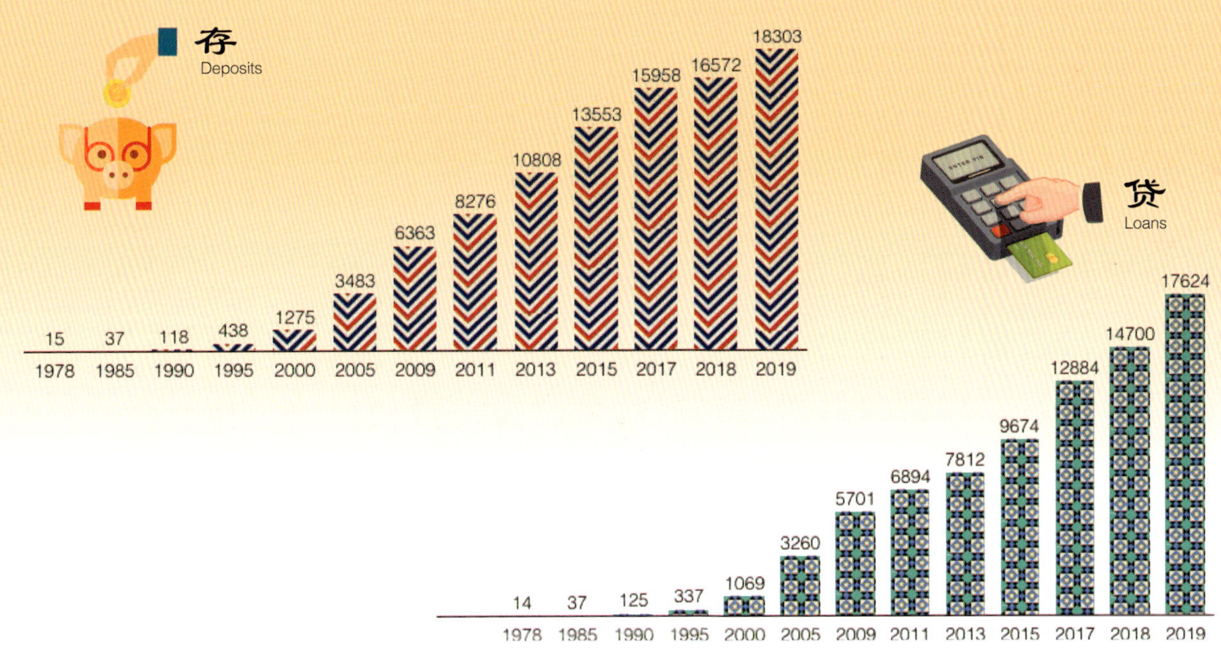

人民生活
People's Livelihood

城乡居民人均可支配收入（元）
Per Capita Disposable Income of Urban and Rural Inhabitant（yuan）

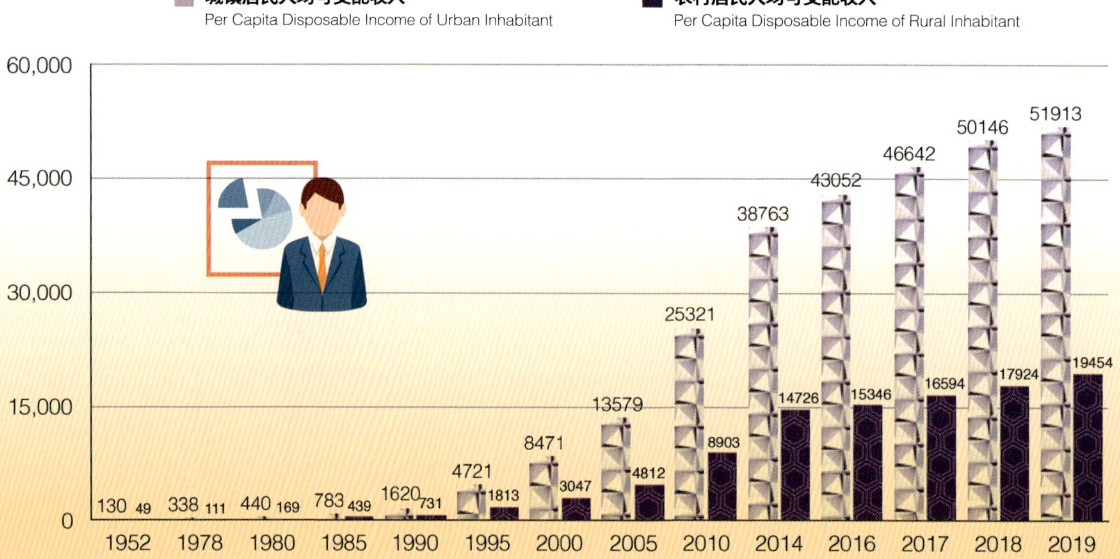

注 城乡一体化改革，2015年起为城镇居民人均支配收入和农村居民人均可支配收入口径 之前年份为城市居民人均可支配收入和农民人均纯收入口径。
Notes:The urban-rural integration reform has been based on the caliber of per capita disposable income of urban and rural residents since 2015; the urban-rural integration reform in previous years was based on the caliber of per capita disposable income of urban residents and the per capita net income of farmers.

城乡居民人均生活消费支出（元）
Per Capita Consumer Expenditure of Urban and Rural Inhabitant（yuan）

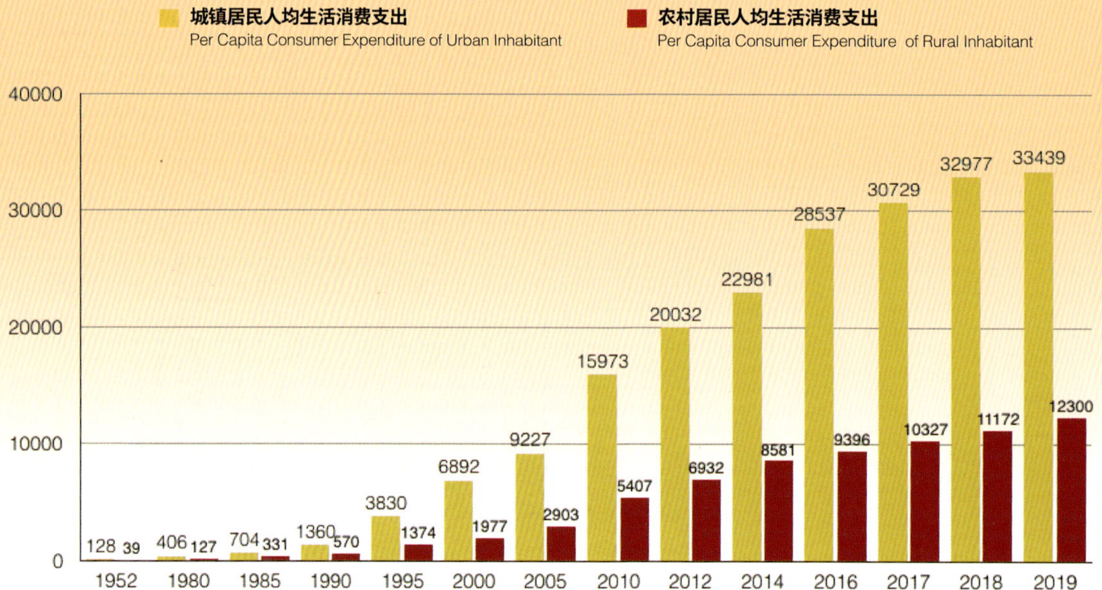

注：从2015年年开始，本市居民收支调查指标采用新口径。“农村居民人均生活消费支出”2014年以前为农民人均生活费支出口径。
Notes: Starting from 2015, the city's residents' income and expenditure survey indicators adopt a new caliber. "Per capita consumption expenditure of Rural Residents" was the "per capita living expenses of farmers" before 2014.

城镇居民与农村居民恩格尔系数（%）
Engel's Coefficient of Urban and Rural Inhabitant (%)

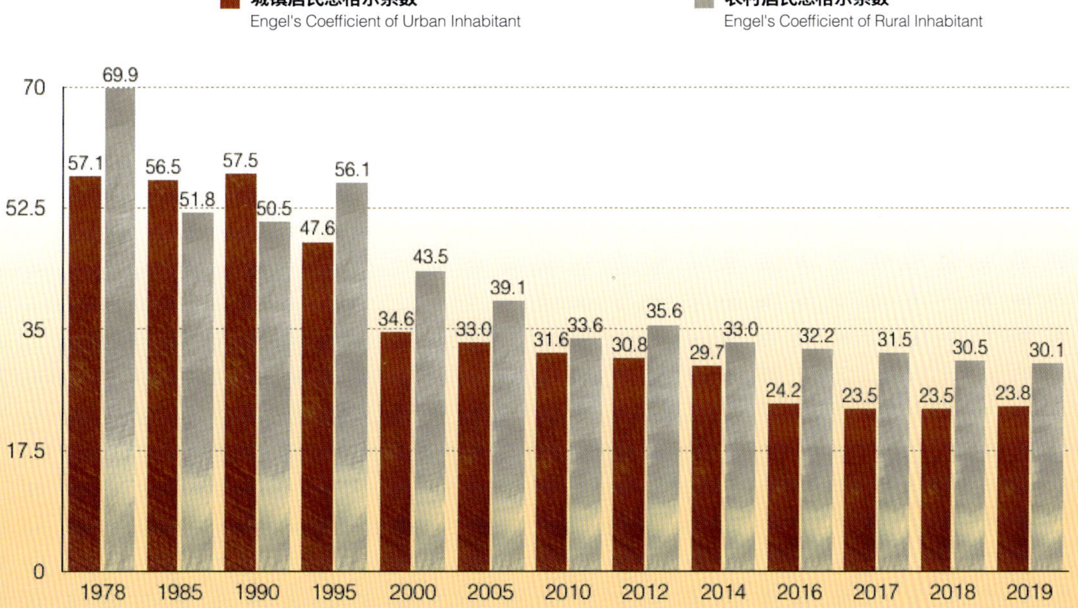

人民币住户存款余额（亿元）
The Balance RMB Household Deposits（100 millon yuan）

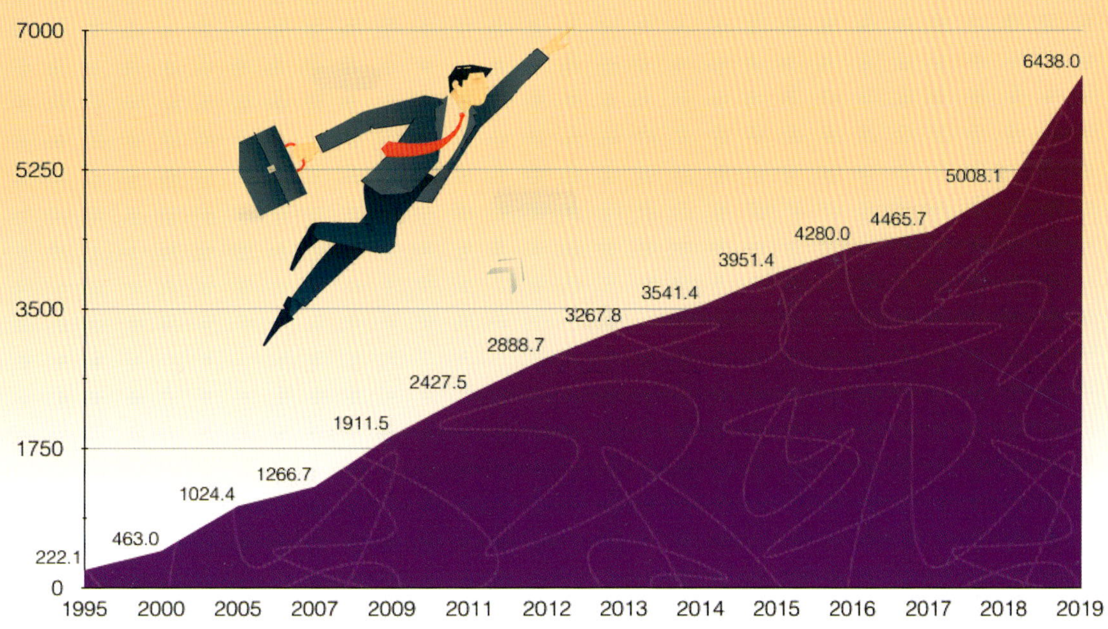

注：2015 年之前为城乡居民人民币储蓄存款余额口径，2015 年调整为住户存款余额口径。
Notes: Before 2015, the caliber was the balance of saving deposit (RMB) of urban and rural residents, and has been adjusted to balance held on deposit of households since 2015.

物 价
Prices

居民消费价格指数与商品零售价格指数（以上年为 100）
Consumer Price Index and Retail Price Index (Preceding Last Year=100)

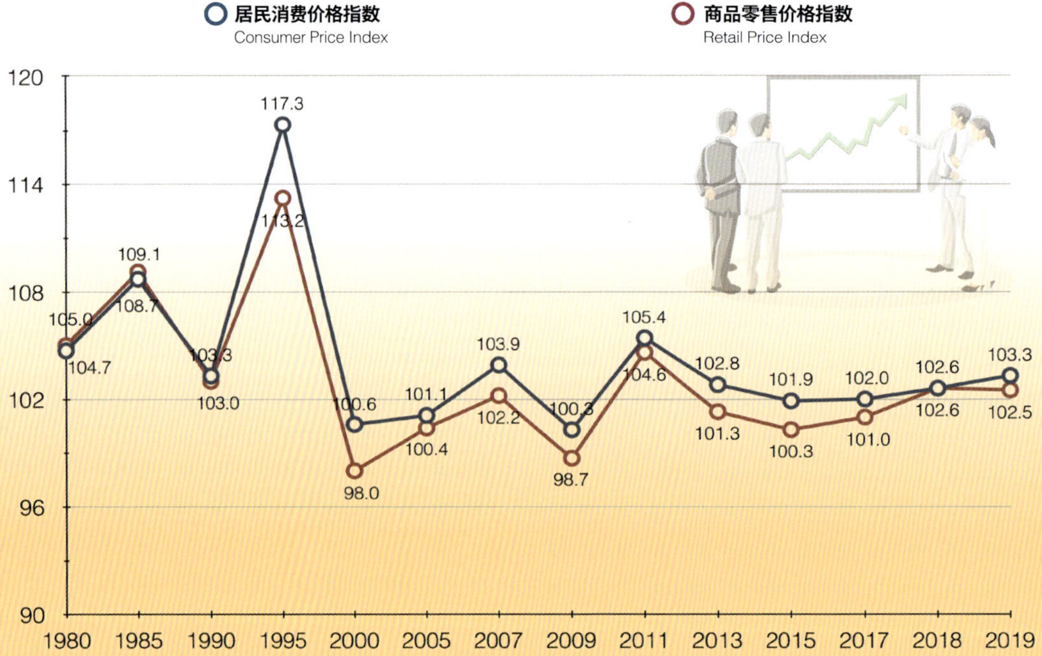

工业生产者出厂价格指数与工业生产者购进价格指数（以上年为 100）
Producer Price Index and Purchasing Price Index for Industrial Products (Preceding Last Year=100)

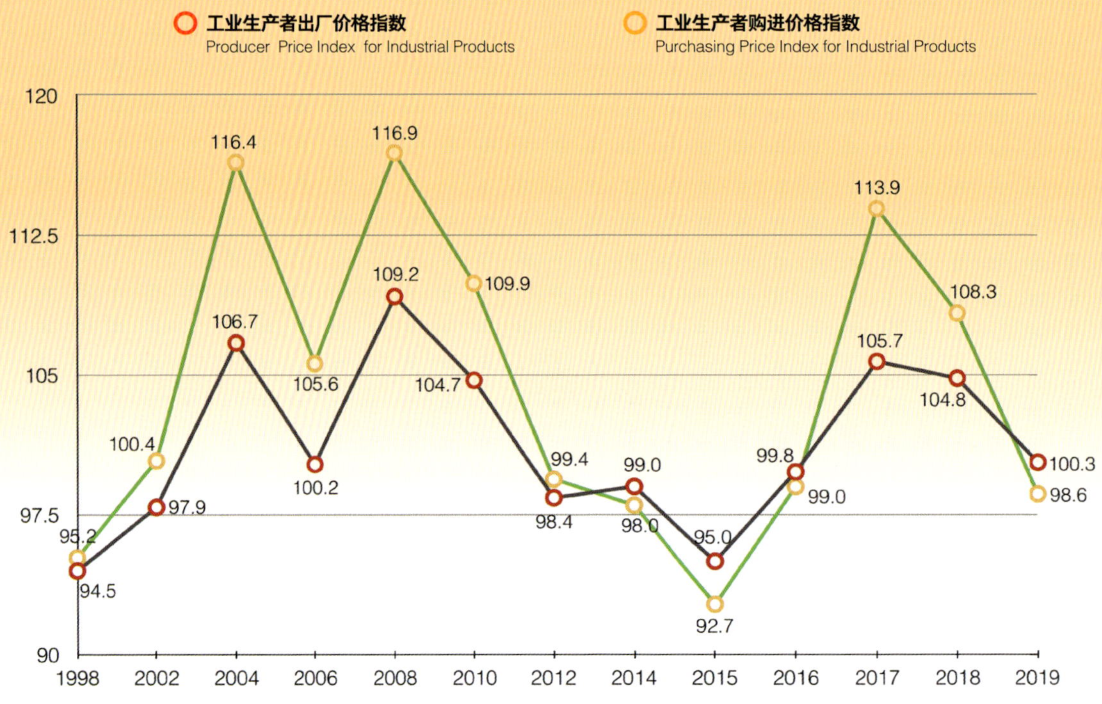

外经外贸
Foreign Trade

实际使用外资金额（万美元）
Actual Use of Foreign Capital'(USD 10 000)

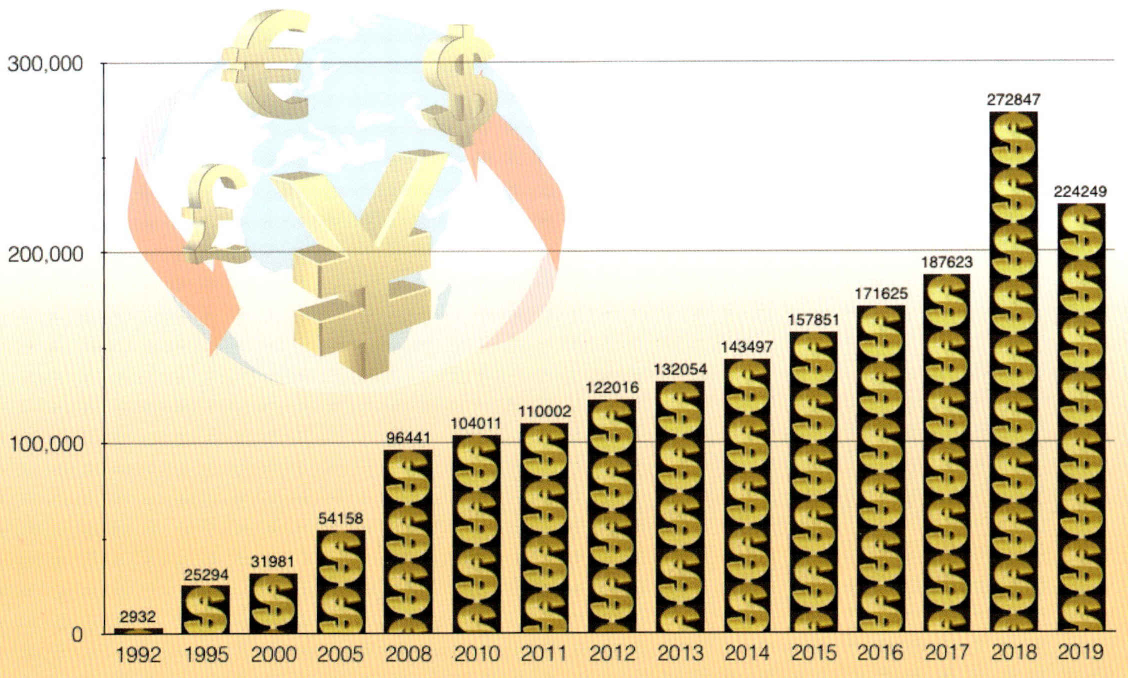

海关进出口总额（万美元）
Total Value of Imports and Exports (USD 10 000)

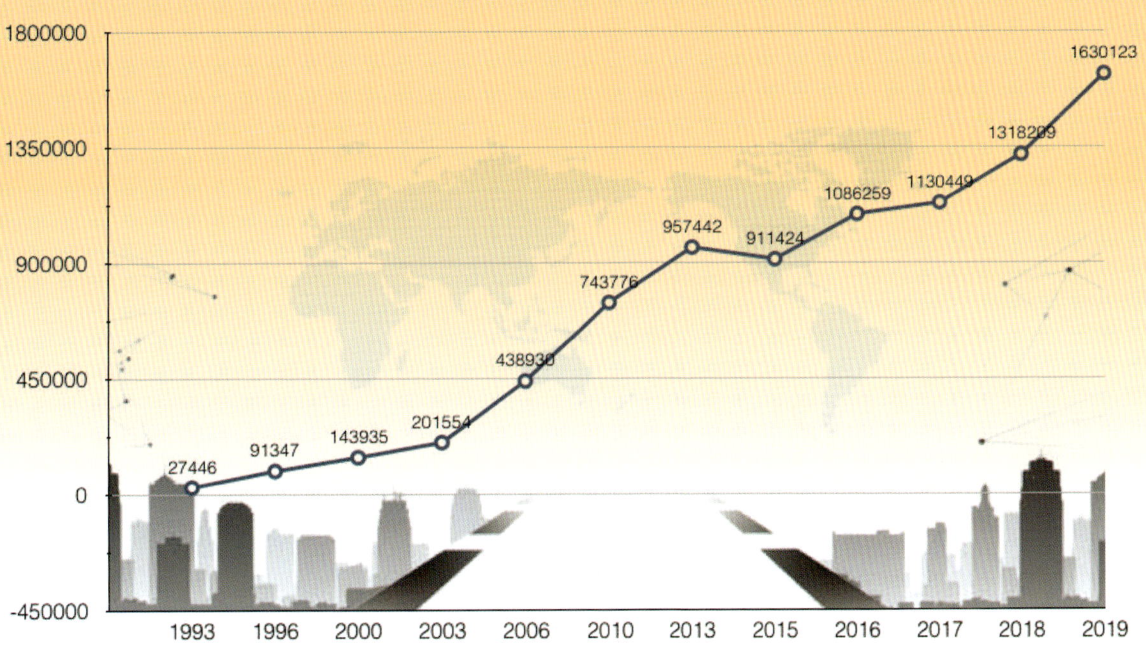

工 业
Industry

规模以上工业营业收入（亿元）
Business Revenue of Industrial Enterprises Above Designated Size (100 million yuan)

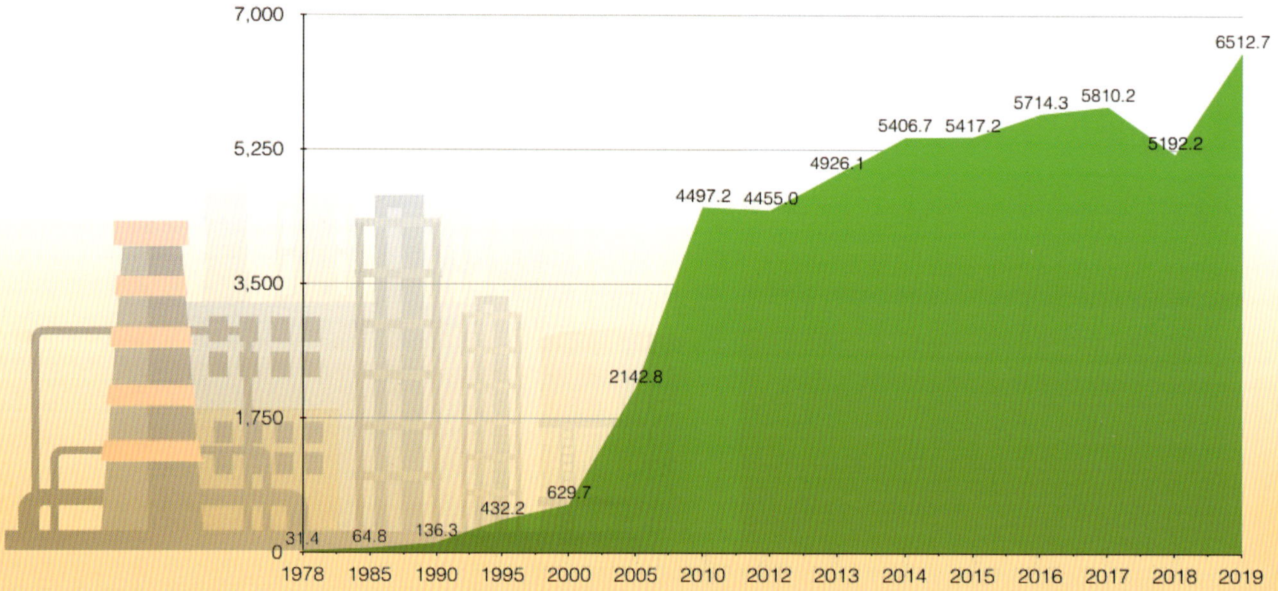

注：2018 年以前为主营业务收入口径。
Notes: Before 2018, the caliber was revenue from principal business.Revenue from principal business.

规模以上工业利税总额（亿元）
Total Profits and Taxes of Industrial Enterprises Above Designated Size (100 million yuan)

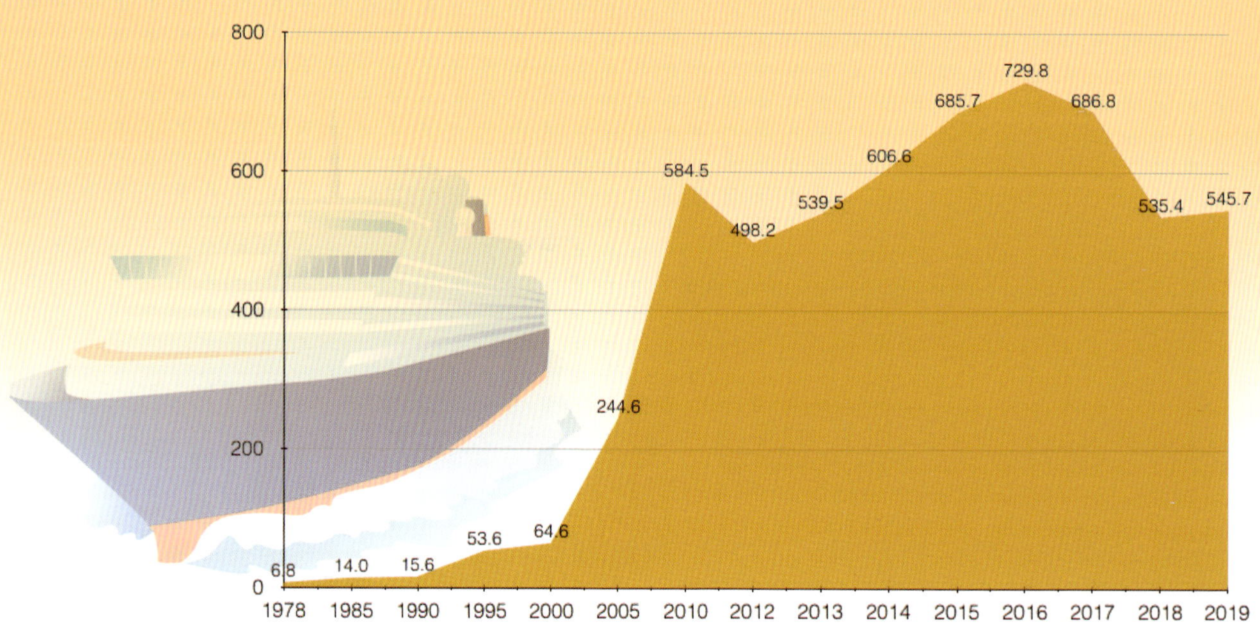

规模以上工业利润总额（亿元）

Total Profits of Industrial Enterprises Above Designated Size (100 million yuan)

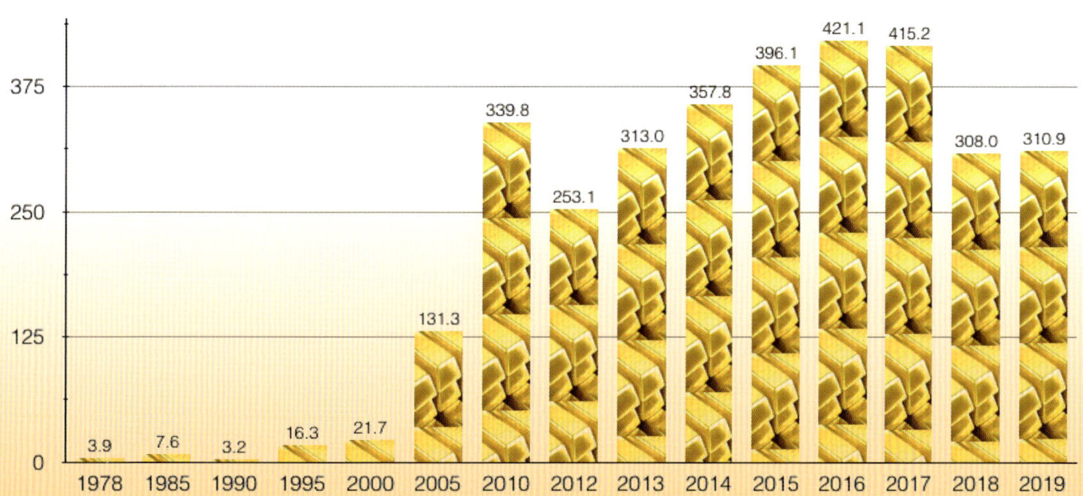

主要工业产品产量

Output of Major Industrial Products

发电量（亿千瓦时）
Power Generating Capacity (100 million kwh)

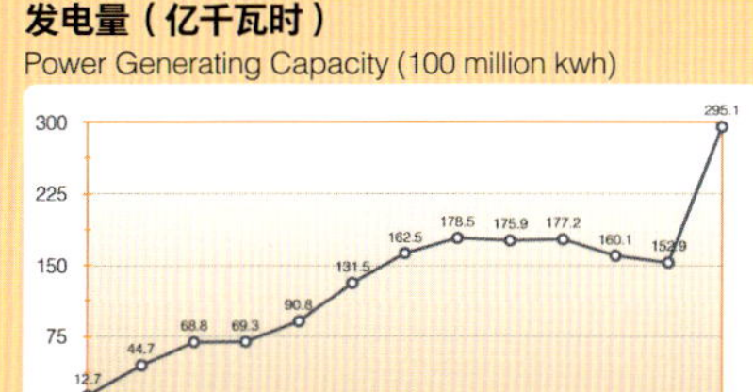

服务器（万台）
Servers (10 000 unit)

原油加工量（万吨）
Crude Processing Volume (10 000 tons)

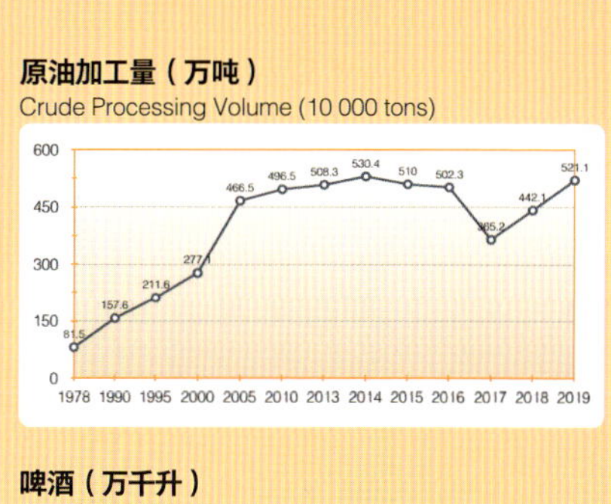

化肥（万吨）
Chemical Fertilizer (10 000 tons)

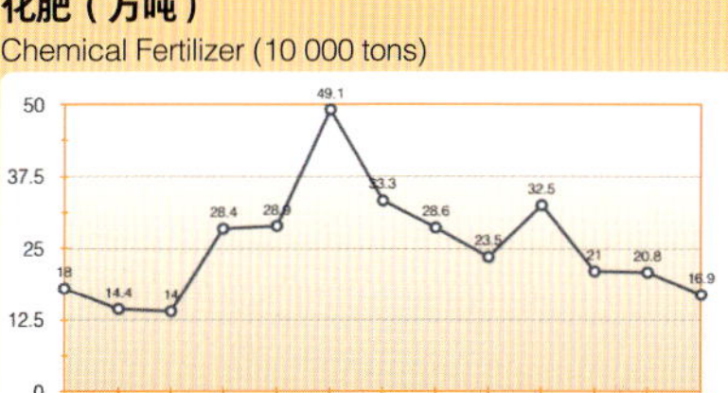

水泥（万吨）
Cement (10 000 tons)

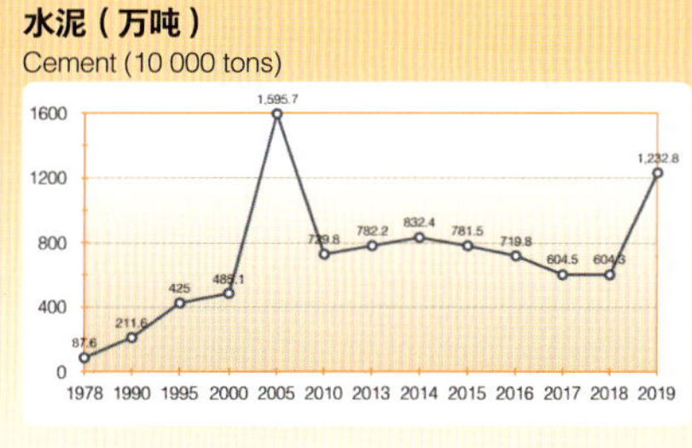

啤酒（万千升）
Beer (10 000 kiloliter)

汽车（辆）
Motor Vehicles (unit)

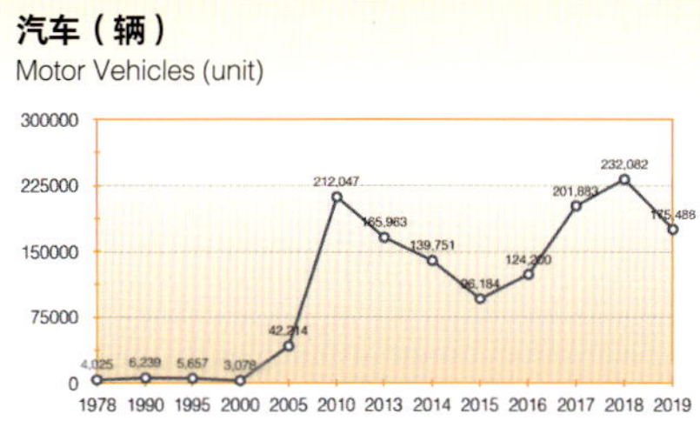

钢（万吨）
Steel (10 000 tons)

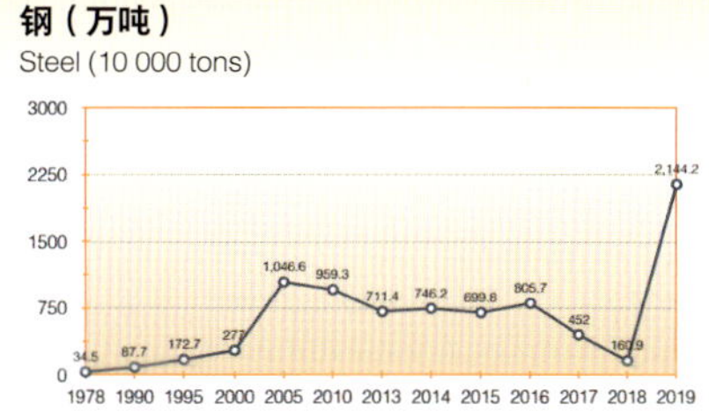

初级形态塑料（万吨）
Primary Plastic (10 000 tons)

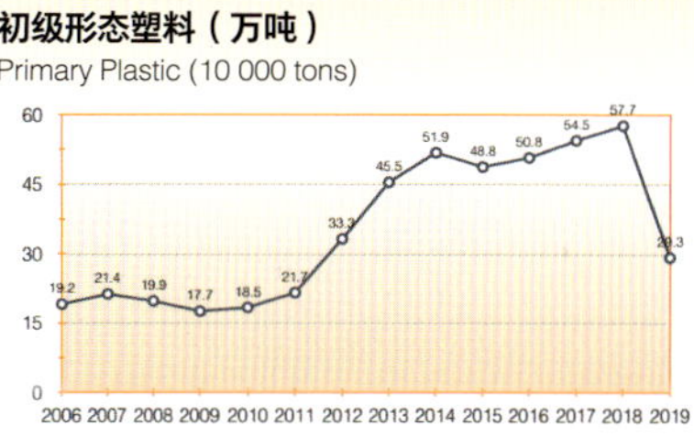

国内贸易 投资
Domestic Trade Investment

社会消费品零售总额及构成（亿元）
Total Retail Sales of Consumer Goods and Composition (100 million yuan)

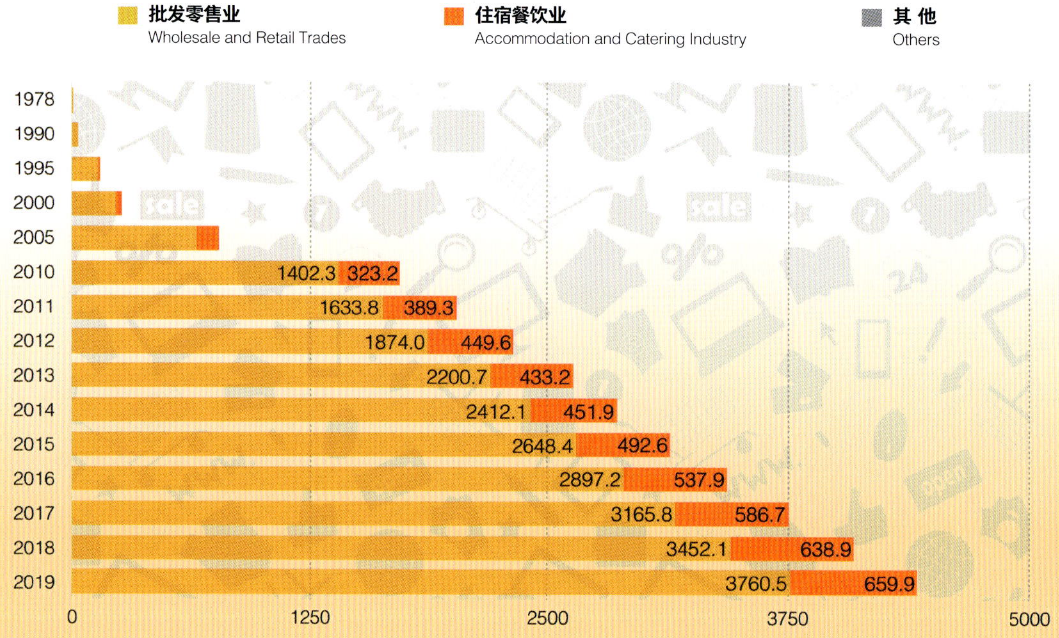

固定资产投资及构成（亿元）
Total Investment in Fixed Assets and Composition (100 million yuan)

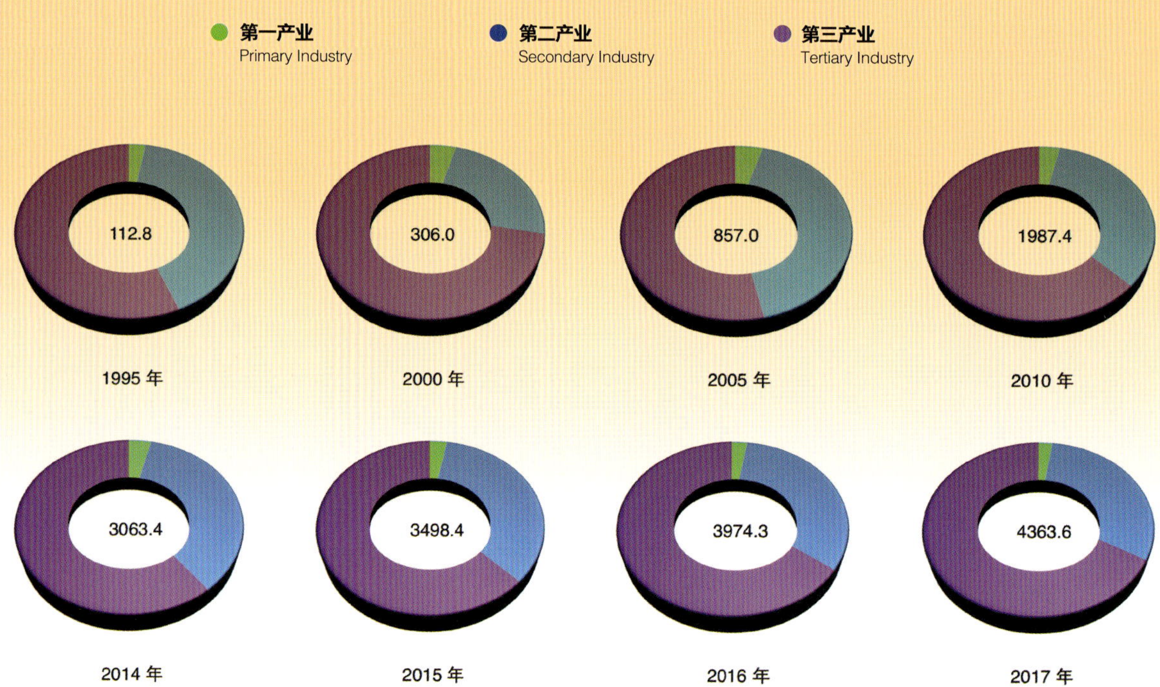

农 业
Agriculture

农林牧渔业增加值（亿元）
Added Value of Agriculture, Forestry, Animal Husbandry and Fishery (100 million yuan)

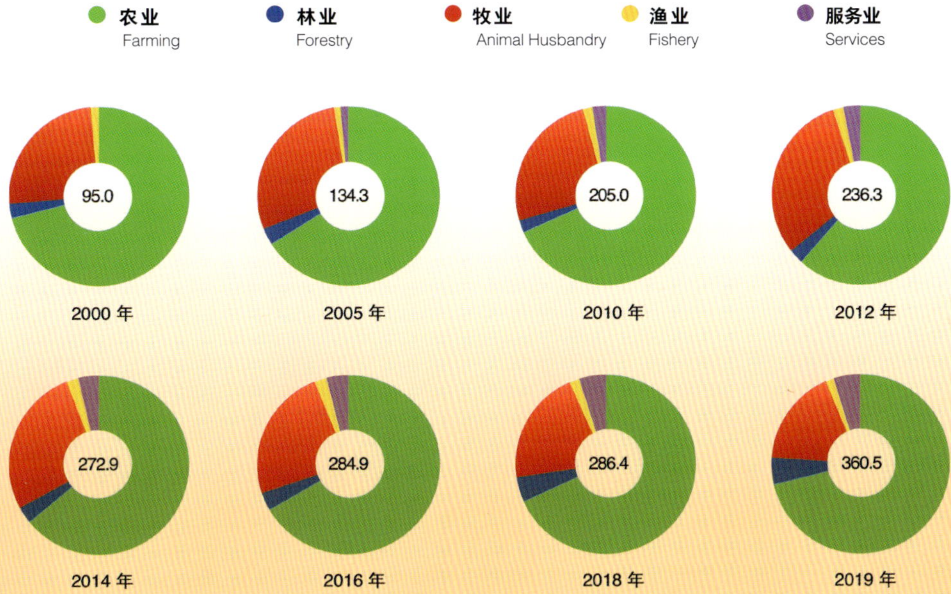

主要农产品产量（万吨）
Output of Main Agricultural Products (10 000 tons)

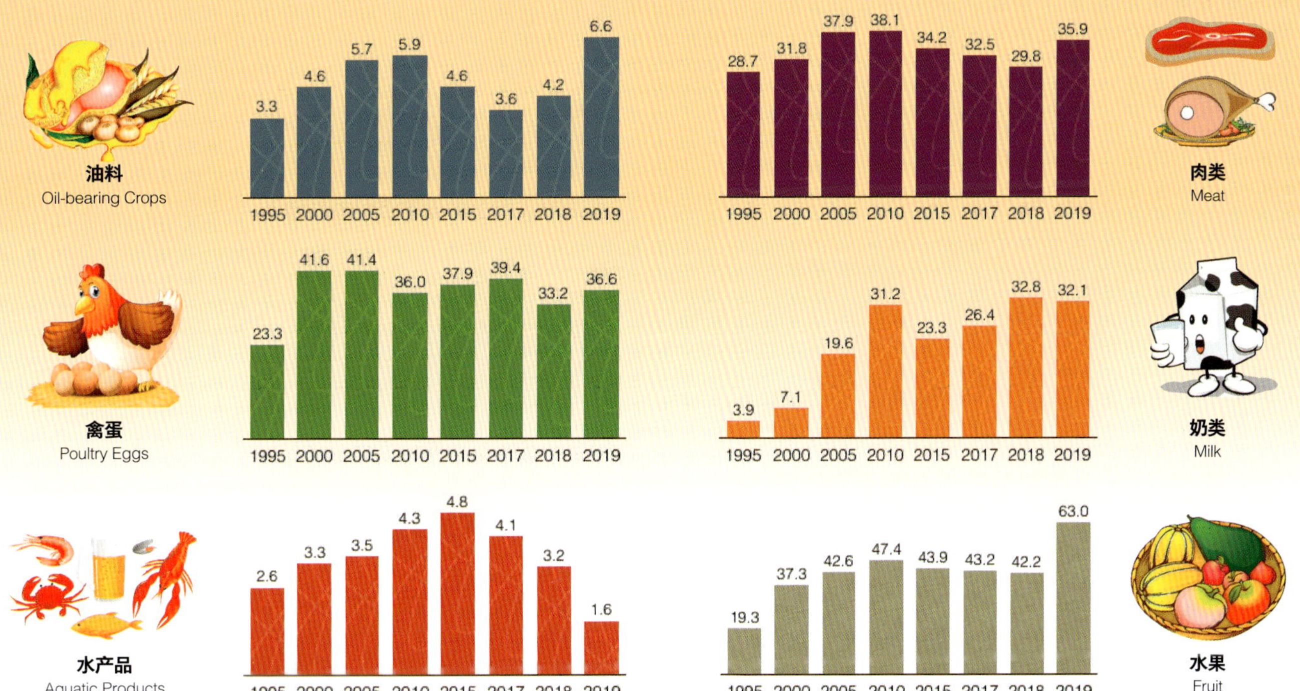

城市建设
Urban Public

供热面积（万平方米）
Area of Central Heating (10 000 sq.m)

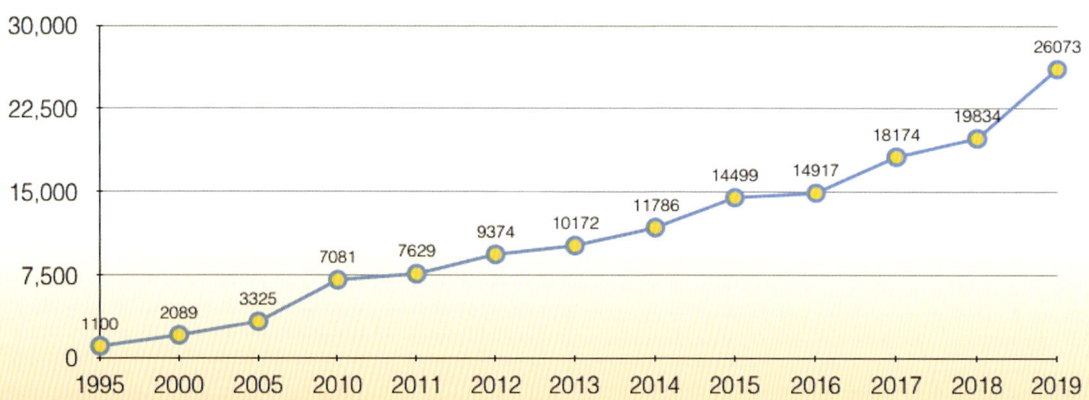

公共交通客运量（万人次）
Public Transportation of Passenger Traffic (10 000 person-times)

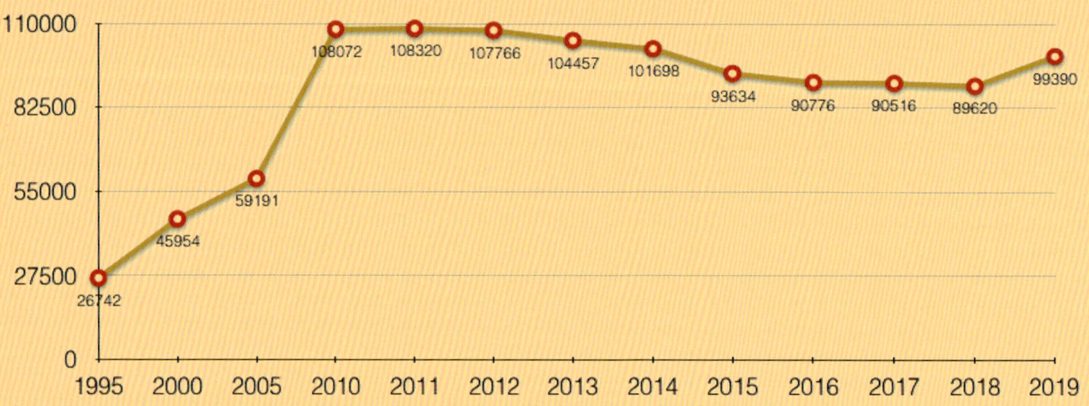

人均公园绿地面积（平方米/人）
Per Capita Public Green Area (sq.m/person)

全社会用电量（万千瓦时）
Electricity Consumption (10 000 kwh)

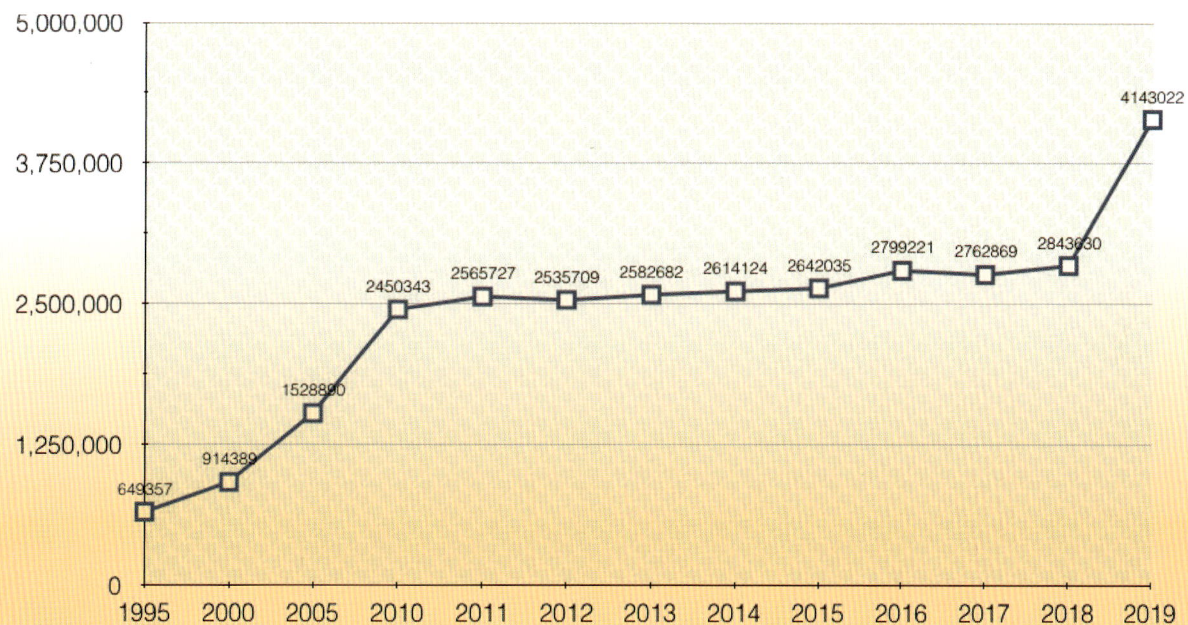

全社会供气量
Total Social Gas Supply

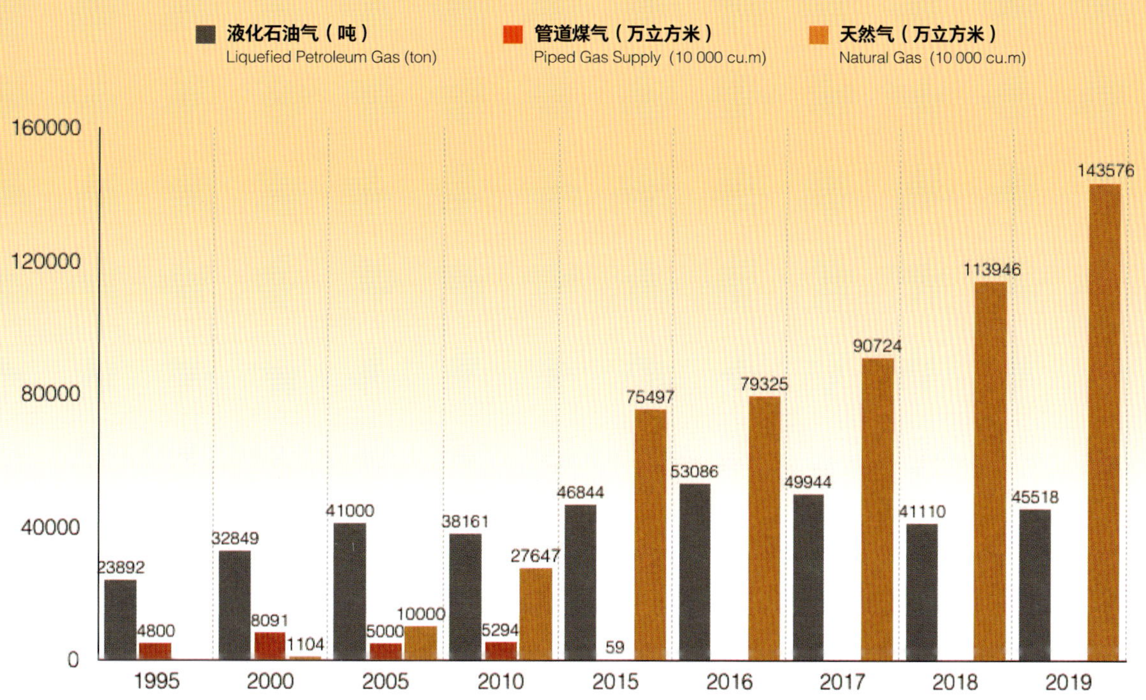

邮电 交通
Transportation Post and Telecommunication

移动电话用户、 宽带互联网接入用户数（万户）
Number of Mobile Telephone Subscribers, Subscribers of Broad Band Internet(10 000 subscribers)

■ 移动电话用户（万户） Number of Mobile Telephone Subscribers (10 000 subscribers)
■ 宽带互联网接入用户数（万户） Subscribers of Broad Band Internet (10 000 subscribers)

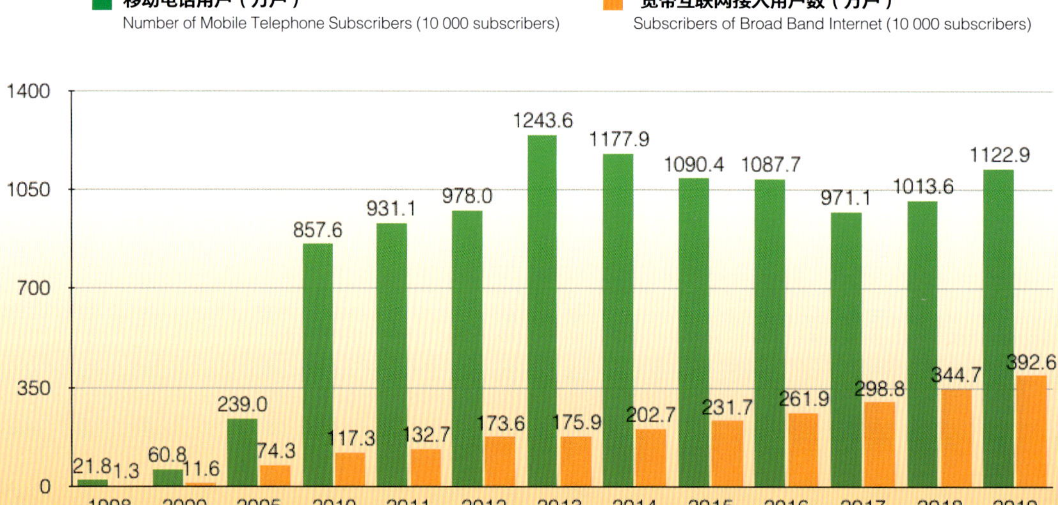

客运量（万人）
Passenger Traffic(10 000 persons)

货运量（万吨）
Freight Traffic(10 000 tons)

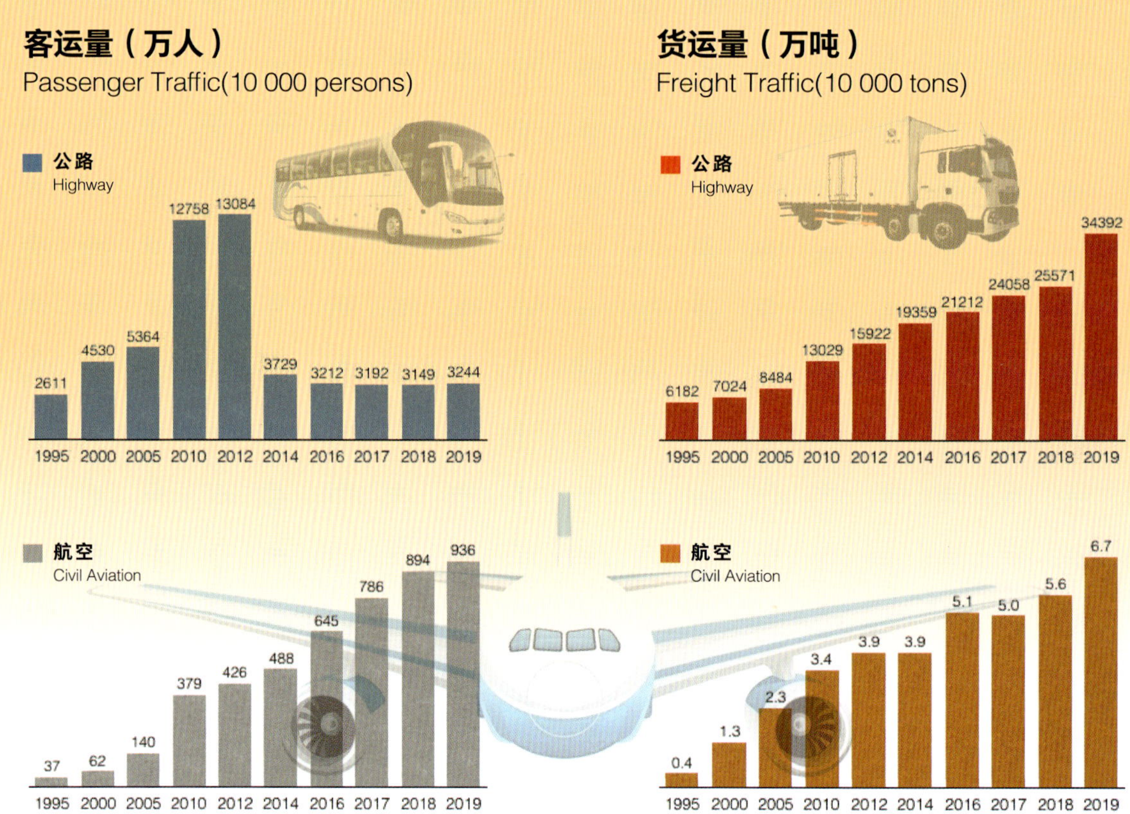

教育 卫生
Education Public Health

各类学校专任教师(人)
Full-time Teachers (person)

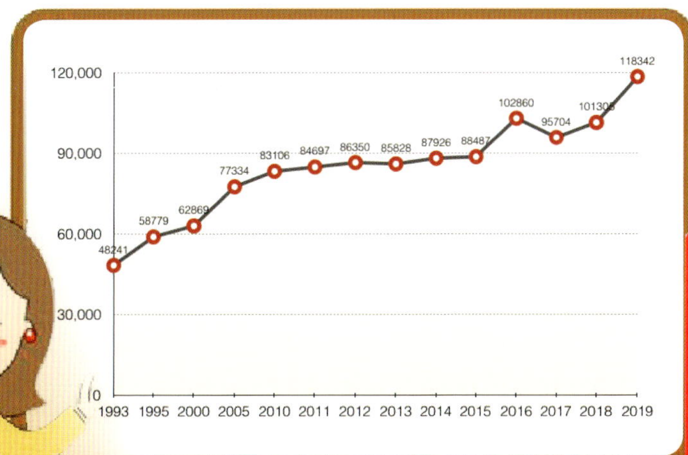

各类学校在校学生（万人）
Total Enrollment (10 000 persons)

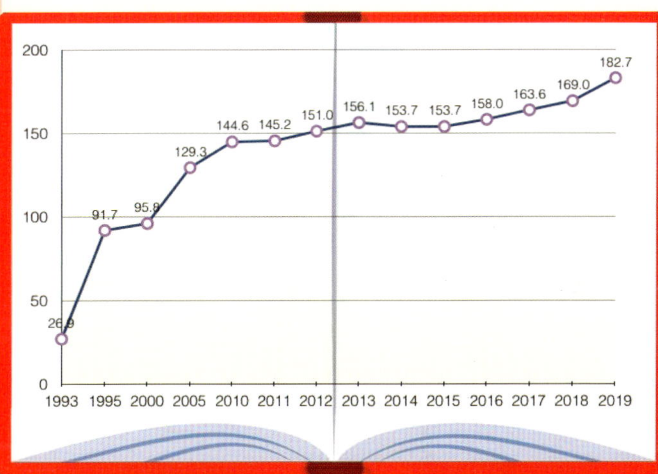

每万人拥有医院床位数（张）
Number of Hospitals Beds per 10000 Population (set)

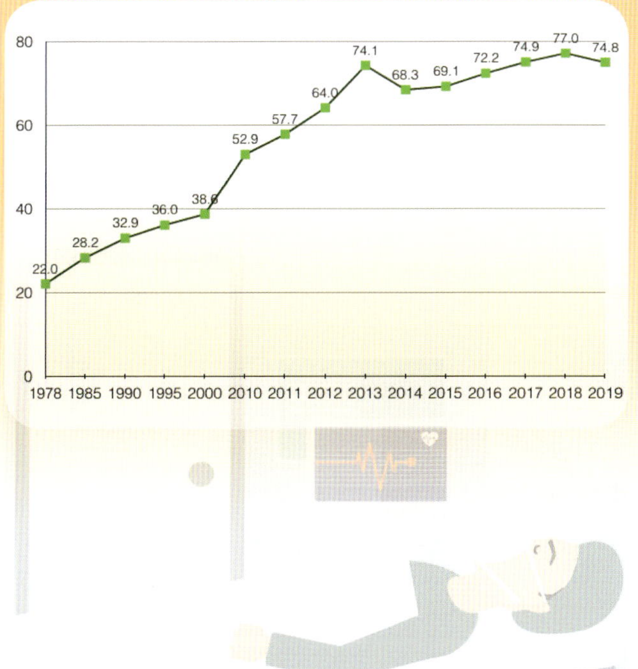

每万人拥有医生数（人）
Number of Doctors per 10000 Population (person)

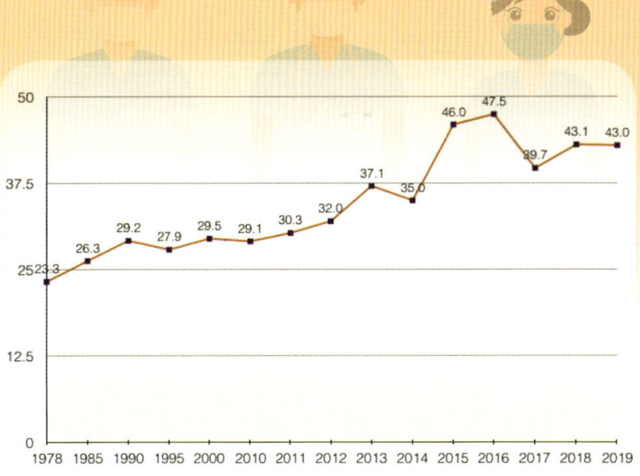

新时代·新黄河
New Era·New Yellow River Civilization

黄河的故事灿若繁星
黄河的文化源远流长
黄河的精神振奋人心

Grand Stories of Yellow River as a Multitude of Stars
Profound Cultures of Yellow River with a Long History
Impressive Spirits of Yellow River with Inspiring Enthusiasm

1

行 政 区 划

DIVISIONS OF ADMINISTRATIVE AREAS

1-1 行政区划
Divisions of Administrative Areas

单位：个 (unit)

年份地区	Year and Region	乡 Townships	镇 Towns	街道 Street Communities	村 Village	居委会 Neighborhood Committee	土地面积（平方公里）Land Area (sq.km)
全市主要年份							
1989		57	54	53	4710	702	8227
1990		57	54	48	4752	669	8227
1991		57	54	48	4752	670	8227
1992		57	54	48	4759	670	8227
1993		56	55	48	4756	670	8227
1994		55	56	48	4759	670	8227
1995		48	63	49	4723	721	8227
1996		42	68	49	4704	685	8154
1997		42	68	50	4696	616	8154
1998		42	69	50	4711	505	8154
1999		42	69	50	4714	468	8154
2000		42	69	50	4702	416	8154
2001		28	64	54	4677	417	8177
2002		27	65	54	4657	487	8177
2003		27	61	58	4657	487	8177
2004		27	61	58	4657	487	8177
2005		12	53	64	4628	400	8177
2006		11	53	64	4604	487	8177
2007		11	50	73	4563	500	8177
2008		11	50	73	4551	521	8177
2009		11	50	75	4553	522	8177
2010		6	49	86	4552	532	8177
2011		4	51	86	4538	556	8177
2012		4	51	86	4532	586	8177
2013		2	51	90	4548	597	7998
2014		2	51	90	4547	627	7998
2015		2	46	95	4546	641	7998
2016			39	104	4547	669	7998
2017			29	112	4548	711	7998
2018			29	112	4546	740	7998
2019			40	121	5551	847	10244
2019 年分地区							
市　区	Districts unber City		23	118	4267	809	8367
历下区	Li xia			13	20	114	101
市中区	Shi zhong			17	77	116	281
槐荫区	Huai yin			16	92	94	152
天桥区	Tian qiao			15	120	153	259
历城区	Li cheng			14	266	81	1301
长清区	Chang qing		3	7	580	59	1209
章丘区	Zhang qiu		3	15	890	35	1719
济阳区	Ji yang		4	6	811	46	1099
莱芜区	Lai wu		11	3	738	33	1740
钢城区	Gang cheng		2	3	211	24	506
济南高新区	Ji' nan Gao xin			5	152	40	
莱芜高新区	Laiwu Gao xin			1	56	14	
济南先行区	JN Pioneer Area						
南部山区	Nan shan			3	254		
平阴县	Ping yin		6	2	336	24	715
商河县	Shang he		11	1	948	14	1162

注：1. 指标“土地面积”2013 年起为第二次全市土地调查数据。
2. 本表内数据由相关主管部门提供。

Note: 1.Indicator “land area” is the city land survey data for the second time as of 2013.
2.The data in this table are provided by the relevant authority departments.

1-2 县区所辖镇、街道办事处(2019年末)
Town and Street Communities Under the Jurisdiction(End of 2019)

县区	Region	镇、街道办事处数量(个) Number of Towns and Street Communities (unit)	镇、街道办事处名称 Name of Towns and Street Communities
历下区	Li xia	14	大明湖街道 千佛山街道 燕山街道 泉城路街道 趵突泉街道 东关街道 解放路街道 建筑新村街道 文化东路街道 甸柳新村街道 姚家街道 智远街道 龙洞街道 舜华路街道
市中区	Shi zhong	17	泺源街道 杆石桥街道 魏家庄街道 大观园街道 四里村街道 六里山街道 七里山街道 二七新村街道 舜玉路街道 舜耕街道 王官庄街道 七贤街道 白马山街道 十六里河街道 兴隆街道 党家街道 陡沟街道
槐荫区	Huai yin	16	西市场街道 五里沟街道 道德街街道 营市街街道 青年公园街道 中大槐树街道 振兴街街道 南辛庄街道 段店北路街道 匡山街道 张庄路街道 美里湖街道 兴福街道 玉清湖街道 腊山街道 吴家堡街道
天桥区	Tian qiao	15	无影山街道 堤口路街道 宝华街街道 工人新村南村街道 工人新村北村街道 官扎营街道 北坦街道 天桥东街街道 纬北路街道 制锦市街道 北园街道 泺口街道 药山街道 桑梓店街道 大桥街道
历城区	Li cheng	21	洪家楼街道 山大路街道 东风街道 全福街道 华山街道 荷花路街道 王舍人街道 鲍山街道 郭店街道 唐冶街道 港沟街道 董家街道 彩石街道 唐王街道 孙村街道 巨野河街 临港街道 遥墙街道 仲宫街道 柳埠街道 西营镇
长清区	Chang qing	10	文昌街道 平安街道 崮云湖街道 五峰山街道 归德街道 张夏街道 万德街道 孝里镇 马山镇 双泉镇
章丘区	Zhang qiu	18	明水街道 双山街道 龙山街道 枣园街道 埠村街道 圣井街道 绣惠街道 相公庄街道 文祖街道 普集街道 官庄街道 高官寨街道 白云湖街道 宁家埠街道 曹范街道 垛庄镇 刁镇 黄河镇
济阳区	Ji yang	10	济阳街道 济北街道 回河街道 垛石镇 曲堤镇 仁风镇 新市镇 孙耿街道 太平街道 崔寨街道
莱芜区	Lai wu	15	凤城街道 张家洼街道 高庄街道 口镇 洋里镇 方下镇 牛泉镇 苗山镇 雪野镇 大王庄镇 寨里镇 杨庄镇 茶叶口镇 和庄镇 鹏泉街道
钢城区	Gang cheng	5	艾山街道 里辛街道 汶源街道 颜庄镇 辛庄镇
平阴县	Ping yin	8	榆山街道 锦水街道 洪范池镇 东阿镇 孔村镇 孝直镇 玫瑰镇 安城镇
商河县	Shang he	12	许商街道 玉皇庙镇 龙桑寺镇 贾庄镇 殷巷镇 郑路镇 怀仁镇 白桥镇 孙集镇 韩庙镇 张坊镇 沙河镇

人 口

POPULATION

2-1 主要年份总户数、总人口（户籍人口）
Total Household and Population in Major Years(registered population)

年份 Year	年末总户数 （万户） Total year-end Households (10 000 households)	年末总人口 （万人） Total year-end Population (10 000 persons)	按性别分（万人） Grouped by Sex (10 000 persons)		性别比 （女＝100） Sex Ratio (Femal=100)	年平均人口 （万人） Annual Average Population (10 000 persons)	比上年增长 （‰） Growth Rate （‰）	人口密度 （人/平方公里） Density of Population (Person/sq.km)
			男性 Male	女性 Femal				
1952	70.19	318.66	157.68	160.98	97.95	315.94	3.30	387
1957	76.44	346.38	170.30	176.09	96.71	343.25	17.40	421
1962	81.45	351.44	174.55	176.89	98.68	350.18	-4.60	427
1965	83.01	373.22	186.08	187.14	99.43	370.24	19.50	454
1970	89.48	407.50	203.16	204.34	99.42	404.17	16.60	495
1975	96.54	437.73	217.82	219.91	99.05	435.15	9.90	532
1976	98.63	442.09	220.89	221.20	99.86	439.91	10.90	537
1977	100.60	445.05	222.46	222.59	99.94	443.57	8.30	541
1978	102.93	450.67	226.31	224.36	100.87	447.86	9.70	548
1979	105.34	456.37	228.57	227.80	100.34	453.52	12.60	555
1980	106.83	458.61	230.47	228.15	101.02	457.49	8.80	557
1981	110.52	467.93	235.35	232.58	101.19	463.27	12.60	569
1982	112.51	474.23	238.99	235.26	101.59	471.08	16.80	576
1983	114.92	479.38	242.02	237.36	101.54	476.81	12.20	583
1984	116.92	483.85	244.32	239.53	102.00	481.62	10.10	588
1985	120.19	488.39	246.86	241.53	102.21	486.12	9.30	594
1986	122.67	494.06	250.09	243.97	102.51	491.23	10.50	601
1987	125.43	501.03	253.95	247.08	102.78	497.55	12.90	609
1988	130.32	507.18	257.22	249.86	102.95	504.11	13.20	616
1989	134.77	513.39	260.79	252.61	103.24	510.29	12.30	624
1990	140.36	523.60	265.91	257.69	103.19	518.50	16.10	636
1991	143.42	527.43	267.78	259.65	103.13	525.52	13.50	641
1992	147.50	530.70	269.46	261.25	103.14	529.07	6.70	645
1993	149.42	533.53	270.77	262.76	103.05	532.12	5.80	649

2-1 续表 continued

年份 Year	年末总户数 (万户) Total year-end Households (10 000 households)	年末总人口 (万人) Total year-end Population (10 000 persons)	按性别分 (万人) Grouped by Sex (10 000 persons)		性别比 (女=100) Sex Ratio (Femal=100)	年平均人口 (万人) Annual Average Population (10 000 persons)	比上年增长 (‰) Growth Rate (‰)	人口密度 (人/平方公里) Density of Population (Person/sq.km)
			男性 Male	女性 Femal				
1994	153.60	537.31	272.76	264.54	103.11	535.42	6.20	653
1995	156.45	542.12	274.98	267.14	102.93	539.72	8.00	656
1996	156.42	543.45	275.59	267.86	102.89	542.79	5.70	666
1997	157.66	549.20	278.30	270.90	102.73	546.33	6.50	674
1998	160.93	553.54	279.91	273.63	102.30	551.37	9.20	679
1999	163.52	557.63	281.71	275.93	102.09	555.59	7.70	684
2000	166.63	562.65	284.19	278.46	102.06	560.14	8.20	690
2001	168.46	569.00	287.39	281.61	102.06	565.83	10.20	696
2002	170.10	575.01	290.58	284.43	102.16	572.00	10.90	703
2003	172.18	582.56	294.04	288.52	101.91	578.78	11.90	712
2004	173.24	590.08	297.25	292.82	101.51	586.32	13.03	722
2005	177.69	597.44	300.42	297.02	101.15	593.76	12.69	731
2006	179.48	603.35	302.72	300.63	100.70	600.39	11.17	738
2007	181.88	604.85	302.87	301.98	100.29	604.10	6.17	740
2008	184.63	603.99	302.00	301.99	100.00	604.42	0.53	739
2009	187.70	603.27	301.26	302.01	99.75	603.63	-1.30	738
2010	190.65	604.08	301.28	302.80	99.50	603.68	0.08	739
2011	193.61	606.64	302.19	304.44	99.26	605.36	2.78	742
2012	195.79	609.21	303.30	305.91	99.15	607.92	4.23	745
2013	199.67	613.25	304.93	308.32	98.90	611.23	5.44	767
2014	201.93	621.61	309.09	312.52	98.90	617.43	15.64	777
2015	203.59	625.73	310.92	314.80	98.77	623.67	10.11	782
2016	205.45	632.83	314.28	318.55	98.66	629.28	9.00	791
2017	208.08	643.62	319.21	324.41	98.40	638.22	14.21	805
2018	216.64	655.90	324.74	331.15	98.06	649.76	19.08	820
2019	270.26	796.74	395.30	401.44	98.47	726.32	21.47	778

2-2 主要年份市区总户数、总人口（户籍人口）
Total Household and Population of Urban in Major Years(registered population)

年份 Year	年末总户数 （万户） Total year-end Households (10 000 households)	年末总人口 （万人） Total year-end Population (10 000 persons)	按性别分（万人） Grouped by Sex (10 000 persons)		年平均人口 （万人） Annual Average Population (10 000 persons)
			男性 Male	女性 Femal	
1952	26.46	124.96	63.95	61.01	123.83
1957	29.13	143.17	72.05	71.13	140.11
1962	32.25	153.35	78.52	74.83	154.18
1965	34.03	162.82	83.20	79.62	161.90
1970	37.21	167.82	85.61	82.21	168.51
1975	40.67	178.78	90.83	87.95	177.74
1976	41.59	180.99	91.83	89.16	179.88
1977	42.34	181.49	91.92	89.57	181.24
1978	43.79	186.43	94.70	91.73	183.96
1979	45.33	189.26	96.22	93.04	187.84
1980	46.12	190.01	97.22	92.79	189.63
1981	48.64	194.05	99.37	94.69	192.03
1982	50.60	201.31	101.44	99.87	197.68
1983	52.32	205.48	103.42	102.07	203.39
1984	54.30	209.55	105.57	103.99	207.52
1985	56.88	213.28	107.96	105.33	211.42
1986	58.65	216.98	111.54	105.43	215.13
1987	60.54	221.49	113.79	107.70	219.23
1988	63.03	225.00	115.51	109.39	223.25
1989	65.29	228.88	117.49	111.39	226.94
1990	81.22	283.66	145.29	138.36	
1991	83.30	286.20	146.55	139.65	284.93
1992	85.87	288.52	145.19	143.33	287.36
1993	88.02	291.24	149.07	142.17	289.88
1994	90.10	294.60	150.75	143.85	292.92
1995	92.04	299.20	152.97	146.23	296.90

2-2 续表 continued

年份 Year	年末总户数 (万户) Total year-end Households (10 000 households)	年末总人口 (万人) Total year-end Population (10 000 persons)	按性别分 (万人) Grouped by Sex (10 000 persons)		年平均人口 (万人) Annual Average Population (10 000 persons)
			男性 Male	女性 Femal	
1996	93.12	302.78	154.58	148.20	300.99
1997	93.90	306.98	156.54	150.44	304.88
1998	96.65	309.90	157.58	152.32	308.44
1999	97.74	313.18	159.19	153.99	311.54
2000	99.25	317.20	161.03	156.17	315.19
2001	100.53	322.45	163.73	158.72	319.83
2002	101.62	327.55	166.43	161.12	325.00
2003	102.71	334.80	169.84	164.96	331.18
2004	102.68	341.73	172.91	168.82	338.27
2005	104.87	347.87	175.41	172.45	344.80
2006	106.19	352.29	177.10	175.19	350.08
2007	107.55	352.71	176.70	176.01	352.50
2008	109.26	350.23	175.08	175.15	351.47
2009	111.07	348.24	173.71	174.53	349.24
2010	112.91	348.02	173.19	174.83	348.13
2011	114.75	349.44	173.51	175.93	348.73
2012	116.49	352.17	174.55	177.62	350.81
2013	118.50	355.38	175.86	179.52	353.78
2014	120.33	360.99	178.55	182.44	358.19
2015	121.96	364.54	180.12	184.42	362.77
2016	154.64	473.33	233.74	239.59	418.94
2017	157.42	483.75	238.48	245.27	478.54
2018	182.76	554.13	273.31	280.82	518.94
2019	236.31	695.09	343.90	351.19	68 9.31

注：1990 年以前的数据中不包括长清区。2016 年起数据包括章丘区。2018 年起数据包括济阳区。2019 年起数据包括莱芜区、钢城区。

Note: The data before 1990 excludes Changqing District. The data as of 2016 includes Zhangqiu District The data as of 2018 includes Jiyang District. Data after the year of 2019 involves Laiwu District and Gangcheng District.

2-3 主要年份人口自然变动情况
Natural Changes of Population in Major Years

年份 Year	申报出生人口 （人） Population of Birth (person)	申报出生率 (‰) Birth Rate (‰)	申报死亡人口 （人） Population of Death (person)	申报死亡率 (‰) Death Rate (‰)	人口自然增长 （人） Population of Natural Growth (person)	人口自然增长率 (‰) Natural Growth Rate (‰)
1952	72861	23.06	29949	9.48	42912	13.58
1957	108432	31.59	38082	11.09	70350	20.50
1962	108029	30.85	44464	12.70	63565	18.15
1965	121364	32.78	39355	10.63	82009	22.15
1970	111861	27.68	29965	7.41	81896	20.27
1975	82939	19.06	33837	7.78	49102	11.28
1976	70065	15.93	34693	7.89	35372	8.04
1977	67413	15.20	33723	7.60	33690	7.60
1978	69541	15.53	31343	7.00	38198	8.53
1979	72596	16.01	30205	6.66	42391	9.35
1980	60336	13.19	32004	7.00	28332	6.19
1981	70327	15.18	31671	6.84	38656	8.34
1982	74147	15.74	28679	6.09	45468	9.65
1983	56454	11.84	30080	6.31	26374	5.53
1984	61156	12.70	32277	6.70	28879	6.00
1985	55386	11.39	31678	6.52	23708	4.87
1986	69901	14.23	30790	6.27	39111	7.96
1987	86752	17.44	30007	6.03	56745	11.41
1988	78922	15.66	32850	6.52	46072	9.14
1989	76380	14.97	30721	6.02	45659	8.95
1990	66806	12.88	33916	6.54	32890	6.34
1991	59374	11.30	32675	6.20	26699	5.10
1992	52825	9.98	34969	6.61	17856	3.37
1993	46007	8.65	35317	6.64	10690	2.01
1994	49940	9.30	35308	6.60	14632	2.70
1995	54132	10.03	34107	6.32	20025	3.71

2-3 续表 continued

年份 Year	申报出生人口 (人) Population of Birth (person)	申报出生率 (‰) Birth Rate (‰)	申报死亡人口 (人) Population of Death (person)	申报死亡率 (‰) Death Rate (‰)	人口自然增长 (人) Population of Natural Growth (person)	人口自然增长率 (‰) Natural Growth Rate (‰)
1996	58254	10.73	36452	6.71	21802	4.02
1997	62245	11.39	35768	6.55	26477	4.84
1998	62490	11.33	36497	6.64	25893	4.69
1999	55931	10.07	34956	6.29	20975	3.78
2000	62059	11.08	39499	7.05	22560	4.03
2001	55536	9.82	33816	5.98	21720	3.84
2002	57317	10.02	36234	6.33	21083	3.69
2003	54599	9.43	42539	7.35	12060	2.08
2004	60670	10.35	38158	6.51	22512	3.84
2005	60240	10.15	37782	6.36	22458	3.78
2006	57706	9.61	39040	6.50	18666	3.11
2007	58367	9.66	39752	6.58	18615	3.08
2008	59600	9.86	39887	6.60	19713	3.26
2009	56694	9.39	40911	6.78	15783	2.61
2010	67162	11.13	50380	8.35	16782	2.78
2011	66563	11.00	40310	6.66	26253	4.34
2012	71449	11.75	49148	8.08	22301	3.67
2013	69351	11.35	41713	6.82	27638	4.53
2014	110503	17.90	41887	6.78	68616	11.11
2015	73688	11.82	41999	6.73	31689	5.09
2016	91941	14.61	39460	6.27	52481	8.34
2017	113766	17.83	62958	9.86	50808	7.96
2018	94694	14.57	45374	6.98	49320	7.59
2019	101723	12.86	52396	6.62	49327	6.24

2-4 分地区户数、人口数(2019年)(户籍人口)
Household and Population by Region(2019)(registered population)

地区	Region	户数（万户）Households (10 000 households)	人口数（万人）Population (10 000 persons)	按性别分（万人）Grouped by Sex (10 000 persons)	
				男性 Male	女性 Femal
全 市	Total City	270.26	796.74	395.30	401.44
市 区	Districts unber City	236.31	695.09	343.9	351.19
历下区	Li xia	24.43	71.36	34.90	36.46
市中区	Shi zhong	24.31	66.46	32.41	34.05
槐荫区	Huai yin	16.43	45.14	21.87	23.27
天桥区	Tian qiao	19.31	53.19	25.99	27.20
历城区	Li cheng	35.77	106.93	52.71	54.22
长清区	Chang qing	18.26	57.19	28.48	28.72
章丘区	Zhang qiu	31.70	105.53	52.18	53.35
济阳区	Ji yang	17.45	59.72	30.03	29.69
莱芜区	Lai wu	37.58	99.48	49.87	49.62
钢城区	Gang cheng	11.07	30.09	15.48	14.61
平阴县	Ping yin	13.56	37.38	18.73	18.66
商河县	Shang he	20.40	64.27	32.67	31.60

2-5 计划生育情况 (2019)
Basic Statistics of Family Planning (2019)

地区	Region	合法生育（人）Legal Childbearing (person)			出生政策符合率 (%) Legitimate Fertility (%)	违法生育（人）Illegal Childbearing (person)		
		一孩 First Child	二孩 Second Child	三孩 Third Child		一孩 First Child	二孩 Second Child	三孩 Third Child
总　计	Total	29344	41082	1323	95.19	410	77	3000
市　区	Districts unber City	26385	35348	1055	95.70	296	49	2202
历下区	Li xia	2947	2823	76	99.93	1	0	3
市中区	Shi zhong	1952	2259	61	97.92	4	0	85
槐荫区	Huai yin	1728	2143	53	98.13	3	0	72
天桥区	Tian qiao	1863	2071	44	97.17	13	4	92
历城区	Li cheng	3353	3946	105	97.55	7	2	171
长清区	Chang qing	2326	3159	70	95.15	36	5	237
章丘区	Zhang qiu	3827	4906	119	96.02	62	2	288
济阳区	Ji yang	1353	2679	149	90.34	69	8	350
莱芜区	Lai wu	2800	4582	141	95.73	33	8	295
钢城区	Gang cheng	748	1543	53	94.56	10	4	120
济南高新区	Ji’ nan Gao xin	1724	1924	47	97.93	6	3	66
济南先行区	JN Pioneer Area	973	1999	83	88.71	50	7	319
南部山区	Nan shan	791	1314	54	94.98	2	6	104
平阴县	Ping yin	1297	2216	69	96.11	13	1	122
商河县	Shang he	1662	3518	199	86.50	101	27	676

2-6 分地区人口机械变动情况(2019年)

Un-Natural Changes of Population by Region (2019)

地区	Region	迁入人口（人）Move Into the Population (person)	迁入率（‰）Move In Rate (‰)	迁出人口（人）Move Out the Population (person)	迁出率（‰）Move Out Rate (‰)	人口机械增长（人）Mechanical Growth of Population (person)	人口机械增长率（‰）Mechanical Growth Rates of Population (‰)
全 市	Total	100434	12.61	34433	4.32	66001	8.28
市 区	Districts unber City	95392	13.72	25189	3.62	70203	10.10
历下区	Li xia	20868	29.24	4753	6.66	16115	22.58
市中区	Shi zhong	12823	19.29	2970	4.47	9853	14.83
槐荫区	Huai yin	13618	30.17	1727	3.83	11891	26.34
天桥区	Tian qiao	10052	18.90	1781	3.35	8271	15.55
历城区	Li cheng	23543	22.02	3452	3.23	20091	18.79
长清区	Chang qing	4382	7.66	1480	2.59	2902	5.07
章丘区	Zhang qiu	3776	3.58	2512	2.38	1264	1.20
济阳区	Ji yang	3127	5.24	2298	3.85	829	1.39
莱芜区	Lai wu	2378	2.39	2759	2.77	–381	–0.38
钢城区	Gang cheng	825	2.74	1457	4.84	–632	–2.10
平阴县	Ping yin	2100	5.62	4144	11.08	–2044	–5.47
商河县	Shang he	2942	4.58	5100	7.93	–2158	–3.36

2-7 分地区人口自然变动情况(2019年)

Natural Changes of Population by Region (2019)

地区	Region	申报出生人口（人）Population of Birth (person)	申报出生率（‰）Birth Rate (‰)	申报死亡人口（人）Population of Death (person)	申报死亡率（‰）Death Rate (‰)	人口自然增长（人）Population of Natural Growth (person)	人口自然增长率（‰）Natural Growth Rate (‰)
全 市	Total	101723	12.86	52396	6.62	49327	6.24
市 区	Districts unber City	90406	13.01	44517	6.40	45889	6.60
历下区	Li xia	10720	15.02	3031	4.25	7689	10.78
市中区	Shi zhong	9091	13.68	3511	5.28	5580	8.40
槐荫区	Huai yin	7318	16.21	2647	5.86	4671	10.35
天桥区	Tian qiao	6752	12.69	3637	6.84	3115	5.86
历城区	Li cheng	17933	16.77	6516	6.09	11417	10.68
长清区	Chang qing	6743	11.79	4438	7.76	2305	4.03
章丘区	Zhang qiu	11437	10.84	7904	7.49	3533	3.35
济阳区	Ji yang	7932	13.28	3629	6.08	4303	7.21
莱芜区	Lai wu	9618	9.67	7301	7.34	2317	2.33
钢城区	Gang cheng	2862	9.51	1903	6.32	959	3.19
平阴县	Ping yin	3931	10.52	2939	7.86	992	2.65
商河县	Shang he	7386	11.49	4940	7.69	2446	3.81

2-8 结婚情况
Number of Marriages

单位：对 (couple)

地区	Region	2014 年	2015 年	2016 年	2017 年	2018 年	2019 年
总　计	Total	55475	50300	47457	52663	51383	52300
市　直	Departments Directiy Under the Municipal Government	114	88	82	67	90	0
历下区	Li xia	7139	6594	5742	5830	5763	5456
市中区	Shi zhong	6315	5975	5364	5973	5699	5092
槐荫区	Huai yin	4179	3772	3445	3728	3863	3452
天桥区	Tian qiao	5472	4953	4447	4563	4874	4287
历城区	Li cheng	7816	7163	7296	7551	7419	6809
长清区	Chang qing	4270	3777	3649	4331	4003	3930
章丘区	Zhang qiu	6811	6119	6135	7613	6840	6000
济阳区	Ji yang	4484	3938	3615	4023	4248	3629
莱芜区	Lai wu						4514
钢城区	Gang cheng						1183
济南高新区	Ji’ nan Gao xin	1707	1577	1593	2516	2621	2533
平阴县	Ping yin	2893	2550	2563	2564	2330	1974
商河县	Shang he	4275	3794	3526	3904	3633	3441

2-9 离婚情况
Number of Divorces

单位：对 (couple)

地　区	Region	2014 年	2015 年	2016 年	2017 年	2018 年	2019 年
总　计	Total	25899	25399	26915	32491	31611	35932
法院数	Divorce Case Handled	6995	7395	6909	6024	6228	7034
民政数	Divorces Handled through Civil	18904	18004	20006	26467	25383	28898
市　直	Departments Directiy Under the Municipal Government	14	12	17	25	19	0
历下区	Li xia	2517	2382	2800	3474	3322	3644
市中区	Shi zhong	2458	2262	2327	3448	3288	3441
槐荫区	Huai yin	1681	1510	1720	2223	2362	2416
天桥区	Tian qiao	2251	2104	2224	2834	2810	3031
历城区	Li cheng	3110	2666	3177	4337	3664	4195
长清区	Chang qing	1319	1301	1422	1549	1801	1864
章丘区	Zhang qiu	1967	2026	2171	3303	2916	2793
济阳区	Ji yang	1281	1344	1434	1733	1783	1745
莱芜区	Lai wu						1418
钢城区	Gang cheng						502
济南高新区	Ji’ nan Gao xin	566	502	557	1097	1127	1322
平阴县	Ping yin	764	880	938	993	839	968
商河县	Shang he	976	1015	1219	1451	1452	1559

主要统计指标解释

人口统计资料主要有三个来源 人口普查、人口抽样调查和人口经常性登记。

人口普查 是在国家规定的统一时间内，用统一的方法，统一的调查项目，对全国或某一地区的人口进行的一种专门调查。

人口抽样调查 是从所要研究的总人口中，随机抽取部分人口，并根据对这些人口调查所得到的数据来推算该人口总体相应指标的方法。

人口经常性登记 是指对人口出生、死亡、婚姻、迁移等事件进行连续的、持久的、强制的全面登记制度。

人口数 指一定时点、一定地区范围内的有生命的个人的总和。

年度统计的年末人口数 指每年12月31日24时的人口数。

出生率（又称出生率） 指在一定时期内（通常为一年）平均每千人所出生的人数的比率，一般用千分率表示。计算公式为：

出生率 = 年出生人数 / 年平均人数 ×1000‰

式中：出生人数指活产婴儿，即胎儿脱离母体时（不管怀孕月数），有过呼吸或其他生命现象。

出生人数 是指活产婴儿，即胎儿脱离母体时（不管怀孕月数），有过呼吸或其他生命现象。

年平均人数 是指年初、年底人口数的平均数，也可用年中人口数代替。

死亡率（又称粗死亡率） 指在一定时期内（通常为一年）一定地区的死亡人数与同期平均人数（或期中人数）之比，一般用千分率表示。计算公式为：

死亡率 = 年死亡人数 / 年平均人数 ×1000‰

人口自然增长率 指在一定时期内（通常为一年）人口自然增加数（出生人数减死亡人数）与该时期内平均人数（或期中人数）之比，一般用千分率表示。计算公式为：

人口自然增长率 =（本年出生人数 - 本年死亡人数）/ 年平均人数 ×1000‰

人口自然增长率 = 人口出生率 - 人口死亡率

机械增长率 是反映迁移变动的一个相对指标。它表明一个地区在一定时间内迁入人口数与迁出人口数相抵后的差额与总人口数的比率，一般用千分率表示。计算公式为：

机械增长率 = 一定时期的迁入迁出人口差额 / 该时期的平均人口 ×100%

人口密度 指一定时点，一定地区的人口数与该时点、该地区的面积之比，即一定时点的单位土地面积上的人口数，通常以每平方公里的居民人数来表示：

$$\text{人口密度} = \frac{\text{该地区人口数}}{\text{该地区土地面积}} \times 100\%$$

性别比 反映两性人口间比例的指标，指在总人口中或各年龄组人口中，男性人数与女性人数之比。通常以每100个女性人口相对应的男性人口数。计算公式：

$$\text{性别比} = \frac{\text{男性人口}}{\text{女生人口}} \times 100\%$$

Explanatory Notes on Main Statistical Indicators

Source of Demographic Data population census, sample survey of population and recurrent registration of population.

Population Census refers to an official survey of total population nationwide or in a given region by an official method within a given period of time in China.

Sample Survey of Population refers to the method of calculating corresponding indicators of total population pursuant to the data originated from the survey of partial population randomly extracted from the total population to be researched.

Recurrent registration of population refers to continuous, persistent and enforced registration system for population birth, death, marriage, and migration , etc.

Total Population refers to the total number of people alive at a certain point of time within a given area.

The Annual Statistics on Total Population is taken at midnight, the 31st of December.

Birth Rate (or Crude Birth Rate) refers to the ratio of births per one thousand people during a certain period of time (generally a year), expressed in permillage. The following formula is used:

Birth rate = number of births/annual average population *1,000‰

Wherein: Births refer to liveborn infants, namely those with breath or other vital signs when breaking away from the mother (regardless of number of months of pregnancy).

Births refer to liveborn infants, namely those with breath or other vital signs when breaking away from the mother (regardless of number of months of pregnancy).

Annual Average Population refers to the mean value of the number of people at the beginning and ending of the year, which can be replaced with the number of people in the middle of the year.

Death Rate (or Crude Death Rate) refers to the ratio of the number of deaths to the average population (or mid period population) during a certain period of time (usually a year), expressed in ‰ . The following formula is used:

Death rate = number of deaths/annual average population *1,000‰

Natural Growth Rate of Population refers to the ratio of natural increase in population (number of births minus number of deaths) in a certain period of time (usually a year) to the average population (or mid period population) of the same period, expressed in ‰ . The following formula is used:

Natural Growth Rate of Population=(number of births – number of deaths)/ annual average population * 1,000‰

Natural Growth Rate of Population=Birth Rate–Death Rate

Mechanical Growth Rate is a relative indicator that reflects changes in the population migration. It shows the ratio of the balance (between the people count moving in and out of a given area) to total population during a certain period of time, expressed in permillage. The following formula is used:

Mechanical growth rate = the balance between people count moving in and out of a given area during a certain period of time/average population * 100%

Population Density refers to the ratio of total population in a given area at a certain point of time to the area at this point of time, namely total population per area of land at a certain point of time, expressed in number of residents per square kilometers:

$$\text{Population density} = \frac{\text{Total population in the region}}{\text{Land area in the region}} \times 100\%$$

Sex ratio refers to the ratio of male to female population in total population or age groups, male population to per 100 female populations. The following formula is used:

$$\text{Sex ratio} = \frac{\text{Male n population}}{\text{Female population}} \times 100\%$$

3

综合

GENERAL SURVEY

3-1 国民经济和社会发展总量指标
Principal Aggregate Indicators on National Economic and Social Development

指 标	Indicators	单位 Unit	1978
面 积	Area		
土地面积	Land Area	平方公里 (sq.km)	
#市内十区建成区面积	Built-up Area of Ten Districts in the City	平方公里 (sq.km)	85
人 口	Population		
年末总户数(户籍人口)	Total year-end Households(Household Population)	万户 (10 000 households)	102.93
年末总人口	Total year-end Population	万人 (10 000 persons)	450.67
#市区	Population	万人 (10 000 persons)	186.43
#男性	Male	万人 (10 000 persons)	226.31
年末常住总人口	Total Resident Population at the Year-end	万人 (10 000 persons)	
就 业	Employment		
全社会从业人员	Employed Persons	万人 (10 000 persons)	204.04
第一产业	Primary Industry	万人 (10 000 persons)	136.30
第二产业	Secondary Industry	万人 (10 000 persons)	46.06
第三产业	Tertiary Industry	万人 (10 000 persons)	21.68
职工平均工资	Average Wage of Staff and Workers	元 (yuan)	578
城镇非私营单位就业人员平均工资	Average Wage of Employed Persons in Urban Non Private Entities	元 (yuan)	
城镇非私营单位在岗职工平均工资	Average Wage of Staff and Workers in Urban Non Private Entities	元 (yuan)	
城镇私营单位就业人员平均工资	Average Wage of Employed Persons in Urban Private Entities	元 (yuan)	
城镇登记失业人员数	Registered Urban Unemployed Persons	万人 (10 000 persons)	
城镇登记失业率	Registered Urban Unemployment Rate	%	
国民经济核算	National Accounting		
地区生产总值	Gross Domestic Product	亿元 (100 million yuan)	23.60
#非公有制经济	Non-ppublic Economy	亿元 (100 million yuan)	
第一产业	Primary Industry	亿元 (100 million yuan)	4.16
第二产业	Secondary Industry	亿元 (100 million yuan)	13.32
第三产业	Tertiary Industry	亿元 (100 million yuan)	6.12
人均地区生产总值	Per Capita GDP	元 (yuan)	527
固定资产投资	Investment in Fixed Assets		
固定资产投资	Investment in Fixed Assets	亿元 (100 million yuan)	3.19
第一产业	Primary Industry	亿元 (100 million yuan)	0.55
第二产业	Secondary Industry	亿元 (100 million yuan)	1.15
#工业	Industry	亿元 (100 million yuan)	0.75
第三产业	Tertiary Industry	亿元 (100 million yuan)	1.29
#房地产投资	Real Estate Investment	亿元 (100 million yuan)	
财政税收	Fiscal Tax Revenue		
一般公共预算收入	General Pubilic Budget Revenue	亿元 (100 million yuan)	5.90
一般公共预算支出	General Pubilic Budget Expenditure	亿元 (100 million yuan)	1.50
地域税收收入	Regional Tax Revenue	亿元 (100 million yuan)	
国税税收收入	National Tax Revenue	亿元 (100 million yuan)	
地税税收收入	Land Tax Revenue	亿元 (100 million yuan)	

1990	1995	2000	2005	2010	2015	2017	2018	2019
8227	8227	8154	8177	8177	7998	7998	7998	10244
103	114	120	295	347	393	464	524	761
140.36	156.45	166.63	177.69	190.65	203.59	208.08	216.64	270.26
523.60	542.12	562.65	597.44	604.08	625.73	643.62	655.90	796.74
232.30	247.57	317.20	347.87	348.02	458.16	483.75	554.13	695.09
265.91	274.98	284.19	300.42	301.28	310.92	319.21	324.74	395.30
				681.80	713.20	732.12	746.04	890.87
270.54	324.22	347.37	360.00	373.70	388.70	405.38	419.27	492.36
125.73	116.13	109.98	99.10	76.66	71.80	69.50	68.80	77.42
87.75	106.68	110.81	114.20	120.20	124.70	129.35	132.17	154.27
57.06	101.41	126.58	146.70	176.84	192.20	206.53	218.30	260.67
2211	5851	10422	20866	31096	58578	70196	71142	–
								97482
								100593
								51530
	2.45	3.90	5.75	5.97	3.20	3.23	3.49	3.53
	2.30	3.70	3.86	3.84	2.04	2.08	2.06	2.01
138.24	473.52	944.13	1846.28	3910.53	6100.23	7201.96	7856.56	9443.37
		238.32	768.50	1664.43	2599.60	3075.08	3237.50	
23.93	67.64	96.02	134.34	215.17	305.39	317.40	272.42	343.06
67.36	220.37	414.74	847.47	1637.45	2307.00	2569.22	2829.31	3265.22
46.95	185.51	433.38	864.47	2057.90	3487.84	4315.34	4754.83	5835.09
2666	8773	16855	28900	57947	85919	98967	106302	106416
30.60	112.76	305.95	857.00	1987.44	3498.42	4363.58	–	–
0.52	3.24	13.57	38.28	68.08	102.52	97.54	–	–
14.62	46.26	73.14	362.05	677.28	1217.39	1441.82	–	–
2.05	45.35	67.72	352.27	667.35	1147.87	1317.64	–	–
13.94	63.27	219.24	456.67	1242.08	2178.51	2824.22	–	–
2.18	16.46	50.53	121.09	484.50	1014.14	1232.57	1369.35	1576.93
12.40	16.99	49.05	106.15	266.13	614.32	677.21	752.82	874.19
8.20	19.63	54.72	120.66	336.80	658.20	834.06	1018.32	1197.32
	53.49	112.35	231.34	527.70	959.33	1134.93	1240.20	1419.58
	39.55	72.54	144.20	309.87	494.43	745.63	755.63	–
	13.94	39.80	87.14	217.82	464.90	389.30	484.58	–

3-1 续表 1 continued 1

指 标	Indicators	单位 Unit	1978
金融保险	Finance and Insurance		
金融机构人民币存款余额	RMB Deposits Balance of Financial Institutions	亿元 (100 million yuan)	15.43
# 住户存款	Deposits of Households	亿元 (100 million yuan)	1.14
金融机构人民币贷款余额	RMB Loans Balance of Financial Institutions	亿元 (100 million yuan)	14.08
# 短期贷款	Short-term Loans	亿元 (100 million yuan)	-
保险承保额	Insurance Premium	亿元 (100 million yuan)	
保险业务收入	Premium	万元 (10 000 yuan)	
保险业务支出	Payment	万元 (10 000 yuan)	
农 业	Agriculture		
农林牧渔业总产值	Gross Output Value of Farming Forestry,Animal Husbandry and Fishery	亿元 (100 million yuan)	6.57
农用机械总动力	total power of agricultural machinery	万千瓦 (10 000kw)	69.70
年末实有耕地面积	Actural cultivated Area at Year-end	千公顷 (1000 ha)	373.19
粮食总产量	Total Output of Grain	万吨 (10 000 tons)	115.38
蔬菜总产量	Total Output of Vegetable	万吨 (10 000 tons)	49.19
肉类总产量	Total Output of meat	万吨 (10 000 tons)	2.50
奶类总产量	Total Output of Milk	万吨 (10 000 tons)	0.40
棉花总产量	Total Output of Cotton	万吨 (10 000 tons)	0.51
规模以上工业	Industry Enterprises above Designated Size		
单位数	Number of Enterprises	个 (unit)	1319
工业总产值	Gross Industrial Output Value	亿元 (100 million yuan)	37.67
营业收入	Revenue from Principal Business	亿元 (100 million yuan)	31.39
利税总额	Total Profits and Taxes	亿元 (100 million yuan)	6.80
利润总额	Total Profits	亿元 (100 million yuan)	3.88
资产总计	Total Assets	亿元 (100 million yuan)	25.68
所有者权益	Owner's Equities	亿元 (100 million yuan)	7.47
建筑业	Construction		
资质以上企业个数	Number of Qualification Enterprises	个 (unit)	10
建筑业总产值	Gross Output Value of Construction Enterprises	亿元 (100 million yuan)	0.68
施工面积	Floor Space under Construction	万平方米 (10 000 sq.m)	
竣工面积	Floor Space of Completed	万平方米 (10 000 sq.m)	49
其中：住宅	Residential	万平方米 (10 000 sq.m)	
交通运输	Transport		
货运量	Freight Traffic		
铁路	Railways	万吨 (10 000 tons)	2191
公路	Highways	万吨 (10 000 tons)	1670
航空	Airways	万吨 (10 000 tons)	
客运量	Passenger Traffic		
铁路	Railways	万人 (10 000 persons)	1302
公路	Highways	万人 (10 000 persons)	505
航空	Airways	万人 (10 000 persons)	

1990	1995	2000	2005	2010	2015	2017	2018	2019
117.95	438.01	1274.96	3483.34	7510.44	14174.72	15957.74	16571.87	18303.20
51.08	222.06	463.04	1024.42	2187.68	3951.42	4465.73	5008.08	6438.09
124.76	337.26	1069.31	3259.86	6319.09	11356.78	12883.66	14700.07	17624.21
98.50	239.31	527.31	1240.49	1898.61	2692.81	2929.73	2865.97	3400.21
		2169	5295	16802	97665	162712	256415	438422
		124982	415338	1223791	2227474	3810660	4155535	5322643
		59618	141353	437708	656570	886699	1033980	1219250
36.92	114.07	154.30	230.46	361.24	493.04	505.08	514.90	637.30
183.40	241.20	349.47	426.76	509.68	584.98	442.90	454.62	543.48
347.56	339.30	333.72	366.99	362.30	358.57	355.66	353.65	
181.47	252.48	240.27	260.11	289.43	264.55	255.57	251.42	285.46
126.09	253.54	405.95	529.37	572.05	626.23	591.63	527.22	671.24
11.38	28.68	31.82	37.93	31.79	34.18	32.50	29.82	35.86
1.87	3.48	7.09	19.61	31.20	23.27	26.36	32.84	32.13
5.00	2.91	2.73	3.55	2.94	0.74	0.20	0.29	0.54
2008	2648	1038	1670	2021	2021	2051	1889	2153
174.89	526.48	680.04	2237.51	4485.61	5339.97	5770.91	4992.28	5839.18
136.29	432.17	629.72	2142.84	4497.17	5417.16	5810.16	5192.15	6512.66
15.57	53.59	64.62	244.61	584.53	685.71	686.80	535.39	545.70
3.23	16.30	21.69	131.30	339.76	396.13	415.23	307.98	310.86
125.25	578.55	958.10	1868.06	3904.42	4987.76	6319.64	5892.64	6663.13
36.82	180.86	363.37	630.06	1481.75	2159.78	2268.27	2386.75	2743.28
46	141	569	737	739	463	504	507	895
12.56	58.78	141.92	462.65	894.30	1663.83	2218.93	2823.47	3513.98
269	1030	1611	3298	4655	10189	11363	12984	14955
170	306	701	1400	1306	2039	2280	2366	3418
77	141	396	884	773	1178	1258	1502	2170
3416	3877	5168	7211	9913	15794	17865	18728	20870
3970	6182	7024	8484	13029	20419	24058	25571	34392
	0.4	1.3	2.0	3.4	4.2	5.0	5.6	6.7
1438	1519	1693	1924	3327	10681	13412	14548	15745
1801	2611	4530	5364	12758	3663	3192	3149	3244
2.6	37.0	62.0	140.0	379.2	533.1	785.6	894.1	936.1

3-1 续表 2 continued 2

指 标	Indicators	单位 Unit	1978
民用汽车拥有量	Possession of Private Vehicles	辆 (unit)	1684
# 载客	Passenger Vehicles	辆 (unit)	1353
# 载货	Trucks	辆 (unit)	224
邮电通信	**Post and Telecommunication Services**		
固定电话	Fixed Telephone	万户 (10 000 households)	2.68
# 城市	Urban	万户 (10 000 households)	2.27
移动电话	Mobile Telephone	万户 (10 000 households)	
互联网用户	Internet Broad Band	万户 (10 000 households)	
国内贸易	**Domestic Trade**		
社会消费品零售总额	Total Retail Sales of Consumer Goods	亿元 (100 million yuan)	8.13
# 批发零售业	Wholesale and Retail Trade	亿元 (100 million yuan)	7.07
# 餐饮业	Catering Services	亿元 (100 million yuan)	0.29
对外经济和国际旅游	**Foreign Economy and Trade,Tourism**		
全年货物进出口总额（海关）	Total Value of Imports and Exports(Customs)	万美元 (10 000 USD)	
进口	Imports	万美元 (10 000 USD)	
出口	Exports	万美元 (10 000 USD)	
全年货物进出口总额	Total Value of Imports and Exports	亿元 (100 million yuan)	
进口	Imports	亿元 (100 million yuan)	
出口	Exports	亿元 (100 million yuan)	
全年实际使用外资	Total Amount of Foreign Capital Actually Utilized	万美元 (10 000 USD)	
全年实现合同外资	Total Amount of Contracted Foreign Capital	万美元 (10 000 USD)	
入境游客人数	International Tourists	人 (person)	
外国人	Foreigners	人 (person)	
港澳台同胞	Compatriots from Hong Kong Macao and Taiwan	人 (person)	
国际旅游（外汇）收入	Foreign Exchange Earnings	亿美元 (100 million USD)	
教 育	**Education**		
普通高等学校在校生	Total Enrollment of Regular Institutions of Higher Education	万人 (10 000 persons)	1.09
普通高等学校专任教师	Full-time Teachers of Regular Institutions of Higher Education	人 (person)	2947
中等专业学校在校生	Total Enrollment of Secondary Professional Schools	万人 (10 000 persons)	0.68
中等专业学校专任教师	Full-time Teachers of Secondary Professional Schools	人 (person)	1020
普通中学在校生	Total Enrollment of Regular Senior Secondary Schools	万人 (10 000 persons)	30.61
普通中学专任教师	Full-time Teachers of Regular Senior Secondary Schools	人 (person)	19275
小学在校生	Total Enrollment of Regular Primary Schools	万人 (10 000 persons)	60.91
小学专任教师	Full-time Teachers of Regular Primary Schools	人 (person)	24926
文 化	**Culture**		
图书馆藏书量	Number of Books in Library	万册 (10 000 copies)	341.0
图书出版种数	Number of Publication	种 (kind)	389
图书量	Books	万册 (10 000 copies)	20166
报纸量	Newspapers	万份 (10 000 copies)	25055
杂志量	Magazines	万份 (10 000 copies)	2209

1990	1995	2000	2005	2010	2015	2017	2018	2019
39748	86766	129204	347687	807378	1541045	1949707	2160748	2584278
26032	33968	68625	196415	627849	1400588	1783848	1978951	2370437
12141	47790	56627	71588	117994	123801	151141	166277	194957
9.87	39.18	106.34	258.90	213.30	165.30	153.10	135.27	148.82
9.12	36.48	83.08	206.30	177.40	141.00	132.55	118.70	136.30
	2.3	60.8	239.0	857.6	1090.4	971.1	1013.7	1122.9
		11.57	74.34	117.30	231.66	298.75	344.70	392.62
52.82	183.76	344.45	772.65	1725.46	3141.04	3752.52	4091.08	4420.41
38.20	134.53	228.75	657.55	1402.27	2648.44	3165.82	3452.14	3760.47
2.56	13.35	37.76	108.44	308.11	473.23	563.82	614.10	632.37
	66587	143935	376213	743776	911424	1130449	1318209	1630123
	29812	143935	198370	338888	311763	379887	463119	695064
	36775	143935	177843	404888	599661	750562	855090	935059
						708.1	825.0	1103.3
						257.1	305.7	480.8
						451.0	519.3	622.5
	25294	31981	54158	104011	157851	187623	272847	224249
	47449	44074	112072	120903	303100	218692	556119	683441
20583	54468	103990	120164	230985	332942	375469	398721	456585
12705	30011	40990	69762	153327	205477	232260	247086	285071
7878	24457	63000	50402	77658	127465	143209	151635	171514
0.15	0.19	0.32	0.42	1.14	1.84	2.08	2.23	2.75
3.73	5.66	9.30	38.04	50.53	53.62	54.44	79.63	76.20
7245	7500	8267	18434	26870	30873	32559	37539	40627
2.51	4.79	5.75	4.79	2.12	1.57	1.28	5.16	5.68
2890	2890	2916	1578	1334	763	716	3711	4058
22.45	27.15	33.82	30.91	30.18	30.16	30.56	31.18	39.35
16065	17621	20585	21915	21943	23643	25676	26588	34177
47.57	49.23	41.40	37.88	38.40	41.44	44.66	46.66	54.14
26922	27417	27417	25201	24801	25795	29109	30605	36067
476.0	524.6	591.7	725.1	941.2	1195.0	1363.3	1442.3	–
2001	2603	3851	5389	6586	10234	12364	–	–
31685	39025	38471	27919	26603	43860	45501	–	–
46930	54460	109199	113751	184706	136480	99089	–	–
3321	4579	11177	7195	6995	8572	7809	–	–

3-1 续表 3 continued 3

指 标	Indicators	单位 Unit	1978
卫 生	Public Health		
卫生机构数	Number of Health Institutions	个 (unit)	1017
# 医院及卫生院	Hospitals and Township Hospitals	个 (unit)	148
卫生机构床位数	Number of Beds	张 (bed)	11496
# 医院及卫生院	Hospitals and Township Hospitals	张 (bed)	9856
卫生工作人员	Medical Personnel	人 (person)	24949
# 卫生技术人员	Medical Technical Personnel	人 (person)	19198
人民生活	People's Livelihood		
城镇居民人均可支配收入	Per Capita Disposable Income of Urban Residents	元 (yuan)	337.8
城镇居民人均生活消费支出	Per Capita Life Consumption Expenditure of Urban Residents	元 (yuan)	317.9
# 食品	Food	元 (yuan)	181.6
农村居民人均可支配收入	Per Capita Disposable Income of Rural Residents	元 (yuan)	110.5
农村居民人均生活消费支出	Per Capita Life Consumption Expenditure of Rural Residents	元 (yuan)	83.2
# 食品	Food	元 (yuan)	58.2
农民人均住宅居住面积	Rural Residential Area Per Capita	平方米 (sq.m)	9.6
社会治安	Public security		
交通事故起数	Number of Traffic Accidents	起 (case)	
交通事故死伤人数	Deaths and Injuries from Traffic Accidents	人 (person)	
交通事故损失折款	Property Losses from Traffic Accidents	万元 (10 000 yuan)	
火灾事故起数	Number of Fire Accidents	起 (case)	
火灾事故死伤人数	Deaths and Injuries from Fire Accidents	人 (person)	
火灾事故损失折款	Property Losses from Fire Accidents	万元 (10 000 yuan)	

注：1.“职工平均工资”2006 年以前为在岗职工口径，2006 年及以后为法人单位在岗职工口径。
2.“市内十区建成区面积”，2018 年为市内八区口径，2017 年以前为市内七区口径，2015 年以前为市内六区口径。
3. 工业统计指标 1997 年及以前统计口径为乡及乡以上工业企业，1998 年及以后为全部国有及年销售收入 500 万元以上工业企业，2011 年及以后为年主营业务收入 2000 万元及以上工业法人单位。
4. 货运量、客运量中的“铁路”指标，2013 年 3 月铁路系统改革，铁路系统统计数据按新口径执行；“公路指标”自 2014 年起交通部门执行新的公路运输量统计方案，调查范围较老口径有所缩小，2014 年及 2013 年数据均为新口径下交通部反馈数据。
5. 从 2015 年起，全市居民收支调查指标采用新口径。“农村居民人均可支配收入”2014 年以前为农民人均纯收入口径；“农村居民人均生活消费支出”2014 年以前为农民人均生活费支出口径。
6. 规模以上工业“营业收入”，2018 年以前为“主营业务收入”口径。

1990	1995	2000	2005	2010	2015	2017	2018	2019
1300	1185	1414	2138	5086	5947	5770	6030	7487
178	216	231	246	277	269	289	293	351
18214	20747	21698	24695	31947	49311	54855	57460	66623
17216	19534	20830	23524	29844	45195	50142	51207	59697
41444	43648	45166	41499	54711	89117	97663	104347	122370
31130	32848	35669	34129	39366	71778	76273	82834	97532
1619.5	4720.6	8471.3	13578.5	25321.1	39888.7	46642.4	50146.5	51912.6
1360.1	3830.4	6891.8	9226.6	15973.3	26318.7	30728.6	32977.1	33438.7
781.6	1823.6	2387.1	3046.9	5051.2	6415.0	7229.3	7758.0	7956.3
731.1	1812.7	3046.8	4812.3	8903.3	14231.8	16593.8	17924.4	19454.2
569.8	1373.6	1976.8	2902.8	5406.6	8597.2	10327.3	11172.3	12300.3
287.7	770.8	860.0	1134.8	1818.3	2775.5	3253.2	3409.0	3702.6
22.5	24.7	28.6	33.8	40.2	52.6	55.2	54.3	51.1
509	1231	1306	911	774	2946	3075	3071	3334
518	1345	1364	1186	1121	3885	3219	3618	3925
64	369	357	316	189	840	1020	947	905
309	110	1281	1071	791	2609	1752	1539	4577
67	87	26	3	9	12	11	12	12
166	925	471	76	462	1571	599	827	1529

Note: 1. The average salary of employees is the caliber data of employees in the post before 2006, and the caliber data of employees in the legal entity in 2006 and later.

2. "The area of the built-up area in the eight districts of the city" , before 2017 adopts the statistical scale of the seven districts in the city, six districts in the city before 2015, and eight districts in the city in 2018.

3. Industrial statistical indicators In 1997 and before, the statistical caliber was industrial enterprises at or above the township level. In 1998 and after, they were all state-owned and with an annual sales income of more than 5 million yuan. In 2011 and beyond, the annual main business income was 20 million yuan and above industrial enterprises legal entities.

4. The "railway" indicator in freight volume and passenger volume, the railway system reform in March 2013, the railway system statistics are implemented according to the new caliber; the "road indicators" since 2014, the transportation department has implemented a new road traffic statistics program. The scope of the survey has been narrower than that of the old one. The data for 2014 and 2013 are the feedback data of the Ministry of Communications under the new caliber.

5. Starting from 2015, the city's residents' income and expenditure survey indicators adopt a new caliber. "per capita disposable income of Rural Residents" was the "per capita net income of Rural Residents" before 2014; "Per capita consumption expenditure of Rural Residents "was the "per capita living expenses of farmers" before 2014.

6."Main operating revenue" of industrial enterprises above designated size adopts the statistical scale of "main operating revenue" before 2018.

3-2 国民经济和社会发展比例和效益指标
Indicators on Proportions and Efficiency in National Economic and Social Development

指　标	Indicators	单位 Unit	1978 年	1985 年
人　口	Population			
申报出生率	Birth Rate	‰	15.53	11.39
申报死亡率	Death Rate	‰	7.00	6.52
自然增长率	Natural Growth Rate	‰	8.53	4.87
就　业	Employment			
就业者负担人口	Dependency of Employed Population	人 (person)	2.21	1.99
三次产业从业者比例	Composition of Employed Population			
第一产业	Primary Industry	%	66.8	47.5
第二产业	Secondary Industry	%	22.6	31.0
第三产业	Tertiary Industry	%	10.6	21.5
城镇登记失业率	Registered Unemployment Rate in Urban Areas	%		
国民经济核算	National Accounting			
三次产业增加值比例	Composition of Gross Domestic Product			
第一产业	Primary Industry	%		21.1
第二产业	Secondary Industry	%		51.8
第三产业	Tertiary Industry	%		27.1
人均生产总值	Per Capita GDP	元 (yuan)		1263
资本形成率（投资率）	Capital Formation Rate	%		
最终消费率（消费率）	Final Consumption Rate	%		
固定资产投资	Investment in Fixed Assets			
固定资产投资占生产总值比重	Proportion of Fixed Assets Investment in GDP	%		23.7
财　政	Finance			
一般公共预算收入占生产总值比重	Proportion of General Public Budget Revenue in GDP	%	25.2	14.5
一般公共预算支出占生产总值比重	Proportion of General Public Budget Expenditure in GDP	%	6.3	5.6
农　业	Agriculture			
人均耕地面积	Per Cultivated Area	亩 (mu)	1.24	1.10
每公顷耕地化肥施用量（折纯）	Consumption of Chemical Fertilizers per Hectare	千克 (kg)		225
每公顷播种面积粮食产量	Grain Yield Per Hectare of Sown Area	千克 (kg)	2475	3864
机耕率	Machine-cultivated Rate	%		

1990 年	1995 年	2000 年	2010 年	2015 年	2017 年	2018 年	2019 年
12.88	10.03	11.08	11.13	11.82	17.83	14.57	12.86
6.54	6.32	7.05	8.35	6.73	9.86	6.98	6.62
6.34	3.71	4.03	2.78	5.09	7.96	7.59	6.24
1.94	1.67	1.62	1.62	1.61	1.34	1.4	1.5
46.5	35.8	31.7	20.5	18.5	17.1	16.4	15.7
32.4	32.9	31.9	32.2	32.1	31.9	31.5	31.3
21.1	31.3	36.4	47.3	49.4	51.0	52.1	52.9
	2.45	3.70	3.84	2.04	2.08	2.06	2.01
17.3	14.3	10.0	5.5	5.0	4.4	3.5	3.6
48.7	46.5	43.9	41.9	37.8	35.7	36.0	34.6
34.0	39.2	46.1	52.6	57.2	59.9	60.5	61.8
2666	8773	16999	57966	85919	98967	106302	106416
39.1	39.5	40.2	52.6	63.0	66.8	–	–
37.8	41.9	56.9	46.9	52.3	52.5	–	–
22.1	23.8	32.1	50.8	57.3	60.6	–	–
9.0	3.6	5.2	15.2	10.1	9.4	9.6	9.3
5.9	4.1	5.8	16.9	10.8	11.6	13.0	12.7
1.00	0.94	0.88	0.90	0.87	0.83	0.82	
330	569	641	646	626	589	564	
4273	5512	5354	6192	6117	5660	5659	5956
					87.3	96.7	92.0

3-2 续表 continued

指　标	Indicators	单 位 Unit	1978 年	1985 年
规模以上工业	Industry Enterprises above Designated Size			
产品销售率	Product Sales Rate	%		
总资产贡献率	Total Asset Contribution Rate	%		
流动资产周转次数	Turnover of Current Asset	次（times）		
邮电通讯业	Post and Telecommunication Services			
每百人拥有电话机	Number of phones Per 100 Population	部 (unit)	0.60	1.26
国内商业	Domestic Commerce			
人均消费品零售总额	Total Sales of Consumption Good Per Capita	元 (yuan)	182	500
教 育	Education			
学龄儿童入学率	School-age Children Enrollment Rate	%		99.44
学校教师负担人数	Teacher-student Ratio	人 (person)	21.28	16.75
高等教育	Higher Education	人 (person)	2.47	6.55
中等教育	Secondary Education	人 (person)	16.65	14.46
小学	Primary Schools	人 (person)	34.99	20.33
卫 生	Public Health			
每万人拥有医院卫生院数	Number of Health Institutes per 10000 Population	个 (unit)	0.33	0.34
每万人拥有医生数	Number of Doctors per 10000 Population	人 (person)	23.3	26.3
每万人拥有医院床位数	Number of Hospitals Beds per 10000 Population	张 (bed)	22.0	28.2
市政建设	City Construction			
城市人口用水普及率	Coverage Rate of Water Supply	%	99.0	100.0
城市用气普及率	Coverage Rate of Natural Gas Supply	%	17.8	26.3
建成区绿化覆盖率	Coverage Rate of Urban Green Areas	%	12.0	23.0
生 活	Life			
城镇居民恩格尔系数	Engel's Coefficient of Urban Residents	%	57.1	56.5
农村居民恩格尔系数	Engel's Coefficient of Rural Residents	%	69.9	51.8

注：1.“一般公共预算收入占生产总值比重”2012 年(含)以前为“地方财政收入”口径；“一般公共预算支出占生产总值比重”2012 年(含)以前为“地方财政支出”口径。
2. 由于第三次全国土地调查数据未反馈，“人均耕地面积”“每公顷耕地化肥施用量”相关数据空缺。

1990 年	1995 年	2000 年	2010 年	2015 年	2017 年	2018 年	2019 年
	97.12	98.24	98.71	98.23	98.40	97.50	96.80
	12.25	8.45	15.98	13.37	17.63	9.93	8.90
	1.69	1.52	2.11	1.82	1.62	1.38	1.65
1.89	7.23	18.98	35.31	26.48	23.99	20.82	18.81
1009	3389	6149	27343	50369	58797	62963	55882
99.03	99.40	99.93	100.00	100.00	100.00	100.00	100.00
14.20	15.60	15.24	17.40	17.37	17.09	16.68	15.44
5.15	7.55	11.25	21.76	22.53	23.79	21.21	18.76
12.99	15.30	16.78	14.72	13.33	12.04	12.87	12.71
17.67	18.20	15.10	15.48	16.07	15.35	15.25	15.01
0.34	0.40	0.41	0.46	0.43	0.45	0.45	0.44
29.2	27.9	29.5	29.1	46.0	39.7	43.1	43.0
32.9	36.0	38.6	52.9	69.1	74.9	77.0	74.8
100.0	100.0	100.0	100.0	99.00	99.64	99.78	100.00
45.7	72.2	90.7	95.5	97.73	99.85	99.87	99.97
30.0	30.5	36.1	36.9	39.94	40.57	40.52	41.18
57.5	47.6	34.6	31.6	24.4	23.5	23.5	23.8
50.5	56.1	43.5	33.6	32.3	31.5	30.5	30.1

Notes:1. "The proportion of general public budget revenue in total output value" was the caliber of "local financial revenue" before 2012 (inclusive); "The proportion of general public budget expenditure in total output value" was the caliber of "local financial expenditure"

2. Because the third national land survery data have not been released, the data of "arable land per capita" and "fertilizers per hectare of cultivated land" are blank.

3-3 平均每天主要社会经济活动
Selected Indicators on Average Daily Social and Economic Activities

指　标	Indicators	单 位 Unit	1978 年	1985 年
每天创造的财富				
地区生产总值(当年价)	Gross Domestic Product	万元 (10 000 yuan)	646	1682
第一产业	Primary Industry	万元 (10 000 yuan)	114	354
第二产业	Secondary Industry	万元 (10 000 yuan)	365	872
第三产业	Tertiary Industry	万元 (10 000 yuan)	167	456
一般公共预算收入	General Pubilic Budget Revenue	万元 (10 000 yuan)	163	244
一般公共预算支出	General Pubilic Budget Expenditure	万元 (10 000 yuan)	41	94
固定资产投资	Investment in Fixed Assets	万元 (10 000 yuan)		399
每天生产主要工、农业产品	Production of Major Industrial Product and Agricultural Products on Average Daily			
粮 食	Grain	吨 (ton)	3161	4479
棉 花	Cotton	吨 (ton)	14	136.2
蔬 菜	Vegetables	吨 (ton)	1348	2304
猪 肉	Pork	吨 (ton)	67	138
奶 类	Milk	吨 (ton)	11	23
钢 材	Steel	吨 (ton)	689	1197
发电量	Electric Energy Capacity	万千瓦时 (10 000 kwh)	347	724
水 泥	Cement	吨 (ton)	2399	3699
化 肥	Chemical Fertilizer	吨 (ton)	494	313
金切机床	Metal-cutting Machine Tools	台 (unit)	10	18
汽 车	Motor Vehicles	辆 (unit)	12	31
服务器	Server	台 (unit)	—	—
布	Cloth	万米 (10 000 m)	38	50

1990年	1995年	2000年	2010年	2015年	2017年	2018年	2019年
3787	12973	26087	107138	167130	197314	215248	258722
656	1853	2603	5895	8367	8696	7464	9399
1845	6257	11469	44862	63205	70390	77515	89458
1286	5082	12015	56381	95557	118228	130269	159865
339	465	1344	7291	16831	18554	20625	23950
224	537	1499	9227	18032	22851	27899	32803
838	3089	8382	54450	95847	119550		
4972	6917	6583	7930	7248	7002	6888	7820
137	79.7	74.7	81	20.2	5.5	8	15
3455	6946	14733	16478	17157	16209	14444	18390
215	390	478	597	508	460	425	467
51	95	194	855	638	722	900	880
1576	2856	6507	26857	19852	11226	6118	61793
1225	1884	1898	3601	4818	4387	4189	8086
5796	11644	13291	19994	21411	16561	16557	35283
396	384	778	1345	644	575	569	463
14	11	8	6	10	16	16	20
17	16	8	581	263	553	636	481
—	—	—	271	1112	1547	2729	3192
55	41	45	22	44	45	11	11

3-3 续表 continued

指 标	Indicators	单 位 Unit	1978 年	1985 年
每天其他经济活动	Other Economic Activity on Average Daily			
最终消费量	Final Consumption	万元 (10 000 yuan)		780
居民消费	Households Expense	万元 (10 000 yuan)		638
农业居民	Rural Households	万元 (10 000 yuan)		367
城镇居民	Urban Households	万元 (10 000 yuan)		271
政府消费	Government Expense	万元 (10 000 yuan)		142
社会消费品零售总额	Total Sales of Consumption Good Per Capita	万元 (10 000 yuan)	261	640
公路货运量	Highways Freight Traffic	万吨 (10 000 tons)	3.2	6.9
公路客运量	Highways Passenger Traffic	万人 (10 000 persons)	1.4	3.1
自来水供水量	Water Supply	万吨 (10 000 tons)	36.9	40
用电量	Electricity Consumption	万千瓦时 (10 000 kwh)	754	747
市内公共车辆乘客人数	Number of City Bus Passengers	万人次 (10 000 person-times)	34.0	62.2
实际使用外资额	Total Amount of Foreign Capital Actually Utilized	万美元 (10 000 USD)		
港澳台及外国来济旅游人数	Compatriots from Hong Kong Macao and Taiwan	人 (person)		27
每天人口变动和婚姻	Daily Population Changes and Marriages			
出 生	Birth	人 (person)	191	152
死 亡	Death	人 (person)	86	87
结 婚	Marriages	对 (couple)		
离 婚	Divorces	对 (couple)		

注：1.“一般公共预算收入”指标 1978 年到 1995 年为“地方财政收入”口径，“一般公共预算支出”指标 1978 年到 1995 年为“地方财政支出”口径。
2. 按照国家统计局经济普查年度数据使用规定，部分涉及国民经济核算的指标数据空缺。

1990 年	1995 年	2000 年	2010 年	2015 年	2017 年	2018 年	2019 年
1580	5524	14833	50253	87412	103538	–	–
1274	4567	11098	39460	55221	76801	–	–
624	1938	3596	5142	7120	9878	–	–
650	2629	7502	34317	48101	66923	–	–
306	957	3735	10794	32192	26737	–	–
1447	5151	9718	49382	93433	113593	120670	121107
10.9	16.9	19.2	35.7	55.9	65.9	70.1	94.2
4.9	7.2	12.4	35.0	10.0	8.7	8.6	8.9
45.3	57.5	76.7	64.5	87.2	98.3	107.5	121.8
1255	1779	2505	6713.3	7238.5	7569.5	7790.8	11350.8
73.3	73.3	125.9	296.1	256.5	248.0	245.5	232.1
8.5	69.3	87.6	285.0	432.5	514.0	747.5	614.4
56	149	285	633	912.2	1029	1092.0	1251.0
183	148	170	184	202	312	259	279
93	94	108	138	115	172	124	144
103	137	120	153	138	144	141	143
	17	20	50	70	89	87	98

Notes: 1. The indicator–"general public budget revenue" was the caliber of "local financial revenue" from 1978 to 1995 and the indicator–"general public budget expenditure" was the caliber of "local fiscal expenditure" from 1978 to 1995.

2. Part of index data regarding national economic accounting is missing according to economic census year data use provisions of National Bureau of Statistics.

3-4 国民经济人均指标
Per Indicators of National Economic

指　标	Indicator	单　位 Unit	1978 年	1985 年
地区生产总值	Gross Domestic Product	元 (yuan)	527	1263
主要农产品产量	Output of Major Agricultural Products			
粮　食	Grain	千克 (kg)	258	336
棉　花	Cotton	千克 (kg)	1.14	10.22
猪　肉	Pork	千克 (kg)	5.44	10.33
水　果	Fruits	千克 (kg)	12.65	14.70
禽　蛋	Eggs	千克 (kg)		
蔬　菜	Vagatables	千克 (kg)	109.84	173.02
牛　奶	Milk	千克 (kg)	0.88	1.76
水产品	Aquatic Products	千克 (kg)	0.29	0.41
主要工业产品产量	Output of Major Industrial Products			
钢　材	Steel	千克 (kg)	48.1	69.6
发电量	Electric Energy Capacity	千瓦小时 (kwh)	282.5	543.9
水　泥	Cement	千克 (kg)	195.5	277.9
化　肥	Chemical Fertilizer	千克 (kg)	29.5	18.7
服务器	Server	台 (unit)	–	–
布	Cloth	米 (m)	30.8	37.2
其他经济活动	Other Economic Activity			
社会消费品零售总额	Total Sales of Consumption Good Per Capita	元 (yuan)	182	500
一般公共预算收入	General Pubilic Budget Revenue	元 (yuan)	133	183
一般公共预算支出	General Pubilic Budget Expenditure	元 (yuan)	33	70
城乡居民人民币储蓄存款余额	RMB Deposits Balance of Urban and Rural Residents	元 (yuan)	33	236
城镇居民人均可支配收入	Per Capita Disposable Income of Urban Residents	元 (yuan)	338	732
城镇居民人均生活消费支出	Per Capita Life Consumption Expenditure of Urban Residents	元 (yuan)	318	704
农村居民人均可支配收入	Per Capita Disposable Income of Rural Residents	元 (yuan)	111	439
农村居民人均生活消费支出	Per Capita Life Consumption Expenditure of Rural Residents	元 (yuan)	83	330

注：1.“一般公共预算收入”指标 1978 年到 1995 年为“地方财政收入”口径。“一般公共预算支出”指标 1978 年到 1995 年为“地方财政支出”口径。
2. 从 2015 年起，全市发布城乡住户调查一体化改革新口径数据，居民收支调查指标与 2014 年前分别实施的城镇和农村住户调查的调查范围、方法、指标口径、名称有所不同。

1990 年	1995 年	2000 年	2010 年	2015 年	2017 年	2018 年	2019 年
2666	8773	16999	57966	85919	98967	106302	106416
350	468	429	479	424	400	340	322
9.64	5.38	4.87	4.87	2.36	1.49	0.39	0.61
15.13	26.33	31.15	36.10	36.46	32.13	20.97	19.22
12.88	35.81	66.56	78.58	61.89	59.29	57.08	70.93
18.27	41.29	74.29	59.68	56.86	51.83	44.96	41.22
243.10	469.77	960.06	996.29	1041.79	962.34	713.35	756.41
3.46	6.44	12.65	51.68	46.75	48.03	44.43	36.21
1.80	4.72	5.87	7.06	7.63	6.47	4.32	1.82
169.1	195.7	424.0	1623.8	1161.8	642.0	302.1	2541.7
862.3	1237.0	1231.5	2177.5	2819.9	2508.9	2068.8	3326.0
408.0	728.4	866.1	1208.9	1253.1	947.2	817.7	1451.2
23.6	23.0	46.5	80.3	37.7	32.9	28.1	19.1
–	–	–	0.016	0.065	0.088	0.1	0.1
38.9	19.9	29.5	13.6	25.7	25.7	5.5	4.6
1009	3468	6332	25577	44243	51566	55353	49812
239	315	876	4409	9850	10611	10186	9851
158	363	977	5579	10553	13069	13778	13492
985	4115	8266	36239	63358	70889	67761	72550
1620	4721	8471	25321	39889	46642	50146	51913
1369	3830	6892	15973	26319	30729	32977	33439
731	1813	3047	8903	14232	16594	17924	19454
570	1374	1977	5407	8597	10327	11172	12300

Notes: 1. The indicator–"general public budget revenue" was the caliber of "local financial revenue" from 1978 to 1995 and the indicator–"general public budget expenditure" was the caliber of "local fiscal expenditure" from 1978 to 1995.

2. From 2015, new caliber data about urban and rural household survey integration reform was published by the city and the survey index of residents' income and expenditure was different from survey scope, method, indicator caliber and name of urban and rural residents implemented before 2014.

3-5 国民经济主要指标及占全国、全省比重（2019）
Main Indicators of National Economy and Their Proportion in China and Shandong Province(2019)

指 标	Indicator	单位 Unit	全国 Country
区划面积	Area	万平方公里 (10 000 sq.km)	960
年末总人口	Total year-end Population	万人 (10 000 persons)	140005
生产总值（当年价）	Gross Domestic Product	亿元 (100 million yuan)	990865.1
第一产业	Primary Industry	亿元 (100 million yuan)	70466.7
第二产业	Secondary Industry	亿元 (100 million yuan)	386165.3
第三产业	Tertiary Industry	亿元 (100 million yuan)	534233.1
规模以上工业营业收入	Revenue from Business of Industrial Enterprises above Designated Size	亿元 (100 million yuan)	1057824.9
规模以上工业利润总额	Total Profits of Industrial Enterprises above Designated Size	亿元 (100 million yuan)	61995.5
粮食总产量	Total Output of Grain	万吨 (10 000 tons)	66384.3
棉花总产量	Total Output of Cotton	万吨 (10 000 tons)	588.9
固定资产投资额	Investment in Fixed Assets	亿元 (100 million yuan)	560874.3
公路货物周转量	Highways Freight Turnover	亿吨公里 (100 million ton-km)	59636.39
社会消费品零售总额	Total Sales of Consumption Good Per Capita	亿元 (100 million yuan)	411649.0
实际使用外资	Total Amount of Foreign Capital Actually Utilized	亿美元 (100 million USD)	1381.4
一般公共预算收入	General Pubilic Budget Revenue	亿元 (100 million yuan)	101077.0
一般公共预算支出	General Pubilic Budget Expenditure	亿元 (100 million yuan)	203759
普通本专科在校学生	Enrollment of Regular Institutions of Higher Educatio	万人 (10 000persons)	3031.5
中等职业教育在校学生	Enrollment of Secondary Professional Schools	万人 (10 000persons)	1577
卫生机构数	Number of Health Institutions	个 (unit)	1007545.0
卫生技术人员	Medical Technical Personnel	万人 (10 000persons)	1015.4
#执业（助理）医师	Licensed Doctors	万人 (10 000persons)	386.7
城镇居民人均可支配收入	Per Capita Life Consumption Expenditure of Urban Residents	元 (yuan)	42359
农村居民人均可支配收入	Per Capita Disposable Income of Rural Residents	元 (yuan)	16021

全省 Province	济南 Ji'nan	济南占全国比重 (%) Ji'nan Account for Proportion of Country(%)	济南占全省比重 (%) Ji'nan Account for Proportion of Province(%)
15.8	1.024	0.11	6.49
10070.2	796.7	0.57	7.91
71067.5	9443.37	0.95	13.29
5116.4	343.06	0.49	6.71
28310.9	3265.22	0.85	11.53
37640.2	5835.09	1.09	15.50
84541.9	6512.7	0.62	7.70
3669.4	310.9	0.50	8.47
5357.0	285.46	0.43	5.33
19.6	0.5	0.09	2.76
–	–	–	–
7085.90	585.50	0.98	8.26
35770.6	4420.4	1.07	12.36
146.9	22.4	1.62	15.26
6526.6	874.2	0.86	13.39
10736.8	1197.3	0.59	11.15
218.4	76.2	2.51	34.89
73	5.7	0.36	7.78
83627.0	7487.0	0.74	8.95
78.3	9.8	0.96	12.46
31.50	3.83	0.99	12.15
42329	51913		
17775	19454		

主要统计指标解释

几点说明：

1. 生产总值及一、二、三次产业增加值，历史数据有所调整，以本年鉴所列数据为准。

2. 生产总值及一、二、三次产业增加值，全部工业增加值，农业总产值等指标的增长速度均以可比价格计算。

3. 由于国家在1994 年开始财税体制改革，1994 年及以后各年的财政收支与以前年份不可比。另外，2000 年财政收入统计口径也有微调。

4. 工业统计口径调整。1998年以前工业统计范围为乡及乡以上独立核算工业企业，1998年，统计范围调整为规模以上工业，即全部国有及年销售收入500万元以上的非国有工业单位，2011年，调整为年主营业务收入2000万元以上。

5. 建筑业统计范围变化。建筑业统计范围1994-1995 年为县及县以上单位，1996-1997年为资质等级四级及以上独立核算建筑业企业，1998 年起为资质等级五级及以上独立核算建筑业企业。

企业（单位）登记注册类型 是以在工商行政管理机关登记注册的具有法人资格的各类企业为划分对象。行政机关、事业单位和社会团体及其他经济组织参照执行。

本项以工商行政管理部门对企业（单位）登记注册的类型为依据，将企业（单位）登记注册类型分为以下几种：

（1）国有企业是指企业全部资产归国家所有，并按《中华人民共和国企业法人登记管理条例》规定登记注册的非公司制的经济组织。不包括有限责任公司中的国有独资公司。

（2）集体企业是指企业资产归集体所有，并按《中华人民共和国企业法人登记管理条例》规定登记注册的经济组织。

（3）股份合作企业是指以合作制为基础，由企业职工共同出资入股，吸收一定比例的社会资产投资组建，实行自主经营，自负盈亏，共同劳动，民主管理，按劳分配与按股分红相结合的一种集体经济组织。

（4）联营企业是指两个及两个以上相同或不同所有制性质的企业法人或事业单位法人，按自愿、平等、互利的原则，共同投资组成的经济组织。

联营企业包括国有联营企业、集体联营企业、国有与集体联营企业和其他联营企业。

（5）有限责任公司是指根据《中华人民共和国登记管理条例》规定登记注册，由两个以上，五十个以下的股东共同出资，每个股东以其所认缴的出资额对公司承担有限责任，公司以其全部资产对其债务承担责任的经济组织。

有限责任公司包括国有独资公司以及其他有限责任公司。

①国有独资公司是指国家授权的投资机构或者国家授权的部门单独投资设立的有限责任公司。

②其他有限责任公司是指国有独资公司以外的其他有限责任公司。

（6）股份有限公司是指根据《中华人民共和国登记管理条例》规定登记注册，其全部注册资本由等额股份构成并通过发行股票筹集资本，股东以其认购的股份对公司承担有限责任，公司以其全部资产对其债务承担责任的经济组织。

（7）私营企业是指由自然人投资设立或由自然人控股，以雇佣劳动为基础的营利性经济组织。包括按照《公司法》、《合伙企业法》、《私营企业暂行条件》规定登记注册的私营有限责任公司、私营股份有限公司、私营合伙企业和私营独资企业。

①私营独资企业是指按《私营企业暂行条例》的规定，由一名自然人投资经营，以雇佣劳动为基础，投资者对企业债务承担无限责任的企业。

②私营合伙企业是指按《合伙企业法》或《私营企业暂行条例》的规定，由两个以上自然人按照协议共同投资、共同经营、共负盈亏，以雇佣劳动为基础，对债务承担无限责任的企业。

③私营有限责任公司是指按《公司法》、《私营企业暂行条例》的规定，由两个以上自然人投资或由单个自然人控股的有限责任公司。

④私营股份有限公司是指按《公司法》的规定，由五个以上自然人投资，或由单个自然人控股的有限公司。

（8）其他内资企业是指上述第（1）条至第（7）条之外的其他内资经济组织。

（9）与港澳台商合资经营企业是指港澳台地区投资者与内地的企业依照《中华人民共和国中外合资经营企业法》及有关法律的规定，按合同规定的比例投资设立、分享利润和分担风险的企业。

（10）与港澳台商合作经营企业是指港澳台地区投资者与内地企业依照《中华人民共和国中外合作经营企业法》及有关法律的规定，依照合作合同的约定进行投资或提供条件设立、分配利润和分担风险的企业。

（11）港澳台商独资经营企业是指依照《中华人民共和国外资企业法》及有关法律的规定，在内地由港澳台地区投资者全额投资设立的企业。

（12）港澳台商投资股份有限公司是指根据国家有关规定，经外经贸部依法批准设立，其中港、澳、台商的股本占公司注册资本的比例达25%以上的股份有限公司。凡其中港、澳、台商的股本占公司注册资本的比例小于25%的，属于内资企业中的股份有限公司。

（13）中外合资经营企业是指外国企业或外国人与中国内地企业依照《中华人民共和国中外合资经营企业法》及有关法律的规定，按合同规定的比例投资设立、分享利润和分担风险的企业。

（14）中外合作经营企业是指外国企业或外国人与中国内地企业依照《中华人民共和国中外合作经营企业法》及有关法律的规定，依照合作合同的约定进行投资或提供条件设立、分配利润和分担风险的企业。

（15）外资企业是指依照《中华人民共和国外资企业法》

及有关法律的规定，在中国内地由外国投资者全额投资设立的企业。

（16）外商投资股份有限公司是指根据国家有关规定，经外经贸部依法批准设立，其中外资的股本占公司注册资本的比例达 25% 以上的股份有限公司。凡其中外资股本占公司注册资本的比例小于 25% 的，属于内资企业中的股份有限公司。

机关、事业单位和社会团体参照《企业登记注册类型与代码》，主要按其经费来源和管理方式划分。具体规定如下：

（1）机关包括国家机关和政党机关，原则上均列为"国有"。但有特殊规定的，如供销社等，则列为"集体"。

（2）事业单位包括经国家机构编制部门和有关业务主管部门批准成立的各类事业单位，不包括实行企业化管理的事业单位。事业单位的划分办法如下：

①由国家财政预算拨款或列入财政预算外资金管理以及经费主要来源于国有主管部门或国有上级单位的事业单位，列为"国有"。

②经费主要来源于集体单位的事业单位，列为"集体"。

③公民个人（或个人合伙）开办的事业单位，列为"私营"。

④上述以外的其他事业单位，如果其经费来源不明确，按管理方式进行归类。

（3）社会团体包括经民政部门批准成立以及未纳入社会团体管理条例范围的工会、妇联等各类社会团体。社会团体的划分办法如下：

①未纳入民政部社会团体管理条例范围的工会、妇联、共青团、青联、工商联、科协、侨联等社会团体，国家拨款设立的基金会或基金管理组织以及经费主要来源于国有业务主管部门或国有上级单位的社会团体，列为"国有"。

②经费主要来源于集体单位的社会团体，列为"集体"。

③公民个人（或个人合伙）开办的社会团体，划为"私营"。

④上述以外的其他社会团体，如果其经费来源不明确，改按管理方式进行归类。

平均增长速度 我国计算平均增长速度有两种方法：一种是习惯上经常使用的"水平法"，又称几何平均法，是以间隔期最后一年的水平同基期水平对比来计算平均每年增长（或下降）速度；另一种是"累计法"，又称代数平均法或方程法，是以间隔期内各年水平的总和同基期水平对比来计算平均每年增长（或下降）速度。在一般正常情况下，两种方法计算的平均每年增长速度比较接近；但在经济发展不平衡、出现大起大落时，两种方法计算的结果差别较大。

本《年鉴》内所列的平均增长速度，除固定资产投资用"累计法"计算外，其余均用"水平法"计算。从某年到某年平均增长速度的年份，均不包括基期年在内。如建国四十三年的平均增长速度是以 1949 年为基期计算的，则写为 1950-1992 年平均增长速度，其余类推。

Explanatory Notes on Main Statistical Indicators

Some explanations:

1. Historical data regarding total output value and value added of the primary industry, the secondary industry and the tertiary industry is adjusted and the data listed in the yearbooks shall prevail.

2. The growth rate of such indicators as total output value, value added of the primary industry, the secondary industry and the tertiary industry, total industrial added value and total value of agricultural output is calculated as per comparable price.

3. Because China started reform of fiscal and tax system from 1994, financial revenue and expenditure in 1994 and later are incomparable to those of previous years. Furthermore, fiscal revenue statistical caliber in 2000 was slightly adjusted.

4. Adjustment of industrial statistical caliber. Industrial statistical range before 1998 covered independent accounting industrial enterprises of township and above. The statistical range was adjusted to industrial enterprises above designated size in 1998, namely all state-owned industrial units and non-state-owned industrial units with annual sales revenue of above RMB 5 million and those with annual main business income of above RMB 20 million in 2011.

5. Change in statistical range in the construction industry. The statistical range in the construction industry covered county and above units from 1994 to 1995, construction enterprises with independent accounting whose qualification level was Level IV and above from 1996 to 1997 or construction enterprises with independent accounting whose qualification level was Level V and above from 1998.

Registration Status of Enterprises (Units) Enterprises are classified according to the registration status of an enterprise with the qualifications of legal person in industrial and commercial administration agencies. Government agencies, institutions, social organizations and other economic organizations shall follow the above classification.

Enterprises (units) are classified into the following categories according to the registration status of an enterprise in industrial and commercial administration agencies:

(1) State-owned Enterprises refer to non-corporation economic units that registered in accordance with the regulations of the people's republic of china for controlling the registration of enterprises as legal persons, where the entire assets are owned by the state. Excluded from this category are solely state-owned companies in the limited liability corporations.

(2) Collective-owned Enterprises refer to economic units where the enterprise assets are owned collectively and which have registered in accordance with the regulations of the people's republic of china for controlling the registration of enterprises as legal persons.

(3) Cooperative Enterprises refer to a form of collective economic units (enterprises) where capitals come mainly from employees as their shares, with certain proportion of capital from the outside, where production is organized on the basis of independent operation, independent accounting for profits and losses, joint work, democratic management, and a distribution system that integrates remuneration according to work with dividend according to capital share.

(4) Joint Ownership Enterprises refer to economic units established by two or more corporate enterprises or corporate institutions of the same or different ownership, through joint investment on the basis of equality, voluntary participation and mutual benefits. They include state joint ownership enterprises, collective joint ownership enterprises, joint state-collective enterprises, other joint ownership enterprises.

They include state joint ownership enterprise, collective joint ownership, joint state-collective enterprises and other joint operation enterprises.

(5) Limited Liability Corporations refer to economic units established with investment from 2-50 investors and registered in accordance with the Regulation of the People' s Republic of China on the Management of Registration of Corporations, each investor bearing limited liability to the corporation depending on its share of investment, and the corporation bearing liability to its debt to the maximum of its total assets.

Limited Liability Corporations include exclusive state funded limited liability corporations and other limited liability corporations.

① State-owned Exclusive Corporations refer to limited liability corporations established with sole investment by the investment organizations or departments authorized by the State.

② Other Limited Liability Corporations refer to other limited liability corporations other than the state-owned exclusive corporations .

(6) Share-holding Corporations Ltd. refer to economic units registered in accordance with the Regulation of the People' s Republic of China on the Management of Registration of Corporations, with total registered capitals divided into equal shares and raised through issuing stocks. Each investor bears limited liability to the corporation depending on the holding of shares, and the corporation bears liability to its debt to the maximum of its total assets.

(7) Private Enterprises refer to profit-making economic units invested and established by natural persons, or controlled by natural persons using employed labour. Included in this category are private limited liability corporations, private share-holding corporations Ltd., private partnership enterprises and private-funded enterprises registered in accordance with the Corporation Law, Partnership Enterprises Law and Interim Regulations on Private Enterprises.

① Private Exclusive Enterprises refer to enterprises invested and operated by one person using employed labour in accordance with Interim Regulations on Private Enterprises , where the investor bears unlimited liability for enterprise debts.

② Private Cooperative Enterprises refer to enterprises jointly invested and managed by more than two natural persons in accordance with Partnership Enterprises Law or Interim Regulations on Private Enterprises using employed labour, where sharing of investment, operation, profits and debts is stipulated under contract. They bear unlimited liabilities for the enterprise debts.

③ Private Limited Liability Corporations refer to the limited liability corporations invested by more than two natural persons or controlled by one natural person according to the stipulations of the Corporations Law and Interim Regulations on Private Enterprises.

④ Private Stock Corporations Ltd. refer to the limited corporations invested by more than five natural persons, or controlled by one natural person in accordance with Corporations Law.

(8) Other Domestic–funded Enterprises refer to other domestic–funded economic organizations other than those specified from Article (1) to Article (7).

(9) Joint Venture Enterprises with Funds from Hong Kong, Macau and Taiwan established by investors from Hong Kong, Macau and Taiwan with enterprises in the mainland of China in accordance with the Law of the People's Republic of China on Sino–foreign Cooperative Enterprises and other relevant laws, where the establishment of investment and the sharing of profits and risks are stipulated under the joint venture contracts.

(10) Cooperative Enterprises with Funds from Hong Kong, Macau and Taiwan established by investors from Hong Kong, Macau and Taiwan with enterprises in the mainland of China in accordance with the Law of the People's Republic of China on Sino–foreign Cooperative Enterprises and other relevant laws, where the investment or provision of facilities, and the sharing of profits and risks are stipulated in the cooperative contracts.

(11) Enterprises with Sole (exclusive) Investment from Hong Kong, Macau and Taiwan refer to enterprises established in the mainland of China with exclusive investment from investors from Hong Kong, Macau and Taiwan in accordance with the Law of the People's Republic of China on Wholly Foreign–owned Enterprises and other relevant laws.

(12) Share–holding Corporations Ltd. with Investment from Hong Kong, Macau and Taiwan refer to share–holding corporations Ltd. established with the approved from the Ministry of Foreign Trade and Economic Cooperation in line with relevant State regulations, where the share of investment from Hong Kong, Macau and Taiwan exceeds 25% of the total registered capital of the corporation. In case the share of foreign investment is less than 25% of the total registered capital, the enterprise is to be classified as domestic–funded share–holding corporation Ltd..

(13) Joint Venture Enterprises with Foreign Investment refer to enterprises jointly established by foreign enterprises or foreigners with enterprises in the mainland of China in accordance with the Law of the People's Republic of China on Sino–Foreign Equity Joint Ventures and other relevant laws, where the sharing of investment, profits and risks is stipulated under contract.

(14) Cooperative Enterprises with Foreign Investment refer to enterprises jointly established by foreign enterprises or foreigners with enterprises in the mainland of China in accordance with the Law of the People's Republic of China on Sino–Foreign Contractual Joint Ventures and other relevant laws, where the investment or provision of facilities and the sharing of profits and risks are stipulated under cooperative contracts.

(15) Enterprises with Sole (exclusive) Foreign Investment refer to enterprises established in the mainland of China with exclusive investment from foreign investors in accordance with the Law of the People's Republic of China on Wholly Foreign–owned Enterprises and other relevant laws.

(16) Share–holding Corporations Ltd. with Foreign Investment refer to share–holding corporations Ltd. established with the approval from the Ministry of Foreign Trade and Economic Cooperation in line with relevant State regulations, where the share of investment from foreign investors exceeds 25% of the total registered capital of the corporation. In case the share of foreign investment is less than 25% of the total registered capital, the enterprise is to be classified as domestic–funded share–holding corporation Ltd.

Government Agencies, Institutions and Social Organizations are classified into the following categories by source of funds and manner of management taking reference of the registration status and code of enterprises:

(1) Government agencies: include State and party agencies, classified in principle as State–owned. There are exceptions, such as supply and marketing cooperatives which are classified as collective–owned.

(2) Institutions: include institutions of various types established with the approval by organization and staffing departments of the government, but exclude institutions where enterprise management system is introduced. Institutions are further classified as follows:

① Institutions for which their main budgets are from government budget appropriations or extra–budget funds, or allocated from the budget of their competent government agencies. Such institutions are classified as state–owned.

② Institutions for which their budget mainly come from collective units are classified as collective–owned.

③ Social institutions established by individual or a group of citizens, which are classified as private.

④ Institutions other than those mentioned above for which their sources of budget are not clear are classified by the manner of management.

(3) Social organizations: include social organizations established with the approved from the Ministry of Civil Affairs and organizations that are not covered by social organization management regulations such as trade unions, women's federations etc. Such organizations are further classified as follows:

① Social organizations that are not covered by social organization management regulations of the Ministry of Civil Affairs such as labor union, women federations, communist youth leagues, youth federation, industrial and commerce associations, scientist associations, overseas Chinese associations,etc., foundations and fund management organizations established with funds from the state, and social organizations whose funds mainly come from the budget of their competent government agencies. Such institutions are classified as State-owned.

② Social organizations for which their budget mainly come from collective units are classified as collective-owned.

③ Social organizations established by individual or a group of citizens are classified as private.

④ Social organizations other than those mentioned above for which their sources of budget are not clear are classified by the manner of management.

Average speed of growth The average speed of growth in China is calculated based on two methods: Customarily, one method -- "level method" (also called as geometric method) is often used to calculate average annual growth (or decline) speed by comparing the level of the final year of the interval with the level during the base period; The other method is "cumulative method" (also called as method of algebraic or equation method) which is used to calculate average annual growth (decline) speed by comparing total level of all years within the interval with the level during the base period. In normal circumstances, average annual growth rates calculated based on these two method are relatively close; However, in case of unbalanced economic development and changing radically, big difference happens to results calculated based on these two methods.

Average speed of growth listed in the Yearbooks of fixed investments is calculated as per "cumulative method" and the rest is calculated pursuant to "level method". Years of average speed of growth from one year to one year are not included into the base period. For example, the average speed of growth in the 43 years after founding of China is calculated based on base period in 1949; average speed of growth from 1950 to 1992 is written down and the rest is analogized.

国民经济核算

NATIONAL ACCOUNTS

4-1 各时期生产总值（按当年价格计算）
Gross Domestic Product in Each Period(Calculated at Current Prices)

年份 Year	地区生产总值（万元）Gross Domestic Product (10 000 yuan)	其中 of which				
		第一产业 Primary Industry	第二产业 Secondary Industry	第三产业 Tertiary Industry	#工业 Industry	人均生产总值（元）Per Capita GDP (yuan)
1952	38282	14464	11300	12518	10907	121
1957	66616	19282	22378	24956	21840	194
1962	62056	10271	24346	27439	23610	177
1965	96827	18837	44395	33595	43388	262
1970	136085	21582	76949	37554	75571	337
1975	162427	28985	86500	46942	84614	373
"五五"时期						
1976	181751	33447	99797	48507	97215	413
1977	199814	35831	112347	51636	109811	450
1978	235993	41633	133172	61188	128910	527
1979	265619	50144	147679	67796	141048	586
1980	288001	59580	158591	69830	142369	630
"六五"时期						
1981	315623	65646	176516	73461	151131	681
1982	360552	88026	185548	86978	157894	765
1983	420075	116162	204758	99155	179572	881
1984	479948	103502	254684	121762	201017	997
1985	613741	129221	318193	166327	275447	1263
"七五"时期						
1986	712831	148165	344782	219884	286895	1451
1987	845431	175195	402857	267379	328783	1699
1988	1142249	222330	570722	349197	474895	2266
1989	1258319	237692	615209	405418	546591	2466
1990	1382350	239283	673593	469474	604274	2666
"八五"时期						
1991	1633920	253797	765582	614541	677340	3109
1992	2078386	277408	983638	817340	868539	3928
1993	2707637	326614	1331453	1049570	1153600	5088
1994	3718760	494413	1768214	1456133	1544940	6946
1995	4735176	676399	2203700	1855077	1941631	8773

4-1 续表 continued

年份 Year	地区生产总值（万元） Gross Domestic Product (10 000 yuan)	其中 of which				
		第一产业 Primary Industry	第二产业 Secondary Industry	第三产业 Tertiary Industry	# 工业 Industry	人均生产总值（元） Per Capita GDP (yuan)
"九五"时期						
1996	5808366	742400	2749300	2316666	2383100	10701
1997	7099490	825200	3279700	2994590	2788668	12995
1998	8021619	902000	3664300	3455319	2984090	14549
1999	8813156	925171	3998006	3889979	3188000	15863
2000（调整前）	9521798	950125	4186077	4385596	3366075	16999
2000	9441315	960185	4147355	4333775	3319701	16855
"十五"时期						
2001	10579155	983242	4380564	5215349	3507175	18697
2002	11901167	1000514	5016352	5884300	4023830	20807
2003	13521540	1048068	5886754	6586718	4822007	23362
2004	16002700	1205800	7219300	7577600	6034000	27293
2005	18462792	1343400	8474679	8644713	7158669	28900
"十一五"时期						
2006	21615316	1451210	9971161	10192945	8441795	33480
2007	25001427	1502995	11287598	12210834	9548644	38301
2008	30067703	1750100	13130913	15186690	11152190	45563
2009	33409059	1870700	14335100	17203259	11913600	50219
2010	39105271	2151700	16374544	20579027	13524244	57947
"十二五"时期						
2011	44062889	2378573	18289700	23394616	15078800	64310
2012	48036696	2529161	19381399	26126136	16030799	69444
2013	52301948	2847088	20532400	28922460	16906300	74994
2013（新行业）	52301948	2769911	20950832	28581205	16906300	74994
2014	57705966	2902894	22616579	32186493	18221072	82052
2015	61002320	3053916	23070000	34878404	18443700	85919
"十三五"时期						
2016	65361165	3173113	23689000	38499052	18788300	90999
2017	72019553	3173969	25692200	43153384	20031000	98967
2018	78565600	2724200	28293100	47548300	21450700	106302
2019	94433700	3430600	32652200	58350900	21678700	106416

注：1. 2013 年始使用新口径、新行业分类标准（GB–2011）。新行业中：第一产业不再包括 农林牧渔服务业；第二产业不再包括开采辅助活动，金属制品、机械和设备修理业；农林牧渔服务业，开采辅助活动，金属制品、机械和设备修理业归入第三产业。后同。
2. 2013 年（新行业）、2014 年为普查口径数据，后同。
3. 2005 年后人均生产总值为常住人口口径，后同。
4. 经济普查年度，2018 年相关指标为快报数据。

Note: 1.New caliber and industry classification standard started to be used from 2013 (GB–2011). In the new industries: The primary industry doesn't include agriculture,forestry, animal husbandry and fishery service industry any longer; The secondary industry doesn't include mining auxiliary activities, metalware and machinery and equipment repair industry; Agriculture, forestry, animal husbandry and fishery service industry, mining auxiliary activities, metalware and machinery and equipment repair industry fall into the tertiary industry. Similarly hereinafter.
2.Economic census survey caliber data in 2013 (new industry) and 2014 arises (the same below).
3.After 2005, the per capita gross domestic product (GDP) of the permanent population caliber(the same below).
4.In the economic census year, related indicator in 2018 is the express data.

4-2 各时期生产总值环比指数(以上年为100)

Circle Indices of Gross Domestic Product (Preceding Last Year=100)

年份 Year	地区生产总值 Gross Domestic Product	其中 of which				
		第一产业 Primary Industry	第二产 Secondary Industry	第三产业 Tertiary Industry	工业 Industry	人均生产总值 Per Capita GDP
1952	123.9	119.1	153.2	132.7	126.2	118.0
1957	97.5	91.7	89.0	112.7	92.3	95.7
1962	105.6	116.7	82.7	121.9	81.3	105.9
1965	120.8	120.4	138.8	105.3	132.9	120.7
1970	113.7	95.9	131.9	100.5	130.8	108.7
1975	139.0	121.5	160.4	117.6	167.8	133.9
"五五"时期						
1976	104.9	93.2	114.6	104.5	113.1	104.6
1977	106.8	95.0	112.3	106.3	113.9	104.7
1978	113.0	99.3	114.2	119.0	111.9	109.1
1979	112.1	120.0	110.5	110.4	109.0	110.8
1980	113.6	124.5	112.5	107.9	105.7	112.6
"六五"时期						
1981	109.5	110.1	111.2	105.1	106.1	108.0
1982	116.0	136.2	106.7	120.2	106.1	114.1
1983	117.0	132.5	110.8	114.5	114.2	115.6
1984	118.4	92.3	128.9	127.3	116.0	117.3
1985	105.4	102.9	103.0	112.6	112.9	104.4
"七五"时期						
1986	110.8	109.4	103.4	126.1	99.4	109.6
1987	112.2	111.9	110.5	115.0	108.4	110.8
1988	119.0	111.8	124.8	115.0	127.2	117.5
1989	103.2	100.1	101.0	108.8	107.8	101.9
1990	108.3	99.2	107.9	114.2	109.0	106.6
"八五"时期						
1991	112.8	101.2	108.5	124.9	107.0	111.3
1992	122.8	105.5	124.0	128.4	123.8	122.0
1993	121.4	109.7	126.1	119.7	123.8	120.7
1994	118.9	131.0	115.0	120.1	115.9	118.2
1995	113.3	121.7	110.9	112.3	111.8	112.4

4-2 续表 continued

年份 Year	地区生产总值 Gross Domestic Product	其中 of which				
		第一产业 Primary Industry	第二产 Secondary Industry	第三产业 Tertiary Industry	工业 Industry	人均生产总值 Per Capita GDP
"九五"时期						
1996	114.9	102.8	116.9	117.0	115.0	114.3
1997	119.6	108.8	116.7	126.3	114.5	118.8
1998	113.8	110.1	112.6	116.3	107.8	112.8
1999	113.1	109.5	111.8	115.4	110.6	112.2
2000	112.1	106.1	110.8	114.9	112.2	111.2
"十五"时期						
2001	112.1	104.0	109.8	115.9	111.0	110.9
2002	113.2	102.6	114.8	113.9	115.2	112.0
2003	114.5	104.6	118.2	113.0	121.9	113.2
2004	115.6	107.8	119.8	113.0	121.9	114.1
2005	115.6	106.0	117.4	115.4	119.8	114.2
"十一五"时期						
2006	115.7	106.0	117.2	115.6	119.3	114.4
2007	115.8	100.0	115.3	118.5	116.0	114.5
2008	113.0	105.0	110.0	116.8	110.7	111.8
2009	112.2	105.1	112.1	113.1	110.5	111.3
2010	112.7	104.9	111.0	114.9	110.7	111.1
"十二五"时期						
2011	110.6	104.4	111.7	110.3	112.2	108.9
2012	109.5	104.7	109.2	110.1	109.7	108.4
2013	109.6	103.9	110.1	109.7	110.6	108.7
2013(新行业)	109.6	103.7	110.1	109.7	110.6	108.7
2014	108.8	103.9	108.8	109.1	108.9	107.9
2015	108.1	104.1	107.4	108.9	107.1	107.0
"十三五"时期						
2016	107.8	104.1	106.9	108.7	106.9	106.5
2017	108.0	103.3	108.4	108.2	108.9	106.6
2018	107.4	102.5	107.8	107.5	107.0	105.7
2019	107.0	101.3	107.8	107.0	104.1	105.7

4-3 资本形成总额（按当年价格计算）
Gross Capital Formation(Calculated at Current Prices)

单位：万元 (10 000 yuan)

指标	Indicator	2012 年	2013 年	2014 年	2015 年	2016 年	2017 年
资本形成总额	Gross Capital Formation	24140144	30182535	34417750	38457600	40333673	48134888
一、固定资本形成总额	Gross Fixed Capital Formation	21390653	27194510	31268206	33457249	37051965	44000633
1. 住宅	Residential	4209797	6274201	6617872	7438000	9945598	11719804
2. 非住宅建筑物	Non-residential Buildings	9748694	13011712	15557997	14780097	15626960	17892869
3. 机器和设备	Machinery and Equipment	3984376	4499778	5067899	6450000	5880359	6674207
4. 土地改良支出	Land Improvement Expenditure	44788	62574	92567	136928	83868	51369
5. 矿藏勘探费	Mineral Exploration Expenditure	4730	5198	6049	6979	6899	6821
6. 计算机软件	Computer Software	2130000	2276970	2590812	2970366	3407010	3815852
7. 其他	Others	1268268	1064077	1335012	1674879	2101270	2636211
二、存货增加	Changes in Inventories	2749492	2988025	3149544	5000351	3281707	4134254
1. 农林牧渔业	Agriculture, Forestry, Animal Husbandry and Fishery	161773	163227	-1100	-16200	-31854	-13992
2. 工业	Industry	248136	670461	685047	733000	8376	3468105
3. 建筑业	Construction	188246	-532	-603	514751	399574	976845
4. 交通运输、仓储和邮政业	Transport, Storage and Postal Services	1791	2508	2115	-17600	116139	-5000
5. 批发和零售业	Wholesale and Retail Trade	175842	31828	110839	-79000	-104495	869398
6. 住宿和餐饮业	Accommodations and Catering Services	157	-1866	-523	-26000	-21754	-23786
7. 房地产业	Real Estate	1973546	2122399	2347812	4010000	2090306	-1226316
8. 其他服务业	Other Services			5957	-118600	825415	89000

4-4 最终消费支出（按当年价格计算）
Final Consumption Expenditure(Calculated at Current Prices)

单位：亿元 (100 million yuan)

指　标	Indicator	2012 年	2013 年	2014 年	2015 年	2016 年	2017 年
最终消费支出	**Final Consumption Expenditures**	**2448.32**	**2728.45**	**2936.20**	**3190.55**	**3466.81**	**3779.14**
居民消费支出	Expense on Consumption of All Households	1574.06	1747.52	1856.00	2015.55	2227.92	2396.54
农村居民	Rural Households	206.67	226.28	243.72	259.87	282.02	299.67
食品类支出	Food,Tobacco and Liquor	60.81	64.14	67.29	68.50	74.73	80.26
衣着类支出	Clothing	10.16	10.98	12.95	11.73	12.78	13.48
居住类支出	Residence	30.13	33.68	31.54	38.73	43.34	48.89
家庭设备、用品及服务类支出	Supplies and Services	10.88	13.45	15.99	13.94	15.32	16.17
医疗保健类支出	Health Care	23.83	20.54	19.78	17.73	18.81	18.37
交通和通信类支出	Transport and Communications	24.73	30.40	36.10	36.83	39.26	40.44
文教娱乐用品及服务类支出	Recreation,Education and Cultural	10.75	14.17	16.18	21.61	23.93	24.50
金融中介服务虚拟支出	FIinancial Intermediary Services Virtual Expenditure	1.92	2.14	2.33	2.54	2.88	3.12
保险服务消费支出	Insurance Services Expenditure	7.74	8.03	9.42	11.05	11.56	12.68
自有住房服务虚拟支出	Private Housing Service Virtual Expenditure	24.03	26.68	28.02	29.42	30.89	32.43
其他商品和服务类支出	Other Goods and Services Expenditure	1.69	2.06	4.12	7.78	8.52	9.33
城镇居民	Urban Households	1367.39	1521.23	1612.27	1755.68	1945.90	2096.86
食品类支出	Food,Tobacco and Liquor	336.42	367.27	377.92	415.71	447.72	468.76
衣着类支出	Clothing	138.84	152.42	152.72	155.01	136.57	138.61
居住类支出	Residence	123.43	138.63	172.32	181.63	232.57	266.76
家庭设备、用品及服务类支出	Supplies and Services	96.57	105.23	111.02	126.11	130.78	134.26
医疗保健类支出	Health Care	100.39	110.48	110.26	125.36	144.54	155.09
交通和通信类支出	Transport and Communications	220.64	253.86	261.73	288.43	345.54	356.59
文教娱乐用品及服务类支出	Recreation,Education and Cultural	143.21	155.17	170.23	197.80	199.58	211.76
金融中介服务虚拟支出	FIinancial Intermediary Services Virtual Expenditure	38.25	47.12	51.26	55.78	68.43	79.89
保险服务消费支出	Insurance Services Expenditure	14.61	15.17	17.79	20.87	36.04	42.70
自有住房服务虚拟支出	Private Housing Service Virtual Expenditure	98.38	114.15	119.85	125.85	142.71	174.78
实物消费支出	Reality Consumption	5.71	6.18	6.56	9.67	14.28	22.75
其他商品和服务类支出	Other Goods and Services Expenditure	50.94	55.56	60.62	53.46	47.14	44.90
政府消费支出	Government Consumption Expenditure	874.26	980.93	1080.20	1175.00	1238.89	1382.60

4-5 实际最终消费(按当年价格计算)
Final Real Consumption(Calculated at Current Prices)

单位：亿元 (100 million yuan)

指　标	Indicator	2012 年	2013 年	2014 年	2015 年	2016 年	2017 年
最终消费	Final Consumption	2448.32	2728.45	2936.20	3190.55	3466.81	3779.14
居民消费	Expense on Consumption of All Households	1907.56	2066.16	2189.96	2378.21	2610.94	2803.24
农村居民	Rural Households	245.83	272.82	292.65	312.03	342.28	360.56
食品类消费	Food, Tobacco and Liquor	61.32	65.67	68.89	70.13	76.51	82.17
衣着类消费	Clothing	10.24	11.24	13.26	12.01	13.08	13.80
居住类消费	Residence	30.24	34.32	32.14	39.46	44.16	49.81
家庭设备、用品及服务类消费	Supplies and Services	10.97	13.76	16.36	14.26	15.67	16.54
医疗保健类消费	Health Care	42.55	40.63	39.13	35.07	37.21	36.34
交通和通信类消费	Transport and Communcations	24.95	31.14	36.99	37.73	40.22	41.43
文教娱乐用品及服务类消费	Recreation,Education and Cultural	29.90	37.62	42.95	57.39	63.53	65.06
金融中介服务虚拟消费	Flinancial Intermediary Services Virtual Expenditure	1.94	2.14	2.33	2.53	2.88	3.11
保险服务消费支出	Insurance Services Expenditure	7.80	8.03	9.42	11.05	11.56	12.68
自有住房服务虚拟消费	Private Housing Service Virtual Expenditure	24.21	26.68	28.01	29.41	30.89	32.43
其他商品和服务类消费	Other Goods and Services Expenditure	1.71	1.59	3.18	6.01	6.58	7.21
城镇居民	Urban Households	1661.73	1793.34	1897.31	2066.06	2268.66	2442.68
食品类消费	Food, Tobacco and Liquor	339.16	364.59	375.17	412.68	444.46	465.35
衣着类消费	Clothing	139.75	151.07	151.37	153.64	135.36	137.39
居住类消费	Residence	124.48	137.67	171.13	180.37	209.96	240.82
家庭设备、用品及服务类消费	Supplies and Services	97.28	104.39	110.13	125.10	129.73	133.19
医疗保健类消费	Health Care	230.37	251.57	251.07	285.46	329.14	353.16
交通和通信类消费	Transport and Communications	222.24	251.79	259.60	286.08	322.30	332.62
文教娱乐用品及服务类消费	Recreation,Education and Cultural	298.85	318.87	349.80	406.47	410.13	435.15
金融中介服务虚拟消费	Flinancial Intermediary ServicesVirtual Expenditure	38.54	47.12	51.27	55.78	68.43	79.89
保险服务消费支出	Insurance Services Expenditure	14.73	15.17	17.79	20.87	36.05	42.71
自有住房服务虚拟消费	Private Housing Service Virtual Expenditure	99.33	114.15	119.86	125.85	142.71	174.79
实物消费消费	Reality Consumption	5.76	6.18	6.56	9.68	14.28	22.75
其他商品和服务类消费	Other Goods and Services Expenditure	51.24	30.77	33.57	29.60	26.11	24.87
政府消费	Government Consumption	540.76	662.28	746.25	811.74	855.87	975.90

4-6 生产总值分布
Distribution of Gross Domestic Product

单位：亿元 (100 million yuan)

年份 Year	政府最终消费 Government Final Consumption	居民最终消费 Household Final Consumption	国内总投资 Total Domestic Investment	国内储蓄总额 Gross Domestic Savings	资金差额 Funding Gap
GDP分布					
1990	14.63	52.28	54.12	71.36	17.24
“八五”时期					
1991	16.43	60.70	56.35	86.26	29.91
1992	20.06	71.02	80.23	116.76	36.53
1993	22.75	90.63	122.66	157.38	34.71
1994	25.57	122.10	152.31	224.21	71.90
1995	34.93	197.61	190.05	240.98	50.93
“九五”时期					
1996	50.21	240.49	236.98	290.14	53.16
1997	98.69	291.30	246.44	319.96	73.52
1998	100.52	347.78	285.39	353.86	68.47
1999	126.27	362.71	347.37	392.34	44.97
2000	132.05	332.70	398.13	479.38	81.25
“十五”时期					
2001	146.90	357.84	418.38	553.18	134.79
2002	161.84	401.23	500.89	627.04	126.16
2003	184.97	430.62	562.41	736.57	174.15
2004	206.80	457.71	760.12	935.75	175.63
2005	223.46	522.10	1017.39	1100.72	83.33
“十一五”时期					
2006	285.51	621.65	1126.39	1254.37	127.98
2007	350.33	820.82	1286.16	1328.99	42.83
2008	431.26	940.61	1577.87	1634.90	57.03
2009	495.31	1022.07	1749.05	1823.53	74.48
2010	636.91	1197.34	2055.73	2076.28	20.55
“十二五”时期					
2011	747.23	1391.82	2360.99	2267.24	-93.75
2012	874.26	1574.06	2414.01	2355.35	-58.66
2013	980.93	1747.52	3018.25	3042.14	23.88
2014	1080.20	1856.00	3441.78	2834.40	-561.73
2015	1175.00	2015.55	3845.76	2909.68	-936.08
“十三五”时期					
2016	1238.89	2227.92	4033.37	3069.31	-964.06
2017	1382.60	2396.54	4813.49	3422.82	-1390.67

4-7 生产总值(2009年—2013年)(分行业、按当年价格计算)

Value of Gross Domestic Product(2009—2013)(Sub Industry, Calculated at Current Prices)

单位：亿元(100 million yuan)

指　标	Indicator	2009年	2010年	2011年	2012年	2013年
地区生产总值	Gross Domestic Product	3340.91	3910.53	4406.29	4803.67	5230.19
第一产业	Primary Industry	187.07	215.17	237.86	252.92	284.71
农林牧渔业	Agriculture, Forestry, Animal Husbandry and Fishery	187.07	215.17	237.86	252.92	284.71
农业	Farming	120.34	149.43	152.55	160.77	186.98
林业	Forestry	8.34	4.73	5.69	6.68	7.89
畜牧业	Animal Husbandry	51.22	53.08	70.61	75.28	78.08
渔业	Fishery	2.88	3.02	3.35	3.54	4.04
农林牧渔服务业	Services of Agriculture,Forestry,Animal Husbandry and Fishing	4.29	4.91	5.66	6.65	7.72
第二产业	Secondary Industry	1433.51	1637.45	1828.97	1938.14	2053.24
工业	Industry	1191.36	1352.42	1507.88	1603.08	1690.63
采矿业	Mining	26.60	31.64	34.11	33.21	56.03
制造业	Manufacture	1073.42	1194.23	1299.80	1490.91	1539.44
电力、燃气及水的生产和供应业	Production and Supply of Electric,Gas and Water	91.34	126.56	173.98	78.96	95.16
建筑业	Construction	242.15	285.03	321.09	335.06	362.61
房屋和土木工程建筑业	Building Construction	193.94	233.87	265.87	279.09	280.86
建筑安装业	Construction Installment	36.02	38.26	38.41	40.22	59.54
建筑装饰业	Construction Decoration	7.51	7.78	11.77	13.03	19.00
其他建筑业	Others	4.69	5.12	5.04	2.72	3.21
第三产业	Tertiary Industry	1720.33	2057.90	2339.46	2612.61	2892.24
交通运输、仓储和邮政业	Transport,Storage and Postal Services	200.27	236.81	296.61	320.41	332.97
铁路运输业	Railway Transport	52.01	56.18	60.70	65.55	63.12
道路运输业	Road Transport	96.68	118.25	152.71	170.27	172.42
城市公共交通业	Public Transportation by City	13.62	14.71	17.08	18.99	18.28
水上运输业	Waterway Transport	0.60	0.73	0.94	1.05	1.18
航空运输业	Air Transport	17.01	24.76	33.73	27.71	31.87
管道运输业	Pipeline Transport	1.20	1.36	1.37	1.40	1.65
装卸搬运和其他运输服务业	Loading and Unloading and Other Transport Services	11.84	13.55	21.59	21.64	26.47

4-7 续表 1 continued 1

指　标	Indicator	2009 年	2010 年	2011 年	2012 年	2013 年
仓储业	Storage	5.79	6.09	7.18	10.97	15.00
邮政业	Postal Services	1.52	1.19	1.30	2.83	2.98
信息传输、计算机服务和软件业	Information Transmission, Computer Services and Software	66.24	116.38	136.70	152.10	162.58
电信和其他信息传输服务业	Telecommunications, Radio and Television and Satellite Transmission Services	30.95	31.15	29.93	28.80	33.11
计算机服务业	Internet and Related Services	17.95	25.14	31.67	37.99	44.56
软件业	Software and Information Technology Services	17.33	60.09	75.10	85.31	84.90
批发和零售业	Wholesale and Retail Trade	416.50	476.43	522.96	588.50	671.63
批发业	Wholesale	234.13	288.90	335.52	381.87	437.59
零售业	Retail Trade	182.37	187.53	187.44	206.64	234.04
住宿和餐饮业	Accommodations and Catering Services	125.55	142.81	143.73	149.52	168.18
住宿业	Accommodations	12.43	16.44	16.77	17.68	20.76
餐饮业	Catering Services	113.12	126.37	126.96	131.84	147.42
金融业	Financial Intermediation	240.21	288.33	330.14	411.34	461.00
银行业	Banking Sector	164.58	226.00	278.34	357.71	387.31
证券业	Securities Industry	60.51	47.28	32.05	26.87	33.74
保险业	Insurance	10.02	5.37	6.43	6.99	8.16
其他金融活动	Others	5.10	9.68	13.32	19.77	31.80
房地产业	Real Estate	172.63	220.79	254.98	273.94	320.56
房地产开发经营业	Real Estate Development and Management	62.40	83.08	99.19	100.31	124.98
物业管理业	Property Management	18.69	28.65	31.55	32.35	38.34
房地产中介服务业	Real Estate Intermediary Services	10.13	15.53	17.11	17.62	17.62
其他房地产活动	Other Real Estate Activity	7.21	11.05	12.20	13.03	22.87
居民自有住房服务业	Private Housing Service	74.20	82.48	94.94	110.62	116.74
租赁和商务服务业	Leasing and Business Services	88.71	107.32	131.18	145.29	153.19
租赁业	Leasing Services	4.92	7.01	8.39	12.30	15.05
商务服务业	Business Services	83.78	100.31	122.79	132.99	138.14
科学研究、技术服务和地质勘查业	Scientific Research, Technical Services and Geeological Prospecting Industry	57.79	63.63	69.22	69.36	75.62

4–7 续表 2 continued 2

指　标	Indicator	2009 年	2010 年	2011 年	2012 年	2013 年
研究与试验发展	Research and Experimental Development	19.95	18.95	22.14	22.85	27.12
专业技术服务业	Special Technical Services	27.36	32.94	33.95	33.78	32.72
科技交流和推广服务业	Science and Technology Promotion and Application Services	6.74	7.16	7.87	7.46	9.79
地质勘查业	Geeological Prospecting Industry	3.74	4.58	5.27	5.27	5.98
水利、环境和公共设施管理业	Management of Water Conservancy, Environment and Public Facilities	12.18	13.84	13.62	14.05	17.26
水利管理业	Management of Water Conservancy	5.06	6.06	5.91	6.21	9.06
环境管理业	Environmental Management	2.46	2.90	2.54	0.07	0.09
公共设施管理业	Management of Public Facilities	4.67	4.87	5.17	7.77	8.11
居民服务和其他服务业	Services to Households and Other Services	32.95	40.75	46.88	52.01	57.49
居民服务业	Services to Households	18.41	22.77	26.18	29.03	30.26
其他服务业	Other Services	14.53	17.98	20.70	22.98	27.24
教育	Education	109.66	116.49	123.09	128.09	140.75
卫生、社会保障和社会福利业	Health,Social Security and Social Welfare	64.87	87.30	105.00	127.60	134.11
卫生	Public Health	56.31	74.52	95.70	117.78	124.11
社会保障业	Social Security	6.37	9.46	7.11	7.48	7.60
社会福利业	Social Welfare	2.19	3.32	2.19	2.34	2.40
文化、体育和娱乐业	Culture, Sports and Recreation	23.60	28.01	28.40	32.21	36.29
新闻出版业	News and Publication	9.99	10.94	11.82	11.59	12.35
广播、电视、电影和音像业	Radio, Television, Film and Video	5.27	6.65	6.97	10.52	11.24
文化艺术业	Culture and Arts	4.26	5.84	4.46	4.19	5.04
体育	Sports	2.08	2.21	2.47	2.55	4.01
娱乐业	Recreation	2.01	2.37	2.68	3.37	3.65
公共管理和社会组织	Public Management and Social Organizations	109.18	119.01	136.93	148.19	160.61

4-8 生产总值(2013年—2017年)(分行业，按当年价格计算)

Value of Gross Domestic Product(2013-2017)(Sub Industry，Calculated at Current Prices)

单位：亿元(100 million yuan)

指标	Indicator	2013年	2014年	2015年	2016年	2017年
地区生产总值	Gross Domestic Product	5230.19	5770.60	6100.23	6536.12	7201.96
农、林、牧、渔业	Agriculture, Forestry, Animal Husbandry and Fishery	284.71	299.11	314.99	328.24	330.24
农业	Farming	186.98	199.53	210.14	215.11	215.11
林业	Forestry	7.89	8.85	9.96	11.19	11.19
畜牧业	Animal Husbandry	78.08	77.57	80.82	86.47	86.47
渔业	Fishery	4.04	4.33	4.47	4.55	4.63
农、林、牧、渔服务业	Services of Agriculture, Forestry, Animal Husbandry and Fishing	7.72	8.82	9.60	10.93	12.84
工业	Industry	1690.63	1822.11	1844.37	1878.83	2003.10
采矿业	Mining	27.95	30.13	36.89	45.80	49.88
#开采辅助活动	Mining Support Activities	0.03	0.03	0.03	0.03	0.03
制造业	Manufacture	1471.81	1586.27	1715.26	1749.57	1877.08
#金属制品、机械和设备修理业	Metal Products, Machinery and Equipment Repair Industry	3.08	3.32	3.40	3.46	3.60
电力、燃气及水的生产和供应业	Production and Supply of Electric, Gas and Water	190.87	205.71	92.22	83.46	76.14
建筑业	Construction	407.56	442.90	466.06	493.56	569.75
房屋建筑业	Building Construction	236.10	252.57	241.65	279.93	316.15
土木工程建筑业	Civil Engineering Construction	107.82	121.17	178.83	172.85	215.22
建筑安装业	Construction Installment	25.22	27.40	21.12	13.47	15.97
建筑装饰业和其他建筑业	Construction Decoration and Others	38.43	41.76	24.47	27.32	22.41
批发和零售业	Wholesale and Retail Trade	626.68	691.65	715.54	760.76	976.87
批发业	Wholesale	397.64	441.38	453.30	482.02	620.82
零售业	Retail Trade	229.04	250.27	262.24	278.74	356.05
交通运输、仓储和邮政业	Transport, Storage and Post	332.97	364.29	371.63	392.18	415.61
铁路运输业	Railway Transport	63.12	69.06	68.40	72.50	72.40
道路运输业	Road Transport	166.88	181.18	186.88	191.92	198.29

4-8 续表 1 continued 1

指标	Indicator	2013 年	2014 年	2015 年	2016 年	2017 年
水上运输业	Waterway Transport	1.18	1.29	1.32	1.50	1.42
航空运输业	Air Transport	31.87	34.87	35.57	41.51	44.62
管道运输业	Pipeline Transport	21.47	23.49	23.96	24.35	29.71
装卸搬运和运输代理业	Loading, Unloading and Forwarding Agency	26.47	28.96	29.54	27.33	28.63
仓储业	Storage	15.00	16.41	16.74	21.68	27.20
邮政业	Postal Services	6.98	9.04	9.22	11.38	13.33
住宿和餐饮业	**Accommodations and Catering Services**	**168.18**	**180.96**	**188.45**	**202.85**	**218.71**
住宿业	Accommodations	20.76	22.45	22.68	23.99	25.21
餐饮业	Catering Services	147.42	158.51	165.77	178.86	193.50
信息传输、软件和信息技术服务和业	**Information Transmission, Soft ware and Information Technology**	**162.58**	**190.17**	**201.95**	**232.78**	**276.11**
电信、广播电视和卫星传输服务	Telecommunications, Radio and Television and Satellite Transmission Services	101.79	119.07	126.45	125.49	164.15
互联网和相关服务	Internet and related Services	4.35	5.09	5.40	18.21	20.24
软件和信息技术服务业	Software and Information Technology Services	56.44	66.02	70.11	89.08	91.72
金融业	**Financial Intermediation**	**461.00**	**541.88**	**641.86**	**719.98**	**776.01**
货币金融服务	Monetary and Financial Services	387.31	437.25	517.93	589.41	657.35
资本市场服务	Capital Market Services	33.74	48.65	57.63	36.42	41.05
保险业	Insurance	8.16	9.59	11.36	23.06	26.76
其他金融业	Others	31.80	46.38	54.94	71.10	50.85
房地产业	**Real Estate**	**320.56**	**369.23**	**415.00**	**463.21**	**500.05**
房地产开发经营业	Real Estate Development and Management	136.61	169.38	190.37	218.55	220.66
物业管理业	Property Management	26.72	25.46	28.62	33.66	35.55
房地产中介服务业	Real Estate Intermediary Services	17.62	17.44	19.60	25.72	29.89
自有房地产经营活动	Own Real Estate Operating Activities	116.74	132.83	134.73	140.19	160.01
其他房地产业	Other Real Estate Industry	22.87	24.13	41.68	45.09	53.94
租赁和商务服务业	**Leasing and Business Services**	**153.19**	**172.19**	**182.86**	**214.29**	**192.31**
租赁业	Leasing Services	15.05	16.92	17.97	25.15	28.46
商务服务业	Business Services	138.14	155.27	164.90	189.14	163.85

4-8 续表 2 continued 2

指标	Indicator	2013 年	2014 年	2015 年	2016 年	2017 年
科学研究和技术服务业	**Scientific Research and Technical Services**	75.62	82.35	90.00	103.15	136.89
研究和试验发展	Research and Experimental Development	6.39	6.96	7.60	10.15	14.42
专业技术服务业	Special Technical Services	50.38	54.86	59.96	68.00	94.49
科技推广和应用服务业	Science and Technology Promotion and Application Services	18.85	20.53	22.43	25.00	27.98
水利、环境和公共设施管理业	**Management of Water Conservancy, Environment and Public Facilities**	17.26	18.80	20.54	24.95	28.81
水利管理业	Management of Water Conservancy	1.88	2.05	2.24	2.50	2.70
生态保护和环境治理业	Ecological Protection and Environmental Management	0.61	0.74	0.80	1.45	2.07
公共设施管理业	Management of PublicFacilities	14.77	16.01	17.50	21.00	24.04
居民服务、修理和其他服务业	**Services to Households, Repair and Other Services**	57.49	64.63	68.63	80.79	78.46
居民服务业	Services to Households	30.26	32.21	34.21	39.47	36.39
机动车、电子产品和日用产品修理业	Repair of Motor Vehicle, Electronics and Household Products	9.12	10.25	10.89	13.07	13.44
其他服务业	Other Services	18.11	22.16	23.53	28.25	28.62
教育	**Education**	140.75	153.27	167.51	196.78	232.09
卫生和社会工作	**Health,Social Security and Social Welfare**	134.11	146.04	159.60	176.10	179.89
卫生	Public Health	124.11	135.15	147.70	161.56	164.89
社会工作	Social Work	10.00	10.89	11.90	14.53	15.00
文化、体育和娱乐业	**Culture, Sports and Recreation**	36.29	40.79	43.32	48.60	52.29
新闻和出版业	Journalism and Publishing Activities	12.35	13.88	14.74	17.30	20.63
广播、电视、电影和影视录音	Radio, Television, Motion Picture and Videotape Programme	11.24	14.43	15.33	15.50	15.47
文化艺术业	Culture and Arts	5.04	4.37	4.64	5.69	6.11
体育	Sports	4.01	4.51	4.79	5.55	5.74
娱乐业	Recreation	3.65	3.60	3.83	4.57	4.34
公共管理、社会保障和社会组织	**Public Management, Social Security and Social Organization**	160.61	190.24	207.91	219.08	234.78
第一产业	**Primary Industry**	276.99	290.29	305.39	317.31	317.40
第二产业	**Secondary Industry**	2095.08	2261.66	2307.00	2368.90	2569.22
第三产业	**Tertiary Industry**	2858.12	3218.65	3487.84	3849.91	4315.34

注：新行业分组 (GB–2011)。
Note: Grouping of new industries (GB–2011).

4-9 生产总值贡献率(2009年—2013年)(分行业、按不变价格计算)

Distribution Rate of Gross Domestic Product(Calculated at Fixed Prices)(2009—2013) (Sub Industry, Calculated at Constant Prices)

单位：%(%)

指 标	Indicator	2009年	2010年	2011年	2012年	2013年
地区生产总值贡献率	**Gross Domestic Product**	100.0	100.0	100.0	100.0	100.0
第一产业	Primary Industry	2.3	1.9	2.3	2.6	2.0
农林牧渔业	Agriculture, Forestry, Animal Husbandry and Fishery	2.3	1.9	2.3	2.6	2.0
农业	Farming	1.3	2.3	-1.3	1.4	1.1
林业	Forestry	0.0	-0.6	0.2	0.2	0.2
畜牧业	Animal Husbandry	1.0	0.2	3.3	0.8	0.5
渔业	Fishery	0.0	0.0		0.0	0.0
农林牧渔服务业	Services of Agriculture,Forestry,Animal Husbandry and Fishing	0.0	0.1	0.1	0.2	0.2
第二产业	Secondary Industry	44.6	39.1	46.2	41.2	44.5
工业	Industry	33.8	32.6	39.9	36.0	38.8
采矿业	Mining	3.9	1.1	0.6	0.0	5.9
制造业	Manufacture	15.0	23.3	27.5	58.7	30.6
电力、燃气及水的生产和供应业	Production and Supply of Electric, Gas and Water	14.8	8.2	11.7	-22.7	2.4
建筑业	Construction	10.8	6.5	6.3	5.2	5.6
房屋和土木工程建筑业	Building Construction	11.5	6.3	5.8	4.7	-6.3
建筑安装业	Construction Installment	0.6	0.1	-0.2	0.6	10.5
建筑装饰业	Construction Decoration	-0.9	0.0	0.9	0.4	1.3
其他建筑业	Others	-0.4	0.0	-0.1	-0.5	0.1
第三产业	Tertiary Industry	53.1	59.0	51.5	56.2	53.5
交通运输、仓储和邮政业	Transport, Storage and Postal Services	12.4	6.4	13.0	5.4	2.9
铁路运输业	Railway Transport	1.2	1.1	0.8	1.1	-0.4
道路运输业	Road Transport	9.7	3.1	7.6	4.1	0.9
城市公共交通业	Public Transportation by City	0.1	0.2	0.5	0.4	-0.1
水上运输业	Waterway Transport	0.1	0.2		0.0	0.0
航空运输业	Air Transport	0.9	1.2	2.0	-1.5	0.8

4-9 续表 1 continued 1

指　标	Indicator	2009 年	2010 年	2011 年	2012 年	2013 年
管道运输业	Pipeline Transport	0.1	0.0		0.0	0.1
装卸搬运和其他运输服务业	Loading and Unloading and Other Transport Services	0.5	0.4	1.8	0.0	0.8
仓储业	Storage	-0.1	0.1	0.2	0.9	0.7
邮政业	Postal Services	0.0	0.1		0.4	0.0
信息传输、计算机服务和软件业	Information Transmission, Computer Services and Software	2.9	7.7	4.7	3.5	2.3
电信和其他信息传输服务业	Telecommunications, Radio and Television and Satellite Transmission Services	-0.3	0.1	-0.3	-0.3	0.9
计算机服务业	Internet and related Services	2.9	2.6	1.5	1.5	1.4
软件业	Software and Information Technology Services	0.3	5.1	3.5	2.3	-0.1
批发和零售业	Wholesale and Retail Trade	10.5	12.4	7.6	13.5	15.7
批发业	Wholesale	10.6	11.8	9.5	9.4	11.2
零售业	Retail Trade	-0.1	0.6	-1.8	4.1	4.5
住宿和餐饮业	Accommodations and Catering Services	2.0	3.4	-0.6	1.0	2.5
住宿业	Accommodations	-0.1	1.1	0.1	0.2	0.3
餐饮业	Catering Services	2.1	2.4	-0.7	0.8	2.1
金融业	Financial Intermediation	8.7	8.8	7.0	17.5	13.9
银行业	Banking Sector	9.4	11.9	10.0	17.3	9.1
证券业	Securities Industry	0.1	-3.0	-4.0	-1.3	1.7
保险业	Insurance	-0.4	-1.0	0.2	0.1	0.3
其他金融活动	Others	-0.4	0.9	0.8	1.4	2.8
房地产业	Real Estate	5.3	8.3	4.9	3.5	8.3
房地产开发经营业	Real Estate Development and Management	0.7	3.6	3.1	0.0	4.4
物业管理业	Property Management	1.3	2.1	0.4	0.1	1.0
房地产中介服务业	Real Estate Intermediary Services	0.7	1.2	0.2	0.1	-0.1
其他房地产活动	Other Real Estate Activity	0.4	0.7	0.2	0.2	1.9
居民自有住房服务业	Private Housing Service	2.1	0.6	10.0	3.1	1.1
租赁和商务服务业	Leasing and Business Services	5.4	3.6	5.2	2.6	0.8

4-9 续表 2 continued 2

指　标	Indicator	2009 年	2010 年	2011 年	2012 年	2013 年
租赁业	Leasing Services	0.4	0.3	0.3	0.9	0.5
商务服务业	Business Services	5.1	3.2	4.9	1.7	0.3
科学研究、技术服务和地质勘查业	Scientific Research, Technical Servicesand Geeological Prospecting Industry	1.0	0.5	1.0	−0.4	0.9
研究与试验发展	Research and Experimental Development	0.4	−0.6	0.7	0.0	0.7
专业技术服务业	Special Technical Services	0.1	1.0	0.1	−0.3	−0.4
科技交流和推广服务业	Science and Technology Promotion and Application Services	0.4	0.1	0.1	−0.1	0.4
地质勘查业	Geeological Prospecting Industry	0.0	0.0	0.1	0.0	0.1
水利、环境和公共设施管理业	Management of Water Conservancy, Environment and Public Facilities	−0.3	−0.2	−0.1	0.0	0.6
水利管理业	Management of Water Conservancy	0.1	−0.1	−0.1	0.0	0.6
环境管理业	Environmental Management	0.1	0.0	−0.1	−0.6	0.0
公共设施管理业	Management of Public Facilities	−0.5	−0.1		0.6	0.0
居民服务和其他服务业	Services to Households and Other Services	0.7	1.8	1.3	0.9	0.9
居民服务业	Services to Households	0.4	1.0	0.7	0.5	0.1
其他服务业	Other Services	0.3	0.8	0.6	0.4	0.8
教育	Education	2.8	1.1	1.0	0.5	1.9
卫生、社会保障和社会福利业	Health, Social Security and Social Welfare	0.9	3.5	3.8	4.7	0.6
卫生	Public Health	0.6	2.6	4.7	4.7	0.6
社会保障业	Social Security	0.3	0.6	−0.6	0.0	0.0
社会福利业	Social Welfare	0.1	0.2	−0.3	0.0	0.0
文化、体育和娱乐业	Culture, Sports and Recreation	0.7	1.1		0.7	0.7
新闻出版业	Newsand Publication	0.3	0.2	0.2	−0.1	0.1
广播、电视、电影和音像业	Radio, Television, Film and Video	0.1	0.3		0.8	0.1
文化艺术业	Culture and Arts	0.1	0.4	−0.4	−0.1	0.2
体育	Sports	0.2	0.0	0.1	0.0	0.3
娱乐业	Recreation	0.0	0.1	0.1	0.1	0.0
公共管理和社会组织	Public Management and Social Organizations	0.1	0.7	2.6	2.8	1.7

注：旧行业分组 (GB−2002)。
Note: Grouping of old industries (GB−2002).

4-10 生产总值贡献率(2013年—2017年)(分行业，按不变价格计算)

Contribution Rate of Gross Domestic Product(2013–2017)(Sub Industry, Calculated at Constant Prices)

单位：%(%)

指标	Indicator	2013年	2014年	2015年	2016年	2017年
地区生产总值贡献率	Contribution Rate of Gross Domestic Product	100.00	100.00	100.00	100.00	100.00
农、林、牧、渔业	Agriculture, Forestry, Animal Husbandry and Fishery	2.03	2.26	2.37	2.89	2.28
农业	Farming	1.13	3.36	3.51	1.85	0.94
林业	Forestry	0.20	0.09	0.09	0.29	0.31
畜牧业	Animal Husbandry	0.49	−1.36	−1.43	0.48	0.69
渔业	Fishery	0.03	0.05	0.05	0.03	0.03
农、林、牧、渔服务业	Services of Agriculture,Forestry,Animal Husbandry and Fishing	0.17	0.12	0.16	0.24	0.30
工业	Industry	38.69	36.05	31.40	26.92	33.80
采矿业	Mining	2.91	0.60	−0.36	2.41	1.00
#开采辅助活动	Mining Support Activities	0.00	0.00	0.00	0.00	0.00
制造业	Manufacture	31.06	26.58	26.89	25.49	33.95
#金属制品、机械和设备修理业	Metal Products, Machinery and Equipment Repair Industry	0.06	0.07	0.06	0.05	0.06
电力、燃气及水的生产和供应业	Production and Supply of Electric, Gas and Water	4.73	8.88	4.86	−0.98	−1.15
建筑业	Construction	6.70	7.52	8.58	6.75	5.77
房屋建筑业	Building Construction	4.31	−1.08	4.04	8.60	2.08
土木工程建筑业	Civil Engineering Construction	−3.32	7.07	9.30	−0.92	4.73
建筑安装业	Construction Installment	3.42	0.47	−1.20	−1.59	0.23
建筑装饰业和其他建筑业	Construction Decoration and Others	2.29	1.06	−3.56	0.66	−1.27
批发和零售业	Wholesale and Retail Trade	15.34	10.65	6.58	11.42	17.71
批发业	Wholesale	10.89	7.51	3.55	7.35	13.68
零售业	Retail Trade	4.44	3.13	3.03	4.07	4.02
交通运输、仓储和邮政业	Transport, Storage and Post	2.87	3.58	2.33	3.54	6.29
铁路运输业	Railway Transport	−0.35	−0.78	1.34	0.73	0.31
道路运输业	Road Transport	0.72	2.00	−0.55	0.67	2.11
水上运输业	Waterway Transport	0.03	0.02	−0.01	0.04	−0.01
航空运输业	Air Transport	0.76	0.72	1.00	1.17	0.79

4-10 续表 1 continued 1

指标	Indicator	2013 年	2014 年	2015 年	2016 年	2017 年
管道运输业	Pipeline Transport	0.57	0.16	0.11	0.03	1.13
装卸搬运和运输代理业	Loading, Unloading and Forwarding Agency	0.59	0.47	0.14	–0.52	0.38
仓储业	Storage	0.47	0.35	0.11	1.00	1.15
邮政业	Postal Services	0.10	0.65	0.21	0.43	0.42
住宿和餐饮业	**Accommodations and Catering Services**	**2.45**	**2.28**	**1.16**	**2.04**	**2.05**
住宿业	Accommodations	0.35	0.21	0.22	0.22	0.34
餐饮业	Catering Services	2.10	2.06	0.95	1.82	1.71
信息传输、软件和信息技术服务和业	**Information Transmission, Software and Information Technology**	**2.27**	**3.82**	**1.92**	**5.69**	**13.79**
电信、广播电视和卫星传输服务	Telecommunications, Radio and Television and Satellite Transmission Services	2.19	3.39	1.76	–0.65	10.70
互联网和相关服务	Internet and related Services	0.14	0.10	–0.01	2.64	0.79
软件和信息技术服务业	Software and Information Technology Services	–0.06	0.33	0.18	3.69	2.30
金融业	**Financial Intermediation**	**13.84**	**16.01**	**22.21**	**15.56**	**6.25**
货币金融服务	Monetary and Financial Services	9.10	7.35	13.63	14.35	9.08
资本市场服务	Capital Market Services	1.68	4.13	5.86	–4.52	0.64
保险业	Insurance	0.30	0.30	0.59	2.44	0.54
其他金融业	Others	2.74	4.23	2.13	3.29	–4.01
房地产业	**Real Estate**	**8.28**	**6.70**	**10.89**	**7.55**	**–2.19**
房地产开发经营业	Real Estate Development and Management	4.79	5.87	8.17	3.97	–3.86
物业管理业	Property Management	0.71	–0.37	0.67	0.76	–0.34
房地产中介服务业	Real Estate Intermediary Services	–0.11	–0.12	0.44	1.06	0.17
自有房地产经营活动	Own Real Estate Operating Activities	1.10	1.15	1.21	1.42	1.32
其他房地产业	Other Real Estate Industry	1.80	0.17	0.41	0.34	0.52
租赁和商务服务业	**Leasing and Business Services**	**0.77**	**2.49**	**1.67**	**5.85**	**1.67**
租赁业	Leasing Services	0.49	–0.10	0.37	1.43	1.45
商务服务业	Business Services	0.28	2.58	1.30	4.43	0.22

4-10 续表 2 continued 2

指标	Indicator	2013 年	2014 年	2015 年	2016 年	2017 年
科学研究和技术服务业	Scientific Research and Technical Services	0.89	0.81	1.40	1.75	3.77
研究和试验发展	Research and Experimental Development	0.18	0.24	0.24	0.44	0.54
专业技术服务业	Special Technical Services	-0.13	-0.36	0.74	1.02	3.22
科技推广和应用服务业	Science and Technology Promotion and Application Services	0.84	0.92	0.41	0.29	0.02
水利、环境和公共设施管理业	Management of Water Conservancy, Environmentand Public Facilities	0.19	0.18	0.32	0.68	0.52
水利管理业	Management of Water Conservancy	0.11	0.02	0.01	0.03	0.02
生态保护和环境治理业	Ecological Protection and Environmental Management	0.03	0.04	0.01	0.12	0.10
公共设施管理业	Management of Public Facilities	0.05	0.12	0.29	0.53	0.40
居民服务、修理和其他服务业	Services to Households, Repair and Other Services	0.85	0.93	0.63	2.28	1.90
居民服务业	Services to Households	0.10	-0.22	0.51	0.97	0.51
机动车、电子产品和日用产品修理业	Repair of Motor Vehicle, Electronics and Household Products	0.33	0.10	-0.01	0.41	0.47
其他服务业	Other Services	0.42	1.05	0.12	0.90	0.92
教育	Education	1.85	1.51	2.60	4.23	3.51
卫生和社会工作	Health, Social Security and Social Welfare	0.62	1.42	2.48	1.49	-0.59
卫生	Public Health	0.64	1.05	2.38	1.08	-0.55
社会工作	Social Work	-0.02	0.37	0.10	0.41	-0.04
文化、体育和娱乐业	Culture,Sports and Recreation	0.67	0.59	0.40	0.94	2.23
新闻和出版业	Journalism and Publishing Activities	0.09	-0.10	-0.06	0.48	1.22
广播、电视、电影和影视录音	Radio, Television, Motion Picture and Videotape Programme	0.09	0.92	-0.01	-0.02	0.46
文化艺术业	Culture and Arts	0.15	-0.21	0.22	0.20	0.26
体育	Sports	0.29	0.03	0.13	0.14	0.21
娱乐业	Recreation	0.04	-0.05	0.12	0.14	0.09
公共管理、社会保障和社会组织	Public Management, Social Security and Social Organization	1.69	3.21	3.08	0.40	1.24
第一产业	Primary Industry	1.86	2.14	2.21	2.65	1.97
第二产业	Secondary Industry	45.33	43.50	39.92	33.63	39.52
第三产业	Tertiary Industry	52.81	54.36	57.88	63.72	58.51

注：新行业分组 (GB-2011)。
Note: Grouping of new industries (GB-2011).

4-11 生产总值行业比重(2009年—2013年)(按当年价格计算)

Ratio of Gross Domestic Product by Sector(2009—2013)(Calculated at Current Prices)

单位：%(%)

指　标	Indicator	2009年	2010年	2011年	2012年	2013年
生产总值比重	Ratio of Gross Domestic Product	100.0	100.0	100.0	100.0	100.0
第一产业	Primary Industry	5.6	5.5	5.4	5.3	5.4
农林牧渔业	Agriculture, Forestry, Animal Husbandry and Fishery	5.6	5.5	5.4	5.3	5.4
农业	Farming	3.6	3.8	3.5	3.4	3.6
林业	Forestry	0.2	0.1	0.1	0.1	0.2
畜牧业	Animal Husbandry	1.5	1.4	1.6	1.6	1.5
渔业	Fishery	0.1	0.1	0.1	0.1	0.1
农林牧渔服务业	Services of Agriculture,Forestry,Animal Husbandry and Fishing	0.1	0.1	0.1	0.1	0.1
第二产业	Secondary Industry	42.9	41.9	41.5	40.3	39.3
工业	Industry	35.7	34.6	34.2	33.3	32.3
采矿业	Mining	0.8	0.8	0.8	0.7	1.1
制造业	Manufacture	32.1	30.5	29.5	31.0	29.4
电力、燃气及水的生产和供应业	Production and Supply of Electric, Gas and Water	2.7	3.2	3.9	1.6	1.8
建筑业	Construction	7.2	7.3	7.3	7.0	6.9
房屋和土木工程建筑业	Building Construction	5.8	6.0	6.0	5.8	5.4
建筑安装业	Construction Installment	1.1	1.0	0.9	0.8	1.1
建筑装饰业	Construction Decoration	0.2	0.2	0.3	0.3	0.4
其他建筑业	Others	0.1	0.1	0.1	0.1	0.1
第三产业	Tertiary Industry	51.5	52.6	53.1	54.4	55.3
交通运输、仓储和邮政业	Transport, Storage and Postal Services	6.0	6.1	6.7	6.7	6.4
铁路运输业	Railway Transport	1.6	1.4	1.4	1.4	1.2
道路运输业	Road Transport	2.9	3.0	3.5	3.5	3.3
城市公共交通业	Public Transportation by City	0.4	0.4	0.4	0.4	0.3
水上运输业	Waterway Transport	0.0	0.0	0.0	0.0	0.0
航空运输业	Air Transport	0.5	0.6	0.8	0.6	0.6

4–11 续表 1 continued 1

指　标	Indicator	2009 年	2010 年	2011 年	2012 年	2013 年
管道运输业	Pipeline Transport	0.0	0.0	0.0	0.0	0.0
装卸搬运和其他运输服务业	Loading and Unloading and Other Transport Services	0.4	0.3	0.5	0.5	0.5
仓储业	Storage	0.2	0.2	0.2	0.2	0.3
邮政业	Postal Services	0.0	0.0	0.0	0.1	0.1
信息传输、计算机服务和软件业	Information Transmission, Computer Services and Software	2.0	3.0	3.1	3.2	3.1
电信和其他信息传输服务业	Telecommunications, Radio and Television and Satellite Transmission Services	0.9	0.8	0.7	0.6	0.6
计算机服务业	Internet and related Services	0.5	0.6	0.7	0.8	0.9
软件业	Software and Information Technology Services	0.5	1.5	1.7	1.8	1.6
批发和零售业	Wholesale and Retail Trade	12.5	12.2	11.9	12.2	12.8
批发业	Wholesale	7.0	7.4	7.6	7.9	8.4
零售业	Retail Trade	5.5	4.8	4.3	4.3	4.5
住宿和餐饮业	Accommodations and Catering Services	3.8	3.7	3.3	3.1	3.2
住宿业	Accommodations	0.4	0.4	0.4	0.4	0.4
餐饮业	Catering Services	3.4	3.2	2.9	2.7	2.8
金融业	Financial Intermediation	7.2	7.4	7.5	8.5	8.8
银行业	Banking Sector	4.9	5.8	6.3	7.4	7.4
证券业	Securities Industry	1.8	1.2	0.7	0.6	0.6
保险业	Insurance	0.3	0.1	0.1	0.1	0.2
其他金融活动	Others	0.2	0.2	0.3	0.4	0.6
房地产业	Real Estate	5.2	5.6	5.8	5.7	6.1
房地产开发经营业	Real Estate Development and Management	1.9	2.1	2.3	2.1	2.4
物业管理业	Property Management	0.6	0.7	0.7	0.7	0.7
房地产中介服务业	Real Estate Intermediary Services	0.3	0.4	0.4	0.4	0.3
其他房地产活动	Other Real Estate Activity	0.2	0.3	0.3	0.3	0.4
居民自有住房服务业	Private Housing Service	2.2	2.1	2.2	2.2	2.2
租赁和商务服务业	Leasing and Business Services	2.7	2.7	3.0	3.0	2.9

4-11 续表 2 continued 2

指　标	Indicator	2009 年	2010 年	2011 年	2012 年	2013 年
租赁业	Leasing Services	0.1	0.2	0.2	0.3	0.3
商务服务业	Business Services	2.5	2.6	2.8	2.7	2.6
科学研究、技术服务和地质勘查业	Scientific Research,Technical Services and Geeological Prospecting Industry	1.7	1.6	1.6	1.4	1.4
研究与试验发展	Research and Experimental Development	0.6	0.5	0.5	0.5	0.5
专业技术服务业	Special Technical Services	0.8	0.8	0.8	0.6	0.6
科技交流和推广服务业	Science and Technology Promotion and Application Services	0.2	0.2	0.2	0.2	0.2
地质勘查业	Geeological Prospecting Industry	0.1	0.1	0.1	0.1	0.1
水利、环境和公共设施管理业	Management of Water Conservancy, Environment and Public Facilities	0.4	0.4	0.3	0.3	0.3
水利管理业	Management of Water Conservancy	0.2	0.2	0.1	0.1	0.2
环境管理业	Environmental Management	0.1	0.1	0.1	0.0	0.0
公共设施管理业	Management of Public Facilities	0.1	0.1	0.1	0.2	0.2
居民服务和其他服务业	Services to Households and Other Services	1.0	1.0	1.1	1.1	1.1
居民服务业	Services to Households	0.6	0.6	0.6	0.6	0.6
其他服务业	Other Services	0.4	0.5	0.5	0.5	0.5
教育	Education	3.3	3.0	2.8	2.7	2.7
卫生、社会保障和社会福利业	Health,Social Security and Social Welfare	1.9	2.2	2.4	2.7	2.6
卫生	Public Health	1.7	1.9	2.2	2.5	2.4
社会保障业	Social Security	0.2	0.2	0.2	0.2	0.1
社会福利业	Social Welfare	0.1	0.1	0.0	0.0	0.0
文化、体育和娱乐业	Culture, Sports and Recreation	0.7	0.7	0.6	0.7	0.7
新闻出版业	News and Publication	0.3	0.3	0.3	0.2	0.2
广播、电视、电影和音像业	Radio, Television, Film and Video	0.2	0.2	0.2	0.2	0.2
文化艺术业	Culture and Arts	0.1	0.1	0.1	0.1	0.1
体育	Sports	0.1	0.1	0.1	0.1	0.1
娱乐业	Recreation	0.1	0.1	0.1	0.1	0.1
公共管理和社会组织	Public Management and Social Organizations	3.3	3.0	3.1	3.1	3.1

注：旧行业分组 (GB–2002)。
Note: Grouping of old industries (GB–2002).

4-12 生产总值行业比重 (2013 年—2017 年)(按当年价格计算)
Ratio of Gross Domestic Product by Sector(2013—2017)(Calculated at Current Prices)

单位：%(%)

指标	Indicator	2013 年	2014 年	2015 年	2016 年	2017 年
地区生产总值比重	Ratio of Gross Domestic Product	100.00	100.00	100.00	100.00	100.00
农、林、牧、渔业	Agriculture, Forestry, Animal Husbandry and Fishery	5.44	5.18	5.16	5.02	4.59
农业	Farming	3.57	3.46	3.44	3.29	2.99
林业	Forestry	0.15	0.15	0.16	0.17	0.16
畜牧业	Animal Husbandry	1.49	1.34	1.32	1.32	1.20
渔业	Fishery	0.08	0.08	0.07	0.07	0.06
农、林、牧、渔服务业	Services of Agriculture,Forestry,Animal Husbandry and Fishing	0.15	0.15	0.16	0.17	0.18
工业	Industry	32.32	31.58	30.23	28.75	27.81
采矿业	Mining	0.53	0.52	0.60	0.70	0.69
# 开采辅助活动	Mining Support Activities	0.00	0.00	0.00	0.00	0.00
制造业	Manufacture	28.14	27.49	28.12	26.77	26.06
# 金属制品、机械和设备修理业	Metal Products, Machinery and Equipment Repair Industry	0.06	0.06	0.06	0.05	0.05
电力、燃气及水的生产和供应业	Production and Supply of Electric, Gas and Water	3.65	3.56	1.51	1.28	1.06
建筑业	Construction	7.79	7.68	7.64	7.55	7.91
房屋建筑业	Building Construction	4.51	4.38	3.96	4.28	4.39
土木工程建筑业	Civil Engineering Construction	2.06	2.10	2.93	2.64	2.99
建筑安装业	Construction Installment	0.48	0.47	0.35	0.21	0.22
建筑装饰业和其他建筑业	Construction Decoration and Others	0.73	0.72	0.40	0.42	0.31
批发和零售业	Wholesale and Retail Trade	11.98	11.99	11.73	11.64	13.56
批发业	Wholesale	7.60	7.65	7.43	7.37	8.62
零售业	Retail Trade	4.38	4.34	4.30	4.26	4.94
交通运输、仓储和邮政业	Transport, Storage and Post	6.37	6.31	6.09	6.00	5.77
铁路运输业	Railway Transport	1.21	1.20	1.12	1.11	1.01
道路运输业	Road Transport	3.19	3.14	3.06	2.94	2.75

4-12 续表 1 continued 1

指标	Indicator	2013 年	2014 年	2015 年	2016 年	2017 年
水上运输业	Waterway Transport	0.02	0.02	0.02	0.02	0.02
航空运输业	Air Transport	0.61	0.60	0.58	0.64	0.62
管道运输业	Pipeline Transport	0.41	0.41	0.39	0.37	0.41
装卸搬运和运输代理业	Loading, Unloading and Forwarding Agency	0.51	0.50	0.48	0.42	0.40
仓储业	Storage	0.29	0.28	0.27	0.33	0.38
邮政业	Postal Services	0.13	0.16	0.15	0.17	0.19
住宿和餐饮业	**Accommodations and Catering Services**	**3.22**	**3.14**	**3.09**	**3.10**	**3.04**
住宿业	Accommodations	0.40	0.39	0.37	0.37	0.35
餐饮业	Catering Services	2.82	2.75	2.72	2.74	2.69
信息传输、软件和信息技术服务和业	**Information Transmission,Software and Information Technology**	**3.11**	**3.30**	**3.31**	**3.56**	**3.83**
电信、广播电视和卫星传输服务	Telecommunications, Radio and Television and Satellite Transmission Services	1.95	2.06	2.07	1.92	2.28
互联网和相关服务	Internet and related Services	0.08	0.09	0.09	0.28	0.28
软件和信息技术服务业	Software and Information Technology Services	1.08	1.14	1.15	1.36	1.27
金融业	**Financial Intermediation**	**8.81**	**9.39**	**10.52**	**11.02**	**10.77**
货币金融服务	Monetary and Financial Services	7.41	7.58	8.49	9.02	9.13
资本市场服务	Capital Market Services	0.65	0.84	0.94	0.56	0.57
保险业	Insurance	0.16	0.17	0.19	0.35	0.37
其他金融业	Others	0.61	0.80	0.90	1.09	0.71
房地产业	**Real Estate**	**6.13**	**6.40**	**6.80**	**7.09**	**6.94**
房地产开发经营业	Real Estate Development and Management	2.61	2.94	3.12	3.34	3.06
物业管理业	Property Management	0.51	0.44	0.47	0.51	0.49
房地产中介服务业	Real Estate Intermediary Services	0.34	0.30	0.32	0.39	0.42
自有房地产经营活动	Own Real Estate Operating Activities	2.23	2.30	2.21	2.14	2.22
其他房地产业	Other Real Estate Industry	0.44	0.42	0.68	0.69	0.75
租赁和商务服务业	**Leasing and Business Services**	**2.93**	**2.98**	**3.00**	**3.28**	**2.67**
租赁业	Leasing Services	0.29	0.29	0.29	0.38	0.40
商务服务业	Business Services	2.64	2.69	2.70	2.89	2.28

4-12 续表 2 continued 2

指标	Indicator	2013 年	2014 年	2015 年	2016 年	2017 年
科学研究和技术服务业	Scientific Research and Technical Services	1.45	1.43	1.48	1.58	1.90
研究和试验发展	Research and Experimental Development	0.12	0.12	0.12	0.16	0.20
专业技术服务业	Special Technical Services	0.96	0.95	0.98	1.04	1.31
科技推广和应用服务业	Science and Technology Promotion and Application Services	0.36	0.36	0.37	0.38	0.39
水利、环境和公共设施管理业	Management of Water Conservancy, Environment and Public Facilities	0.33	0.33	0.34	0.38	0.40
水利管理业	Management of Water Conservancy	0.04	0.04	0.04	0.04	0.04
生态保护和环境治理业	Ecological Protection and Environmental Management	0.01	0.01	0.01	0.02	0.03
公共设施管理业	Management of Public Facilities	0.28	0.28	0.29	0.32	0.33
居民服务、修理和其他服务业	Services to Households, Repair and Other Services	1.10	1.12	1.13	1.24	1.09
居民服务业	Services to Households	0.58	0.56	0.56	0.60	0.51
机动车、电子产品和日用产品修理业	Repair of Motor Vehicle, Electronics and Household Products	0.17	0.18	0.18	0.20	0.19
其他服务业	Other Services	0.35	0.38	0.39	0.43	0.40
教育	Education	2.69	2.66	2.75	3.01	3.22
卫生和社会工作	Health,Social Security and Social Welfare	2.56	2.53	2.62	2.69	2.50
卫生	Public Health	2.37	2.34	2.42	2.47	2.29
社会工作	Social Work	0.19	0.19	0.20	0.22	0.21
文化、体育和娱乐业	Culture, Sports and Recreation	0.69	0.71	0.71	0.74	0.73
新闻和出版业	Journalism and Publishing Activities	0.24	0.24	0.24	0.26	0.29
广播、电视、电影和影视录音	Radio, Television, Motion Picture and Videotape Programme	0.21	0.25	0.25	0.24	0.21
文化艺术业	Culture and Arts	0.10	0.08	0.08	0.09	0.08
体育	Sports	0.08	0.08	0.08	0.08	0.08
娱乐业	Recreation	0.07	0.06	0.06	0.07	0.06
公共管理、社会保障和社会组织	Public Management, Social Security and Social Organization	3.07	3.30	3.41	3.35	3.26
第一产业	Primary Industry	5.30	5.03	5.01	4.85	4.41
第二产业	Secondary Industry	40.06	39.19	37.82	36.24	35.67
第三产业	Tertiary Industry	54.65	55.78	57.18	58.90	59.92

注：新行业分组 (GB–2011)。
Note: Grouping of new industries (GB–2011).

4-13 分地区生产总值（2019 年）
Value of Gross Domestic Product by Region(2019)

单位：亿元 (100 million yuan)

指　标	Indicator	济南市 Total City	历下区 Li xia	市中区 Shi zhong	槐荫区 Huai yin	天桥区 Tian qiao	历城区 Li cheng	长清区 Chang qing	章丘区 Zhang qiu	济阳区 Ji yang
地区生产总值	Gross Domestic Product	9443.4	1685.4	1060.5	605.1	541.3	921.3	317.9	911.0	190.1
第一产业	Primary Industry	343.1		1.8	2.3	1.3	19.8	32.0	76.9	29.3
第二产业	Secondary Industry	3265.2	320.9	288.7	182.6	187.4	242.9	152.9	467.3	92.1
第三产业	Tertiary Industry	5835.1	1364.5	770.0	420.2	352.6	658.6	133.0	366.9	68.7

4-13 续表 continued

指　标	Indicator	莱芜区 Lai wu	钢城区 Gang cheng	济南高新区 Ji'nan Gao xin	莱芜高新区 Lai wu Gao xin	济南先行区 JN Pioneer Area	南部山区 Nan shan	平阴县 Ping yin	商河县 Shang he
地区生产总值	Gross Domestic Product	593.5	278.1	1150.2	162.3	52.5	61.4	223.2	163.0
第一产业	Primary Industry	55.9	9.9	4.0	1.6	15.1	16.6	31.9	44.7
第二产业	Secondary Industry	250.3	184.0	552.9	43.4	21.9	11.0	128.0	46.1
第三产业	Tertiary Industry	287.3	84.2	593.3	117.3	15.5	33.9	63.3	72.2

4-14 生产总值(2019年)(分行业，按当年价格计算)

Value of Gross Domestic Product(2019)(Sub Industry，Calculated at Current Prices)

单位：亿元 (100 million yuan)

指标	Indicator	2019年
地区生产总值	Gross Domestic Product	9443.37
农、林、牧、渔业	Agriculture, Forestry, Animal Husbandry and Fishery	360.51
农、林、牧、渔服务业	Services of Agriculture,Forestry,Animal Husbandry and Fishing	17.45
工业	Industry	2167.87
#开采辅助活动	Mining Support Activities	0.02
#金属制品、机械和设备修理业	Metal Products, Machinery and Equipment Repair Industry	10.61
建筑业	Construction	1107.98
批发和零售业	Wholesale and Retail Trade	1271.70
批发业	Wholesale	683.48
零售业	Retail Trade	588.22
交通运输、仓储和邮政业	Transport, Storage and Post	547.97
住宿和餐饮业	Accommodations and Catering Services	138.86
住宿业	Accommodations	20.47
餐饮业	Catering Services	118.39
金融业	Financial Intermediation	839.64
房地产业	Real Estate	764.83
房地产业(K门类)	Real Estate Industry(K category)	579.90
自有房地产经营活动	Own Real Estate Operating Activities	184.93
其他服务业	Other Services	2244.01
营利性服务业	Profit Service Industry	1336.63
非营利性服务业	Non-Profit Service Industry	907.38
第一产业	Primary Industry	343.06
第二产业	Secondary Industry	3265.22
第三产业	Tertiary Industry	5835.09

4-15 规模以上服务业企业分行业主要经济指标(2019年)

Main Economic Indicators of Service Enterpriese Above Designated Size by Sector(2019)

指标	Indicator	单位数（个）Number of Enterprises (unit)	固定资产原价 Original Value of Fixed Assets	本年折旧 Depreciation in the Year
合计	Total	1524	34374855	1613627
交通运输、仓储和邮政业	Transport, Storage and Postal Services	323	24355409	980233
信息传输、软件和信息技术服务业	Information Transmission, Softwareand Information Technology	211	4411614	307660
房地产业	Real Estate	174	874438	45917
租赁和商务服务业	Leasing and Business Services	307	2608744	112455
科学研究和技术服务业	Scientific Research,Technical Services	300	1053952	97895
水利、环境和公共设施管理业	Management of Water Conservancy,Environment and Public Facilities	27	461883	29016
居民服务、修理和其他服务业	Services to Households, Repair and Other Services	49	74086	4101
教育	Education	29	146102	12944
卫生和社会工作	Health and Social Work	44	109662	8194
文化、体育和娱乐业	Culture, Sports and Recreation	60	278966	15213

单位：万元 (10 000 yuan)

折旧率 (%) Depreciation Rate(%)	营业收入 Business Revenue	税金及附加 Taxes and Other Surcharges	营业利润 Profits from Business	利润总额 Total Profits	应付职工薪酬（本年贷方累计发生额） Total Wages Payable	从业人员平均人数（人） Average Number of Employees (person)	人均工资（元） Per Capita Wages (yuan)	应交增值税 Value Added Tax Payable
4.7	23676909	123852	1760194	1778460	5267402	448754	117378	668253
4.0	11828713	26057	712549	671678	2578456	168831	152724	280187
7.0	3535402	19287	702	29643	917211	77686	118066	163174
5.3	901486	19008	50216	52376	274764	49336	55692	37799
4.3	2609687	30109	403590	405707	457916	60108	76182	62176
9.3	3213093	16557	340404	349379	693536	47970	144577	88877
6.3	297204	2351	85018	88547	52849	11799	44791	11846
5.5	168283	928	11552	10165	52175	13508	38625	3921
8.9	202031	1256	6541	13389	72193	5825	123937	5256
7.5	299652	92	25817	25444	77137	7858	98164	282
5.5	621359	8207	123806	132133	91165	5833	156291	14735

主要统计指标解释

国内生产总值（GDP） 指一个国家（或地区）所有常住单位在一定时期内生产活动的最终成果。国内生产总值有三种表现形态，即价值形态、收入形态和产品形态。从价值形态看，它是所有常住单位在一定时期内生产的全部货物和服务价值超过同期中间投入的全部非固定资产货物和服务价值的差额，即所有常住单位的增加值之和；从收入形态看，它是所有常住单位在一定时期内创造并分配给常住单位和非常住单位的初次收入分配之和；从产品形态看，它是所有常住单位在一定时期内最终使用的货物和服务价值与货物和服务净出口价值之和。在实际核算中，国内生产总值有三种计算方法，即生产法、收入法和支出法。三种方法分别从不同的方面反映国内生产总值及其构成。国统字〔2004〕4号文规定：地区GDP的中文名称改为“地区生产总值”。

生产法 生产法是从生产过程中生产的货物和服务总产品价值入手，剔除生产过程中投入的中间产品的价值，得到增加价值的一种方法。计算公式为：

增加值=总产出－中间投入

将国民经济各行业的增加值相加，得到国内生产总值。

总产出、中间投入和增加值具有相同的生产范围，即常住生产单位货物和服务的生产。它不仅包括常住生产单位为其他单位提供的货物和服务的生产，而且包括为本单位使用的货物和服务的生产，但是，住户为自己最终消费生产的服务，只计算自有住房服务和付酬家庭雇员提供的服务，不包括住户成员为本住户最终消费而生产的自给性家庭服务。

收入法 收入法也称为分配法。按收入法计算生产总值是从生产过程创造收入的角度，对常住单位的生产活动成果进行核算。按照这种计算方法，增加值由劳动者报酬、生产税净额、固定资产折旧和营业盈余四个部分组成。计算公式为：

增加值=劳动者报酬+生产税净额+固定资产折旧+营业盈余

国民经济各部门的增加值之和等于生产总值。

在计算劳动者报酬时，需要注意作为劳动者报酬的实物性收入与中间消耗的界限。如果生产单位为其从事生产活动的劳动者提供的货物或服务，可以由劳动者在自己闲暇的时间里满足他们的需要，并且可以改善和提高他们的实际生活水平，同时，其他普通消费者也可以在市场上购买到这些货物和服务，那么就属于劳动者的实物收入。生产单位为了生产能正常进行，为劳动者购买的货物和提供的服务，如因特殊工作需要提供的服装或鞋，因公出差提供的运输和旅馆服务费用等，属于中间投入。

支出法 支出法是从最终使用的角度反映国内生产总值最终使用去向的一种方法。最终使用包括货物和服务的最终消费支出、资本形成总额、货物和服务净出口三部分，计算公式为：

国内生产总值=最终消费支出+资本形成总额+货物和服务净出口

按支出法计算的生产总值，在计算最终消费支出，包括居民消费支出和政府消费支出时，是从支出的最终承担者的角度计算的，而不是从最终实际消费者的角度计算的；在计算资本形成总额时，固定资本形成总额只包括通过生产活动生产出来的固定资产，不包括自然资产，存货增加不包括由于价格因素影响产生的持有收益。

按三种方法计算的国内生产总值反映的是同一经济总体在同一时期的生产活动成果，因此，从理论上讲，三种计算方法所得到的结果应该是一致的。但是，在实践中，由于受资料来源的口径限制和计算方法的影响，要保证这三种计算方法所得到的结果完全相等几乎是不可能的。在国内生产总值的三种计算方法中，生产法和收入法都是对各产业部门的增加值进行核算，为了就每一产业部门取得一致的增加值数据，根据资料来源状况，我国在核算实践中，有的产业部门，如农业、工业的增加值，确定以生产法的计算结果为准，有的产业部门，如部分服务业增加值，确定以收入法的计算结果为准，因此，我国的生产法国内生产总值等于收入法国内生产总值。但是，支出法国内生产总值与生产法和收入法国内生产总值之间存在统计误差，有的年份支出法国内生产总值大于生产法和收入法国内生产总值，有的年份结果相反。我国通常以生产法和收入法国内生产总值数据为准，将上述统计误差控制在一定范围。各种公开发表的国内生产总值总量和增长速度数据均是生产法和收入法的计算结果。按三种方法计算的国内生产总值数据之间具有如下关系：

国内生产总值=生产法国内生产总值

=收入法国内生产总值

=支出法国内生产总值+统计误差

可比价格 指计算各种总量指标所采用的扣除了价格变动因素的价格，可进行不同时期总量指标的对比。按可比价格计算总量指标有两种方法：一种是直接用产品产量乘某一年的不变价格计算；另一种是用价格指数进行缩减。

不变价格 指以同类产品某年的平均价格作为固定价格，用于计算各年的产品价值。按不变价格计算的产品价值消除了价格变动因素，不同时期对比可以反映生产的发展速度。新中国成立后，随着工农业产品价格水平的变化，国家统计局先后九次制定了全国统一的工业产品不变价格和农业产品不变价格。从1952年到1957年使用1952年工（农）业产品不变价格，从1957年到1970年使用1957年不变价格，从1971年到1980年使用1970年不变价格，从1981年到1990年使用1980年不变价格，从1991年到2000年使用1990年不变价格，从2001年到2005年使用2000年不变价格，从2006年到2010年使用2005年不变价格，从2011年到2015年使用2010年不变价格，从2016年开始使用2015年不变价格。

三次产业 根据社会生产活动历史发展的顺序对产业结构的划分，产品直接取自自然界的部门称为第一产业，对初级产品进行再加工的部门称为第二产业。为生产和消费提供各种服

务的部门称为第三产业。它是世界上通用的产业结构分类，但各国的划分不尽一致。我国的三次产业划分是:

第一产业是指农、林、牧、渔业(不含农、林、牧、渔服务业)。

第二产业是指采矿业（不含开采辅助活动），制造业（不含金属制品、机械和设备修理业），电力、热力、燃气及水生产和供应业，建筑业。

第三产业即服务业，是指除第一产业、第二产业以外的其他行业。第三产业包括: 批发和零售业，交通运输、仓储和邮政业，住宿和餐饮业，信息传输、软件和信息技术服务业，金融业，房地产业，租赁和商务服务业，科学研究和技术服务业，水利、环境和公共设施管理业，居民服务、修理和其他服务业，教育，卫生和社会工作，文化、体育和娱乐业，公共管理、社会保障和社会组织，国际组织，以及农、林、牧、渔业中的农、林、牧、渔服务业，采矿业中的开采辅助活动，制造业中的金属制品、机械和设备修理业。

国内支出总额 指一个国家（或地区）所有常住单位在一定时期内用于最终消费和投资，以及净出口的货物和服务支出总额，它反映本期生产的国内生产总值的使用构成。这一总量就是支出法测算的国内生产总值，具体包括最终消费支出、资本形成总额、货物和服务净出口。

最终消费 指常住单位在一定时期内的货物和服务的全部最终消费。总消费分为居民消费和政府消费。

居民实际最终消费 指常住住户获得的所有消费品和消费服务的价值。包括以下二类 (1) 居民自身通过支出所得到的个人货物和服务，其价值即居民在个人消费品和消费服务上承担的支出，包括虚拟支出。(2) 作为为居民服务的非营利机构和政府的实物转移得到的个人货物和服务。其价值即为居民非营利机构和政府在个人消费品和服务上的支出。包括虚拟支出。

资本形成总额 指常住单位在一定时期内获得减去处置的固定资产和存货的净额，包括固定资本形成总额和存货增加。

居民消费支出 居民消费支出包括居民实际最终消费中第 (1) 项内容。所以居民实际最终消费大于居民消费支出。

政府实际最终消费 指政府向社会或社会中某些部门提供的公共消费服务的价值。其价值即政府在公共服务上的支出。

政府消费支出 指(1)政府在个人消费品和消费服务。(2)在公共消费服务上承担的支出，包括虚拟支出。

总投资 指常住单位在一定时期内对固定资产和库存的投资支出合计，分为固定资产形成和库存增加两项。

（1）固定资本形成总额 指从常住单位在一定时期内购置、转入和自产自用的固定资产中，扣除已有固定资产的销售和转出后的价值。固定资产形成包括在一定时期内完成的建筑工程、安装工程和设备器具购置价值，以及新增役、种、奶、毛、娱乐用牲畜和新增经济林价值等。

（2）库存增加 指常住单位一定时期内库存实物量变动的市场价值。期初与期末差额为正值表示库存增加，负值表示库存减少。具体包括本期购买的原材料、燃料和储备物资等商品库存；本期生产的产成品、半成品和在制品等产品库存。

货物和服务净出口 指货物和服务出口减货物和服务进口的差额。出口包括常住单位向非常住单位出售或无偿转让的各种货物和服务的价值；进口包括常住单位从非常住单位购买或无偿得到的各种货物和服务的价值。由于服务活动的提供与使用同时发生，因此服务的进出口业务并不发生出入境现象，一般把常住单位从国外得到的服务作为进口，非常住单位从本国得到的服务作为出口。货物的出口和进口都按离岸价格计算。

来自国外的净要素收入 指一定国家（或地区）来自国外（地区外）的生产税及进口税（扣除生产及进口补贴）、劳动者报酬和财产收入，减去支付给国外（地区外）的生产税及进口税（扣除生产及进口补贴）、劳动者报酬和财产收入的差额。国内生产总值加上来自国外的净要素收入等于国民生产总值。

总产出 总产出是指一定时期内一个国家（或地区）常住单位生产的所有货物和服务的价值，即包括新增价值，也包括转移价值。它反映常住单位生产活动的总规模。总产出按生产者价格计算。

中间投入 中间投入是指常住单位在生产或提供货物与服务过程中，消耗和使用的所有非固定资产货物和服务的价值，中间投入也称为中间消耗。一般按购买者价格计算。

增加值 增加值是指常住单位生产过程创造的新增价值和固定资产的转移价值。它可以按生产法计算，也可以按收入法计算，按生产法计算，它等于总产出减去中间投入；按收入法计算，它等于劳动者报酬、生产税净额、固定资产折旧和营业盈余之和。

固定资产折旧 指一定时期内为弥补固定资产损耗而应提取的补偿价值，它反映了全部固定资产在本期生产中的资产转移价值。各类企业的固定资产折旧是指从成本费用中提取的折旧费。对不计提折旧的单位，如政府机关、事业单位、学校医院、部队和居民住房则应进行虚拟折旧。

劳动者报酬 指劳动者为常住单位提供劳务而获得的各种报酬，它反映劳动者参与增加值创造而获得的原始收入。具体包括从各种来源开支的货币工资和实物工资，即单位以工资、福利、社会保险等形式，从成本、费用和利润中为劳动者支付的各种开支，以及个体和其他劳动者通过参加社会生产活动所获得的各种劳动报酬。

生产税净额 指生产税与补贴之差，它反映政府从本期创造的增加值中所得到的原始收入份额。生产税是指政府对生产单位的生产经营活动所征收的各种税、附加和规费，具体包括销售（营业）税金及附加、增值税、管理费开支的税、应交纳的养路费、排污费和水电附加等，以及烟酒专卖上缴政府的专项收入。补贴与生产税相反，是政府对生产单位的单方面收入转移，因此视为负税处理，包括政策亏损补贴、粮食系统价格补贴、外贸企业出口退税收入等。

营业盈余 指常住单位创造的增加值扣除固定资产折旧价值、支付劳动者报酬和上缴政府生产税净额后的余额，它反映企业参与增加值创造而应得到的原始收入份额。该指标相当于企业的营业利润，但要扣除利税后项目中支付的工资、福利及公益金等。

非金融企业部门 非金融企业部门是指由以营利为目的、

从事非金融经济活动的所有常住非金融企业组成的集合。包括农业企业、工业、建筑业企业、流通企业、服务企业、执行企业会计制度的事业单位；行政事业单位下属的独立核算单位（即企业化管理的事业单位）亦划入本部门。

金融机构部门 金融机构部门是指由从事金融活动的所有常住独立核算单位组成的集合。在我国的新国民经济核算体系中，将其分为三大类：银行机构、保险机构和非银行金融机构。

银行机构为中央银行（中国人民银行）、政策性银行（国家开发银行、农业开发银行、进出口银行）和商业银行（中国工商银行、中国农业银行、中国银行、中国建设银行、交通银行、中信实业银行、中国投资银行、光大银行、城市合作银行等），以及若干区域性银行或私营银行（如华夏银行、民生银行等）。

政府部门 政府部门是指由行使国家管理职能的行政单位和为社会提供非市场化服务的事业单位（即所谓非盈利性机构单位）组成的集合。包括国家机关、政党机关、社会团体及执行预算会计制度的事业单位等。军事单位及所属的非独立核算单位也包括在本部门中。由于目前在我国非盈利机构主要是由国家拨款资助的事业单位，因此我国将为政府和为居民服务的非盈利机构统一归进政府部门。

我国的政府部门由行政单位和非盈利的事业单位组成。其中“财政”作为一个特殊的部门归列于政府部门。

住户部门 住户部门是指由所有常住居民户组成的集体。包括城镇常住居民户、农村常住居民户和城乡个体经营单位。由于个体经营单位的资产负债及财务收支还不能完全独立于所属住户，因此把个体经营单位也划入住户部门。

住户内的成员共同享用其生活设施、共同消费一些货物和服务，其收入和财产的部门或全部被集中起来，因此他们也有权利参与或影响整个住户的经济活动。

国外部门 国外部门指与我国常住机构单位发生经济往来的所有非常住机构单位组成的集合，增列国外部门并不要求编制其整个资产负债表，而只限于记录常住机构单位与非常住机构单位之间所进行的交易及往来活动的累计存量，即仅仅是为了反映我国经济总体与国外进行经济往来活动及结果的总规模和结构关系。

非金融资产 根据我国新国民经济核算体系中有关资产负债项目的基本定义和联合国1993 年SNA 的定义，“非金融资产”是指机构单位单独或共同对其执行所有权或处置权，并通过在核算期内持有或使用它们可从中获得经济利益的，除金融资产以外的经济资产。

非金融资产按是否具有物质形态划分为有形资产和无形资产，按产生的方式或过程可划分为生产资产和非生产资产。在非金融资产中，“生产资产”由固定资产、存货和珍贵物品组成。“非生产资产”可大致分为两类，一类是资源资产，即有形非生产资产，由土地资产、水资源资产、地下资产和非培育生物资产组成；另一类是无形非生产资产，如专利权、租约和其他可转让合同、购买的商誉等。

由于我国目前在资产负债核算中所面临的资料来源和技术条件的限制，我们仅将非金融资产简单地划分为固定资产、存货和其他非金融资产三类。

贡献率 各产业的贡献率是分析经济效益的一个指标，它是指第一、二、三产业增量与生产总值增量之比。

规模以上服务业法人单位 包括：交通运输、仓储和邮政业，信息传输、软件和信息技术服务业，租赁和商务服务业，科学研究和技术服务业，水利、环境和公共设施管理业，居民服务业、修理和其他服务业，教育，卫生和社会工作，文化、体育和娱乐业；以及物业管理、房地产中介服务等行业。

Explanatory Notes on Main Statistical Indicators

GDP refers to the final products at market prices produced by all residents in a country (or a region) during a certain period of time. Gross domestic product is expressed in three different forms, i.e., value, income, and products respectively. GDP in its value form refers to the total value of all goods and services produced by all resident units during a certain period of time, minus the total value of input of goods of non-fixed assets and services; in other term, it is the sum of the value-added of all resident units. GDP in the form of income includes the income created by all resident units and distributed to resident and non-resident units. GDP in the form of products refers to the value of all goods and services for final consumption by all resident units minus the net exports of goods and services during a given period of time. In the practice of national accounting, gross domestic product is calculated with three approaches, i.e., production approach, income approach and expenditure approach, which reflect gross domestic product and its composition from different aspects. In the actual calculation, GDP is based on three calculation methods-production approach, income approach and expenditure approach. These three methods reflect GDP and its composition from different aspects. GTZi (2004) No. 4 document prescribes: Chinese name of regional GDP is "regional gross domestic product".

Production Approach focuses on the total value of goods and services produced in production activities. GDP by Production Approach equals the value of total output minus that of input consumed in production process. The calculation formula is:

GDP by Production Approach= gross output– intermediate input

The sum of value added made by different industries is GDP.

Gross output, intermediate input and value added have the same production scope, i.e., production of goods and services by resident units. It not only includes the production of goods and services by resident units for other units, but that used for the unit. However, services finally consumed and produced by households only include own housing services and services provided by paid family employees (excluding self-supporting family services produced by the household member for final consumption of the household).

Income Approach (also known as distribution approach): refers to the method measuring the final results of production activities from the perspective of income made by all residents. GDP of income approach includes laborers' remuneration, net taxes on production, depreciation of fixed assets and operating surplus. The calculation formula is:

GDP by income approach= laborers' remuneration + net taxes on production + depreciation of fixed assets+ operating surplus

The sum of value added made by different industries is GDP.

In the calculation of labourers' remunerations, it's necessary to define the limit between material incomes and intermediate consumption among labourers' remunerations. If goods or units provided by production units for its labourers engaging in production activity can be met by such labourers in their spare time, improve and raise their actual living level, and other ordinary consumers can purchase such goods and services in the market, these goods and services are classified into material incomes of labourers. Goods purchased by production units for labourers and relevant services for the purpose of successful production, such as clothes or shoes provided due to special work need and transportation and hotel service charges in the business trip, are classified into intermediate input.

Expenditure Approach refers to the method measuring the final results of production activities of a country during a given period from the perspective of final use. It includes final consumption expenditure, total capital formation and net export of goods and services.

GDP by expenditure approach = final consumption expenditure+ gross capital formation+ net export of goods and services

For GDP by expenditure approach, the final consumption expenditure, including household consumption expenditure and government consumption expenditure, is calculated from the perspective of final bearer of expenditure, not from the perspective of final consumers; in the calculation of gross capital formation, gross fixed capital formation only includes fixed assets produced by production activities, excluding natural assets, where increases in inventories do not include holding gains.

GDP by three approaches reflects the results of production activities of the same economic entity during the same period, so theoretically results from three calculation approaches shall be consistent. However, in practice, it's almost impossible to ensure results from these three approaches are completely equal due to the caliber limit of data source and the influence of calculation approaches. Among three calculation approaches of GDP, production approach and income approach are used for business accounting of the value added of each industry sector. For the purpose of consistent data regarding value added of each industrial sector, the value added of some industrial sectors (such as agriculture and industry) is subject to the calculation result of the production approach and the value added of some industry sectors (such as some service industries) is subject to the calculation result of the income approach in the accounting practice in China according to data source, thus China's GDP by production approach is equal to that by income approach. However, statistical error exists between GDP by expenditure approach and that by production approach and income approach. GDP by expenditure approach is more than that by production approach and income approach in some years and it turns out just the opposite in some other years. GDP by production approach and income approach prevail in China generally and the above statistical error shall be controlled to a certain range. Various data regarding total volume and growth rate of GDP published is the calculation result based on production approach and income approach.

The following relationships between data regarding GDP calculated based on above-mentioned three methods are as follows:

GDP= GDP by production approach

= GDP by income approach

= GDP by expenditure approach+ statistical error

Constant Price refers to the price without the effect of price change. By using constant price, total amount of indices of different periods can be compared. There are two methods in which total amount indices are obtained, one using current price of some year to multiply the physical volume of certain products and the other using price index.

Fixed Price refers to the average price of similar products in a given period, with which the product value of different period can be calculated. The product value calculated at fixed price can show the growth rate of production in different periods. Since 1949, NBS has framed the united industrial and agricultural fixed price 8 times, including the fixed price of 1952 used from 1952 to 1957, the fixed price of 1957 used from 1957 to 1970, the fixed price of 1970 used from 1971 to 1980, the fixed price of 1980 used from 1981 to 1990, the fixed price of 1990 used from 1991 to 2000, the fixed price of 2000 used from 2001 to 2005, the fixed price of 2005 used from 2006 to 2010, the fixed price of 2010 used from 2011 to 2015, and the fixed price of 2015 used from 2016.

Three Industries Classification of economic activities into three branches of industries is based on the development of production. Primary industry refers to the production activities that obtain products from nature. Secondary industry refers to the production activities that process primary goods. Tertiary industry refers to the production activities that provide primary and secondary industries with services. Classification of economic activities into three branches of industries is a common practice in the world, although the grouping varies to some extent from country to country.

Economic activities of China are categorized into following industries:

Primary industry refers to agriculture, forestry, animal husbandry and fishery (not contain agriculture, forestry, animal husbandry and fishery service industry).

Secondary industry refers to mining industry (not contain mining auxiliary activities), manufacturing industry (not contain metal products, machinery and equipment repair industry), electricity, heat, gas and water production and supply industry and construction industry.

The tertiary industry is the service industry, refers to all other economic activities not included in primary or secondary industry. According to the economic condition in China, tertiary industry includes Wholesale and Retail Trades, Transport, Storage and Post, Information Transmission, Computer Services and Software, Hotels and Catering Services, Financial Intermediation, Real Estate, Leasing and Business Services, Scientific Research, Technical Services and Geologic Prospecting, Management of Water Conservancy, Environment and Public Facilities, Services to Households and Other Services, Education, Health and Social Security and Social Welfare, Culture, Sports and Entertainment, Public Management and Social Organization, and International Organizations, as well as agriculture, forestry, animal husbandry and fishery services in the agriculture, forestry, animal husbandry and fishery, mining auxiliary activities in the mining industry, metalware, machinery and equipment repair industry in the manufacturing industry.

Gross Domestic Expenditure refers to total expenditures on goods and services of all resident units used for final consumption and investment and net export in a certain period of time in a country (or region) and reflects usage composition of GDP produced in the current period. The gross domestic expenditure is GDP by expenditure approach, including final consumption expenditure, gross capital formation and net export value of such goods and services.

Final Consumption refers to the final consumption of all goods and services of the resident unit within a certain period of time. Total consumption is classified into household consumption and government consumption.

Final Consumption of Households refers to the value of all consumer goods and consumption services obtained by permanent households, including two categories below (1) personal goods and services obtained by the resident based on expenditure whose value is the expenditure regarding individual consumer's goods and consumption services borne by the resident, including virtual expenditure and (2) personal goods and services obtained by physical transfer of non-profit organization and government serving the resident whose value is the expenditure regarding individual consumer's goods and consumption service borne by non-profit organization and government serving the resident, including virtual expenditure.

Total Capital Formation refers to the fixed assets acquired minus those disposed of and the net value of inventory, including the total fixed capital formation and the increase in inventory.

Household Consumption Expenditure includes Item (1) content in the residents' actual final consumption, so the residents' actual final consumption is more than household consumption expenditure.

Actual Final Consumption of Government refers to the value of public consumption services provided by the government to the society or some departments in the society whose value is the public service expenditure of the government.

Government Consumption Expenditure refers to the expenditure regarding (1) individual consumer's goods and consumption services and (2) public consumption services borne by the government, including virtual expenditure.

Total Investment refers to total investment expenditures of resident unit relating to fixed assets and inventories within a certain period of time, divided into formation of fixed assets and increase in inventories.

(1) Gross fixed capital formation refers to the value arising after deduction of sales and roll-out of existing fixed assets from fixed assets of the resident unit purchased, transferred in and produced independently

within a certain period of time. Gross fixed capital formation includes the value of constructional engineering and installation project and equipment purchase completed within a certain period of time and the value of new livestock for service, breeding, milk, wool and recreation and economic forest.

(2) Increase in Inventory refers to the market value of the change in physical quantity of inventory of resident units within a certain period of time. In case that the difference between the beginning and the end is positive, it means an increase in inventories; in case that the difference between the beginning and the end is negative, it means decrease in inventories, including inventory of commodities such as raw material, fuel and restock purchased in the current period and inventory of such products as finished products, semi-finished products and products in process produced in the current period.

Net Export of Goods and Services refers to the difference of the exports of goods and services minus imports of goods and services. The exports include the value of various goods and services sold or gratuitously transferred by the resident units to the non- resident units; The imports include the value of various goods and services purchased or gratuitously obtained by the resident units from the non- resident units; Because the provision of services and the use of them happen simultaneously, the acquisition of services by the resident units from abroad is usually treated as import while the acquisition of services by non-resident units in this country is usually treated as export. The export and import of goods are calculated at FOB.

Net Factor Income from Abroad refers to the difference of net production tax and import tax (deducting production and import subsidies), labourers' remunerations and property income of a country (or region) from abroad minus production and import duties (deducting production and import subsidies), remuneration for labourers and property income paid to foreign country (region). The result after GDP plus foreign net factor income equals to GNP.

Gross Output Gross output refers to the value of all goods and services produced by resident units in a country (or region) within a certain period of time, including newly-increased value and transfer value which reflects the total scale of production activities of resident units. Gross output is calculated in line with producer's price.

Intermediate Input Intermediate input refers to the value of all non-permanent asset goods and services consumed and used in the process of resident units producing or providing goods and services, which is also called as intermediate consumption and is generally calculated pursuant to purchaser price.

Value Added refers to the newly-increased value created by the resident unit in the production process and transfer value of fixed assets which can be calculated based on production approach or income approach. The added value equals to the result after grass output is deducted by intermediate input in case of being calculated based on production approach or the sum of remuneration for labourers, net production tax, depreciation of fixed assets and operating surplus in case of being calculated based on income approach.

Depreciation of Fixed Assets refers to the compensated value extracted to make up for losses of fixed assets within a certain period of time which reflects the asset transfer value of all fixed assets in the production in the current period. Depreciation of fixed assets of various enterprises refers to the depreciation cost extracted from the cost. Units of no calculation of depreciation (such as government agency, public institution, school and hospital, troops and residents' housing) shall be subject to virtual depreciation.

Remuneration for Labourers refers to various remunerations because the worker provides the resident unit with labor service which reflects original income obtained by the worker due to participate in creation of value added, including monetary wages and wages in kind from various sources (namely various expenditures paid by the unit to the worker based on costs, expenses and profits in the form of salary, welfare and social insurance as well as various remunerations of labor obtained by individual and other labourers by participating in social production activity.

Net Production Tax refers to the balance between production tax and subsidy which reflects the original income share obtained by the government from the added value which is created in the current period. Net production tax refers to various taxes additional taxes and levies and charges levied against production and operation activities of production units by the government, including sales (business) taxes and surcharges, added-value tax, tax on overhead expenses, road toll, sewage charge and utility surcharge which shall be paid and special revenue of the government paid for a state monopoly of sales of tobacco and alcoholic drinks. The subsidy is contrary to the net production tax. The former is unilateral transfer of income of the government to the production unit, thus it's deemed negative tax, including policy loss subsidies, food system price subsidies, export tax rebate income of foreign trade enterprises.

Operating Surplus refers to the balance after the value added which is created by resident units is deducted by value of depreciation of fixed assets and used for payment of remuneration for labourers and net production tax of the government which reflects the original income share to be obtained after the enterprise participates in creating the value added. The indicator is equivalent to operating profit of the enterprise but deduction of salary, welfare and welfare fund paid in the after-tax project.

Non-Financial Institutions Sector refer to all resident non-financial businesses for a lucrative purpose which engage in non-financial economic activities, including agricultural enterprises, industrial enterprises, construction enterprises, circulation enterprises, service enterprises and public institutions implementing the enterprise accounting system; Independent accounting units (namely public institutions based on enterprise-style management) subordinate to the administrative institution are included into non-financial corporate sectors.

Financial Institutions Sector refer to all resident independent accounting units engaging in financial activities. In the new national economic accounting system in China, financial institutions sector are divided into three categories: banking institution, insurance institute and non–bank financial institution.

Banking institutions include central bank (The People's Bank of China), policy banks (China Development Bank, Agricultural Development Bank of China and The Export–Import Bank of China), commercial banks (ICBC, ABC, Bank of China, CCB, Bank of Communications, China CITIC Bank, China Investment Bank, China Everbright Bank and Urban Partnership Bank) as well as several regional banks and private banks (such as Huaxia Bank and China Minsheng Bank).

Government Departments Government departments refer to administrative units exercising state administration functions and public institutions providing the society with non–market service (namely so–called non–profit organization), including state organs, Party organs, social organization and public institution implementing the budget accounting system. The military unit and non–independent accounting unit subordinate to the military unit are also included into government departments. Non–profit organizations in China are mainly public institution subsidized by state appropriation, so China uniformly classy non–profit organizations serving the government and residents into government departments.

Government departments in China are composed by administrative units and non–profit public institutions. "Financial department" (special department) is classified as government department.

Household Sector refers to the collective constituted by all resident households, including permanent urban households, permanent rural households and urban and rural self–employed units. Because assets and liabilities and financial revenues of individual business unit fail to be completely independent from corresponding household, the individual business unit is included into household sector.

Members in the household share domestic installation as well as consume some goods and services together whose income and property departments may be collected, so they also have the right to participate in or affect economic activities of the whole household.

Foreign Departments Foreign departments refer to all non–resident institutional units with economic exchanges with resident institutional units in China. In case of increasing foreign departments, preparation of the whole balance sheet isn't required, but it's necessary to record the cumulative stock of transactions and exchanges between resident institutional unit and non–resident institutional unit, namely only reflecting economic exchange between China's economic entity and foreign entity and total scale and structural relationship of corresponding results.

Non–financial Assets "Non–financial assets" refer to economic assets against which the institutional unit executes the ownership or disposal right independently or together with an economic interest obtained by holding or usage within the accounting period except for financial assets according to basic definition about assets and liabilities in the new national economic accounting system in China and definition regarding SNA of UN in 1993.

Non–financial assets can be classified into tangible assets and intangible assets based on whether physical form exists or productive assets and non–productive assets based on production way or process. In the non–financial assets, "productive assets" are constituted by fixed assets, inventories and valuables. "Non–productive assets" can be roughly divided into two categories, including resource assets (namely tangible non–productive assets, consisting of land assets, water resource assets, underground assets and non–breeding biological assets) and intangible non–productive assets (such as patent right, rental agreement and other transferrable contract and goodwill purchased).

Due to the restriction of data source and technical conditions in the assets and liabilities, accounting in China now, we only simply divide non–financial assets into three categories–fixed assets, inventories and other non–financial assets.

Rate of Contribution Rate of contribution of each industry is an indicator for analyzing economic benefit which refers to the ratio between the increment of primary, secondary and tertiary industries and increment of total output value.

Above State Designated Scale Service Industry Legal Entities include: transportation, warehousing and postal services, information transmission, software, and information technology service industry, leasing and business service, scientific research and technological services, water conservancy, environment and public facility management, resident service, repair and other service industries, education, health and social work, culture, sports and entertainment as well as property management, real estate agency service.

5

劳动就业

LABOR AND EMPLOYMENT

5-1 按三次产业分从业人员及构成
Number of Employed Persons and Structure by Type of Industry

年份 Year	从业人员（万人） Total Employed Persons(10 000 persons)				构成（合计=100） Composition in Percentage(Total=100)		
	合计 Total	第一产业 Primary Industry	第二产业 Secondary Industry	第三产业 Tertiary Industry	第一产业 Primary Industry	第二产业 Secondary Industry	第三产业 Tertiary Industry
1952	134.26	109.87	5.86	18.53	81.8	4.4	13.8
1957	144.29	118.65	13.12	12.52	82.2	9.1	8.7
1962	137.58	106.50	16.45	14.63	77.4	12.0	10.6
1965	143.67	107.68	20.96	15.03	74.9	14.6	10.5
1970	161.18	118.15	30.32	12.71	73.3	18.8	7.9
1975	192.59	135.95	41.56	15.08	70.6	21.6	7.8
1978	204.04	136.30	46.06	21.68	66.8	22.6	10.6
1980	214.21	135.16	51.30	27.75	63.1	23.9	13.0
1985	245.32	116.59	76.08	52.65	47.5	31.0	21.5
1990	270.54	125.73	87.75	57.06	46.5	32.4	21.1
1991	276.18	130.36	87.99	57.83	47.2	31.9	20.9
1992	280.19	127.09	85.59	67.51	45.4	30.5	24.1
1993	285.69	124.25	89.91	71.53	43.5	31.5	25.0
1994	303.46	122.62	91.64	89.20	40.4	30.2	29.4
1995	324.22	116.13	106.68	101.41	35.8	32.9	31.3
1996	332.33	107.70	113.91	110.72	32.4	34.3	33.3
1997	337.43	108.17	113.93	115.33	32.0	33.8	34.2
1998	341.63	109.32	113.38	118.93	31.9	33.2	34.9
1999	344.48	109.56	112.98	121.94	31.8	32.8	35.4
2000	347.37	109.98	110.81	126.58	31.7	31.9	36.4
2001	350.10	109.99	109.24	130.87	31.4	31.2	37.4
2002	352.70	108.01	109.14	135.55	30.6	30.9	38.5
2003	355.30	104.90	110.60	139.80	29.5	31.1	39.4
2004	358.50	99.30	113.30	145.90	27.7	31.6	40.7
2005	360.00	99.10	114.20	146.70	27.5	31.7	40.8
2006	361.80	99.00	115.20	147.60	27.4	31.8	40.8
2007	364.30	98.80	116.30	149.20	27.1	31.9	41.0
2008	367.36	98.01	116.95	152.40	26.7	31.8	41.5
2009	372.25	97.80	119.15	155.30	26.3	32.0	41.7
2010	373.70	76.66	120.20	176.84	20.5	32.2	47.3
2011	375.50	74.95	120.70	179.85	20.0	32.1	47.9
2012	379.30	74.30	123.10	181.90	19.6	32.5	47.9
2013	382.30	73.40	122.19	186.71	19.20	32.00	48.80
2014	385.70	72.50	123.30	189.90	18.80	31.97	49.24
2015	388.70	71.80	124.70	192.20	18.47	32.08	49.45
2016	394.93	70.90	126.90	197.13	17.95	32.13	49.92
2017	405.38	69.50	129.35	206.53	17.14	31.91	50.95
2018	419.27	68.80	132.17	218.30	16.41	31.52	52.07
2019	492.36	77.42	154.27	260.67	15.72	31.33	52.94

5-2 主要年份职工工资
Wage of Staff and Workers in Major Years

年份 Year	职工工资总额(万元) Total Wages of Staff and Workers(10 000yuan)				职工平均工资(元) Average Wage of Staff and Workers(yuan)			
	合计 Total	国有经济 State-owned Units	城镇集体经济 Urban Collective-owned Units	其他经济 Others	合计 Total	国有经济 State-owned Units	城镇集体经济 Urban Collective-owned Units	其他经济 Others
1952	4881	4587	294	—	442	453	324	—
1957	14553	11654	2899	—	586	621	480	—
1962	19412	16409	3003	—	577	607	451	—
1965	20367	16821	3546	—	617	664	461	—
1970	21226	17314	3912	—	549	578	449	—
1975	29239	22662	6577	—	557	615	420	—
1978	37840	28733	9107	—	578	626	465	—
1980	55900	41809	14091	—	776	821	668	—
1985	92092	67756	24330	6	1104	1169	954	894
1986	111934	84269	27643	22	1298	1384	1092	882
1987	126263	96322	29673	268	1422	1515	1185	1603
1988	166206	130287	35515	404	1806	1946	1427	2304
1989	190106	150899	38654	553	2037	2199	1577	2614
1990	210618	166250	43003	1365	2211	2370	1751	2460
1991	229540	181185	46091	2264	2368	2535	1872	2658
1992	267295	214311	49565	3419	2710	2938	2020	2919
1993	327226	264252	54442	8532	3323	3547	2524	3553
1994	465966	371403	67351	27212	4736	5209	2975	4922
1995	581432	465311	79932	36189	5851	6561	3623	5663
1996	700636	562645	89126	48865	7031	7839	4290	6875
1997	792368	636694	67999	57675	7896	8761	4954	7303
1998	717927	578788	68455	70684	8326	9022	5459	7410
1999	756696	608052	67273	81371	9083	9929	5766	7818
2000	857337	639312	59468	158557	10422	11761	6211	8651
2001	950851	713222	60818	176811	11980	13462	7061	9945
2002	1120837	846978	74672	199187	14395	16362	8188	11729
2003	1256160	930392	69554	256214	16027	18197	9331	12942
2004	1420491	1049033	73150	298308	18029	20759	10587	13974
2005	1966782	1126918	77722	762142	20866	24626	11890	18164
2006	2459044	1326412	140974	991658	21808	26550	12332	19305
2007	3086928	1680494	166960	1239474	26085	31910	15763	22500
2008	3735956	2049453	202995	1483509	30798	37191	19296	26645
2009	4241838	2227992	177020	1836825	34544	41239	21365	30368
2010	4695402	2462874	179365	2053164	36833	43339	22593	32740
2011	5569118	2647111	169476	2752531	41959	49342	26646	37851
2012	6458632	2811390	161513	3485729	45924	52845	32180	42294
2013	7927677	2766005	170176	4991497	53650	58842	37264	51891
2014	8464904	2912941	148424	5403539	59534	66810	40170	56945
2015	8885256	3282169	143078	5460009	67112	78733	47013	62283
2016	10068893	3715397	162695	6190800	74834	88887	51370	69107
2017	10694345	3776127	124702	6793516	82192	98770	54790	75814
2018	11496722	3869498	98327	7528898	89168	109052	62941	81935
2019	14170697	4846897	87776	9236024	97482	123249	66047	88204

注：本表中1998年及以后年份数据均为在岗职工口径，国有、集体、其他分组按1998年新标准。2006年及以后年份数据为非私营单位从业人员口径。

Note: In this table, the data for 1998 and subsequent years are the caliber of on-the-job workers, and the data of state-owned, collective and other groups base the new standard in 1998. Data for 2006 and subsequent years are the caliber of employees in non-private units.

5-3 城镇非私营单位从业人员人数 (2019 年)

Number of Employed Persons in Urban Non Private Entities(2019)

单位：人 (person)

指 标	Indicator	从业人员 Employed Persons	其中 of which 在岗职工 Staff and Workers	劳务派遣人员 Labor Dispatch Personnel	其他从业人员 Others
合计	Total	1465324	1204137	136155	125032
按隶属关系分组	By Affiliation	220291	146826	17633	55832
中央	Central	741901	616367	87467	38067
地方	Local	503132	440944	31055	31133
其他	Others				
按国民经济行业分组	Grouped by Sector				
农、林、牧、渔业	Agriculture, Forestry, Animal Husbandry and Fishing	774	706	50	18
农业	Agriculture	54	36		18
林业	Forestry	73	73		
畜牧业	Animal Husbandry	162	162		
渔业	Fishing	124	105	19	
农、林、牧、渔专业及辅助性活动	Service Activities for Agriculture, Forestry, Animal Production and Hunting, Fishing	361	330	31	
采矿业	Mining	10630	8895	1252	483
煤炭开采和洗选业	Mining and Washing of Coal	930	815		115
石油和天然气开采业	Extraction of Petroleum and Natural Gas	706	386	114	206
黑色金属矿采选业	Mining of Ferrous Metal Ores	8598	7298	1138	162
有色金属矿采选业	Mining of Non-ferrous Metal Ores				
非金属矿采选业	Mining and Processing of Nonmetal Ores	384	384		
开采专业及辅助性活动	Mining Support Service Activities				
其他采矿业	Mining of Other Ores	12	12		
制造业	Manufacturing	240736	223178	12642	4916
农副食品加工业	Processing of Food from Agricultural Products	3298	2890	61	347
食品制造业	Manufacture of Foods	10145	9845	178	122
酒、饮料和精制茶制造业	Manufacture of Wine, Drinks and Refined Tea	6117	5850	201	66
烟草制品业	Manufacture of Tobacco	2390	2348	42	
纺织业	Manufacture of Textile	3421	3322	92	7
纺织服装、服饰业	Manufacture of Textile Wearing Apparel and Finery	5818	5775		43
皮革、毛皮、羽毛及其制品业和制鞋业	Manufacture of Leather, Fur, Feather and Its Products, and Footwear	410	409		1
木材加工和木、竹、藤、棕、草制品业	Processing of Timbers, Manufacture of Wood, Bamboo, Rattan, Palm and Straw Products	80	80		
家具制造业	Manufacture of Furniture				

5-3 续表 1 continued 1

指 标	Indicator	从业人员 Employed Persons	其中 of which 在岗职工 Staff and Workers	劳务派遣人员 Labor Dispatch Personnel	其他从业人员 Others
造纸和纸制品业	Manufacture of Paper and Paper Products	1419	1337	79	3
印刷和记录媒介复制业	Printing, Reproduction of Recording Media	5563	5440	80	43
文教、工美、体育和娱乐用品制造业	Manufacture of Articles for Culture, Education, Artwork, Sport and Entertainment Activities	544	532		12
石油、煤炭及其他燃料加工业	Processing of Petroleum, Coking, Processing of Nucleus Fuels	2212	2066	67	79
化学原料和化学制品制造业	Manufacture of Chemical Raw Material and Chemical Products	4836	4711	34	91
医药制造业	Manufacture of Medicines	22715	22634	34	47
化学纤维制造业	Manufacture of Chemical Fiber	823	822		1
橡胶和塑料制品业	Manufacture of Rubber and Plastic	2155	2096	11	48
非金属矿物制品业	Manufacture of Non-metallic Mineral Products	17634	14312	2908	414
黑色金属冶炼和压延加工业	Manufacture and Processing of Ferrous Metals	25479	25405	20	54
有色金属冶炼和压延加工业	Manufacture & Processing of Non-ferrous Metals	1254	1254		
金属制品业	Manufacture of Metal Products	16729	16265	403	61
通用设备制造业	Manufacture of General Purpose Machinery	24229	21792	1760	677
专用设备制造业	Manufacture of Special Purpose Machinery	10306	10131	105	70
汽车制造业	Manufacture of Automotive	34932	28475	4502	1955
铁路、船舶、航空航天和其他运输设备制造业	Manufacture of Railway Locomotives, Building of Ships and Boats, Manufacture of Air and Spacecrafts and Other Transportation Equipments	7895	6895	532	468
电气机械和器材制造业	Manufacture of Electrical Machinery & Equipment	15153	14083	919	151
计算机、通信和其他电子设备制造业	Manufacture of Computers, Communication Equipment and Other Electronic Equipment	10545	10204	284	57
仪器仪表制造业	Manufacture of Measuring Instrument	4126	3812	219	95
其他制造业	Other Manufacture	164	164		
废弃资源综合利用业	Comprehensive Utilization of Waste	338	226	111	1
金属制品、机械和设备修理业	Metal Products, Machinery and Equipment Repair Industry	6	3		3
电力、热力、燃气及水生产和供应业	Production and Distribution of Electricity, Heating Power, Gas and Water	16356	15266	951	139
电力、热力生产和供应业	Production and Supply of Electric Power and Heat Power	9490	8804	625	61
燃气生产和供应业	Production and Supply of Gas	3185	2921	200	64
水的生产和供应业	Production and Supply of Water	3681	3541	126	14
建筑业	Construction	314179	196153	60330	57696
房屋建筑业	Construction of Building	171191	89724	35457	46010

5-3 续表 2 continued 2

指　标	Indicator	从业人员 Employed Persons	其中 of which 在岗职工 Staff and Workers	劳务派遣人员 Labor Dispatch Personnel	其他从业人员 Others
土木工程建筑业	Civil Engineering Construction	109565	82703	16968	9894
建筑安装业	Construction Installation	18465	16450	1328	687
建筑装饰、装修和其他建筑业	Building Completion, Finishing and Other Construction	14958	7276	6577	1105
批发和零售业	Wholesale and Retail Trade	83267	77419	4328	1520
批发业	Wholesale Trade	41653	39484	1445	724
零售业	Retail Trade	41614	37935	2883	796
交通运输、仓储和邮政业	Traffic, Transport, Storage and Post	59354	47602	6177	5575
铁路运输业	Railway Transport	1806	1449	286	71
道路运输业	Road Transport	29241	25336	3094	811
水上运输业	Waterway Transport	547	460	61	26
航空运输业	Air Transport	12157	10235	1175	747
管道运输业	Pipeline Transport	1057	930	84	43
多式联运和运输代理业	Multimodal transport and transportation agency	1308	1099	167	42
装卸搬运和仓储业	Loading, Unloading, Portage and Storage	1254	1139	42	73
邮政业	Postal Services	11984	6954	1268	3762
住宿和餐饮业	Hotels and Catering Services	25114	21703	485	2926
住宿业	Hotels	13262	12552	372	338
餐饮业	Catering Services	11852	9151	113	2588
信息传输、软件和信息技术服务业	Information Transfer, Software and Information Technology Services	68991	63141	4072	1778
电信、广播电视和卫星传输服务	Telecommunications, Radio and Television and Satellite Transmission Services	10141	8421	1693	27
互联网和相关服务	Internet and related Services	4276	2952	116	1208
软件和信息技术服务业	Software and Information Technology Services	54574	51768	2263	543
金融业	Financial Intermediation	80920	48549	1694	30677
货币金融服务	Monetary and Financial Services	34461	33123	1070	268
资本市场服务	Capital Market Services	1880	1879	1	
保险业	Insurance	43452	12444	602	30406
其他金融业	Others	1127	1103	21	3
房地产业	Real Estate	61904	57457	2889	1558
房地产开发经营	Real Estate Development and Management	19614	18334	955	325
物业管理	Property Management	32401	30027	1739	635
房地产中介服务	Real Estate Intermediary Services	3085	2864	77	144
房地产租赁经营	Real Estate Leasing Business	6515	5952	117	446
其他房地产业	Others				
租赁和商务服务业	Leasing and Business Services	45044	41656	2404	984

5-3 续表 3 continued 3

指 标	Indicator	从业人员 Employed Persons	其中 of which 在岗职工 Staff and Workers	劳务派遣人员 Labor Dispatch Personnel	其他从业人员 Others
租赁业	Leasing Services	1745	1612	128	5
商务服务业	Business Services	43299	40044	2276	979
科学研究和技术服务业	Scientific Research and Development,Technical Services	63737	56261	4613	2863
研究和试验发展	Research and Experimental Development	8675	7930	243	502
专业技术服务业	Special Technical Services	50330	43747	4301	2282
科技推广和应用服务业	Science and Technology Promotion and Application Services	4732	4584	69	79
水利、环境和公共设施管理业	Management of Water Conservancy, Environment and Public Facilities	31041	27532	2888	621
水利管理业	Management of Water Conservancy	18337	18252	68	17
生态保护和环境治理业	Ecological Protection and Environmental Management	858	793	18	47
公共设施管理业	Management of Public Facilities	11718	8360	2802	556
土地管理业	Land Mangement	128	127		1
居民服务、修理和其他服务业	Services to Households, Repair and Other Services	6678	3544	3097	37
居民服务业	Services to Households	5329	2393	2899	37
机动车、电子产品和日用产品修理业	Repair of Motor Vehicles, Electronics and Household Appliances	323	323	0	0
其他服务业	Other Services	1026	828	198	0
教育	Education	143690	129482	8980	5228
卫生和社会工作	Health and Social Work	82455	75818	4182	2455
卫生	Health Care	80329	73840	4115	2374
社会工作	Social Work	2126	1978	67	81
文化、体育和娱乐业	Culture, Sports and Entertainment	14201	12822	744	635
新闻和出版业	Journalism and Publishing	4461	4150	208	103
广播、电视、电影和录音制作业	Radio Broadcasting, Television,Movies, Videos and Sound Recording	3021	2896	79	46
文化艺术业	Culture and Arts	4236	3644	281	311
体育	Sports	938	857	78	3
娱乐业	Recreation	1545	1275	98	172
公共管理、社会保障和社会组织	Public Administration, Social Security and Social Organizations	116253	96953	14377	4923
中国共产党机关	Organs of Communist Party of China	10280	9884	377	19
国家机构	Organs of State	103484	84894	13791	4799
人民政协、民主党派	People's Political Consultative Conference and Democratic Parties	879	748	94	37
社会保障	Social Security	428	376	52	0
群众团体、社会团体和其他成员组织	Mass Communities, Social Organizations and Other Membership Organizations	1182	1051	63	68
基层群众自治组织	Grass Roots Self-Government Organization				

5-4 城镇非私营单位从业人员工资总额（2019 年）
Total Wage of Employed Persons in Urban Non Private Entities(2019)

单位：千元 (1000 yuan)

指　标	Indicator	从业人员工资总额 Wage Bill of Employed Persons	其中 of which		
			在岗职工工资总额 Total Wage of Staff and Workers	劳务派遣人员工资总额 Total Wage of Labor Dispatch Personnel	其他从业人员工资总额 Total Wage of Other Staff
合计	Total	141706967	124511618	9309503	7885846
按隶属关系分组	By Affiliation				
中央	Central	25567196	20078707	1359060	4129429
地方	Local	75487969	67207392	6011240	2269337
其他	Others	40651802	37225519	1939203	1487080
按国民经济行业分组	Grouped by Sector				
农、林、牧、渔业	Agriculture, Forestry, Animal Husbandry and Fishing	86414	83264	2810	340
农业	Agriculture	1452	1112		340
林业	Forestry	7918	7918		
畜牧业	Animal Husbandry	18060	18060		
渔业	Fishing	14503	13408	1095	
农、林、牧、渔专业及辅助性活动	Service Activities for Agriculture, Forestry, Animal Production and Hunting, Fishing	44481	42766	1715	
采矿业	Mining	844828	723532	82384	38912
煤炭开采和洗选业	Mining and Washing of Coal	83740	80674		3066
石油和天然气开采业	Extraction of Petroleum and Natural Gas	119048	73386	14683	30979
黑色金属矿采选业	Mining of Ferrous Metal Ores	634390	561822	67701	4867
有色金属矿采选业	Mining of Non-ferrous Metal Ores				
非金属矿采选业	Mining and Processing of Nonmetal Ores	6570	6570		
开采专业及辅助性活动	Mining Support Service Activities				
其他采矿业	Mining of Other Ores	1080	1080		
制造业	Manufacturing	19842641	18647383	958384	236874
农副食品加工业	Processing of Food from Agricultural Products	155125	143838	2216	9071
食品制造业	Manufacture of Foods	560293	543085	14035	3173
酒、饮料和精制茶制造业	Manufacture of Wine, Drinks and Refined Tea	450549	441001	6915	2633
烟草制品业	Manufacture of Tobacco	141848	140196	1652	
纺织业	Manufacture of Textile	202619	198099	4420	100
纺织服装、服饰业	Manufacture of Textile Wearing Apparel and Finery	287391	283513		3878
皮革、毛皮、羽毛及其制品业和制鞋业	Manufacture of Leather, Fur, Feather and Its Products, and Footwear	14212	14205		7
木材加工和木、竹、藤、棕、草制品业	Processing of Timbers, Manufacture of Wood, Bamboo, Rattan, Palm and Straw Products	4074	4074		
家具制造业	Manufacture of Furniture				
造纸和纸制品业	Manufacture of Paper and Paper Products	92149	90839	1148	162

5-4 续表 1 continued 1

指　标	Indicator	从业人员工资总额 Wage Bill of Employed Persons	其中 of which 在岗职工工资总额 Total Wage of Staff and Workers	劳务派遣人员工资总额 Total Wage of Labor Dispatch Personnel	其他从业人员工资总额 Total Wage of Other Staff
印刷和记录媒介复制业	Printing, Reproduction of Recording Media	339626	332489	4917	2220
文教、工美、体育和娱乐用品制造业	Manufacture of Articles for Culture, Education, Artwork, Sport and Entertainment Activities	24912	24332		580
石油、煤炭及其他燃料加工业	Processing of Petroleum, Coking Processing of Nucleus Fuels	291982	280292	5853	5837
化学原料和化学制品制造业	Manufacture of Chemical Raw Material and Chemical Products	370350	362235	3648	4467
医药制造业	Manufacture of Medicines	2110697	2103929	1395	5373
化学纤维制造业	Manufacture of Chemical Fiber	54240	54130		110
橡胶和塑料制品业	Manufacture of Rubber and Plastic	106923	104634	764	1525
非金属矿物制品业	Manufacture of Non-metallic Mineral Products	1236990	1035566	184565	16859
黑色金属冶炼和压延加工业	Manufacture and Processing of Ferrous Metals	2417874	2408674	1740	7460
有色金属冶炼和压延加工业	Manufacture & Processing of Non-ferrous Metals	85347	85347		
金属制品业	Manufacture of Metal Products	1106960	1079694	23004	4262
通用设备制造业	Manufacture of General Purpose Machinery	2003350	1851447	120879	31024
专用设备制造业	Manufacture of Special Purpose Machinery	696930	686601	5722	4607
汽车制造业	Manufacture of Automotive	3312674	2766381	450380	95913
铁路、船舶、航空航天和其他运输设备制造业	Manufacture of Railway Locomotives,Building of Ships and Boats, Manufacture of Air and Spacecrafts and Other Transportation Equipments	652138	613102	26076	12960
电气机械和器材制造业	Manufacture of Electrical Machinery & Equipment	1286563	1215631	62695	8237
计算机、通信和其他电子设备制造业	Manufacture of Computers, Communication Equipment and Other Electronic Equipment	1412906	1386024	19795	7087
仪器仪表制造业	Manufacture of Measuring Instrument	382477	360873	12348	9256
其他制造业	Other Manufacture	20481	20481		
废弃资源综合利用业	Comprehensive Utilization of Waste	20505	16263	4217	25
金属制品、机械和设备修理业	Metal Products, Machinery and Equipment Repair Industry	456	408		48
电力、热力、燃气及水生产和供应业	Production and Distribution of Electricity, Heating Power, Gas and Water	1661735	1607277	46698	7760
电力、热力生产和供应业	Production and Supply of Electric Power and Heat Power	926410	894880	29733	1797
燃气生产和供应业	Production and Supply of Gas	374830	357248	12123	5459
水的生产和供应业	Production and Supply of Water	360495	355149	4842	504
建筑业	Construction	26698215	17264400	4680496	4753319
房屋建筑业	Construction of Building	13372944	6425699	2926929	4020316
土木工程建筑业	Civil Engineering Construction	11499263	9403930	1430147	665186

5-4 续表 2 continued 2

指　标	Indicator	从业人员工资总额 Wage Bill of Employed Persons	其中 of which		
			在岗职工工资总额 Total Wage of Staff and Workers	劳务派遣人员工资总额 Total Wage of Labor Dispatch Personnel	其他从业人员工资总额 Total Wage of Other Staff
建筑安装业	Construction Installation	1080989	970913	80724	29352
建筑装饰、装修和其他建筑业	Building Completion, Finishing and Other Construction	745019	463858	242696	38465
批发和零售业	Wholesale and Retail Trade	6227468	5863052	273859	90557
批发业	Wholesale Trade	3781712	3624230	108677	48805
零售业	Retail Trade	2445756	2238822	165182	41752
交通运输、仓储和邮政业	Traffic, Transport, Storage and Post	6589643	5887825	417053	284765
铁路运输业	Railway Transport	224882	203739	17080	4063
道路运输业	Road Transport	2319038	2098833	174392	45813
水上运输业	Waterway Transport	43645	37661	3219	2765
航空运输业	Air Transport	2662024	2536716	101926	23382
管道运输业	Pipeline Transport	145593	130187	7128	8278
多式联运和运输代理业	Multimodal transport and transportation agency	162389	144614	13515	4260
装卸搬运和仓储业	Loading, Unloading, Portage and Storage	88032	83694	2016	2322
邮政业	Postal Services	944040	652381	97777	193882
住宿和餐饮业	Hotels and Catering Services	1162031	1098274	23225	40532
住宿业	Hotels	694370	665029	18134	11207
餐饮业	Catering Services	467661	433245	5091	29325
信息传输、软件和信息技术服务业	Information Transfer, Software and Information Technology Services	7222905	6788360	329835	104710
电信、广播电视和卫星传输服务	Telecommunications, Radio and Television and Satellite Transmission Services	1411083	1285384	119537	6162
互联网和相关服务	Internet and related Services	466155	389268	12356	64531
软件和信息技术服务业	Software and Information Technology Services	5345667	5113708	197942	34017
金融业	Financial Intermediation	10283285	8723710	123575	1436000
货币金融服务	Monetary and Financial Services	6214985	6126155	77425	11405
资本市场服务	Capital Market Services	502063	501703	360	
保险业	Insurance	3340144	1870879	44870	1424395
其他金融业	Others	226093	224973	920	200
房地产业	Real Estate	4196069	3979955	151392	64722
房地产开发经营	Real Estate Development and Management	2289858	2196647	63741	29470
物业管理	Property Management	1290865	1198837	74382	17646
房地产中介服务	Real Estate Intermediary Services	229309	211821	7657	9831
房地产租赁经营	Real Estate Leasing Business	352858	339896	5535	7427
其他房地产业	Others				
租赁和商务服务业	Leasing and Business Services	4125131	3848895	236851	39385
租赁业	Leasing Services	150286	142622	7042	622

5-4 续表 3 continued 3

指　标	Indicator	从业人员工资总额 Wage Bill of Employed Persons	其中 of which		
			在岗职工工资总额 Total Wage of Staff and Workers	劳务派遣人员工资总额 Total Wage of Labor Dispatch Personnel	其他从业人员工资总额 Total Wage of Other Staff
商务服务业	Business Services	3974845	3706273	229809	38763
科学研究和技术服务业	Scientific Research and Development, Technical Services	7126769	6623335	293951	209483
研究和试验发展	Research and Experimental Development	1022203	959243	22033	40927
专业技术服务业	Special Technical Services	5585896	5157021	268163	160712
科技推广和应用服务业	Science and Technology Promotion and Application Services	518670	507071	3755	7844
水利、环境和公共设施管理业	Management of Water Conservancy,Environment and Public Facilities	2703014	2568397	120795	13822
水利管理业	Management of Water Conservancy	1836185	1832739	3127	319
生态保护和环境治理业	Ecological Protection and Environmental Management	77101	74599	1124	1378
公共设施管理业	Management of Public Facilities	776262	647773	116544	11945
土地管理业	Land Mangement	13466	13286		180
居民服务、修理和其他服务业	Services to Households, Repair and Other Services	368326	272641	94118	1567
居民服务业	Services to Households	299468	212778	85123	1567
机动车、电子产品和日用产品修理业	Repair of Motor Vehicles, Electronics and Household Appliances	20976	20976		
其他服务业	Other Services	47882	38887	8995	
教育	Education	15882646	15195373	482468	204805
卫生和社会工作	Health and Social Work	11400973	10925844	307259	167870
卫生	Health Care	11267860	10798264	304307	165289
社会工作	Social Work	133113	127580	2952	2581
文化、体育和娱乐业	Culture, Sports and Entertainment	1661404	1591339	37035	33030
新闻和出版业	Journalism and Publishing	644751	628387	11826	4538
广播、电视、电影和录音制作业	Radio Broadcasting, Television, Movies, Videos and Sound Recording	353373	346113	5825	1435
文化艺术业	Culture and Arts	440119	411532	11167	17420
体育	Sports	94579	91100	3384	95
娱乐业	Recreation	128582	114207	4833	9542
公共管理、社会保障和社会组织	Public Administration, Social Security and Social Organizations	13623470	12818762	647315	157393
中国共产党机关	Organs of Communist Party of China	1526399	1510107	15775	517
国家机构	Organs of State	11756579	10980584	623523	152472
人民政协、民主党派	People's Political Consultative Conference and Democratic Parties	141172	135568	4027	1577
社会保障	Social Security	54996	53036	1960	
群众团体、社会团体和其他成员组织	Mass Communities, Social Organizations and Other Membership Organizations	144324	139467	2030	2827
基层群众自治组织	Grass Roots Self-Government Organization				

5-5 城镇非私营单位从业人员平均工资（2019 年）
Average Wage of Employed Persons in Urban Non Private Entities(2019)

单位：元 (yuan)

指标	Indicator	从业人员平均工资 Average Wage of Employed Persons	其中 of which 在岗职工平均工资 Average Wage of Total Wage of Staff	劳务派遣人员平均工资 Average Wage of Labor Dispatch Personnel	其他从业人员平均工资 Average Wage of Other Staff
合计	Total	97482	104586	66591	63930
按隶属关系分组	By Affiliation				
中央	Central	117293	137220	77215	76399
地方	Local	102148	110333	65895	58714
其他	Others	81846	85564	62603	48518
按国民经济行业分组	Grouped by Sector				
农、林、牧、渔业	Agriculture, Forestry, Animal Husbandry and Fishing	111358	117605	56200	18889
农业	Agriculture	26889	30889		18889
林业	Forestry	109972	109972		
畜牧业	Animal Husbandry	108144	108144		
渔业	Fishing	116960	127695	57632	
农、林、牧、渔专业及辅助性活动	Service Activities for Agriculture, Forestry, Animal Production and Hunting, Fishing	123903	130384	55323	
采矿业	Mining	80698	83356	66332	71137
煤炭开采和洗选业	Mining and Washing of Coal	89657	99108		25550
石油和天然气开采业	Extraction of Petroleum and Natural Gas	166036	188169	128798	145441
黑色金属矿采选业	Mining of Ferrous Metal Ores	72776	76179	60019	22743
有色金属矿采选业	Mining of Non-ferrous Metal Ores				
非金属矿采选业	Mining and Processing of Nonmetal Ores	73820	73820		
开采专业及辅助性活动	Mining Support Service Activities				
其他采矿业	Mining of Other Ores	90000	90000		
制造业	Manufacturing	82668	83964	69843	56158
农副食品加工业	Processing of Food from Agricultural Products	47439	49892	29158	29167
食品制造业	Manufacture of Foods	57331	58296	43997	22993
酒、饮料和精制茶制造业	Manufacture of Wine, Drinks and Refined Tea	76093	76950	59612	35581
烟草制品业	Manufacture of Tobacco	61247	61652	39333	
纺织业	Manufacture of Textile	60375	60954	43762	20000
纺织服装、服饰业	Manufacture of Textile Wearing Apparel and Finery	47160	46862		88136
皮革、毛皮、羽毛及其制品业和制鞋业	Manufacture of Leather, Fur,Feather and Its Products,and Footwear	33128	33189		7000
木材加工和木、竹、藤、棕、草制品业	Processing of Timbers, Manufacture of Wood, Bamboo, Rattan, Palm and Straw Products	47929	47929		
家具制造业	Manufacture of Furniture				
造纸和纸制品业	Manufacture of Paper and Paper Products	63948	66695	15307	40500

5-5 续表 1 continued 1

指　标	Indicator	从业人员平均工资 Average Wage of Employed Persons	其中 of which		
			在岗职工平均工资 Average Wage of Total Wage of Staff	劳务派遣人员平均工资 Average Wage of Labor Dispatch Personnel	其他从业人员平均工资 Average Wage of Other Staff
印刷和记录媒介复制业	Printing, Reproduction of Recording Media	62719	62876	60704	48261
文教、工美、体育和娱乐用品制造业	Manufacture of Articles for Culture, Education, Artwork,Sport and Entertainment Activities	47093	46973		52727
石油、煤炭及其他燃料加工业	Processing of Petroleum, Coking, Processing of Nucleus Fuels	130875	134691	86074	71183
化学原料和化学制品制造业	Manufacture of Chemical Raw Material and Chemical Products	75412	76196	68830	42952
医药制造业	Manufacture of Medicines	95498	95585	41029	94263
化学纤维制造业	Manufacture of Chemical Fiber	68832	68780		110000
橡胶和塑料制品业	Manufacture of Rubber and Plastic	52697	53033	95500	31771
非金属矿物制品业	Manufacture of Non-metallic Mineral Products	70782	72927	64241	41834
黑色金属冶炼和压延加工业	Manufacture and Processing of Ferrous Metals	93676	93603	69600	140755
有色金属冶炼和压延加工业	Manufacture & Processing of Non-ferrous Metals	68717	68717		
金属制品业	Manufacture of Metal Products	67958	68236	55565	81962
通用设备制造业	Manufacture of General Purpose Machinery	83843	86371	69034	43881
专用设备制造业	Manufacture of Special Purpose Machinery	67109	67334	56098	53570
汽车制造业	Manufacture of Automotive	92260	95567	81164	68023
铁路、船舶、航空航天和其他运输设备制造业	Manufacture of Railway Locomotives, Building of Ships and Boats, Manufacture of Air and Spacecrafts and Other Transportation Equipments	85347	88971	53216	49846
电气机械和器材制造业	Manufacture of Electrical Machinery & Equipment	85350	86911	68295	48740
计算机、通信和其他电子设备制造业	Manufacture of Computers, Communication Equipment and Other Electronic Equipment	133697	135659	67330	124333
仪器仪表制造业	Manufacture of Measuring Instrument	84024	85272	53921	101714
其他制造业	Other Manufacture	124127	124127		
废弃资源综合利用业	Comprehensive Utilization of Waste	62325	72603	40548	25000
金属制品、机械和设备修理业	Metal Products, Machinery and Equipment Repair Industry	76000	136000		16000
电力、热力、燃气及水生产和供应业	Production and Distribution of Electricity, Heating Power, Gas and Water	103085	106294	53800	59237
电力、热力生产和供应业	Production and Supply of Electric Power and Heat Power	100055	103228	53670	49917
燃气生产和供应业	Production and Supply of Gas	117834	123019	61852	67395
水的生产和供应业	Production and Supply of Water	97961	100098	41034	36000
建筑业	Construction	85786	89913	74006	84940
房屋建筑业	Construction of Building	79319	74098	76451	92224
土木工程建筑业	Civil Engineering Construction	104981	114962	83801	62336

5-5 续表 2 continued 2

指　标	Indicator	从业人员平均工资 Average Wage of Employed Persons	其中 of which		
			在岗职工平均工资 Average Wage of Total Wage of Staff	劳务派遣人员平均工资 Average Wage of Labor Dispatch Personnel	其他从业人员平均工资 Average Wage of Other Staff
建筑安装业	Construction Installation	59480	59481	65048	48118
建筑装饰、装修和其他建筑业	Building Completion, Finishing and Other Construction	49964	64685	36479	35386
批发和零售业	Wholesale and Retail Trade	72711	73846	59034	56177
批发业	Wholesale Trade	91080	92632	65905	65335
零售业	Retail Trade	55427	55594	55245	48268
交通运输、仓储和邮政业	Traffic, Transport, Storage and Post	110633	123999	68651	47421
铁路运输业	Railway Transport	124382	140607	59720	55658
道路运输业	Road Transport	79183	82638	58482	50510
水上运输业	Waterway Transport	78498	80301	52770	106346
航空运输业	Air Transport	225806	255769	86968	33451
管道运输业	Pipeline NTransport	121530	139089	83859	46768
多式联运和运输代理业	Multimodal Transport and Transportation Agency	129911	138652	80928	106500
装卸搬运和仓储业	Loading, Unloading, Portage and Storage	69922	72777	48000	34657
邮政业	Postal Services	76034	91627	76388	48277
住宿和餐饮业	Hotels and Catering Services	46383	51271	48486	12855
住宿业	Hotels	53213	53753	50233	35465
餐饮业	Catering Services	38959	47878	43144	10337
信息传输、软件和信息技术服务业	Information Transfer, Software and Information Technology Services	105858	108955	82110	54793
电信、广播电视和卫星传输服务	Telecommunications, Radio and Television and Satellite Transmission Services	137640	152804	65861	246480
互联网和相关服务	Internet and related Services	115072	141862	116566	53731
软件和信息技术服务业	Software and Information Technology Services	99124	99979	94438	49660
金融业	Financial Intermediation	126956	180735	72224	46293
货币金融服务	Monetary and Financial Services	181497	186149	72158	43865
资本市场服务	Capital Market Services	270362	270314	360000	
保险业	Insurance	76221	150380	71907	46311
其他金融业	Others	209929	212039	70769	66667
房地产业	Real Estate	68606	70495	48994	40076
房地产开发经营	Real Estate Development and Management	116124	118558	76889	81409
物业管理	Property Management	40964	41631	36213	26696
房地产中介服务	Real Estate Intermediary Services	76006	75542	98167	72822
房地产租赁经营	Real Estate Leasing Business	53536	56517	43242	16541
其他房地产业	Others				
租赁和商务服务业	Leasing and Business Services	96027	98959	78014	38312
租赁业	Leasing Services	86371	88972	53756	103667

5-5 续表 3 continued 3

指　标	Indicator	从业人员平均工资 Average Wage of Employed Persons	其中 of which 在岗职工平均工资 Average Wage of Total Wage of Staff	劳务派遣人员平均工资 Average Wage of Labor Dispatch Personnel	其他从业人员平均工资 Average Wage of Other Staff
商务服务业	Business Services	96435	99388	79108	37929
科学研究和技术服务业	Scientific Research and Development, Technical Services	115507	120315	69149	87321
研究和试验发展	Research and Experimental Development	120500	124142	85399	82183
专业技术服务业	Special Technical Services	115071	120491	68391	88206
科技推广和应用服务业	Science and Technology Promotion and Application Services	110969	112109	52153	99291
水利、环境和公共设施管理业	Management of Water Conservancy, Environment and Public Facilities	86710	92796	41870	22659
水利管理业	Management of Water Conservancy	100190	100402	55839	18765
生态保护和环境治理业	Ecological Protection and Environmental Management	93117	97771	62444	29319
公共设施管理业	Management of Public Facilities	65270	75878	41460	21917
土地管理业	Land Mangement	107728	107145		180000
居民服务、修理和其他服务业	Services to Households, Repair and Other Services	55205	76952	30439	42351
居民服务业	Services to Households	56143	88917	29312	42351
机动车、电子产品和日用产品修理业	Repair of Motor Vehicles, Electronics and Household Appliances	64741	64741		
其他服务业	Other Services	47221	47079	47846	
教育	Education	112845	119522	56245	40668
卫生和社会工作	Health and Social Work	140085	145723	77886	68129
卫生	Health Care	142172	147940	78470	69275
社会工作	Social Work	62465	64240	44060	33090
文化、体育和娱乐业	Culture, Sports and Entertainment	116386	124217	50663	45061
新闻和出版业	Journalism and Publishing	145083	152558	57408	38134
广播、电视、电影和录音制作业	Radio Broadcasting, Television, Movies, Videos and Sound Recording	117634	120976	67733	25175
文化艺术业	Culture and Arts	104047	112934	41207	55302
体育	Sports	100723	106177	43385	31667
娱乐业	Recreation	77552	85935	53700	39925
公共管理、社会保障和社会组织	Public Administration, Social Security and Social Organizations	117962	132851	45760	32425
中国共产党机关	Organs of Communist Party of China	149691	154093	41844	25850
国家机构	Organs of State	114292	129895	45854	32221
人民政协、民主党派	People' s Political Consultative Conference and Democratic Parties	160971	181727	41948	45057
社会保障	Social Security	137490	145304	56000	
群众团体、社会团体和其他成员组织	Mass Communities, Social Organizations and Other Membership Organizations	125281	133461	50750	42194
基层群众自治组织	Grass Roots Self-Government Organization				

5-6 国有单位从业人员和工资(2019年)

Number and Wage of Employed Persons in State-owned Units(2019)

指 标	Indicator	从业人员（人）Number of Employed Persons (person)	从业人员工资总额（千元）Wage of Employed Persons (1000 yuan)	从业人员平均工资（元）Average Wage of Employed Persons(yuan)
总计	Total	397707	48468972	123249
按隶属关系分组	By Affiliation			
中央	Central Investment	46998	7230326	156072
地方	Local	299215	35649973	120505
其他	Others	51494	5588673	109380
按国民经济行业分组	Grouped by Sector			
农、林、牧、渔业	Agriculture, Forestry, Animal Husbandry and Fishing	639	80013	125807
采矿业	Mining	71	3210	45211
制造业	Manufacturing	1644	159502	99131
电力、热力、燃气及水生产和供应业	Production and Distribution of Electricity, Heating Power, Gas and Water	1583	113114	74712
建筑业	Construction	6370	596999	94208
批发和零售业	Wholesale and Retail Trade	2452	207422	81566
交通运输、仓储和邮政业	Transport, Storage and Post	20950	1984035	95194
住宿和餐饮业	Accommodation and Restaurants	5016	292605	59041
信息传输、软件和信息技术服务业	Information Transmission, Software and Information Technology Services	1022	139648	138677
金融业	Financial Intermediation	8542	1523226	179287
房地产业	Real Estate	3355	255820	75731
租赁和商务服务业	Leasing and Business Services	6750	921708	136894
科学研究和技术服务业	Scientific Research and Development, Technical Services	23363	2849694	125609
水利、环境和公共设施管理业	Management of Water Conservancy, Environment and Public Facilities	7631	794873	103459
居民服务、修理和其他服务业	Resident Services, Repair and Other Services	581	59686	102730
教育	Education	113343	13640706	122336
卫生和社会工作	Health Care and Social Works	71609	10514119	148898
文化、体育和娱乐业	Culture, Sports and Entertainment	7771	839717	107808
公共管理、社会保障和社会组织	Public Administration, Social Security and Social Organizations	115015	13492875	118066

5-7 城镇集体单位从业人员和工资（2019年）
Number and Wage of Employed Persons in Urban Collective-owned Units (2019)

指 标	Indicator	从业人员（人）Number of Employed Persons (person)	从业人员工资总额（千元）Wage of Employed Persons (1000 yuan)	从业人员平均工资（元）Average Wage of Employed Persons(yuan)
总计	Total	13840	877760	66047
按隶属关系分组	By Affiliation			
中央	Central Investment	115	6634	57190
地方	Local	8027	599126	77910
其他	Others	5698	272000	49599
按国民经济行业分组	Grouped by Sector			
农、林、牧、渔业	Agriculture, Forestry, Animal Husbandry and Fishing	2	46	23000
采矿业	Mining			
制造业	Manufacturing	542	24238	44637
电力、热力、燃气及水生产和供应业	Production and Distribution of Electricity, Heating Power, Gas and Water	85	3726	43835
建筑业	Construction	4238	201100	53527
批发和零售业	Wholesale and Retail Trade	882	36625	41762
交通运输、仓储和邮政业	Transport, Storage and Post	250	11105	46271
住宿和餐饮业	Accommodation and Restaurants	344	17168	49476
信息传输、软件和信息技术服务业	Information Transmission, Software and Information Technology Services	8	721	90125
金融业	Financial Intermediation	106	27724	274495
房地产业	Real Estate	1138	48178	42523
租赁和商务服务业	Leasing and Business Services	506	34269	68129
科学研究和技术服务业	Scientific Research and Development, Technical Services	369	33533	92377
水利、环境和公共设施管理业	Management of Water Conservancy, Environment and Public Facilities	116	5148	44000
居民服务、修理和其他服务业	Resident Services, Repair and Other Services	28	1061	37893
教育	Education	2489	221836	89667
卫生和社会工作	Health Care and Social Works	2488	189861	76464
文化、体育和娱乐业	Culture, Sports and Entertainment	7	454	64857
公共管理、社会保障和社会组织	Public Administration, Social Security and Social Organizations	242	20967	94446

5-8 城镇其他单位从业人员和工资（2019 年）

Number and Wage of Employed Persons in Other Urban Collective-owned Units(2019)

指　标	Indicator	从业人员（人）Number of Employed Persons (person)	从业人员工资总额（千元）Wage of Employed Persons (1000 yuan)	从业人员平均工资（元）Average Wage of Employed Persons(yuan)
总计	Total	1053777	92360235	88204
按隶属关系分组	By Affiliation			
中央	Central Investment	173178	18330236	106861
地方	Local	434659	39238870	90105
其他	Others	445940	34791129	79052
按国民经济行业分组	Grouped by Sector			
农、林、牧、渔业	Agriculture, Forestry, Animal Husbandry and Fishing	133	6355	46051
采矿业	Mining	10559	841618	80940
制造业	Manufacturing	238550	19658901	82643
电力、热力、燃气及水生产和供应业	Production and Distribution of Electricity, Heating Power, Gas and Water	14688	1544895	106390
建筑业	Construction	303571	25900116	86011
批发和零售业	Wholesale and Retail Trade	79933	5983421	72767
交通运输、仓储和邮政业	Transport, Storage and Post	38154	4594503	119397
住宿和餐饮业	Accommodation and Restaurants	19754	852258	43152
信息传输、软件和信息技术服务业	Information Transmission, Software and Information Technology Services	67961	7082536	105368
金融业	Financial Intermediation	72272	8732335	120609
房地产业	Real Estate	57411	3892071	68703
租赁和商务服务业	Leasing and Business Services	37788	3169154	88717
科学研究和技术服务业	Scientific Research and Development, Technical Services	40005	4243542	109794
水利、环境和公共设施管理业	Management of Water Conservancy, Environment and Public Facilities	23294	1902993	81418
居民服务、修理和其他服务业	Resident Services, Repair and Other Services	6069	307579	50730
教育	Education	27858	2020104	75456
卫生和社会工作	Health Care and Social Works	8358	696993	84076
文化、体育和娱乐业	Culture, Sports and Entertainment	6423	821233	126753
公共管理、社会保障和社会组织	Public Administration, Social Security and Social Organizations	996	109628	111185

5-9 社会保障基本情况
Basic Conditions of Social Sewrity

单位：万人 (10 000 persons)

指标	Indicator	2014 年	2015 年	2016 年	2017 年	2018 年	2019 年
职工基本养老保险参保人数	Urban Basic Pension Insurance	250.63	266.14	284.28	304.63	331.66	408.33
# 企业	Enterpris	225.63	241.07	259.26	279.65	306.59	378.63
事业机关	Institution and Government Agency	25.01	25.08	25.02	24.98	25.06	297.00
职工基本医疗保险参保人数	Medcial Care Insurance	196.50	208.09	214.48	228.68	241.54	288.04
参加失业保险人数	Unemployment Insurance	125.04	130.08	135.78	147.19	158.29	189.70
工伤保险参保人数	Work Injury Insurance	139.42	144.46	161.22	187.51	220.47	262.56
生育保险参保人数	Maternity Insurance	129.43	136.43	142.17	152.73	163.97	201.24

注：“职工基本养老保险参保人数”“企业”及“事业机关”包含离退休人员。
Note: The caliber "number of employees with basic endowment insurance" "enterprise" and "business organ" contains the retired after.

主要统计指标解释

从业人员 指在本单位工作，并取得工资或其他形式劳动报酬的人员。

城镇登记失业人员 是指具有本地城镇户口，有劳动能力，目前无业，有求职愿望并在街道（乡镇）劳动保障部门办理了求职登记的人员。

城镇登记失业率 指报告期末，登记失业人员期末实有人数占期末从业人员总数与登记失业人员期末实有人数之和的比重。

在岗职工 指在本单位工作且与本单位签订劳动合同，并由单位支付各项工资和社会保险、住房公积金的人员，以及上述人员中由于学习、病伤、产假等原因暂未工作仍由单位支付工资的人员。

在岗职工工资总额 指本单位在报告期内直接支付给本单位全部在岗职工的劳动报酬总额。

在岗职工平均工资 指本单位在岗职工在报告期内平均每人所得的工资额。

Explanatory Notes on Main Statistical Indicators

Employees refer to persons who work in the unit and receive remuneration payment or other forms of payment.

Registered Urban Unemployed Persons refer to persons with local urban registration and labor capacity who are unemployed currently, have the job-hunting desire and handle registering at an employment agency at the street (town) labor security department.

Registered Urban Unemployment Rate refers to the ratio of the actual number of unemployed people registered at the end of the reporting period to the sum of the total number of employees at the end of the reporting period and the sum of the actual number of unemployed people registered at the end of the reporting period.

Fully Employed staff and Workers refer to persons who work in the unit and sign a labor contract with working units for whom working units pays various wages, social insurances and housing provident fund, and persons who have their work posts, but are temporarily absent from work for reasons of study or on sick, injury or maternal leave and still receive wages from their working units.

Total Wages Bill refers to the total remuneration payment to staff and workers in working units during the reporting period.

Average Wage refers to average wage per person within the reporting period for staff and workers in working units.

6

固定资产投资

INVESTMENT IN FIXED ASSETS

6-1 固定资产投资
Total Investment in Fixed Assets

单位：万元 (10 000 yuan)

指 标	Indicator	2011 年	2012 年	2013 年	2014 年	2015 年	2016 年	2017 年
固定资产投资额	**Investment in Fixed Assets**	19343389	21860756	26383337	30634425	34984158	39743278	43635821
按管理渠道分	**By Management Channels**							
城镇集体以上投资	Above Urban Collective Investment	13059328	14005706	18189147	20297503	23817574	27091510	30334660
房地产开发投资	Real Estate Development Investment	5271575	6633153	7211744	9173706	10141433	11639381	12325712
农村投资	Rural Investment	1012486	1221898	982446	1163216	1025151	1012387	975449
按经济类型分	**Registration Status**							
国有经济	State-owned	7334983	6595774	8770551	6421555	8236033	7175934	8700130
集体经济	Collective-owned	1802483	1920132	2165782	2309282	1809902	1298005	1458316
联营经济	Joint Ownership Units		195897	100213	17820	30882	1808	
股份制经济	Share-holding	5682038	1234405	1448535	5814573	7403146	10826143	12722943
外商投资经济	Fund from Overseas	408736	466383	336618	384940	284944	771449	410019
港澳台投资经济	Fund from Hong Kong, Macao and Taiwan	586347	634574	546675	177167	270022	961601	1129955
个体经济	Self-employed	2956158	3318099	30342	4423319	4447149	6788160	39804
其他经济	Others	572644	1169661	2044857	1912063	2360647	1683680	1002734
按投资用途分	**By Investment Purpose**							
第一产业	Primary Industry	486482	624114	982446	1163216	1025151	1012387	975449
第二产业	Secondary Industry	6073178	7337047	9078831	10985386	12173905	13019930	14418169
#工 业	Industry	5767374	7018465	8060463	10410562	11478708	12373806	13176351
第三产业	Tertiary Industry	12783729	13899596	16322060	18485823	21785102	25710961	28242203
投资资金来源	**Fund of Different Sources**							
国家资金	State Appropriations	1317777	1693582	1302138	1240862	691574	1360695	1353707
国内贷款	Domestic Loans	1579846	517431	2173131	341374	73212	3656032	3343213
债券	Bond							40902
利用外资	Overseas Funds	68300	226374	262823	32757	44835	327727	250555
自筹资金	Self-raised Fund	14843051	16405182	19166006	19058000	23594834	28216931	28042143
其他资金	Others	3469710	4139026	5741361	454265	342083	10839004	10267805

注：自 2011 年起固定资产投资统计口径由 50 万元调整为 500 万元。
Note: Statistical caliber of fixed-asset investment as of 2011 was adjusted to RMB 5 million from 0.5 million.

6-2 固定资产投资分类(2019年)
Classification of Fixed Assets Investment(2019)

指 标	Indicator	固定资产投资额比上年增长(%) Growth Rate of Investment in Fixed Assets(%)
本年完成投资	Investment Completed This Year	12.6
按构成分	Investment by Structure	
建筑安装工程	Construction and Installation	12.4
设备工器具购置	Purchase of Equipment and Instruments	-3.2
#购置旧设备	Purchase of Second-hand Equipment	-85.2
其他费用	Others	20.8
按产业分	Grouped by Three Strata of Industry	
第一产业	Primary Industry	-49.6
第二产业	Secondary Industry	-23.5
第三产业	Tertiary Industry	22.6
按单位登记注册类型分	Registration Status	
内资	Domestically-invested	11.5
国有	State-owned	39.2
集体	Collective-owned	-82.7
股份合作	Joint-equity Cooperative	34.7
私营个体	Private Enterprises	-39.9
港澳台投资	Fund from Hong Kong, Macao and Taiwan	67.8
#港澳台股份有限公司	Share-holding	-
外商投资	Fund from Overseas	-23.2
#外商合资经营	Joint Venture	-
#外商独资	Foreign Funded	-26.8
其他	Others	-60.5
按建设性质分	Investment by Type of Construction	
新建	New Construction	14.7
扩建	Expansion	26.2
改建和技术改造	Reconstruction and Technical Transformation	-2.1
其他	Others	11.0
按国民经济行业分	Investments in Fixed Assets by Sector	

6-2 续表 continued

指　标	Indicator	固定资产投资额 比上年增长 (%) Growth Rate of Investment in Fixed Assets(%)
农、林、牧、渔业	Farming, Forestry, Animal Husbandry and Fishery	-50.5
采矿业	Mining	-44.7
制造业	Manufacture	-15.3
电力、热力、燃气及水生产和供应业	Production and Supply of Electric, Heat, Gas and Water	-34.7
建筑业	Construction	-90.7
批发和零售业	Wholesale and Retail Trade	-6.4
交通运输、仓储和邮政业	Transport, Storage and Postal Services	30.5
住宿和餐饮业	Accommodations and Catering Services	216.6
信息传输、软件和信息技术服务业	Information Transmission, Computer Services and Software	186.3
金融业	Finance	22.5
房地产业	Real Estate	18.1
租赁和商务服务业	Leasing and Business Services	5.9
科学研究和技术服务业	Scientific Research and Technical Services	15.0
水利、环境和公共设施管理业	Management of Water Conservancy, Environment and Public Facilities	32.3
居民服务、修理和其他服务业	Households services, Repair and Other Service	-31.0
教育	Education	110.2
卫生和社会工作	Health and Social Work	10.5
文化、体育和娱乐业	Culture, Sports and Recreation	-8.5
公共管理、社会保障和社会组织	Public Management, Social Security and Social Organizations	-57.9
新增固定资产（万元）	Newly Increased Fixed Assets(10 000 yuan)	13405475
施工项目个数（个）	Number of Project under Construction(unit)	1959
# 新开工	Started This Year	949
竣工项目个数（个）	Number of Buildings Completed(unit)	734
施工房屋面积（万平方米）	Project under Construction(10 000 sq.m)	10801.6
# 住宅	Residential Buildings	6859.3
竣工房屋面积（万平方米）	Project Completed and Put into Use(10 000 sq.m)	1194.6
# 住宅	Residential Buildings	819.1

6-3 房地产开发投资分类（2019 年）
Classification of Estate Development Investment(2019)

指 标	Indicator	房地产开发投资 Estate Development Investment
本年完成投资额（万元）	Investment Completed This Year(10 000 yuan)	15769302
按构成分	Investment by Structure	
建筑工程	Construction	9183871
安装工程	Installation	1606223
设备、工器具购置	Purchase of Equipment and Instruments	406018
其他费用	Others	4573190
按单位登记注册类型分	Registration Status	
内资	Domestic Fund	14664919
国有	State-owned	127871
集体	Collective-owned	
股份合作	Cooperative	
联营	Joint Ownership Units	
国有联营	State-owned Joint	
集体联营	Collective-owned Joint	
其他联营企业	Other Joint Ownership Units	
有限责任公司	Limited Liability	10733229
国有独资公司	Solely State-owned Company	1501295
其他有限责任公司	Other Limited Liability Company	9231934
股份有限公司	Share-holding Corporations Ltd.	367642
私营	Private	3429191
其它内资	Other Domestic Fund	6986
港澳台投资	Fund from Hong Kong,Macao and Taiwan	1037813
港澳台商合资经营	Joint Venture	294742
港澳台商合作经营	Collaborative Operation	23870
港澳台商独资	Solely Foreign-owned	719201
港澳台股份有限公司	Share-holding	
外商投资	Fund from Overseas	66570
外商合资经营	Joint Venture	5530
外商合作经营	Collaborative Operation	
外商独资	Foreign Funded	7254
外商股份有限公司	Share-holding	
其他外商投资企业	Other Fund from Overseas	53786
个体经营	Self-employed	
新增固定资产（万元）	Newly Increased Fixed Assets (10 000 yuan)	3988646
施工项目个数（个）	Number of Project under Construction(unit)	790
施工房屋面积（万平方米）	Project under Construction(10 000 sq.m)	9979.96
# 住 宅	Residential Buildings	6524.82
竣工房屋面积（万平方米）	Project Completed and Put into Use(10 000 sq.m)	1070.03
# 住宅	Residential Buildings	770.69

6-4 固定资产投资资金来源(2019 年)
Investment by Source of Funds (2019)

指 标	Indicator	固定资产投资额比上年增长 (%) Growth Rate of Investment in Fixed Assets (%)	房地产开发投资（万元）Estate Development Investment (10 000 yuan)
本年资金来源合计	Total Funds of All Sources	6.0	30290452
上年末结余资金	Fund Left from Last Year	-4.6	7085557
本年资金来源小计	Fund of All Sources in Currrent Year	8.5	23204895
国家预算资金	State Budgetary Funds	58.4	
国内贷款	Domestic Loans	10.7	4766901
债券	Bond	13.1	
利用外资	Foreign Investment	-35.7	
其中：外商直接投资	Foreign Direct Investment		
自筹资金	Self-Raising Funds	8.9	6767608
其中：企、事业单位 自有资金	Enterprise and Intitutions Own Funds		
其他资金来源	Others Capital Source	3.1	1001504

6-5 新增主要生产能力和效益(2019 年)
Newly Increased Production Capacity and Administrative(2019)

项目 Item	单位 Unit	新增生产能力 Newly Increased This Year
县级道路改造提升工程	公里（km.）	102
青兰高速平阴段	公里（km.）	25
国电投商河一期 100MW 风电场项目	万千瓦（MKW）	6
济南至乐陵高速公路南延线工程	公里（km.）	5.9
G220 至济青高速公路王舍人互通立交连接线工程	公里（km.）	1.5
高庄街道办事处 2019 年三年集中攻坚计划项目	公里（km.）	52.5
生物质热电联产项目	万千瓦（MKW）	3
高强度轻量化异型结构件项目	万吨 / 年（MT/year）	1

6-6 历年房地产开发建设情况
Basic Situations of Real Estate Development in Major Years

指 标	Indicator	单位 Unit	2014 年	2015 年	2016 年	2017 年	2018 年	2019 年
计划总投资	Intended Investment	万元 (10 000 yuan)	47123834	55571721	65080572	75662272	90392774	111989855
本年完成投资	Investment Completed in Current Year	万元 (10 000 yuan)	9173706	10141433	11639381	12325712	13693456	15769302
按构成分	Grouped by Use of Funds							
建筑工程	Construction	万元 (10 000 yuan)	5444613	6083337	7329570	8643701	7920264	9183871
安装工程	Installation	万元 (10 000 yuan)	922515	1126053	1614742	1446801	1409538	1606223
设备、工器具购置	Purchase of Equipment and Instruments	万元 (10 000 yuan)	116907	78310	152443	172327	178895	406018
其他费用	Others	万元 (10 000 yuan)	2689671	2853733	2542621	2062883	4184759	4573190
#旧建筑物购置费	Purchase of Used Building	万元 (10 000 yuan)	18696	1892	35444	4742	196	9701
土地购置	Purchase of Land	万元 (10 000 yuan)	2356776	2545842	2241602	1683185	3780143	4231601
按工程用途分	Grouped by Use of Buildings							
住宅	Residential Buildings	万元 (10 000 yuan)	6136895	7254184	8055689	8227871	9285419	11356997
#安居工程	Comfortable Housing Project	万元 (10 000 yuan)						
办公楼	Office Buildings	万元 (10 000 yuan)	1267961	1379919	1112954	1058113	1047097	1312853
商业营业用房	Buildings for Business	万元 (10 000 yuan)	1115138	833683	1665634	1907938	1879155	1662057
其他	Others	万元 (10 000 yuan)	653712	673647	805104	1131790	1481785	1437395
本年新增固定资产	Newly Increased Fixed Assets	万元 (10 000 yuan)	1865035	1815666	3770747	3061175	4698943	3988646
待开发土地面积	Space of Land to be Developed	万平方米 (10 000 sq.m)	179.81	291.87	225.80	138.80	302.35	455.29
本年购置土地面积	Space of Land Purchased in Current Year	万平方米 (10 000 sq.m)	273.89	274.45	170.34	144.77	265.91	280.44
房屋施工面积	Floor Space Under Construction	万平方米 (10 000 sq.m)	5257.57	6625.90	7912.30	8006.85	9112.05	9979.96
房屋竣工面积	Area of buildings completed	万平方米 (10 000 sq.m)	516.76	579.05	1134.10	631.29	1203.81	1070.03
竣工房屋价值	Value of Buildings Completed	万元 (10 000 yuan)	1204331	1389148	2639414	1615213	3172322	2844724
竣工住宅	Residential Buildings Completed	套 (unit)	29976	27877	68682	45775	70120	60422

6-7 历年房地产开发公司经营情况
Real Estate Development and Managment in Major Years

指　标	Indicator	单位 Unit	2014 年	2015 年	2016 年	2017 年	2018 年	2019 年
开发公司家数	Number of Real Estate Enterprises	家 (unit)	524	570	622	646	706	710
企业资本金	Enterprises Funds	万元 (10 000 yuan)	6756174	7612830	9270991	10505186	12994960	14920358
资产与负债	Property debt							
资产总计	Assets	万元 (10 000 yuan)	47284278	57218796	72602423	85586496	113393735	128868654
负债总计	Liabilities	万元 (10 000 yuan)	38185924	46478285	58406976	68738188	93511277	106654306
所有者权益	Owners' Equity	万元 (10 000 yuan)	9098353	10740511	14195447	16848309	19882458	22214348
损益情况	Net Income or Loss							
经营收入	Revenues from Business	万元 (10 000 yuan)	7146915	7076463	11913217	11218828	12495191	14411472
土地转让收入	Revenues from Land Transfer	万元 (10 000 yuan)	15595	14820	2409	1501	952885	150739
商品房销售收入	Revenues from Commercial Housing Sale	万元 (10 000 yuan)	6709472	6265506	11227539	10803498	11087179	11656310
房屋出租收入	Housing Rental Income	万元 (10 000 yuan)	86836	79458	106425	109982	90017	99996
其他收入	Others	万元 (10 000 yuan)	335012	716679	576844	302963	126592	134461
经营成本	Business Cost	万元 (10 000 yuan)	5416141	5515583	968896	8352620	8570149	10131040
经营税金及附加	Business Tax and Extra Charges	万元 (10 000 yuan)	569221	573637	706161	658995	951196	1036931
利润总额	Total Profits	万元 (10 000 yuan)	525409	401995	606344	875949	2177983	2287980
房屋销售与出租								
本年实际销售房屋面积	Floor Space of Buildings to Lease	平方米 (sq.m)	8648934	11911661	14242514	12152665	12346236	12464708
#住　宅	Residential Buildings	平方米 (sq.m)	7234582	9234805	12316804	9737162	9636143	10206808
本年房屋实际销售额	Total Sales of Buildings	万元 (10 000 yuan)	6374593	9159131	111750932	11725660	14737908	13807789
#住　宅	Residential Buildings	万元 (10 000 yuan)	5179753	6954738	10357228	9462791	11728181	11738543
待售房屋面积	Floor Space of Waiting For Sale	平方米 (sq.m)	1173463	1694588	1720232	1398451	980301	1064915
#住　宅	Residential Buildings	平方米 (sq.m)	607336	864938	931437	740636	542047	635088
出租房屋面积	Floor Space of Buildings to Lease	平方米 (sq.m)	61250	229415	182137	66089	1794	39132

6-8 房地产开发公司经营情况 (2019 年)
Real Estate Development and Management(2019)

单位：万元 (10 000 yuan)

指 标	Indicator	合计 Total	内资企业 Domestic Enterprise		外资企业 Foreign-owned Enterprise	
			小计 Total	# 国有 State-owned	小计 Total	# 港澳台商 Hong kong,Macao and Taiwan Investment
开发公司家数（个）	Number of Real Estate Enterprises(unit)	710	680	15	30	22
按资质分	by Qualification Criteria					
# 一级资质	First Grade	23	23	1		
二级资质	Second Grade	59	57	5	2	2
三级资质	Third Grade	88	85	6	3	2
四级资质	Forth Grade	12	10	1	2	1
企业资本金	Enterprises Funds	14920358	13040938	49666	1879420	1859563
资产与负债	Property debt					
资产总计	Assets	128868654	124129885	4432996	4738770	2417661
负债总计	Liabilities	106654306	104020515	4399021	2633791	1456295
所有者权益	Owners' Equity	22214348	20109370	33976	2104978	961366
损益情况	Net Income or Loss					
经营收入	Revenues from Business	14411472	13843972	386816	567500	281271
土地转让收入	Revenues from Land Transfer	150739	150739			
商品房销售收入	Revenues from Commercial Housing Sale	11656310	11145817	202182	510493	225359
房屋出租收入	Housing Rental Income	99996	46981	220	53015	51920
其他收入	Others	134461	134408	518	53	53
经营成本	Business Cost	10131040	9771250	356185	359790	145283
经营税金及附加	Business Tax and Extra Charges	1036931	955469	5968	81462	36875
利润总额	Total Profits	2287980	2223460	-964	64520	53795

主要统计指标解释

固定资产投资额 指以货币形式表现的在一定时期内建造和购置固定资产的工作量以及与此有关的费用的总称。

房地产开发投资 指各种登记注册类型的房地产开发法人单位统一开发的住宅、厂房、仓库、饭店、宾馆、度假村、写字楼、办公楼等房屋建筑物，配套的服务设施，土地开发工程（如道路、给水、排水、供电、供热、通讯、平整场地等基础设施工程）和土地购置的投资；不包括单纯的土地开发和交易活动。

固定资产投资的资金来源 根据固定资产投资的资金来源不同，分为国家预算内资金、国内贷款、债券、利用外资、自筹资金和其他资金来源。

（1）国家预算内资金：指各级政府用于固定资产投资的财政资金，包括中央预算资金和地方预算资金。

（2）国内贷款：指报告期固定资产投资项目单位向银行及非银行金融机构借入用于固定资产投资的各种国内借款，包括银行利用自有资金及吸收存款发放的贷款、上级拨入的国内贷款、国家专项贷款，地方财政专项资金安排的贷款、国内储备贷款、周转贷款等。

（3）债券：指企业或金融机构为筹集用于固定资产投资的资金向投资者出具的承诺按一定发行条件还本付息的债务凭证，包括金融债券和企业债券。

（4）利用外资：指报告期收到的境外（包括外国及港澳台地区）资金（包括设备、材料、技术在内）。包括对外借款（外国政府贷款、国际金融组织贷款、出口信贷、外国银行商业贷款、对外发行债券和股票）、外商直接投资、外商其他投资（包括补偿贸易、加工装配由外商提供的设备价款、国际租赁，外商投资收益的再投资资金）。不包括我国自有外汇资金（国家外汇、地方外汇、留成外汇、调济外汇和中国境内银行自有资金发放的外汇贷款等）。各类外资按报告期的外汇牌价（中间价）折成人民币计算。

（5）自筹资金：指在报告期内筹集的用于项目建设和购置的资金。包括自有资金、股东投入资金和借入资金，但不包括各类财政性资金、从各类金融机构借入资金和国外资金。

（6）其他资金来源：指在报告期收到的除以上各种资金之外的用于固定资产投资的资金。包括社会集资、个人资金、无偿捐赠的资金及其他单位拨入的资金等。

固定资产投资按建设性质分 建设项目的性质一般分为新建、扩建、改建和技术改造、单纯建造生活设施、迁建、恢复、单纯购置。

（1）新建：指从无到有“平地起家”开始建设的项目。现有企业、事业、行政单位投资的项目一般不属于新建。但如有的单位原有基础很小，经过建设后新增的固定资产价值超过该企业、事业、行政单位原有固定资产价值（原值）三倍以上的，也应作为新建。

（2）扩建：指为扩大原有产品的生产能力（或效益）或增加新的产品生产能力，而增建的生产车间（或主要工程）、分厂、独立的生产线等项目。行政、事业单位在原单位增建业务性用房（如学校增建教学用房、医院增建门诊部、病房等）也作为扩建。

（3）改建和技术改造：指对原有设施进行技术改造或更新（包括相应配套的辅助性生产、生活福利设施）的建设项目。

（4）单纯建造生活设施：指在不扩建、改建生产性工程和业务用房的情况下，单纯建造职工住宅、托儿所、子弟学校、医务室、浴室、食堂等生活设施的项目。

（5）迁建：指为改变生产能力布局或由于城市环境保护和安全生产的需要等原因而搬迁到另地建设的项目。在搬迁另地的建设过程中，不论是维持原来规模还是扩大规模都按迁建来统计。

（6）恢复：指因自然灾害、战争等原因，使原有固定资产全部或部分报废，以后又投资恢复建设的项目。不论是按原规模恢复还是在恢复的同时进行扩建的都按恢复项目统计。尚未建成投产的建设项目因自然灾害而损坏重建的，仍按原有建设性质划分。

（7）单纯购置：指单纯购置不需要安装的设备、工具、器具而不进行工程建设的项目。有些调查单位当年虽然只从事一些购置活动，但其设计中规定有建筑安装活动，应根据设计文件的内容来确定建设性质，不得作为单纯购置统计。

固定资产投资按构成分 固定资产投资活动按其工作内容和实现方式分为建筑工程、安装工程、设备工器具购置、其他费用三个部分。

（1）建筑工程：指各种房屋、建筑物的建造工程，又称建筑工作量。这部分投资额必须兴工动料，通过施工活动才能实现，是固定资产投资额的重要组成部分。

（2）安装工程：指各种设备、装置的安装工程，又称安装工作量。

（3）设备工器具购置：指报告期内购置或自制的，达到固定资产标准的设备、工具、器具的价值。

（4）其他费用：指在固定资产建造和购置过程中发生的，除建筑安装工程和设备、工器具购置投资完成额以外的应当分摊计入固定资产投资项目的费用，不指经营中财务上的其他费用。

新增生产能力（或工程效益）名称 指建成投产项目或工程新增生产能力（或工程效益）的名称。

建设规模 指建设项目或工程设计文件中规定的全部设计能力（或工程效益）。包括已经建成投产和尚未建成投产的工程的生产能力（或工程效益）。它是以实物形态表示固定资产投资规模的指标，反映建设项目或工程全部建成投产（或交付使用）后，能够为社会提供多少设计能力（或工程效益）。

房屋施工面积 指报告期内施工的全部房屋建筑面积。

房屋竣工面积 指报告期内房屋建筑按照设计要求已全部完工，达到住人和使用条件，经验收鉴定合格或达到竣工验收标准，可正式移交使用的各栋房屋建筑面积的总和。

本年新增固定资产 指在报告期已经完成建造和购置过程，并已交付生产或使用单位的固定资产的价值，包括已经建成投入生产或交付使用的工程投资和达到固定资产标准的设备、工具、器具的投资及有关应摊入的费用。属于增加固定资产价值的其他建设费用，应随同交付使用的工程一并计入新增固定资产。

房地产开发本年完成投资 指各种登记注册类型的房地产开发法人单位本年内统一开发的住宅、厂房、仓库、饭店、宾馆、度假村、写字楼、办公楼等房屋建筑物，配套的服务设施，土地开发工程（如道路、给水、排水、供电、供热、通讯、平整场地等基础设施工程）和土地购置的投资；不包括单纯的土地开发和交易活动。

土地购置和开发情况

（1）待开发土地面积：指经有关部门批准，通过各种方式获得土地使用权，但尚未开工建设的土地面积。

（2）本年土地购置面积：指在本年内通过各种方式获得土地使用权的土地面积。

商品房屋销售与出租情况

（1）商品房销售面积：指报告期内出售商品房屋的合同总面积（即双方签署的正式买卖合同中所确定的建筑面积）。商品房销售面积由现房销售面积和期房销售面积两部分组成。

①现房销售面积：指在报告期内正式签订买卖合同、已经竣工达到入住条件的商品房屋建筑面积。包括以一次性付款方式和分期付款方式销售的现房建筑面积。

②期房销售面积：指在报告期内正式签订买卖合同、正在建设尚未竣工交付使用的商品房屋建筑面积。包括以一次性付款方式和分期付款方式销售的商品房屋建筑面积。期房销售建筑面积竣工后不再结转为现房销售建筑面积。

（2）待售面积：指报告期末已竣工的可供销售或出租的商品房屋建筑面积中，尚未销售或出租的商品房屋建筑面积，包括以前年度竣工和本期竣工的房屋面积，但不包括报告期已竣工的拆迁还建、统建代建、公共配套建筑、房地产公司自用及周转房等不可销售或出租的房屋面积。按照商品房待售时间的长短可以划分为待售一年以下、待售一到三年（含一年）和待售三年以上（含三年）。

（3）房屋出租面积：指在报告期末房屋开发单位出租的商品房屋的全部面积。

（4）商品房销售额：指报告期内出售商品房屋的合同总价款（即双方签署的正式买卖合同中所确定的合同总价）。该指标与商品房销售面积同口径，由现房销售额和期房销售额两部分组成。

①现房销售额：指报告期内销售的已竣工商品房屋的合同总价款。包括现房销售前期预收的定金、预收款、首付款及全部按揭贷款的本金等款项。该指标与现房销售面积同口径。

②期房销售额：指报告期内销售的正在建设尚未竣工的商品房屋的合同总价款。包括预售房屋前期预收的定金、预收款、首付款及全部按揭贷款的本金等项。该指标与期房销售面积同口径。

Explanatory Notes on Main Statistical Indicators

Total Investment in Fixed Assets refers to the volume of activities in construction and purchases of fixed assets and related fees during a certain period of time, expressed in monetary terms.

Investment in Real Estate Development refers to the investment by real estate development units of various types of ownership in buildings and structures (such as residence, factory, warehouse, restaurant, hotel, resort, office building and administration building), supporting service facilities and land development engineering (including infrastructure projects such as road, water supply, drainage, power supply, heat supply, communication and land grading) excluding activities in pure land transactions.

Source of Funds for Investment in Fixed Assets include national budgetary funds, domestic loans, foreign investment, self–raised funds, and others depending on the source of investment.

(1) National budgetary funds refers to financial funds used by governments at all levels for fixed–asset investment, including central budget funds and local budget funds.

(2) Domestic loans refer to loans of various forms borrowed by investing units from banks and non–bank financial institutions during the reference period for the purpose of investment in fixed assets, including the loan issued by the bank by self–owned funds and deposit taking, domestic loans appropriated by superior, national special loan, loan arranged by special funds for local finance, domestic reserve loan and revolving credit.

(3) Bonds: refer to the certificate of indebtedness issued by the enterprise or the financial institution to the investor for raising the capital of fixed–asset investment with capital and interest promised to be repaid as per certain issue terms, including financial bond and enterprise bond.

(4) Foreign investment: refer to overseas (including foreign countries, Hong Kong, Macau and Taiwan) funds (including equipment, materials and technology) received in the reporting period, including foreign borrowings (loans from foreign governments and international financial organizations, export credit, commercial loans from foreign banks and issue of bonds and stocks overseas), foreign direct investment and other foreign investments (including compensation trade, the price of processing and assembling the equipment provided by foreign business, international leasing, funds from foreign direct investment income that are reinvested in fixed assets domestically). Excluded from this category is capital in foreign exchanges owned by China (foreign exchanges owned by the central and local governments, foreign exchanges retained by enterprises, foreign exchanges by enterprises through the regulating mechanism, loans in foreign exchanges issued by the Bank of China with its own fund, etc.). In calculating the utilization of foreign capital, foreign currencies are converted into CNY applying the exchange rate (central parity rate) at the end of the reference period. .

(5) Self–raised funds: refer to the fund raised in the reporting period and used for construction and purchase of the project, including self–owned funds, capital invested by shareholders and borrowed funds other than various financial funds, capital borrowed from various financing institutions and offshore funds.

(6) Other refer to funds for investment in fixed assets received in the reporting period, except for the above–mentioned various capitals, including funds raised in society, personal money, voluntary donations and capital from other units.

Investment in Fixed Assets by Type of Construction The construction projects in general can be classified, by the type of construction, into new construction, expansion, reconstruction and technical transformation, simple construction of living facilities, relocation, recovery and simple purchase.

(1) New construction: refers to the project that started construction from scratch. Projects invested by the existing enterprises, institutions or agencies is not considered as new construction. In case the assets of the existing unit are quite small, and the value of newly added fixed assets exceeds the original value of assets by three times, the expansion will be considered as new construction.

(2) Expansion: refers to construction of new production workshops (or major projects), branch factories or independent production lines, for the purpose of increasing the production capacity (or improving efficiency) of the original products. Newly constructed houses for the operation of institutions and administrative organizations (such as the newly constructed buildings for teaching in schools, buildings for clinics or wards in hospitals, etc.) are also classified as expansion.

(3) Reconstruction and technical transformation: refer to the construction project for technical transformation or renewal for original facilities (including corresponding supporting auxiliary production and living welfare facilities).

(4) Simple construction of living facilities: refers to the project of simply constructing living facilities such as staff houses, nurseries, schools for children of employees, medical rooms, shower rooms and canteens, etc. without expanding or reconstructing productive engineering and business housing.

(5) Relocation: refer to the project moved to other place for construction for the purpose of changing production capacity layout or urban environment protection and safety production requirements. In the process of being moved to other places for construction, whether it is to maintain the original scale or augment the scale, it will be counted as relocation.

(6) Recovery: refers to the project with original fixed assets scrapped in whole or in part due to natural disaster or war which is invested to recover construction later. Regardless of recovery as per

original size or expansion at the time of recovery, it will be counted as recovery. If the construction project which has not been completed and gone into operation is reconstructed due to being damaged by natural disaster, it is still classified according to the original type of construction.

(7) Simple purchase: refers to the project of simply purchasing equipment, tools and appliances which do not need to be installed without engineering construction. Although some investigating units only engaged in some purchase activities in that year, construction and installation activities were specified in their design, so it is necessary to confirm the type of construction in line with the content of the design document, and should not be counted as simple purchase.

Investment in fixed assets by Structure Fixed-asset investment activities are divided into construction engineering, installation engineering, purchase of equipment & tools and other expenses in terms of working content and implementation model.

(1) Construction engineering: refers to the construction of various houses and buildings, also called as construction workload. Such investment volume must be implemented through construction activities based on utilization of materials, which is an important part of fixed investments.

(2) Installation engineering: refers to installation of various equipment and devices, also called as installation workload.

(3) Purchase of equipment and tools: refers to the value of purchased or home-made equipment, tools and appliances within the reporting period, which reach to fixed-asset standards.

(4) Other expenses: refer to expenses incurred in the construction and purchase process of fixed assets which shall be allocated and included into the fixed-asset investment project, except for the expenses of construction and installation engineering and purchase of equipment & tools, and not refer to other financial expenses in the operation.

Newly Increased Production Capacity (or Project Efficiency) refers to the name of new production capacity (or project benefit) of the project or the engineering completed and put into operation.

Scale of Construction refers to all design ability (or project benefit) specified in the design document for construction project or engineering, including production capacity (or project benefit) completed and put into production and not yet be completed and put into production. It is an indicator showing the scale of investment in fixed assets in the matter form and reflects the design capability (or project benefit) provided for the society after the construction project or engineering is completed and put into production (or delivered for use).

Construction area of the house refers to building area of all houses constructed in the reporting period.

Housing completion area refers to total building areas of all houses which have been completed in accordance with design requirements in the reporting period, reach to living and using conditions, pass acceptance and verification or reach to the completion acceptance standards and can be formally handed over for use.

New fixed assets in this year refer to the value of fixed assets having been delivered to the production or use unit with construction and purchase process completed in the reporting period, including investment in projects completed and put into production or delivered for use and investment in equipment, tools and appliances reaching to fixed-asset standards and related expenses which shall be included. Other construction costs falling into the added fixed-asset value shall be included into new fixed assets together with the project delivered for use.

Investment completed in current year in real estate development refers to buildings and structures (such as residence, factory, warehouse, restaurant, hotel, resort, office building and administration building), supporting service facilities and land development engineering (including infrastructure projects such as road, water supply, drainage, power supply, heat supply, communication and land grading) and investment in land purchase uniformly developed by real estate development legal entity in the current year based on all kinds of businesses; excluding simple land development and trading activities.

Land purchase and development

(1) Land area to be developed: refers to the area of the land approved by related department with land use right obtained by all means but not yet under construction.

(2) Land acquisition area in the current year: refers to the area of the land with land use right obtained by all means in the current year.

Sales and rental of the residential property

(1) Sales area of residential property: refers to the total area in the contract of residential properties sold within the reporting period (namely the building area set forth in the sales contract formally signed by both parties). Sales area of the residential property is composed by two parts -- sales area of completed houses and sales area of the property under construction.

① Sales area of completed houses: refers to the building area of the residential property which has been completed and reached to living conditions with the sales contract formally signed within the reporting period, including the building area of completed houses sold by one-off payment and installment payment.

② Sales area of property under construction: refer to the building area of residential properties under construction which has not yet been delivered for use with the sales contract formally signed within the reporting period, including the building area of residential properties sold by one-off payment and installment payment. The sales building area of the property under construction will not be transfered to the sales building area of the competed house after being completed.

(2) Area to be sold: refers to the building area of residential properties not sold or rented in the building area of residential properties available for sale or renting which has been completed at the end of the reporting period, including the area of houses completed before and in the current period, and other than the area of housings not available for sale or renting such as the housing built due to demolition, the housing uniformly

built by the government, public matching buildings, the housing used by the real estate company and the relocation housing in the reporting period. As per the waiting time for sales of the residential property, the housings can be divided into the one waiting for sales for less than one year, the one waiting for sales for more than one year (one year included) but less than three years and the one waiting for sales for more than three years (three years included).

(3) Area of rental housing: refers to all areas of the residential property rented out by the house development unit at the end of the reporting period.

(4) Sales amount of residential property: refers to the total price in the contract of residential properties sold within the reporting period (namely the total contract price set forth in the sales contract formally signed by both parties). The indicator shares the same caliber with the sales area of the residential property, and it consists two parts -- sales amount of completed houses and sales amount of the property under construction.

① Sales amount of completed houses: refer to total contract price of residential properties completed and sold within the reporting period, including deposits, prepayments and down payment as well as all principal of all mortgage loans. The indicator shares the same caliber with the sales area of the completed houses.

② Sales amount of property under construction: refer to total contract price of residential properties under construction sold within the reporting period, including deposits, prepayments and down payment as well as all principal of all mortgage loans. The indicator shares the same caliber with the sales area of the property under construction.

7

城市公用事业和环境保护

URBAN PUBLIC UTILITIES AND ENVIRONMENTAL PROTECTION

7-1 城市道路与公共交通
Basic Statistics on Muncipal Engineering and Public Transportation

指 标	Indicator	2014 年	2015 年	2016 年	2017 年	2018 年	2019 年
城市道路	City Roads						
道路长度（公里）	Length of Roads (km)	5264	5350	5422	5663	5788	6987
道路面积（万平方米）	Area of Roads(10 000 sq.m)	9116	9523	9724	10224	10529	12653
城市桥梁（座）	Number of Bridges(unit)	836	845	927	935	1021	1136
# 立交桥（座）	Interchange(unit)	76	77	82	82	85	95
路灯（盏）	Number of Streetlights(unit)	162590	167462	170314	188598	195014	213259
人均拥有道路面积（平方米）	Per Capita Road Arae(sq.m)	25.19	26.10	26.20	22.96	23.03	20.30
公共交通	Public Transportation						
年末营运车辆（辆）	Number of Operating Vehicles(unit)	14650	15236	15539	16850	16644	19676
公共汽车	Buses	5099	5537	5846	7157	6951	8383
# 无轨电车	Trolley Buses	139	140	121	121	106	109
出租汽车	Number of Taxis	9551	9699	9693	9693	9693	11293
客运总量（万人次）	Total Passenger Traffic(10 000 person– times)	101698	93634	90776.1	90515.6	89619.7	99389.9
轨道交通	Rail Traffic						
配属车辆数（辆）	Number of Vehicles(unit)						204
运营里程（公里）	Length in Operation(km)						47.7
客运总量（万人次）	Total Passenger Traffic(10 000 person– times)						573.5

7-2 水、电、气、热供应情况

Basic Statistics on Water, Electricity, Gas and Heating in Cities

指 标	Indicator	单位 Unit	2014 年	2015 年	2016 年	2017 年	2018 年	2019 年
自来水	**Water**							
年末水厂生产能力	Production Capacity of Water Supply	万吨 / 日 (10 000 tons/day)	201.74	201.74	211.47	215.57	220.27	241.00
年末管线长度	Length of Water Supply Pioelines	公里 (km)	4222	4325.56	4241.04	4779.01	5277.13	5703.60
全年供水量	Volume of Water Supply	万吨 (10 000 tons)	31158	31826.63	33191.11	35865.07	39226.16	44452.30
人均日生活用水	Per Capita Daily Water Consumption	升 (litre)	143.9	138.95	142.78	139.58	140.37	134.79
城市人口用水普及率	Coverage Rate of Water Supply	%(%)	98.92	99	99.57	99.64	99.78	100.00
用电量	**Electricity Consumption**							
全社会用电量	Electricity Consumption	万千瓦时 (10 000 kwh)	2614124	2642035	2799221	2762869	2843630	4143022
工 业	Industrial Electricity Consumption	万千瓦时 (10 000 kwh)	1507683	1420304	1470794	1319975	1215034	2215281
城乡居民生活用电	Household Electricity Consumption	万千瓦时 (10 000 kwh)	488075	522513	554853	598578	667505	776162
液化石油气和管道煤气	**Liquefied Petroleum Gas and Piped Gas**							
液化石油气全年供气量	Total Liquefied Petroleum Gas Supply	吨 (tons)	46693	46844.2	53086.2	49944.0	41110.0	45518.0
生活用	Residential Use	吨 (tons)	21960	21866	19771	23462	20458	25935
居民用气人口	Population Uses Gas	万人 (10 000 persons)	85	87.1	77.39	55.93	46.81	59.90
天然气供气量	Total Natural Gas Supply	万立方米 (10 000 cu.m)	64904	75496.75	79325.47	90724.36	113945.56	143576.00
生产用	Production Use	万立方米 (10 000 cu.m)	45937	58196.06	60994.42	69361.61	88821.02	96706.80
生活用	Residential Use	万立方米 (10 000 cu.m)	17967	17300.69	18331.05	21362.75	25124.54	46869.20
居民用气人口	Population Uses Gas	万人 (10 000 persons)	264	269.44	291.56	388.63	409.70	560.90
管道煤气供气量	Piped Gas Supply	万立方米 (10 000 cu.m)	940	59	-	-	-	-
生产用	Production Use	万立方米 (10 000 cu.m)	796	59	-	-	-	-
生活用	Residential Use	万立方米 (10 000 cu.m)	144		-	-	-	-
居民用气人口	Population Uses Gas	万人 (10 000 persons)	2		-	-	-	-
用气普及率	Coverage Rate of Gas Supply	%(%)	96.88	97.73	99.42	99.85	99.87	99.97
集中供热	**Central Heating**							
管道长度	Pipe Length	公里 (km)	2488	3277	2742	6104	7010	8893
供热面积	Heating Area	万平方米 (10 000 sq.m)	11785.6	14498.50	14917.00	18174.10	19833.80	26073.30

注：本表指标为“-”的，是指济南市已不再使用“管道煤气”。
Notes: The indicator"-",in this table refers Jinan no Longer Use Piped Gas.

7-3 环境状况及污染治理情况
Basic Statistics on Environment and Treatment of Pollution

指　标	Indicator	单位 Unit	2014 年	2015 年	2016 年	2017 年	2018 年	2019 年
环境质量状况	Environment Condition							
环境空气细颗粒物 (PM2.5) 浓度年均值	Annual Average Concentration of PM2.5	mg/m^3	0.090	0.087	0.073	0.063	0.052	0.053
环境空气二氧化硫浓度年均值	Annual Average Concentration of SO_2	mg/m^3	0.072	0.050	0.038	0.025	0.017	0.015
环境空气二氧化氮浓度年均值	Annual Average Concentration of NO_2	mg/m^3	0.053	0.048	0.045	0.046	0.045	0.041
环境空气可吸入颗粒物 (PM10) 浓度年均值	Annual Average Concentration of PM10	mg/m^3	0.172	0.157	0.141	0.130	0.112	0.103
集中式饮用水源地水质达标率	Standard Rate of Concentrate Water Source Area	%(%)	100.00	100.00	100.00	100.00	100.00	100.00
区域环境噪声昼间平均等效声级	Area Whole-day Average Noise Value	分贝 (db)	54.2	53.7	53.1	53.7	53.3	54.9
道路交通噪声平均等效声级	Traffic Average Noise Value	分贝 (db)	69.7	70.0	69.8	69.7	69.5	69.6
污染物排放情况	Discharge of Major Pollutants							
废水排放总量	Volume of Waste Water Discharged	万吨 (10 000 tons)	38904	39454	34530	34693	34693	
# 工业废水排放量	Volume of Industrial Waste Water Discharged	万吨 (10 000 tons)	7880	7415	5993	5949	5949	
化学需氧量排放量	Volume of COD Emission	吨 (tons)	104876	107743	30202	28701	28701	
# 工业化学需氧量排放量	Volume of Industrial COD Emission	吨 (tons)	5289	5515	2777	2594	2594	
氨氮排放量	Volume of Ammonia Nitrogen	吨 (tons)	8224	9050	4306	4255	4255	
# 工业氨氮排放量	Volume of Industrial Ammonia Nitrogen	吨 (tons)	346	360	186	197	197	
二氧化硫排放量	Volume of Sulphur Dioxide Discharged	吨 (tons)	97171	99653	44403	32502	32502	
# 工业二氧化硫排放量	Volume of Industrial Sulphur Dioxide Discharged	吨 (tons)	67842	70327	28458	16545	16545	
氮氧化物排放量	Volume of Nitrogen Oxides Discharged	吨 (tons)	95295	91614	61075	23316	23316	
# 工业氮氧化物排放量	Volume of Industrial Nitrogen Oxides Discharged	吨 (tons)	64861	63781	34502	21254	21254	
机动车氮氧化物排放量	Volume of Vehicle Nitrogen Oxides	吨 (tons)	26703	24080	24472			
烟 (粉) 尘排放量	Volume of Soot and Dust Discharged	吨 (tons)	100899	108643	64253	32794	32794	
# 工业烟 (粉) 尘排放量	Volume of Industrial Soot and Dust Discharged	吨 (tons)	90082	92900	54677	25060	25060	

注：1. 从 2014 年工业烟 (粉) 统计口径增加钢铁、水泥等行业无组织排放量。
2. “机动车氮氧化物排放量”指标，自 2017 年起，国家只核定到省级数据。
3. 污染物排放情况数据，根据生态环境部统一工作安排，暂时使用 2017 年已公布数据，2018 年数据待第二次全国污染源普查完成后统一发布。
4. 截至年鉴出版刊印前，国家尚未发布第二次全国污染源普查和 2019 年环境统计年报数据。

Notes:1.Industry unorganized emission (including steel and cement, etc.) was added to the statistical caliber of industrial smoke (powder) from 2014.
2.The indicator-"nitrogen oxide emission from motor vehicles" was only verified to provincial data by the state from 2017.
3.As for data on pollutant discharge, the data published in 2017 is temporarily used as per the unified arrangement of Ministry of Ecology and Environment and the data in 2018 will be uniformly published after completion of the 2nd national census of pollution sources.
4.Before the yearbooks were published and printed, the national authority had not released the second national pollution source census and annaul report of environmental statistics in 2019.

7-4 城市园林绿化、环境卫生及其他
Basic Statistics on Parks, Gardens, Green Areas and Urban Sanitation in Cities

指　标	Indicator	单位 Unit	2014 年	2015 年	2016 年	2017 年	2018 年	2019 年
园林绿化	Parks Gardens and Green Areas							
年末园林绿地面积	Garden Green Area at Year-end	公顷 (ha)	17002	17561	18162.9	19528.6	20701.0	28199.3
#公园面积	Area of Parks	万平方米 (10 000 sq.m)	3116	3190	3190	3414	3930	3688
人均公园绿地面积	Per Capita Public Green Areas	平方米 / 人 (sq.m/person)	11.5	11.6	11.8	11.8	12.6	13.2
建成区绿化覆盖率	Coverage of Green Area	%	39.62	39.94	40.12	40.57	40.52	41.18
城市卫生	Urban Health							
污水集中处理率	Centralized Sewage Treatment Rate	%	95.33	95.85	96.33	95.98	96.59	97.73
清运垃圾	Garbage Clearance	万吨 (10 000 tons)	114	158	179.68	192.22	202.64	278.75
清运粪便	Garbage Disposal	万吨 (10 000 tons)	58.5	48.2	10.5	-	-	-
公共厕所	Public Lavatory	座 (unit)	1026	1060	1077	1075	1086	1122
城市维护费收支	Expenditure and Earning for City Maintenance							
维护费收入	Earning for City Maintenance	万元 (10 000 yuan)	1546397	1693759	1843784	-	-	-
维护费支出	Expenditure for City Maintenance	万元 (10 000 yuan)	1559055	1681108	1571443	-	-	-

注：本表指标为“-”的，部门相关统计制度中已经不在进行统计。

Notes: The indicator "-" in this table means statistics are no longer in the relevant statistical system of the department.

主要统计指标解释

年末自来水生产能力 指年底城建部门管理的自来水厂和自备水源的社会单位取水、净化、送水、出厂输水干管等环节的实际生产能力。

年末供水管道长度 指从送水泵到用户水表之间所有管道的长度。

全年供水总量 指公用自来水厂和自备水源的社会单位全年的供水总量，包括有效供水量及损失水量。

生活用水量 指居民日常生活与公共福利设施的用水量，包括居民、饮食店、旅馆、医院、理发店、浴池、洗衣店、游泳池、商店、学校、机关、部队等单位的用水量。

城市人口用水普及率 指城市用水的非农业人口数（不包括临时人口和流动人口）与城市非农业人口总数之比。计算公式为:

用水普及率＝城市用水的非农业人口数／城市非农业人口数 ×100％

城市用气普及率 指使用煤气（包括人工煤气、液化石油气、天然气）的城市非农业人口数（不包括临时人口和流动口）与城市非农业人口总数之比。计算公式为:

城市用气普及率＝城市用气的非农业人口数／城市非农业人口总数 ×100％

年底实有铺装道路长度 指除土路外，路面经过铺装宽度在 3.5 米以上的道路，包括高级、次高级道路和普通道路。

城市桥梁 指城市范围内，修建在河道上的桥梁和道路与道路立交、道路跨越铁路的立交桥及人行天桥。包括永久性桥和半永久性桥，不包括临时性桥、铁路桥、涵洞。

城市污水日处理能力 指污水处理厂每昼夜处理污水量的设计能力。

年末实有公共汽（电）车 指年底可参加营运的全部车辆数，包括营运车辆数和库存查封未参加营运的车辆。不包括非营运车辆，如架线车、油罐车、工程车、货车及其他专用车辆和借入的客运车辆。

绿地面积 指报告期末用作园林和绿化的各种绿地面积。包括公园绿地、生产绿地、防护绿地、附属绿地和其他绿地的面积。

公园绿地 城市中向公众开放的、以游憩为主要功能，有一定的游憩设施和服务设施，同时兼有健全生态、美化景观、防灾减灾等综合作用的绿化用地。它是城市建设用地、城市绿地系统和城市市政公用设施的重要组成部分。

工业废水排放量 指报告期内经过企业厂区所有排放口排到企业外部的工业废水量。包括生产废水、外排的直接冷却水、废气治理设施废水、超标排放的矿井地下水和与工业废水混排的厂区生活污水，不包括独立外排的间接冷却水（清浊不分流的间接冷却水应计算在内）。

化学需氧量（COD） 测量有机和无机物质化学分解所消耗氧的质量浓度的水污染指数。废气排放总量 指燃料燃烧和生产工艺过程中排放的各种废气总量，以标准状态下每年万标立方米表示。

二氧化硫排放量 指报告期内企业在燃料燃烧和生产工艺过程中排入大气的二氧化硫总质量。工业中二氧化硫主要来源于化石燃料（煤、石油等）的燃烧，还包括含硫矿石的冶炼或含硫酸、磷肥等生产的工业废气排放。

氮氧化物排放量 指报告期内企业在燃料燃烧和生产工艺过程中排入大气的氮氧化物总质量。

烟（粉）尘排放量 指报告期内企业在燃料燃烧和生产工艺过程中排入大气的烟尘及工业粉尘的总质量之和。烟尘或工业粉尘排放量可以通过除尘系统的排风量和除尘设备出口烟尘浓度相乘求得。

工业粉尘排放量 指企业在生产工艺过程中排放的颗粒物重量。如钢铁企业的耐火材料粉尘、焦化企业的筛焦系统粉尘、烧结机的粉尘、石灰窑的粉尘、建材企业的水泥粉尘等。不包括电厂排放大气的烟尘。

Explanatory Notes on Main Statistical Indicators

Year-end Tap Water Production Capacity refers to actual capacity of such links as water intaking, purification, water carriage and leaving factory water main pipe of the waterworks managed by urban construction department and social unit water source prepared at the end of the year.

Length of Water Supply Pipelines at the Year-end refers to the total length of all the pipelines between the water pumps and the user water meters.

Annual Volume of water supply refers to annual total water supply of public waterworks and social unit with water source prepared, including both the effective water supply and loss during the water supply.

Consumption of Water for Residential Use refers to water consumption in the daily life of residents and by public amenities and facilities, including water consumption by residents, eateries, hotels, hospitals, barber shops, common bathing pools, laundries, swimming pools, shops, schools, organs and troops, etc..

Urban Population Water Penetration Rate refers to the ratio between non-agricultural population of municipal water (excluding temporary and floating population) and total urban non-agricultural population. The calculation formula is:

Water penetration rate = non-agricultural population of municipal water / urban non-agricultural population * 100%

Urban Gas Popularizing Rate refers to the ratio between urban non-agricultural population (excluding temporary population and migrant population) using the coal gas (including manufactured gas, liquefied petroleum gas and natural gas) and total urban non-agricultural population. The calculation formula is:

Urban gas popularizing rate = non-agricultural population of municipal gas / total urban non-agricultural population * 100%

Year-end Actual Length of Paved Road refers to roads whose pavement width exceeds 3.5 m except for unsurfaced road (including senior, sub-senior and ordinary roads).

Urban Bridges refer to bridge and road built above the river, interchange between roads, highway interchange based on road spanning railway and pedestrian overpass, both permanent and semi-permanent bridges are included, other than temporary bridge, railway bridge and culvert in the scope of the city.

Daily Urban Sewage Treatment Capacity refers to the design capability of the sewage quantity treated by sewage treatment works every day and night.

Year-end Existing Buses (Public Trolleys) refer to all vehicles which can be put into operation at the end of the year, including number of vehicles put into operation and vehicles with inventory sealed up which are not put into operation other than non-operating vehicles, such as overhead line vehicle, oil tank truck, engineering vehicle, truck, other special vehicle and borrowed passenger service vehicle.

Green Area refers to a green area for gardening and greening. Including parks, green spaces, protective green, the accessory Greenbelt and other green areas at the end of referenced period.

Park Green Land refers to the green land which is open to the public for relaxation and has services facilities and is used for ecological protection, landscaping and disaster reduction. It is an important part of construction land, urban green space and municipal public facilities. public facilities.

Industrial Waste Water Discharged refers to the volume of industrial waste water discharged through all of the drainage system to the outside of factory complex by enterprises during the report period. It includes discharged waste water from production, direct cooling water, waste gas treatment facilities, mine groundwater beyond the standard and domestic sewage mixed with industrial waste water, does not include independently discharged indirect cooling water (voicing split-less indirect cooling water should be taken into account).

Chemical Oxygen Demand (COD) refers to index of water pollution measuring the mass concentration of oxygen consumed by the chemical breakdown of organic and inorganic matter. Total exhaust emission refers to total quantity of various exhaust gases discharged in the process of fuel burning and production which is expressed with 10,000 standard cubic meters each year under the standard state.

SO2 Emission refers to total volume of SO2 discharged into air during the process of fuel combustion and industrial production in enterprises in a given time, and is mainly caused by the combustion of fossil fuel, ore smelting and the discharge of industrial waste gas during the production of sulfuric acid and phosphate fertilizers.

Nitrogen Oxides Emission refers to total volume of nitrogen oxides discharged into air during the process of fuel combustion and industrial production.

Industrial Soot and Dust Emission refers to volume of soot and dust in smoke emitted in process of fuel burning and industrial production in premises of enterprises in the report period. It is calculated by multiplying exhaust volume of dust removal system by dust concentration.

Emission Load of Industrial Dust refers to the weight of particulate matters discharged in the process of production (such as fireproofing dust of the iron and steel enterprise, coke screening system dust of the coke making enterprise, dust of the sintering machine, dust of the lime kiln and cement dust of the building material industry), excluding smoke discharged by the power plant in to the atmosphere.

财政和金融保险

GOVERNMENT FINANCE AND FINANCIAL INSURANCE

8-1 各时期地方财政收支及指数
Expenditures and Indices of Major Years

年份 Year	一般公共预算收入（万元）General Pubilic Budget Revenue (10 000yuan)	一般公共预算支出（万元）General Pubilic Budget Expenditure (10 000yuan)	指数 (%)(以上年为 100)(%) (Preceding Year=100)	
			一般公共预算收入 General Pubilic Budget Revenue	一般公共预算支出 General Pubilic Budget Expenditure
1999	460690	497667	119.9	110.8
2000	490485	547210	110.5	110.4
"十五" 时期				
2001	596061	703720	121.5	128.6
2002	662511	775046	115.4	110.2
2003	761064	884597	119.6	114.3
2004	890364	1016953	120.9	115.0
2005	1061547	1206643	120.7	118.7
"十一五" 时期				
2006	1284388	1469762	121.0	121.8
2007	1570192	1799787	122.3	122.5
2008	1860155	2213190	118.5	123.1
2009	2101923	2599178	113.0	117.4
2010	2661314	3368037	126.6	129.6
"十二五" 时期				
2011	3249315	3968831	122.1	117.8
2012	3808218	4656731	117.0	117.3
2013	4820722	5193190	113.9	111.5
2014	5431278	5714138	112.7	110.0
2015	6143172	6581813	113.1	115.2
"十三五" 时期				
2016	6412167	7412641	104.4	112.6
2017	6772100	8340600	105.6	112.5
2018	7528162	10183179	111.2	122.1
2019	8741898	11973158	107.2	107.0

注：2013 年财政部门对一般公共预算收入口径进行调整，2013 年一般公共预算收入指数为可比口径。
Note: In 2013, the financial department adjusted the caliber of general public budget revenue. In 2013, the index of general public budget income index was comparable caliber.

8-2 地方财政收入(2019年)
Local Financial Revenue(2019)

单位：万元 (10 000yuan)

指标	Indicator	全市合计 Total	市本级 Cities				县区级 Counties
			小计 Total	市直 Departments Directiy Under the Municipal Government	莱芜高新区 Lai wu Gao xin	南部山区 Nan shan	
一般公共预算收入	General Pubilic Budget Revenue	8741898	911461	804197	100755	6509	7830437
增值税	Value-added Tax	2681265	42656		38392	4264	2638609
企业所得税	Enterprise Income Tax	1231592	10151		9753	398	1221441
个人所得税	Personal Income Tax	312135	1611		1511	100	310524
资源税	Resource Tax	56443	599		580	19	55844
城市维护建设税	Tax on City Maintenance and Construction	464189	10013	2451	6860	702	454176
房产税	Tax on Real Estates	234482	2742		2553	189	231740
印花税	Stamp Tax	127825	1473		1416	57	126352
城镇土地使用税	Holding Tax on Urban and County Land	266211	8987		8758	229	257224
土地增值税	Land Value Added Tax	677329	8232		8195	37	669097
车船税	Tax on Vehicles and Their Registration	116668	1725		1724	1	114943
耕地占用税	Farmland Occupation Tax	80701	616		616		80085
契税	Contract Tax	721393	8336		8316	20	713057
环境保护税	Environmental Protection Tax	25472	85		83	2	25387
专项收入	Specific Revenue	647174	315817	309063	6287	467	331357
行政事业性收费收入	Income from Administrative Fees	346470	166367	161357	5010		180103
罚没收入	Penalty and Confiscatory Income	149621	86962	86693	269		62659
国有资本经营收入	Profits of State-owned Enterprises	-931	-6735	-6735			5804
国有资源(资产)有偿使用收入	Revenue of Compensable Use of State-owned Resources (Assets)	467113	148417	147955	438	24	318696
捐赠收入	Donation Income	20701	457	446	11		20244
政府住房基金收入	Government Housing Fund Income	107542	102967	102967			4575
其他收入	Others	2728					2728
政府性基金收入	Government Funds Income	10191789	7933730	7910088	23642		2258059
# 城市基础设施配套收入	Urban Infrastructure Supporting Income	862671	570368	547858	22510		292303

8-3 各区财政收入(2019年)
Financial Revenue by District(2019)

指　标	Indicator	合计 Total	历下区 Li xia	市中区 Shi zhong
一般公共预算收入	General Pubilic Budget Revenue	7465177	1479133	1002551
增值税	Value-added Tax	2538083	511883	299862
企业所得税	Enterprise Income Tax	1193120	263458	212554
个人所得税	Personal Income Tax	302525	86869	51990
资源税	Resource Tax	47356	1015	9147
城市维护建设税	Tax on City Maintenance and Construction	442726	92437	46142
房产税	Tax on Real Estates	224733	61959	32316
印花税	Stamp Tax	122958	34170	17370
城镇土地使用税	Holding Tax on Urban and CountyLand	233208	15628	15089
土地增值税	Land Value Added Tax	652970	183555	88976
车船税	Tax on Vehicles and Their Registration	68995	24121	4103
耕地占用税	Farmland Occupation Tax	73300		273
契税	Contract Tax	696448	95968	89550
环境保护税	Environmental Protection Tax	23942	269	294
专项收入	Specific Revenue	317045	69967	31712
行政事业性收费收入	Income from Administrative Fees	152161	10369	27912
罚没收入	Penalty and Confiscatory Income	46687	2353	2694
国有资本经营收入	Profits of State-owned Enterprises	1272		
国有资源(资产)有偿使用收入	Revenue of Compensable Use of State-owned Resources (Assets)	303892	24368	70589
捐赠收入	Donation Income	12423		150
政府住房基金收入	Government Housing Fund Income	4561	721	
其他收入	Others	1006		
政府性基金收入	Government Funds Income	2041964		
#城市基础设施配套收入	Urban Infrastructure Supporting Income	261542		

单位：万元 (10 000yuan)

槐荫区 Huai yin	天桥区 Tian qiao	历城区 Li cheng	长清区 Chang qing	章丘区 Zhang qiu	济阳区 Ji yang	莱芜区 Lai wu	钢城区 Gang cheng	济南高新区 Ji'nan Gao xin
529037	441005	1089641	256307	642171	269518	301435	208397	1245982
178909	140446	318361	83201	218949	87007	135230	99896	464339
49822	71475	175405	19797	61026	30592	23190	17838	267963
17930	19352	31304	4970	14806	4000	5525	4195	61584
231	770	1828	2146	6794	2126	11541	7303	4455
25669	19305	53933	11987	31752	12932	21147	15711	111711
18105	16548	14033	6895	13535	5189	7950	6744	41459
7235	5372	11837	2858	10099	2759	6143	3932	21183
14714	14364	31328	19954	47641	14841	20205	14124	25320
87512	29204	140261	15856	31241	16791	7280	122	52172
1010	1311	1614	1554	3062	26647	4243	1002	328
8479	1478	28864	16133	5479	6106	1308	687	4493
61974	47981	170591	25885	81598	22070	15286	1064	84481
54	152	642	102	1514	133	8183	12559	40
17537	12961	38395	11214	24896	11331	18656	12917	67459
6876	4142	30875	26683	29743	4833	2884	1117	6727
1104	2180	6254	2131	15062	4288	4222	4975	1424
							1272	
28246	53769	24435	4506	44730	17366	6917	1787	27179
105	120	9552	435		507	1554		
				241				3599
				1			1005	
	3722		36941	1524473	311630	26727	13	138458
	3722		35654	44302	29957	9615	640	137652

8-4 各县财政收入（2019年）
Financial Revenue by County(2019)

单位：万元 (10 000yuan)

指标	Indicator	合计 Totl	平阴县 Ping yin	商河县 Shang he
一般公共预算收入	**General Pubilic Budget Revenue**	365260	230135	135125
增值税	Value-added Tax	100526	67465	33061
企业所得税	Enterprise Income Tax	28321	22870	5451
个人所得税	Personal Income Tax	7999	6012	1987
资源税	Resource Tax	8488	7503	985
城市维护建设税	Tax on City Maintenance and Construction	11450	7164	4286
房产税	Tax on Real Estates	7007	4219	2788
印花税	Stamp Tax	3394	2283	1111
城镇土地使用税	Holding Tax on Urban and County Land	24016	9272	14744
土地增值税	Land Value Added Tax	16127	5773	10354
车船税	Tax on Vehicles and Their Registration	45948	18851	27097
耕地占用税	Farmland Occupation Tax	6785	3432	3353
契税	Contract Tax	16609	10214	6395
环境保护税	Environmental Protection Tax	1445	1397	48
专项收入	Specific Revenue	14312	8757	5555
行政事业性收费收入	Income from Administrative Fees	27942	21191	6751
罚没收入	Penalty and Confiscatory Income	15972	10231	5741
国有资本经营收入	Profits of State-owned Enterprises	4532	4532	
国有资源（资产）有偿使用收入	Revenue of Compensable Use of State-owned Resources (Assets)	14804	11176	3628
捐赠收入	Donation Income	7821	7759	62
政府住房基金收入	Government Housing Fund Income	14	14	
其他收入	Others	1722		1722
政府性基金收入	**Government Funds Income**	216095	86448	129647
#城市基础设施配套收入	Urban Infrastructure Supporting Income	30761	11089	19672

8-5 地方财政支出(2019年)
Local Financial Expenditures(2019)

指 标	Indicator	全市合计 Total	市本级 Cities				县区级 Counties
			小计 Total	市直 Departments Directiy Under the Municipal Government	莱芜高新区 Lai wu Gao xin	南部山区 Nan shan	
一般公共预算支出	**General Pubilic Budget Expenditure**	**11973158**	**4727223**	**4423246**	**90517**	**213460**	**7245935**
一般公共服务支出	General Public Service	1276024	324789	292369	7751	24669	951235
国防支出	Defence Expenditure	25857	20567	20489		78	5290
公共安全支出	Public Security	659048	449402	447720	525	1157	209646
教育支出	Education	1858212	380866	329594	12446	38826	1477346
科学技术	Science and Technology	431785	209876	203356	6516	4	221909
文化体育与传媒支出	Culture, Sports and Media	296205	224571	222898	49	1624	71634
社会保障和就业支出	Social Security and Employment	1639065	621932	594335	4561	23036	1017133
医疗卫生与计划生育支出	Health and Family Planning	822826	374463	361672	3010	9781	448363
节能环保支出	Energy-saving and Environment Protection	451780	219897	183505	2744	33648	231883
城乡社区支出	Urban and Rural Community Affairs	2531826	1263704	1204306	28896	30502	1268122
农林水支出	Farming, Forestry and Irrigation Affairs	802952	197773	158249	1873	37651	605179
交通运输支出	Transport	212782	123757	122610	228	919	89025
资源勘探信息等支出	Exploration and Information Affairs	202065	40365	25511	14722	132	161700
商业服务业等支出	Commerce and Services Affairs	53865	10895	10254	275	366	42970
金融支出	Financial Supervision Affairs	51482	20330	20294	36		31152
援助其他地区支出	Aid to Other Area	30266	14775	14639	136		15491
自然资源海洋气象等支出	Natural Resources Marine Meteorological	226013	130030	124026	155	5849	95983
住房保障支出	Housing Security Affairs	238320	26208	21459	1210	3539	212112
粮油物资储备支出	Grain and Oil Reserves	11285	6367	4767	1600		4918
债务付息支出	Pay Principle and Interest for Public Debt	82044	28042	27042	1000		54002
其他支出	Other Expenditure	27966	14775	14639	136		13191
政府性基金支出	**Government Funds Expenditure**	**11045717**	**4244420**	**4091486**	**122367**	**30567**	**6801297**
#城乡社区支出	Urban and Rural Community Affairs	2531826	1263704	1204306	28896	30502	1268122

8-6 各区地方财政支出(2019年)
Local Financial Expenditures by District(2019)

指　标	Indicator	合计 Total	历下区 Li xia	市中区 Shi zhong
一般公共预算支出	**General Pubilic Budget Expenditure**	6481619	868189	615581
一般公共服务支出	General Public Service	871893	136953	111892
国防支出	Defence Expenditure	4436	1151	1560
公共安全支出	Public Security	176700	27154	26708
教育支出	Education	1306155	185086	163477
科学技术	Science and Technology	217702	18129	8238
文化体育与传媒支出	Culture, Sports and Media	65520	22734	2762
社会保障和就业支出	Social Security and Employment	906096	170135	76933
医疗卫生与计划生育支出	Health and Family Planning	397439	47477	36259
节能环保支出	Energy-saving and Environment Protection	196581	9955	18751
城乡社区支出	Urban and Rural Community Affairs	1168274	201849	108835
农林水支出	Farming, Forestry and Irrigation Affairs	489262	4353	19533
交通运输支出	Transport	78273		1651
资源勘探信息等支出	Exploration and Information Affairs	156253	5582	8317
商业服务业等支出	Commerce and Services Affairs	41001	2046	1500
金融支出	Financial Supervision Affairs	30074	18210	670
援助其他地区支出	Aid to Other Area	15155	3174	2296
国土海洋气象等支出	Land and Weather Affairs	78837	2350	7928
住房保障支出	Housing Security Affairs	203617	8067	15008
粮油物资储备支出	Grain and Oil Reserves	4223		
国债还本付息支出	Pay Principle and Interest for Public Debt	46054		1292
其他支出	Other Expenditure	12855	3074	2296
政府性基金支出	**Government Funds Expenditure**	6419697	312192	726713
#城乡社区支出	Urban and Rural Community Affairs	1168274	201849	108835

槐荫区 Huai yin	天桥区 Tian qiao	历城区 Li cheng	长清区 Chang qing	章丘区 Zhang qiu	济阳区 Ji yang	莱芜区 Lai wu	钢城区 Gang cheng	济南高新区 Ji'nan Gao xin
453693	380016	726269	585007	729543	508122	515811	186508	912880
82099	62610	117470	65262	83219	50310	49181	15945	96952
37	160	136	474	242	536	71	37	32
18449	13169	19417	11455	15778	16932	9772	4343	13523
83216	96115	155337	115929	203433	78588	120018	36934	68022
6125	8731	32809	4026	10959	6169	2694	1168	118654
2861	1990	5580	9576	11204	4506	2337	1797	173
86356	73822	85125	67622	108555	86338	89158	30946	31106
35598	34008	33925	36825	59705	33670	46909	17415	15648
16637	17778	20378	25954	23046	15766	27971	6984	13361
66277	40242	165034	48009	40981	89330	29615	14013	364089
20770	10905	32014	151702	83255	62555	66179	20571	17425
250	298	9086	16744	10487	10827	10315	11883	6732
7200	2583	4175	1863	9658	3405	3781	799	108890
4524	2865	5643	975	1979	1453	3515	664	15837
148	89	77	81	103	57	93		10546
700	621	2240		3846	247	315	213	1503
1759	1174	7867	11140	6309	14864	13594	8122	3730
16481	8198	25383	12616	45739	27270	21929	4528	18398
		1044	2645	378	156			
2142	2930	806	786	5431	3678	16313	8295	4381
700	621	2240		1646	247	315	213	1503
211178	86237	1422391	517899	1590909	322400	188244	10774	1030760
66277	40242	165034	48009	40981	89330	29615	14013	364089

8-7 各县地方财政支出(2019年)
Local Financial Expenditures by County(2019)

单位：万元(10 000yuan)

指　标	Indicator	合计 Total	平阴县 Ping yin	商河县 Shang he
一般公共预算支出	General Pubilic Budget Expenditure	764316	325176	439140
一般公共服务支出	General Public Service	79342	34446	44896
国防支出	Defence Expenditure	854	303	551
公共安全支出	Public Security	32946	15325	17621
教育支出	Education	171191	71811	99380
科学技术	Science and Technology	4207	3096	1111
文化体育与传媒支出	Culture, Sports and Media	6114	2580	3534
社会保障和就业支出	Social Security and Employment	111037	45443	65594
医疗卫生与计划生育支出	Health and Family Planning	50924	21404	29520
节能环保支出	Energy-saving and Environment Protection	35302	14165	21137
城乡社区支出	Urban and Rural Community Affairs	99848	45408	54440
农林水支出	Farming, Forestry and Irrigation Affairs	115917	43014	72903
交通运输支出	Transport	10752	2552	8200
资源勘探信息等支出	Exploration and Information Affairs	5447	2447	3000
商业服务业等支出	Commerce and Services Affairs	1969	626	1343
金融支出	Financial Supervision Affairs	1078	974	104
援助其他地区支出	Aid to Other Area	336	214	122
自然资源海洋气象等支出	Natural Resources Marine Meteorological	17146	11670	5476
住房保障支出	Housing Security Affairs	8495	4098	4397
粮油物资储备支出	Grain and Oil Reserves	695	271	424
国债还本付息支出	Pay Principle and Interest for Public Debt	7948	4831	3117
其他支出	Other Expenditure	336	214	122
政府性基金支出	Government Funds Expenditure	381600	173760	207840
#城乡社区支出	Urban and Rural Community Affairs	99848	45408	54440

8-8 金融机构本外币各项存、贷款期末余额

The Ending Balance of all Deposits and Loans in RMB and Foreign Currencies of Financial Institutions

单位：万元 (10 000yuan)

指　标	Indicator	2016 年	2017 年	2018 年	2019 年
金融机构本外币各项存款余额	The Balance of RMB and Foreign Currencies Deposits in Financial Institutions	155374463	165605979	170601377	186460860
# 住户存款	Household Deposits	43448420	45241390	50672701	64970029
非金融企业存款	Non-financial Corporate Deposits	69796525	73973987	72213088	77067935
广义政府存款	General Government Deposits	30738367	35586733	36530329	35087861
非银行业金融机构存款	Non-bank Financial Intermediary Deposits	8457783	7083306	6729522	7629436
金融机构本外币各项贷款余额	The Balance of RMB and Foreign Currencies Loans in Financial Institutions	130961411	143502995	160599213	187687420
# 住户贷款	Household Loans	24694440	31418600	37617608	47041192
非金融企业及机关团体贷款	Non-financial Corporate and Institution Loans	90455320	98004377	109865593	129406853
短期贷款	Short-term Loans	27912544	30184576	29398790	34665784
中长期贷款	Medium and Long-term Loans	51574175	61606175	72421049	82655910
票据融资	Bill Financing	9670794	3896507	4995957	8682607
融资租赁	Finance Lease	1129383	2181289	2870478	3240815
各项垫款	Bill Financing	168425	135831	179319	161737
非银行业金融机构贷款	Non-bank Financial Intermediary Loans	73	50000	0	200000

8-9 金融机构人民币各项存、贷款期末余额

The Ending Balance of all Deposits and Loans in RMB of Financial Institutions

单位：万元 (10 000yuan)

指 标	Indicator	2016 年	2017 年	2018 年	2019 年
金融机构人民币各项存款余额	The Balance of RMB Deposits in Financial Institutions	150327948	159577448	165718671	183032033
# 住户存款	Household Deposits	42799454	44657303	50080833	64380943
非金融企业存款	Non-financial Corporate Deposits	68394947	72288512	70776618	75805636
广义政府存款	General Government Deposits	30735405	35426387	36493478	34923450
非银行业金融机构存款	Non-bank Financial Intermediary Deposits	8232449	6942272	6630358	7571079
金融机构人民币各项贷款余额	The Balance of RMB Loans in Financial Institutions	113701787	128836570	147000678	176242063
# 住户贷款	Household Loans	24693431	31417225	37616195	47038338
非金融企业及机关团体贷款	Non-financial Corporate and Institution Loans	88019574	96407415	108452714	128277535
短期贷款	Short-term Loans	27188058	29297325	28659735	34002100
中长期贷款	Medium and Long-term Loans	49896069	60896806	71747225	82190276
票据融资	Bill Financing	9670794	3896507	4995957	8682607
融资租赁	Finance Lease	1129383	2181289	2870478	3240815
各项垫款	Bill Financing	135271	135488	179319	161737
非银行业金融机构贷款	Non-bank Financial Intermediary Loans	0	50000	-	200000

8-10 保险业务情况
Insurance Business

指 标	Indicator	2014 年	2015 年	2016 年	2017 年	2018 年	2019 年
承保额(亿元)	Insurance Value(100 million yuan)	63675	97665	112875	162712	256415	438422
企业财产险	Enterprise Property Insurance	17723	36178	26150	32210	37263	69122
家庭财产险	Family Property Insurance	321	1744	1568	3825	7799	14815
运输工具及责任险	Motor Vehicle and Third Party Liability	10470	13920	14443	17555	36906	73457
货物运输险	Freight Transport Insurance	2021	1955	2769	2227	2590	4510
养老金险	Pension Insurance	1017	1800	7187	6758	4262	6045
人身意外伤害险	Accident Injury Insurance	24686	34112	43834	66079	125189	129331
简易人身险	Simple Life Insurance	3620	4239	10871	29390	32027	117371
农业险	Agriculture Insurance	28	30	36	52	138	320
其他险	Other Property Insurance	3788	3687	6017	4617	10242	23451
保险业务收入(万元)	Insurance Revenue(10 000yuan)	1628650	2227474	3474988	3810660	4155535	5322643
企业财产险	Enterprise Property Insurance	30479	42535	53352	53503	52896	75594
家庭财产险	Family Property Insurance	726	1757	2761	4997	5115	7685
运输工具及责任险	Motor Vehicle and Third Party Liability	386898	487124	547370	538780	554548	587532
货物运输险	Freight Transport Insurance	3042	4260	4035	3359	3118	4358
养老金险	Pension Insurance	809083	1322141	1818536	2470364	2579988	3090172
人身意外伤害险	Accident Injury Insurance	56249	74259	71613	78836	146634	219280
简易人身险	Simple Life Insurance	120282	245598	827557	574080	638398	868888
农业险	Agriculture Insurance	5527	9389	9036	11121	23767	35742
其他险	Other Property Insurance	216365	40411	140728	75619	151071	433393
保险业务支出(万元)	Insurance Expenses(10 000yuan)	529707	656570	786752	886699	1033980	1219250
企业财产险	Enterprise Property Insurance	860	7184	8843	7488	8186	15821
家庭财产险	Family Property Insurance	15	80	705	1542	1539	2871
运输工具及责任险	Motor Vehicle and Third Party Liability	17016	151723	187490	170705	138639	169420
货物运输险	Freight Transport Insurance	204	1954	3455	1437	934	1576
养老金险	Pension Insurance	451243	392111	426820	545380	702446	626575
人身意外伤害险	Accident Injury Insurance	7389	16613	16603	15393	19719	22686
简易人身险	Simple Life Insurance	47425	69165	101695	110349	124070	228314
农业险	Agriculture Insurance	218	1795	6021	5199	11603	20217
其他险	Other Property Insurance	5337	15946	35120	29207	26846	131770

注：2018 年以前为区划调整前数据。
Note: Data before the year of 2018 are the data of administrative division before the adjustment.

8-11 证券机构及证券交易情况
Institution and Trading Summary for Stocks

单位：亿元 (100 million yuan)

指　标	Indicator	2014 年	2015 年	2016 年	2017 年	2018 年	2019 年
注册地在济南证券公司数(个)	Stocks Institutions in Ji'nan(Unit)	1	1	1	1	1	1
证券营业部(个)	Securities Business Department(Unit)	72	78	83	92	87	92
证券交易额	Trading Volume of Securities Business Department	16077	54575	34687	30975	28482	36453
股　票	Stock	10165	38091	19183	15987	12126	18621
基　金	Fund	1044	4568	1449	2361	2111	2197
债　券	Bond	4857	11899	14045	12602	14119	15536
其　他	Others	11	17	10	25	126	99

注：1. 数据由金融办提供。
2.2018 年以前为区划调整前数据。
Note: 1.Data are provided by the Municipal financial office.
2. Data before the year of 2018 are the data of administrative division before the adjustment.

主要统计指标解释

一般公共预算收入　指国家财政参与社会产品分配所取得的收入，是实现国家职能的财力保证。主要包括：（1）各项税收：包括国内增值税、国内消费税、进口货物增值税和消费税、出口货物退增值税和消费税、营业税、企业所得税、个人所得税、资源税、城市维护建设税、房产税、印花税、城镇土地使用税、土地增值税、车船税、船舶吨税、车辆购置税、关税、耕地占用税、契税、烟叶税等。（2）非税收入：包括专项收入、行政事业性收费、罚没收入和其他收入。财政收入按现行分税制财政体制划分为中央本级收入和地方本级收入。

一般公共预算支出　指国家财政将筹集起来的资金进行分配使用，以满足经济建设和各项事业的需要。主要包括：一般公共服务、外交、国防、公共安全、教育、科学技术、文化体育与传媒、社会保障和就业、医疗卫生与计划生育、节能环保、城乡社区、农林水、交通运输、资源勘探信息等、商业服务业等、金融、援助其他地区、国土海洋气象等、住房保障、粮油物资储备、政府债务付息等方面的支出。财政支出根据政府在经济和社会活动中的不同职权，划分为中央财政支出和地方财政支出。

存款　指企业、机关、团体或居民根据资金必须收回的原则，把货币资金存入银行或其他信贷机构保管并取得一定利息的一种信用活动形式。根据存款对象或性质的不同可划分为企业存款、财政存款、机关团体存款、基本建设存款、储蓄存款、农村存款、委托存款、其他存款等科目。它是银行信贷资金的主要来源。

贷款　指银行或其他信贷机构根据资金必须归还的原则，按一定利率，为企业、个人等提供资金的一种信用活动形式。我国银行贷款分为短期贷款、中期流动资金贷款、中长期贷款、信托贷款、融资租赁、委托贷款、票据融资、各项垫款等。

保险金额　指保险人承担赔偿或者给付保险金责任的最高限额。

保费　指投保人为取得保险人在约定范围内所承担赔偿责任而支付给保险人的费用。

赔款　指保险人根据保险合同的规定，向被保险人支付的赔偿保险责任损失的金额。

给付　包括死伤医疗给付和满期给付。死伤医疗给付是指保险人根据人寿保险及长期健康保险合同的规定，因被保险人在保险期内发生保险责任范围内的保险事故支付给被保险人（或受益人）的金额。满期给付是指被保险人生存期满，保险人按人寿保险合同规定支付给被保险人的满期保险金额。

Explanatory Notes on Main Statistical Indicators

General Public Budget Revenue refers to the revenue of the government finance by means of participating in the distribution of the social products, which is the financial resources for ensuring the government to function. The contents of government revenue have been changed several times. Now it includes the following main items : (1) Various tax revenues: Include domestic value–added tax, domestic excise duty, value–added tax and consumption tax on imported goods, VAT refund and consumption tax on exports, business tax, corporate income tax, individual income tax, resource tax, urban maintenance and construction tax, building taxes, stamp duty, city and town land use tax, land value increment tax, vehicle and vessel tax, tonnage tax, vehicle purchase tax, tariff, farmland conversion tax, deed tax and tobacco taxes. (2) Non–tax revenues: Included in this category are special revenue, revenue from administrative and institutional fees, confiscated income and other income. Fiscal revenues are divided into revenue at the central level and local income pursuant to the current tax–sharing financial system.

General Public Budget Expenditure refers to the distribution and use of the funds the government finances has raised, so as to meet the needs of economic construction and various causes. It includes the following main items: expenditures regarding general public service, diplomacy, national defense, public security, education, science and technology, culture, sports and media, social security and employment, health care and family planning, energy conservation and environment protection, urban and rural communities, agroforestry water, transportation, resource exploration information, commercial service industry, finance, assistance to other areas, territorial marine meteorology, housing security, reserves of grain, oil and materials and payment of government debt interest, etc. Fiscal expenditure is divided into central fiscal expenditure and local fiscal expenditure in accordance with different function and power of government in economic and social activities.

Deposit is a form of credit by which enterprises, institutions, organizations or households can put money into banks and other credit institutions for safekeeping and interest earning under the principle of free withdrawal. According to different depositors, deposits are divided into enterprise deposits, treasury deposits, deposits of government agencies and organizations, capital construction deposits, savings deposits, rural saving deposits, entrusted deposits and other deposits. Deposits are major sources of the credit funds of banks.

Loan is a form of credit by which banks and other credit institutions provide funds at certain interest rate to enterprises and individuals in the light of the principle of unconditional repayment. Loans from Chinese Banks include circulating capital loans, fixed assets loans, loans to urban and rural individuals engaged in industrial and commercial business and agricultural loans.

Amount Insured refers to the maximum that the insurant will get for the claim of the case insured.

Premium is the fee paid by the insurant to the insurer to obtain the obligation of compensation from the insurance within the agreed terms.

Settled Claim is the compensation paid by the insurer to the insurant in accordance with the insurance contract.

Payment includes payment for death, injury or medical treatment and mature payment. Payment for death, injury or medical treatment refers to the money paid to the insurant (or the beneficiary) in accordance with the life or health insurance contract when the insurant encounters accidents within the insured period covered in the contract. Mature payment refers to the mature payment to the insurant in accordance with the life insurance contract at the end of the insured period.

物价

PRICE

9-1 主要年份物价指数(以上年价格为100)
Price Indices of Major Years(Preceding Last Year=100)

年份 Year	居民消费价格指数 Consumer Price Index	#食品 Food	#服务项目 Services	零售物价指数 Retail Price Index
1951	108.5	105.3	98.7	109.8
1952	101.5	103.9	101.0	101.2
1955	101.6	101.3	103.4	101.4
1956	100.5	100.7	100.6	100.5
1965	107.3	111.5	97.5	108.0
1970	98.4	99.0	100.0	98.3
1971	100.0	100.5	100.0	100.0
1972	100.1	100.3	100.0	100.1
1973	99.5	99.6	97.9	99.7
1974	99.4	99.1	99.9	99.5
1975	100.2	100.0	100.0	100.2
1976	100.4	100.0	100.0	100.4
1977	99.2	99.9	91.2	100.0
1978	100.3	100.3	100.0	100.3
1979	101.1	101.7	100.5	101.1
1980	104.7	107.9	100.0	105.0
1981	101.9	102.2	100.1	102.0
1982	101.1	101.6	100.3	101.2
1983	100.1	100.3	100.9	100.1
1984	101.9	101.1	109.8	101.3
1985	108.7	112.2	103.3	109.1
1986	106.2	107.6	104.9	106.3
1987	109.5	111.9	104.9	109.8
1988	122.4	128.0	108.8	123.4
1989	116.2	111.2	113.5	116.4
1990	103.3	102.6	108.0	103.0
1991	106.7	107.6	106.9	106.7
1992	110.4	108.7	122.2	109.3
1993	114.7	109.8	138.0	112.1
1994	124.8	133.9	114.5	122.7
1995	117.3	123.0	115.1	113.2
1996	109.1	109.7	116.2	106.3
1997	102.9	101.8	107.8	101.5
1998	100.9	99.4	119.0	98.9
1999	99.1	97.3	127.6	96.9
2000	100.6	97.9	129.0	98.0
2001	100.3	100.8	106.1	98.8
2002	98.8	100.2	101.3	97.8
2003	99.9	103.6	100.3	98.0
2004	102.5	107.4	101.2	100.6
2005	101.1	102.7	101.2	100.4
2006	100.9	102.4	100.9	100.3
2007	103.9	111.6	101.8	102.2
2008	105.7	115.5	101.8	104.5
2009	100.3	102.7	102.4	98.7
2010	102.1	107.3	100.6	101.3
2011	105.4	111.3	104.4	104.6
2012	102.4	103.6	102.2	101.8
2013	102.8	104.9	102.7	101.3
2014	102.2	103.2	102.9	101.2
2015	101.9	101.4	101.6	100.3
2016	102.7	103.9	103.5	100.8
2017	102.0	98.5	104.2	101.0
2018	102.6	102.8	102.1	102.6
2019	103.3	112.0	101.4	102.5

9-2 主要年份物价指数(以1950年价格为100)
Price Indices of Major Years(Preceding 1950=100)

年份 Year	居民消费价格指数 Consumer Price Index	#食品 Food	#服务项目 Services	零售物价指数 Retail Price Index
1951	108.5	105.3	98.7	109.8
1952	110.1	109.4	103.7	111.1
1955	117.2	123.7	108.2	118.4
1956	117.8	124.6	108.8	119.0
1965	127.7	141.5	116.9	130.7
1970	123.0	141.6	110.1	126.0
1971	123.0	142.3	110.1	126.0
1972	123.1	142.7	110.1	126.1
1973	122.5	142.1	107.8	125.8
1974	121.8	140.9	107.7	125.1
1975	122.0	140.9	107.7	125.4
1976	122.5	140.9	107.7	125.9
1977	121.5	140.7	98.2	125.9
1978	121.9	141.1	98.2	126.3
1979	123.2	143.5	98.6	127.6
1980	129.0	154.9	98.6	134.0
1981	131.5	158.3	98.7	136.7
1982	132.9	160.8	99.0	138.3
1983	133.0	161.3	99.9	138.5
1984	135.6	163.1	109.7	140.3
1985	147.4	183.0	113.3	153.0
1986	156.5	195.8	118.9	162.7
1987	171.4	219.1	124.7	178.6
1988	209.8	280.4	135.7	220.4
1989	234.8	311.8	154.0	256.5
1990	251.8	319.9	166.3	264.2
1991	268.7	344.2	177.8	281.9

9-2 续表 continued

年份 Year	居民消费价格指数 Consumer Price Index	# 食品 Food	# 服务项目 Services	零售物价指数 Retail Price Index
1992	296.6	376.2	217.3	308.1
1993	340.2	413.1	299.8	345.4
1994	424.6	570.4	343.3	423.8
1995	498.1	709.7	395.1	479.7
1996	543.4	797.7	459.1	509.9
1997	559.2	782.5	494.9	551.6
1998	564.2	777.8	588.9	545.5
1999	559.1	756.8	751.4	528.6
2000	562.4	740.9	969.3	518.0
2001	564.1	746.8	1028.4	511.8
2002	557.3	748.3	1041.8	500.5
2003	556.7	775.2	1044.9	490.5
2004	570.6	832.6	1057.4	493.4
2005	576.9	855.1	1070.1	495.4
2006	582.1	875.6	1079.7	496.9
2007	604.8	977.2	1099.1	507.8
2008	639.3	1128.7	1118.9	530.7
2009	641.2	1159.2	1145.8	523.8
2010	654.7	1243.8	1152.7	530.6
2011	690.2	1384.7	1203.1	555.1
2012	706.8	1434.5	1229.5	565.1
2013	726.6	1504.8	1262.7	572.4
2014	742.6	1553.0	1299.3	579.3
2015	756.7	1574.7	1320.1	581.0
2016	777.1	1636.1	1366.3	585.6
2017	792.6	1611.6	1423.7	591.5
2018	813.3	1656.7	1453.6	606.8
2019	840.1	1855.5	1473.9	622.0

9-3 分月居民消费价格指数（2019年，以上年同期价格为100）
Consumer Price Indices by Month(2019，Preceding Last Year=100)

指 标	Indicator	全年 Total	1月 January	2月 February
居民消费价格总指数	Consumer Price Index	103.3	102.3	101.9
非食品烟酒价格指数	Non-food,Tobacco and Alcohol Price Index	101.0	101.4	101.4
服务价格指数	Services Price Index	101.4	101.2	101.0
工业品价格指数	Industrial Products Price Index	100.5	101.7	101.8
消费品价格指数	Consumer Goods Price Index	104.5	103.0	102.5
扣除食品和能源价格指数	Excluding Food and Energy Price Index	101.5	101.9	101.7
一、食品烟酒	Food,Tobacco and Liquor	109.1	104.5	103.3
1. 食品	Food	112.0	104.8	103.3
(1) 粮食	Grain	101.5	101.4	101.8
(2) 薯类	Tuber	108.4	114.2	105.2
(3) 豆类	Beans	100.4	105.4	105.1
(4) 食用油	Edible Oil	104.3	104.9	104.1
食用植物油	Edible Vegetable Oil	103.2	105.0	104.3
(5) 菜	Vegetables	104.4	119.8	109.3
鲜 菜	Fresh Vegetables	104.7	121.2	109.8
(6) 畜肉类	Livestock Meat	140.2	100.9	103.7
猪 肉	Pork	158.9	99.6	102.7
(7) 禽肉类	Poultry	111.7	112.2	112.6
(8) 水产品	Aquatic Products	101.1	102.0	98.7
(9) 蛋类	Eggs	104.8	104.6	94.6
鸡 蛋	Hen's Eggs	104.7	103.0	91.4
(10) 奶类	Milk	103.1	101.4	102.0
(11) 干鲜瓜果类	Dried and Fresh Melons and Fruits	104.9	100.6	99.1
鲜瓜果	Fresh Melons and Fruits	104.8	100.7	96.9
(12) 糖果糕点类	Candy and Cakes	103.6	105.3	105.2
(13) 调味品	Condiment	104.3	106.1	106.1
(14) 其他食品类	Other Foods	96.6	97.5	96.3
2. 茶及饮料	Tea and Beverages	101.8	101.8	102.1
3. 烟酒	Tobacco and Liquor	103.3	103.8	102.9
(1) 烟草	Tobacco	100.0	100.0	100.0
(2) 酒类	Liquor	107.0	108.2	106.2
4. 在外餐饮	Outside Catering	104.5	104.2	103.6
二、衣着	Clothing	101.3	102.5	102.4
1. 服装	Garments	101.5	102.8	102.3
(1) 男式服装	Men's Clothing	100.2	101.3	100.4
(2) 女式服装	Women's Clothing	102.4	103.3	103.2
(3) 儿童服装	Children's Clothing	102.2	105.1	104.1
2. 服装材料	Clothing Material	103.6	107.8	106.3
3. 其他衣着及配件	Other Clothing and Accessories	102.2	104.2	104.3
4. 衣着加工服务费	Clothing Processing Service Fee	103.7	103.1	103.1

3月 March	4月 April	5月 May	6月 June	7月 July	8月 August	9月 September	10月 October	11月 November	12月 December
102.8	102.5	102.5	102.7	103.2	102.8	103.1	104.4	105.7	105.5
101.6	101.2	100.9	100.9	101.3	101.1	100.5	100.3	100.3	100.8
101.6	101.3	101.2	101.4	102.1	101.9	101.0	101.2	101.1	101.2
101.6	101.1	100.6	100.2	100.3	100.1	99.9	99.4	99.3	100.4
103.5	103.2	103.3	103.6	103.9	103.4	104.4	106.5	108.7	108.3
101.7	101.4	101.1	101.3	101.7	101.5	101.2	101.3	101.6	101.7
105.7	105.6	106.5	107.6	108.1	107.2	109.6	114.6	119.5	117.1
107.0	107.1	108.5	110.1	111.1	109.6	112.9	120.2	126.7	123.1
99.8	100.0	102.5	99.5	102.4	102.7	103.2	102.9	99.2	102.0
100.9	106.8	102.6	102.2	111.8	113.9	109.1	117.1	111.7	109.5
97.9	101.4	99.9	98.6	97.3	98.4	98.9	99.0	100.9	102.2
103.8	103.7	104.3	105.2	104.2	104.1	104.4	103.5	104.7	104.3
103.7	103.3	103.8	104.6	103.6	103.3	102.9	101.5	101.6	101.3
116.9	112.0	103.9	103.5	107.6	94.8	80.8	86.8	107.2	115.1
118.1	113.0	104.3	103.7	108.3	94.5	79.7	85.8	107.9	116.2
117.4	119.5	118.9	121.6	124.6	131.9	160.4	186.0	203.0	190.3
124.7	127.7	125.9	131.5	135.3	146.8	188.8	229.8	252.5	235.2
108.2	109.1	108.8	105.6	102.8	108.2	114.3	121.7	125.3	110.7
98.7	98.5	98.8	100.8	101.8	100.5	102.1	102.0	104.7	105.7
98.4	103.5	106.7	103.1	110.1	102.4	108.9	110.6	109.2	105.2
95.8	102.1	106.0	101.7	110.6	102.7	111.1	113.9	111.1	106.4
103.9	102.5	102.1	103.9	103.2	103.9	103.6	102.3	103.3	105.3
99.7	102.2	121.5	130.2	125.1	114.0	98.2	96.5	91.5	86.5
98.1	100.8	125.6	137.1	131.2	117.2	95.2	93.8	88.2	82.5
106.9	104.4	101.2	104.3	103.8	102.2	103.2	102.7	101.5	102.6
105.7	104.8	105.1	104.3	104.7	104.6	103.1	100.9	104.4	101.7
96.6	97.1	93.8	94.3	95.6	98.0	97.1	97.2	98.0	97.3
102.6	102.8	102.5	102.4	102.3	101.8	101.3	100.9	100.0	100.6
103.3	102.3	101.5	102.1	103.6	104.1	103.9	104.1	104.2	104.3
100.0	100.0	100.0	100.0	100.0	100.0	100.0	100.0	100.0	100.0
107.0	105.0	103.2	104.3	107.5	108.5	108.2	108.5	108.7	108.8
103.2	103.3	103.6	104.0	103.1	102.7	103.8	105.4	109.1	108.3
102.1	101.4	101.3	101.2	101.2	100.6	100.6	100.8	100.8	100.7
102.5	101.9	101.4	101.1	100.9	100.6	100.8	101.5	101.3	101.6
100.5	99.8	99.7	99.6	99.8	99.6	99.3	100.2	100.4	101.1
103.2	102.9	102.1	101.5	101.2	100.7	101.8	102.9	102.7	102.8
105.2	103.9	103.9	103.5	102.8	102.8	100.8	99.7	97.7	97.8
106.3	106.3	104.6	103.1	103.1	104.8	101.1	101.1	100.0	100.0
103.1	102.9	102.1	102.1	102.6	101.6	101.9	101.8	101.7	97.9
103.1	103.1	103.8	103.8	103.8	103.8	103.8	105.2	105.2	102.0

9-3 续表 1 continued 1

指 标	Indicator	全年 Total	1月 January	2月 February
5. 鞋类	Footwear	100.0	100.8	102.0
(1) 鞋	Shoes	99.7	100.5	101.7
(2) 鞋类加工服务	Footwear Processing Services	121.0	121.6	121.6
三、居住	Residence	101.3	101.1	100.4
1. 租赁房房租	Rental Housing Rent	106.0	98.5	96.5
2. 住房保养维修及管理	Housing Maintenance	101.0	102.0	101.9
(1) 住房装潢材料	Housing Decoration Materials	100.8	103.5	103.4
(2) 物业管理费	Property Management Fee	100.0	100.0	100.0
(3) 住房装潢维修	Housing Decoration Maintenance	101.8	101.3	101.3
3. 水电燃料	Water, Electricity and Fuels	101.8	102.2	101.8
(1) 水	Water	100.0	100.0	100.0
(2) 电	Electricity	100.0	100.0	100.0
(3) 燃气	Gas	106.2	107.5	107.5
(4) 取暖费	Heating Fee	100.0	100.0	100.0
(5) 其他燃料	Other Fuel	112.0	116.1	109.7
4. 自有住房	Self-owned House	100.5	100.8	100.0
四、生活用品及服务	Daily Necessities and Services	100.3	101.7	101.9
1. 家具及室内装饰品	Furniture and Interior Decorations	100.2	100.9	100.5
(1) 家具	Furniture and Interior Decorations	100.2	99.6	99.6
(2) 室内装饰品	Interior Decorations	100.3	105.2	103.6
2. 家用器具	Household Appliances	99.1	100.4	102.0
(1) 大型家用器具	Large Household Appliances	99.5	100.8	102.5
(2) 小家电	Small Household Appliances	97.3	98.5	99.7
3. 家用纺织品	Home Textiles	97.2	108.2	106.7
(1) 床上用品	Bedding Article	96.6	108.6	106.9
(2) 窗帘门帘	Curtain	100.6	103.2	103.2
(3) 其他家用纺织品	Other Household Textiles	102.5	108.8	108.7
4. 家庭日用杂品	The Family Daily Sundry Goods	100.2	100.8	100.6
(1) 洗涤卫生用品	Washing Sanitary Articles	99.7	101.4	100.4
(2) 厨具餐具茶具	Kitchenware, Tableware, Tea Set	101.3	100.7	101.5
(3) 家用手工工具	Home Hand Tools	97.5	95.9	95.9
(4) 其他家庭日用杂品	Other Household Articles For Daily Use	101.3	100.3	101.4
5. 个人护理用品	Personal Care Products	102.2	102.0	100.6
(1) 化妆品	Cosmetics	104.5	104.7	102.6
(2) 其他护理用品类	Other Nursing Products	99.9	99.3	98.6
6. 家庭服务	Family Services	103.1	101.7	104.4
五、交通和通信	Transport and Communication	97.3	99.1	99.3
1. 交通	Transport	96.4	97.3	97.5
(1) 交通工具	Transport Tools	96.2	94.1	94.2
(2) 交通工具用燃料	Transport Fuels	94.1	93.9	97.2

3月 March	4月 April	5月 May	6月 June	7月 July	8月 August	9月 September	10月 October	11月 November	12月 December
100.4	99.4	100.2	101.2	101.5	100.0	99.2	98.1	98.8	98.1
100.1	99.1	99.9	100.9	101.3	99.7	98.8	97.8	98.6	97.9
121.6	121.6	121.6	121.6	121.6	123.0	124.4	124.4	114.8	114.8
100.7	100.4	101.2	101.1	102.0	102.0	101.7	101.6	101.4	101.3
96.5	95.7	99.2	101.4	112.9	116.0	113.0	113.1	114.8	115.0
101.7	101.3	100.7	100.7	100.4	100.3	100.2	100.4	101.1	101.7
102.9	102.0	100.5	100.5	99.7	99.6	99.4	98.8	98.9	100.7
100.0	100.0	100.0	100.0	100.0	100.0	100.0	100.0	100.0	100.0
101.3	101.3	101.3	101.3	101.3	101.3	101.3	102.4	104.3	103.8
101.9	101.9	102.1	102.1	102.4	102.4	102.4	101.7	100.1	100.4
100.0	100.0	100.0	100.0	100.0	100.0	100.0	100.0	100.0	100.0
100.0	100.0	100.0	100.0	100.0	100.0	100.0	100.0	100.0	100.0
107.5	107.5	107.5	107.5	107.5	107.5	107.5	107.5	100.0	100.0
100.0	100.0	100.0	100.0	100.0	100.0	100.0	100.0	100.0	100.0
110.4	110.4	115.1	115.1	119.3	119.3	119.3	106.7	100.8	105.6
100.5	100.2	101.1	100.7	100.9	100.6	100.3	100.5	100.4	100.1
101.9	101.3	100.8	99.5	99.8	99.7	99.2	99.6	98.9	99.3
101.5	101.5	101.5	101.2	101.2	98.6	98.0	98.0	100.5	99.6
101.0	100.9	100.9	100.9	100.9	99.4	98.9	99.7	100.5	100.3
103.2	103.5	103.5	102.3	102.3	96.2	95.0	92.5	100.3	97.2
100.7	100.3	100.0	100.0	99.0	98.2	97.7	98.2	95.4	97.6
101.0	100.7	100.4	100.3	99.2	98.6	98.4	98.9	95.5	97.7
99.5	98.6	97.9	98.3	97.8	96.4	94.3	95.2	94.6	96.7
102.8	101.0	97.4	86.9	90.9	95.7	94.4	96.8	94.0	94.3
102.4	100.3	97.1	84.9	89.5	95.1	93.7	96.2	92.9	93.3
103.2	103.2	99.6	99.6	99.6	99.6	98.0	98.0	98.4	102.1
106.9	107.0	98.6	98.6	98.8	98.6	98.3	104.5	104.5	98.4
101.3	100.8	99.8	98.9	99.3	99.6	100.4	100.1	100.1	100.5
101.8	100.4	98.7	97.7	98.2	98.6	99.7	99.2	99.7	100.9
100.8	103.6	103.1	101.4	102.1	101.1	100.4	100.8	100.9	99.9
95.9	95.9	95.9	95.9	95.9	100.0	100.0	100.0	100.0	100.0
101.6	100.6	101.3	101.3	101.1	101.7	103.3	102.4	100.8	99.8
102.2	103.0	103.7	103.3	103.3	103.4	101.8	102.5	100.5	100.4
105.4	106.4	106.7	107.3	106.4	107.0	102.5	104.6	100.6	100.5
99.0	99.6	100.7	99.3	100.2	99.8	101.0	100.3	100.4	100.2
105.4	102.4	102.4	102.4	102.9	102.9	102.9	102.9	103.3	103.3
100.6	99.5	97.5	96.6	96.5	95.7	95.2	94.0	95.5	97.9
99.6	98.5	96.9	95.3	95.1	94.7	94.5	92.8	95.7	99.5
95.0	95.0	95.0	95.3	96.3	96.1	97.5	96.0	99.7	100.0
103.4	100.4	98.9	93.8	91.3	90.0	88.0	84.9	89.4	100.6

9-3 续表 2 continued 2

指　标	Indicator	全年 Total	1月 January	2月 February
(3) 交通工具使用和维修	Vehicle Use and Maintenance	101.4	110.6	102.4
(4) 交通费	Travelling Expenses	98.9	106.9	105.9
2. 通信	Signal Communication	98.8	102.4	102.6
(1) 通信工具	Communication Tools	103.6	110.5	112.1
(2) 通信服务	Communication Services	97.6	100.0	100.0
(3) 邮递服务	Mailing Service	100.1	110.0	110.0
六、教育文化和娱乐	Education Culture and Recreation	102.7	100.9	101.8
1. 教育	Education	102.4	102.9	102.9
(1) 教育用品	Educational Supplies	104.3	100.3	100.3
(2) 教育服务	Education Services	102.3	103.0	103.0
2. 文化娱乐	Culture and Entertainment	102.9	99.1	100.8
(1) 文娱耐用消费品	Recreational Consumer Durables	99.7	102.0	102.5
(2) 其他文娱用品	Other Entertainment Products	102.1	103.6	103.2
(3) 文化娱乐服务	Cultural and Recreational Services	102.4	99.2	103.2
(4) 旅游	Tourism	104.4	97.1	99.0
七、医疗保健	Health Care	101.7	105.1	104.3
1. 药品及医疗器具	Drugs and Medical Devices	102.0	108.6	107.0
(1) 中药	Traditional Chinese Medicine	104.9	108.5	108.4
(2) 西药	West Medicine	103.9	114.7	115.2
(3) 滋补保健品	Western Medicine	97.6	101.9	94.3
(4) 医疗卫生器具	Medical and Health Equipment	100.4	101.4	101.4
(5) 保健器具	Healthcare Apparatus	95.2	100.9	100.9
2. 医疗服务	Medical Services	101.5	101.8	101.8
(1) 综合医疗类	Comprehensive Health Care	106.6	107.6	107.6
(2) 诊断类	Diagnostic	99.9	100.0	100.0
(3) 治疗类	Therapeutic	100.0	100.0	100.0
(4) 康复类	Rehabilitation	100.0	100.0	100.0
(5) 中医医疗服务类	Chinese Medicine Services	100.0	100.0	100.0
(6) 其他医疗服务	Other Medical Services	100.0	100.0	100.0
八、其他用品和服务	Other Supplies and Services	104.5	102.0	103.3
1. 其他用品类	Other Products	107.1	100.8	103.5
(1) 首饰手表	Jewelry Watches	108.6	100.8	104.0
(2) 其他杂项用品	Other Miscellaneous Supplies	103.0	100.8	102.0
2. 其他服务类	Other Services	102.1	103.2	103.1
(1) 旅馆住宿	Hotel Accommodation	106.9	106.6	112.5
(2) 美容美发洗浴	Hairdressing Bath	97.6	100.3	99.1
(3) 养老服务	Pension Services	117.4	121.7	121.7
(4) 金融保险	Finance and Insurance	99.7	100.0	99.3
(5) 其他服务类	Other Service	121.4	121.4	121.4

3月 March	4月 April	5月 May	6月 June	7月 July	8月 August	9月 September	10月 October	11月 November	12月 December
100.9	100.1	100.1	100.1	100.1	100.9	100.9	100.9	99.4	100.9
107.3	105.9	96.2	94.8	96.2	96.1	95.0	95.4	94.3	93.7
102.3	101.4	98.7	99.1	98.9	97.6	96.4	96.3	95.0	95.2
110.3	104.7	104.8	107.3	112.2	105.1	98.1	98.1	90.7	92.1
100.0	100.0	96.4	96.4	96.4	96.4	96.4	96.4	96.4	96.4
110.0	110.0	110.0	110.0	91.2	91.2	91.2	89.2	89.2	89.2
103. 4	102. 9	103. 0	104. 0	104. 6	103. 5	101. 3	102. 1	101. 9	102. 6
102.4	102.9	102.2	102.2	102.1	101.6	101.9	102.5	102.5	102.5
100.5	100.5	100.5	100.5	100.1	100.2	109.0	114.2	113.4	112.7
102.5	103.0	102.3	102.3	102.2	101.7	101.6	102.1	102.1	102.1
104.3	102.9	103.8	105.7	107.0	105.3	100.7	101.6	101.4	102.8
102.6	101.6	100.5	100.4	100.2	99.9	98.3	96.8	94.6	97.1
104.3	101.7	103.4	103.6	103.5	100.6	101.0	100.4	100.5	99.6
100.5	100.9	99.5	104.4	103.7	100.7	103.8	104.2	103.8	105.2
106.4	104.4	106.8	108.5	111.5	110.1	100.3	102.6	103.0	104.8
102. 2	102. 4	101. 3	101. 4	101. 3	101. 2	101. 1	100. 2	100. 3	100. 3
102.6	103.0	100.8	101.1	100.9	100.7	100.5	99.8	99.9	99.6
103.9	103.9	103.9	107.1	104.2	103.9	103.9	103.9	103.9	103.1
104.6	104.2	103.7	101.2	101.3	101.1	100.5	100.9	101.1	100.9
100.1	101.9	94.3	98.1	99.1	99.3	99.3	94.3	94.3	93.8
100.0	101.9	100.0	100.0	100.0	100.0	100.0	100.0	100.0	100.0
93.7	93.7	91.0	91.0	91.0	91.0	91.0	100.0	100.0	100.0
101.8	101.8	101.8	101.8	101.8	101.8	101.8	100.6	100.6	101.0
107.6	107.6	107.6	107.6	107.6	107.6	107.6	102.5	102.5	105.4
100.0	100.0	100.0	100.0	100.0	100.0	100.0	100.0	100.0	98.7
100.0	100.0	100.0	100.0	100.0	100.0	100.0	100.0	100.0	100.6
100.0	100.0	100.0	100.0	100.0	100.0	100.0	100.0	100.0	100.0
100.0	100.0	100.0	100.0	100.0	100.0	100.0	100.0	100.0	100.0
100.0	100.0	100.0	100.0	100.0	100.0	100.0	100.0	100.0	100.0
102. 2	103. 0	102. 4	103. 3	104. 4	107. 2	108. 4	107. 6	105. 3	105. 3
102.0	102.9	103.2	104.9	106.9	112.6	113.7	114.1	110.8	110.4
101.2	102.7	103.0	105.5	108.0	115.7	117.3	118.5	113.7	112.5
104.3	103.6	103.7	103.1	103.6	103.4	103.3	101.3	102.3	104.2
102.3	103.0	101.7	101.8	102.1	102.1	103.4	101.5	100.1	100.4
110.4	117.0	104.3	105.4	105.3	105.1	116.7	99.8	101.0	100.0
97.0	97.0	97.0	97.0	97.0	97.0	97.0	97.0	97.0	98.4
121.7	121.7	121.7	121.7	121.7	121.7	121.7	121.7	100.0	100.0
99.3	99.3	99.3	99.3	99.3	99.3	99.3	99.3	101.2	101.2
123.0	123.0	123.0	123.0	129.6	129.6	129.6	129.6	105.4	105.4

9-4 分月商品零售价格指数 (2019 年，以上年同期价格为 100)
Retail Price Indices by Month(2019，Preceding Last Year=100)

指 标	Indicator	全 年 Total	1 月 January	2 月 February
商品零售价格指数	Retail Price Indices	102.5	102.3	102.2
一、食品	Food	110.4	104.9	103.5
二、饮料、烟酒	Beverages, Tobacco and Liquor	102.8	103.1	102.6
三、服装、鞋帽	Garments, Shoes and Hats	101.2	102.5	102.4
四、纺织品	Textiles	97.6	108.5	106.8
五、家用电器及音像器材	Household Appliances, Music and Video Equipment	98.5	100.4	101.1
六、文化办公用品	Cultural and Office Appliances	101.9	102.8	103.3
七、日用品	Articles for Daily Use	100.0	100.4	100.4
八、体育娱乐用品	Sports and Recreation Articles	100.8	101.6	101.1
九、交通、通信用品	Transportation and Communication Appliances	99.4	99.4	99.7
十、家具	Furniture	100.2	99.6	99.6
十一、化妆品	Cosmetics	104.0	103.6	102.3
十二、金银饰品	Gold and Silver Ornaments	109.4	99.7	103.7
十三、中西药品及医疗保健用品	Traditional Chinese and Western Medicines and Health Care Articles	102.0	108.8	107.1
十四、书报杂志及电子出版物	Books, Newspapers, Magazines and Electronic Publications	104.9	104.4	104.4
十五、燃料	Fuels	96.5	96.7	99.4
十六、建筑材料及五金电料	Building Materials and Hardware	100.6	102.8	102.8

3月 March	4月 April	5月 May	6月 June	7月 July	8月 August	9月 September	10月 October	11月 November	12月 December
102.8	102.2	102.0	101.7	102.0	101.6	101.9	102.7	103.8	104.4
106.4	106.4	107.4	108.6	109.2	108.0	110.7	116.8	122.9	120.0
102.9	102.3	101.7	102.1	103.1	103.3	103.1	103.2	103.0	103.2
102.1	101.3	101.1	101.0	101.0	100.4	100.4	100.7	100.7	100.7
103.0	101.3	98.2	87.6	91.5	96.5	94.8	96.9	93.9	94.3
100.2	99.8	99.3	99.4	98.8	98.5	97.4	96.7	94.5	96.2
103.8	102.2	102.6	102.4	103.0	101.8	101.1	100.9	99.2	99.2
100.9	100.8	100.2	99.5	99.6	99.4	100.9	99.4	98.8	99.4
102.4	100.3	101.4	101.7	100.8	99.3	100.7	100.2	100.5	99.9
99.8	98.9	98.9	99.6	101.0	100.1	99.2	98.4	98.7	99.0
101.0	100.9	100.9	100.9	100.9	99.4	98.9	99.7	100.5	100.3
103.9	104.6	105.9	105.6	105.6	105.6	103.9	104.1	101.5	101.4
100.4	102.1	102.5	105.5	108.5	117.4	120.8	122.2	116.4	114.8
102.7	103.1	100.8	101.1	100.9	100.8	100.5	99.7	99.8	99.4
104.6	104.6	104.6	104.6	104.3	103.0	105.0	106.7	106.4	106.1
104.3	101.9	100.6	96.5	94.5	93.4	91.7	89.0	91.5	100.5
102.4	101.3	100.3	100.2	99.6	99.7	99.5	99.1	99.1	100.5

9-5 主要年份零售商品和服务项目年平均价格
Per Retail and Services Price of Major Years

商品名称	Name	规格等级牌 Grade	单位 Unit	1978年	1980年	1985年
面粉	Flour	特一	元/千克 (yuan/kg)	0.50	0.50	0.50
粳米	Japonica	标一	元/千克 (yuan/kg)	0.34	0.34	0.40
小米	Millet	一等	元/千克 (yuan/kg)	0.27	0.27	0.44
土豆	Potato		元/千克 (yuan/kg)	0.19	0.22	0.30
豆腐	Doufu	水豆腐	元/千克 (yuan/kg)	0.16	0.18	0.26
猪肉	Pork	净肉	元/千克 (yuan/kg)	1.72	1.95	2.65
牛肉	Beef	净肉	元/千克 (yuan/kg)	1.26	1.76	2.91
羊肉	Mutton	净肉	元/千克 (yuan/kg)	1.38	1.88	2.80
鸡蛋	Hen's Egg	新鲜完整	元/千克 (yuan/kg)	1.58	2.20	2.60
海带	Kelp	盐干一级	元/千克 (yuan/kg)	1.18	1.26	1.32
大白菜	Chinese Cabbage	一等	元/千克 (yuan/kg)	0.11	0.07	0.09
菠菜	Spinage	一等	元/千克 (yuan/kg)	0.08	0.09	0.28
油菜	Oilseed rape	一等	元/千克 (yuan/kg)	0.05	0.07	0.26
芹菜	Celery	一等	元/千克 (yuan/kg)	1.13	0.11	0.39
韭菜	Chinese Chives	一等	元/千克 (yuan/kg)	0.15	0.16	0.54
黄瓜	Cucumber	一等	元/千克 (yuan/kg)	0.19	0.18	0.47
西红柿	Tomato	一等	元/千克 (yuan/kg)	0.15	0.18	0.53
茄子	Eggplant	一等	元/千克 (yuan/kg)	0.14	0.11	0.27
青椒	Green Pepper	一等	元/千克 (yuan/kg)	0.23	0.20	0.47
大葱	Allium Fistulosum	一等	元/千克 (yuan/kg)	0.11	0.12	0.28
黑木耳	Black Fungus	甲级	元/千克 (yuan/kg)	30.00	32.00	34.86
精盐	Salt	再制盐	元/千克 (yuan/500g)	0.16	0.16	0.14
酱油	Soy Sauce	二级	元/千克 (yuan/kg)	0.22	0.22	0.34
味精	Aginomoto	含麸酸钠80%以上	元/千克 (yuan/kg)	10.80	9.68	12.60
绵白糖	Soft Sugar	国产机制一级	元/千克 (yuan/kg)	1.60	1.70	1.70
红糖	Brown Sugar	一级	元/千克 (yuan/kg)	1.30	1.30	1.30
啤酒	Beer	熟12度瓶装	元/瓶 (yuan/unit)	0.58	0.58	0.73
苹果	Apple	一级	元/千克 (yuan/kg)	0.82	0.90	1.19
桔子	Orange	一级	元/千克 (yuan/kg)	1.30	1.52	2.35
西瓜	Watermelon	一级	元/千克 (yuan/kg)	0.24	0.28	0.32
香蕉	Banana	一级	元/千克 (yuan/kg)	1.46	1.65	1.82
自来水	Tap Water	生活用水	元/吨 (yuan/tons)	0.08	0.08	0.09
照明用电	Lighting Electricity	民用220V	元/度 (yuan/kwh)	0.18	0.18	0.18
平信	Ordinary Mail	外埠	元/封 (yuan/unit)	0.08	0.08	0.08
注射费	Injection Fees	肌肉注射	元/次 (yuan/unit)	0.10	0.10	0.10
住院费	Hospitalization Fees	普通床位	元/天 (yuan/day)			
学杂费	Tuition and Fees	高中学生	元/学期 (yuan/semester)	2.50	2.50	2.50
公园门票	Park Tickets	大明湖	元/张 (yuan/unit)	0.03	0.03	0.03
理发	Haircut	男理一级全活	元/次 (yuan/unit)	0.30	0.30	0.45
洗澡	Bath		元/次 (yuan/unit)	0.24	0.24	0.30
课本	Textbook	高中语文一年级	元/本 (yuan/unit)			
银花	Silver	一等	元/千克 (yuan/kg)	6.65	8.00	18.00

注：1. 大明湖景区2017年开始免费入园。
2. 由于居民消费价格是指数比较，所以理发和洗澡所选的规格品与上年不一致，绝对价格无可比性。
3. 因消费升级，商品和服务规格变化较大，零售商品和服务项目年平均价格自2019年起停止更新。

1990 年	1995 年	2000 年	2005 年	2010 年	2013 年	2014 年	2015 年	2016 年	2017 年	2018 年
0.50	2.24	1.78	2.86	4.14	5.07	5.41	5.43	5.46	5.64	8.54
1.04	3.33	2.03	3.08	4.76	5.91	5.91	6.04	6.05	6.00	6.06
1.32	2.66	2.07	3.26	6.99	8.58	14.10	14.63	10.51	11.49	10.87
0.36	1.48	1.48	1.92	4.53	3.61	3.72	3.80	3.84	3.53	3.84
0.70	1.43	1.55	2.14	4.31	5.21	5.99	6.24	5.97	5.88	6.11
5.52	12.91	12.87	14.90	25.18	33.04	30.57	32.37	35.78	35.49	32.88
5.43	12.06	10.99	16.34	36.47	64.52	65.00	66.58	69.02	69.46	69.25
5.91	15.49	15.04	22.07	44.80	75.33	79.23	76.29	76.85	69.67	79.86
4.96	5.99	3.99	5.72	7.48	8.52	10.87	9.25	8.41	8.18	9.75
3.60	5.35	5.36	8.76	19.29	30.35	33.43	32.50	28.87	27.15	25.51
0.13	0.72	0.91	1.64	3.23	2.77	2.29	2.84	2.80	2.41	2.93
0.50	0.90	1.57	2.21	6.69	7.61	6.53	7.91	8.53	7.41	8.81
0.63	1.11	1.26	1.83	5.05	5.84	5.17	6.43	7.14	6.08	7.46
0.60	1.22	1.25	2.28	4.99	5.46	4.07	5.62	5.06	5.13	5.68
1.01	1.80	1.98	2.99	6.55	7.05	6.47	7.42	5.33	4.97	5.59
0.99	2.45	2.53	3.16	5.67	6.26	5.36	5.96	6.03	5.67	7.53
1.02	2.66	2.07	2.90	6.01	6.60	6.37	7.02	6.97	7.24	7.69
0.89	2.67	2.51	3.07	6.05	6.34	5.60	6.14	6.66	6.14	7.48
1.34	4.13	3.15	4.10	6.45	7.48	6.38	8.07	7.61	7.00	9.03
0.54	1.46	1.31	2.51	6.16	6.95	5.94	6.56	9.59	6.44	6.19
48.95	59.16	68.57	65.13	86.80	121.45	128.14	122.59	118.11	122.67	128.34
0.31	0.70	1.10	2.02	1.50	3.83	3.84	4.28	5.17	5.97	6.18
0.68	1.83	2.40	4.53	6.74	7.04	6.75	6.61	7.14	7.05	8.69
16.50	22.81	14.26	15.67	19.33	21.02	21.34	22.19	21.94	22.56	22.92
2.60	6.89	6.12	5.43	9.75	15.15	15.89	16.08	14.38	14.25	15.39
2.21	6.32	5.90	5.54	9.80	15.62	15.54	14.70	15.68	18.29	21.07
1.41	2.13	2.30	2.42	2.61	2.68	2.77	2.76	2.72	2.49	2.62
2.48	3.86	2.72	3.19	8.93	12.04	14.96	15.11	10.86	11.86	11.85
2.27	3.37	2.35	3.30	7.45	10.29	11.97	9.06	10.72	13.86	11.96
0.58	3.20	2.70	3.06	4.72	5.56	5.88	5.57	5.16	5.60	5.26
2.93	4.78	4.05	4.02	6.39	7.28	9.70	7.01	7.04	6.63	8.24
0.19	0.51	1.60	2.78	3.15	3.15	3.15	4.00	4.21	4.21	4.21
0.18	0.29	0.43	0.53	0.55	0.55	0.56	0.56	0.56	0.56	0.56
0.13	0.20	0.80	0.80	1.20	1.20	1.20	1.20	1.20	1.20	1.20
0.20	0.25	1.67	2.00	2.00	2.00	2.00	2.00	2.00	2.00	2.00
2.50	4.00	7.67	15.00	26.67	26.67	23.33	23.33	33.89	36.67	36.67
12.00	49.00	600.00	800.00	800.00	800.00	800.00	800.00	800.00	800.00	800.00
0.30	4.33	13.48	15.63	30.00	30.00	30.00	30.00	30.00		
1.30	5.63	10.00	17.50	20.50	25.00	25.21	25.21	32.38	25.10	27.70
0.58	5.00	8.00	12.00	30.00	38.00	53.00	58.00	58.00	68.00	68.00
2.00	2.55	6.41	4.60	6.47	6.47	6.47	6.47	6.47	6.44	6.39
28.00	70.00	93.00	87.22	325.00	314.10	361.17	352.71	325.00	324.39	403.83

Note: 1. Daming Lake Scenic spot has been free since 2017.
2. Because the consumer price of residents is an index comparison, the standard products selected for haircut and bath are inconsistent with the previous year, and the absolute price is incomparable."
3. Because of consumption upgrading and large exchanges in commodity and service specifications, the annual average price of retail commodity and service items has not been updated since 2019.

9-6 工业生产者出厂价格总指数(2019年，以上月价格为100)
Producer Price Index for Manufactured Goods (2019,Preceding Last Month=100)

项目名称	Indicator	1月 January	2月 February	3月 March
总指数	Total Price Indices	99.4	100.0	100.1
核心指数	Core Indices	99.4	99.8	99.9
高技术	High Technology	100.3	100.4	98.8
能源	Energy	98.3	101.8	102.4
(一)按轻重工业分	By Light and Heavy Industry			
(1)轻工业	Light Industry	100.2	99.6	100.5
1.以农产品为原料	Agricultural Products as Raw Materials	100.4	99.6	100.1
2.以非农产品为原料	Non-agricultural Products as Raw Materials	100.1	99.6	101.0
(2)重工业	Heavy Industry	99.2	100.2	100.0
1.采掘	Mining	100.0	100.0	100.0
2.原料	Raw Materials	98.7	101.9	100.6
3.加工	Processing	99.3	99.7	99.9
(二)按生产生活资料分	By Means of Production and Consumer Goods			
(1)生产资料	Means of Production	99.1	100.1	100.1
1.采掘	Mining	100.0	100.0	100.0
2.原料	Raw Materials	98.5	101.5	101.1
3.加工	Processing	99.3	99.8	99.9
(2)生活资料	Consumer Goods	100.7	99.8	100.1
1.食品	Food	100.9	100.1	99.2
2.衣着	Clothing	101.0	99.0	100.0
3.一般日用品	Articles for Daily Use	100.8	100.0	100.3
4.耐用消费品	Durable Consumer Goods	99.8	98.8	102.4
(三)按初级中间最终产品分	By Primary, Intermediate and Final Products			
(1)初级产品	Primary Products	100.0	100.0	100.0
1.矿产品	Minerals	100.0	100.0	100.0
2.废料	Scrap			
(2)中间产品	Intermediate Products	99.1	100.2	100.1
(3)最终产品	Final Products	99.4	100.1	100.3
1.最终投资品	Investment Goods	99.0	100.2	100.3
2.最终消费品	Consumer Goods	100.6	99.7	100.2
(四)按工业门类分	Classification by Industrial Category			
(1)采矿业	Mining	100.0	100.0	100.0
(2)制造业	Manufacture	99.3	100.1	100.1
(3)电力、燃气及水生产和供应业	Production and Supply of Electric, Gas and Wate	100.6	99.4	100.2
(五)按工业部门分	By Industrial Department			
(1)冶金工业	Metallurgical Industry	96.3	99.4	100.7
(2)电力工业	Power Industry	100.0	99.3	100.3
(3)煤炭及炼焦工业	Coal Industry			
(4)石油工业	Petroleum Industry	97.2	103.4	103.7
(5)化学工业	Chemical Industry	99.5	100.9	98.7
(6)机械工业	Machine Building Industry	99.6	99.7	100.0
(7)建筑材料工业	Building Materials Industry	102.5	100.9	101.2
(8)森林工业	Timber Industry	100.0	100.0	100.0
(9)食品工业	Food Industry	100.9	99.8	100.2
(10)纺织工业	Textile Industry	99.6	100.3	99.7
(11)缝纫工业	Tailoring Industry	101.0	99.0	100.0
(12)皮革工业	Leather Industry			
(13)造纸工业	Paper Industry	94.6	93.8	100.0
(14)文教艺术用品工业	Industry of Cultural, Educational & Handicrafts Articles	99.5	100.4	97.8
(15)其它工业	Others	100.3	99.1	99.7

4月 April	5月 May	6月 June	7月 July	8月 August	9月 September	10月 October	11月 November	12月 December
100.6	100.1	99.7	99.8	100.2	100.5	100.4	100.1	99.8
100.6	100.0	99.8	100.0	100.0	100.3	100.1	100.0	99.8
102.3	100.0	98.3	100.1	100.0	100.7	99.7	99.8	99.8
101.7	101.5	98.5	98.0	100.4	99.3	100.5	100.0	100.2
99.8	99.6	100.4	100.1	101.0	101.7	101.4	100.5	99.3
99.6	99.3	100.7	100.2	101.4	102.7	102.5	100.8	99.1
100.2	100.1	100.0	100.0	100.4	100.5	99.8	100.3	99.6
100.8	100.2	99.6	99.8	100.0	100.2	100.2	100.0	99.9
100.0	100.0	100.0	100.0	100.0	100.0	100.0	100.0	100.0
101.0	100.7	98.8	98.8	99.7	99.6	101.0	99.8	99.7
100.8	100.0	99.8	100.0	100.1	100.3	100.0	100.1	100.0
100.7	100.2	99.6	99.8	100.0	100.2	100.2	100.0	99.9
100.0	100.0	100.0	100.0	100.0	100.0	100.0	100.0	100.0
101.1	100.9	98.7	98.5	100.3	99.5	100.7	99.7	99.7
100.6	100.0	99.9	100.1	99.9	100.3	100.1	100.1	100.0
100.3	99.7	100.2	100.1	101.0	101.8	101.5	100.4	99.3
100.7	99.1	100.6	100.4	101.8	103.4	103.6	100.8	98.9
100.0	100.0	100.4	99.8	101.3	99.8	100.2	99.8	99.6
100.2	100.1	99.8	100.2	99.8	100.8	99.9	100.0	100.0
99.9	100.1	100.1	99.0	101.5	100.3	99.7	100.1	99.1
100.0	100.0	100.0	100.0	100.0	100.0	100.0	100.0	100.0
100.0	100.0	100.0	100.0	100.0	100.0	100.0	100.0	100.0
100.8	100.2	99.6	99.8	100.1	100.6	100.6	100.3	99.8
100.6	100.1	99.9	99.9	100.3	100.6	100.4	100.2	99.9
100.7	100.3	99.7	99.8	100.1	100.3	100.2	100.2	100.0
100.5	99.6	100.2	100.1	100.9	101.4	101.2	100.3	99.4
100.0	100.0	100.0	100.0	100.0	100.0	100.0	100.0	100.0
100.6	100.1	99.7	99.8	100.2	100.5	100.5	100.1	99.8
101.2	99.6	100.1	99.9	100.3	99.8	100.1	99.9	99.9
100.4	100.8	99.8	100.6	100.1	100.4	100.8	100.1	99.6
101.4	99.5	100.1	99.8	100.4	99.8	100.2	99.9	99.9
101.8	102.7	97.5	96.9	100.3	99.0	100.7	100.0	100.4
100.5	99.9	99.2	99.7	99.2	100.2	100.8	99.3	99.6
100.9	100.0	99.7	100.1	100.1	100.4	99.8	100.0	100.1
100.2	100.1	101.7	99.9	100.7	101.0	100.8	102.3	100.1
100.0	100.0	100.0	100.0	100.0	100.0	100.0	100.0	100.0
99.6	99.0	101.2	100.4	101.9	103.7	103.6	101.2	98.8
100.3	100.1	99.4	99.7	99.9	100.6	99.8	99.6	100.2
100.0	100.0	100.4	99.8	101.3	99.8	100.2	99.8	99.6
95.7	98.9	97.9	100.1	99.4	97.6	98.1	99.5	100.0
99.1	100.2	100.1	100.1	100.3	101.0	99.8	99.4	96.9
99.2	99.3	100.6	99.5	100.2	99.6	99.9	100.1	99.4

9-7 工业生产者出厂价格总指数（2019 年，以上年同期价格为 100）

Producer Price Index for Manufactured Goods(2019,Preceding Last Year=100)

项目名称	Indicator	全年 Total	1月 January	2月 February
总指数	Total Price Indices	100.3	100.3	100.3
核心指数	Core Indices	100.3	100.8	100.6
高技术	High Technology	99.9	101.4	101.6
能源	Energy	98.3	97.4	98.0
㈠按轻重工业分	By Light and Heavy Industry			
⑴轻工业	Light Industry	102.4	101.4	101.6
1.以农产品为原料	Agricultural Products as Raw Materials	103.4	101.1	102.3
2.以非农产品为原料	Non-agricultural Products as Raw Materials	101.0	101.8	100.8
⑵重工业	Heavy Industry	99.8	100.1	100.0
1.采掘	Mining	100.0	100.0	100.0
2.原料	Raw Materials	97.7	96.3	97.8
3.加工	Processing	100.4	101.1	100.7
㈡按生产生活资料分	By Means of Production and Consumer Goods			
⑴生产资料	Means of Production	99.7	100.1	100.0
1.采掘	Mining	100.0	100.0	100.0
2.原料	Raw Materials	97.5	95.7	96.9
3.加工	Processing	100.3	101.1	100.7
⑵生活资料	Consumer Goods	103.2	101.7	102.1
1.食品	Food	104.3	99.1	101.4
2.衣着	Clothing	105.0	107.1	106.1
3.一般日用品	Articles for Daily Use	102.2	104.3	103.4
4.耐用消费品	Durable Consumer Goods	102.1	101.0	100.1
㈢按初级中间最终产品分	By Primary 、Intermediate and Final Products			
⑴初级产品	Primary Products	100.0	100.0	100.0
1.矿产品	Minerals	100.0	100.0	100.0
2.废料	Scrap			
⑵中间产品	Intermediate Products	100.2	100.5	100.5
⑶最终产品	Final Products	100.5	100.4	100.4
1.最终投资品	Investment Goods	99.9	100.0	99.9
2.最终消费品	Consumer Goods	102.7	101.7	101.6
㈣按工业门类分	Classification by Industrial Category			
⑴采矿业	Mining	100.0	100.0	100.0
⑵制造业	Manufacture	100.2	100.2	100.3
⑶电力、燃气及水生产和供应业	Production and Supply of Electric, Gas and Wate	101.3	102.5	100.3
㈤按工业部门分	By Industrial Department			
⑴冶金工业	Metallurgical Industry	98.4	98.0	97.7
⑵电力工业	Power Industry	99.9	101.0	98.4
⑶煤炭及炼焦工业	Coal Industry			
⑷石油工业	Petroleum Industry	97.6	95.4	97.8
⑸化学工业	Chemical Industry	98.2	99.0	99.8
⑹机械工业	Machine Building Industry	100.0	100.5	100.0
⑺建筑材料工业	Building Materials Industry	117.1	116.4	117.1
⑻森林工业	Timber Industry	98.9	96.8	96.8
⑼食品工业	Food Industry	105.3	100.1	102.2
⑽纺织工业	Textile Industry	102.4	103.7	105.2
⑾缝纫工业	Tailoring Industry	105.0	107.1	106.1
⑿皮革工业	Leather Industry			
⒀造纸工业	Paper Industry	81.0	97.4	89.3
⒁文教艺术用品工业	Industry of Cultural, Educational & Handicrafts Articles	97.8	99.7	99.9
⒂其它工业	Others	98.0	99.5	98.9

3月 March	4月 April	5月 May	6月 June	7月 July	8月 August	9月 September	10月 October	11月 November	12月 December
100.7	101.0	100.9	99.8	99.9	100.0	100.0	99.9	99.9	100.8
100.5	101.0	101.1	99.8	100.2	100.0	100.0	99.8	99.6	99.8
100.3	101.6	101.1	97.7	98.4	98.6	98.6	100.0	100.0	100.0
102.5	102.7	101.7	99.7	96.9	96.9	94.4	92.2	95.6	102.4
101.8	101.2	100.5	100.6	100.7	102.5	104.3	105.5	103.9	104.3
102.3	101.7	100.8	101.6	101.4	103.7	106.2	108.4	105.4	106.4
101.2	100.6	100.2	99.5	100.0	101.0	102.0	101.8	101.8	101.5
100.4	101.0	101.0	99.6	99.7	99.5	99.1	98.6	99.0	100.1
100.0	100.0	100.0	100.0	100.0	100.0	100.0	100.0	100.0	100.0
100.4	100.4	99.7	98.6	97.8	96.9	95.2	94.2	95.8	100.2
100.4	101.2	101.4	99.9	100.2	100.2	100.2	99.9	99.9	100.0
100.4	100.9	100.9	99.5	99.5	99.3	98.9	98.5	98.8	100.0
100.0	100.0	100.0	100.0	100.0	100.0	100.0	100.0	100.0	100.0
100.0	100.2	99.5	98.4	97.4	97.1	95.2	93.8	95.5	100.3
100.5	101.0	101.2	99.8	100.0	99.9	99.8	99.7	99.7	99.9
102.1	101.9	101.3	101.5	101.7	103.5	105.5	106.8	105.1	105.0
100.8	101.3	100.7	102.0	102.1	105.5	108.6	111.9	108.3	109.7
105.3	105.5	105.2	105.6	105.1	105.9	106.0	106.2	101.3	100.8
103.3	102.4	100.9	99.9	101.0	101.1	102.6	102.8	102.9	101.8
102.0	101.9	102.8	102.8	101.8	103.4	103.8	102.7	102.0	100.7
100.0	100.0	100.0	100.0	100.0	100.0	100.0	100.0	100.0	100.0
100.0	100.0	100.0	100.0	100.0	100.0	100.0	100.0	100.0	100.0
100.9	101.3	101.2	99.4	99.5	99.6	99.5	99.4	100.0	101.1
100.8	101.1	101.0	99.9	99.8	100.2	100.4	100.4	100.6	101.5
100.5	100.9	101.0	99.5	99.3	99.3	99.1	98.8	99.4	100.6
101.6	101.7	101.0	101.4	101.6	103.1	104.6	105.6	104.1	104.2
100.0	100.0	100.0	100.0	100.0	100.0	100.0	100.0	100.0	100.0
100.7	101.0	100.9	99.7	99.8	99.9	99.9	99.8	99.9	100.8
100.6	101.5	100.8	101.5	101.9	102.0	101.6	101.3	100.8	101.2
98.1	98.0	99.0	98.4	98.8	98.4	98.3	98.4	98.7	99.1
98.7	99.7	98.9	99.7	100.2	100.6	100.1	100.8	100.1	100.6
104.9	104.6	103.6	99.9	95.3	95.1	91.6	88.2	93.4	103.6
99.0	99.1	98.4	97.2	98.6	97.8	97.5	97.4	96.6	97.5
100.0	100.8	100.9	99.0	99.4	99.6	99.9	100.0	100.0	100.2
117.5	118.8	120.1	120.7	118.5	118.5	117.5	114.5	114.6	112.0
96.8	96.8	100.0	100.0	100.0	100.0	100.0	100.0	100.0	100.0
102.6	102.0	101.3	103.2	102.9	106.3	109.9	113.0	109.4	110.8
104.9	105.8	103.2	101.8	101.5	101.4	101.8	101.6	98.8	99.1
105.3	105.5	105.2	105.6	105.1	105.9	106.0	106.2	101.3	100.8
87.2	81.5	81.4	77.9	78.3	76.5	75.3	75.2	76.2	78.0
98.1	97.2	97.2	97.1	97.2	97.5	98.6	98.2	97.8	94.6
97.7	97.5	97.3	98.9	99.0	98.9	97.7	97.0	96.5	97.0

9-8 工业生产者购进价格指数(2019 年，以上月价格为 100)

Purchasing Price Index for Industrial Producers(2019，Preceding Last Month=100)

项目名称	Category	1 月 January	2 月 February	3 月 March	4 月 April
总指数	Total Price Indices	97.8	99.6	100.5	100.3
(一)按初级中间最终产品分	By Primary and Intermediate Products				
(1)初级产品	Primary Products	93.6	98.6	102.9	100.6
1.农产品	Farm Produce	99.5	100.3	99.3	99.0
2.矿产品	Minerals	92.0	98.1	103.9	101.1
3.废料	Scrap				
(2)中间产品	Intermediate Products	99.2	99.9	99.8	100.2
(二)九大类原材料购进价格指数	By Nine Categories of Raw Material				
(1)燃料、动力类	Fuel and Power	95.8	98.8	101.7	101.4
(2)黑色金属材料类	Ferrous Metals	98.4	99.5	99.8	100.4
1.钢材	Steel	100.0	99.2	99.3	101.3
2.其它	Others	96.8	99.9	100.3	99.6
(3)有色金属材料及电线类	Nonferrous Metals	99.3	99.7	101.3	99.8
(4)化工原料类	Raw Chemical Materials	96.7	102.2	99.7	99.9
(5)木材及纸浆类	Timber and Paper Pulp	95.7	100.7	99.2	96.3
(6)建筑材料及非金属类	Building Materials and Nonmetal Ores	102.4	99.3	99.2	98.8
(7)其它工业原材料及半成品类	Other Industrial Raw Materials and Semi-finished Products	99.7	99.9	99.9	99.8
(8)农副产品类	Agricultural Products	99.5	100.3	99.3	99.0
(9)纺织原料类	Textile Materials	99.4	100.1	99.9	99.8

5月 May	6月 June	7月 July	8月 August	9月 September	10月 October	11月 November	12月 December
100.0	99.9	99.1	100.0	98.9	100.4	99.5	99.0
101.5	101.9	95.6	100.6	98.2	101.5	99.8	100.1
101.3	103.2	101.2	101.4	100.5	100.8	99.5	99.2
101.6	101.5	94.1	100.4	97.5	101.6	99.9	100.4
99.5	99.3	100.3	99.7	99.1	100.1	99.4	98.6
100.2	100.6	97.0	99.9	97.8	100.6	98.4	97.7
100.9	99.7	100.6	100.0	98.5	99.9	99.2	100.2
100.6	100.3	100.5	99.6	99.5	100.4	99.6	100.3
101.3	99.2	100.7	100.4	97.4	99.3	98.8	100.2
99.4	98.5	99.4	99.1	99.5	100.5	100.0	99.9
95.5	95.9	101.2	97.8	99.0	99.7	101.5	98.1
98.1	96.3	98.3	99.5	99.4	100.3	99.8	101.3
101.8	100.9	101.3	100.4	99.6	99.8	101.8	100.1
100.2	99.6	100.1	100.4	100.2	100.8	100.3	99.4
101.3	103.2	101.2	101.4	100.5	100.8	99.5	99.2
99.9	100.3	99.9	100.1	98.2	99.9	99.9	102.8

9-9 工业生产者购进价格指数(2019年，以上年同期价格为100)

Purchasing Price Index for Industrial Producers(2019,Preceding Last Year=100)

项目名称	Category	全年 Total	1月 January	2月 February	3月 March	4月 April
总指数	Total Price Indices	98.6	101.6	100.6	101.6	102.3
(一)按初级中间最终产品分	By Primary and Intermediate Products					
(1)初级产品	Primary Products	98.0	102.9	98.6	104.8	107.2
1.农产品	Farm Produce	103.2	100.4	100.8	99.8	97.7
2.矿产品	Minerals	96.5	103.3	97.8	105.8	109.5
3.废料	Scrap					
(2)中间产品	Intermediate Products	98.7	101.0	101.1	100.4	100.5
(二)九大类原材料购进价格指数	By Nine Categories of Raw Material					
(1)燃料、动力类	Fuel and Power	97.9	103.4	99.7	102.8	105.7
(2)黑色金属材料类	Ferrous Metals	96.7	96.9	97.1	96.7	97.9
1.钢材	Steel	98.2	99.2	98.5	97.3	98.8
2.其它	Others	95.1	94.7	95.7	96.2	97.1
(3)有色金属材料及电线类	Nonferrous Metals	96.0	95.0	94.4	96.8	98.7
(4)化工原料类	Raw Chemical Materials	89.6	91.6	96.1	95.6	96.5
(5)木材及纸浆类	Timber and Paper Pulp	89.5	104.8	104.2	101.8	96.7
(6)建筑材料及非金属类	Building Materials and Nonmetal Ores	108.9	109.8	109.1	106.2	107.5
(7)其它工业原材料及半成品类	Other Industrial Raw Materials and Semi-finished Products	101.7	104.1	104.4	104.5	101.8
(8)农副产品类	Agricultural Products	103.2	100.4	100.8	99.8	97.7
(9)纺织原料类	Textile Materials	99.2	99.5	99.8	100.1	100.2

5月 May	6月 June	7月 July	8月 August	9月 September	10月 October	11月 November	12月 December
101.7	100.0	98.9	97.9	96.2	94.9	93.2	95.1
105.7	102.0	96.3	95.0	93.3	91.6	88.1	94.5
100.4	103.0	104.6	105.6	106.0	107.4	107.0	105.3
106.8	101.6	94.0	92.3	90.1	87.9	83.9	91.7
100.4	99.4	99.7	98.9	97.1	96.1	95.0	95.3
104.4	102.1	97.9	96.5	94.5	92.3	88.1	90.2
98.3	97.6	98.1	96.9	94.2	94.5	94.6	97.2
98.7	98.5	98.4	97.6	96.6	97.3	97.7	100.5
97.9	96.6	97.8	96.3	91.8	91.7	91.6	94.0
97.7	94.9	94.2	96.1	96.8	95.1	96.0	96.4
93.7	86.6	92.7	88.8	85.2	81.7	80.7	87.8
88.9	85.6	82.1	81.8	81.7	82.6	83.1	85.7
112.2	113.5	111.1	112.0	109.1	105.9	106.2	105.4
101.8	101.3	101.0	100.6	100.1	100.3	100.4	100.3
100.4	103.0	104.6	105.6	106.0	107.4	107.0	105.3
99.5	99.2	100.3	100.0	97.9	96.8	97.2	100.0

9-10 住宅销售价格指数(2019年，以上月价格为100)

Sales Price of Residential Buildings(2019,Preceding Last Month=100)

指 标	Indicator	1月 January	2月 February	3月 March	4月 April	5月 May	6月 June
新建住宅	New Residential Buildings	100.4	100.6	100.8	101.0	100.4	100.3
新建商品住宅	New Commercial Residential Buildings	100.4	100.6	100.8	101.0	100.4	100.3
90平方米及以下	Buildings below 90sq.m	100.6	100.0	100.5	100.5	100.5	100.0
90-144平方米	Buildings 90-144 sq.m	100.3	100.6	100.9	101.1	100.4	100.4
144平方米以上	Buildings above 144sq.m	100.5	100.6	100.9	100.8	100.3	100.4
二手住宅	Second-hand House	100.6	100.4	100.5	99.7	99.8	99.8
90平方米及以下	Buildings below 90sq.m	100.8	100.4	100.7	99.9	100.2	100.0
90-144平方米	Buildings 90-144 sq.m	100.3	100.5	100.3	99.3	99.4	99.8
144平方米以上	Buildings above 144sq.m	100.7	100.5	100.4	100.0	99.9	99.0

9-10 续表 continued

指 标	Indicator	7月 July	8月 August	9月 September	10月 October	11月 November	12月 December
新建住宅	New Residential Buildings	100.3	99.8	99.6	99.0	99.3	99.2
新建商品住宅	New Commercial Residential Buildings	100.3	99.8	99.6	99.0	99.3	99.2
90平方米及以下	Buildings below 90sq.m	100.4	100.4	100.0	99.2	100.1	100.3
90-144平方米	Buildings 90-144 sq.m	100.3	100.4	99.5	98.8	99.0	99.0
144平方米以上	Buildings above 144sq.m	100.3	100.0	100.0	99.5	99.9	99.3
二手住宅	Second-hand House	99.9	99.1	99.7	99.3	99.4	99.7
90平方米及以下	Buildings below 90sq.m	100.1	98.5	99.2	99.5	99.4	99.5
90-144平方米	Buildings 90-144 sq.m	99.7	99.5	100.1	99.1	99.3	99.9
144平方米以上	Buildings above 144sq.m	100.0	99.7	100.4	99.6	99.5	99.7

9-11 住宅销售价格指数 (2019 年，以上年同期价格为 100)
Sales Price of Residential Buildings (2019,Preceding Last Year=100)

指 标	Indicator	1 月 January	2 月 February	3 月 March	4 月 April	5 月 May	6 月 June
新建住宅	New Residential Buildings	115.7	116.4	117.2	118.2	118.3	114.5
新建商品住宅	New Commercial Residential Buildings	115.7	116.4	117.2	118.2	118.3	114.5
90 平方米及以下	Buildings below 90sq.m	117.2	117.1	117.5	117.9	118.1	113.5
90–144 平方米	Buildings 90–144 sq.m	115.4	116.3	117.1	118.3	118.3	114.9
144 平方米以上	Buildings above 144sq.m	115.8	116.4	117.3	118.0	118.1	113.9
二手住宅	Second-hand House	111.2	111.6	111.8	111.3	110.5	109.3
90 平方米及以下	Buildings below 90sq.m	110.6	111.2	111.7	111.2	111.1	109.9
90–144 平方米	Buildings 90–144 sq.m	111.6	111.9	111.8	111.1	109.8	108.5
144 平方米以上	Buildings above 144sq.m	111.5	112.1	112.1	112.0	111.2	109.5

9-11 续表 continued

指 标	Indicator	7 月 July	8 月 August	9 月 September	10 月 October	11 月 November	12 月 December
新建住宅	New Residential Buildings	111.6	108.2	106.4	104.6	102.1	100.5
新建商品住宅	New Commercial Residential Buildings	111.6	108.2	106.4	104.6	102.1	100.5
90 平方米及以下	Buildings below 90sq.m	110.2	107.3	106.5	104.7	103.0	102.4
90–144 平方米	Buildings 90–144 sq.m	112.0	108.4	106.1	104.2	101.5	99.7
144 平方米以上	Buildings above 144sq.m	110.9	108.3	107.4	105.7	103.7	102.4
二手住宅	Second-hand House	106.5	102.6	101.1	99.9	98.7	98.0
90 平方米及以下	Buildings below 90sq.m	107.5	103.5	101.8	100.7	99.2	98.2
90–144 平方米	Buildings 90–144 sq.m	105.2	101.5	100.0	98.5	97.7	97.3
144 平方米以上	Buildings above 144sq.m	107.1	103.4	102.3	101.5	100.4	99.4

9-12 主要年份工业生产者出厂、购进价格指数（以上年价格为 100）
Purchasing Price Index for Industrial Producers and Producer Price Index for Manufactured Goods in Main Years (Preceding Last Year=100)

年份 Year	工业生产者出厂价格指数 Producer Price Indices for Industrial Products	工业生产者购进价格指数 Industrial Producer Purchasing Price Indices
1998	94.5	95.2
1999	98.9	97.6
2000	104.8	114.5
2001	99.8	101.4
2002	97.9	100.4
2003	103.2	111.2
2004	106.7	116.4
2005	102.3	111.3
2006	100.2	105.6
2007	103.9	105.0
2008	109.2	116.9
2009	96.2	94.3
2010	104.7	109.9
2011	105.3	108.2
2012	98.4	99.4
2013	98.8	97.8
2014	99.0	98.0
2015	95.0	92.7
2016	99.8	99.0
2017	105.7	113.9
2018	104.8	108.3
2019	100.3	98.6

主要统计指标解释

居民消费价格　是指城乡居民购买并用于日常生活消费的商品和服务项目的价格。

居民消费价格指数　是反映一定时期内城乡居民所购买的生活消费品价格和服务项目价格变动趋势和程度的相对数，是对城市居民消费价格指数和农村居民消费价格指数进行综合汇总计算的结果。利用居民消费价格指数，可以观察和分析消费品的零售价格和服务价格变动对城乡居民实际生活费支出的影响程度。

调查内容是城乡居民购买并用于日常生活消费的商品和服务项目的价格。调查内容根据全国城乡居民家庭消费支出调查资料以及居民消费结构和消费习惯确定,按用途划分为8个大类，262个基本分类，包括食品烟酒、衣着、居住、生活用品及服务、交通和通信、教育文化和娱乐、医疗保健、其他用品和服务。

商品零售价格　是商品在流通过程中最后一个环节的价格，是工业、商业、餐饮业和其他零售企业向城乡居民、机关团体出售生活消费品和办公用品的价格。

商品零售价格指数　是反映一定时期内城乡商品零售价格变动趋势和程度的相对数。商品零售价格的变动与国家的财政收入、市场供需的平衡、消费与积累的比例关系有关。因此，该指数可以从一个侧面对上述经济活动进行观察和分析。

调查内容是工业、商业、餐饮业和其他行业的零售商品以及农民对非农业居民出售商品的价格。包括食品、饮料烟酒、服装鞋帽、纺织品、家用电器及音像器材、文化办公用品、日用品、体育娱乐用品、交通通信用品、家具、化妆品、金银饰品、中西药品及医疗保健用品、书报杂志及电子出版物、燃料、建筑材料及五金电料等16个大类，197个基本分类的商品零售价格。

工业生产者价格　工业生产者价格包括工业企业产品第一次出售时的出厂价格和企业作为中间投入的原材料、燃料、动力购进价格（简称工业生产者购进价格）。工业生产者价格调查的目的在于及时、准确、科学地反映各工业行业产品价格水平及其变动趋势和幅度，为国民经济核算、计算工业发展速度、宏观经济分析和调控、理顺价格体系等提供科学、准确的依据。

工业生产者价格指数　是由工业生产者出厂价格指数和工业生产者购进价格指数两部分组成。

工业生产者出厂价格指数　是反映一定时期内全部工业产品第一次出售时的出厂价格总水平的变动趋势和变动幅度的相对数。

工业生产者购进价格指数　是反映作为中间投入的原材料、燃料、动力购进价格总水平的变动趋势和变动幅度的相对数。

住宅销售价格　指房产所有权转移时买卖双方实际成交的价格(合同价格)。房产买卖时，买房人购买的是房产的所有权，卖房人将房产所有权出让，同时要获得房产所有权出让的价格补偿。它主要包括新建住宅销售和二手住宅销售两部分。

住宅销售价格指数　是综合反映住宅商品价格总体变化趋势和变化幅度的相对数。各市住宅销售价格指数是由新建住宅销售价格指数和二手住宅销售价格指数组成。

Explanatory Notes on Main Statistical Indicators

Consumer Price refers to the price of goods and services purchased and used for daily life consumption by urban and rural residents.

Consumer Price index reflects the trend and degree of changes in prices of consumer goods and services purchased by urban households during a given period. It is the result after comprehensive summary and calculation of urban consumer price index and rural consumer price index. It can be used to observe and analyze the impact of price changes in consumer goods and services on the actual expenditure of urban and rural residents.

The investigation content is the price of goods and services purchased and used for daily life consumption by urban and rural residents. The investigation content is confirmed pursuant to survey data regarding national urban and rural residents' household consumption expenditure and resident consumption structure as well as consumption habit which is divided into 8 categories (262 basic types) as per purpose, including food, alcohol and tobacco, clothing, housing, daily necessities and services, transportation and communication, education, culture and entertainment, health care and other goods and services.

Retail Price refers to the prices in the last link of the production circulation process. It is the prices that industrial, commercial, catering and other retail enterprises sell daily consumer goods and products for office use to urban and rural residents and institutions and social organizations.

Retail Price Indices reflect the trend and degree of change in retail prices of commodities during a given period. The change in retail prices of commodities is related to government revenue, the equilibrium of market supply and demand, and the ratio of consumption to accumulation. Therefore, the retail price indices are useful from an oblique perspective for observing and analyzing the changes of the above economic activities.

The research content involves the prices of retail goods in industry, business, catering and other industries as well as the prices of goods sold by the farmer to the non–agricultural residents, including the commodities of 16 categories (including 197 basic types) -- food, beverage alcohol & tobacco, clothing & shoes, textile, household appliances and audio & video equipment, cultural & office goods, daily necessities, sports & entertainment goods, transportation & communication supplies, furniture, cosmetics, gold & silver accessories, traditional Chinese and western medicines & healthcare supplies, newspapers & magazines and electronic publications, fuel, building materials & hardware.

Industrial Producer Price covers the ex–factory price when products of industrial enterprises are sold for the first time and the purchase price (called as industrial producer purchase price for short) of raw materials, fuels and power which are intermediate inputs of the enterprise. The investigation of industrial producer price is aimed at timely, accurately and scientifically reflecting the price level of products and the corresponding trend and range of changing in various industries, and providing scientific and accurate basis for national economic accounting, computing industry development speed, macroeconomic analysis and regulation and straightening out the price system, etc.

Industrial Producer Price Index is constituted by Producer Price Indices for Industrial Products and Purchasing Price Indices for Industrial Producers.

Producer Price Indices for Industrial Products reflect the trend and degree of changes in general ex–factory prices of all manufactured goods for first sale during a given period.

Purchasing Price Indices for Industrial Producers reflect changes in the level and degree of purchasing prices such as intermediate input such as raw materials, fuels and power.

The Sales Price of Residential refers to the actual price (contract price) of the transaction between the buyer and the seller when the house ownership is transferred. When the house property is sold, the house buyer purchases the ownership of the house property and the house seller transfers the ownership of the house property with price compensation for house property ownership transfer obtained at the same time. Housing sales mainly include sales of newly built house and sales of second–hand house.

Price Index for Residential reflects the trend and degree of changes in prices of real estate. The price index for real estate is constituted by the price index for the new houses and the price index for the second–hand house.

10

人民生活

PEOPLE′ S LIVELIHOOD

10-1 人民物质文化生活提高情况
Improvement in People`s Material and Cultural Life

指　　标	Indicator	单位 Unit	1978 年	1990 年
就　业	Employment			
每一农村劳动力负担人数	Average Dependents Per Labor Force	人 (person)	1.70	1.61
每一城镇就业者负担人数	Dependents Per Urban Employee	人 (person)	1.89	1.72
城镇登记失业率	Registered Urban Unemployment Rate	%(%)		
收入与支出	Income and Expenditure			
农村居民人均可支配收入	Per Capita Disposable Income of Rural Inhabitant	元 (yuan)	111	731
农村居民人均生活消费支出	Per Capita Consumer Expenditure of Rural Inhabitant	元 (yuan)	83	570
农村居民恩格尔系数	Engel's Coefficient of Rural Inhabitant	%(%)	69.9	50.5
城镇居民人均可支配收入	Per Capita Disposable Income of Urban Inhabitant	元 (yuan)	338	1620
城镇居民人均生活消费支出	Per Capita Consumer Expenditure of Urban Inhabitant	元 (yuan)	318	1360
城镇居民恩格尔系数	Engel's Coefficient of Urban Inhabitant	%(%)	57.1	57.5
居民储蓄	Household Savings			
城乡居民年末储蓄存款余额	Deposits of Urban and Rural Residents	亿元 (100 million yuan)	1.3	51.1
人均储蓄存款余额	Per Capita Savings Balance	元 (yuan)	28.5	975.5
住房面积	Area of Building			
农村人均住房建筑面积	Rural Per Capita Living Space	平方米 (sq.m)	9.6	22.5
城镇人均住房建筑面积	Urban Per Capita Living Space	平方米 (sq.m)	4.1	7.5
交通通讯	Traffic and Communication			
农村每百户拥有摩托车	Number of Motorcycles Owned by Per 100 Rural Households	辆 (unit)		4.0
城市每百户拥有摩托车	Number of Motorcycles Owned by Per 100 Urban Households	辆 (unit)		7.7
城市公用事业	Urban Utilities			
城市人口用水普及率	Urban Water Penetration Rate	%(%)	99	100
每万人拥有公园绿地面积	Green Area of Park Per 10000 Population	公顷 (ha)	1.6	4
文化生活	Culture Life			
城市每百户拥有彩色电视机	Number of Color TV Sets Owned by Per 100 Rural Households	台 (set)	-	61.3
农村每百户拥有彩色电视机	Number of Color TV Sets Owned by Per 100 Urban Households	台 (set)	-	70.0
教育卫生	Education and Public Health			
每万人口中在校大学生数	Number of College Students Per 10 000 Population	人 (person)	22	71
每万人拥有卫生技术人员	Number of Health Technical Personnel Per 10 000 Population	人 (person)	10.98	59.45
每万人拥有医院病床	Number of Beds of Hospitals and Health Centers Per 10 000 Population	张 (unit)	22.01	32.88

注：1. “城镇居民人均生活消费支出” 1990 年以前为 “生活费支出”。
2. “人均住宅建筑面积”，2009 年以前（不含）为 “使用面积” 口径，2002 年以前（不含）为 “居住面积” 口径。
3. 从 2015 年起，全市发布城乡住户调查一体化改革新口径数据，居民收支调查指标与 2014 年前分别实施的城镇和农村住户调查的调查范围、方法、指标口径、名称有所不同。（以下相关表同）。
4. “农村居民人均可支配收入” 2014 年以前为 “农民人均纯收入” 口径。

2000 年	2010 年	2015 年	2016 年	2017 年	2018 年	2019 年
1.40	1.35	1.38	1.42	1.31	1.4	1.4
1.71	1.67	1.80	1.87	1.35	1.4	1.5
3.70	3.84	2.04	2.17	2.08	2.06	2.01
3047	8903	14232	15346	16594	17924	19454
1977	5407	8597	9396	10327	11172	12300
43.5	33.6	32.3	32.2	31.5	30.5	30.1
8471	25321	39889	43052	46642	50146	51913
6892	15973	26319	28537	30729	32977	33439
34.6	31.6	24.4	24.2	23.5	23.5	23.8
463.0	2187.7	3951.4	4279.9	4465.7	5008.1	6438.1
8229.6	36239.0	63358.0	68012.6	69971.2	77076.2	81389.8
28.6	40.2	52.6	53.8	55.2	54.3	51.1
10.5	29.7	44.9	45.5	47.8	46.5	39.0
61.0	84.9	79.1	75.8	76.3	51.7	58.5
34.3	13.3	15.1	13.5	16.1	11.6	12.9
100	100	99.00	99.57	99.64	99.78	100.00
7.2	11.3	11.55	11.81	11.79	12.59	13.20
132.3	115.5	110.5	110.6	111.1	106.0	105.1
125.0	122.2	114.0	118.3	118.4	114.1	113.0
165	1064	1141	1154	1241	1226	96.3
63.40	65.2	100.6	105.6	104.2	111.0	109.5
38.57	52.9	69.1	72.2	74.9	77.0	74.8

Note: 1. "Per capita living expenditure of urban residents" was "cost of living expenses" before 1990.

2. "Per capita housing area" was the caliber of "usable area" before 2009 (excluding) and was the caliber of "living area" before 2002 .

3. Since 2015, the city has released new caliber data for the integrated reform of urban and rural household surveys. The survey indicator of residents' income and expenditure was different from the survey scope, method, index caliber and name of urban and rural households carried out before 2014. (The same below).

4. "Per capita disposable income of rural residents" was the caliber of "rural per capita net income" before 2014.

10-2 各时期城镇居民生活情况
Basic Conditions of Urban Households in Each Period

年 份 Year	人均可支配收入（元） Per Capita Annual Disposable Income (yuan)	人均生活消费支出（元） Per Capita Consumer Expenditure(yuan)		就业者负担人数（人） Average Dependents Per Employee (person)	人均住宅建筑面积（平方米） Per Capita Floor Space (sq.m)
		小 计 Total	# 人均食品支出 Per Capita Food Expenditure		
1949	64.53	61.30	37.39		4.09
1952	130.00	127.84	77.98		4.11
1957	206.50	194.15	117.69		3.64
1962	201.74	209.84	131.42		3.48
1965	219.51	212.82	131.59		3.31
1970					3.51
1975					3.66
1978	337.80	317.88	181.56	1.89	4.06
1980	440.09	405.53	230.11	1.67	4.22
“六五”时期					
1981	487.19	452.77	256.67	1.73	4.40
1982	502.97	468.03	275.30	1.70	4.57
1983	552.37	484.87	293.32	1.66	4.93
1984	671.89	537.27	326.97	1.69	5.10
1985	783.00	703.82	397.33	1.68	5.21
“七五”时期					
1986	946.46	836.50	474.62	1.70	7.40
1987	1057.48	943.58	534.12	1.73	7.30
1988	1272.83	1150.44	635.11	1.70	7.50
1989	1487.91	1355.64	745.32	1.71	7.50
1990	1619.50	1360.08	781.58	1.72	7.50
“八五”时期					
1991	1854.33	1569.26	896.62	1.71	7.60
1992	2148.49	1781.21	979.03	1.73	7.65
1993	2873.94	2394.03	1146.02	1.74	7.80
1994	3951.94	3224.73	1566.59	1.72	7.90
1995	4720.55	3830.38	1823.64	1.80	8.00
“九五”时期					
1996	5681.49	4422.91	2161.00	1.71	8.00

10-2 续表 continued

年 份 Year	人均可支配收入（元） Per Capita Annual Disposable Income (yuan)	人均生活消费支出（元） Per Capita Consumer Expenditure(yuan)		就业者负担人数（人） Average Dependents Per Employee (person)	人均住宅建筑面积（平方米） Per Capita Floor Space (sq.m)
		小 计 Total	# 人均食品支出 Per Capita Food Expenditure		
1997	6261.21	5210.40	2185.11	1.62	8.10
1998	6757.12	5440.10	2179.99	1.61	9.89
1999	7162.48	6415.39	2204.76	1.66	10.00
2000	8471.32	6891.75	2387.06	1.71	10.50
"十五"时期					
2001	9564.99	7465.04	2386.84	1.74	10.70
2002	10094.13	7818.33	2575.21	1.72	17.83
2003	11012.86	8395.36	2610.75	1.68	18.85
2004	12005.06	8580.54	2784.87	1.65	19.50
2005	13578.46	9226.61	3046.93	1.73	19.55
"十一五"时期					
2006	15340.17	10713.13	3335.31	1.74	20.1
2007	18005.10	12389.69	3900.91	1.72	21.0
2008	20802.17	13904.59	4466.18	1.87	21.5
2009	22721.65	14764.28	4836.78	1.86	29.4
2010	25321.06	15973.32	5051.18	1.67	29.7
"十二五"时期					
2011	28891.97	18045.58	5722.65	1.71	30.3
2012	32569.75	20031.67	6162.16	1.72	–
2013	35647.59	21666.94	6624.32	–	–
2014	38762.77	22980.67	6814.14	2.04	–
2015	39888.71	26318.72	6415.00	1.80	44.9
"十三五"时期					
2016	43052.16	28536.93	6908.01	1.87	45.5
2017	46642.40	30728.60	7229.30	1.35	47.8
2018	50146	32977	7758	1.4	46.5
2019	51913	33439	7956	1.5	39.0

注：1. 可支配收入 1983 年以前为生活费收入，消费性支出 1992 年以前为生活费支出。
2. "人均住宅建筑面积"，2009 年以前（不含）为"使用面积"口径，2002 年以前（不含）为"居住面积"口径。

Note: 1. The disposable income was living expenditure income before 1983, and the consumption expenditure was previously the cost-of-living expenditure before 1992.
2. "Per capita housing area", was the caliber of "usable area" before 2009 (excluding) and was the caliber of "living area"before 2002.

10-3 主要年份农村居民生活情况
Basic Conditions of Rural Households in Major Years

年份 Year	人均可支配收入（元） Per Capita Annual Disposable Income (yuan)	人均生活消费支出（元） Per Capita Consumer Expenditure(yuan)		每一劳动力负担人数（人） Average Dependents Per Labor Force (person)	人均住宅建筑面积（平方米） Per Capita Floor Space (sq.m)
		小计 Total	# 人均食品支出 Per Capita Food Expenditure		
1952	49.4	39.2	29.2	1.8	7.5
1957	63.6	57.9	34.8	1.8	7.8
1962	67.7	59.9	36.3	1.8	8.0
1965	92.6	69.7	46.1	1.8	8.2
1970	82.7	67.2	42.2	1.7	8.5
1975	79.1	59.5	40.8	1.7	9.0
1978	110.5	83.2	58.2	1.7	9.6
1980	168.9	127.1	85.8	1.6	10.5
1985	439.2	330.5	171.1	1.6	16.9
1990	731.1	569.8	287.7	1.6	22.5
1991	810.1	610.6	303.7	1.6	23.7
1992	865.3	660.5	335.1	1.6	21.1
1993	1031.4	724.8	371.4	1.6	22.9
1994	1401.0	942.5	511.0	1.6	24.1
1995	1812.7	1373.6	770.8	1.4	24.7
1996	2328.1	1728.1	926.2	1.4	26.9
1997	2600.0	1799.7	922.0	1.4	27.1
1998	2826.4	1872.5	935.9	1.4	27.4
1999	2943.7	1841.2	876.7	1.4	28.3
2000	3046.8	1976.8	860.0	1.4	28.6
2001	3215.7	2057.8	852.5	1.5	29.9
2002	3355.8	2133.9	849.5	1.4	30.6
2003	3619.3	2316.2	900.7	1.4	32.5
2004	4198.7	2543.1	1040.4	1.4	32.9
2005	4812.3	2902.8	1134.8	1.4	33.8
2006	5480.0	3415.3	1199.8	1.4	35.3
2007	6300.1	3789.8	1423.0	1.4	37.3
2008	7180.2	4385.4	1628.2	1.4	38.7
2009	7804.8	4733.1	1686.3	1.4	39.4
2010	8903.3	5406.6	1818.3	1.4	40.2
2011	10411.8	5905.1	2147.3	1.4	41.2
2012	11786.2	6932.2	2465.4	1.4	42.9
2013	13247.6	7798.7	2640.8	1.4	43.9
2014	14726.0	8581.4	2831.4	1.4	–
2015	14231.8	8597.2	2775.5	1.4	52.6
2016	15345.6	9396.3	3028.0	1.4	53.8
2017	16593.8	10327.3	3253.2	1.3	55.2
2018	17924	11172	3409	1.4	54.3
2019	19454	12300	3703	1.4	51.1

注：1. “人均可支配收入”2014 年以前为“农民人均纯收入”口径。
2. “人均住宅建筑面积”，2009 年以前（不含）为“使用面积”口径，2002 年以前（不含）为“居住面积”口径。

Note: 1. "Per capita disposable income" was the caliber of "rural per capita net income" before 2014.
2. "Per capita housing area" was the caliber of "usable area" before 2009 (excluding) and was the caliber of "living area" before 2002 (excluding).

10-4 每百户城镇居民家庭主要耐用消费品拥有量
Number of Durable Consumer Goods Owned Per 100 Urban Households in Major Years

商品名称	Indicator	单位 Unit	1995 年	2000 年	2005 年	2010 年	2015 年	2017 年	2018 年	2019 年
摩托车	Motorcycles	辆 (Unit)	13.0	34.3	30.1	13.3	15.1	16.1	11.6	12.9
助力车	Moped	辆 (Unit)			18.1	40.2	72.0	75.7	80.8	78.5
家用汽车	Automobiles	辆 (Unit)			5.4	22.7	47.6	53.7	53.7	54.0
洗衣机	Washing Machines	台 (set)	91.5	100.0	97.0	93.2	98.5	99.5	99.3	98.6
电冰箱	Refrigerators	台 (set)	92.0	99.3	97.0	96.7	101.8	101.9	103.2	104.0
彩色电视机	Color TV Sets	台 (set)	95.0	132.3	126.8	115.5	110.5	111.1	106.0	105.1
家用电脑	Computers	台 (set)		20.0	54.2	81.0	90.8	91.3	80.6	81.8
组合音响	Music Center	台 (set)	10.5	29.0	26.8	16.2	–	0.0	0.0	0.0
摄像机	Pickup Cameras	台 (set)		2.3	4.0	10.8	16.9	0.0	0.0	0.0
照相机	Cameras	台 (set)	40.5	76.0	59.2	54.0	56.1	52.3	36.4	32.9
其它中高档乐器	High-grade Instruments	件 (Unit)	6.5	12.3	6.4	3.5	5.7	7.9	13.1	16.3
微波炉	Microwave Oven	台 (set)		32.3	53.2	55.8	58.7	63.6	61.0	59.2
空调器	Air Conditioner	台 (set)	16.0	65.0	104.4	121.5	146.3	156.4	172.8	166.6
淋浴热水器	Water Heaters	台 (set)	36.5	81.3	79.3	82.0	100.3	101.4	101.1	99.0
消毒碗柜	Sterilized Cupboard	台 (set)			5.4	6.5	6.2	0.0	0.0	0.0
洗碗机	Dish-washing Machine	台 (set)			1.0	0.3	2.1	4.9	2.6	3.1
健身器材	Fitness Equipment	台 (set)		4.7	6.4	4.3	10.2	11.7	7.8	8.2
住宅电话	Fixed-line Phones	台 (set)	38.0	86.7	88.6	46.3	54.7	54.8	26.5	20.8
移动电话	Mobile Phones	台 (set)		28.7	145.2	179.7	213.5	212.5	219.5	222.9

10-5 农村每百户居民家庭主要耐用消费品拥有量

Number of Major Durable Consumer Goods Owend Per 100 Rural Households

商品名称	Indicator	单位 Unit	2011 年	2012 年	2013 年	2015 年	2016 年	2017 年	2018 年	2019 年
洗 衣 机	Washing Machines	台 (set)	82	86	88	86	90	90	95	93
电 冰 箱	Refrigerators	台 (set)	88	91	92	91	97	97	97	99
摩 托 车	Motorcycles	辆 (unit)	71	62	65	79	76	76	52	58
家用汽车	Automobiles	辆 (unit)						44	42	39
彩色电视机	Color TV Sets	台 (set)	116	118	119	114	118	118	114	113
照 相 机	Cameras	台 (set)	15	14	16	8	9	9	6	6
抽油烟机	Range Hoods	台 (set)	27	28	34	28	36	38	45	56
空 调 器	Air Conditioner	台 (set)	36	39	46	56	67	74	87	93
热 水 器	Water Heaters	台 (set)	64	69	69	74	79	82	87	82
电 话 机	Phones	部 (set)	60	58	55	47	48	46	26	21
移动电话	Mobile Phones	部 (set)	175	186	195	214	224	231	245	232
家用计算机	Computers	台 (set)	36	39	43	40	43	43	41	39

10-6 居民人均可支配收入和消费性支出 (2019 年)

Per Capital Annual Income and Per Capital Annual Expenditure(2019)

单位：元 (yuan)

指标名称	Item	全体居民 All Households	城镇居民 Urban Households	农村居民 Rural Households
可支配收入	**Disposable Income**	**41472**	**51913**	**19454**
工资性收入	Income of Wages and Salaries	24010	30344	10653
经营净收入	Net Business Income	4229	2823	7193
财产净收入	Income from Properties	6279	9050	435
转移净收入	Income from Transfer	6954	9695	1174
消费支出	**Consumption Expenditure**	**26639**	**33439**	**12300**
食品烟酒	Food, Tobacco and Liquor	6588	7956	3703
衣着	Clothing	1522	1947	625
居住	Residence	7948	10374	2832
生活用品及服务	Household Appliances and Services	1900	2431	780
交通通信	Transport and Communications	3513	4303	1847
教育文化娱乐	Recreation,Education and Cultural Services	2804	3575	1178
医疗保健	Health Care and Medical Services	1841	2166	1154
其他用品和服务	Miscellaneous Goods and Services	524	686	182

主要统计指标解释

可支配收入 指调查户在调查期内获得的、可用于最终消费支出和储蓄的总和，即调查户可以用来自由支配的收入。可支配收入既包括现金，也包括实物收入。按照收入的来源，可支配收入包含四项，分别为：工资性收入、经营净收入、财产净收入、转移净收入。计算公式为：

可支配收入 = 工资性收入 + 经营净收入 + 财产净其中:经营净收入 = 经营收入 - 经营费用 - 生产性固定资产折旧 - 生产税净额（生产税 - 生产补贴）

财产净收入 = 财产性收入 - 财产性支出

转移净收入 = 转移性收入 - 转移性支出

工资性收入 指就业人员通过各种途径得到的全部劳动报酬和各种福利，包括受雇于单位或个人、从事各种自由职业、兼职和零星劳动得到的全部劳动报酬和福利。

经营净收入 指住户或住户成员从事生产经营活动所获得的净收入，是全部经营收入中扣除经营费用、生产性固定资产折旧和生产税之后得到的净收入。

财产净收入 指住户或住户成员将其所拥有的金融资产、住房等非金融资产和自然资源交由其他机构单位、住户或个人支配而获得的回报并扣除相关的费用之后得到的净收入。财产净收入包括利息净收入、红利收入、储蓄性保险净收益、转让承包土地经营权租金净收入、出租房屋净收入、出租其他资产净收入和自有住房折算净租金等。

转移性收入 指国家、单位、社会团体对住户的各种经常性转移支付和住户之间的经常性收入转移。包括政府、非行政事业单位、社会团体对居民转移的养老金或退休金、社会救济和补助、惠农补贴、政策性生活补贴、救灾款、经常性捐赠和赔偿以及报销医疗费等；住户之间的赡养收入、经常性捐赠和赔偿以及农村地区（村委会）在外（含国外）工作的本住户非常住成员寄回带回的收入等。转移性收入不包括住户之间的实物馈赠。

转移性支出 指调查户对国家、单位、住户或个人的经常性或义务性转移支付。包括缴纳的税款、各项社会保障支出、赡养支出、经常性捐赠和赔偿支出以及其他经常转移支出等。

消费支出 指住户用于满足家庭日常生活消费需要的全部支出，包括用于消费品的支出和用于服务性消费的支出。根据用途不同，消费支出可划分为食品烟酒、衣着、居住、生活用品及服务、交通通信、教育文化娱乐、医疗保健、其他用品及服务八大类。根据来源不同，消费支出可划分为现金消费支出、实物消费支出（含自产自用、来自单位、来自政府和其他社会组织）。

食品烟酒 指用于各种食品和烟草、酒类的支出，包括食品和烟酒两个中类。

衣着 指与居民穿着有关的支出，包括服装、服装材料、鞋类、其他衣类及配件、衣着相关加工服务的支出。

居住 指与居住有关的支出，包括房租、水、电、燃料、物业管理等方面的支出，也包括自有住房折算租金。

生活用品及服务 指家庭及个人的各类生活品及家庭服务。包括家具及室内装饰品、家用器具、家用纺织品、家庭日用杂品、个人用品和家庭服务。

交通通信 指用于交通和通信工具及相关的各种服务费、维修费和车辆保险等支出。

教育文化和娱乐 指用于教育和文化娱乐方面的支出。

医疗保健 指用于医疗和保健的药品、用品和服务的总费用。包括医疗器具及药品，以及医疗服务。

其他用品及服务 指无法直接归入上述各类支出的其他用品与服务支出。

就业者负担人数 指家庭人口与就业人口之比。

城镇家庭可支配收入（老口径） 指家庭成员得到可用于最终消费支出和其它非义务性支出以及储蓄的总和，即居民家庭可以用来自由支配的收入。它是家庭总收入扣除交纳的所得税、个人交纳的社会保障支出以及记账补贴后的收入。计算公式为：

可支配收入＝家庭总收入－交纳所得税－个人交纳的社会保障支出－记帐补贴

农村居民纯收入（老口径） 指农村住户当年从各个来源得到的总收入相应地扣除所发生的费用后的收入总和。计算方法：

纯收入＝总收入－家庭经营费用支出－税费支出－生产性固定资产折旧

纯收入主要用于再生产投入和当年生活消费支出，也可用于储蓄和各种非义务性支出。“农民人均纯收入”按人口平均的纯收入水平，反映的是一个地区或一个农户农村居民的平均收入水平。

农村居民人均可支配收入与改革前的农民纯收入指标的主要区别是：可支配收入扣除了赠送农村以外亲友支出、农村居民用于购买住房、汽车等生活性贷款的利息支出，以及个人交纳的养老、医疗等社会保障支出，纯收入则不扣。同时，计算农村居民人均收入的分母调整为农村常住人口，调整了外出农民工寄带回收入的归类。

Explanatory Notes on Main Statistical Indicators

Disposable Income refers to the sum of households income that can be used for final consumption expenditure and savings during the period of investigation. Disposable income includes cash and real income. According to sources of income, disposable income includes the wage income, net operating income, net property income, and net transfer income. The formula for computing:

Disposable income = the wage income + net operating income + net property income + net transfer income

Net operating income = Income – operating costs – depreciation of productive fixed assets – net taxes on production (production tax – production subsidies)

Net property income = income from property – property expenditure

The transfer of net income = income from transfer – transfer expenditure

Wage Income refers to income and all kinds of welfare obtained by labors employed by different establishments, working independently or part–time.

Net Operating Income refers to the net income from operation run by the members of households, and it equals to total income minus operating costs and depreciation of productive fixed assets and taxes on production.

Net Property Income refers to the net income obtained from the financial assets, non–financial assets such as housing and natural resources provided by its owners to other establishments, households or individuals. It includes net interest income, bonus, net income from saving insurance, net income from the transfer of the right to land contractual management, income from house renting, income from renting of other assets and net rental income of home ownership.

Income from Transfer refers to the current transaction between government, establishments, social organization and households, and to the income transaction between households. It includes annuity, pension, social relief, agricultural subsidy, disaster relief fund, and medical expense, which are provided by governments, institutions, social organizations. It also includes supporting expense, regular donations, and income provided by non–permanent population. It does not include donations between households.

Transfer Expenditure refers to the regular or obligatory expenditure provided by the households to governments, institutions, other households or residents. It includes taxes, social security expenditure, supporting expenditure, regular donation and compensation expenditure, etc.

Expenditure refers to the consumption of all expenditures needs to meet the family daily life, including the expenditures on consumer goods and services. According to different purposes, consumption can be divided into tobacco & food, clothing, housing, daily necessities & services, transportation & communication, education & culture & entertainment, health care, and other goods & services. According to different sources, consumption expenditures can be divided into cash consumption and physical consumption expenditures (including self–occupied, from the unit, from the government and other social organizations).

Tobacco & Food refers to all kinds of expenditure on foods, tobaccos and beverages, including food and tobacco.

Clothing refers to the expenditure on clothes, clothing materials, shoes, accessories and charges for clothing production process.

Housing refers to the expenditure related to residing, including the expenditure on rent, water, fuel, power and real estate management and net rental income of home ownership.

Daily Necessities & Services refer to the expenditure on daily necessities and home service, including the expenditure on furniture, decoration, appliance, textile, personal items and home service.

Transportation & Communication refer to the expenditure on transportation, communication, related service, maintenance, and vehicle insurance.

Education & Culture & Entertainment refer to the expenditure on education, culture and entertainment.

Health Care refers to the sum of the expenditure on health care, medicine, related products and service, including the medical devices, drug as well as medical services.

Other Services refer to the expenditure on the goods and services that cannot be included in the categories mentioned above.

Number of Dependents per Employee refers to the ratio between number of persons in households and the number of employers in the household.

Urban Households Disposable Income (in previous cope) refers to the sum of households' income used for final consumption expenditure and savings during the period of investigation, meaning the income that is disposable for households. Disposable income is the general income of households minus income tax, social security expenditure and subsidy for account–keeping. The formula for computing:

Disposable Income of Households = General income – income tax – personal social security expenditure – subsidy for account keeping

Rural Households Net Income (in previous cope) refers to the total income of rural households from all sources minus all corresponding expenses. The formula for calculation is as follows:

Net income = total income – household operation expenses – taxes and fees – depreciation of fixed assets for production

Net income is mainly used as input for reproduction and as consumption expenditure of the year, and also used for savings and non–compulsory expenses of various forms. "Per capita net income of farmers" is the level of net income averaged by population which reflects the average income level of rural households in a given area.

The main difference between rural household disposable income and rural household net income is that the disposable income does not include the expenditure of donations to urban relatives, the expenditure on houses and vehicles purchasing, interest expenditure on consumer loans, and expenditure on pension and health care, but the net income includes all the expenditure mentioned above. When calculating the average income of rural household, the denominator is changed to permanent rural residents, and the classification of income brought back by migrant workers is also changed.

11

农　业

AGRICULTURE

11-1 各时期农业主要经济指标
Major Economic Indicators of Agriculture in Each Period

年份 Year	农村劳动力（万人） Rural Labor (10 000 persons)	农林牧渔业总产值（亿元） Gross Output Value of Farming,Forestry, Animal Husbandry and Fishery (100 million yuan)	农业机械总动力（万千瓦） Total Power of Agricultural Machinery (10 000 kw)	年末实有耕地面积（千公顷） Actual Cultivated Area (1000 ha)	粮食总产量（万吨） Output of Grain (10 000 tons)	蔬菜总产量（万吨） Output of Vegetables (10 000 tons)	肉类总产量（万吨） Output of Meat (10 000 tons)	粮食单产（千克/公顷） Output Per Hectare of Grain (kg/ha)
1949	106.51	1.50	–	469.85	51.63	10.72	0.24	825
1952	112.35	1.91	–	481.17	62.75	8.61	0.40	960
1957	121.09	2.79	0.32	479.58	67.92	15.86	0.66	1065
1962	108.44	1.33	2.98	412.34	39.74	27.67	0.72	765
1965	111.74	2.61	4.84	410.02	73.80	29.12	1.12	1350
1970	123.91	2.75	14.32	396.49	75.47	31.81	1.21	1470
1975	141.00	4.07	48.04	382.05	100.46	42.00	2.07	2025
1978	140.05	6.57	69.70	373.19	115.38	49.19	2.50	2475
1979	141.60	7.48	80.63	372.45	122.56	49.42	2.92	2610
1980	143.19	7.79	88.45	370.87	116.54	58.13	3.69	2565
"六五"时期								
1981	146.52	11.73	94.47	369.80	121.27	49.85	3.99	2865
1982	149.07	14.47	106.60	369.22	121.13	63.45	4.31	3060
1983	152.39	18.07	112.19	368.45	147.41	65.66	4.66	3570
1984	158.23	19.00	123.92	367.35	160.60	86.91	5.03	3915
1985	162.51	18.36	130.41	357.41	163.50	84.11	5.43	3915
"七五"时期								
1986	165.86	20.91	147.36	353.96	168.16	118.86	6.44	3855
1987	168.56	24.65	156.23	352.18	167.25	101.52	7.13	3945
1988	171.44	34.24	172.89	350.56	167.95	122.83	8.68	4080
1989	173.38	35.14	182.40	349.59	162.45	117.99	9.70	3945
1990	176.83	36.92	183.40	347.56	181.47	126.09	11.38	4273
"八五"时期								
1991	180.09	40.13	191.00	344.76	207.55	146.87	13.50	4779
1992	182.51	45.14	191.50	343.29	198.29	170.61	15.36	4655
1993	183.78	57.81	194.40	341.54	232.21	205.62	19.12	4963
1994	183.42	85.37	207.40	339.97	237.66	226.39	26.14	5237
1995	183.55	114.07	241.20	339.30	252.48	253.54	28.68	5512

注：1. 自 2005 年始年末实有耕地面积有国土资源局提供，暂无 2009 年数据。
2. 依据 2006 年农业普查数据，对 1997 年至 2007 年蔬菜面积、产量做了相应调整。
3. 粮食作物产量、播种面积自 2012 年开始由山东调查总队反馈。
4. 按照国务院农普办要求，由国家统计局山东调查总队根据第三次农业普查数据，对 2016–2017 年市县（区）粮食播种面积 . 单产和总产量等数据进行了修订。
5. 依据 2016 年农业普查数据，对 2007 年至 2017 年农林牧渔业总产值做了相应调整。
6. 依据 2016 年农业普查数据，对 2008 年至 2017 年蔬菜总产量、肉类总产量做了相应调整。
7. 2019 年农业数据为区划调整后的数据，以下各表同。
8. 由于第三次全国土地调查数据未反馈，“年末实有耕地面积”2019 年相关数据延用 2018 年数据。

11-1 续表 continued

年份 Year	农村劳动力(万人) Rural Labor (10 000 persons)	农林牧渔业总产值(亿元) Gross Output Value of Farming,Forestry, Animal Husbandry and Fishery (100 million yuan)	农业机械总动力(万千瓦) Total Power of Agricultural Machinery (10 000 kw)	年末实有耕地面积(千公顷) Actual Cultivated Area (1000 ha)	粮食总产量(万吨) Output of Grain (10 000 tons)	蔬菜总产量(万吨) Output of Vegetables (10 000 tons)	肉类总产量(万吨) Output of Meat (10 000 tons)	粮食单产(千克/公顷) Output Per Hectare of Grain (kg/ha)
"九五"时期								
1996	184.68	117.65	247.07	337.25	267.08	350.36	30.43	5602
1997	186.68	131.69	258.50	335.90	240.34	328.64	24.75	5064
1998	186.54	141.45	273.30	334.83	273.10	344.67	27.38	5634
1999	188.27	148.61	297.55	333.72	279.01	366.78	29.89	5752
2000	189.15	154.30	349.47	333.72	240.27	405.95	31.82	5354
"十五"时期								
2001	189.87	162.27	409.07	331.75	239.08	435.20	33.23	5480
2002	190.98	167.99	410.17	329.35	189.86	478.34	31.87	4440
2003	192.71	180.30	417.43	325.18	220.56	504.81	33.29	5448
2004	191.31	204.39	418.54	324.89	242.74	515.26	35.35	5807
2005	190.21	230.46	426.76	366.99	260.11	529.37	37.93	5932
"十一五"时期								
2006	190.80	247.70	429.62	361.74	267.91	536.28	38.74	6042
2007	191.16	262.51	446.60	358.80	268.01	522.24	31.85	6064
2008	190.45	302.00	466.00	361.33	281.50	520.25	30.22	6230
2009	195.56	318.06	486.00		289.47	560.83	31.39	6246
2010	196.85	361.24	509.68	362.30	289.43	572.05	31.79	6192
"十二五"时期								
2011	197.38	399.90	527.39	361.25	295.84	590.02	32.43	6315
2012	198.74	422.75	538.66	360.28	286.03	606.11	33.22	6285
2013	199.80	470.55	552.06	361.01	266.60	629.54	33.59	5997
2014	199.73	479.50	567.02	360.24	271.19	638.22	34.10	6109
2015	200.45	493.04	584.98	358.57	264.55	626.23	34.18	6117
"十三五"时期								
2016	200.46	501.72	447.83	357.60	275.43	611.25	31.72	5778
2017	198.91	505.08	442.90	355.66	255.57	591.63	32.50	5660
2018	189.10	514.90	454.62	353.65	251.42	527.22	29.82	5659
2019	239.03	637.30	543.48	353.65	285.46	671.24	35.86	5956

Note: 1. Since 2005, the actual cultivated area has been provided by Land Resources Bureau. No data for 2009.
2. According to the data of the agricultural census in 2006, the area and yield of the vegetables from 1997 to 2007 were adjusted accordingly.
3. Grain crop yield and sown area have been reported by Shandong Survey Team since 2012.
4. According to the requirements of Agricultural Census Office of the State Council, Shandong Survey Team of National Bureau of Statistics revised the grain sown area, yield per unit and total yield of each city and country (district) from 2016-2017 based on the data from the third agricultural census.
5. According to the data of the agricultural census in 2016, the total output value of agriculture, forestry, animal husbandry and fishery in the period from 2007 to 2017 was adjusted accordingly.
6. According to the data of the agricultural census in 2016, the total output value of vegetable and meat in the period from 2008 to 2017 was adjusted accordingly.
7. The data of agriculture in 2019 is the adjusted data by the administrative division (the same below).
8. "Actual cultivated area at the end of year " in 2019 uses the data in the year of 2018 because no data of the third national land survey has been reflected.

11-2 农村基层组织和农业基本情况
Basic Conditions of Rural Grassroots Units and Agriculture

指 标	Indicator	单位 Unit	2014 年	2015 年	2016 年	2017 年	2018 年	2019 年
乡镇数量	Number of Towns	个 (Unit)	53	48	39	29	29	40
#镇	Towns	个 (Unit)	51	46	39	29	29	40
村民委员会	Village Committee	个 (Unit)	4547	4546	4547	4548	4546	5551
乡村户数	Rural Households	万户 (10 000 households)	101.31	101.96	103.14	102.31	101.96	139.19
乡村人口	Rural Numbers	万人 (10 000 persons)	357.42	360.29	362.55	359.18	355.74	456.10
家庭从业人员	Family Practitioner	万人 (10 000 persons)	199.73	200.45	200.46	198.91	189.10	239.03
男	Male	万人 (10 000 persons)	105.89	106.07	106.06	105.38	99.96	127.55
女	Female	万人 (10 000 persons)	93.84	94.38	94.40	93.52	89.15	111.48
地类面积	Land Category Area	公顷 (ha)	799841	799841	799841	799841	799841	799841
耕地	Cultivated Land	公顷 (ha)	360241	358568	357601	355659	353652	353652
其中水浇地	Irrigated Land	公顷 (ha)	265119	264016	263310	261894	263885	263885
园地	Garden Land	公顷 (ha)	26180	26054	25957	25801	25675	25675
林地	Forest Land	公顷 (ha)	84963	84676	84484	84175	83947	83947
草地	Grazing and Pasture Land	公顷 (ha)	57430	57250	57151	57018	56879	56879
城镇村及工矿用地	Land for Urban Village, Mining and Manufacturing	公顷 (ha)	140772	142969	144219	146819	149020	149020
交通运输用地	Land for Transport Facilities	公顷 (ha)	29068	29135	29319	29617	30216	30216
水域及水利设施用地	Land for Water Conservancy Facilities	公顷 (ha)	51039	50962	50875	50696	50531	50531
其它土地	Other Land	公顷 (ha)	50150	50227	50236	50055	49921	49921
年末耕地总资源	Total Cultivated Area	公顷 (ha)	398132	396365	395292	393224	391040	391040
农业机械总动力	Total Power of Agricultural Machinery	万千瓦 (10 000 kw)	567.02	584.98	447.83	442.90	454.62	543.48
农用大中型拖拉机	Large and Medium-sized Tractors	台 (set)	23906	24328	25574	24329	20208	23553
农用小型拖拉机	Small Tractors	台 (set)	37503	36964	35492	27179	30152	49911
谷物联合收割机	Combine Harvester	台 (set)	12734	12933	14365	13948	14380	15746
柴油机	Diesel Engine	台 (set)	85395	85775	84583	82173		
割晒机	Cutter-Rower	台 (set)	3768	3357	3103	2935		
脱粒机	Thresher	台 (set)	20901	20178	20450	19917	19660	27007
农村用电量	Electricity Consumption in Rural Area	亿千瓦小时 (100 million kwh)	26.42	26.51	25.66	24.40	23.58	32.87
农作物总播种面积	Total Sown Area of Farm Crops	千公顷 (1000 ha)	578.1	562.4	598.9	566.1	549.0	615.6

注：1. 按照国务院农普办要求，由国家统计局山东调查总队根据第三次农业普查数据，对 2016-2017 年市、县(区)粮食播种面积数据进行了修订。
2. 由于第三次全国土地调查数据未反馈，"地类面积"2019 年相关数据延用 2018 年数据，以下相关各表同。

Note:1. According to the requirements of Agricultural Census Office of the State Council, Shandong Survey Team of National Bureau of Statistics revised the grain sown area, of each city and country (district) from 2016-2017 based on the data from the third agricultural census.
2. "Land Category Area" data in 2019 uses the data of year 2018 because no data of the third national land survey has been reflected (the same below).

11-3 分地区农村基层组织和农业基本情况 (2019 年)
Basic Conditions of Rural Grassroots Units and Agriculture by Region(2019)

指 标	Indicator	单 位 Unit	济南市 Ji'nan	历下区 Li xia
乡镇数量	Number of Towns	个 (Unit)	40	
#镇	Towns	个 (Unit)	40	
村民委员会	Village Committee	个 (Unit)	5551	20
乡村户数	Rural Households	万户 (10 000 households)	139.19	
乡村总人口	Rural Numbers	万人 (10 000 persons)	456.10	
乡村劳动力	Family Practitioner	万人 (10 001 persons)	239.03	
男	Male	万人 (10 002 persons)	127.55	
女	Female	万人 (10 003 persons)	111.48	
地类面积	Land Category Area	公顷 (ha)	799841	10118
耕地	Cultivated Land	公顷 (ha)	353652	276
其中水浇地	Irrigated Land	公顷 (ha)	263885	78
园地	Garden Land	公顷 (ha)	25675	25
林地	Forest Land	公顷 (ha)	83947	1901
草地	Grazing and Pasture Land	公顷 (ha)	56879	436
城镇村及工矿用地	Land for Urban Village, Mining and Manufacturing	公顷 (ha)	149020	7262
交通运输用地	Land for Transport Facilities	公顷 (ha)	30216	59
水域及水利设施用地	Land for Water Conservancy Facilities	公顷 (ha)	50531	38
其它土地	Other Land	公顷 (ha)	49921	120
年末耕地总资源	Total Cultivated Area	公顷 (ha)	391040	276
农业机械总动力	Total Power of Agricultural Machinery	万千瓦 (10 000 kw)	543	3.31
农用大中型拖拉机	Large and Medium-sized Tractors	台 (set)	23553	55
农用小型拖拉机	Small Tractors	台 (set)	49911	565
谷物联合收割机	Combine Harvester	台 (set)	15746	31
柴油机	Diesel Engine	台 (set)		
割晒机	Cutter-Rower	台 (set)		
脱粒机	Thresher	台 (set)	27007	20
农村用电量	Electricity Consumption in Rural Area	亿千瓦小时 (100 million kwh)	32.87	
农作物总播种面积	Total Sown Area of Farm Crops	千公顷 (1000 ha)	612.80	

市中区 Shi zhong	槐荫区 Huai yin	天桥区 Tian qiao	历城区 Li cheng	长清区 Chang qing	章丘区 Zhang qiu	济阳区 Ji yang	莱芜区 Lai wu	钢城区 Gang cheng	平阴县 Ping yin	商河县 Shang he
				3	3	4	11	2	6	11
				3	3	4	11	2	6	11
77	92	120	672	580	890	811	794	211	336	948
4.53	1.24	1.10	22.18	13.59	24.63	15.65	26.78	6.18	8.82	14.49
15.52	4.64	3.93	71.15	46.37	82.04	57.32	73.08	17.80	30.02	54.24
7.01	2.44	1.89	34.96	20.86	47.26	30.00	40.00	9.77	16.21	28.63
3.78	1.25	1.13	18.22	10.42	25.02	16.76	21.47	5.40	8.42	15.68
3.23	1.20	0.75	16.73	10.44	22.24	13.24	18.53	4.38	7.79	12.95
28149	15161	25897	130121	120859	171909	109881			71506	116240
5401	3263	9477	31801	46147	78263	70253			33201	75570
1436	1416	8940	17390	20489	52301	67022			19745	75067
1104	40	88	13632	4392	3782	377			1949	286
3698	431	1767	23091	20691	14624	4391			10398	2954
4149	118	130	15628	15154	16428	494			3997	345
10163	7783	9066	29872	14746	28793	15852			9747	15736
867	723	1337	5033	3772	6205	4130			2806	5284
358	2625	3773	4600	4911	8011	11563			3207	11446
2411	179	258	6465	11046	15802	2820			6200	4619
6659	3549	10716	39401	52628	90141	73396			37036	77238
12.71	4	16.26	50.42	49.18	93.40	99.37	63.61	18.58	43.42	89.00
364	266	542	1645	2876	3371	4693	2070	458	1678	5535
386	333	2261	5368	3489	2243	3299	16060	4525	5013	6369
114	158	344	1235	1339	3739	2601	825	153	731	4476
121	2634	1158	1227	886	2193	6053	6320	1291	705	4399
1.50	0.52	0.33	4.11	2.91	8.59	2.62	7.01	0.68	2.35	2.24
4.15	2.55	13.44	25.58	56.33	139.18	115.58	61.47	10.81	47.22	136.50

11-4 各时期农林牧渔业增加值(按当年价格计算)

Added Value of Agriculture, Forestry, Animal Husbandry and Fishery in Each Period(Calculated at Current Prices)

单位:亿元 (100 million yuan)

年份 Year	合计 Total	其中 of which 农业 Farming	林业 Forestry	牧业 Animal Husbandry	渔业 Fishery	农林牧渔服务业 Services of Agriculture,Forestry,Animal Husbandry and Fishing
1957	1.89	1.42	–	0.47	–	–
1962	1.01	0.76	–	0.25	–	–
1965	1.85	1.39	–	0.46	–	–
1970	2.11	1.58	–	0.53	–	–
1975	2.84	2.13	–	0.71	–	–
1978	4.08	2.94	0.19	0.89	0.06	–
1980	5.84	4.21	0.27	1.28	0.08	–
1985	12.16	8.75	0.57	2.66	0.18	–
"七五"时期						
1986	13.94	10.03	0.65	3.05	0.21	–
1987	16.21	11.66	0.76	3.55	0.24	–
1988	22.05	15.87	1.03	4.83	0.32	–
1989	22.74	16.37	1.06	4.98	0.33	–
1990	22.70	16.34	1.06	4.97	0.33	–
"八五"时期						
1991	24.68	18.00	0.95	5.31	0.42	–
1992	27.74	19.52	1.31	6.38	0.53	–
1993	35.66	23.83	1.45	9.72	0.66	–
1994	49.44	33.39	2.02	13.48	0.55	–
1995	67.24	49.59	1.97	14.95	0.75	–
"九五"时期						
1996	72.74	55.35	2.68	13.49	1.22	–
1997	81.07	62.25	2.95	14.66	1.21	–
1998	88.06	67.07	2.67	16.92	1.40	–
1999	92.52	67.30	2.21	21.33	1.68	–
2000	95.01	67.57	2.51	23.56	1.37	–
"十五"时期						
2001	97.17	68.96	2.25	24.49	1.47	–
2002	98.74	68.88	2.44	25.99	1.43	–
2003	104.90	70.71	2.87	28.51	1.22	1.60
2004	120.47	80.17	3.15	33.86	1.50	1.77
2005	134.34	88.66	4.05	38.14	1.59	1.90

11-4 续表 continued

年份 Year	合计 Total	其中 of which 农业 Farming	林业 Forestry	牧业 Animal Husbandry	渔业 Fishery	农林牧渔服务业 Services of Agriculture,Forestry,Animal Husbandry and Fishing
"十一五" 时期						
2006	145.12	95.80	4.54	40.32	1.77	2.69
2007	148.53	95.54	5.26	42.19	1.98	3.56
2008	171.05	105.38	7.58	51.14	3.11	3.83
2009	180.67	114.54	8.12	50.27	3.24	4.50
2010	205.01	139.90	4.57	51.77	3.53	5.24
"十二五" 时期						
2011	224.58	140.49	5.45	68.43	4.08	6.14
2012	236.29	145.64	6.34	72.50	4.48	7.33
2013	262.72	166.61	7.42	74.73	5.30	8.65
2014	272.90	174.90	8.25	73.78	5.93	10.05
2015	284.25	181.19	9.20	76.39	6.36	11.11
"十三五" 时期						
2016	284.92	189.87	9.28	68.36	6.16	11.26
2017	279.91	185.71	10.72	66.27	4.86	12.36
2018	286.44	195.16	12.86	59.27	5.13	14.02
2019	360.51	256.98	17.49	63.16	5.44	17.45
2019 年分地区 Region						
历下区 Li xia						
市中区 Shi zhong	1.86	0.98	0.47	0.33		0.09
槐荫区 Huai yin	2.38	1.57	0.39	0.14	0.23	0.05
天桥区 Tian qiao	3.85	2.79	0.19	0.67	0.16	0.03
历城区 Li cheng	42.48	32.76	4.16	2.87	0.64	2.06
长清区 Chang qing	33.13	22.85	1.60	7.38	0.20	1.09
章丘区 Zhang qiu	81.72	57.33	2.96	15.60	0.97	4.86
济阳区 Ji yang	42.98	32.23	1.61	7.03	0.93	1.19
莱芜区 Lai wu	59.14	44.35	1.87	10.36	0.89	1.66
钢城区 Gang cheng	10.34	7.12	0.98	1.81	0.03	0.40
平阴县 Ping yin	34.38	24.20	1.40	6.02	0.26	2.50
商河县 Shang he	48.26	30.80	1.86	10.95	1.12	3.54

注：依据 2016 年农业普查数据，对 2007 年至 2017 年农林牧渔业增加值做了相应调整。
Note: According to the data of the agricultural census in 2016, the value added of agriculture, forestry, animal husbandry and fishery in the period from 2007 to 2017 was adjusted accordingly.

11-5 各时期农林牧渔业总产值（按当年价格计算）
Gross Output Value of Agriculture, Forestry, Animal Husbandry and Fishery in Each Period(Calculated at Current Prices)

单位：亿元 (100 million yuan)

年份 Year	合计 Total	其中 of which 农业 Farming	林业 Forestry	牧业 Animal Husbandry	渔业 Fishery	农林牧渔服务业 Services of Agriculture,Forestry,Animal Husbandry and Fishing
1952	1.91	1.67	0.04	0.18	0.02	–
1957	2.79	2.41	0.09	0.28	0.01	–
1962	1.33	1.18	0.03	0.12	–	–
1965	2.61	2.25	0.07	0.28	0.01	–
1970	2.75	2.32	0.10	0.32	0.01	–
1975	4.07	3.48	0.13	0.44	0.02	–
1978	6.57	5.63	0.20	0.72	0.02	–
1980	7.78	6.66	0.18	0.93	0.01	–
1985	18.36	14.63	0.75	2.93	0.05	–
"七五"时期						
1986	20.91	16.81	0.79	3.23	0.08	–
1987	24.65	19.50	0.99	4.05	0.11	–
1988	34.24	24.83	1.42	7.67	0.32	–
1989	35.14	25.04	1.24	8.47	0.39	–
1990	36.92	24.70	1.41	10.36	0.45	–
"八五"时期						
1991	40.13	26.44	1.47	11.64	0.58	–
1992	45.14	29.01	1.70	13.71	0.72	–
1993	57.81	36.00	1.98	18.86	0.97	–
1994	85.37	52.36	2.80	29.38	0.83	–
1995	114.07	71.48	2.71	38.69	1.19	–
"九五"时期						
1996	117.65	77.16	3.35	35.25	1.89	–
1997	131.69	87.91	3.86	38.04	1.88	–
1998	141.45	93.56	3.55	42.17	2.17	–
1999	148.61	96.81	3.12	46.27	2.41	–
2000	154.30	100.18	3.64	48.34	2.14	–
"十五"时期						
2001	162.27	105.54	3.27	51.16	2.30	–
2002	167.99	106.27	3.51	55.84	2.37	–
2003	180.30	109.41	4.11	60.90	2.05	3.83
2004	204.39	121.28	4.49	71.87	2.50	4.25
2005	230.46	137.01	5.56	80.56	2.69	4.64

11-5 续表 continued

年 份 Year	合计 Total	其中 of which 农业 Farming	林业 Forestry	牧业 Animal Husbandry	渔业 Fishery	农林牧渔服务业 Services of Agriculture,Forestry,Animal Husbandry and Fishing
"十一五"时期						
2006	247.72	147.98	6.44	84.86	2.89	5.55
2007	262.51	154.32	7.28	91.33	3.18	6.41
2008	302.00	173.32	10.63	104.53	4.54	8.97
2009	318.06	192.96	11.16	98.96	4.79	10.18
2010	361.24	231.08	6.87	106.40	5.31	11.58
"十二五"时期						
2011	399.90	240.80	7.98	131.55	6.05	13.51
2012	422.75	251.57	9.00	139.90	6.88	15.39
2013	470.55	284.66	10.34	149.46	8.01	18.07
2014	479.50	291.94	11.19	147.57	8.76	20.03
2015	493.04	296.93	12.15	153.12	9.32	21.52
"十三五"时期						
2016	501.72	298.63	13.20	156.28	9.88	23.74
2017	505.08	296.75	15.25	159.23	7.80	26.06
2018	514.90	318.55	17.72	141.48	7.28	29.88
2019	637.30	424.04	24.99	144.53	6.79	36.96
2019 年分地区 Region						
历下区 Li xia						
市中区 Shi zhong	3.30	1.77	0.66	0.71		0.17
槐荫区 Huai yin	4.21	2.95	0.53	0.33	0.28	0.11
天桥区 Tian qiao	6.78	4.70	0.27	1.54	0.19	0.07
历城区 Li cheng	76.65	59.10	5.83	6.56	0.80	4.35
长清区 Chang qing	58.57	36.70	2.30	17.08	0.24	2.25
章丘区 Zhang qiu	144.46	93.92	4.36	34.77	1.30	10.11
济阳区 Ji yang	75.98	53.25	3.32	16.74	1.11	2.57
莱芜区 Lai wu	102.98	72.50	2.65	23.21	1.11	3.51
钢城区 Gang cheng	18.28	11.90	1.40	4.15	0.03	0.81
平阴县 Ping yin	60.77	39.38	1.94	13.78	0.34	5.33
商河县 Shang he	85.32	47.87	2.73	25.66	1.37	7.69

注：依据 2016 年农业普查数据，对 2007 年至 2017 年农林牧渔业总产值做了相应调整。
Note: According to the data of the agricultural census in 2016, the total output value of agriculture, forestry, animal husbandry and fishery in the period from 2007 to 2017 was adjusted accordingly.

11-6 各时期农林牧渔业总产值定基指数(以1952年为100)

Gross Output Value and Indices of Farming, Forestry, Animal Husbandry in Each Period(1952=100)

年份 Year	合计 Total	农业 Farming	林业 Forestry	牧业 Animal Husbandry	渔业 Fishery
1952	100.00	100.00	100.00	100.00	100.00
1957	116.18	114.55	170.35	119.90	109.96
1962	73.32	74.42	69.10	69.25	20.68
1965	123.31	121.76	147.34	141.38	28.95
1970	151.35	146.28	254.82	184.02	58.65
1975	201.09	196.80	317.61	226.74	78.38
"五五"时期					
1976	198.67	185.64	340.19	269.52	118.70
1977	197.95	190.19	373.20	218.87	56.26
1978	208.10	203.90	304.32	239.93	57.89
1979	233.93	224.05	316.47	293.89	53.70
1980	264.53	259.07	286.30	330.80	43.98
"六五"时期					
1981	279.36	279.29	281.28	377.56	55.36
1982	312.68	308.75	346.83	460.13	51.95
1983	402.03	369.18	434.91	460.59	57.98
1984	493.28	436.59	572.67	651.29	69.52
1985	505.48	460.68	992.56	841.94	161.47
"七五"时期					
1986	531.29	488.47	964.62	857.25	229.32
1987	560.14	506.85	1075.00	960.76	291.92
1988	585.14	510.86	992.11	1191.92	383.08
1989	571.95	483.32	886.96	1320.55	495.30
1990	607.77	449.63	1126.99	1931.15	695.49
"八五"时期					
1991	670.19	488.17	1189.04	2204.93	830.45
1992	712.62	491.78	1298.34	2574.55	1007.33
1993	844.31	566.55	1420.51	3221.58	1209.21
1994	945.74	603.90	1671.10	2864.71	1064.29
1995	1093.57	657.49	1508.72	4905.57	1945.11

11-6 续表 continued

年 份 Year	合计 Total	农业 Farming	林业 Forestry	牧业 Animal Husbandry	渔业 Fishery
"九五"时期					
1996	1197.20	727.03	1818.36	5258.95	2224.25
1997	1273.56	820.27	2002.99	5116.96	2202.07
1998	1426.28	914.05	1858.14	5907.41	2516.54
1999	1486.09	934.64	2110.21	6277.65	2639.47
2000	1569.90	991.58	2255.81	6620.62	2441.73
"十五"时期					
2001	1599.32	1005.16	1700.16	6905.18	2646.43
2002	1638.09	997.16	1826.57	7349.57	2712.97
2003	1711.88	1072.24	1977.78	7726.93	2324.25
2004	1804.32	1132.29	1979.76	8121.00	2803.05
2005	1930.62	1188.90	2237.13	8770.68	2802.30
"十一五"时期					
2006	2046.15	1249.31	2454.25	9245.35	3003.10
2007	2046.15	1334.26	2610.83	9006.43	3540.65
2008	2148.45	1422.32	2783.14	9231.59	3204.85
2009	2260.17	1524.73	2964.04	9342.35	3323.43
2010	2367.76	1584.02	1815.08	10311.68	3416.48
"十二五"时期					
2011	2471.94	1658.47	2016.56	10600.40	3508.72
2012	2588.12	1724.80	2216.20	11151.62	3768.36
2013	2689.05	1762.74	2491.01	11809.56	3877.64
2014	2801.99	1845.58	2724.66	12116.60	3916.41
2015	2919.67	1924.93	2986.23	12540.68	4033.90
"十三五"时期					
2016	3045.21	2007.70	3317.70	12967.06	4187.19
2017	3157.88	2126.15	3689.28	13278.26	4203.93
2018	3095.96	2215.44	4105.56	12733.85	4330.04
2019	3123.82	2290.76	5037.52	11587.80	3814.77

11-7 主要农作物播种面积及产量
Sown Areas and Output of Main Farm Crops

指 标	Indicator	2013 年	2014 年	2015 年	2016 年	2017 年	2018 年	2019 年
农作物总播种面积（万公顷）	Total Sown Area of Crops(10 000 ha)	58.34	57.81	56.24	59.89	56.61	54.90	61.56
粮食作物	Grain	44.47	44.39	43.25	47.67	45.15	44.43	47.93
谷物	Cereals	42.94	42.80	41.65	46.05	43.79	43.25	46.33
小麦	Wheat	21.04	21.05	20.99	22.00	21.58	21.38	21.89
稻谷	Rice	0.45	0.34	0.21	0.20	0.18	0.14	0.14
玉米	Corn	20.85	20.81	19.82	22.93	21.07	20.84	23.18
谷子	Millet	0.50	0.49	0.54	0.86	0.91	0.86	1.09
高粱	Chinese Sorghum	0.09	0.09	0.09	0.05	0.05	0.02	0.01
其他	Others	0.01	0.01	0.01	0.01	0.00	0.01	0.01
豆类	Beans	0.69	0.69	0.71	0.85	0.70	0.62	0.77
薯类	Tubers	0.84	0.91	0.88	0.77	0.66	0.56	0.83
油料作物	Oil-bearing Crops	1.52	1.36	1.30	1.00	1.00	1.02	1.92
#花生	Peanuts	1.33	1.21	1.13	0.88	0.87	0.90	1.81
棉花	Cotton	1.17	0.89	0.71	0.62	0.20	0.28	0.38
蔬菜	Vegetable	9.61	9.61	9.42	9.13	8.86	7.89	10.03
果用瓜	Melon	1.31	1.29	1.28	1.20	1.16	1.07	0.98
其他作物	Other Farm Crops	0.26	0.27	0.28	0.26	0.25	0.21	0.32
果园种植面积（万公顷）	Orchard Area(10 000 ha)	3.42	3.41	3.35	3.20	3.16	3.09	3.89
#苹果	Apple	1.33	1.33	1.29	1.18	1.18	1.13	1.24
梨	Pear	0.17	0.16	0.16	0.14	0.14	0.16	0.18
葡萄	Grape	0.10	0.10	0.10	0.10	0.10	0.11	0.11
桃	Peach	0.47	0.49	0.47	0.49	0.49	0.72	1.00
农作物总产量（万吨）	Total Output of Farm Crops(10 000 tons)							
粮食作物产量	Output of Grain Crops	266.61	271.19	264.55	275.43	255.57	251.42	285.46
谷物	Cereals	259.98	264.64	257.65	268.30	249.47	246.12	276.48
小麦	Wheat	123.86	126.37	129.75	127.31	123.79	121.78	135.31
稻谷	Rice	2.89	2.33	1.52	1.55	1.36	1.18	1.21
玉米	Corn	131.40	134.26	124.39	136.65	121.25	119.82	136.11
谷子	Millet	1.59	1.45	1.74	2.64	2.97	3.27	3.80
高粱	Chinese Sorghum	0.20	0.19	0.22	0.11	0.11	0.04	0.03
其他	Other Cereals	0.04	0.04	0.03	0.04	0.00	0.03	0.03
豆类	Beans	1.87	1.71	1.92	2.25	1.82	1.67	2.12
薯类	Tubers	4.76	4.85	4.99	4.87	4.28	3.63	6.86
油料作物	Oil-bearing Crops	5.69	4.95	4.59	3.53	3.59	4.15	6.57
#花生	Peanuts	5.33	4.63	4.23	3.25	3.31	3.87	6.31

11-7 续表 continued

指 标	Indicator	2013 年	2014 年	2015 年	2016 年	2017 年	2018 年	2019 年
棉花	Cotton	1.16	0.97	0.74	0.69	0.20	0.29	0.54
蔬菜	Vegetable	629.54	638.22	626.23	611.25	591.63	527.22	671.24
果用瓜	Melon	78.75	77.79	77.00	70.74	67.51	59.65	48.02
水果总产量（万吨）	**Output of Fruits(10 000 tons)**	**43.29**	**44.11**	**43.94**	**41.08**	**43.15**	**42.19**	**62.95**
# 苹果	Apple	20.65	20.98	20.62	18.33	18.59	16.00	20.22
梨	Pear	4.76	4.70	4.83	4.26	3.98	3.40	4.19
葡萄	Grape	3.08	3.10	3.16	2.86	3.00	3.00	3.13
桃	Peach	11.02	10.82	10.71	11.08	13.10	11.86	21.40
杏	Apricot	0.73	0.85	0.83	0.78	0.75	3.02	4.11
枣（鲜）	Jujube	0.98	1.02	1.00	1.02	1.02	0.89	1.21
柿子（鲜）	Persimmon	0.26	0.26	0.24	0.23	0.23	1.24	2.29
山楂	Hawthorn	0.54	0.54	0.54	0.55	0.55	0.63	2.19
樱桃	Cherry	0.95	1.05	1.59	1.49	1.45	1.51	2.78
其他	Others	0.50	0.50	0.50	0.48	0.47	0.64	1.19
农作物单位面积产量（公斤 / 公顷）	**Output Per Hectare of Farm Crops (kg/ha)**							
粮食作物单位面积产量	Output per Hectare of Grain Crops	5995	6109	6117	5778	5660	5659	5956
谷物	Cereals	6054	6184	6186	5826	5697	5690	5968
小麦	Wheat	5887	6002	6182	5787	5736	5696	6181
稻谷	Rice	6422	6799	7259	7698	7645	8288	8334
玉米	Corn	6302	6452	6276	5960	5754	5748	5872
谷子	Millet	3180	2965	3220	3071	3252	3809	3490
高粱	Chinese Sorghum	2222	2149	2497	2097	2228	2074	1941
其他	Others	4000	2974	3000	2716	0.00	3062	2750
豆类	Beans	2710	2474	2683	2659	2614	2716	2747
薯类	Tubers	5667	5341	5673	6371	6462	6462	8248
油料作物	Oil-bearing Crops	3753	3627	3545	3531	3609	4083	3418
# 花生	Peanuts	4004	3830	3747	3713	3795	4327	3495
棉花	Cotton	995	1080	1040	1106	1037	1029	1410
蔬菜	Vegetable	65495	66434	66460	66918	66798	66852	66895
果用瓜	Melon	60056	60506	60263	46939	58724	55628	48797

注：1. 依据 2006 年农业普查数据，对 1997 年至 2007 年蔬菜面积、产量做了相应调整。
2. 按照国务院农普办要求，由国家统计局山东调查总队根据第三次农业普查数据，对 2016–2017 年市、县（区）粮食播种面积、单产和总产量等数据进行修订。
3. 依据 2016 年农业普查数据，对 2008 年至 2017 年种植业相关品种面积、产量做了相应调整。

Note: 1. According to the data of the agricultural census in 2006, the area and yield of the vegetables from 1997 to 2007 were adjusted.
2. According to the requirements of Agricultural Census Office of the State Council, Shandong Survey Team of National Bureau of Statistics revised the grain sown area, yield per unit and total yield of each city and country (district) from 2016–2017 based on the data from the third agricultural census.
3. According to the agricultural census data in 2016, the area and yield of planting related varieties from 2008 to 2017 were adjusted.

11-8 林、牧、渔业生产情况
Basic Statistics on Forestry，Animal Husbandry and Fishery

指 标	Indicator	单位 Unit	2013年	2014年	2015年	2016年	2017年	2018年	2019年
林业生产	Production of Forestry								
造林面积	Forested Area	公顷 (ha)	13637	14881	12013	3504	3809	4902	10758
四旁植树	Surrounding Tree Planting	万株 (10000 trees)	1377	1366	1311	1312	1301	1306	1576
育苗面积	Area of Nursery Garden	公顷 (ha)	8900	12073	14439	11773	10645	10174	11579
果品产量	Output of Fruits	吨 (tons)	535625	574248	573064	539475	596994	555042	686868
木材采伐量	Timber Cut	立方米 (stere)	167433	143896	132014	157238	214946	283354	355596
牧业生产	Production of Animal Husbandry								
大牲畜存栏	Stocked Large Livestock	万头 (10 000 heads)	26.05	26.30	28.11	28.97	31.63	26.30	24.42
#役畜	Draught Animal	万头 (10 000 heads)	1.49	1.37	0.26	0.19	0.02	0.02	
#牛	Cattle	万头 (10 000 heads)	25.46	25.71	27.86	28.69	31.36	26.17	24.27
猪存栏	Stocked Pigs	万头 (10 000 heads)	136.26	136.56	128.51	116.73	120.13	102.95	129.26
羊存栏	Stocked Sheep	万只 (10 000 heads)	88.04	88.78	89.71	93.27	96.60	87.61	100.13
家禽存栏	Stocked Poultry	万只 (10 000 heads)	2701.65	2723.53	2784.87	2743.90	2467.54	2300.42	3440.94
猪出栏数	Slaughtered Pigs	万头 (10 000 heads)	214.59	223.04	214.97	194.15	198.43	185.59	217.66
羊出栏数	Slaughtered Sheep and Goats	万只 (10 000 heads)	121.14	129.91	132.07	149.03	153.23	143.84	164.26
肉类总产量	Output of Meat	吨 (tons)	335868	340975	341829	317201	325036	298180	358655
#猪牛羊肉	Meat	吨 (tons)	248845	259678	259954	235990	246561	223735	236601

11-8 续表 continued

指　标	Indicator	单位 Unit	2013 年	2014 年	2015 年	2016 年	2017 年	2018 年	2019 年
猪肉	Pork	吨 (tons)	180114	188921	185546	162114	168054	155005	170584
牛肉	Beef	吨 (tons)	51272	51902	55852	53203	57206	46438	40698
羊肉	Mutton	吨 (tons)	17459	18854	18557	20673	21301	22292	25319
禽肉	Poultry Meat	吨 (tons)	83473	76781	81113	80447	77809	74164	120194
奶类	Milk	吨 (tons)	243649	258085	232705	214620	263642	328412	321323
# 牛奶	Cow Milk	吨 (tons)	243649	258082	232702	214617	263638	328410	321321
禽蛋	Poultry Eggs	吨 (tons)	342797	347254	378577	386440	394001	332303	365810
# 鸡蛋	Hen's Eggs	吨 (tons)	327293	332092	362017	368636	375517	313234	343650
渔业生产	Aquatic Products								
水产品产量	Total Aquatic Products	吨 (tons)	46048	47018	47565	46709	41279	31911	16167
捕捞	Fishing	吨 (tons)	905	759	650	465	186	289	3513
养殖	Cultured	吨 (tons)	45143	46259	46915	46244	41093	31622	12654
养殖面积	Breeding Area of Aquatic Products	公顷 (ha)	7428	7360	7285	7079	6673	5228	4380
养殖单产	Aquaculture Yield	公斤 / 公顷 (kg/ha)	6077	6285	6440	6533	6158	6049	2889

注：依据 2016 年农业普查数据，对 2008 年至 2017 年牧业生产有关指标做了相应调整。
Note: According to the data of agricultural census in 2016, the relevant indicators of animal husbandry production from 2008 to 2017 were adjusted accordingly.

11-9 分地区主要农作物播种面积及产量(2019年)
Sown Areas and Output of Main Farm Crops by Region(2019)

指 标	Indicator	济南市 Total City	历下区 Li xia	市中区 Shi zhong
农作物播种总面积(公顷)	Total Sown Area of Crops(ha)	612801		4147
粮食	Grain	479308		3973
谷物	Cereals	463284		3932
小麦	Wheat	218917		1486
稻谷	Rice	1449		
玉米	Corn	231773		2278
谷子	Millet	10892		168
高粱	Chinese Sorghum	141		
其他	Others	110		
豆类	Beans	7705		35
薯类	Tubers	8320		6
油料作物	Oil-bearing Crops	19228		11
#花生	Peanuts	18054		11
棉花	Cotton	3841		9
蔬菜	Vegetable	100343		141
果用瓜	Melon	9842		13
其他作物	Other Farm Crops	239		
果园种植面积(公顷)	Orchard Area(ha)	38905		249
#苹果	Apple	12423		49
梨	Pear	1805		
葡萄	Grape	1081		13
桃	Peach	10040		125
农作物产量(吨)	Total Output of Farm Crops (tons)			
粮食作物产量	Output of Grain Crops	2854598		18975
谷物	Cereals	2764805		18872
小麦	Wheat	1353076		8015
稻谷	Rice	12079		
玉米	Corn	1361059		10539
谷子	Millet	38014		319
高粱	Chinese Sorghum	273		
其他	Other Cereals	304		
豆类	Beans	21167		52
薯类	Tubers	68625		51

槐荫区 Huai yin	天桥区 Tian qiao	历城区 Li cheng	长清区 Chang qing	章丘区 Zhang qiu	济阳区 Ji yang	莱芜区 Lai wu	钢城区 Gang cheng	平阴县 Ping yin	商河县 Shang he
2554	**13436**	**25576**	**56332**	**139179**	**115585**	**61466**	**10811**	**47220**	**136497**
2255	12940	19660	43718	106967	98481	31238	4505	34773	120800
2201	12873	19079	41278	102488	97509	28717	3990	30548	120668
1186	6745	7575	16314	53023	51690	5983	670	15910	58335
301	35		56	115	944				
715	6093	10064	21074	46706	44875	21515	3125	12996	62334
		1437	3723	2528		1207	194	1634	
		1	3	116		12	1	8	
		1	109						
54	67	287	1059	2645	939	385	58	2076	102
		294	1381	1834	33	2136	457	2149	30
67	47	384	4173	1885	487	6220	3628	2291	35
	47	380	4000	1708	481	6204	3628	1560	35
	61	48	177	816	121	962	237	668	742
229	382	4181	8164	24540	14230	22880	2379	8498	14719
3	6	1215	86	4971	2179	125	56	987	201
		88	14		87	41	6	3	
	97	**11265**	**3212**	**6308**	**595**	**5195**	**3715**	**7752**	**517**
	10	2834	109	2635	144	842	635	5049	117
	50	872	56	273	84	194	74	57	143
	6	48	15	378	59	145	44	301	71
	14	4501	922	882	162	993	2163	210	70
13063	68024	102727	260990	604249	597458	191225	25835	191813	780240
12941	67865	99741	244362	581710	594508	170630	22168	172412	779597
7193	40149	44795	95765	318306	325146	36737	3812	88919	384240
2324	239		492	980	8044				
3425	27476	50333	129844	255908	261318	131004	17793	78062	395357
		4606	17955	6300		2859	560	5415	
		2	8	217		29	2	16	
		4	299						
121	159	814	2961	7773	2689	925	159	5148	366
		2173	13667	14766	260	19670	3508	14253	277

11-9 续表 continued

指 标	Indicator	济南市 Total City	历下区 Li xia	市中区 Shi zhong
油料作物	Oil-bearing Crops	65709		22
#花生	Peanuts	63093		22
棉花	Cotton	5417		9
蔬菜	Vegetable	6712425		7570
果用瓜	Melon	480214		438
水果总产量（吨）	**Output of Fruits(tons)**	**629485**		**3548**
#苹果	Apple	202192		1361
梨	Pear	41880		
葡萄	Grape	31263		435
桃	Peach	214017		1186
杏	Apricot	41112		303
枣（鲜）	Jujube	12104		26
柿子（鲜）	Persimmon	22949		7
山楂	Hawthorn	21943		25
樱桃	Cherry	27830		204
其他	Others	11930		1
农作物单位面积产量（公斤/公顷）	**Output per Hectare of Farm Crops(kg/ha)**			
粮食作物单位面积产量	Output per Hectare of Grain Crops	5956		4776
谷物	Cereals	5968		4799
小麦	Wheat	6181		5393
稻谷	Rice	8334		
玉米	Corn	5872		4626
谷子	Millet	3490		1899
高粱	Chinese Sorghum	1941		
其他	Others	2750		
豆类	Beans	2747		1512
薯类	Tubers	8248		7865
油料作物	Oil-bearing Crops	3417		1970
#花生	Peanuts	3495		1970
棉花	Cotton	1410		1061
蔬菜	Vegetable	66896		53736
果用瓜	Melon	48797		34235

注：粮食作物产量、播种面积自 2012 年开始由山东调查总队反馈。
Note: Grain crop yield and sown area have been reported by Shandong Survey Team since 2012.

槐荫区 Huai yin	天桥区 Tian qiao	历城区 Li cheng	长清区 Chang qing	章丘区 Zhang qiu	济阳区 Ji yang	莱芜区 Lai wu	钢城区 Gang cheng	平阴县 Ping yin	商河县 Shang he
120	214	1758	17976	6145	2292	18340	9588	9083	172
	214	1754	17464	5874	2273	18285	9588	7448	172
	183	86	162	872	178	2113	304	706	805
11346	15570	257833	521563	1772527	1081591	1236667	194469	639485	973805
157	174	56731	3700	248992	89002	6255	2911	65575	6279
	1060	142126	54776	71786	25401	106588	104747	100864	18589
	72	22250	2582	37877	6195	29255	18602	81107	2891
	590	18339	1750	2664	2784	5682	1163	1762	7148
	233	1335	641	10566	3210	1888	571	7717	4667
	97	76278	11920	10843	7324	26128	74798	3578	1864
	10	14387	15015	495	344	9386	424	266	481
	8	372	229	5606	2679	1240	211	414	1320
	1	2226	7103	136	1510	9382	2068	423	95
	0	4313	106	592	529	12004	3675	688	11
	30	772	15336	2782	41	7012	1098	516	39
	20	1758	10	57	723	3090	1818	4378	75
5791	5257	5225	5970	5649	6067	6122	5735	5516	6459
5879	5272	5228	5920	5676	6097	5942	5556	5644	6461
6066	5952	5913	5870	6003	6290	6140	5691	5589	6587
7731	6917		8855	8553	8521				
4792	4509	5001	6161	5479	5823	6089	5694	6007	6343
		3205	4822	2492		2368	2887	3313	
		2001	2826	1865		2475	2061	1939	
		3989	2738						
2235	2379	2834	2796	2939	2865	2407	2757	2480	3592
		7378	9899	8053	7965	9208	7672	6633	9368
1800	4500	4584	4308	3260	4704	2949	2643	3966	4950
	4500	4613	4365	3440	4725	2948	2643	4775	4950
	3002	1781	915	1068	1464	2196	1284	1056	1085
49461	40710	61671	63887	72231	76008	54051	81756	75252	66159
48062	30636	46706	42990	50085	40850	50121	51920	66452	31280

11-10 分地区林、牧、渔业生产情况(2019年)
Basic Statistics on Forestry, Animal Husbandry and Fishery by Region(2019)

指 标	Indicator	单 位 Unit	济南市 Total City	历下区 Li xia
林业生产	Production of Forestry			
造林面积	Forested Area	公顷 (ha)	10758	134
四旁植树	Surrounding Tree Planting	万株 (10000 trees)	1576	114
育苗面积	Area of Nurs ery Garden	公顷 (ha)	11579	
果品产量	Output of Fruits	吨 (tons)	686868	
木材采伐量	Timber Cut	立方米 (stere)	355596	
牧业生产	Production of Animal Husbandry			
大牲畜存栏	Stocked Large Livestock	万头 (10 000 heads)	24.42	
#役畜	Draught Animal	万头 (10 000 heads)		
#牛	Cattle	万头 (10 000 heads)	24.27	
猪存栏	Stocked Pigs	万头 (10 000 heads)	129.26	
羊存栏	Stocked Sheep	万只 (10 000 heads)	100.13	
家禽存栏	Stocked Poultry	万只 (10 000 heads)	3440.94	
猪出栏数	Slaughtered Pigs	万头 (10 000 heads)	217.66	
羊出栏数	Slaughtered Sheep and Goats	万只 (10 000 heads)	164.26	
肉类总产量	Output of Meat	吨 (tons)	358655	
#猪牛羊肉	Meat	吨 (tons)	236601	
猪肉	Pork	吨 (tons)	170584	
牛肉	Beef	吨 (tons)	40698	
羊肉	Mutton	吨 (tons)	25319	
禽肉	Poultry Meat	吨 (tons)	120194	
奶类	Milk	吨 (tons)	321323	
#牛奶	Cow Milk	吨 (tons)	321321	
禽蛋	Poultry Eggs	吨 (tons)	365810	
#鸡蛋	Hen's Eggs	吨 (tons)	343650	
渔业生产	Aquatic Products			
水产品产量	Total Aquatic Products	吨 (tons)	16167	
捕捞	Fishing	吨 (tons)	3513	
养殖	Cultured	吨 (tons)	12654	
养殖面积	Breeding Area of Aquatic Products	公顷 (ha)	4380	
养殖单产	Aquaculture Yield	公斤/公顷 (kg/ha)	2889	

市中区 Shi zhong	槐荫区 Huai yin	天桥区 Tian qiao	历城区 Li cheng	长清区 Chang qing	章丘区 Zhang qiu	济阳区 Ji yang	莱芜区 Lai wu	钢城区 Gang cheng	平阴县 Ping yin	商河县 Shang he
724	68	80	2771	704	1255	489	1973	972	687	901
120	70	21	197	160	320	100	141	63	120	150
69	33		4103	3244	800	587	515	40	183	2005
7932			364130	53021	23918	9351	99814	61752	47100	19850
	1126	2174	8700	96595	34100	77074	25508		27019	83300
0.05	0.01	0.06	0.27	3.90	10.79	1.77	1.23	0.19	2.39	3.76
0.05	0.01	0.06	0.26	3.81	10.76	1.76	1.23	0.19	2.38	3.76
0.17	0.03	0.30	2.05	16.49	33.56	8.10	30.28	9.34	9.83	19.11
0.39	0.11	0.63	2.29	16.44	22.59	7.09	15.91	6.06	15.72	12.90
10.01	3.00	28.21	109.66	239.58	872.47	328.13	804.60	155.62	317.34	572.32
0.42	0.13	0.69	2.85	25.36	57.96	8.88	55.87	12.27	20.39	32.84
0.43	0.31	0.70	2.49	21.58	32.01	8.98	23.24	6.90	44.59	23.03
1095	189	1200	6829	35051	97753	24329	80814	14862	39929	56604
682	149	690	2610	28495	70841	12827	42413	9763	29215	38916
377	111	551	2046	20011	48856	7692	37459	8621	16292	28568
231	3	53	293	5835	17458	3574	1962	245	5597	5447
74	35	86	271	2649	4527	1561	2992	897	7326	4901
412	39	509	4197	6407	26866	11469	37093	4874	10640	17688
194			2160	36583	82128	27485	2071	1224	40527	128951
194			2160	36580	82128	27486	2071	1224	40527	128951
701	375	4082	9268	25236	172220	13002	40489	7891	39038	53508
701	375	4082	9259	23843	168432	10985	40116	7739	38802	39316
	1500	1925	431	1250	1590	3078	3466	196	1173	1558
				210		28	3133	128		14
	1500	1925	431	1040	1590	3050	333	68	1173	1544
	140	220	42	345	360	551	1710	270	446	296
	10714	8750	10262	3014	4417	16151	195	252	2630	5216

11-11 农业"四化"情况(2019年)

Basic Statistics on Four Modernization of Agriculture(2019)

指 标 Indicator	机耕面积(千公顷) Machine-cultivated Area (1000 hectares)	有效灌溉面积(千公顷) Effective Irrigated Area (1000 hectares)	农用化肥施用量(吨折纯) Consumption of Chemical Fertilizer (tons convert to pure volume)	每公顷耕地化肥施用量(公斤折纯) Consumption of Chemical Fertilizers Per Hectare (kg convert to pure volume)	农药施用量(吨) Pesticides Mption (tons)	每公顷耕地农药施用量(公斤) Consumption of Pesticides Per Hectare (kg)
全市 Total City	393.5	294.0	214814		3477.5	
历下区 Li xia						
市中区 Shi zhong	1.4	2.7	970		34.4	
槐荫区 Huai yin	1.5	2.1	196		4.5	
天桥区 Tian qiao	12.6	8.5	2810		28.9	
历城区 Li cheng	14.8	25.0	13813		394.2	
长清区 Chang qing	22.0	25.1	12184		328.5	
章丘区 Zhang qiu	70.4	57.5	46819		404.0	
济阳区 Ji yang	53.8	53.0	31750		769.3	
莱芜区 Lai wu	38.5	32.9	29907		745.5	
钢城区 Gang cheng	13.6	4.6	4130		239.3	
平阴县 Ping yin	36.8	18.7	14412		136.2	
商河县 Shang he	73.2	63.9	57823		392.6	

注：由于第三次全国土地调查数据未反馈，"每公顷耕地化肥施用量""每公顷耕地农药施用量"相关数据空缺。

Note: "As required by the agricultural census office of the State Council, NBS general investigation office of Shandong Province revises the grain acreage, output per hectare and total output in cities and counties (districts) based on the data of the third agricultural census" and "Consumption of Pesticides per Hectare" are blank because these data are not reflected in the third national land survey.

11-12 主要农副产品产量与上年和历史最高年份比较

Output of Major Agricultral Products in Comparision with Last Year and Maximum Year

指 标	Indicator	2019年	2018年	历史最高年 Maximum Year		2019年为历史最高年的% 2019 Account for Historic High	2019年为2018年的% 2019 Account for 2018
				年份 Year	产量 Output		
农产品产量(万吨)	Total Output of Farm Crops(10 000 tons)						
粮食总产量	Output of Grain Crops	285.46	251.42	2011	295.84	96.5	113.5
#小麦	Wheat	135.31	121.78	2019	135.31	100.0	111.1
稻谷	Rice	1.21	1.18	2000	9.89	12.2	102.1
玉米	Corn	136.11	119.82	2011	143.96	94.5	113.6
薯类	Tubers	6.86	3.63	1995	23.10	29.7	189.2
经济作物(万吨)	Commercial Crop(10 000 tons)						
#棉花	Cotton	0.54	0.29	1999	5.00	10.8	186.8
油料花生	Peanuts	6.31	3.87	2019	6.31	100.0	163.0
蔬菜总产量	Output of Vegetables	671.24	527.22	2019	671.24	100.0	127.3
水果总产量	Output of Fruits	62.95	42.19	2019	62.95	100.0	149.2
水产品总产量(万吨)	Total Aquatic Products(10 000 tons)	1.6	3.2	2015	4.80	33.3	50.0

主要统计指标解释

农林牧渔业总产值 是以货币表现的农、林、牧、渔业全部产品的总量，它反映一定时期内农林牧渔业生产的总规模和总成果。

农、林、牧、渔四业的统计范围是辖区内各种经济组织类型、各个系统的全部农林牧渔业生产单位和非农行业单位附属的农林牧渔业生产活动单位。不包括农业科学试验机构进行的农业生产。

农林牧渔业总产值的核算范围是本辖区内在一定时期内生产的农业、林业、牧业、渔业产品的价值和对农林牧渔业生产活动进行的各种支持性服务活动的价值总和，执行日历年度。

（1）农业产值，包括谷物和其他作物产值：蔬菜，园艺作物产值：水果，坚果，饮料和香料产值；中药材产值。其中谷物和其他作物产值包括谷物、薯类、豆类、棉花、油料，糖料，麻类、烟叶和其他农作物的产值。其他农作物包括青饲料，绿肥、牧草、桑叶及采集的野生植物。

（2）林业，包括林木的培育和种植（不包括茶园、桑园和果园的栽培，管理和收获等活动）。林产品的采集和竹木采伐。

（3）牧业，包括除渔业养殖以外的一切动物饲养和放牧以及捕猎野兽野禽产值。

（4）渔业，包括水生动物和海藻类植物的养殖和捕捞。

（5）农林牧渔服务业，包括灌溉，农产品初加工。农机服务，病虫害防治、森林防火、兽医服务、鱼苗及鱼种场等对农林牧渔业生产活动进行的各种支持性服务活动。但不包括各种科学技术和专业技术服务活动。农林牧渔业总产值核算采用“产品法”进行计算，即用产品产量乘以价格以求出各种产品产值，然后加总求得各业产值，最后各业相加求得农林牧渔业总产值。

1957 年以前的农业总产值中包括了厩肥和农民自给性手工业（如农民自制衣服、鞋、袜，自己从事粮食初步加工等）。1958 年及以后的农业总产值，林业中增加了村及村以下竹木采伐产值；牧业中取消了厩肥产值；副业中取消了农民自给性手工业产值，增加了村及村以下办的工业产值；渔业中增加了海洋捕捞水产品产值。1980 年及以后的农业总产值，在副业中增加了农民家庭兼营工业商品性部分的产值。从 1984 年起村及村以下办工业产值划归工业。从 1993 年起取消副业，将采集野生植物产值和农民家庭兼营商品性工业产值划归农业产值，捕猎野兽、野禽产值划入牧业产值。2003 年根据新的国民经济行业分类，农林牧渔服务业划归第一产业。原农业产值中的农民家庭兼营商品性工业产值划归工业产值；林业中竹木采伐产值统计范围由村及村以下改为全社会。

农林牧渔业增加值 是指农、林、牧、渔及农林牧渔服务业生产货物或提供服务活动而增加的价值，为农林牧渔业现价总产值扣除农林渔业现价中间投入后的余额。

农林牧渔业增加值的核算范围同农林牧渔业总产值的核算范围相同。

农林牧渔业增加值的计算方法：采用生产法和分配法（收入法）两种。

1. 生产法计算公式：

农林牧渔业增加值 = 农林牧渔业总产值 - 农林牧渔业中间消耗

2. 分配法计算公式：

农林牧渔业增加值 = 固定资产折旧 + 劳动者报酬 + 生产税净额 + 营业盈余

其中：生产税净额 = 生产税收 - 生产补贴

粮食产量 指全社会的粮食作物产量。包括国营农场等全民所有制经营的、集体统一经营和农民家庭经营的粮食产量，还包括工矿企业家属办的农场和其他生产单位的产量粮食除包括稻谷、小麦、玉米、高粱、谷子及其他杂粮外，还包括薯类和大豆。其产量计算方法，豆类按去豆荚后的干豆计算；薯类包括甘薯和马铃薯，不包括芋头和木薯。1963 年以前按每 4 公斤鲜薯 1 公斤粮食计算，从 1964 年以后按 5 公斤鲜薯折 1 公斤粮食计算。其他粮食一律按脱粒后的原粮计算。

油料产量 指全部油料作物的生产量。包括花生、油菜籽、芝麻、向日葵籽、胡麻籽（亚麻籽）和其他油料。不包括大豆、木本油料和野生油料。花生以带壳干花生计算。

水产品产量 指人工养殖的水产品和天然生长的水产的捕捞量。包括海水的鱼类、虾蟹类、贝类和藻类以及淡水的鱼类、虾蟹类和贝类，不包括淡水水生植物。

猪、牛、羊肉产量 指当年出栏并已屠宰的猪、牛、羊的肉产量。即屠宰后除去头蹄下水后带骨肉（即胴体重）的重量。

耕地面积 指年初可以用来种植农作物、经常进行耕锄的田地，包括熟地、当年新开荒地、连续撂荒未满三年的耕地和当年的休闲地（轮歇地），还包括以种植农作物为主并附带种植桑树、茶树、果树和其他林木的土地，以及沿海、沿湖地区已围垦利用的“海涂”、“湖田”等面积。

不包括属于专业性的桑园、茶园、果园、果木苗圃、林地、芦苇地、天然或人工草地面积。

农作物播种面积 指实际播种或移植有农作物的面积。凡是实际种植有农作物的面积，不论种植在耕地上还是种植在非耕地上，均包括在农作物播种面积中。在播种季节基本结束后，因遭灾而重新改种和补种的农作物面积，也包括在内。

灌溉面积 有效灌溉面积，指具有一定的水源，地块比较平整，灌溉工程或设备已经配套，在一般年景下半年能够进行正常灌溉的耕地面积。

农用化肥施用量 指本年内实际用于农业生产的化肥数量，包括氮肥、磷肥、钾肥和复合肥。化肥施用量要求按折纯量计算数量。折纯量是指把氮肥、磷肥、钾肥分别按含氮、含五氧化二磷、含氧化钾的百分之一百成份进行折算后的数量。复合肥按其所含主要成分折算。

农业机械总动力 指主要用于农、林、牧、渔业的各种动力机械的动力总和。包括耕作机械、排灌机械、收获机械、农产品加工机械、运输机械、植物保护机械、牧业机械、林业机械、渔业机械和其他农业机械（内燃机按引擎马力折成瓦（特）计算），电动机按功率折成瓦特计算。不包括专门用于乡办工业、基本建设、非农业运输、科学试验和教学等非农业生产方面用的动力机械与作业机械。

Explanatory Notes on Main Statistical Indicators

Gross Output Value of Farming, Forestry, Animal Husbandry and Fishery refers to the total volume of products of farming, forestry, animal husbandry and fishery in monetary expression, which reflects the total scale and the total result of farming, forestry, animal husbandry and fishery production during a given period.

The scope of statistics of farming, forestry, animal husbandry and fishing covers various economic organizations in the area under administration as well as agriculture, forestry, animal husbandry and fishery production activity units which all agriculture, forestry, animal husbandry and fishing production units and units in non-agricultural industries of all systems are subordinate to, excluding agricultural production by agricultural science experiment organization.

The scope of accounting of the gross output value of farming, forestry, animal husbandry and fishery is the sum of the value of agriculture, forestry, animal husbandry and fishery products produced in the area under administration within a certain period and the value of various supportive service activities in agriculture, forestry, animal husbandry and fishery production activities based on a calendar year.

(1) The value of agricultural production includes the output value of cereal and other crop: output value of vegetables and horticultural plants: output value of fruits, nuts, beverages and spices; output value of traditional Chinese medicinal materials. Output value of cereal and other crops includes that of cereal, potato, bean, cotton, oil plants, sugar, bast fiber plants, tobacco and other crops. Other crops include green feed, green manure, pasture, folium mori and collected wild plants.

(2) Forestry includes cultivation and plantation of the forest (excluding cultivation, management and harvesting of tea plantation, mulberry plantation and orchard). Acquisition of forest products and bamboo and wood cutting.

(3) Animal husbandry includes output value of animal feeding and grazing and hunting wild animals and wildfowls except for fishery breeding.

(4) Fishery includes breeding and fishing of aquatic animals and seaweed plants.

(5) Farming, forestry, animal husbandry and fishery service industry include irrigation and primary processing of agricultural products. Various supportive service activities (such as agricultural machinery service, pest control, forest fire prevention, veterinary service and fry and seed farm) for agriculture, forestry, animal husbandry and fishery production activities, excluding various service activities of scientific technology and professional technology. The gross output value of farming, forestry, animal husbandry and fishery is calculated by "product approach", which means the gross output value of agriculture, forestry, animal husbandry and fishery is obtained after adding the output value of all industries obtained by adding the output value of various products originating from the production output multiplying by the price.

Gross output value of farming before 1957 includes animal manure and peasant self-catering handicraft industry (including homemade clothes, shoes and socks of farmers as well as preliminary processing of grain by farmers). As for the gross output value of agriculture in 1958 and later, the output value of bamboo and wood cutting of the village and below is added in the forestry; output value of animal manure is cancelled in the animal husbandry; output value of peasant self-catering handicraft industry is cancelled and output value of the industry of the village and below is added in the sideline; output value of aquatic products based on marine fishing is added in the fishery. As for gross output value of agriculture in 1980 and later, output value of industrial commodities concurrently operated by the peasant family is added in the sideline. Output value of the industry of the village and below from 1984 was incorporated into value of industrial output. The sideline was cancelled from 1993. The output value of wild plants acquired and output of commercial industry concurrently operated by peasant family are classified into value of agricultural production and output of wild animals and wild birds hunted is included into output of animal husbandry. Agriculture, forestry, animal husbandry and fishery service industry was classified into the primary industry in 2003 pursuant to the new classification of national economy industries. Output value of the commercial industry concurrently operated by the peasant family in the original value of agricultural production is included into value of industrial output; the scope of statistics of the output value of bamboo and wood cutting in the forestry is changed to the whole society.

Value added of agriculture, forestry, animal husbandry and fishery refers to the value added due to production of goods or provision of service in agriculture, forestry, animal husbandry and fishing and agriculture, it is the balance of the total output value at the current price of agriculture, forestry, animal husbandry and fishery minus by intermediate input at the current price of agriculture, fishing and forestry.

The scope of accounting of the value added of agriculture, forestry, animal husbandry and fishery is the same to the gross output value of farming, forestry, animal husbandry and fishery.

The method for computing the value added of farming, forestry, animal husbandry and fishery: Production approach and distribution approach (income approach) are adopted:

1. Calculation formula of production approach:

Value added of agriculture, forestry, animal husbandry and fishery = gross output value of agriculture, forestry, animal husbandry and fishery – intermediate consumption of agriculture, forestry, animal husbandry and fishery

2. Calculation formula of distribution approach:

Value added of agriculture, forestry, animal husbandry and fishery

= depreciation of fixed assets + remuneration for workers + net production tax + operating surplus

Wherein: Net production tax = production tax – production subsidy

Grain output refers to food crop yield of the whole society, including output of grain operated by ownership by the whole people (such as state farm), based on collective unified management and operated by peasant family and output of the farm operated by family members of industrial and mining enterprises and other production units. Grains include rice, wheat, corn, sorghum, millet and other coarse cereals as well as potato and soybean. As for output calculation method, bean shall be calculated as per dried bean after removal of the pod; potatoes include sweet potato and potato other than taro and cassava. Calculation was conducted based on 4kg fresh potatoes regarding as 1kg grain before 1963 and calculation was conducted based on 5kg fresh potatoes regarding as 1kg grain from 1964. Other grain shall be calculated after threshing.

Output of Oil–bearing Crops refers to the total production of oil bearing crops of various kinds, including peanuts, sesame, sunflower seeds, flax seeds, and other oil bearing crops. Soybeans, oil bearing woody plants, and wild oil–bearing crops are not included. Only shelled dry peanuts are included.

Output of Aquatic Products refers to catches of both artificially cultured and naturally grown aquatic products, including fish, shrimps, crabs, shellfish and algae in sea and fish, shrimps, crabs and shellfish in fresh water. Freshwater plants are not included.

Output of Pork, Beef, and Mutton refers to the output of meat of slaughtered hogs, cattle, sheep and goats with head, feet, and offal taken away.

Cultivated Area refers to area of the farmland used to plant crops at the beginning of the year which is often plowed, including cultivated land, new cultivated land that very year, arable land abandoned for less than three years consecutively, fallow land (rotation land) that very year, the land mainly planting crops complemented by plantation of white mulberry, tea tree, fruit tree and other forest as well as "shoal" and "shoaly land" having been subject to reclamation and utilization in coastal and lake–side areas.

Excluded from this category are professional mulberry field, tea garden, orchard, nurseries of young plants, woods, reeds, natural or artificial grass area.

Sown Area of Crops refers to area of land sown or transplanted with crops regardless of being in cultivated area or non–cultivated area. Area of land re–sown due to natural disasters is also included.

Irrigation effective irrigation area refers to cultivated area with some water sources, which is smooth, provided with irrigation engineering or equipment and capable of normal irrigation in the latter half of general year.

Consumption of Chemical Fertilizers in Agriculture refers to the quantity of chemical fertilizers applied in agriculture in the year, including nitrogenous fertilizer, phosphate fertilizer, potash fertilizer, and compound fertilizer. The consumption of chemical fertilizers is required in calculation to convert the gross weight into weight containing 100% effective component (e.g. 100% nitrogen content in nitrogenous fertilizer, 100% phosphorous pent oxide contents in phosphate fertilizer, 100% potassium oxide contents in potash fertilizer). Compound fertilizer is converted with its major component.

Total Power of Farm Machinery refers to total mechanical power of machinery used in farming, forestry, animal husbandry, and fishery, including ploughing, irrigation and drainage, harvesting, transport, plant protection, stock breeding, forestry and fishery. The power of internal combustion engines is required to convert horsepower into watts and the power of electric motors is required to be converted into watts. Machinery employed for non– agricultural purposes, such as the machines used in township run and village run industry, construction, non–agricultural transport, scientific experiments and teaching, is excluded.

工 业

INDUSTRY

12-1 各时期全部工业基本情况
Basic Statistics on Total Industry in Each Period

年份 Year	全部工业单位数 (个) Number of Industial Enterprises (Unit)		工业总产值 (亿元) Gross Industrial Output Value (100 million yuan)		工业增加值 (亿元) Value Added of Industry Enterprises (100 million yuan)		国有独立核算工业 (万元) State-owned Independent Accounting Industrial (10 000 yuan)	
	合 计 Total	# 国有单位 State-owned	合 计 Total	# 国有单位 State-owned	合计 Total	# 国有单位 State-owned	利润总额 Total Profits	利税总额 Total Profits and Taxes
1949	52	—	1.20	0.52	0.40	0.15	190	541
1952	92	—	2.97	1.65	1.09	0.52	1616	2761
1957	399	—	6.90	6.13	2.18	1.84	5742	10065
1962	847	286	6.67	5.61	2.36	1.80	3293	8242
1965	724	247	11.99	10.09	4.34	3.39	16246	22906
1970	828	285	23.12	17.93	7.56	5.64	19347	31834
1975	1041	326	26.41	18.87	8.46	5.50	11555	27846
1978	1319	398	39.06	25.87	12.89	7.11	28852	53031
1979	1353	359	42.95	28.90	14.10	8.01	31875	57532
1980	1535	356	45.31	30.37	14.24	8.85	32909	59572
“六五”时期								
1981	1538	350	47.61	31.72	15.11	9.47	35077	62657
1982	1619	357	51.98	33.91	15.79	10.01	32062	64673
1983	1674	369	59.06	36.99	17.96	11.49	35870	60308
1984	1981	325	66.96	39.78	20.10	13.17	45869	83520
1985	2584	477	74.41	44.66	27.54	16.97	61274	112154
“七五”时期								
1986	3005	369	86.93	48.71	28.69	17.53	54804	115006
1987	3957	361	107.63	56.16	32.88	19.40	58715	125775
1988	5252	372	138.05	68.58	47.49	25.09	80173	156056
1989	7655	380	158.53	76.19	54.66	30.51	76571	170703
1990	11020	394	222.63	116.92	60.43	37.11	25084	125522
“八五”时期								
1991	12211	376	245.73	131.35	67.73	43.35	36715	151718
1992	15374	373	303.33	162.35	86.85	48.97	55463	193000
1993	19392	376	448.25	230.93	115.36	69.65	57984	223445
1994	22009	366	614.08	236.40	154.49	69.64	60393	240473
1995	24621	495	752.23	279.16	194.16	83.12	65335	316289

12–1 续表 continued

年份 Year	全部工业单位数（个）Number of Industial Enterprises (Unit)		工业总产值（亿元）Gross Industrial Output Value (100 million yuan)		工业增加值（亿元）Value Added of Industry Enterprises (100 million yuan)		国有独立核算工业（万元）State-owned Independent Accounting Industrial (10 000 yuan)	
	合 计 Total	# 国有单位 State-owned	合 计 Total	# 国有单位 State-owned	合计 Total	# 国有单位 State-owned	利润总额 Total Profits	利税总额 Total Profits and Taxes
"九五" 时期								
1996	32902	425	834.45	260.16	238.31	91.30	79615	337807
1997	33000	325	897.59	263.34	278.87	92.99	95267	343426
1998	32793	227	966.62	234.03	298.41	94.28	42152	292991
1999	29319	211	981.78	212.95	318.80	79.51	–2340	254619
2000	30899	195	994.00	237.14	336.61	81.00	34824	292198
"十五" 时期								
2001	34135	169	1090.70	140.44	356.72	64.69	49222	226242
2002	30064	155	1302.00	144.78	410.98	49.16	28011	234986
2003	30258	126	1544.50	167.30	494.55	68.80	53363	302975
2004	31163	115	1981.80	150.70	620.14	37.21	–3943	72684
2005	31370	102	2447.51	177.00	786.11	66.49	268573	354111
"十一五" 时期								
2006	35370	86	2806.94	193.10	861.48	73.95	315323	458191
2007	36112	76	3389.09	283.32	985.78	103.65	364790	751182
2008	36416	80	4829.16	338.24	1140.14	136.55	418265	853091
2009	37656	77	5096.98	345.44	1191.36	166.36	422898	885006
2010	37521	66	5800.39	404.38	1352.42	284.75	643216	1162785
"十二五" 时期								
2011	36750	54	5544.60	478.10	1507.88		561683	1217350
2012	35917	52	5535.25	491.20	1603.08		646193	1401892
2013	38443	30	5711.48	280.63	1690.63		551967	665206
2014	38753	25	5861.98	246.26	1822.11		507491	611865
2015	38793	24	5877.28	204.79	1844.37		517575	571354
"十三五" 时期								
2016	34310	16	6059.16	157.83	1878.83		540739	622714
2017	33725	12	6395.21	147.27	2003.10		583734	589999
2018	31270	13	5641.61	15.50	2145.10			5014
2019					2167.87			

注：1. 工业增加值、工业总产值按当年价格计算。
2. 1985、1995 年因工业普查对教育局校办工厂统计方法的规定，故国有单位较多。
3. 2001 年后炼油、浪潮、将军等原国有企业陆续改制，故国有数字较以前年份有所减小。
4. 2004 年第一次经济普查后，统计年鉴包含济南供电公司年报数据。
5. 非经济普查年度，除"工业增加值"外，其它指标空缺。

Note: 1. Industrial value added and total industrial output value are calculated according to the current year' s prices.
2. There were many state–owned units in 1985 and 1995 due to the provisions regarding statistical approach for school–run factories of Education Bureau from industrial census.
3. Original state–owned enterprises such as Oil Refining, Inspur and General were subject to restructuring in succession after 2001, so the quantity of state–owned enterprises decreased in comparison to that of previous years.
4. After the economic census for the first time in 2004, statistical yearbook includes annual report data of Ji' nan Power Supply Company.
5.In years other than the year of economic census, indicators are blank, excluding "Value Added of Industrial Enterprises".

12-2 各时期规模以上工业基本情况

Basic Statistics of Industrial Enterprises Above Designated Size in Each Period

单位：亿元 (100 million yuan)

年份 Year	单位数（个） Number of Industial Enterprises (unit)	工业总产值 Gross Industrial Output Value	工业增加值 Value Added of Industry Enterprises	营业收入 Revenue from Principal Business	利税总额 Total Profits and Taxes	利润总额 Total Profits	资产总计 Total Assets	所有者权益 Owner's Equities
1949	52	1.06	0.40	0.91	0.07	0.03	0.58	0.17
1952	92	2.83	1.02	2.40	0.32	0.18	1.89	0.55
1957	399	6.04	2.08	5.85	1.04	0.60	2.85	0.83
1962	847	6.65	2.15	6.87	0.92	0.39	5.66	1.65
1965	724	11.89	4.07	9.49	2.47	1.73	5.93	1.73
1970	828	22.94	7.29	19.30	3.66	2.22	10.67	3.10
1975	1041	26.16	7.94	19.70	3.47	1.55	17.21	5.01
1978	1319	37.67	9.94	31.39	6.80	3.88	25.68	7.47
1979	1353	38.79	11.18	35.51	7.21	4.13	27.19	7.91
1980	1535	43.60	12.15	36.90	7.51	4.26	29.22	8.50
“六五”时期								
1981	1538	42.26	12.77	39.84	7.98	4.37	31.49	9.20
1982	1619	45.58	13.63	42.94	8.13	4.18	34.52	10.08
1983	1674	49.64	14.86	46.38	8.84	4.74	38.09	11.12
1984	1981	55.95	17.91	52.16	10.46	5.82	41.66	12.16
1985	1915	66.98	23.10	64.76	13.98	7.62	47.09	13.75
“七五”时期								
1986	2036	75.67	24.54	73.98	14.38	7.07	56.79	16.70
1987	2004	88.17	27.24	86.19	15.88	7.52	64.21	18.88
1988	1984	107.76	35.39	113.84	19.65	10.37	81.67	24.01
1989	1993	118.88	43.20	131.86	20.88	9.73	104.34	30.68
1990	2008	174.89	41.63	136.29	15.57	3.23	125.25	36.82
“八五”时期								
1991	1985	194.29	44.84	160.58	18.46	4.97	138.34	40.81
1992	1941	236.37	60.16	200.54	23.48	7.84	167.44	49.39
1993	2156	319.49	104.43	309.91	31.88	10.26	338.15	99.61
1994	2202	414.81	113.71	346.13	41.69	13.61	462.34	136.14
1995	2648	526.48	130.88	432.17	53.59	16.30	578.55	180.86

注：1. 工业增加值、工业总产值按当年价格计算。
2. 1997 年及以前统计口径为乡及乡以上工业企业，1998 年及以后为全部国有及年销售收入 500 万元以上工业企业，2011 年及以后为年主营业务收入 2000 万元以上工业企业。
3. 1991 年及以前“工业增加值”指标为“工业净产值”指标。
4. 2018 年及以前“营业收入”“营业成本”“税金及附加”指标为“主营业务收入”“主营业务成本”及“主营业务税金及附加”指标。以下相关各表同。
5. 自 2019 年起，不再包含省直单位相关数据。以下相关各表同。
6. 自 2019 年起，数据为济南市、莱芜市区划调整后合并数据，之前年度数据为原济南市数据。以下相关各表同。
7. 表中的合计数和部分计算数据因小数取舍而产生的误差，均未作机械调整。以下相关各表同。

12-2 续表 continued

年份 Year	单位数（个） Number of Industial Enterprises (unit)	工业总产值 Gross Industrial Output Value	工业增加值 Value Added of Industry Enterprises	营业收入 Revenue from Principal Business	利税总额 Total Profits and Taxes	利润总额 Total Profits	资产总计 Total Assets	所有者权益 Owner's Equities
“九五”时期								
1996	2301	549.40	175.21	494.99	66.82	27.83	705.50	225.53
1997	1843	603.30	194.42	605.81	70.12	26.99	882.36	286.59
1998	1060	593.83	189.88	539.29	58.56	18.62	882.38	297.81
1999	1064	628.59	201.38	579.64	59.17	15.97	931.22	302.21
2000	1038	680.04	219.19	629.72	64.62	21.69	958.10	363.37
“十五”时期								
2001	1015	786.70	252.61	746.92	77.79	28.45	984.71	369.40
2002	1125	1009.04	325.98	917.31	92.71	32.13	1120.60	407.36
2003	1319	1318.54	426.30	1223.76	132.84	54.71	1312.97	440.85
2004	1512	1781.78	560.15	1677.93	175.98	83.68	1473.90	507.63
2005	1670	2237.51	722.11	2142.84	244.61	131.30	1868.06	630.06
“十一五”时期								
2006	1752	2591.65	797.70	2490.94	289.78	153.74	2000.62	702.78
2007	1820	3189.09	926.58	3086.85	358.87	199.73	2337.09	903.87
2008	2016	3862.64	1052.48	3766.93	425.72	220.79	2899.47	1123.03
2009	2156	3950.77	1154.01	3868.70	500.63	275.85	3478.94	1572.11
2010	2021	4485.61	1313.00	4497.17	584.53	339.76	3904.42	1481.75
“十二五”时期								
2011	1417	4028.49	–	4165.19	453.47	242.63	3932.90	1407.89
2012	1647	4248.29	–	4454.97	498.24	253.06	4109.29	1582.77
2013	1901	4777.47	–	4926.11	539.49	312.95	4249.79	1671.91
2014	1984	5253.05	–	5406.67	606.60	357.82	4564.86	1846.32
2015	2021	5339.97	–	5417.16	685.71	396.13	4987.76	2159.78
“十三五”时期								
2016	1962	5486.56	–	5714.29	729.75	421.11	5501.88	2301.94
2017	2051	5770.91	–	5810.16	686.80	415.23	6319.64	2268.27
2018	1889	4992.28	–	5192.15	535.39	307.98	5892.64	2386.75
2019	2153	5839.18	–	6512.66	545.70	310.86	6663.13	2743.28

Note: 1. The value added and total output of industrial enterprises are calculated as per the price of the years.

2. The statistic scale of year 1997 and before involves industrial enterprises in rural areas and above level, that of year 1998 and onwards involves all state-owned industrial enterprises and industrial enterprises with the annual sales revenue of RMB 5 million, and that of year 2011 and onwards involves industrial enterprises with the annual main operating income of RMB 20 million.

3. "Value added of industrial enterprises" in year 1991 and before refers to the indicator of "net value of industiral output".

4. "Operating income", "operating cost" and "taxes and surcharges" indicators in year 2019 and before refer to "main operating income", "main operating cost" and "main operating taxes and surcharges" (the same below).

5. Since 2019, statistics does not include data of units directly under provincial jurisdiction (the same below).

6. Since 2019, the data used refer to the combined data after the adjustment of administrative division between Jinan City and Laiwu City, and the data before 2019 are data of original Jinan City (the same below).

7.Errors in totals and part of calculations in the table are produced by decimal trade-offs, not mechanically adjusted (the same below).

12-3 各时期主要工业产品产量
Output of Major Industrial Products in Each Period

年份 Year	钢 （万吨） Steel (10 000 tons)	发电量 （亿千瓦小时） Electric Energy Production (100 million kwh)	水泥 （万吨） Cement (10 000 tons)	化肥 （万吨） Chemical Fertilizer (10 000 tons)	金切机床 （台） Metal-cutting Machine Tools(unit)	汽车 （辆） Motor Vehicles (unit)	服务器 （万台） Servers (10 000 unit)	布 （万米） Cloth (10 000 m)
1949	—	0.29	0.15	—	40	—	—	2682
1952	—	0.55	1.08	1.62	565	—	—	5104
1957	0.03	1.07	1.29	0.48	2312	—	—	5573
1962	0.57	4.20	4.85	0.81	1140	12	—	2160
1965	0.54	5.65	19.24	3.79	2061	335	—	4853
1970	7.01	11.28	38.06	4.87	4718	1775	—	11665
1975	22.81	11.07	58.48	9.06	3994	3507	—	12547
1978	34.54	12.65	87.55	18.02	3610	4025	—	13806
1979	33.19	11.92	93.77	11.07	3771	4515	—	14300
1980	36.34	11.95	98.86	12.78	4414	5641	—	15236
“六五”时期							—	
1981	34.23	11.12	96.50	11.62	3336	5099		16290
1982	34.96	11.15	104.64	13.23	4262	5993	—	17657
1983	41.24	13.01	112.38	15.37	4816	7249	—	17963
1984	43.80	23.49	117.17	14.53	5533	7947	—	16522
1985	52.64	26.44	135.10	11.44	6686	9400	—	18082
“七五”时期							—	
1986	57.24	27.01	154.51	12.31	7472	7600		12346
1987	64.09	28.83	158.92	13.00	7007	5225	—	20137
1988	75.23	42.97	182.80	13.69	7280	6741	—	19374
1989	81.58	43.98	198.95	14.48	6806	7701	—	21744
1990	87.68	44.71	211.56	14.44	5121	6239	—	20155
“八五”时期								
1991	105.42	56.43	248.33	14.90	5330	7096		20119
1992	113.34	61.46	335.61	14.64	7443	8544	—	14896
1993	139.35	69.00	340.35	14.47	6724	10132	—	13205
1994	166.19	66.87	384.00	15.62	3297	9380	—	16062
1995	172.72	68.75	425.02	14.03	4109	5657	—	15046

12-3 续表 continued

年份 Year	钢 （万吨） Steel (10 000 tons)	发电量 （亿千瓦小时） Electric Energy Production (100 million kwh)	水泥 （万吨） Cement (10 000 tons)	化肥 （万吨） Chemical Fertilizer (10 000 tons)	金切机床 （台） Metal-cutting Machine Tools(unit)	汽车 （辆） Motor Vehicles (unit)	服务器 （万台） Servers (10 000 unit)	布 （万米） Cloth (10 000 m)
“九五” 时期								
1996	205.49	63.50	379.32	13.73	3855	7125	—	13710
1997	237.70	59.14	392.23	13.89	2526	5656	—	14213
1998	267.33	60.06	379.40	17.29	1508	3615	—	11286
1999	265.29	64.24	474.47	22.91	1955	3738	—	14782
2000	277.04	69.29	485.12	28.41	2908	3078	—	16493
“十五” 时期								
2001	293.83	69.81	572.28	28.71	3528	7395	—	14107
2002	394.41	69.12	867.71	28.29	4522	12152		16027
2003	507.70	77.60	925.20	28.50	6751	19989	—	17040
2004	688.30	74.70	1343.90	40.30	8904	29648	—	16336
2005	1046.60	90.80	1595.70	28.90	7166	42214	—	14018
“十一五” 时期							—	
2006	1131.26	100.14	1960.64	31.44	10057	59242	—	22852
2007	1214.90	130.37	733.98	40.31	9473	100133	—	27469
2008	1123.20	124.25	734.58	48.52	5110	109107	8.3	11786
2009	1051.67	128.76	761.72	57.77	2400	129900	9.7	7500
2010	959.33	131.45	729.79	49.09	2165	212047	9.9	8191
“十二五” 时期								
2011	835.80	154.48	824.70	44.20	2024	170717	13.0	11461
2012	694.50	156.60	776.00	55.20	4237	141269	14.7	14908
2013	711.14	162.55	782.20	33.29	4297	165963	17.1	14574
2014	746.20	178.47	832.40	28.60	4902	139751	28.1	14070
2015	699.80	175.87	781.50	23.50	3807	96184	40.6	15539
“十三五” 时期								
2016	805.70	177.20	719.80	32.50	4679	124200	46.8	15585
2017	452.03	160.12	604.48	21.00	6013	201883	56.5	16407
2018	160.92	152.90	604.32	20.77	5964	232082	99.6	4032
2019	2144.18	295.1	1287.82	16.91	7237	175488	116.5	4095

注：按经济普查规定汽车产量不含底盘。
Note: The automotive output excludes chassis in line with the provisions of economic census.

12-4 规模以上工业主要经济指标(2019 年)
Main Economic Indicators of Industrial Enterprises Above Designated Size(2019)

指标	Indicator	企业单位数(个) Number of Industial Enterprises (unit)	亏损企业数(个) Loss Enterpriss (unit)	工业总产值(现价)(亿元) Gross Indutrial Output Value (Current Prices) (100 million yuan)	平均用工人数(万人) Average of Employed Persons (10 000 persons)
总计	Total	2153	390	5839.18	39.70
按登记注册类型分组	by Status of Registration				
内资企业	Domestic Funded Enterprises	2006	365	5037.63	33.11
国有企业	State-owned Enterprises	12	2	14.38	0.18
中央企业	Central Enterprises	1		0.39	0.03
地方企业	Local Enterprises	11	2	13.99	0.15
集体企业	Collective-owned Enterprises	7	2	5.77	0.15
股份合作企业	Cooperative Enterprises	4		2.25	0.06
联营企业	Joint Ownership Enterprises	1		0.04	0.02
国有联	State Joint Ownership Enterprises				
集体联营企业	Collective Joint Ownership Enterprises	1		0.04	0.02
国有与集体联营企业	Joint State-collective Enterprises				
其他联营企业	Other Joint Ownership Enterprises				
有限责任公司	Limited Liability Corporations	691	156	2053.75	16.28
国有独资公司	State Sole Funded Corporations	38	11	194.21	1.97
其他有限责任公司	Other Limited Liability Corporations	653	145	1859.54	14.31
股份有限公司	Share-holding Corporations Ltd.	102	21	1658.23	5.11
私营企业	Private Enterprises	1189	184	1303.20	11.31
私营独资企业	Private-funded Enterprises	32	5	9.37	0.15
私营合伙企业	Private Partnership Enterprises				
私营有限责任公司	Private Limited Liability Corporations	1098	168	1224.51	10.49
私营股份有限公司	Private Share-holding Corporations Ltd.	59	11	69.33	0.67
其他企业	Other Enterprises				
港、澳、台商投资企业	Enterprises with Funds from Hong Kong, Macao and Taiwan	62	8	560.50	4.28
合资经营企业(港或澳、台资)	Joint-venture Enterprises	30	6	203.80	1.87
合作经营企业(港或澳、台资)	Cooperative Enterprises	1		12.48	0.13
港澳台商独资经营企业	Enterprises with Sole Investment	28	1	326.32	2.09
港澳台商投资股份有限公司	Share-holding Corporations Ltd.	2		17.59	0.17
其他港澳台商投资企业	Other Enterprises with Funds from Hong Kong,Macao and Taiwan	1	1	0.30	0.01

12-4 续表 1 continued 1

指标	Indicator	企业单位数（个）Number of Industial Enterprises (unit)	亏损企业数（个）Loss Enterpriss (unit)	工业总产值（现价）(亿元) Gross Indutrial Output Value (Current Prices) (100 million yuan)	平均用工人数（万人）Average of Employed Persons (10 000 persons)
外商投资企业	Foreign Funded Enterprises	85	17	241.05	2.31
中外合资经营企业	Joint-venture Enterprises	38	7	95.37	1.06
中外合作经营企业	Cooperation Enterprises	3		3.04	0.04
外资企业	Enterprises with Sole Fund	43	10	121.53	1.12
外商投资股份有限公司	Share-holding Corporations Ltd. with Foreign Investment	1		21.12	0.10
其他外商投资企业	Other Foreign Funded Enterprises				
按轻重工业分	by Light & Heavy Industry				
轻工业	Light Industry	587	123	894.25	10.73
重工业	Heavy Industry	1566	267	4944.93	28.97
按企业规模分	by Enterprise Size				
大型企业	Large-sized Enterprises	56	4	3047.71	14.59
中型企业	Medium-sized Enterprises	181	29	1218.71	9.28
小型企业	Small-sized Enterprises	1722	326	1508.58	15.47
微型企业	Micro-sized Enterprises	194	31	64.18	0.36
按工业行业分	by Sector				
煤炭开采和洗选业	Mining and Washing of Coal	5	2	9.60	0.35
石油和天然气开采业	Extraction of Petroleum and Natural Gas	3		8.93	0.07
黑色金属矿采选业	Mining and Processing of Ferrous Metal Ores	12	2	64.18	0.92
有色金属矿采选业	Mining and Processing of Non-Ferrous Metal Ores				
非金属矿采选业	Mining and Processing of Non-metal Ores	9	1	10.46	0.05
开采专业及辅助性活动	Professional and Support Activities for Mining				
其他采矿业	Mining of Other Ores				
农副食品加工业	Processing of Food from Agricultural Products	95	22	108.42	0.95
食品制造业	Manufacture of Foods	67	15	119.88	1.76
酒、饮料和精制茶制造业	Manufacture of Liquor, Beverages and Refined Tea	21	5	65.52	0.55
烟草制品业	Manufacture of Tobacco	1		1.19	0.02
纺织业	Manufacture of Textile	51	9	39.21	0.53
纺织服装、服饰业	Manufacture of Textile, Wearing Apparel and Accessories	22	7	16.14	0.68
皮革、毛皮、羽毛及其制品和制鞋业	Manufacture of Leather, Fur, Feather and Related Products and Footwear	5		2.39	0.04
木材加工和木、竹、藤、棕、草制品业	Processing of Timber, Manufacture of Wood, Bamboo, Rattan,Palm and Straw Product	14	1	6.45	0.08

12–4 续表 2 continued 2

指标	Indicator	企业单位数（个）Number of Industial Enterprises (unit)	亏损企业数（个）Loss Enterprise (unit)	工业总产值（现价）(亿元) Gross Indutrial Output Value (Current Prices) (100 million yuan)	平均用工人数（万人）Average of Employed Persons (10 000 persons)
家具制造业	Manufacture of Furniture	13	5	8.14	0.19
造纸和纸制品业	Manufacture of Paper and Paper Products	33	10	32.03	0.38
印刷和记录媒介复制业	Printing and Reproduction of Recording Media	53	12	44.60	0.72
文教、工美、体育和娱乐用品制造业	Manufacture of Articles for Culture, Education, Arts and Crafts,Sport and Entertainment Activities	24	3	11.19	0.29
石油、煤炭及其他燃料加工业	Processing of Petroleum, Coal and Other Fuels	14	2	362.41	0.34
化学原料和化学制品制造业	Manufacture of Raw Chemical Materials and Chemical Products	105	17	257.96	1.95
医药制造业	Manufacture of Medicines	60	8	226.72	2.43
化学纤维制造业	Manufacture of Chemical Fibres	8	2	10.11	0.10
橡胶和塑料制品业	Manufacture of Rubber and Plastics Products	61	7	31.62	0.55
非金属矿物制品业	Manufacture of Non–metallic Mineral Products	260	32	459.46	3.36
黑色金属冶炼和压延加工业	Smelting and Pressing of Ferrous Metals	31	7	1131.52	3.35
有色金属冶炼和压延加工业	Smelting and Pressing of Non–ferrous Metals	25	5	12.92	0.20
金属制品业	Manufacture of Metal Products	242	35	282.51	2.97
通用设备制造业	Manufacture of General Purpose Machinery	256	50	296.54	3.88
专用设备制造业	Manufacture of Special Purpose Machinery	189	36	207.74	2.09
汽车制造业	Manufacture of Automobiles	107	13	783.30	4.21
铁路、船舶、航空航天和其他运输设备制造业	Manufacture of Railway, Ship, Aerospace and Other Transport Equipments	27	7	63.66	0.67
电气机械和器材制造业	Manufacture of Electrical Machinery and Apparatus	127	27	323.66	1.85
计算机、通信和其他电子设备制造业	Manufacture of Computers, Communication and Other Electronic Equipment	65	18	535.38	1.36
仪器仪表制造业	Manufacture of Measuring Instruments and Machinery	60	6	64.09	0.87
其他制造业	Other Manufacture	6	1	3.41	0.03
废弃资源综合利用业	Utilization of Waste Resources	7	3	9.60	0.05
金属制品、机械和设备修理业	Repair Service of Metal Products, Machinery and Equipment	4		8.88	0.20
电力、热力生产和供应业	Production and Supply of Electric Power and Heat Power	39	14	150.89	1.02
燃气生产和供应业	Production and Supply of Gas	19	4	45.43	0.32
水的生产和供应业	Production and Supply of Water	13	2	23.07	0.31

注：2019 年年报起，取消“工业销售产值”指标。后续各表同。
Note: From 2019 onwards, "Sales Output of Industrial Enterprises" is cancelled (the same below).

12-5 规模以上国有及国有控股工业主要经济指标(2019年)
Main Economic Indicators of State-Owned and State-Controlled Industrial Enterprises Above Designated Size(2019)

指标	Indicator	企业单位数(个) Number of Industial Enterprises (unit)	亏损企业数(个) Loss Enterpriss (unit)	工业总产值(现价)(亿元) Gross Indutrial Output Value (Current Prices) (100 million yuan)	平均用工人数(万人) Average of Employed Persons (10 000 persons)
总计	Total	183	35	2454.00	9.94
按登记注册类型分组	by Status of Registration				
内资企业	Domestic Funded Enterprises	170	34	2305.86	9.06
国有企业	State-owned Enterprises	12	2	14.38	0.18
中央企业	Central Enterprises	1		0.39	0.03
地方企业	Local Enterprises	11	2	13.99	0.15
集体企业	Collective-owned Enterprises				
股份合作企业	Cooperative Enterprises				
联营企业	Joint Ownership Enterprises				
有限责任公司	Limited Liability Corporations	140	26	891.05	5.89
国有独资公司	State Sole Funded Corporations	38	11	194.21	1.97
其他有限责任公司	Other Limited Liability Corporations	102	15	696.84	3.92
股份有限公司	Share-holding Corporations Ltd.	18	6	1400.43	2.99
私营企业	Private Enterprises				
其他企业	Other Enterprises				
港、澳、台商投资企业	Enterprises with Funds from Hong Kong,Macao and Taiwan	5		112.23	0.60
合资经营企业(港或澳、台资)	Joint-venture Enterprises	4		99.75	0.47
合作经营企业(港或澳、台资)	Cooperative Enterprises	1		12.48	0.13
港澳台商独资	Enterprises with Sole Investment				
港澳台商投资股份有限公司	Share-holding Corporations Ltd.				
其他港澳台商投资企业	Other Enterprises with Funds from Hong Kong, Macao and Taiwan				
外商投资企业	Foreign Funded Enterprises	8	1	35.91	0.27
中外合资经营企业	Joint-venture Enterprises	6	1	33.22	0.25
中外合作经营企业	Cooperation Enterprises	2		2.69	0.03
外资企业	Enterprises with Sole Fund				
外商投资股份有限公司	Share-holding Corporations Ltd. with Foreign Investment				
其他外商投资企业	Other Foreign Funded Enterprises				
按轻重工业分	by Light & Heavy Industry				

12-5 续表 1 continued 1

指标	Indicator	企业单位数（个）Number of Industial Enterprises (unit)	亏损企业数（个）Loss Enterpriss (unit)	工业总产值（现价）(亿元) Gross Indutrial Output Value (Current Prices) (100 million yuan)	平均用工人数（万人）Average of Employed Persons (10 000 persons)
轻工业	Light Industry	36	9	66.60	1.05
重工业	Heavy Industry	147	26	2387.41	8.89
按企业规模分	by Enterprise Size				
大型企业	Large-sized Enterprises	21	3	1926.24	6.09
中型企业	Medium-sized Enterprises	44	5	299.47	2.33
小型企业	Small-sized Enterprises	112	26	224.26	1.51
微型企业	Micro-sized Enterprises	6	1	4.03	0.02
按工业行业分	by Sector				
煤炭开采和洗选业	Mining and Washing of Coal	1		3.52	0.09
石油和天然气开采业	Extraction of Petroleum and Natural Gas	2		7.35	0.05
黑色金属矿采选业	Mining and Processing of Ferrous Metal Ores	2		20.68	0.44
有色金属矿采选业	Mining and Processing of Non-Ferrous Metal Ores				
非金属矿采选业	Mining and Processing of Non-metal Ores	1		0.70	0.01
开采专业及辅助性活动	Professional and Support Activities for Mining				
其他采矿业	Mining of Other Ores				
农副食品加工业	Processing of Food from Agricultural Products	3	1	0.98	0.02
食品制造业	Manufacture of Foods	4		2.49	0.08
酒、饮料和精制茶制造业	Manufacture of Liquor, Beverages and Refined Tea	3		24.44	0.23
烟草制品业	Manufacture of Tobacco	1		1.19	0.02
纺织业	Manufacture of Textile	2	2	1.09	0.04
纺织服装、服饰业	Manufacture of Textile, Wearing Apparel and Accessories	4	2	3.08	0.16
皮革、毛皮、羽毛及其制品和制鞋业	Manufacture of Leather, Fur, Feather and Related Products and Footwear				
木材加工和木、竹、藤、棕、草制品业	Processing of Timber, Manufacture of Wood, Bamboo, Rattan,Palm and Straw Products				
家具制造业	Manufacture of Furniture				
造纸和纸制品业	Manufacture of Paper and Paper Products	1		1.93	
印刷和记录媒介复制业	Printing and Reproduction of Recording Media	7	2	8.61	0.18

12-5 续表 2 continued 2

指标	Indicator	企业单位数（个）Number of Industial Enterprises (unit)	亏损企业数（个）Loss Enterpriss (unit)	工业总产值（现价）(亿元) Gross Indutrial Output Value (Current Prices) (100 million yuan)	平均用工人数（万人）Average of Employed Persons (10 000 persons)
文教、工美、体育和娱乐用品制造业	Manufacture of Articles for Culture, Education, Arts and Crafts,Sport and Entertainment Activities				
石油、煤炭及其他燃料加工业	Processing of Petroleum, Coal and Other Fuels	1		272.87	0.15
化学原料和化学制品制造业	Manufacture of Raw Chemical Materials and Chemical Products	7	2	46.35	0.29
医药制造业	Manufacture of Medicines	3		7.08	0.12
化学纤维制造业	Manufacture of Chemical Fibres	1		1.97	0.03
橡胶和塑料制品业	Manufacture of Rubber and Plastics Products				
非金属矿物制品业	Manufacture of Non-metallic Mineral Products	15	1	57.89	0.42
黑色金属冶炼和压延加工业	Smelting and Pressing of Ferrous Metals	4		609.50	1.69
有色金属冶炼和压延加工业	Smelting and Pressing of Non-ferrous Metals				
金属制品业	Manufacture of Metal Products	11	2	34.20	0.25
通用设备制造业	Manufacture of General Purpose Machinery	10	1	75.19	0.95
专用设备制造业	Manufacture of Special Purpose Machinery	11	2	27.56	0.33
汽车制造业	Manufacture of Automobiles	9	1	398.25	1.33
铁路、船舶、航空航天和其他运输设备制造业	Manufacture of Railway, Ship, Aerospace and Other Transport Equipments	8	1	44.27	0.41
电气机械和器材制造业	Manufacture of Electrical Machinery and Apparatus	21	8	129.17	0.51
计算机、通信和其他电子设备制造业	Manufacture of Computers, Communication and Other Electronic Equipment	8	2	476.84	0.55
仪器仪表制造业	Manufacture of Measuring Instruments and Machinery	6		18.51	0.21
其他制造业	Other Manufacture	2	1	2.55	0.02
废弃资源综合利用业	Utilization of Waste Resources				
金属制品、机械和设备修理业	Repair Service of Metal Products, Machinery and Equipment	1		1.46	0.02
电力、热力生产和供应业	Production and Supply of Electric Power and Heat Power	18	3	130.48	0.83
燃气生产和供应业	Production and Supply of Gas	8	2	28.40	0.23
水的生产和供应业	Production and Supply of Water	8	2.00	15.41	0.27

12-6 规模以上私营工业企业主要经济指标(2019 年)

Main Economic Indicators of Private Industrial Enterprises Above Designated Size(2019)

指标	Indicator	企业单位数(个) Number of Industial Enterprises (unit)	亏损企业数(个) Loss Enterpriss (unit)	工业总产值(现价)(亿元) Gross Indutrial Output Value (Current Prices) (100 million yuan)	平均用工人数(万人) Average of Employed Persons (10 000 persons)
总计	Total	1189	184	1303.20	11.31
按登记注册类型分组	by Status of Registration				
内资企业	Domestic Funded Enterprises	1189	184	1303.20	11.31
私营企业	Private Enterprises	1189	184	1303.20	11.31
私营独资企业	Private-funded Enterprises	32	5	9.37	0.15
私营合伙企业	Private Partnership Enterprises				
私营有限责任公司	Private Limited Liability Corporations	1098	168	1224.51	10.49
私营股份有限公司	Private Share-holding Corporations Ltd.	59	11	69.33	0.67
其他企业	Other Enterprises				
按轻重工业分	by Light & Heavy Industry				
轻工业	Light Industry	320	62	219.43	3.19
重工业	Heavy Industry	869	122	1083.77	8.12
按企业规模分	by Enterprise Size				
大型企业	Large-sized Enterprises	5	0	204.70	1.40
中型企业	Medium-sized Enterprises	38	6	334.69	1.80
小型企业	Small-sized Enterprises	1009	155	724.92	7.86
微型企业	Micro-sized Enterprises	137	23	38.90	0.26
按工业行业分	by Sector				
煤炭开采和洗选业	Mining and Washing of Coal	2	1	1.17	0.00
石油和天然气开采业	Extraction of Petroleum and Natural Gas	0	0	0.00	0.00

12-6 续表 1 continued 1

指标	Indicator	企业单位数（个）Number of Industial Enterprises (unit)	亏损企业数（个）Loss Enterpriss (unit)	工业总产值（现价）(亿元) Gross Indutrial Output Value (Current Prices) (100 million yuan)	平均用工人数（万人）Average of Employed Persons (10 000 persons)
黑色金属矿采选业	Mining and Processing of Ferrous Metal Ores	3	2	6.08	0.06
有色金属矿采选业	Mining and Processing of Non-Ferrous Metal Ores				
非金属矿采选业	Mining and Processing of Non-metal Ores	5	1	3.95	0.02
开采专业及辅助性活动	Professional and Support Activities for Mining				
其他采矿业	Mining of Other Ores				
农副食品加工业	Processing of Food from Agricultural Products	58	13	63.07	0.55
食品制造业	Manufacture of Foods	35	10	38.08	0.66
酒、饮料和精制茶制造业	Manufacture of Liquor, Beverages and Refined Tea	3	1	0.79	0.01
烟草制品业	Manufacture of Tobacco				
纺织业	Manufacture of Textile	26	2	9.83	0.18
纺织服装、服饰业	Manufacture of Textile, Wearing Apparel and Accessories	11	3	3.95	0.11
皮革、毛皮、羽毛及其制品和制鞋业	Manufacture of Leather, Fur, Feather and Related Products and Footwear	4		1.22	0.03
木材加工和木、竹、藤、棕、草制品业	Processing of Timber, Manufacture of Wood, Bamboo, Rattan,Palm and Straw Products	11	1	5.99	0.07
家具制造业	Manufacture of Furniture	13	5	8.14	0.19
造纸和纸制品业	Manufacture of Paper and Paper Products	24	7	16.46	0.25
印刷和记录媒介复制业	Printing and Reproduction of Recording Media	23	3	10.52	0.16
文教、工美、体育和娱乐用品制造业	Manufacture of Articles for Culture, Education, Arts and Crafts,Sport and Entertainment Activities	20	1	9.02	0.25
石油、煤炭及其他燃料加工业	Processing of Petroleum, Coal and Other Fuels	9	2	65.12	0.13
化学原料和化学制品制造业	Manufacture of Raw Chemical Materials and Chemical Products	52	7	69.15	0.50
医药制造业	Manufacture of Medicines	25	4	20.69	0.21

12-6 续表 2 continued 2

指标	Indicator	企业单位数 (个) Number of Industial Enterprises (unit)	亏损企业数 (个) Loss Enterpriss (unit)	工业总产值 (现价)(亿元) Gross Indutrial Output Value (Current Prices) (100 million yuan)	平均用工人数 (万人) Average of Employed Persons (10 000 persons)
化学纤维制造业	Manufacture of Chemical Fibres	3	1	1.04	0.02
橡胶和塑料制品业	Manufacture of Rubber and Plastics Products	39	4	18.18	0.30
非金属矿物制品业	Manufacture of Non-metallic Mineral Products	160	19	214.42	1.43
黑色金属冶炼和压延加工业	Smelting and Pressing of Ferrous Metals	16	4	266.95	0.77
有色金属冶炼和压延加工业	Smelting and Pressing of Non-ferrous Metals	16	1	5.07	0.06
金属制品业	Manufacture of Metal Products	147	20	92.40	1.15
通用设备制造业	Manufacture of General Purpose Machinery	164	25	89.50	1.48
专用设备制造业	Manufacture of Special Purpose Machinery	112	22	134.08	1.06
汽车制造业	Manufacture of Automobiles	59	3	30.89	0.45
铁路、船舶、航空航天和其他运输设备制造业	Manufacture of Railway, Ship, Aerospace and Other Transport Equipments	10	3	8.85	0.07
电气机械和器材制造业	Manufacture of Electrical Machinery and Apparatus	57	8	38.11	0.30
计算机、通信和其他电子设备制造业	Manufacture of Computers, Communication and Other Electronic Equipment	25	5	27.57	0.32
仪器仪表制造业	Manufacture of Measuring Instruments and Machinery	40	2	29.35	0.43
其他制造业	Other Manufacture	4		0.86	0.01
废弃资源综合利用业	Utilization of Waste Resources	2	1	1.01	0.01
金属制品、机械和设备修理业	Repair Service of Metal Products, Machinery and Equipment	2		0.80	0.01
电力、热力生产和供应业	Production and Supply of Electric Power and Heat Power	3	2	3.28	0.03
燃气生产和供应业	Production and Supply of Gas	4	1	6.01	0.01
水的生产和供应业	Production and Supply of Water	2		1.61	0.01

12-7 规模以上工业资产实力(2019年)
Capital Power of Industrial Enterprises Above Designated Size(2019)

指 标	Indicator	流动资产合计 Total Current Assets	其中 of which 应收账款 Receivable	存货 Inventory
总计	Total	3945.34	1163.80	807.12
按登记注册类型分组	by Status of Registration			
内资企业	Domestic Funded Enterprises	3347.70	1073.22	703.22
国有企业	State-owned Enterprises	17.25	6.35	2.36
中央企业	Central Enterprises	1.58	0.20	0.66
地方企业	Local Enterprises	15.67	6.16	1.70
集体企业	Collective-owned Enterprises	3.09	1.03	0.91
股份合作企业	Cooperative Enterprises	2.30	0.74	0.38
联营企业	Joint Ownership Enterprises	0.11	0.06	0.01
国有联营企业	State Joint Ownership Enterprises			
集体联营企业	Collective Joint Ownership Enterprises	0.11	0.06	0.01
国有与集体联营企业	Joint State-collective Enterprises			
其他联营企业	Other Joint Ownership Enterprises			
有限责任公司	Limited Liability Corporations	1686.72	412.82	323.36
国有独资公司	State Sole Funded Corporations	268.65	65.91	37.17
其他有限责任公司	Other Limited Liability Corporations	1418.07	346.91	286.20
股份有限公司	Share-holding Corporations Ltd.	763.76	208.24	187.63
私营企业	Private Enterprises	874.48	443.98	188.57
私营独资企业	Private-funded Enterprises	3.35	1.75	0.56
私营合伙企业	Private Partnership Enterprises			
私营有限责任公司	Private Limited Liability Corporations	808.49	422.28	173.74
私营股份有限公司	Private Share-holding Corporations Ltd.	62.64	19.96	14.27
其他企业	Other Enterprises			
港、澳、台商投资企业	Enterprises with Funds from Hong Kong,Macao and Taiwan	444.77	47.84	65.30
合资经营企业(港或澳、台资)	Joint-venture Enterprises	193.50	28.39	20.91
合作经营企业(港或澳、台资)	Cooperative Enterprises	4.34	0.39	1.46
港澳台商独资经营企业	Enterprises with Sole Investment	231.65	15.83	40.40
港澳台商投资股份有限公司	Share-holding Corporations Ltd.	14.81	3.16	2.26
其他港澳台商投资企业	Other Enterprises with Funds from Hong Kong,Macao and Taiwan	0.47	0.07	0.27
外商投资企业	Foreign Funded Enterprises	152.87	42.74	38.60
中外合资经营企业	Joint-venture Enterprises	66.01	18.43	17.84
中外合作经营企业	Cooperation Enterprises	3.65	0.70	0.82
外资企业	Enterprises with Sole Fund	75.41	20.49	17.26
外商投资股份有限公司	Share-holding Corporations Ltd. with Foreign Investment	7.80	3.12	2.67
其他外商投资企业	Other Foreign Funded Enterprises			
按轻重工业分	by Light & Heavy Industry			
轻工业	Light Industry	705.06	161.53	142.81
重工业	Heavy Industry	3240.28	1002.27	664.30
按企业规模分	by Enterprise Size			
大型企业	Large-sized Enterprises	1700.44	347.81	353.20
中型企业	Medium-sized Enterprises	1006.80	403.60	195.19
小型企业	Small-sized Enterprises	1197.26	395.18	253.41
微型企业	Micro-sized Enterprises	40.84	17.20	5.32

单位：亿元 (100 million yuan)

固定资产净额 Net Fixed Assets	固定资产原价 Original Value of Fixed Assets	流动负债合计 Current Liabilities Total	非流动负债合计 Non-Current Liabilities Total	所有者权益合计 Total Owner's Equities	其中 of which: 实收资本 Paid-up Capital	其中 of which: 国家资本 Official Capital
1548.68	2910.55	3441.11	478.76	2743.28	1295.84	413.70
1362.79	2542.88	2998.24	421.50	2255.71	1026.35	393.74
13.18	21.57	23.07	2.21	8.24	3.64	3.64
1.12	1.77	1.32		1.38	0.12	0.12
12.06	19.80	21.75	2.20	6.86	3.52	3.52
2.29	4.42	1.75	0.69	3.07	0.54	
0.48	0.81	1.34	0.04	1.56	0.16	
0.42	0.89	0.26	0.08	0.25	0.02	
0.42	0.89	0.26	0.08	0.25	0.02	
925.60	1584.44	1570.14	285.23	1328.20	614.02	285.31
137.42	244.96	260.96	84.95	202.04	114.45	104.64
788.18	1339.48	1309.18	200.28	1126.16	499.57	180.66
228.86	534.22	601.52	86.29	517.85	188.86	103.15
191.97	396.53	800.17	46.96	396.54	219.10	1.65
1.23	2.73	3.10	0.29	1.64	1.13	
174.42	365.02	756.92	37.49	330.03	191.71	1.63
16.32	28.78	40.15	9.18	64.87	26.26	0.02
120.21	236.65	335.17	34.80	348.66	183.75	11.86
44.78	93.37	113.31	18.21	157.42	69.53	11.55
3.82	6.00	5.30	0.15	3.28	0.40	0.30
62.98	122.80	207.62	12.00	176.69	112.15	
8.62	14.42	8.86	4.45	10.85	1.62	
0.01	0.06	0.08		0.41	0.05	
65.68	131.02	107.70	22.46	138.91	85.74	8.11
22.17	48.91	53.45	2.83	43.00	35.59	7.47
0.75	1.78	2.37		2.13	1.12	0.64
34.37	67.58	47.21	16.25	82.32	46.07	
8.40	12.75	4.67	3.38	11.46	2.97	
215.26	404.77	417.44	39.98	700.82	235.61	15.10
1333.42	2505.78	3023.67	438.78	2042.46	1060.23	398.61
842.58	1591.01	1542.09	230.27	1333.54	562.87	271.04
314.64	620.37	812.54	108.69	624.63	239.48	85.91
366.47	665.88	1054.72	122.93	752.10	471.28	53.14
24.98	33.29	31.76	16.86	33.02	22.21	3.62

12-7 续表 continued

指 标	Indicator	流动资产合计 Total Current Assets	其中 of which	
			应收账款 Receivable	存货 Inventory
按工业行业分	by Sector			
煤炭开采和洗选业	Mining and Washing of Coal	7.00	1.84	0.73
石油和天然气开采业	Extraction of Petroleum and Natural Gas	31.57	1.35	0.08
黑色金属矿采选业	Mining and Processing of Ferrous Metal Ores	76.83	2.37	17.55
有色金属矿采选业	Mining and Processing of Non-Ferrous Metal Ores			
非金属矿采选业	Mining and Processing of Non-metal Ores	5.02	1.67	0.55
开采专业及辅助性活动	Professional and Support Activities for Mining			
其他采矿业	Mining of Other Ores			
农副食品加工业	Processing of Food from Agricultural Products	56.01	17.95	17.12
食品制造业	Manufacture of Foods	50.13	10.86	12.43
酒、饮料和精制茶制造业	Manufacture of Liquor, Beverages and Refined Tea	48.46	3.25	8.68
烟草制品业	Manufacture of Tobacco	2.00	0.22	0.09
纺织业	Manufacture of Textile	17.90	5.45	5.96
纺织服装、服饰业	Manufacture of Textile, Wearing Apparel and Accessories	12.95	2.12	3.61
皮革、毛皮、羽毛及其制品和制鞋业	Manufacture of Leather, Fur, Feather and Related Products and Footwear	2.05	0.33	0.51
木材加工和木、竹、藤、棕、草制品业	Processing of Timber, Manufacture of Wood, Bamboo, Rattan,Palm and Straw Products	2.73	0.99	1.00
家具制造业	Manufacture of Furniture	6.54	0.52	4.22
造纸和纸制品业	Manufacture of Paper and Paper Products	16.45	4.42	6.92
印刷和记录媒介复制业	Printing and Reproduction of Recording Media	32.51	8.14	5.79
文教、工美、体育和娱乐用品制造业	Manufacture of Articles for Culture, Education, Arts and Crafts,Sport and Entertainment Activities	6.92	1.32	3.60
石油、煤炭及其他燃料加工业	Processing of Petroleum, Coal and Other Fuels	85.07	52.81	14.96
化学原料和化学制品制造业	Manufacture of Raw Chemical Materials and Chemical Products	175.26	27.90	29.72
医药制造业	Manufacture of Medicines	289.17	68.73	39.84
化学纤维制造业	Manufacture of Chemical Fibres	7.99	1.73	2.27
橡胶和塑料制品业	Manufacture of Rubber and Plastics Products	21.85	8.26	5.20
非金属矿物制品业	Manufacture of Non-metallic Mineral Products	324.39	157.36	39.89
黑色金属冶炼和压延加工业	Smelting and Pressing of Ferrous Metals	465.76	169.10	121.03
有色金属冶炼和压延加工业	Smelting and Pressing of Non-ferrous Metals	11.49	3.83	3.89
金属制品业	Manufacture of Metal Products	207.12	68.60	44.31
通用设备制造业	Manufacture of General Purpose Machinery	280.97	74.09	73.02
专用设备制造业	Manufacture of Special Purpose Machinery	188.10	56.25	52.84
汽车制造业	Manufacture of Automobiles	548.59	96.62	109.01
铁路、船舶、航空航天和其他运输设备制造业	Manufacture of Railway, Ship, Aerospace and Other Transport Equipments	54.41	20.28	6.81
电气机械和器材制造业	Manufacture of Electrical Machinery and Apparatus	313.47	108.99	69.11
计算机、通信和其他电子设备制造业	Manufacture of Computers, Communication and Other Electronic Equipment	289.48	123.35	78.61
仪器仪表制造业	Manufacture of Measuring Instruments and Machinery	63.02	22.19	12.75
其他制造业	Other Manufacture	2.69	1.34	0.27
废弃资源综合利用业	Utilization of Waste Resources	1.05	0.19	0.12
金属制品、机械和设备修理业	Repair Service of Metal Products, Machinery and Equipment	6.29	1.93	1.92
电力、热力生产和供应业	Production and Supply of Electric Power and Heat Power	143.74	27.58	8.30
燃气生产和供应业	Production and Supply of Gas	45.97	4.55	3.41
水的生产和供应业	Production and Supply of Water	44.41	5.31	1.00

固定资产净额 Net Fixed Assets	固定资产原价 Original Value of Fixed Assets	流动负债合计 Current Liabilities Total	非流动负债合计 Non-Current Liabilities Total	所有者权益合计 Total Owner's Equities	其中 of which 实收资本 Paid- up Capital	其中 of which 国家资本 Official Capital
8.28	15.89	24.69	0.04	-7.31	3.98	2.80
7.00	37.43	0.90	2.38	37.40	5.18	0.70
39.12	75.37	74.34	4.65	61.64	33.42	3.25
1.48	2.47	3.19	0.45	3.58	1.98	0.50
10.69	18.71	57.91	4.50	13.02	9.12	0.53
39.02	67.70	46.88	6.18	64.88	30.18	0.19
23.19	50.26	33.78	1.34	55.36	44.12	5.98
0.97	1.32	0.54		2.63	0.95	0.95
11.25	19.52	19.22	2.72	13.93	7.07	0.69
7.41	12.67	9.06	1.53	12.97	4.99	
0.30	0.50	2.04		0.36	0.24	
1.56	2.34	4.48	0.10	1.00	0.52	
1.96	2.70	7.65	0.01	2.85	2.26	
9.19	22.17	16.16	10.80	10.12	6.38	0.80
17.45	38.14	24.43	2.15	34.89	18.64	2.00
2.23	3.79	6.12	0.42	4.58	2.91	
46.48	110.35	101.43	10.62	33.00	32.21	26.56
114.83	186.83	186.10	46.48	133.48	53.34	10.85
62.13	111.30	99.65	7.29	335.80	64.93	0.86
5.53	8.68	9.36		7.70	7.41	
6.76	14.81	12.58	1.35	16.31	7.61	
78.47	153.05	265.28	13.98	163.64	53.75	6.22
389.41	757.95	606.14	65.61	280.87	176.35	119.21
2.11	4.86	9.80	0.11	6.14	2.48	
62.75	108.03	141.05	13.03	175.64	53.61	2.09
63.80	139.61	180.27	18.13	218.04	131.40	64.97
28.52	44.83	146.94	13.85	105.30	45.35	4.35
87.69	194.59	470.31	10.06	268.59	143.02	17.92
13.33	28.87	51.76	5.64	44.80	31.88	22.92
56.26	101.83	277.20	13.68	176.20	109.63	30.61
24.50	42.86	195.73	13.67	156.92	51.37	10.32
9.42	17.15	37.81	1.56	41.98	18.69	4.55
3.19	3.79	3.50	0.09	2.53	2.20	1.00
0.94	1.11	3.06	0.21	2.77	1.65	
2.85	6.09	3.31		6.52	2.47	1.22
252.16	414.80	211.69	140.49	173.59	93.85	56.29
27.98	40.64	40.48	15.73	49.33	16.54	4.77
28.48	47.54	56.27	49.91	32.25	24.14	10.59

12-8 规模以上国有及国有控股工业资产实力(2019年)

Capital Power of State-Owned and State-Controlled Industrial Enterprises Above Designated Size(2019)

指 标	Indicator	流动资产合计 Total Current Assets	其中 of which 应收账款 Receivable	存货 Inventory
总计	Total	1312.08	311.76	273.76
按登记注册类型分组	by Status of Registration			
内资企业	Domestic Funded Enterprises	1201.89	300.95	259.61
国有企业	State-owned Enterprises	17.25	6.35	2.36
中央企业	Central Enterprises	1.58	0.20	0.66
地方企业	Local Enterprises	15.67	6.16	1.70
集体企业	Collective-owned Enterprises			
股份合作企业	Cooperative Enterprises			
联营企业	Joint Ownership Enterprises			
有限责任公司	Limited Liability Corporations	638.81	142.42	113.11
国有独资公司	State Sole Funded Corporations	268.65	65.91	37.17
其他有限责任公司	Other Limited Liability Corporations	370.16	76.51	75.94
股份有限公司	Share-holding Corporations Ltd.	545.83	152.18	144.15
私营企业	Private Enterprises			
其他企业	Other Enterprises			
港、澳、台商投资企业	Enterprises with Funds from Hong Kong,Macao and Taiwan	83.41	4.47	6.91
合资经营企业(港或澳、台资)	Joint-venture Enterprises	79.07	4.08	5.45
合作经营企业(港或澳、台资)	Cooperative Enterprises	4.34	0.39	1.46
港澳台商独资经营企业	Enterprises with Sole Investment			
港澳台商投资股份有限公司	Share-holding Corporations Ltd.			
其他港澳台商投资企业	Other Enterprises with Funds from Hong Kong,Macao and Taiwan			
外商投资企业	Foreign Funded Enterprises	26.79	6.33	7.24
中外合资经营企业	Joint-venture Enterprises	23.41	5.68	6.51
中外合作经营企业	Cooperation Enterprises	3.38	0.65	0.72
外资企业	Enterprises with Sole Fund			
外商投资股份有限公司	Share-holding Corporations Ltd. with Foreign Investment			
其他外商投资企业	Other Foreign Funded Enterprises			
按轻重工业分	by Light & Heavy Industry	1312.08	311.76	273.76
轻工业	Light Industry	52.56	7.27	14.58
重工业	Heavy Industry	1259.52	304.49	259.18
按企业规模分	by Enterprise Size	1312.08	311.76	273.76
大型企业	Large-sized Enterprises	856.54	177.65	177.19
中型企业	Medium-sized Enterprises	252.13	80.68	52.70
小型企业	Small-sized Enterprises	199.04	52.57	43.73
微型企业	Micro-sized Enterprises	4.37	0.87	0.14
按工业行业分	by Sector	1312.08	311.76	273.76
煤炭开采和洗选业	Mining and Washing of Coal	1.01	0.57	0.01
石油和天然气开采业	Extraction of Petroleum and Natural Gas	27.98	0.95	0.08
黑色金属矿采选业	Mining and Processing of Ferrous Metal Ores	13.98	0.61	1.49

单位：亿元 (100 million yuan)

固定资产净额 Net Fixed Assets	固定资产原价 Original Value of Fixed Assets	流动负债合计 Current Liabilities Total	非流动负债合计 Non-Current Liabilities Total	所有者权益合计 Total Owner's Equities	其中 of which	
					实收资本 Paid- up Capital	其中 of which 国家资本 Official Capital
794.18	1499.51	1373.35	289.52	899.42	512.66	380.95
759.51	1435.14	1286.79	270.46	826.13	481.85	366.82
13.18	21.57	23.07	2.21	8.24	3.64	3.64
1.12	1.77	1.32		1.38	0.12	0.12
12.06	19.80	21.75	2.20	6.86	3.52	3.52
573.41	975.56	792.60	206.15	512.14	359.06	263.60
137.42	244.96	260.96	84.95	202.04	114.45	104.64
435.99	730.60	531.64	121.20	310.10	244.61	158.96
172.92	438.01	471.12	62.11	305.75	119.16	99.58
28.16	49.51	62.76	17.11	60.08	22.24	9.40
24.34	43.51	57.46	16.97	56.80	21.83	9.10
3.82	6.00	5.30	0.15	3.28	0.40	0.30
6.51	14.87	23.79	1.94	13.21	8.57	4.74
5.80	13.18	21.45	1.94	11.37	7.52	4.10
0.71	1.69	2.34		1.84	1.06	0.64
794.18	1499.51	1373.35	289.52	899.42	512.66	380.95
21.87	42.74	43.85	3.66	40.82	20.50	12.60
772.31	1456.77	1329.50	285.86	858.60	492.16	368.35
794.18	1499.51	1373.35	289.52	899.42	512.66	380.95
539.87	1044.70	933.96	176.64	588.12	327.94	267.84
145.58	281.05	219.70	69.50	178.28	93.67	68.94
103.64	167.68	216.89	39.56	128.85	88.76	42.20
5.09	6.08	2.80	3.82	4.18	2.29	1.97
794.18	1499.51	1373.35	289.52	899.42	512.66	380.95
5.85	9.85	7.53		0.26	2.50	2.50
5.19	27.74	0.75	1.72	32.66	4.48	
14.59	30.47	19.66	4.38	22.81	24.82	0.14

12-8 续表 continued

指　标	Indicator	流动资产合计 Total Current Assets	其中 of which	
			应收账款 Receivable	存货 Inventory
有色金属矿采选业	Mining and Processing of Non-Ferrous Metal Ores			
非金属矿采选业	Mining and Processing of Non-metal Ores	1.05	0.08	0.05
开采专业及辅助性活动	Professional and Support Activities for Mining			
其他采矿业	Mining of Other Ores			
农副食品加工业	Processing of Food from Agricultural Products	3.02	0.14	1.52
食品制造业	Manufacture of Foods	1.12	0.23	0.07
酒、饮料和精制茶制造业	Manufacture of Liquor, Beverages and Refined Tea	10.47	0.63	2.84
烟草制品业	Manufacture of Tobacco	2.00	0.22	0.09
纺织业	Manufacture of Textile	0.83	0.16	0.54
纺织服装、服饰业	Manufacture of Textile, Wearing Apparel and Accessories	7.25	0.40	1.59
皮革、毛皮、羽毛及其制品和制鞋业	Manufacture of Leather, Fur, Feather and Related Products and Footwear			
木材加工和木、竹、藤、棕、草制品业	Processing of Timber, Manufacture of Wood, Bamboo, Rattan,Palm and Straw Products			
家具制造业	Manufacture of Furniture			
造纸和纸制品业	Manufacture of Paper and Paper Products	1.69	0.12	0.15
印刷和记录媒介复制业	Printing and Reproduction of Recording Media	7.53	1.78	1.43
文教、工美、体育和娱乐用品制造业	Manufacture of Articles for Culture, Education, Arts and Crafts,Sport and Entertainment Activities			
石油、煤炭及其他燃料加工业	Processing of Petroleum, Coal and Other Fuels	20.53	4.37	7.08
化学原料和化学制品制造业	Manufacture of Raw Chemical Materials and Chemical Products	29.22	3.23	4.92
医药制造业	Manufacture of Medicines	7.20	1.20	0.98
化学纤维制造业	Manufacture of Chemical Fibres	2.51	0.04	1.40
橡胶和塑料制品业	Manufacture of Rubber and Plastics Products			
非金属矿物制品业	Manufacture of Non-metallic Mineral Products	37.31	16.64	5.08
黑色金属冶炼和压延加工业	Smelting and Pressing of Ferrous Metals	129.36	1.72	28.75
有色金属冶炼和压延加工业	Smelting and Pressing of Non-ferrous Metals			
金属制品业	Manufacture of Metal Products	26.80	4.62	8.43
通用设备制造业	Manufacture of General Purpose Machinery	100.52	24.00	19.76
专用设备制造业	Manufacture of Special Purpose Machinery	48.68	15.53	11.41
汽车制造业	Manufacture of Automobiles	245.66	39.19	59.14
铁路、船舶、航空航天和其他运输设备制造业	Manufacture of Railway, Ship, Aerospace and Other Transport Equipments	36.30	9.31	4.03
电气机械和器材制造业	Manufacture of Electrical Machinery and Apparatus	137.50	54.33	37.26
计算机、通信和其他电子设备制造业	Manufacture of Computers, Communication and Other Electronic Equipment	233.05	104.15	64.05
仪器仪表制造业	Manufacture of Measuring Instruments and Machinery	17.00	6.84	3.66
其他制造业	Other Manufacture	1.92	1.00	0.02
废弃资源综合利用业	Utilization of Waste Resources			
金属制品、机械和设备修理业	Repair Service of Metal Products, Machinery and Equipment	1.18	0.45	0.60
电力、热力生产和供应业	Production and Supply of Electric Power and Heat Power	89.69	13.30	4.81
燃气生产和供应业	Production and Supply of Gas	34.49	1.74	1.84
水的生产和供应业	Production and Supply of Water	35.21	4.20	0.68

固定资产净额 Net Fixed Assets	固定资产原价 Original Value of Fixed Assets	流动负债合计 Current Liabilities Total	非流动负债合计 Non-Current Liabilities Total	所有者权益合计 Total Owner's Equities	其中 of which	
					实收资本 Paid- up Capital	其中 of which 国家资本 Official Capital
0.46	0.87	0.23	0.40	0.92	0.50	0.50
0.51	0.90	2.19	1.31	0.38	0.46	0.37
0.40	0.83	0.75	0.08	0.71	0.26	0.14
6.75	12.63	7.40	0.64	10.40	6.13	5.97
0.97	1.32	0.54		2.63	0.95	0.95
0.18	0.67	0.93		0.20	0.22	0.19
1.43	4.07	4.84	0.06	5.41	0.78	
	0.21	2.11		0.83	0.80	0.80
4.80	12.70	4.10	0.48	9.03	6.22	1.41
35.51	86.99	37.67	5.14	22.85	26.56	26.56
29.46	46.27	59.01	16.02	-5.53	5.97	3.40
3.21	4.56	7.73	1.09	6.63	1.62	0.81
2.25	2.42	5.28		1.09	1.00	
12.36	24.22	34.00	2.22	20.42	6.06	2.77
291.65	551.53	285.61	52.54	146.59	119.47	118.81
7.14	12.77	25.66	3.16	7.80	4.38	1.84
17.72	58.35	46.84	6.69	93.46	64.86	63.74
7.97	12.24	43.04	5.24	19.79	9.59	3.29
17.79	51.41	182.12	2.31	93.22	20.49	12.11
7.77	18.28	31.30	5.31	32.45	25.56	21.77
35.18	59.17	142.96	6.73	71.97	51.13	29.05
5.82	11.72	161.99	6.61	104.65	24.65	8.37
4.05	6.43	11.86		10.15	5.82	4.53
3.17	3.73	2.90	0.09	2.34	2.00	1.00
0.36	0.69	0.53		1.04	0.20	0.16
224.10	371.82	168.75	109.43	129.22	71.21	54.55
19.21	27.62	29.41	15.20	36.96	11.81	4.64
28.35	46.99	45.68	42.68	18.09	12.17	10.59

12-9 规模以上工业损益及分配(2019年)
Profit，Loss and Distribution of Industrial Enterprises Above Designated Size(2019)

指　标	Indicator	营业收入 Business Revenue	营业成本 Business Cost	税金及附加 Taxes and Other Charges
总计	Total	6512.66	5530.33	106.17
按登记注册类型分组	by Status of Registration			
内资企业	Domestic Funded Enterprises	5686.66	4874.95	100.69
国有企业	State-owned Enterprises	15.65	12.67	0.43
中央企业	Central Enterprises	0.42	0.32	
地方企业	Local Enterprises	15.23	12.35	0.43
集体企业	Collective-owned Enterprises	5.88	5.18	0.03
股份合作企业	Cooperative Enterprises	2.27	1.27	0.02
联营企业	Joint Ownership Enterprises	0.71	0.40	0.02
国有联营企业	State Joint Ownership Enterprises			
集体联营企业	Collective Joint Ownership Enterprises	0.71	0.40	0.02
国有与集体联营企业	Joint State-collective Enterprises			
其他联营企业	Other Joint Ownership Enterprises			
有限责任公司	Limited Liability Corporations	2359.20	1981.90	18.01
国有独资公司	State Sole Funded Corporations	222.93	196.45	2.10
其他有限责任公司	Other Limited Liability Corporations	2136.27	1785.44	15.92
股份有限公司	Share-holding Corporations Ltd.	1859.48	1608.75	75.78
私营企业	Private Enterprises	1443.48	1264.79	6.39
私营独资企业	Private-funded Enterprises	9.09	8.27	0.06
私营合伙企业	Private Partnership Enterprises			
私营有限责任公司	Private Limited Liability Corporations	1362.55	1202.35	5.79
私营股份有限公司	Private Share-holding Corporations Ltd.	71.84	54.17	0.54
其他企业	Other Enterprises			
港、澳、台商投资企业	Enterprises with Funds from Hong Kong,Macao and Taiwan	585.03	465.60	3.77
合资经营企业(港或澳、台资)	Joint-venture Enterprises	226.85	174.19	1.71
合作经营企业(港或澳、台资)	Cooperative Enterprises	14.59	10.45	0.08
港澳台商独资经营企业	Enterprises with Sole Investment	323.47	264.64	1.82
港澳台商投资股份有限公司	Share-holding Corporations Ltd.	19.81	16.09	0.15
其他港澳台商投资企业	Other Enterprises with Funds from Hong Kong,Macao and Taiwan	0.31	0.23	0.01
外商投资企业	Foreign Funded Enterprises	240.96	189.78	1.72
中外合资经营企业	Joint-venture Enterprises	93.04	75.50	0.61
中外合作经营企业	Cooperation Enterprises	3.13	2.35	0.03
外资企业	Enterprises with Sole Fund	123.27	96.64	0.98
外商投资股份有限公司	Share-holding Corporations Ltd. with Foreign Investment	21.53	15.29	0.10
其他外商投资企业	Other Foreign Funded Enterprises			
按轻重工业分	by Light & Heavy Industry	6512.66	5530.33	106.17
轻工业	Light Industry	897.22	644.28	7.28
重工业	Heavy Industry	5615.44	4886.06	98.89
按企业规模分	by Enterprise Size	6512.66	5530.33	106.17
大型企业	Large-sized Enterprises	3624.65	3127.65	86.24
中型企业	Medium-sized Enterprises	1250.61	1022.14	9.46
小型企业	Small-sized Enterprises	1574.34	1322.57	10.14
微型企业	Micro-sized Enterprises	63.05	57.98	0.34

单位：亿元 (100 million yuan)

销售费用 Selling Expenses	管理费用 Administrative Expenses	利息费用 Interest Expenses	利润总额 Total Profits	所得税费用 Income Tax Payable	亏损企业亏损总额 Total Loss of Loss Enterprises	利税总额 Total Profits and Taxes	应交增值税 Value-added Tax Payable
213.27	206.36	57.13	310.86	50.75	39.59	545.70	128.68
179.30	172.17	51.56	240.77	36.90	34.72	448.20	106.74
0.10	1.93	0.24	0.24	0.01	0.41	1.02	0.35
0.02	0.09		0.01			0.02	
0.09	1.84	0.24	0.23	0.01	0.41	1.00	0.34
0.02	0.48		0.18	0.03	0.02	0.36	0.15
0.44	0.44	0.02	0.17	0.02		0.33	0.14
	0.07	0.01	0.21	0.05		0.28	0.06
	0.07	0.01	0.21	0.05		0.28	0.06
86.05	82.90	33.88	128.04	24.55	26.22	194.86	48.81
8.00	13.88	2.11	5.00	1.44	6.17	11.02	3.92
78.05	69.01	31.77	123.04	23.12	20.05	183.84	44.89
48.50	32.59	10.87	60.10	6.54	2.61	168.28	32.40
44.19	53.77	6.53	51.83	5.69	5.47	83.06	24.84
0.37	0.25	0.02	0.08	0.01	0.03	0.34	0.20
39.46	49.09	5.79	45.82	5.15	5.06	75.00	23.39
4.36	4.43	0.72	5.92	0.53	0.38	7.72	1.25
24.69	18.81	3.60	51.74	10.22	2.16	72.42	16.91
8.32	10.01	0.86	26.62	6.41	1.84	36.59	8.26
3.03	0.05		1.05	0.26		1.38	0.25
12.55	7.38	2.54	23.00	3.23	0.13	32.92	8.11
0.73	1.16	0.20	1.27	0.32		1.70	0.29
0.06	0.20		–0.19		0.19	–0.17	0.02
9.28	15.38	1.97	18.35	3.63	2.70	25.08	5.02
4.33	5.48	0.54	4.24	0.71	1.06	6.87	2.01
0.04	0.36	0.01	0.26	0.05		0.36	0.07
4.11	8.73	1.08	10.54	2.40	1.64	14.29	2.78
0.79	0.81	0.34	3.31	0.47		3.56	0.15
213.27	206.36	57.13	310.86	50.75	39.59	545.70	128.68
78.19	42.61	5.55	102.44	15.96	5.71	134.21	24.49
135.08	163.75	51.58	208.42	34.79	33.88	411.50	104.19
213.27	206.36	57.13	310.86	50.75	39.59	545.70	128.68
89.35	78.94	30.88	162.97	26.70	6.98	314.57	65.35
62.03	44.51	12.30	82.55	14.15	14.07	118.29	26.28
60.69	80.76	13.52	64.19	9.77	17.75	110.26	35.93
1.21	2.15	0.42	1.14	0.13	0.77	2.59	1.11

12-9 续表 continued

指　标	Indicator	营业收入 Business Revenue	营业成本 Business Cost	税金及附加 Taxes and Other Charges
按工业行业分	**by Sector**	**6512.66**	**5530.33**	**106.17**
煤炭开采和洗选业	Mining and Washing of Coal	10.37	7.69	0.42
石油和天然气开采业	Extraction of Petroleum and Natural Gas	9.13	5.83	0.69
黑色金属矿采选业	Mining and Processing of Ferrous Metal Ores	102.12	85.37	1.43
有色金属矿采选业	Mining and Processing of Non-Ferrous Metal Ores			
非金属矿采选业	Mining and Processing of Non-metal Ores	10.79	8.33	0.28
开采专业及辅助性活动	Professional and Support Activities for Mining			
其他采矿业	Mining of Other Ores			
农副食品加工业	Processing of Food from Agricultural Products	112.73	104.51	0.27
食品制造业	Manufacture of Foods	118.73	93.44	0.85
酒、饮料和精制茶制造业	Manufacture of Liquor, Beverages and Refined Tea	61.11	48.23	1.92
烟草制品业	Manufacture of Tobacco	1.21	0.61	
纺织业	Manufacture of Textile	43.91	39.77	0.19
纺织服装、服饰业	Manufacture of Textile, Wearing Apparel and Accessories	19.81	15.67	0.22
皮革、毛皮、羽毛及其制品和制鞋业	Manufacture of Leather, Fur, Feather and Related Products and Footwear	2.35	2.12	0.01
木材加工和木、竹、藤、棕、草制品业	Processing of Timber, Manufacture of Wood, Bamboo, Rattan,Palm and Straw Products	6.37	5.77	0.04
家具制造业	Manufacture of Furniture	8.47	6.83	0.10
造纸和纸制品业	Manufacture of Paper and Paper Products	34.23	29.53	0.18
印刷和记录媒介复制业	Printing and Reproduction of Recording Media	45.43	37.37	0.30
文教、工美、体育和娱乐用品制造业	Manufacture of Articles for Culture, Education, Arts and Crafts,Sport and Entertainment Activities	13.99	12.08	0.09
石油、煤炭及其他燃料加工业	Processing of Petroleum, Coal and Other Fuels	366.74	277.69	70.42
化学原料和化学制品制造业	Manufacture of Raw Chemical Materials and Chemical Products	282.47	235.13	1.60
医药制造业	Manufacture of Medicines	227.26	94.06	2.04
化学纤维制造业	Manufacture of Chemical Fibres	9.83	7.67	0.07
橡胶和塑料制品业	Manufacture of Rubber and Plastics Products	39.65	34.83	0.17
非金属矿物制品业	Manufacture of Non-metallic Mineral Products	461.07	387.58	3.11
黑色金属冶炼和压延加工业	Smelting and Pressing of Ferrous Metals	1573.61	1508.59	5.84
有色金属冶炼和压延加工业	Smelting and Pressing of Non-ferrous Metals	13.64	12.04	0.07
金属制品业	Manufacture of Metal Products	289.63	239.11	1.74
通用设备制造业	Manufacture of General Purpose Machinery	300.97	233.31	2.22
专用设备制造业	Manufacture of Special Purpose Machinery	191.33	142.78	1.07
汽车制造业	Manufacture of Automobiles	879.80	761.37	4.08
铁路、船舶、航空航天和其他运输设备制造业	Manufacture of Railway, Ship, Aerospace and Other Transport Equipments	66.44	55.26	0.54
电气机械和器材制造业	Manufacture of Electrical Machinery and Apparatus	322.61	273.68	1.68
计算机、通信和其他电子设备制造业	Manufacture of Computers, Communication and Other Electronic Equipment	561.85	497.82	1.02
仪器仪表制造业	Manufacture of Measuring Instruments and Machinery	61.56	41.12	0.47
其他制造业	Other Manufacture	3.45	2.94	0.01
废弃资源综合利用业	Utilization of Waste Resources	9.43	8.81	0.10
金属制品、机械和设备修理业	Repair Service of Metal Products, Machinery and Equipment	8.29	5.70	0.11
电力、热力生产和供应业	Production and Supply of Electric Power and Heat Power	165.44	142.27	1.56
燃气生产和供应业	Production and Supply of Gas	50.95	43.71	0.15
水的生产和供应业	Production and Supply of Water	25.90	21.72	1.09

销售费用 Selling Expenses	管理费用 Administrative Expenses	利息费用 Interest Expenses	利润总额 Total Profits	所得税费用 Income Tax Payable	亏损企业亏损总额 Total Loss of Loss Enterprises	利税总额 Total Profits and Taxes	应交增值税 Value-added Tax Payable
213.27	206.36	57.13	310.86	50.75	39.59	545.70	128.68
0.08	1.15	0.03	1.12		0.03	2.27	0.73
	0.40	0.03	2.20	0.72		3.71	0.82
0.25	4.82	1.66	8.28	1.13	0.40	13.15	3.44
0.14	0.87		1.13	0.18	0.07	1.80	0.40
3.17	2.43	0.71	1.24	0.11	0.55	2.65	1.14
7.44	6.69	0.65	11.77	2.58	0.76	16.06	3.44
4.14	2.17	0.72	3.22	0.72	1.62	6.95	1.81
0.01	0.21		0.38	0.03		0.48	0.10
0.96	1.66	0.40	0.14	0.04	0.44	0.81	0.48
2.04	1.41	0.09	0.59	0.18	0.24	1.51	0.70
0.03	0.13		0.03			0.09	0.05
0.14	0.26	0.09	0.10			0.23	0.09
0.70	0.42	0.15	0.29	0.06	0.05	0.62	0.23
1.31	1.34	0.42	0.87	0.23	0.18	1.55	0.50
1.59	2.84	0.11	3.81	0.47	0.25	5.37	1.25
0.74	0.67	0.07	0.20	0.02	0.01	0.51	0.22
0.85	8.09	1.25	7.45	1.51	0.18	89.78	11.91
9.63	9.78	8.05	14.89	2.69	2.29	22.32	5.82
39.97	14.91	1.53	56.98	8.73	1.15	68.12	9.10
0.21	0.47	0.08	1.11	0.14	0.02	1.09	–0.10
1.16	1.63	0.17	1.18	0.15	0.10	1.99	0.64
17.92	19.10	3.63	26.37	5.07	1.38	43.16	13.68
6.62	15.86	12.65	23.21	1.53	0.25	42.04	12.99
0.23	0.62	0.10	0.21	0.07	0.24	0.45	0.17
9.33	10.27	2.17	20.08	3.06	1.47	29.61	7.78
16.71	20.58	1.26	22.70	3.10	1.79	32.94	8.02
12.08	11.73	1.79	15.82	2.07	1.08	20.98	4.09
30.33	17.10	5.84	41.80	9.09	9.03	64.16	18.28
1.89	5.32	0.17	2.05	0.37	0.82	4.37	1.78
17.50	13.47	2.72	10.29	1.18	4.39	17.05	5.08
14.53	10.51	2.50	6.81	0.61	3.00	15.05	7.21
6.23	5.63	0.29	5.65	0.80	0.28	8.46	2.34
0.12	0.51		–0.24	0.02	0.34	–0.25	–0.02
0.04	0.20		0.32	0.09	0.11	1.12	0.70
0.05	1.59	0.02	0.85	0.12		1.28	0.32
1.15	7.22	6.87	11.50	2.08	6.29	15.59	2.54
2.74	2.16	0.22	4.65	1.50	0.51	5.13	0.34
1.24	2.11	0.67	1.80	0.30	0.24	3.52	0.62

12-10 规模以上国有及国有控股工业损益及分配（2019 年）
Profit, Loss and Distribution of State-Owned and State-Controlled Industrial Enterprises Above Designated Size(2019)

指标	Indicator	营业收入 Business Revenue	营业成本 Business Cost	税金及附加 Taxes and Other Charges
总计	Total	2739.75	2385.40	85.62
按登记注册类型分组	by Status of Registration			
内资企业	Domestic Funded Enterprises	2583.97	2261.49	84.72
国有企业	State-owned Enterprises	15.65	12.67	0.43
中央企业	Central Enterprises	0.42	0.32	
地方企业	Local Enterprises	15.23	12.35	0.43
集体企业	Collective-owned Enterprises			
股份合作企业	Cooperative Enterprises			
联营企业	Joint Ownership Enterprises			
有限责任公司	Limited Liability Corporations	958.69	828.80	10.08
国有独资公司	State Sole Funded Corporations	222.93	196.45	2.10
其他有限责任公司	Other Limited Liability Corporations	735.76	632.35	7.98
股份有限公司	Share-holding Corporations Ltd.	1609.64	1420.02	74.21
私营企业	Private Enterprises			
其他企业	Other Enterprises			
港、澳、台商投资企业	Enterprises with Funds from Hong Kong, Macao and Taiwan	120.03	94.02	0.65
合资经营企业（港或澳、台资）	Joint-venture Enterprises	105.44	83.57	0.57
合作经营企业（港或澳、台资）	Cooperative Enterprises	14.59	10.45	0.08
港澳台商独资经营企业	Enterprises with Sole Investment			
港澳台商投资股份有限公司	Share-holding Corporations Ltd.			
其他港澳台商投资企业	Other Enterprises with Funds from Hong Kong, Macao and Taiwan			
外商投资企业	Foreign Funded Enterprises	35.75	29.88	0.25
中外合资经营企业	Joint-venture Enterprises	32.99	27.77	0.22
中外合作经营企业	Cooperation Enterprises	2.77	2.11	0.03
外资企业	Enterprises with Sole Fund			
外商投资股份有限公司	Share-holding Corporations Ltd. with Foreign Investment			
其他外商投资企业	Other Foreign Funded Enterprises			
按轻重工业分	by Light & Heavy Industry	2739.75	2385.40	85.62
轻工业	Light Industry	65.65	47.23	1.53
重工业	Heavy Industry	2674.10	2338.17	84.09
按企业规模分	by Enterprise Size	2739.75	2385.40	85.62
大型企业	Large-sized Enterprises	2182.46	1930.05	79.31
中型企业	Medium-sized Enterprises	314.59	255.63	3.89
小型企业	Small-sized Enterprises	238.86	196.17	2.40
微型企业	Micro-sized Enterprises	3.83	3.55	0.02
按工业行业分	by Sector	2739.75	2385.40	85.62
煤炭开采和洗选业	Mining and Washing of Coal	4.62	2.69	0.19
石油和天然气开采业	Extraction of Petroleum and Natural Gas	7.54	4.88	0.55
黑色金属矿采选业	Mining and Processing of Ferrous Metal Ores	20.60	14.51	0.67

单位：亿元 (100 million yuan)

销售费用 Selling Expenses	管理费用 Administrative Expenses	利息费用 Interest Expenses	利润总额 Total Profits	所得税费用 Income Tax Payable	亏损企业亏损总额 Total Loss of Loss Enterprises	利税总额 Total Profits and Taxes	应交增值税 Value-added Tax Payable
60.30	63.10	28.31	89.47	15.46	11.08	227.04	51.95
51.19	58.33	27.86	74.56	11.81	11.02	207.54	48.26
0.10	1.93	0.24	0.24	0.01	0.41	1.02	0.35
0.02	0.09		0.01			0.02	
0.09	1.84	0.24	0.23	0.01	0.41	1.00	0.34
23.74	36.56	18.77	38.81	7.79	9.69	69.46	20.58
8.00	13.88	2.11	5.00	1.44	6.17	11.02	3.92
15.74	22.68	16.65	33.81	6.35	3.52	58.44	16.65
27.35	19.84	8.85	35.52	4.01	0.92	137.06	27.33
7.73	2.21	0.35	13.43	3.49		17.25	3.18
4.70	2.16	0.35	12.37	3.23		15.87	2.93
3.03	0.05		1.05	0.26		1.38	0.25
1.38	2.56	0.10	1.49	0.17	0.06	2.25	0.52
1.34	2.26	0.09	1.28	0.13	0.06	1.97	0.47
0.04	0.30	0.01	0.21	0.03		0.29	0.05
60.30	63.10	28.31	89.47	15.46	11.08	227.04	51.95
8.89	4.29	0.40	4.16	0.75	0.58	8.03	2.35
51.41	58.81	27.90	85.32	14.71	10.50	219.01	49.61
60.30	63.10	28.31	89.47	15.46	11.08	227.04	51.95
37.85	38.40	20.09	58.07	10.50	6.07	175.24	37.86
14.45	12.27	5.01	17.88	3.63	0.92	30.09	8.33
7.76	12.00	3.08	13.74	1.30	3.77	22.05	5.91
0.23	0.43	0.12	–0.22	0.02	0.31	–0.35	–0.15
60.30	63.10	28.31	89.47	15.46	11.08	227.04	51.95
0.02	0.58		1.13			1.73	0.42
	0.30	0.01	1.81	0.51		3.04	0.68
0.12	2.49	0.44	2.66	0.08		4.63	1.31

12-10 续表 continued

指标	Indicator	营业收入 Business Revenue	营业成本 Business Cost	税金及附加 Taxes and Other Charges
有色金属矿采选业	Mining and Processing of Non-Ferrous Metal Ores			
非金属矿采选业	Mining and Processing of Non-metal Ores	1.04	0.50	0.08
开采专业及辅助性活动	Professional and Support Activities for Mining			
其他采矿业	Mining of Other Ores			
农副食品加工业	Processing of Food from Agricultural Products	1.37	1.15	0.01
食品制造业	Manufacture of Foods	2.49	1.86	0.01
酒、饮料和精制茶制造业	Manufacture of Liquor, Beverages and Refined Tea	24.92	18.05	1.11
烟草制品业	Manufacture of Tobacco	1.21	0.61	
纺织业	Manufacture of Textile	1.07	1.04	
纺织服装、服饰业	Manufacture of Textile, Wearing Apparel and Accessories	3.29	2.66	0.04
皮革、毛皮、羽毛及其制品和制鞋业	Manufacture of Leather, Fur, Feather and Related Products and Footwear			
木材加工和木、竹、藤、棕、草制品业	Processing of Timber, Manufacture of Wood, Bamboo, Rattan,Palm and Straw Products			
家具制造业	Manufacture of Furniture			
造纸和纸制品业	Manufacture of Paper and Paper Products	1.93	1.79	
印刷和记录媒介复制业	Printing and Reproduction of Recording Media	8.95	6.94	0.11
文教、工美、体育和娱乐用品制造业	Manufacture of Articles for Culture, Education, Arts and Crafts,Sport and Entertainment Activities			
石油、煤炭及其他燃料加工业	Processing of Petroleum, Coal and Other Fuels	273.67	191.54	70.02
化学原料和化学制品制造业	Manufacture of Raw Chemical Materials and Chemical Products	42.32	35.00	0.38
医药制造业	Manufacture of Medicines	6.89	2.58	0.12
化学纤维制造业	Manufacture of Chemical Fibres	1.62	1.81	0.03
橡胶和塑料制品业	Manufacture of Rubber and Plastics Products			
非金属矿物制品业	Manufacture of Non-metallic Mineral Products	58.27	44.12	0.66
黑色金属冶炼和压延加工业	Smelting and Pressing of Ferrous Metals	728.04	694.28	3.93
有色金属冶炼和压延加工业	Smelting and Pressing of Non-ferrous Metals			
金属制品业	Manufacture of Metal Products	40.06	36.87	0.25
通用设备制造业	Manufacture of General Purpose Machinery	77.98	57.98	0.78
专用设备制造业	Manufacture of Special Purpose Machinery	26.66	20.17	0.19
汽车制造业	Manufacture of Automobiles	498.66	444.49	1.95
铁路、船舶、航空航天和其他运输设备制造业	Manufacture of Railway, Ship, Aerospace and Other Transport Equipments	47.23	38.59	0.42
电气机械和器材制造业	Manufacture of Electrical Machinery and Apparatus	135.70	118.07	0.83
计算机、通信和其他电子设备制造业	Manufacture of Computers, Communication and Other Electronic Equipment	508.54	458.19	0.69
仪器仪表制造业	Manufacture of Measuring Instruments and Machinery	17.01	12.18	0.14
其他制造业	Other Manufacture	2.59	2.23	0.01
废弃资源综合利用业	Utilization of Waste Resources			
金属制品、机械和设备修理业	Repair Service of Metal Products, Machinery and Equipment	1.46	1.02	0.01
电力、热力生产和供应业	Production and Supply of Electric Power and Heat Power	143.96	125.01	1.38
燃气生产和供应业	Production and Supply of Gas	31.87	27.96	0.08
水的生产和供应业	Production and Supply of Water	18.18	16.62	0.95

销售费用 Selling Expenses	管理费用 Administrative Expenses	利息费用 Interest Expenses	利润总额 Total Profits	所得税费用 Income Tax Payable	亏损企业亏损总额 Total Loss of Loss Enterprises	利税总额 Total Profits and Taxes	应交增值税 Value–added Tax Payable
0.05	0.23		0.20	0.06		0.38	0.11
0.14	0.18	0.02	–0.07		0.08	–0.02	0.03
0.22	0.28		0.13	0.02		0.27	0.13
3.32	0.53	0.05	2.02	0.50		3.83	0.69
0.01	0.21		0.38	0.03		0.48	0.10
0.03	0.08		–0.12		0.12	–0.09	0.03
0.13	0.69		–0.09		0.12	0.11	0.16
0.06	0.07		0.01			0.02	
0.30	0.95	0.03	0.63	0.11	0.10	1.15	0.41
0.20	4.91	0.66	6.31	1.45		87.47	11.14
1.90	1.53	3.62	–0.66	0.11	1.37	0.49	0.77
2.99	0.67	0.23	0.89	0.03		1.58	0.57
0.01	0.05		0.01			–0.09	–0.14
2.16	2.90	0.43	8.09	1.70	0.02	10.87	2.11
3.83	7.76	9.59	6.54	–0.25		17.43	6.97
0.93	1.03	0.53	0.18	0.06	0.23	1.07	0.64
4.03	5.34	0.05	8.36	1.11		12.30	3.15
1.15	1.63	0.94	1.08	0.12	0.08	1.81	0.55
15.10	4.66	2.25	27.53	6.12	0.02	38.16	8.68
1.59	4.07	0.14	1.58	0.25	0.65	3.15	1.14
5.80	5.35	1.61	0.31	0.11	2.11	3.37	2.23
10.82	6.09	1.68	5.98	0.37	0.31	12.70	6.03
1.43	1.05	0.06	1.61	0.15		2.33	0.58
0.07	0.48		–0.26	0.02	0.34	–0.29	–0.03
0.01	0.09	0.02	0.20	0.02		0.24	0.03
0.26	5.84	5.56	10.48	1.82	4.97	14.58	2.71
2.41	1.43	0.06	2.38	0.88	0.32	2.62	0.17
1.23	1.63	0.30	0.17	0.06	0.24	1.70	0.58

12-11 分地区规模以上工业主要经济指标(2019年)

Main Economic Indicators of Industrial Enterprises Above Designated Size by Region(2019)

指 标	Indicator	全市 Total	历下区 Li xia	市中区 Shi zhong	槐荫区 Huai yin	天桥区 Tian qiao
企业单位数(个)	Number of Industial Enterprises(unit)	2153	37	39	59	87
工业总产值	Gross Industrial Output Value	5839.18	346.57	363.27	193.63	118.35
资产与负债	Assets and Liabilities					
资产总计	Total Assets	6663.13	326.74	389.87	256.77	238.59
流动资产合计	Total Fixed Assets	3945.34	145.21	301.86	179.04	110.45
存货	Inventory	807.12	18.25	64.42	26.38	18.31
应收账款	Receivable	1163.80	30.03	90.99	41.61	27.68
固定资产净额	Net Value of Fixed Assets	1548.68	104.76	37.28	26.43	63.25
流动负债合计	Current Liabilities Total	3441.11	157.45	230.35	110.34	144.37
非流动负债合计	Non-Current Liabilities Total	478.76	53.35	38.07	10.07	33.79
所有者权益合计	Total Owner' s Equities	2743.28	115.94	121.45	136.36	60.44
实收资本	Paid- up Capital	1295.84	53.47	38.36	43.44	36.13
国家资本	Official Capital	413.70	43.32	26.20	23.78	13.89
损益及分配	Profit,Loss and Distribution					
营业收入	Business Revenue	6512.66	357.26	470.47	190.51	124.45
营业成本	Business Cost	5530.33	267.11	422.35	153.68	107.30
税金及附加	Taxes and Other Charges	106.17	70.45	2.02	1.10	0.81
管理费用	Cost of Management	206.36	10.75	7.30	9.54	9.42
利润总额	Total Profits	310.86	5.23	16.80	16.87	1.50
应交所得税	Income Tax Payable	50.75	2.26	3.41	1.93	0.72
亏损企业亏损总额	Total Loss of Loss Enterprises	39.59	4.06	0.48	0.88	4.08
利税总额	Total Profits and Taxes	545.70	87.52	25.85	22.91	4.60
本年应交增值税	Value-added Tax Payable	128.68	11.84	7.03	4.94	2.28

单位：亿元 (100 million yuan)

历城区 Li cheng	长清区 Chang qing	章丘区 Zhang qiu	济阳区 Ji yang	莱芜区 Lai wu	钢城区 Gang cheng	济南高新区 Ji nan Gao xin	莱芜高新区 Lai wu Gao xin	济南先行区 JN Pioneer Area	南部山区 Nan shan	平阴县 Ping yin	商河县 Shang he
126	208	536	91	211	93	277	123	35	12	109	110
255.45	217.12	988.74	137.57	795.50	740.17	1136.76	128.61	44.81	10.69	263.25	98.70
406.43	287.02	1060.44	162.01	962.69	651.58	1234.39	172.54	45.59	14.96	339.17	114.33
266.27	173.31	605.20	100.73	579.93	216.19	860.80	107.97	18.11	9.78	203.37	67.13
33.17	44.19	127.06	17.23	135.81	53.96	183.98	21.91	3.33	4.40	39.50	15.19
87.34	64.67	131.55	16.42	260.50	22.36	281.68	24.83	8.21	2.53	54.46	18.94
58.47	54.95	251.14	42.62	260.58	335.11	151.58	36.34	13.63	2.00	78.60	31.94
220.19	141.84	533.92	58.39	599.85	380.63	580.35	70.96	23.00	9.66	119.28	60.53
22.68	20.57	61.88	9.32	92.66	56.95	37.56	7.54	3.96	0.52	20.71	9.11
163.56	124.61	464.64	94.30	270.20	213.99	616.48	94.04	18.63	4.78	199.17	44.69
96.98	106.76	230.38	36.57	152.55	152.57	201.52	59.43	13.63	1.70	49.08	23.26
5.77	67.11	24.25	2.66	28.27	123.12	43.02	0.50	2.50		5.60	3.72
269.45	215.55	1026.58	133.87	1160.21	863.63	1146.25	126.39	47.65	10.83	256.76	112.81
213.36	173.93	850.75	105.98	1075.69	806.02	899.63	108.89	37.05	8.64	201.45	98.49
1.76	1.39	7.20	1.44	4.88	5.18	5.70	0.68	0.52	0.50	1.75	0.80
14.40	13.47	32.69	7.37	21.18	13.09	44.97	5.00	2.28	0.62	9.77	4.50
16.35	11.61	49.06	12.39	39.98	17.18	82.98	5.00	5.19	0.49	26.18	4.03
3.11	2.16	8.77	3.31	4.33	1.78	12.62	0.42	0.86	0.09	4.35	0.63
2.97	1.49	11.80	1.16	2.35	1.12	5.78	1.06	0.14		1.69	0.52
25.79	18.59	82.35	17.97	57.86	32.81	111.52	7.22	7.78	1.26	35.46	6.21
7.67	5.59	26.09	4.13	13.00	10.45	22.84	1.54	2.08	0.26	7.53	1.39

12-12 规模以上大中型工业企业经营情况 (2019 年)
Main Indicators of Large and Medium-Sized Enterprises(2019)

指 标	Indicator	企业单位数 (个) Number of Industial Enterprises (unit)	亏损企业 (个) Loss Nterprises (unit)	工业总产值 (现价) Gross Industrial Output Value (Current Prices)
总计	Total	237	33	4266.42
按登记注册类型分组	by Status of Registration			
内资企业	Domestic Funded Enterprises	190	25	3588.80
国有企业	State-owned Enterprises	1		7.01
中央企业	Central Enterprises			
地方企业	Local Enterprises	1		7.01
集体企业	Collective-owned Enterprises	2		3.86
股份合作企业	Cooperative Enterprises	1		1.40
联营企业	Joint Ownership Enterprises			
有限责任公司	Limited Liability Corporations	115	16	1467.50
国有独资公司	State Sole Funded Corporations	12	4	139.59
其他有限责任公司	Other Limited Liability Corporations	103	12	1327.91
股份有限公司	Share-holding Corporations Ltd.	28	3	1569.64
私营企业	Private Enterprises	43	6	539.39
私营独资企业	Private-funded Enterprises			
私营合伙企业	Private Partnership Enterprises			
私营有限责任公司	Private Limited Liability Corporations	41	6	515.25
私营股份有限公司	Private Share-holding Corporations Ltd.	2		24.13
其他企业	Other Enterprises			
港、澳、台商投资企业	Enterprises with Funds from Hong Kong,Macao and Taiwan	23	2	509.16
合资经营企业(港或澳、台资)	Joint-venture Enterprises	12	2	173.77
合作经营企业(港或澳、台资)	Cooperative Enterprises	1		12.48
港澳台商独资经营企业	Enterprises with Sole Investment	8		305.32
港澳台商投资股份有限公司	Share-holding Corporations Ltd.	2		17.59
其他港澳台商投资企业	Other Enterprises with Funds from Hong Kong,Macao and Taiwan			
外商投资企业	Foreign Funded Enterprises	24	6	168.46
中外合资经营企业	Joint-venture Enterprises	12	1	72.78
中外合作经营企业	Cooperation Enterprises			
外资企业	Enterprises with Sole Fund	11	5	74.57
外商投资股份有限公司	Share-holding Corporations Ltd. with Foreign Investment	1		21.12
其他外商投资企业	Other Foreign Funded Enterprises			
按轻重工业分	by Light & Heavy Industry			
轻工业	Light Industry	71	8	554.60
重工业	Heavy Industry	166	25	3711.82
按企业规模分	by Enterprise Size			
大型企业	Large-sized Enterprises	56	4	3047.71
中型企业	Medium-sized Enterprises	181	29	1218.71
小型企业	Small-sized Enterprises			
微型企业	Micro-sized Enterprises			
按工业行业分	by Sector			
煤炭开采和洗选业	Mining and Washing of Coal	3	1	8.43

单位：亿元 (100 million yuan)

资产总计 Total Assets	负债合计 Total Liabilities	营业收入 Business Revenue	利润总额 Total Profits	利税总额 Total Profits and Taxes	平均用工人数（万人）Average of Employed Persons (10 000 persons)
4651.76	2693.59	4875.26	245.53	432.85	23.87
3845.77	2278.23	4189.24	187.49	352.20	18.63
10.33	10.01	7.02	0.21	0.44	0.01
10.33	10.01	7.02	0.21	0.44	0.01
2.52	0.45	3.94	0.14	0.26	0.11
2.22	1.24	1.42	0.10	0.21	0.04
2275.31	1274.32	1717.14	109.49	157.91	11.04
456.97	283.22	159.64	4.36	8.98	1.65
1818.35	991.09	1557.50	105.14	148.94	9.39
1047.98	598.90	1771.14	49.05	154.57	4.24
507.42	393.31	688.58	28.50	38.80	3.19
456.54	373.93	658.58	25.12	34.69	3.02
50.88	19.38	30.00	3.38	4.12	0.17
637.45	336.79	519.71	46.06	63.89	3.65
257.18	117.03	183.22	24.37	32.09	1.47
8.73	5.45	14.59	1.05	1.38	0.13
347.38	201.00	302.09	19.37	28.71	1.88
24.15	13.31	19.81	1.27	1.70	0.17
168.53	78.58	166.32	11.98	16.76	1.59
71.64	41.52	70.05	3.88	5.93	0.77
77.39	29.01	74.74	4.79	7.27	0.72
19.51	8.05	21.53	3.31	3.56	0.10
780.12	262.30	557.50	87.91	111.09	6.24
3871.64	2431.29	4317.76	157.62	321.77	17.63
3105.90	1772.37	3624.65	162.97	314.57	14.59
1545.85	921.23	1250.61	82.55	118.29	9.28
16.94	24.43	9.23	1.13	2.26	0.35

12-12 续表 continued

指 标	Indicator	企业单位数（个）Number of Industial Enterprises (unit)	亏损企业（个）Loss Nterprises (unit)	工业总产值（现价）Gross Industrial Output Value (Current Prices)
石油和天然气开采业	Extraction of Petroleum and Natural Gas	1		6.52
黑色金属矿采选业	Mining and Processing of Ferrous Metal Ores	4		38.35
有色金属矿采选业	Mining and Processing of Non-Ferrous Metal Ores			
非金属矿采选业	Mining and Processing of Non-metal Ores			
开采专业及辅助性活动	Professional and Support Activities for Mining			
其他采矿业	Mining of Other Ores			
农副食品加工业	Processing of Food from Agricultural Products	7	1	36.01
食品制造业	Manufacture of Foods	12	1	86.13
酒、饮料和精制茶制造业	Manufacture of Liquor, Beverages and Refined Tea	7	1	48.61
烟草制品业	Manufacture of Tobacco			
纺织业	Manufacture of Textile	3	1	11.14
纺织服装、服饰业	Manufacture of Textile, Wearing Apparel and Accessories	5	2	10.73
皮革、毛皮、羽毛及其制品和制鞋业	Manufacture of Leather, Fur, Feather and Related Products and Footwear			
木材加工和木、竹、藤、棕、草制品业	Processing of Timber, Manufacture of Wood, Bamboo, Rattan,Palm and Straw Products			
家具制造业	Manufacture of Furniture	2		5.28
造纸和纸制品业	Manufacture of Paper and Paper Products	3		11.54
印刷和记录媒介复制业	Printing and Reproduction of Recording Media	5		15.43
文教、工美、体育和娱乐用品制造业	Manufacture of Articles for Culture, Education, Arts and Crafts,Sport and Entertainment Activities	2		2.87
石油、煤炭及其他燃料加工业	Processing of Petroleum, Coal and Other Fuels	3		347.29
化学原料和化学制品制造业	Manufacture of Raw Chemical Materials and Chemical Products	9	2	136.20
医药制造业	Manufacture of Medicines	15	1	191.10
化学纤维制造业	Manufacture of Chemical Fibres			
橡胶和塑料制品业	Manufacture of Rubber and Plastics Products	1	1	2.25
非金属矿物制品业	Manufacture of Non-metallic Mineral Products	25	3	200.56
黑色金属冶炼和压延加工业	Smelting and Pressing of Ferrous Metals	9		1108.99
有色金属冶炼和压延加工业	Smelting and Pressing of Non-ferrous Metals	1		3.98
金属制品业	Manufacture of Metal Products	17	4	127.40
通用设备制造业	Manufacture of General Purpose Machinery	21	3	173.21
专用设备制造业	Manufacture of Special Purpose Machinery	14		94.04
汽车制造业	Manufacture of Automobiles	17	3	699.69
铁路、船舶、航空航天和其他运输设备制造业	Manufacture of Railway, Ship, Aerospace and Other Transport Equipments	5	1	45.17
电气机械和器材制造业	Manufacture of Electrical Machinery and Apparatus	17	4	189.98
计算机、通信和其他电子设备制造业	Manufacture of Computers, Communication and Other Electronic Equipment	10	1	488.09
仪器仪表制造业	Manufacture of Measuring Instruments and Machinery	7	1	24.43
其他制造业	Other Manufacture			
废弃资源综合利用业	Utilization of Waste Resources			
金属制品、机械和设备修理业	Repair Service of Metal Products, Machinery and Equipment	1		6.62
电力、热力生产和供应业	Production and Supply of Electric Power and Heat Power	6	2	112.41
燃气生产和供应业	Production and Supply of Gas	3		24.01
水的生产和供应业	Production and Supply of Water	2		9.97

资产总计 Total Assets	负债合计 Total Liabilities	营业收入 Business Revenue	利润总额 Total Profits	利税总额 Total Profits and Taxes	平均用工人数（万人） Average of Employed Persons (10 000 persons)
33.07	2.26	6.71	1.73	2.84	0.04
85.61	46.52	39.97	6.57	10.53	0.78
29.13	27.45	40.07	0.24	0.57	0.35
75.07	29.18	87.30	10.23	13.56	1.18
34.41	16.17	45.42	2.35	5.60	0.44
12.39	7.96	16.37	-0.12	0.25	0.16
15.96	7.89	14.46	0.67	1.44	0.52
7.50	6.06	5.56	0.26	0.52	0.10
12.36	8.98	13.78	0.69	1.04	0.13
31.98	11.84	16.63	2.70	3.28	0.27
3.14	1.84	3.38	0.09	0.24	0.09
134.20	105.68	352.16	7.29	89.28	0.24
237.76	157.79	153.86	10.10	14.37	0.94
400.52	93.31	192.96	52.99	62.56	1.98
6.84	4.31	2.40	-0.04	0.03	0.06
215.13	109.03	199.87	18.33	25.94	1.69
928.93	653.09	1536.63	23.38	42.08	3.24
6.87	3.75	4.06	0.24	0.28	0.05
176.59	56.78	124.22	17.22	22.64	1.27
263.11	111.61	175.37	17.68	24.30	1.99
125.20	80.46	94.46	8.48	10.41	0.76
655.76	420.15	794.89	37.82	56.24	3.34
61.26	28.49	46.37	1.81	3.08	0.45
234.90	135.68	188.01	8.75	11.62	0.99
286.32	171.63	517.47	6.37	13.40	0.77
29.26	15.82	23.17	2.13	3.17	0.36
7.55	2.38	6.04	0.63	1.00	0.18
363.41	244.26	126.52	3.08	6.61	0.75
77.10	40.23	25.93	2.73	2.90	0.21
83.48	68.56	11.99	0.02	0.80	0.17

12-13 规模以上大中型工业企业一览表(2019年)

Summary of Large and Medium-Sized Enterprises(2019)

企业名称 Number of Industial Enterprises	登记注册类型 Status of Registration	企业规模 Enterprise Size	所属行业 Sector
浪潮电子信息产业股份有限公司	股份有限公司	大型	计算机整机制造
山东钢铁股份有限公司	股份有限公司	大型	钢压延加工
中国重汽集团济南卡车股份有限公司	股份有限公司	大型	汽柴油车整车制造
山东泰山钢铁集团有限公司	其他有限责任公司	大型	钢压延加工
山东富伦钢铁有限公司	私营有限责任公司	大型	炼钢
中国石油化工股份有限公司济南分公司	股份有限公司	大型	原油加工及石油制品制造
莱芜钢铁集团银山型钢有限公司	其他有限责任公司	大型	钢压延加工
中国重汽集团济南商用车有限公司	港澳台商独资	大型	汽柴油车整车制造
济南市九羊福利钢铁有限公司	私营有限责任公司	中型	炼铁
中国重汽集团济南动力有限公司	港澳台商独资	大型	汽车零部件及配件制造
齐鲁制药有限公司	其他有限责任公司	大型	化学药品制剂制造
山东闽源钢铁有限公司	其他有限责任公司	大型	钢压延加工
中国重汽集团济南桥箱有限公司	与港澳台商合资经营	大型	汽车零部件及配件制造
山东宝鼎煤焦化有限公司	私营有限责任公司	中型	煤制液体燃料生产
山东泰山轧钢有限公司	其他有限责任公司	中型	钢压延加工
九阳股份有限公司	股份有限公司	中型	家用厨房电器具制造
华能莱芜发电有限公司	其他有限责任公司	中型	火力发电
山东晋煤明水化工集团有限公司	其他有限责任公司	大型	有机化学原料制造
玫德集团有限公司	其他有限责任公司	大型	建筑装饰及水暖管道零件制造
济南二机床集团有限公司	国有独资公司	大型	金属成形机床制造
山东电力设备有限公司	国有独资公司	中型	变压器、整流器和电感器制造
临工集团济南重机有限公司	私营有限责任公司	中型	矿山机械制造
山东圣泉新材料股份有限公司	股份有限公司	大型	初级形态塑料及合成树脂制造
山东鲁碧建材有限公司	其他有限责任公司	大型	水泥制造
华能济南黄台发电有限公司	其他有限责任公司	大型	火力发电
山东泰山焦化有限公司	其他有限责任公司	中型	炼焦
济南圣泉集团股份有限公司	私营有限股份公司	大型	初级形态塑料及合成树脂制造
中国重汽集团济南橡塑件有限公司	其他有限责任公司	大型	汽车车身、挂车制造
齐鲁安替制药有限公司	与港澳台商合资经营	大型	化学药品原料药制造
伊莱特能源装备股份有限公司	外商投资股份有限公司	大型	锻件及粉末冶金制品制造
济南澳海炭素有限公司	其他有限责任公司	中型	石墨及碳素制品制造
费斯托气动有限公司	外资企业	大型	液压动力机械及元件制造
中车山东机车车辆有限公司	其他有限责任公司	大型	铁路机车车辆制造
中国石油集团济柴动力有限公司	国有独资公司	大型	内燃机及配件制造
山东国舜绿色钢结构有限公司	私营有限责任公司	中型	环境保护专用设备制造
济南热电有限公司	国有独资公司	大型	热力生产和供应
济南伊利乳业有限责任公司	其他有限责任公司	大型	液体乳制造
山东大汉建设机械有限公司	其他有限责任公司	大型	生产专用起重机制造
华电章丘发电有限公司	其他有限责任公司	中型	热电联产
山东旺旺食品有限公司	外资企业	大型	液体乳制造
济南万瑞炭素有限责任公司	私营有限责任公司	大型	石墨及碳素制品制造
浪潮商用机器有限公司	与港澳台商合资经营	中型	计算机整机制造
济南达利食品有限公司	私营有限责任公司	大型	饼干及其他焙烤食品制造
山东晋煤日月化工有限公司	其他有限责任公司	大型	有机化学原料制造
中国重汽集团济南专用车有限公司	其他有限责任公司	中型	改装汽车制造
济南裕兴化工有限责任公司	其他有限责任公司	大型	专项化学用品制造
山东明泉新材料科技有限公司	其他有限责任公司	中型	其他基础化学原料制造

12-13 续表 1 continued 1

企业名称 Number of Industial Enterprises	登记注册类型 Status of Registration	企业规模 Enterprise Size	所属行业 Sector
济南热力集团有限公司	国有独资公司	大型	热力生产和供应
中国重汽集团济南特种车有限公司	其他有限责任公司	中型	汽柴油车整车制造
中粮可口可乐饮料(济南)有限公司	与港澳台商合作经营	大型	果菜汁及果菜汁饮料制造
鲁中矿业有限公司	其他有限责任公司	大型	铁矿采选
济南轻骑铃木摩托车有限公司	中外合资经营	大型	摩托车整车制造
卧龙电气章丘海尔电机有限公司	与港澳台商合资经营	大型	微特电机及组件制造
华熙生物科技股份有限公司	其他有限责任公司	中型	生物药品制造
积成电子股份有限公司	股份有限公司	大型	配电开关控制设备制造
山东水泥厂有限公司	其他有限责任公司	中型	水泥制造
济南邦德激光股份有限公司	股份有限公司	大型	其他金属加工机械制造
济南港华燃气有限公司	与港澳台商合资经营	大型	天然气生产和供应业
华润双鹤利民药业(济南)有限公司	其他有限责任公司	中型	化学药品制剂制造
莱芜钢铁集团泰东实业有限公司	其他有限责任公司	大型	耐火陶瓷制品及其他耐火材料制造
莱钢集团矿山建设有限公司	其他有限责任公司	中型	铁矿采选
平阴山水水泥有限公司	与港澳台商合资经营	中型	水泥制造
山东莱芜金雷风电科技股份有限公司	股份有限公司	中型	锻件及粉末冶金制品制造
齐鲁天和惠世制药有限公司	与港澳台商合资经营	大型	化学药品原料药制造
济南泰山阳光冶金有限公司	其他有限责任公司	中型	炼铁
齐鲁动物保健品有限公司	其他有限责任公司	大型	兽用药品制造
福士汽车零部件(济南)有限公司	外资企业	大型	汽车零部件及配件制造
山东电工电气日立高压开关有限公司	中外合资经营	中型	配电开关控制设备制造
山东省万兴食品有限公司	其他有限责任公司	中型	蔬菜加工
山东山水水泥集团有限公司	港澳台商投资股份有限公司	大型	水泥制造
山东济华燃气有限公司	与港澳台商合资经营	中型	天然气生产和供应业
山东省章丘鼓风机股份有限公司	股份有限公司	大型	风机、风扇制造
东港股份有限公司	股份有限公司	中型	包装装潢及其他印刷
山东正泰电缆有限公司	其他有限责任公司	中型	电线、电缆制造
山东华森建材集团有限公司	其他有限责任公司	中型	水泥制品制造
安莉芳(山东)服装有限公司	港澳台商独资	大型	运动休闲针织服装制造
莱芜钢铁集团莱芜矿业有限公司	其他有限责任公司	大型	铁矿采选
山东宏业纺织股份有限公司	股份有限公司	中型	棉纺纱加工
维达纸业(山东)有限公司	港澳台商投资股份有限公司	中型	机制纸及纸板制造
山东齐发药业有限公司	其他有限责任公司	中型	化学药品原料药制造
济南迈克管道科技股份有限公司	港澳台商独资	中型	金属结构制造
济南鲁冠混凝土有限责任公司	私营有限责任公司	中型	水泥制品制造
济南中海炭素有限公司	其他有限责任公司	中型	石墨及碳素制品制造
济南龙山炭素有限公司	私营有限责任公司	中型	石墨及碳素制品制造
济南锅炉集团有限公司	私营有限责任公司	大型	锅炉及辅助设备制造
济南金麒麟刹车系统有限公司	其他有限责任公司	大型	汽车零部件及配件制造
济南水务集团有限公司	国有独资公司	大型	自来水生产和供应
中国重汽集团济南豪沃客车有限公司	其他有限责任公司	中型	汽柴油车整车制造
山东科兴生物制品有限公司	其他有限责任公司	中型	基因工程药物和疫苗制造
济南黄河特钢有限责任公司	其他有限责任公司	中型	钢压延加工
中电装备山东电子有限公司	其他有限责任公司	中型	电工仪器仪表制造
济南佳宝乳业有限公司	其他有限责任公司	大型	液体乳制造
莱芜泰禾生化有限公司	其他有限责任公司	中型	食品及饲料添加剂制造
济南统一企业有限公司	港澳台商独资	中型	茶饮料及其他饮料制造
济南西门子变压器有限公司	中外合资经营	中型	变压器、整流器和电感器制造

12-13 续表 2 continued 2

企业名称 Number of Industial Enterprises	登记注册类型 Status of Registration	企业规模 Enterprise Size	所属行业 Sector
山东银鹭食品有限公司	外资企业	中型	含乳饮料和植物蛋白饮料制造
西电济南变压器股份有限公司	股份有限公司	中型	变压器、整流器和电感器制造
济南市城建材料开发服务中心	国有	中型	水泥制品制造
济南海川投资集团有限公司	私营有限责任公司	中型	石墨及碳素制品制造
济南市鲁明济北油气开发有限公司	其他有限责任公司	中型	陆地石油开采
莱芜钢铁集团粉末冶金有限公司	其他有限责任公司	中型	锻件及粉末冶金制品制造
泰富特钢悬架(济南)有限公司	其他有限责任公司	中型	汽车零部件及配件制造
山东力诺特种玻璃股份有限公司	股份有限公司	中型	日用玻璃制品制造
青岛啤酒(济南)有限公司	其他有限责任公司	中型	啤酒制造
济南新峨嵋实业有限公司	其他有限责任公司	中型	黑色金属铸造
莱芜新希望六和食品有限公司	私营有限责任公司	中型	禽类屠宰
山东济南发电设备厂有限公司	其他有限责任公司	中型	发电机及发电机组制造
济南宇飞食品有限公司	其他有限责任公司	中型	禽类屠宰
济南黄台煤气炉有限公司	其他有限责任公司	中型	气体、液体分离及纯净设备制造
莱芜市鲁中啤酒原料有限公司	私营有限责任公司	中型	其他未列明农副食品加工
山东太古飞机工程有限公司	与港澳台商合资经营	大型	航空航天器修理
山东桑乐太阳能有限公司	其他有限责任公司	中型	燃气及类似能源家用器具制造
山东力诺瑞特新能源有限公司	中外合资经营	中型	太阳能器具制造
山东博士伦福瑞达制药有限公司	与港澳台商合资经营	中型	化学药品制剂制造
山东温岭精锻科技有限公司	其他有限责任公司	中型	锻件及粉末冶金制品制造
山东力创科技股份有限公司	股份有限公司	中型	电力电子元器件制造
山东奥太电气有限公司	其他有限责任公司	中型	金属切割及焊接设备制造
山东华凌电缆有限公司	私营有限责任公司	中型	电线、电缆制造
济南重工股份有限公司	股份有限公司	中型	矿山机械制造
济南鲁东耐火材料有限公司	中外合资经营	中型	耐火陶瓷制品及其他耐火材料制造
济南沃德汽车零部件有限公司	中外合资经营	大型	汽车零部件及配件制造
山东朗进科技股份有限公司	股份有限公司	中型	制冷、空调设备制造
山推建友机械股份有限公司	股份有限公司	中型	建筑材料生产专用机械制造
济南大阳食品有限公司	私营有限责任公司	中型	禽类屠宰
山东新阳能源有限公司	国有独资公司	中型	烟煤和无烟煤开采洗选
济南金威刻科技发展有限公司	私营有限责任公司	中型	其他非金属加工专用设备制造
山东爱普电气设备有限公司	其他有限责任公司	中型	其他输配电及控制设备制造
济南轻骑标致摩托车有限公司	中外合资经营	中型	摩托车整车制造
济南中燃科技发展有限公司	其他有限责任公司	中型	其他金属加工机械制造
莱芜莱新铁矿有限责任公司	其他有限责任公司	中型	铁矿采选
章丘华明水泥有限公司	其他有限责任公司	中型	水泥制造
山东能源重装集团莱芜装备制造有限公司	其他有限责任公司	中型	矿山机械制造
山东福贞金属包装有限公司	外资企业	中型	金属包装容器及材料制造
济南市琦泉热电有限责任公司	其他有限责任公司	中型	热电联产
济南娃哈哈恒枫饮料有限公司	中外合资经营	中型	含乳饮料和植物蛋白饮料制造
齐鲁宏业纺织集团有限公司	其他有限责任公司	中型	棉纺纱加工
山东小鸭集团家电有限公司	国有独资公司	中型	其他家用电力器具制造
山东福牌阿胶股份有限公司	其他有限责任公司	中型	中成药生产
莱芜万兴果菜食品加工有限公司	港澳台商独资	中型	蔬菜加工
山东宏济堂制药集团股份有限公司	股份有限公司	大型	中成药生产
山东胜邦绿野化学有限公司	其他有限责任公司	中型	化学农药制造
济南市冶金科学研究所有限责任公司	其他有限责任公司	中型	有色金属合金制造
莱芜市万祥矿业有限公司	其他有限责任公司	中型	烟煤和无烟煤开采洗选

12-13 续表 3 continued 3

企业名称 Number of Industial Enterprises	登记注册类型 Status of Registration	企业规模 Enterprise Size	所属行业 Sector
济南迈克阀门科技有限公司	其他有限责任公司	中型	阀门和旋塞制造
济南轻骑大韩摩托车有限责任公司	中外合资经营	中型	摩托车整车制造
济南森峰科技有限公司	私营有限责任公司	中型	其他专用仪器制造
国机铸锻机械有限公司	其他有限责任公司	中型	铸造机械制造
山东百脉泉酒业有限公司	其他有限责任公司	中型	白酒制造
济南泉华包装制品有限公司	与港澳台商合资经营	中型	纸和纸板容器制造
章丘重型锻造有限公司	私营有限责任公司	中型	锻件及粉末冶金制品制造
山东欧克家具有限公司	私营有限责任公司	中型	木质家具制造
济南弘正科技有限公司	港澳台商独资	中型	摩托车零部件及配件制造
迈大食品(山东)有限公司	外资企业	中型	饼干及其他焙烤食品制造
山东上好佳食品工业有限公司	港澳台商独资	中型	饼干及其他焙烤食品制造
济南泓泉制水有限公司	其他有限责任公司	中型	自来水生产和供应
济南世纪创新水泥有限公司	其他有限责任公司	中型	水泥制造
山东福瑞达医药集团有限公司	其他有限责任公司	中型	生物药品制造
济南宜和食品有限公司	中外合资经营	中型	酱油、食醋及类似制品制造
济南中维世纪科技有限公司	私营有限责任公司	中型	集成电路制造
山东汇金股份有限公司	股份有限公司	中型	汽车零部件及配件制造
山东金钟科技集团股份有限公司	股份有限公司	中型	衡器制造
山东山大电力技术股份有限公司	其他有限责任公司	中型	其他专用仪器制造
济南市莱芜燃气热力有限责任公司	其他有限责任公司	中型	天然气生产和供应业
济南市平阴县玛钢厂	集体	中型	建筑装饰及水暖管道零件制造
山东天鹅棉业机械股份有限公司	股份有限公司	中型	棉花加工机械制造
山东北辰机电设备股份有限公司	私营有限股份公司	中型	金属压力容器制造
山东明仁福瑞达制药股份有限公司	股份有限公司	中型	中成药生产
济南华阳炭素有限公司	私营有限责任公司	中型	石墨及碳素制品制造
神思电子技术股份有限公司	股份有限公司	中型	其他计算机制造
山东大旺食品有限公司	外资企业	中型	饼干及其他焙烤食品制造
中集车辆(山东)有限公司	中外合资经营	中型	汽车用发动机制造
中孚信息股份有限公司	股份有限公司	中型	信息安全设备制造
山东博科生物产业有限公司	其他有限责任公司	中型	医疗实验室及医用消毒设备和器具制造
山东华熙海御生物医药有限公司	其他有限责任公司	中型	生物药品制造
山东通发实业有限公司	私营有限责任公司	中型	建筑工程用机械制造
山东大鲁阁织染工业有限公司	外资企业	中型	棉纺纱加工
山东鲁信天一印务有限公司	其他有限责任公司	中型	包装装潢及其他印刷
山东科源制药股份有限公司	股份有限公司	中型	化学药品原料药制造
平阴鲁西装备科技有限公司	其他有限责任公司	中型	其他金属加工机械制造
济南台有玻璃制品有限公司	私营有限责任公司	中型	日用玻璃制品制造
济南冶金化工设备有限公司	其他有限责任公司	中型	冶金专用设备制造
济南桃李面包有限公司	其他有限责任公司	中型	糕点、面包制造
山东莱芜煤矿机械有限公司	国有独资公司	中型	矿山机械制造
山东阿尔普尔节能装备有限公司	其他有限责任公司	中型	制冷、空调设备制造
山东蓝贝思特教装集团股份有限公司	私营有限责任公司	中型	文具制造
山东地矿慧通特种轮胎有限公司	其他有限责任公司	中型	轮胎制造
济南圣泉倍进陶瓷过滤器有限公司	中外合资经营	中型	特种陶瓷制品制造
莱芜永保电子有限公司	私营有限责任公司	中型	其他电子器件制造
山东法因智能设备有限公司	其他有限责任公司	中型	金属切削机床制造
济南实达紧固件有限公司	私营有限责任公司	中型	紧固件制造
济南汇丰炭素有限公司	私营有限责任公司	中型	石墨及碳素制品制造

12-13 续表 4 continued 4

企业名称 Number of Industial Enterprises	登记注册类型 Status of Registration	企业规模 Enterprise Size	所属行业 Sector
山东巧夺天工家具有限公司	私营有限责任公司	中型	木质家具制造
济南晶恒电子有限责任公司	国有独资公司	中型	半导体分立器件制造
济南鑫贝西生物技术有限公司	私营有限责任公司	中型	其他医疗设备及器械制造
山东小鸭精工机械有限公司	其他有限责任公司	中型	汽车零部件及配件制造
济南方圣混凝土构件有限公司	私营有限责任公司	中型	砼结构构件制造
山东银鹰炊事机械有限公司	其他有限责任公司	中型	其他金属加工机械制造
山东汶河新材料有限公司	其他有限责任公司	中型	专项化学用品制造
济南星辉数控机械科技有限公司	其他有限责任公司	中型	其他专用设备制造
济南界龙科技有限公司	外资企业	中型	电阻电容电感元件制造
济南圣都食品有限公司	私营有限责任公司	中型	肉制品及副产品加工
莱芜市九龙耐火材料有限公司	其他有限责任公司	中型	耐火陶瓷制品及其他耐火材料制造
山东耀华玻璃有限公司	私营有限责任公司	中型	其他玻璃制造
济南元首针织股份有限公司	股份有限公司	中型	运动休闲针织服装制造
山东宏达科技集团有限公司	其他有限责任公司	中型	金属压力容器制造
山东华氟化工有限责任公司	其他有限责任公司	中型	化学试剂和助剂制造
济南瑞泉电子有限公司	私营有限责任公司	中型	供应用仪器仪表制造
济南趵突泉酿酒有限责任公司	其他有限责任公司	中型	白酒制造
济南奥图自动化股份有限公司	私营有限责任公司	中型	工业机器人制造
济南二机床铸造有限公司	国有独资公司	中型	黑色金属铸造
海湾电子(山东)有限公司	与港澳台商合资经营	中型	其他电子元件制造
济南科盛电子有限公司	其他有限责任公司	中型	光电子器件制造
山东越宫钢构件有限公司	其他有限责任公司	中型	金属结构制造
济南汇智电力科技有限公司	其他有限责任公司	中型	工业自动控制系统装置制造
山东冠世针织有限公司	外资企业	中型	运动休闲针织服装制造
济南市长清计算机应用公司	股份合作	中型	供应用仪器仪表制造
济南巨鑫机车车辆配件有限公司	私营有限责任公司	中型	锻件及粉末冶金制品制造
济南莱钢钢结构有限公司	其他有限责任公司	中型	金属结构制造
济南双凤耐火材料有限公司	私营有限责任公司	中型	隔热和隔音材料制造
山东晨熙智能科技有限公司	其他有限责任公司	中型	包装装潢及其他印刷
中闻集团山东印务有限公司	其他有限责任公司	中型	书、报刊印刷
莱芜朝阳电子有限公司	其他有限责任公司	中型	电力电子元器件制造
济南银鹰食品机械有限公司	其他有限责任公司	中型	农副食品加工专用设备制造
山东新华印务有限责任公司	国有独资公司	中型	书、报刊印刷
济南润友模塑有限公司	私营有限责任公司	中型	其他工艺美术及礼仪用品制造
金德利餐饮有限公司	其他有限责任公司	中型	米、面制品制造
济南沃德机械制造有限公司	股份有限公司	中型	汽车零部件及配件制造
山东博特生物资源制品有限公司	私营有限责任公司	中型	其他纸制品制造
济阳元首针织有限责任公司	其他有限责任公司	中型	其他针织或钩针编织服装制造
莱芜环球汽车零部件有限公司	外资企业	中型	汽车零部件及配件制造
济南思迈迩制衣有限公司	私营有限责任公司	中型	运动机织服装制造
章丘市铜铝铸造厂	集体	中型	锻件及粉末冶金制品制造
山东省莱芜市辛庄煤矿有限公司	其他有限责任公司	中型	烟煤和无烟煤开采洗选
济南金木铸造有限公司	私营有限责任公司	中型	铸造机械制造
莱芜科林光电有限公司	其他有限责任公司	中型	光伏设备及元器件制造
济南第一机床有限公司	其他有限责任公司	中型	金属切削机床制造
济南野风酥食品有限公司	私营有限责任公司	中型	饼干及其他焙烤食品制造

12-14 主要工业产品生产量(2019年)
Output of Major Industrial Products(2019)

主要工业产品名称	Major Industrial Products above Designated Size	单位 Unit	生产量 Proction
铁矿石原矿	Crude Iron Ore	万吨(10 000 tons)	557.0
铁矿石成品矿	Iron Ore Finished Ore	万吨(10 000 tons)	295.0
铁精矿	Iron Ore Concentrate	万吨(10 000 tons)	292.4
石灰石	Lime Powder	万吨(10 000 tons)	64.0
高岭土(瓷土)	Kaolin	万吨(10 000 tons)	8.9
小麦粉	Wheat Flour	万吨(10 000 tons)	4.1
饲料	Feed	万吨(10 000 tons)	82.5
配合饲料	Formula Feed	万吨(10 000 tons)	21.3
混合饲料	Mixed Feed	万吨(10 000 tons)	12.4
精制食用植物油	Refined Edible Vegetable Oil	万吨(10 000 tons)	6.1
成品糖	Finished Sugar products	吨(ton)	2106
鲜、冷藏肉	Frozen, Fresh Meat	万吨(10 000 tons)	14.9
冻肉	Frozen Meat	万吨(10 000 tons)	4.5
熟肉制品	Cooked Meat Products	吨(ton)	9300
冷冻蔬菜	Frozen Vegetable	吨(ton)	3963
膨化食品	Puffed Foods	万吨(10 000 tons)	1.3
糖果	Candies	万吨(10 000 tons)	1.3
速冻食品	Quick-rozen Food	吨(ton)	3043
速冻米面食品	Quick-frozen Rice and Noodles	吨(ton)	2488
方便面	Instant Noodles	万吨(10 001 tons)	2.2
乳制品	Milk Products	万吨(10 000 tons)	47.7
液体乳	Liquid Milk	万吨(10 000 tons)	46.7
固体及半固体乳制品	Solid and Semi-soild Dairy Products	吨(ton)	9621
罐头	Canned Food	吨(ton)	5
酱油	Soy Sauce	万吨(10 000 tons)	12.0
营养、保健食品	Nutrition and Health Food	吨(ton)	1022
食品添加剂	Food Additives	万吨(10 000 tons)	14.7
饲料添加剂	Feed Additive	万吨(10 000 tons)	3.5
饮料酒	Liquor	万千升(10 000 kiloliter)	31.0
白酒(折65度,商品量)	Liquor (65 degree discount, commercial quantity)	万千升(10 001 kiloliter)	1.6
啤酒	Beer	万千升(10 000 kiloliter)	29.4
饮料	Drinks	万吨(10 000 tons)	156.4
碳酸型饮料(汽水)	Carbonated Drinks	万吨(10 000 tons)	35.9
包装饮用水	Bottled Drinking Water	万吨(10 000 tons)	36.9
果汁和蔬菜汁类饮料	Juice and Vegetable Juice Beverage	万吨(10 000 tons)	32.9
蛋白饮料	Protein Beverage	吨(ton)	1305
精制茶	Refined Tea	吨(ton)	10
纱	Yarn	万吨(10 000 tons)	6.3
棉纱	Cotton Yarn	万吨(10 000 tons)	2.7
棉混纺纱	Cotton Blended Yarn	万吨(10 000 tons)	3.2
化学纤维纱	Chemical Fiber Yarn	吨(ton)	3669
布	Cloth	万米(10 000 m)	4094.8
色织布(含牛仔布)	Yarn-dyed Fabric (including denim)	万米(10 000 m)	102.0
棉布	Cotton Cloth	万米(10 000 m)	653.1
棉混纺布	Cotton Blended Cloth	万米(10 000 m)	169.0
化学纤维短纤布	Chemical Fiber Cloth	万米(10 000 m)	2962.4
毛条	Wool Top	吨(ton)	354
蚕丝	Silk	吨(ton)	35
化纤长丝机织物	Synthetic Filament Woven Fabric	万米(10 000 m)	80.3
非织造布(无纺布)	Nonwovens	万吨(10 000 tons)	11.1

12-14 续表 1 continued 1

主要工业产品名称	Major Industrial Products above Designated Size	单位 Unit	生产量 Proction
服装	Garments	万件 (10 000 pieces)	5563.1
梭织服装	Woven Garments	万件 (10 000 pieces)	2208.7
羽绒服装	Down Garments	万件 (10 000 pieces)	14.5
西服套装	Tailored Suit	万件 (10 000 pieces)	25.0
衬衫	Shirts	万件 (10 000 pieces)	3.4
运动服类服装	Sportswear Category	万件 (10 000 pieces)	35.2
针织服装	Knitted Clothing	万件 (10 000 pieces)	3354.5
天然毛皮服装	Natural Fur Garments	万件 (10 000 pieces)	1.3
人造板	Manmade Plates	万立方米 (10 000 cu.m)	19.2
纤维板	Fiberboard	万立方米 (10 000 cu.m)	13.4
复合木地板	Composite Floor	万平方米 (10 000 sq.m)	6.8
家具	Furniture	万件 (10 000 pieces)	32.7
木质家具	Wood Furniture	万件 (10 000 pieces)	32.1
机制纸及纸板(外购原纸加工除外)	Machine – made Paper and Board (Excluding Outsourced Base Paper Processing)	万吨 (10 000 tons)	17.3
纸制品	Paper Products	万吨 (10 000 tons)	19.8
瓦楞纸箱	Corrugated Box	万吨 (10 000 tons)	7.9
卫生用纸制品	Sanitary Paper Products	吨 (ton)	1401
单色印刷品	Monochrome Print	万令 (10 000 ream)	244.7
多色印刷品	Ploychrome Print	万对开色令 (10 000 color folio ream)	928.8
丙烯	Propylene	吨 (ton)	327
纯苯	Purified Petroleum Benzin(e)	万吨 (10 001 tons)	3.8
精甲醇	Extracted Methanol	万吨 (10 000 tons)	85.0
硅	Silicon	万吨 (10 001 tons)	2.1
合成氨(无水氨)	Synthetic Ammonia	万吨 (10 000 tons)	69.3
农用氮、磷、钾化学肥料(折纯)	Chemical Fertilizer	万吨 (10 000 tons)	16.9
氮肥(折含氮 100%)	Nitrogen Fertilizer	万吨 (10 000 tons)	16.9
尿素(折含氮 100%)	Urea	万吨 (10 000 tons)	16.7
化学农药原药(折有效成分 100%)	Chemical Pesticide	吨 (ton)	9415
杀虫剂(杀螨剂)原药	Insecticides Pesticide	吨 (ton)	337
杀菌剂原药	Fungicides	吨 (ton)	47
除草剂原药	Herbicide	吨 (ton)	5721
涂料	Paint	万吨 (10 000 tons)	2.7
初级形态塑料	Primary Plastic	万吨 (10 000 tons)	29.3
聚丙烯树脂	Polypropylene Colophony	万吨 (10 000 tons)	11.5
聚氯乙烯树脂	PVC Resins	吨 (ton)	6826
聚苯乙烯树脂	Polystyrene Resins	吨 (ton)	2507
合成橡胶	Synthetic Rubber	吨 (ton)	6363
合成纤维聚合物	Synthetic Fiber Polymer	吨 (ton)	7797
聚酯	Polyester	吨 (ton)	7797
化学试剂	Chemical Reagent	万吨 (10 000 tons)	2.9
表面活性剂	Surface Active Agent	万吨 (10 000 tons)	4.3
化学药品原药	Chemical Medicine	吨 (ton)	7572
中成药	Traditional Chemical Medicine	吨 (ton)	3263
兽用药品	Veterinary Drugs	吨 (ton)	3254
化学纤维	Chemical Fiber	万吨 (10 000 tons)	6.0
人造纤维(纤维素纤维)	Artifical Fiber (Cellulosic Fiber)	万吨 (10 000 tons)	1.2
醋酸纤维长丝	Acetate Filament	万吨 (10 000 tons)	1.2
合成纤维	Synthetic Fiber Polymers	万吨 (10 000 tons)	4.9
涤纶纤维	Polyester Fiber	万吨 (10 000 tons)	4.9
橡胶轮胎外胎☆	Rubber Tyre Cover	万条	29.7
工程机械用橡胶轮胎外胎	Rubber Tyre Cover for Construction Machinery	万条	29.7

12–14 续表 2 continued 2

主要工业 产品名称	Major Industrial Products above Designated Size	单 位 Unit	生产量 Proction
塑料制品	Plastic Articles	万吨 (10 000 tons)	9.9
塑料薄膜	Plastic Film	万吨 (10 000 tons)	3.1
农用薄膜	Agricultural Film	吨 (ton)	7037
泡沫塑料	Foam	吨 (ton)	1398
日用塑料制品	Commodity Plastics	吨 (ton)	1750
硅酸盐水泥熟料	Portland Cement Clinker	万吨 (10 000 tons)	538.3
窑外分解窑水泥熟料	Precalciner Kiln Clinker	万吨 (10 000 tons)	396.4
水泥	Cement	万吨 (10 000 tons)	1287.8
强度等级 42.5 水泥 (含 R 型)	Strength Grade42.5Cement	万吨 (10 000 tons)	60.6
石灰	Lime	万吨 (10 000 tons)	77.5
商品混凝土	Concrete	万立方米 (10 000 cu.m)	2607.9
水泥混凝土排水管	Cement and Concrete Drainage Pipes	千米 (km)	67.5
水泥混凝土压力管	Cement and Concrete Pressure Pipes	千米 (km)	0.5
砖	Brick	亿块 (100 million unit)	1.8
天然花岗石建筑板材	Natural Marble Building Block	万平方米 (10 000 sq.m)	1.7
隔热、隔音人造矿物材料及其制品	Insulation and Sound Insulation Materials and Products	万吨 (10 000 tons)	1.1
钢化玻璃	Stalinite	万平方米 (10 000 sq.m)	56.7
夹层玻璃	Sandwich Glass	万平方米 (10 000 sq.m)	30.2
中空玻璃	Hollow Glass	万平方米 (10 000 sq.m)	140.8
日用玻璃制品	Household Glass	万吨 (10 000 tons)	11.6
玻璃包装容器	Glass Container	万吨 (10 000 tons)	30.1
玻璃保温容器	Glass Insulation Vessel	万个 (10 000 unit)	36.1
玻璃纤维纱	Glass Fiber Yarn	吨 (ton)	1820
纤维增强塑料制品	Fiber Reinforced Plastic Products	吨 (ton)	587
耐火材料制品	Refractory Product	万吨 (10 000 tons)	74.5
石墨及碳素制品	Graphite and Carbon Products	万吨 (10 000 tons)	181.0
生铁	Cast Iron	万吨 (10 000 tons)	1961.8
粗钢	Crude Steel	万吨 (10 000 tons)	2144.2
钢材	Steel	万吨 (10 000 tons)	2255.5
大型型钢	Large Steel	万吨 (10 000 tons)	190.3
中小型型钢	Small and Medium Steel	万吨 (10 000 tons)	74.4
棒材	Bar	万吨 (10 000 tons)	464.3
钢筋	Reinforcing Steel Bar	万吨 (10 000 tons)	297.7
线材 (盘条)	Wire Rod (Steel Wire Rod)	万吨 (10 000 tons)	120.4
特厚板	Extra–thick Steel Plate	万吨 (10 000 tons)	15.2
厚钢板	Thick Steel Plate	万吨 (10 000 tons)	73.1
中板	Middle Plate	万吨 (10 000 tons)	54.8
冷轧薄板	Cold–rolled Sheet	万吨 (10 000 tons)	2.1
中厚宽钢带	Medium Thick and Wide Steel Strip	万吨 (10 000 tons)	672.6
热轧薄宽钢带	Hot–rolled Thin Wide Steel Strip	万吨 (10 000 tons)	52.7
冷轧薄宽钢带	Cold–rolled Thin Wide Steel Strip	万吨 (10 000 tons)	128.9
热轧窄钢带	Hot–rolled Narrow Steel Strip	万吨 (10 000 tons)	78.9
冷轧窄钢带	Cold–rolled Narrow Steel Strip	吨 (ton)	3241
无缝钢管	Seamless Steel Tube	万吨 (10 000 tons)	2.3
焊接钢管	Welded Steel Tube	万吨 (10 000 tons)	23.5
其他钢材	Other Steel Profiles	万吨 (10 000 tons)	4.1
用外购钢材再加工生产钢材	Steel in Process of Foreign–purchased Steel	万吨 (10 000 tons)	27.4
用外购国产钢材再加工生产钢材	Steel in Process of Foreign–purchased Domestic Steel	万吨 (10 000 tons)	27.4
高温合金	High Temperature Alloy	吨 (ton)	174
铁合金	Iron Alloy	万吨 (10 000 tons)	8.0
铝合金	Aluminium Alloy	吨 (ton)	4707

12-14 续表 3 continued 3

主要工业产品名称	Major Industrial Products above Designated Size	单位 Unit	生产量 Proction
铜材	Copper Product	吨 (ton)	2532
铝材	Aluminium Product	吨 (ton)	5661
钢结构	Steel Structure	万吨 (10 000 tons)	38.6
金属门窗及类似制品	Metal Doors and Windows and Similar Products	吨 (ton)	4949
金属切削工具	Metal Cutting Tool	万件 (10 000 unit)	284.7
金属压力容器	Metal Pressure Vessel	吨 (ton)	305
金属包装容器	Metal Packaging Container	万吨 (10 000 tons)	3.8
钢丝	Steel Wire	万吨 (10 000 tons)	1.3
钢丝绳	Steel Wire Rope	吨 (ton)	3955
不锈钢日用制品	Stainless Steel Daily Articles	万件 (10 001 unit)	2.7
铸铁件	Iron Casting	万吨 (10 000 tons)	7.0
铸钢件	Steel Casting	万吨 (10 000 tons)	6.4
锻件	Forge Piece	万吨 (10 000 tons)	93.6
粉末冶金零件	Sintered Metal Products	万吨 (10 000 tons)	2.9
电站锅炉	Utility Boilers	蒸发量吨 (evaporation ton)	4730
工业锅炉	Industrial Boilers	蒸发量吨 (evaporation ton)	47
发动机	Engine	万千瓦 (10 000kw)	3583.6
汽车用发动机	Automotive Engine	万千瓦 (10 000kw)	3483.0
金属切削机床	Metal-cutting Machine Tools	台 (unit)	7237
数控金属切削机床	CNC Metal Cutting Machine	台 (unit)	1027
金属成形机床	Metal Forming Machine	台 (unit)	1163
数控金属成形机床 (数控锻压设备)	CNC Metal Forming Machine (CNC Forging Equipment)	台 (unit)	182
铸造机械	Casting Machinery	万台 (10 000 unit)	9.0
电焊机	Electric Welding Machine	万台 (10 000 unit)	7.4
机床数控装置	Machine Tool Control Device	套 (unit)	7465
起重机	Lifting Equipment	万吨 (10 000 tons)	28.2
电梯、自动扶梯及升降机	Elevators, Escalators and Lifts	台 (unit)	5119
电梯	Elevators	台 (unit)	846
升降机	Lifts	台 (unit)	4273
泵	Pumps	万台 (10 000 unit)	1.4
真空泵	Vacuum Pumps	台 (unit)	193
真空应用设备	Vacuum Application Equipment	台 (unit)	339
气体压缩机	Gas Compressor	台 (unit)	195
非制冷设备用压缩机	Compressor for Non-refrigeration Equipment	台 (unit)	195
阀门	Valves	吨 (ton)	9595
液压元件	Hydraulic Components	万件 (10 000 unit)	37.9
气动元件	Pneumatic Components	万件 (10 000 unit)	1675.6
滚动轴承	Rolling Bearings	万套 (10 000 unit)	2433.8
齿轮	Wheel Gear	吨 (ton)	5817
工业电炉	Industrial Furnace	台 (unit)	42
风机	Fans	万台 (10 000 unit)	4.8
鼓风机	Air Blower	万台 (10 000 unit)	3.8
工商用制冷、空调设备	Commercial Refrigeration Equipment	万台 (10 000 unit)	1.9
工商用空调设备	Air-conditioning Equipment for Industrial and Commercial Use	台 (套)(unit)	1864
金属紧固件	Metal Fastener	万吨 (10 000 tons)	3.7
弹簧	Spring	万吨 (10 000 tons)	7.1
矿山专用设备	Mining Equipment	万吨 (10 000 tons)	6.2
石油钻井设备	Oil Drilling Equipment	台 (套)(unit)	2920
建筑工程用机械	Construction Engineering Machinery	台 (unit)	5431
水泥专用设备	Cement Special Equipment	吨 (ton)	2035

12–14 续表 4 continued 4

主要工业 产品名称	Major Industrial Products above Designated Size	单 位 Unit	生产量 Proction
混凝土机械	Concrete Machinery	台 (unit)	6454
金属冶炼设备	Metal Smelting Equipment	万吨 (10 000 tons)	3.9
金属轧制设备	Metal Rolling Equipment	吨 (ton)	1003
炼油、化工生产专用设备	Special Equipment for Oil Refining and Chemical Protection	吨 (ton)	6759
塑料加工专用设备	Special Equipment for Plastic Processing	台 (unit)	1382
模具	Matrix	套 (unit)	38
食品制造机械	Food Manufacturing Machinery	台 (unit)	9708
农产品初加工机械	Agricultural Primary Processing Machinery	万台 (10 000 unit)	4.8
印刷专用设备	Printing Special Equipment	吨 (ton)	1133
电子工业专用设备	Special Equipment for Electrionic Industry	万台 (10 000 unit)	10.6
机械化农业及园艺机具	Mechanized Farming and Gardening Tools	台 (unit)	7900
棉花加工机械	Cotton Processing Machinery	台 (unit)	765
医疗仪器设备及器械	Medical Instruments	万台 (10 000 unit)	18.3
环境污染防治专用设备	Special Equipment for Environmental Protection	台 (套)(unit)	9363
大气污染防治设备	Air Pollution Control Equipment	台 (套)(unit)	937
水质污染防治设备	Water Pollution Control Equipment	台 (套)(unit)	86
固体废弃物处理设备	Soild Waste Dis posal Equipment	台 (套)(unit)	8340
灭火器	Fire Extinguisher	台 (unit)	8931
工业机器人	Industrial Robot	套 (unit)	1074
汽车	Motor Vehicles	万辆 (10 000 unit)	17.5
基本型乘用车 (轿车)	Basic Passenger Car (Car)	辆 (unit)	1500
轿车 (1 升 < 排量≤ 1.6 升)	Car (1 liter < Displacement < 1.6 liter)	辆 (unit)	1500
载货汽车	Trucks	万辆 (10 000 unit)	17.4
改装汽车	Modified Cars	万辆 (10 000 unit)	1.1
铁路货车	Railway Freight Wagons	辆 (unit)	5311
摩托车整车	Motorcycles	万辆 (10 000 unit)	30.2
发电机组 (发电设备)	Power Generating Equipment	万千瓦 (10 000kw)	108.1
汽轮发电机组	Steam Turbogenerator	万千瓦 (10 000kw)	85.0
风力发电机组	Wind Generating Set	万千瓦 (10 000kw)	23.1
电动机	Electromotor	万千瓦 (10 000kw)	257.3
直流电动机	DC Motor	万千瓦 (10 000kw)	5.2
交流电动机	AC Motors	万千瓦 (10 000kw)	252.1
变压器	Transformers	万千伏安 (10 000 KVA)	15448.4
电力变压器，额定容量≥ 8000kVA	Power Transformer, Rated Capacity ≥ 8000kVA	万千伏安 (10 000 KVA)	3560.5
互感器	Mutual Inductor	台 (unit)	57
高压开关板	High Voltage Switch Plate	面 (unit)	370
低压开关板	Low Voltage Switch Plate	面 (unit)	3615
高压开关设备 (11 万伏以上)	High Voltage Switchgear (over 110,000 volts)	万台 (10 000 unit)	1.3
安全、自动化监控设备	Safety and Automatic Monitoring Equipment	台 (套)(unit)	4821
通信及电子网络用电缆	Cable for Communications and Electronic Network	万对千米 (10 000 couples.km)	10.1
电力电缆	Power Cable	万千米 (10 000 km)	6.0
锂离子电池	Lithium Ion Battery	万只 (万自然只)(10 000 unit)	13.2
太阳能电池 (光伏电池)	Solar Cell (Photovoltaic Cell)	万千瓦 (10 000kw)	55.7
房间空气调节器	Room Air Conditioner	万台 (10 000 unit)	1.8
电冷热饮水机	Electric Hot and Cold Water Dispenser	台 (unit)	7199
家用电热水器	Solar Water Heater	万台 (10 000 unit)	1.7
太阳能热水器	Solar Water Heater	万平方米 (10 000 sq.m)	121.2
电光源	Electric Light Source	万只 (10 000 unit)	11.0
白炽灯泡	Incandescent Bulb	万只 (10 000 unit)	11.0

12–14 续表 5 continued 5

主要工业 产品名称	Major Industrial Products above Designated Size	单 位 Unit	生产量 Proction
灯具及照明装置	Lamps and Lighting Fixtures	万套（台个）(10 000 unit)	24.5
电子计算机整机	Computers	万台 (10 000 unit)	118.4
微型计算机设备	Microcomputer Equipment	台 (unit)	8377
服务器	Servers	万台 (10 000 unit)	116.5
显示器	Display	台 (unit)	1099
半导体分立器件	Discrete Semiconductor Devices	亿只 (100 million unit)	114.2
传感器	Transducer	万只 (10 000 unit)	524.0
集成电路	Integrated Circuit	万块 (10 000 unit)	1561.1
电子元件	Eletronic Components	亿只 (100 million unit)	16.9
电声器件	Electroacoustic Device	万只 (10 000 unit)	548.0
印制电路板	Print–circuit Board	万平方米 (10 000 sq.m)	126.8
工业自动调节仪表与控制系统	Industrial Automatic Instrument and Control System	台（套）(unit)	7180
电工仪器仪表	Electrical Instrument	万台 (10 000 unit)	384.2
分析仪器及装置	Analytical Instruments and Devices	台（套）(unit)	9250
试验机	Testing Machine	台 (unit)	6170
环境监测专用仪器仪表	Special Instruments for Environmental Monitoring	台 (unit)	5207
汽车仪器仪表	Automobile Instrument	万台 (10 000 unit)	93.4
钟	Clock	万只 (10 000 unit)	100.5
光学仪器	Opitcal Instrument	台 (unit)	9463
衡器（秤）	Scales	台 (unit)	3880
自来水生产量	Tap Water Production	亿立方米 (100 million cu.m)	6.6
半导体分立器件	Discrete Semiconductor Devices	亿只 (100 million unit)	114.2
传感器	Transducer	万只 (10 000 unit)	524.0
集成电路	Integrated Circuit	万块 (10 000 unit)	1561.1
电子元件	Eletronic Components	亿只 (100 million unit)	16.9
电声器件	Electroacoustic Device	万只 (10 000 unit)	548.0
印制电路板	Print–circuit Board	万平方米 (10 000 sq.m)	126.8
工业自动调节仪表与控制系统	Industrial Automatic Instrument and Control System	台（套）(unit)	7180
电工仪器仪表	Electrical Instrument	万台 (10 000 unit)	384.2
分析仪器及装置	Analytical Instruments and Devices	台（套）(unit)	9250
试验机	Testing Machine	台 (unit)	6170
环境监测专用仪器仪表	Special Instruments for Environmental Monitoring	台 (unit)	5207
汽车仪器仪表	Automobile Instrument	万台 (10 000 unit)	93.4
钟	Clock	万只 (10 000 unit)	100.5
光学仪器	Opitcal Instrument	台 (unit)	9463
衡器（秤）	Scales	台 (unit)	3880
自来水生产量	Tap Water Production	亿立方米 (100 million cu.m)	6.6
原油加工量	Crude Processing Volume	万吨 (10 000 tons)	521.1
汽油	Gasoline	万吨 (10 000 tons)	186.3
柴油	Diesel Oil	万吨 (10 000 tons)	139.0
燃料油	Fuel Oil	万吨 (10 000 tons)	1.3
石脑油	Naphtha	万吨 (10 000 tons)	7.5
液化石油气	Liquefied Petroleum	万吨 (10 000 tons)	33.2
石油焦	Petroleum Coke	万吨 (10 000 tons)	16.6
石油沥青	Asphalt	万吨 (10 000 tons)	18.6
发电量	Power Generating Capacity	亿千瓦时 (100 million kwh)	295.1
其中：火力发电量	Thermal Power Generation	亿千瓦时 (100 million kwh)	285.9
风力发电量	Wind Power Generation	亿千瓦时 (100 million kwh)	7.5
垃圾发电量	Garbage Power Generation	亿千瓦时 (100 million kwh)	3.9
煤气生产量	Gas Power Generation	亿立方米 (100 million cu.m)	269.5

12-15 工业企业能源购进、消费及库存 (2019 年)
Purchases, Consumption and Invetory of Main Energy Source in Industrial Enterprises(2019)

能源名称	Energy	计量单位 Unit	年初库存量 Beginning Stock	本年购进量 Purchases This Year	本年消费 Consumption of This Year 合计 Total	工业生产消费 Industrial Consumption	非工业生产消费 Non-Industrial Consumption	年末库存量 Year-end Stock
能源合计	Total Energy	吨标准煤 (tons of SCE)			50916150	50489034	427115	
原煤	Raw Coal	吨 (ton)	1106950	18026905	18985460	18873763	111697	940427
洗精煤	Cleaned Coal	吨 (ton)	394895	7733535	7794552	7794552		333878
其他洗煤	Other Cleaned Coal	吨 (ton)	142513	3499439	3513684	3513684		141743
煤制品	Coal Product	吨 (ton)	72730	688823	676537	676537		85014
焦炭	Coke	吨 (ton)	94801	3425194	9199600	9199479	121	159982
天然气	Natural Gas	万立方米 (10 000 cu.m)		67636	67601	67110	490	
液化天然气	Liquefied Nutural Gas	吨 (ton)	35	12310	12307	12266	40	38
原油	Crude Oil	吨 (ton)	81102	5211818	5210923	5210923		81997
汽油	Gasoline	吨 (ton)	776	6214	6333	3316	3017	729
煤油	Kerosene	吨 (ton)	4	62	87	87		4
柴油	Diesel Oil	吨 (ton)	3068	45932	46195	36188	10007	2356
燃料油	Fuel Oil	吨 (ton)	237	545	445	445		337
液化石油气	Liquefied Petroleum	吨 (ton)	2	45	45	39	6	2
炼厂干气	Refinery Dry Gas	吨 (ton)			205545	205545		
其他石油制品	Other Petroleum Product	吨 (ton)		63982	553219	553219		
热力	Heating	百万千焦 (mkj)		5309237	8606866	8529224	77642	
电力	Electricity	万千瓦时 (10 000 kwh)		1577402	2079553	2042120	37432	
其他燃料	Other Fuel	吨标准煤 (tons of SCE)	554	2550	2548	2548		2

注：按照经济普查要求，免填能源合计中，年初库存、购进量、年末库存。

Note: According to requirements of economic census, it's unnecessary to fill in inventory and volume of purchase at the beginning of the year and the inventory at the end of the year in the total energy.

12-16 工业分行业主要能源消费量(2019年)

Consumption of Main Energy Source in Industrial Enterprises by Sector(2019)

指 标	Indicator	原煤(吨) Coal (ton)	汽油(吨) Gasoline (ton)	煤油(吨) Kerosene (ton)	柴油(吨) Diesel Oil (ton)	燃料油(吨) Fuel Oil (ton)	热力(百万千焦) Heating (mkj)	电力(万千瓦时) Electricity (10 000 kwh)
总计	Total	18985460	6333	87	46195	445	8606866	2079553
采矿业	Mining							
煤炭开采和洗选业	Mining and Washing of Coal	741110	13		99		45	7883
石油和天然气开采业	Extraction of Petroleum and Natural Gas				12			4052
黑色金属矿采选业	Mining and Processing of Ferrous Metal Ores	25281	104		1957			42229
非金属矿采选业	Mining and Processing of Non-Ferrous Metal Ores				1636			2519
制造业	Manufacture							
农副食品加工业	Processing of Food from Agricultural Products	49198	100		110		55567	12310
食品制造业	Manufacture of Foods	115577	91		638		427456	23639
酒、饮料和精制茶制造业	Manufacture of Wine, Drinks and Refined Tea		23		180		114012	10733
纺织业	Manufacture of Textile		26		22		163497	28817
纺织服装、服饰业	Manufacture of Textile Wearing Apparel and Finery		53		8		39201	3016
皮革、毛皮、羽毛及其制品和制鞋业	Manufacture of Leather, Fur, Feather and Related Products and Footwear		18					433
木材加工及木、竹、藤、棕、草制品业	Processing of Timbers, Manufacture of Wood, Bamboo, Rattan, Palm, and Straw Products		18				269	5961
家具制造业	Manufacture of Furniture		19		28			2214
造纸及纸制品业	Manufacture of Paper and Paper Products	75382	14		6		269930	21644
印刷和记录媒介复制业	Printing and Reproduction of Recording Media		143		226		22769	11526
文教、工美、体育和娱乐用品制造业	Manufacture of Articles for Culture, Education, Arts and Crafts,Sport and Entertainment Activities		20		23			2361
石油、煤炭及其他燃料加工业	Processing of Petroleum, Coal and Other Fuels		118	25	196		248428	50670
化学原料及化学制品制造业	Manufacture of Chemical Raw Material and Chemical Products	2741280	104		961		3710440	162370
医药制造业	Manufacture of Medicines	43854	217		96		2741170	65238

12-16 续表 continued

指 标	Indicator	原煤（吨）Coal (ton)	汽油（吨）Gasoline (ton)	煤油（吨）Kerosene (ton)	柴油（吨）Diesel Oil (ton)	燃料油（吨）Fuel Oil (ton)	热力（百万千焦）Heating (mkj)	电力（万千瓦时）Electricity (10 000 kwh)
化学纤维制造业	Manufacture of Chemical Fiber	8080	18		17		18440	5358
橡胶和塑料制品业	Manufacture of Rubber and Plastic		90		61		59515	15431
非金属矿物制品业	Manufacture of Non-metallic Mineral Products	958197	490		23592		4245	172407
黑色金属冶炼及压延加工业	Manufacture and Processing of Ferrous Metals	2804090	72		7414		242367	813659
有色金属冶炼及压延加工业	Manufacture & Processing of Non-ferrous Metals		17		50			3476
金属制品业	Manufacture of Metal Products	10352	491		1079	35		114135
通用设备制造业	Manufacture of General Purpose Machinery		921	35	2090		38	45444
专用设备制造业	Manufacture of Special Purpose Machinery	59	547		252			25358
汽车制造业	Manufacture of Automotive	124	239	20	3049		403314	87088
铁路、船舶、航空航天和其他运输设备制造业	Manufacture of Railroad,Marine,Aerospace and Other Transportation Equipment		237		225		55034	12938
电气机械及器材制造业	Manufacture of Electrical Machinery & Equipment		648	6	91		27067	16479
计算机、通信和其他电子设备制造业	Manufacture of Computer, Communications and Other Electronic Equipment		460		39		712	14217
仪器仪表制造业	Manufacture of Measuring Instrument		623		51		3348	2472
其他制造业	Other Manufacture		32		15			1747
废弃资源综合利用业	Utilization of Waste Resources				36			376
金属制品、机械和设备修理业	Metal Products, Machinery and Equipment Repair Industry							546
电力、热力、燃气及水生产和供应业	**Production and Supply of Electric Power and Heat Power**							
电力、热力生产和供应业	Production and Supply of Electric Power and Heat Power	11412877	71		1814	410	2	262685
燃气生产和供应业	Production and Supply of Gas		132		62			1678
水的生产和供应业	Production and Supply of Water		162		62			26443

主要统计指标解释

按照国家统计方法制度规定，1998 年独立核算工业统计范围由原乡及乡以上调整为全部国有及年销售收入 500 万元以上非国有工业企业，2011 年规模以上工业企业统计范围调整为年主营业务收入 2000 万元以上。同时，统计分类中的原经济组织类型分组相应地调整为按企业登记注册类型分组。

工业 指从事自然资源的开采，对采掘品和农产品进行加工和再加工的物质生产部门。具体包括：(1) 对自然资源的开采，如采矿、晒盐等（但不包括禽兽捕猎和水产捕捞）；(2) 对农副产品的加工、再加工，如粮油加工、食品加工、缫丝、纺织、制革等；(3) 对采掘品的加工、再加工，如炼铁、炼钢、化工生产、石油加工、机器制造、木材加工等，以及电力、自来水、煤气的生产和供应等；(4) 对工业品的修理、翻新，如机器设备的修理、交通运输工具（如汽车）的修理等。

工业统计调查单位为独立核算法人工业企业。

独立核算法人工业企业指从事工业生产经营活动的单位。独立核算法人工业企业应同时具备以下条件：①依法成立，有自己的名称、组织机构和场所，能够承担民事责任；②独立拥有和使用资产，承担负债，有权与其他单位签订合同；③独立核算盈亏，并能够编制资产负债表。

本年鉴中涉及的企业登记注册类型：

国有及国有控股企业 指国有企业加上国有控股企业。国有企业（即原全民所有制工业或国营工业）指企业全部资产归国家所有，并按《中华人民共和国企业法人登记管理条例》规定登记注册的非公司制的经济组织。包括国有企业、国有独资公司和国有联营企业。1957 年以前的公私合营和私营工业，后均改造为国营工业，1992 年改为国有工业，这部分工业的资料不单独分列时，均包括在国有企业内。国有控股企业是对混合所有制经济的企业进行的“国有控股”分类。它是指这些企业的全部资产中国有资产（股份）相对其他所有者中的任何一个所有者占资（股）最多的企业。该分组反映了国有经济控股情况。

集体企业 指企业资产归集体所有，并按《中华人民共和国企业法人登记管理条例》规定登记注册的经济组织。

股份合作企业 指以合作制为基础，由企业职工共同出资入股，吸收一定比例的社会资产投资组建，实行自主经营，自负盈亏，共同劳动，民主管理，按劳分配与按股分红相结合的一种集体经济组织。

联营企业 指两个及两个以上相同或不同所有制性质的企业法人或事业单位法人，按自愿、平等、互利的原则，共同投资组成的经济组织。联营企业包括：

国有联营企业指国有企业与国有企业间的联营；

集体联营企业指集体企业与集体企业间的联营；

国有与集体联营企业指国有企业与集体企业间的联营。

有限责任公司 指根据《中华人民共和国公司登记管理条例》规定登记注册，由两个以上，五十个以下的股东共同出资，每个股东以其所认缴的出资额对公司承担有限责任，公司以其全部资产对其债务承担责任的经济组织。

有限责任公司包括国有独资公司以及其他有限责任公司。

股份有限公司 指根据《中华人民共和国企业法人登记管理条例》规定登记注册，其全部注册资本由等额股份构成并通过发行股票筹集资本，股东以其认购的股份对公司承担有限责任，公司以其全部资产对其债务承担责任的经济组织。

私营企业 指由自然人投资设立或由自然人控股，以雇佣劳动为基础的营利性经济组织。包括按照《公司法》、《合伙企业法》、《私营企业暂行条例》规定登记注册的私营有限责任公司、私营股份有限公司、私营合伙企业、私营独资企业和个人独资企业。

港、澳、台商投资企业 指企业注册登记类型中的港、澳、台资合资、合作、独资经营企业和股份有限公司之和。

外商投资企业 指企业注册登记类型中的中外合资、合作经营企业、外资企业和外商投资股份有限公司之和。

“三资”企业系指港、澳、台商投资企业和外资企业的简称。

轻工业 指主要提供生活消费品和制作手工工具的工业。按其所使用的原料不同，可分为两大类：(1) 以农产品为原料的轻工业，是指直接或间接以农产品为基本原料的轻工业。主要包括食品制造、饮料制造、烟草加工、纺织、缝纫、皮革和毛皮制作、造纸以及印刷等工业；(2) 以非农产品为原料的轻工业，是指以工业品为原料的轻工业。主要包括文教体育用品、化学药品制造、合成纤维制造、日用化学制品、日用玻璃制品、日用金属制品、手工工具制造、医疗器械制造、文化和办公用机械制造等工业。

重工业 指为国民经济各部门提供物质技术基础的主要生产资料的工业。按其生产性质和产品用途，可以分为下列三类：(1) 采掘（伐）工业，是指对自然资源的开采，包括石油开采、煤炭开采、金属矿开采、非金属矿开采等工业；(2) 原材料工业，指向国民经济各部门提供基本材料、动力和燃料的工业。包括金属冶炼及加工、炼焦及焦炭、化学、化工原料、水泥、人造板以及电力、石油和煤炭加工等工业；(3) 加工工业，是指对工业原材料进行再加工制造的工业。包括装备国民经济各部门的机械设备制造工业、金属结构、水泥制品等工业，以及为农业提供的生产资料如化肥、农药等工业。

根据上述划分原则，修理业中以重工业产品为修理作业对象的划为重工业，反之划为轻工业。

工业总产值 是以货币表现的工业企业在一定时期内生产的已出售或可供出售工业产品总量，它反映一定时间内工业生产的总规模和总水平。它包括：在本企业内不再进行加工，经检验、包装入库（规定不需包装的产品除外）的成品价值，对外加工费收入，自制半成品、在产品期末初差额价值。工业总产值采用“工厂法”计算，即以工业企业作为一个整体，按企业工业生产活动的最终成果来计算，企业内部不允许重复计算，不能把企业内部各个车间（分厂）生产的成果相加。但在企业之间、行业之间、地区之间存在着重复计算。

轻重工业总产值的划分也是按“工厂法”计算的，即一个工业企业在正常情况下生产的主要产品的性质属于轻工业，则该企业的全部总产值作为轻工业总产值。如生产的主要产品的性质属于重工业，则该企业的全部总产值作为重工业总产值。

工业增加值 是指工业行业在报告期内以货币表现的工业生产活动的最终成果。

实收资本 指企业实际收到的投资人投入的资本。按投资主体可分为国家资本、集体资本、法人资本、个人资本、港澳台资本和外商资本等。

资产总计 指企业拥有或控制的能以货币计量的经济资源。包括各种财产、债权和其他权利。资产按其流动性划分为流动资产、长期投资、固定资产、无形及递延资产和其他资产。

（1）流动资产指企业可以在一年内或者超过一年的一个生产周期内变现或耗用的资产合计。包括现金及各种存款、短期投资、应收及预付款项、存货等。

（2）固定资产指企业固定资产净值、固定资产清理、在建工程、待处理固定资产损失所占用的资金合计。

（3）无形资产指企业长期使用而没有实物形态的资产。包括专利权、非专利技术、商标权、著作权、土地使用权、商誉等。

负债合计 指企业承担的能以货币计量，将以资产或劳务偿付的债务。负债一般按偿还期长短分为流动负债和长期负债、递延税项等。

（1）流动负债指企业在一年内或者超过一年的一个营业周期内需要偿还的债务合计，其中包括短期借款、应付及预收款项、应付工资、应交税金和应交利润等。

（2）长期负债指企业在一年以上或者超过一年的一个营业周期以上需要偿还的债务合计，其中包括长期借款、应付债务、长期应付款项等。

所有者权益 指企业投资人对企业净资产的所有权。企业净资产等于企业全部资产减去全部负债后的余额，其中包括投资者对企业的最初投入，以及资本公积金、盈余公积金和未分配利润，对股份制企业即为股东权益。

固定资产原价 指企业在建造、购置、安装、改建、扩建、技术改造某项固定资产时所支出的全部货币总额。它一般包括买价、包装费、运杂费和安装费等。

营业收入 指企业从事销售商品、提供劳务和让渡资产使用权等生产经营活动形成的经济利益流入。包括“主营业务收入”和“其他业务收入”。

营业成本 指企业从事销售商品、提供劳务和让渡资产使用权等生产经营活动发生的实际成本。“营业成本”应当与“营业收入”进行配比。包括“主营业务成本”和“其他业务成本”。根据会计“利润表”中“营业成本”项目的本年累计数填报。

税金及附加 指企业因从事生产经营活动按税法规定应缴纳的消费税、城市维护建设税、资源税、环境保护税、教育费附加及房产税、土地使用税、车船使用税、印花税等相关税费。

利润总额 指企业在一定会计期间的经营成果，是生产经营过程中各种收入扣除各种耗费后的盈余，反映企业在报告期内实现的盈亏总额。

平均用工人数 是指报告期平均实际拥有的，参与本企业生产经营活动的人员数。

利税总额 指企业产品销售税金及附加、利润总额和应交增值税之和。

本年应交增值税 指按照税法规定，以销售货物、服务、无形资产、不动产或提供加工、修理修配劳务的增值额和货物进口金额为计税依据而课征的一种流转税。

Explanatory Notes on Main Statistical Indicators

As per provisions of national system of statistical method, the scope of statistics of the independent accounting industry in 1998 was adjusted to all state–owned enterprises and non–state industrial enterprises with above RMB 5 million annual sales revenue from those of village and above and the scope of statistics of above state designated scale industrial enterprises in 2011 was adjusted to above RMB 20 million annual income of main business. Meanwhile, grouping of original economic organizations in the statistical classification is adjusted to grouping based on enterprise registration type accordingly.

Industry refers to the material production sector which is engaged in extraction of natural resources and processing and reprocessing of minerals and agricultural products, including (1) extraction of natural resources, such as mining, salt production (but not including hunting and fishing); (2) processing and reprocessing of farm and sideline produces, such as rice husking, flour milling, wine making, oil pressing, silk reeling, spinning and weaving, and leather making; (3) manufacture of industrial products, such as steel making, iron smelting, chemicals manufacturing, petroleum processing, machine building, timber processing; water and gas production and electricity generation and supply; (4)repairing of industrial products such as the repairing of machinery and means of transport (including cars).

Units of industrial statistics survey corporate are industrial enterprises with independent accounting system.

Corporate industrial enterprises with independent accounting system refer to enterprises engaging in industrial production activities, which meet the following requirements: (1)They are established legally, having their own names, organizations, location, able to take civil liability; (2)They possess and use their assets independently, assume liabilities, and are entitled to sign contracts with other units; (3)They are financially independent and compile their own balance sheets.

Enterprises covered in the industrial statistics in this Yearbook include following categories by their registration:

State–owned and State–holding Enterprises refer to state owned enterprises plus state holding enterprises. State owned enterprises (originally known as state run enterprises with ownership by the whole society) are non–corporate economic entities registered in accordance with the Regulation of the People's Republic of China on the Management of Registration of Legal Enterprises, where all assets are owned by the state. Included in this category are state owned enterprises, state funded corporations and state owned joint operation enterprises. Public–private partnerships industries and private industries, which existed before 1957, were transformed into state run industries since 1957, and into state owned industries after 1992. Statistics on those enterprises are included in the state owned industries instead of grouping them separately. State–holding enterprise is a sub–classification of enterprises with mixed ownership, referring to enterprises where the percentage of state assets (or shares by the state) is larger than any other single shareholder of the same enterprise. This sub–classification illustrates the control of the state over a particular industry.

Collective–owned Enterprises refer to economic entities registered in accordance with the Regulation of the People's Republic of China on the Management of Registration of Legal Enterprises, where assets are owned by collectively.

Share–holding Cooperative Enterprises refer to economic units set up on cooperative basis, with funding partly from members of the enterprise and partly from outside investment, which are collective economic organizations with characteristics of self–employed, self–financing, working together, democratic management, distributing by work and shares.

Joint Operation Enterprises refer to economic units that are established by joint investment by two or more corporate enterprises or institutions of the same or different types of ownership on voluntary, equal and mutual beneficial basis. They include:

State owned joint operation enterprises (joint operation between state owned enterprises);

Collective joint operation enterprises (joint operation between collective enterprises, and

State collective joint operation enterprises (joint operation between state and collective enterprises)

Limited Liability Corporations refer to economic units registered in accordance with the Regulation of the People's Republic of China on the Management of Registration of Corporations, with capitals from 2 to 49 investors, each investor bears limited liability to the corporation depending on his/her holding of shares, and the corporation bears liability to its debt to the maximum of its total assets.

Limited liability corporations cover state–owned exclusive company and other limited liability corporations.

Share–holding Corporations Ltd. refer to economic units registered in accordance with the Regulation of the People's Republic of China on the Management of Registration of Corporate Enterprises, with total registered capitals divided into equal shares and raised through issuing stocks. Each investor bears limited liability to the corporation depending on the holding of shares, and the corporation bears liability to its debt to the maximum of its total assets.

Private Enterprises refer to economic units invested on controlled (by holding the majority of the shares) by natural persons who hire labors for profit making activities. Included in this category are private limited liability corporations, private share–holding corporations Ltd., private partnership enterprises and private sole investment enterprises registered in accordance with the Corporation Law, Partnership Enterprise Law and

Tentative Regulation on Private Enterprises.

Enterprises with Funds from Hong Kong, Macao and Taiwan refers to all industrial enterprises registered as the joint venture, cooperative, sole investment industrial enterprises and limited liability corporations with funds from Hong Kong, Macao and Taiwan.

Foreign Funded Enterprises refers to all industrial enterprises registered as the joint venture, cooperative, foreign companies and foreign investment Co. Ltd..

Enterprise with Hong Kong, Macao, Taiwan and foreign fund refer to all the enterprises with funds from Hong Kong Macao and Taiwan and foreign funded enterprises.

Light industry refers to the industry that produces consumer goods and hand tools. It consists of two categories, depending on the materials used: (1) Industries using farm products as raw materials. These are branches of light industry which directly or indirectly use farm products as basic raw materials, including the manufacture of food and beverages, tobacco processing, textile, clothing, fur and leather manufacturing, paper making, printing, etc.(2) Industries using non–farm products as raw materials. These are branches of light industry which use manufactured goods as raw materials, including the manufacture of cultural, educational articles and sports goods, chemicals, synthetic fiber, chemical products for daily use, glass products for daily use, metal products for daily use, hand tools, medical apparatus and instruments, and the manufacture of cultural and clerical machinery.

Heavy Industry refers to the industry which produces capital goods, and provides various sectors of the national economy with necessary material and technical basis. It consists of the following three branches according to the purpose of production or the use of products: (1) Mining, quarrying and logging industry refers to the industry that extracts natural resources, including extraction of petroleum, coal, metal and non–metal ores. (2) Raw materials industry refers to the industry that provides various sectors of the national economy with raw materials, fuels and power. It includes smelting and processing of metals, coking and coke chemistry, chemical materials, cement, plywood, power, petroleum refining and coal dressing. (3) Manufacturing industry refers to the industry that processes raw materials. It includes machine building industry which equips sectors of the national economy, industries of metal structure and cement products, industries producing means of agricultural production, such as chemical fertilizers and pesticides.

According to the above principle of classification, the repairing trades, which are engaged primarily in repairing products of heavy industry are classified into heavy industry while these engaged in repairing products of light industry are classified into light industry.

Gross Industrial Output Value refers to total industrial products which were sold or are available for sale produced by industrial enterprise within a certain period of time and expressed with currency and reflects total scale and total level of industrial production within a certain period of time. It includes: value of finished product not processed in the enterprise which are put in storage after inspection and packaging (except products specified not to be packaged), external processing fee income and the value of the difference between the end of the period and the beginning of the period of self–made semi–manufactured goods. Gross industrial output value is calculated as per "factory approach", that is to say that gross industrial output value is calculated according to final result of industrial production activities of enterprises based on industrial enterprise as a whole. Repeated calculation in the enterprise and adding production results of all workshops (branch factories) in the enterprise are forbidden. However, the repeated calculation between enterprises, industries and regions exists.

Gross output value of light and heavy industries is also calculated according to "factory approach", that is to say that total output value of the enterprise is used as gross output of the light industry if major products produced by an industrial enterprise under normal circumstances fall into light industry. Gross output value of the enterprise is use as gross output value of heavy industry if major products produced fall into heavy industry.

Value–added of Industry refers to the final results of industrial production of industrial enterprises in currency during the reference period

Paid–up capital refers to the capital actually received by the enterprise and invested by the investor. Paid–up capital can be divided into national capital, collectively owned capital, corporate capital, personal capital, Hong Kong, Macao and Taiwan capital and foreign capital as per investors.

Total Assets refer to all economic resources, in monetary terms, that is owned or controlled by enterprises, including properties, creditors equity and other economic rights of all forms. Classified by the degree of equitability, total assets include circulating assets, long–term investment, fixed assets, intangible assets and deferred assets, and other assets.

(1)Current assets refer to assets that an enterprise can convert into cash or use during one year or one production cycle that may exceeds one year, including cash and savings deposits of various forms, short–term investment, receivable and prepaid money, inventories, etc..

(2) Fixed assets refer to the total amount of net fixed assets of the enterprise, disposal of fixed assets, project under construction and losses on pending fixed assets.

(3) Intangible assets refer to the assets without physical form used by the enterprise for a long time. It consists of patent right, non–patent technology, trademark right, copyright, chartered right, land use right, etc..

Total Liabilities refer to the liabilities borne by the enterprise which can be measured with currency and repaid by assets or labor services. Liabilities are generally divided into current liabilities, long–term liabilities and deferred tax on the basis of repayment period.

(1) Current liabilities (also called quick liabilities or immediate liabilities) refer to enterprises' total debt payable within an operating cycle of one year or over one year, including short term loans, payables and

advance payments, wages payable, taxes payable and profit payable, etc..

(2) Long–term liabilities refers enterprises' total debt payable within an operating cycle of one year or over one year, including long–term loans, payable liabilities, long–term payables, etc..

Owner's Equity refers to the ownership of net assets of enterprise by its investors. The net assets equal the total assets minus total liabilities of the enterprise, including the actual assets invested into the enterprise by investors, accumulation of capitals and operating surplus and non–distributed profits (namely stockholders' equity for corporate enterprise).

Original Value of Fixed Assets refers to the total value, in monetary terms, that an enterprise spent on fixed assets, through construction, purchase, installation, transformation, expansion or technical upgrading. Generally, it covers cost of purchase, packing, transportation and installation, etc..

Business Revenue refers to the inflow of economic benefits gained by enterprises engaged in production and operation activities, such as selling commodities, providing labor services, and transferring asset use rights, including "main business income" and "other business income."

Business Cost refers to the actual cost incurred by enterprises in production and operation activities, such as selling goods, providing labor services, and transferring asset use rights. "Business costs" should be matched with "business revenue",including "main business cost" and "other business cost". It is filled in the report based on the cumulative number of the current year in "business cost" item of the "profit statement" accounting.

Taxes and Surcharges refers to the consumption tax, urban maintenance and construction tax, resource tax, environmental protection tax, education surcharges, and real estate tax, land use tax, vehicle and vessel use tax, stamp tax and other related taxes and fees due in accordance with the tax law for their production and business activities .

Total Profits refer to the operating result of the enterprise during a certain accounting period, they are the balance of the production and operation process after all incomes are deducted by various costs, reflect the total amount of profit and loss achieved within the reporting period. Total profit is the amount after operating profit plus non–business income and then minus non–business expenditure, which shall be filled in and reported pursuant to the cumulative data in the current year in the item "total profit" in the "profit statement".

Average Number of Workers refers to the average number of personnel actually owned and participating in production and operation activities of the enterprise within the reporting period.

Total Profits and Taxes refer to the sum of sales taxes, charges, revenues and VAT of the products in the enterprise.

VAT payable this year refers to a turnover tax that pursuant to the VAT of goods and services sales, invisible assets, real estate, machining provided, repair services and to the amount of goods import in accordance with the taxes laws.

13

建筑业

CONSTRUCTION

13-1 建筑业主要指标
Main Indicators of Construction Enterprises

指 标	Indicator	单 位 Unit	2014 年	2015 年	2016 年	2017 年	2018 年	2019 年
汇总单位数	Number of Enterprises	个 (unit)	454	463	460	504	507	895
建筑业增加值	Construction Inscreased	万元 (10 000 yuan)	3014387	2826306	2805982	3308084	5136408	5849207
建筑业总产值	Gross Output Value	万元 (10 000 yuan)	15422095	16638332	18647972	22189343	28234734	35139777
按隶属关系分	by Ownership							
中央属	Central	万元 (10 000 yuan)	6781707	7693792	9079591	11379540	14747883	17350365
地方属	Local	万元 (10 000 yuan)						11793174
省属	Provincial	万元 (10 000 yuan)	1549456	1664077	1853736	2391026	3039149	
市属	Region	万元 (10 000 yuan)	2978560	3222554	3676145	5195869	6391344	
县及县以下	County	万元 (10 000 yuan)	1654785	1608569	1711315	570463	641220	
其他	Others	万元 (10 000 yuan)	2457587	2449340	2327185	2652445	3415138	5996238
按工程性质分	by Sector							
建筑工程	Building and Civil Engineering Construction	万元 (10 000 yuan)	13708876	14422832	16291789	19476820	25182882	31199367
安装工程	Construction Installation	万元 (10 000 yuan)	1392597	1744180	1998465	2051423	2329541	3015885
其他产值	Others	万元 (10 000 yuan)	320622	471320	357718	661100	722311	924525
竣工产值	Value of Construction Completed	万元 (10 000 yuan)	6398538	7613104	7415119	7987351	8691856	12943615
房屋施工面积	Floor Space Completed	万平方米 (10 000 sq.cm)	9183	10189	10293	11363	12984	14955
#本年新开工	Startde This year	万平方米 (10 000 sq.cm)	3420	2991	3222	3694	4842	4705
房屋竣工面积	Floor Space Completed	万平方米 (10 000 sq.cm)	1772	2039	2298	2280	2366	3418
#住宅	Residential	万平方米 (10 000 sq.cm)	1157	1178	1379	1258	1502	2170
所有者权益	Creditors'Equity	万元 (10 000 yuan)	3516583	4015082	4433678	5900444	6269077	8130630
利润总额	Total Profits	万元 (10 000 yuan)	516686	568473	573258	836297	810897	1051261
工资总额	Total wages	万元 (10 000 yuan)	1917170	1638141	1812042	2185631	3480056	3793574

注：建筑业增加值 2006 年起采用以企业营业利润为主的收入法计算。
Note: The value added of construction output was calculated as per income method mainly involving enterprise operating profit as of 2006.

13-2 建筑业增加值构成（2019年）
Value Added of Construction by Structure(2019)

单位：万元 (10 000yuan)

指 标（总承包与专业承包）	Indicator	建筑业增加值 Construction Inscreased	本年提取固定资产折旧 Fixed Assets Depreciation in the Year	税金及附加 Taxes and Other Charges	营业利润 Profits from Business	应付职工薪酬（本年贷方累计发生额） Total Wages Payable
总计	Total	5849207	188411	882405	984818	3793574
其中：国有及国有控股企业	State-owned and State-controlled Enterprises	3899480	115565	599845	739386	2444683
一、按登记注册类型分组	Grouped by Registration Status					
内资企业	Domestic Funded	5847077	188407	882229	985396	3791045
国有企业	State-owned	18514	912	3982	2815	10806
集体企业	Collective-owned Enterprises	22733	1004	5290	878	15561
股份合作企业	Cooperative Enterprises	-	87	1566	-5577	3062
联营企业	Joint Ownership Enterprises	354	26	92	25	211
其他联营企业	Other Joint Ownership Enterprises	354	26	92	25	211
有限责任公司	Limited Liability Corporations	4715612	130872	728389	826823	3029528
国有独资公司	State Sole Funded Corporations	1270099	34546	146977	236798	851779
其他有限责任公司	Other Limited Liability Corporations	3445512	96326	581412	590026	2177749
股份有限公司	Share-holding Corporations Ltd.	370003	25396	32596	52332	259680
私营企业	Private Enterprises	720723	30111	110315	108100	472197
私营独资企业	Private-funded Enterprises					
私营有限责任公司	Private Limited Liability Corporations	691821	28839	107412	102067	453502
私营股份有限公司	Private Share-holding Corporations Ltd.	28902	1272	2902	6033	18695
其他企业	Other Enterprises					
港、澳、台商投资企业	Enterprises with Funds from Hong Kong, Macao and Taiwan					
外商投资企业	Foreign Funded Enterprises	2130	4	176	-578	2529
中外合资经营企业	Joint-venture Enterprises	500	4	31	-90	556
外商投资股份有限公司	Foreign Investment limited Liability Company	1629	0	145	-488	1972
二、按国民经济行业分组	by Sector					
房屋建筑业	Building Construction	3043288	47821	469582	498508	2027377
土木工程建筑业	Civil Engineering Construction	2298542	118782	317865	383728	1478167
建筑安装业	Construction Installation	277318	11929	47754	55306	162330
建筑装饰和其他建筑业	Construction Decoration and Others	230059	9879	47204	47276	125700
三、按隶属关系分组	by Ownership					
中央	Central	2426505	81473	435284	438913	1470836
地方	Local	2197667	61366	269600	350961	1515740
其他	Others	1225034	45572	177521	194944	806998
四、按企业资质等级分组	by Qualification Criteria					
施工总承包	Construction Contract	5422056	168760	801947	894928	3556422
特级	Special Grade	3285174	78544	484813	604073	2117744
一级	First Grade	1351543	42991	201405	208233	898914
二级	Second Grade	466895	29457	64542	54645	318252
三级以下	Third Grade and below	318444	17768	51186	27977	221513
专业承包	Professional Contract	427151	19651	80458	89890	237152
一级	First Grade	237358	5785	49370	63009	119195
二级	Second Grade	116070	8191	19138	19390	69350
三级以下	Third Grade and below	73723	5675	11950	7491	48607

13-3 建筑企业资产实力(2019年)
Assets of Construction Enterprises (2019)

指 标 (总承包与专业承包)	Indicator	流动资产合计 Liquid Assets	其中 of which #存货 Inventory
总计	Total	30823249	5449424
其中:国有及国有控股企业	State-owned and State-controlled Enterprises	22614998	3921258
一、按登记注册类型分组	Grouped by Registration Status		
内资企业	Domestic Funded	30810672	5445169
国有企业	State-owned	120460	19312
集体企业	Collective-owned	98063	24213
股份合作企业	Stock-holding Cooperation	150983	106895
联营企业	Joint-owned	8440	517
其他联营企业	Others	8440	517
有限责任公司	Company with Limited Liabilition	23186393	4567048
国有独资公司	State-owned	7003405	1060940
其他有限责任公司	Others	16182988	3506107
股份有限公司	Stock-holding Company limited	4010331	205998
私营企业	Private Enterprises	3236002	521187
私营独资企业	Solely Owned		
私营有限责任公司	Private Limited Liability Corporations	3033239	479356
私营股份有限公司	Private Share-holding Corporations Ltd.	202763	41831
其他企业	Others		
港、澳、台商投资企业	Enterprises with Funds from Hong Kong,Macao and Taiwan		
外商投资企业	Foreign Funded Enterprises	12577	4255
中外合资经营企业	Joint-venture Enterprises	3974	882
外商投资股份有限公司	Foreign Investment limited Liability Company	8603	3373
二、按国民经济行业分组	by Sector		
房屋建筑业	Building Construction	9456746	1554165
土木工程建筑业	Civil Engineering Construction	18704226	3521200
建筑安装业	Construction Installation	1364077	260702
建筑装饰和其他建筑业	Construction Decoration and Others	1298201	113358
三、按隶属关系分组	by Ownership		
中央	Central	12341521	1302624
地方	Local	12307754	2952796
其他	Others	6173974	1194005
四、按企业资质等级分组	by Qualification Criteria		
施工总承包	Construction Contract	28493703	5076318
特级	Special Grade	16391942	2783540
一级	First Grade	8306034	1540699
二级	Second Grade	2529678	524535
三级以下	Third Grade and below	1266049	227545
专业承包	Professional Contract	2329546	373106
一级	First Grade	1479538	280914
二级	Second Grade	510670	55320
三级以下	Third Grade and below	339339	36872

单位：万元 (10 000yuan)

固定资产合计 Fixed Assets	固定资产原价 Original Value of Fixed Assets	流动负债合计 Current Liabilities Total	非流动负债合计 Non–Current Liabilities Total	负债合计 Total Liabilitie	所有者权益合计 Total Creditors' Equity
1249469	2533004	26999173	1438612	29404561	8130630
748641	1635222	20797104	1260487	22905812	5221357
1247279	2529590	26983607	1438612	29387676	8121875
7263	16283	108583	1322	110010	33743
11757	16874	86322	1976	88772	38175
1845	3855	158931		167881	-9796
73	148	8132		8132	382
73	148	8132		8132	382
880612	1823167	20703316	1146289	22737596	5410806
304686	604265	6543405	346977	6890382	1290061
575927	1218902	14159911	799312	15847213	4120744
100302	238478	3790568	218402	4037356	1167858
245427	430784	2127756	70623	2237931	1480709
230823	404568	2008635	28469	2076509	1408155
14604	26216	119121	42153	161422	72554
2190	3415	15566		16885	8755
29	208	1123		2441	1561
2161	3207	14443		14443	7194
364623	630064	6802908	289296	8009755	2643066
717539	1612400	18227862	1066008	19320540	4461655
107713	181992	1028778	24710	1059557	564941
59595	108547	939625	58598	1014709	460968
412883	990461	11646437	632769	13127321	2798955
452002	870550	10650737	708380	11411898	3059469
384585	671993	4701999	97463	4865342	2272206
1107195	2288224	25248262	1371694	27550252	7286717
433397	942360	15004434	1005653	16858202	3904706
384629	815312	7305076	306904	7626400	1925630
177752	336015	1955734	46325	2063127	950117
111417	194538	983019	12811	1002524	506264
142274	244780	1750911	66918	1854308	843913
62541	109190	1181688	14080	1211958	405832
40271	68367	339688	8500	360038	293982
39463	67224	229535	44338	282312	144099

13-4 建筑业施工产值构成 (2019 年)

Output Value of Construction by Structure(2019)

单位：万元 (10 000 yuan)

指 标 (总承包与专业承包)	Indicator	合计 Total	建筑工程 Constructional Engineering	安装工程 Installation Project	其他产值 Other Value	竣工产值 Value of Construction Completed
总计	Total	35139777	31199367	3015885	924525	12943615
其中：国有及国有控股企业	State-owned and State-controlled Enterprises	26231553	23785868	1895469	550217	8538835
一、按登记注册类型分组	Grouped by Registration Status					
内资企业	Domestic Funded	35132775	31199367	3008912	924496	12943615
国有企业	State-owned	111036	107613	0	3423	43710
集体企业	Collective-owned	94169	93477	692	0	44417
股份合作企业	Stock-holding Cooperation	35232	34771	461	0	5461
联营企业	Joint-owned	8899	8899	0	0	0
其他联营企业	Others	8899	8899	0	0	0
有限责任公司	Company with Limited Liabilition	27841271	24868931	2292813	679527	9573819
国有独资公司	State-owned	9393759	8406717	969927	17115	3101515
其他有限责任公司	Others	18447512	16462215	1322886	662411	6472304
股份有限公司	Stock-holding Company limited	3688756	3436415	211961	40380	1539546
私营企业	Private Enterprises	3353413	2649261	502986	201166	1736663
私营有限责任公司	Private Limited Liability Corporations	3218239	2541410	478259	198570	1641307
私营股份有限公司	Private Share-holding Corporations Ltd.	135173	107851	24727	2596	95356
港、澳、台商投资企业	Funded from Hong Kong,Macao and Taiwan	0	0	0	0	0
外商投资企业	Foreign Funded	7002	0	6973	29	0
中外合资经营企业	Chinese-foreign Joint Venture	1905	0	1905	0	0
外商投资股份有限公司	Foreign Investment limited Liability Company	5097	0	5068	29	0
二、按国民经济行业分组	by Sector					
房屋建筑业	Building Construction	16087675	15029049	757595	301030	7558441
土木工程建筑业	Civil Engineering Construction	16424703	14573037	1445739	405926	4232160
建筑安装业	Construction Installation	1104712	330814	694128	79771	571679
建筑装饰和其他建筑业	Construction Decoration and Others	1522687	1266467	118423	137797	581336
三、按隶属关系分组	by Ownership					
中央	Central	17350365	15756569	1355209	238587	5147157
地方	Local	11793174	10861722	640338	291114	4934401
其他	Others	5996238	4581076	1020338	394823	2862057
四、按企业资质等级分组	by Qualification Criteria					
施工总承包	Construction Contract	32596444	29510602	2510459	575384	11785694
特级	Special Grade	20661854	19694164	960006	7684	7463615
一级	First Grade	8820473	7255624	1197573	367276	2721954
二级	Second Grade	1756472	1518435	192210	45827	918266
三级及以下	Third Grade and below	1357645	1042379	160669	154597	681859
专业承包	Professional Contract	2543334	1688766	505427	349141	1157922
一级	First Grade	1623502	1092833	257673	272996	630307
二级	Second Grade	593733	349036	178194	66503	345367
三级及以下	Third Grade and below	326099	246897	69560	9643	182248

13-5 建筑企业损益及分配（2019 年）

Output Value of Construction by Structure(2019)

单位：万元 (10 000yuan)

指标（总承包与专业承包）	Indicator	营业收入 Business Revenue	利税总额 Total Profits and Taxes	营业利润 Profits from Business	利润总额 Total Profits	应付职工薪酬（本年贷方累计发生额）Total Wages Payable
总计	Total	35334369	1933665	984818	1051261	3793574
其中：国有及国有控股企业	State-owned and State-controlled Enterprises	26179754	1391489	739386	791644	2444683
一、按登记注册类型分组	Grouped by Registration Status					
内资企业	Domestic Funded	35326880	1934065	985396	1051836	3791045
国有企业	State-owned	146669	6794	2815	2812	10806
集体企业	Collective-owned	95166	6002	878	712	15561
股份合作企业	Stock-holding Cooperation	50436	2931	-5577	1364	3062
联营企业	Joint-owned	7940	117	25	25	211
其他联营企业	Others	7940	117	25	25	211
有限责任公司	Company with Limited Liabilition	27562430	1609132	826823	880743	3029528
国有独资公司	State-owned	9406066	422858	236798	275881	851779
其他有限责任公司	Others	18156363	1186275	590026	604862	2177749
股份有限公司	Stock-holding Company limited	3641724	88023	52332	55427	259680
私营企业	Private Enterprises	3822515	221066	108100	110752	472197
私营独资企业	Solely Owned					
私营有限责任公司	Private Limited Liability Corporations	3662132	211455	102067	104043	453502
私营股份有限公司	Private Share-holding Corporations Ltd.	160383	9611	6033	6709	18695
其他企业	Others					
港、澳、台商投资企业	Enterprises with Funds from Hong Kong, Macao and Taiwan					
外商投资企业	Foreign Funded Enterprises	7489	-400	-578	-575	2529
中外合资经营企业	Joint-venture Enterprises	1775	-61	-90	-91	556
外商投资股份有限公司	Foreign Investment limited Liability Company	5713	-339	-488	-484	1972
二、按国民经济行业分组	by Sector					
房屋建筑业	BuildingConstruction	15196689	988166	498508	518584	2027377
土木工程建筑业	Civil Engineering Construction	16868408	732909	383728	415044	1478167
建筑安装业	Construction Installation	1583005	116529	55306	68775	162330
建筑装饰和其他建筑业	Construction Decoration and Others	1686268	96061	47276	48858	125700
三、按隶属关系分组	by Ownership					
中央	Central	17836755	894138	438913	458854	1470836
地方	Local	11152149	662345	350961	392745	1515740
其他	Others	6345464	377183	194944	199662	806998
四、按企业资质等级分组	by Qualification Criteria					
施工总承包	Construction Contract	32303326	1761559	894928	959613	3556422
特级	Special Grade	20035088	1121807	604073	636994	2117744
一级	First Grade	8823432	422785	208233	221380	898914
二级	Second Grade	1957128	134749	54645	70207	318252
三级以下	Third Grade and below	1487678	82218	27977	31031	221513
专业承包	Professional Contract	3031043	172106	89890	91648	237152
一级	First Grade	1895747	114604	63009	65235	119195
二级	Second Grade	728417	37636	19390	18498	69350
三级以下	Third Grade and below	406879	19866	7491	7915	48607

13-6 施工工程施工面积 (2019 年)

Number of Floor Space Under Construction(2019)

单位：万平方千米 (10 000sq.m)

指标（总承包与专业承包）	Indicator	房屋建筑施工面积 Floor Space under Construction	#本年新开工面积 Started This Year	房屋建筑竣工面积 Floor Space Completed	#住宅房屋 (Residential)	竣工房屋价值（万元） Value of Construction Completed (10 000 yuan)
总计	Total	14955.4	4704.7	3417.7	2169.6	7087165
其中：国有及国有控股企业	State-owned and State-controlled Enterprises	9312.7	2639.0	1689.9	959.0	4643488
一、按登记注册类型分组	Grouped by Registration Status					
内资企业	Domestic Funded	14955.4	4704.7	3417.7	2169.6	7087165
国有企业	State-owned	88.3	35.0	1.3	1.3	3371
集体企业	Collective-owned	50.3	23.6	12.3	9.0	19752
股份合作企业	Stock-holding Cooperation	8.1	7.8	5.0	5.0	5000
有限责任公司	Company with Limited Liabilition	12585.5	3843.5	2504.3	1569.6	5942984
国有独资公司	State-owned	4157.6	1282.5	687.3	304.0	2033571
其他有限责任公司	Others	8427.8	2561.1	1817.0	1265.5	3909413
股份有限公司	Stock-holding Company limited	796.5	236.0	271.1	200.6	419566
私营企业	Private Enterprises	1426.7	558.8	623.7	384.1	696492
私营有限责任公司	Private Limited Liability Corporations	1400.1	543.7	604.8	376.0	662608
私营股份有限公司	Private Share-holding Corporations Ltd.	26.6	15.1	18.8	8.1	33884
二、按国民经济行业分组	by Sector					
房屋建筑业	Building Construction	14394.7	4393.3	3012.7	1958.7	6788253
土木工程建筑业	Civil Engineering Construction	399.2	226.1	191.2	133.0	220707
建筑安装业	Construction Installation	21.4	14.1	27.4	23.3	23143
建筑装饰和其他建筑业	Construction Decoration and Others	140.0	71.1	186.4	54.7	55062
三、按隶属关系分组	by Ownership					
中央	Central	6741.9	1920.0	1044.7	598.9	3456376
省（自治区、直辖市）	Provincial	6093.0	1883.9	1558.5	1110.1	2591101
地区（州、盟、省辖市）及以下、其他	Region	2120.5	900.8	814.5	460.6	1039687
四、按企业资质等级分组	by Qualification Criteria					
施工总承包	Construction Contract	14718.9	4584.8	3103.2	2001.0	6989074
特级	Special Grade	10000.0	2970.6	1744.4	1022.9	4951965
一级	First Grade	3791.8	1095.7	980.3	768.9	1471665
二级	Second Grade	564.1	276.8	211.6	118.9	367578
三级及以下	Third Grade and below	362.9	241.7	167.0	90.3	197865
专业承包	Professional Contract	236.6	119.9	314.5	168.6	98091
一级	First Grade	194.6	93.3	258.3	135.1	72331
二级	Second Grade	30.1	16.7	49.1	30.7	19223
三级及以下	Third Grade and below	11.9	9.8	7.1	2.7	6537

13-7 济南市建筑业特级、一级资质企业一览表 (2019 年)
Summary of Construction Enterprises with Grade Ⅰ Qualification(2019)

企业名称 Name	隶属关系 Ownership	经济类 Economic Type	所属行业 Sector
山东省建设建工(集团)有限责任公司	地方	其他有限责任公司	住宅房屋建筑
中建八局第一建设有限公司	中央	国有独资公司	住宅房屋建筑
中建八局第二建设有限公司	中央	其他有限责任公司	住宅房屋建筑
济南四建(集团)有限责任公司	地方	其他有限责任公司	住宅房屋建筑
山东平安建设集团有限公司	地方	其他有限责任公司	住宅房屋建筑
济南长兴建设集团有限公司	地方	其他有限责任公司	住宅房屋建筑
山东三箭建设工程股份有限公司	地方	股份有限公司	住宅房屋建筑
山东省路桥集团有限公司	地方	其他有限责任公司	其他道路、隧道和桥梁工程建筑
山东省公路建设(集团)有限公司	地方	其他有限责任公司	公路工程建筑
中铁十四局集团第三工程有限公司	中央	股份有限公司	铁路工程建筑
中铁十四局集团有限公司	中央	股份有限公司	铁路工程建筑
中铁十局集团有限公司	中央	其他有限责任公司	铁路工程建筑
中国电建集团山东电力建设第一工程有限公司	中央	国有独资公司	架线及设备工程建筑
中国电建集团核电工程有限公司	中央	其他有限责任公司	架线及设备工程建筑
济南城建集团有限公司	地方	国有独资公司	铁路工程建筑
山东高速齐鲁建设集团有限公司	地方	其他有限责任公司	其他房屋建筑业
山东天宝建设集团有限公司	其他	私营有限责任公司	住宅房屋建筑
瑞森新建筑有限公司	其他	私营有限责任公司	其他房屋建筑业
山东省城建工程集团公司	地方	股份合作	住宅房屋建筑
山东鲁建工程集团有限公司	地方	其他有限责任公司	住宅房屋建筑
山东泉景建设有限公司	地方	其他有限责任公司	住宅房屋建筑
山东恒霖建设工程有限公司	其他	私营有限责任公司	住宅房屋建筑
济南华海建设集团有限公司	其他	私营有限责任公司	住宅房屋建筑
济南二建集团工程有限公司	地方	其他有限责任公司	住宅房屋建筑
中铁十局集团建筑工程有限公司	中央	其他有限责任公司	住宅房屋建筑
普利置业集团股份有限公司	地方	股份有限公司	住宅房屋建筑
山东浩岳建设工程有限公司	其他	私营有限责任公司	住宅房屋建筑
山东中恒建设集团有限公司	其他	私营有限责任公司	住宅房屋建筑
济南建工总承包集团有限公司	地方	其他有限责任公司	住宅房屋建筑
济南一建集团有限公司	地方	国有独资公司	住宅房屋建筑
山东港基建设集团有限公司	其他	其他有限责任公司	住宅房屋建筑
山东长箭建设集团有限公司	地方	其他有限责任公司	住宅房屋建筑
山东汇富建设集团有限公司	地方	其他有限责任公司	住宅房屋建筑
山东长泰建设集团工程有限公司	其他	私营有限责任公司	住宅房屋建筑
山东泰实建筑工程有限公司	其他	其他有限责任公司	住宅房屋建筑
章丘市第二建筑安装(集团)有限责任公司	地方	其他有限责任公司	住宅房屋建筑
山东莱芜建设集团有限公司	地方	国有独资公司	住宅房屋建筑
山东正顺建设集团有限公司	其他	私营有限责任公司	住宅房屋建筑
山东省莱芜市宏强建筑安装工程有限公司	其他	私营有限责任公司	其他房屋建筑业
济南铸诚建筑工程集团有限公司	地方	其他有限责任公司	住宅房屋建筑
山东科信达建筑安装有限公司	地方	其他有限责任公司	住宅房屋建筑
山东三箭建设工程管理有限公司	地方	国有独资公司	住宅房屋建筑
山东信达建设工程有限公司	其他	私营有限责任公司	其他房屋建筑业
山东省建设集团有限公司	其他	私营有限责任公司	其他房屋建筑业
山东中宝置业有限公司	其他	私营有限责任公司	住宅房屋建筑
山东惠诚建筑有限公司	其他	私营有限责任公司	其他房屋建筑业

13-7 续表 1 continued 1

企业名称 Name	隶属关系 Ownership	经济类 Economic Type	所属行业 Sector
莱芜市庚鑫市政工程有限公司	地方	其他有限责任公司	管道和设备安装
中铁十四局集团第四工程有限公司	中央	国有独资公司	铁路工程建筑
山东省公路桥梁建设有限公司	地方	其他有限责任公司	公路工程建筑
山东省高速路桥养护有限公司	地方	其他有限责任公司	其他道路、隧道和桥梁工程建筑
山东省大通公路工程有限责任公司	地方	其他有限责任公司	公路工程建筑
济南金曰公路工程有限公司	地方	其他有限责任公司	公路工程建筑
山东鲁桥建设有限公司	其他	其他有限责任公司	公路工程建筑
济南通达公路工程有限公司	地方	国有独资公司	公路工程建筑
山东泰东公路工程有限公司	地方	其他有限责任公司	公路工程建筑
山东琴通路桥集团有限公司	地方	其他有限责任公司	公路工程建筑
山东省齐鲁装饰设计院	地方	其他联营	公共建筑装饰和装修
济南舜联建设集团有限公司	其他	私营有限责任公司	其他房屋建筑业
山东济铁工程建设集团有限公司	地方	其他有限责任公司	铁路工程建筑
山东黄河工程集团有限公司	中央	国有独资公司	港口及航运设施工程建筑
山东水总有限公司	地方	国有独资公司	河湖治理及防洪设施工程建筑
山东省水利工程局有限公司	地方	国有独资公司	河湖治理及防洪设施工程建筑
山东黄河顺成水利水电工程有限公司	中央	国有独资公司	管道工程建筑
山东送变电工程有限公司	中央	股份有限公司	架线及设备工程建筑
山东电建建设集团有限公司	其他	其他有限责任公司	架线及设备工程建筑
山东环城城建工程有限公司	其他	其他有限责任公司	市政道路工程建筑
济南易通城市建设集团股份有限公司	地方	股份有限公司	市政道路工程建筑
济南普利供水工程有限公司	地方	其他有限责任公司	管道工程建筑
中铁十四局集团隧道工程有限公司	中央	其他有限责任公司	铁路工程建筑
济南热力工程有限公司	地方	国有独资公司	管道和设备安装
山东汇通建设集团有限公司	地方	国有独资公司	市政道路工程建筑
济南黄河路桥建设集团有限公司	地方	国有独资公司	市政道路工程建筑
山东汇友市政园林集团有限公司	地方	国有独资公司	其他未列明建筑业
中铁十局集团第一工程有限公司	中央	其他有限责任公司	公路工程建筑
济南昊兴市政工程有限公司	其他	其他有限责任公司	管道工程建筑
山东亿威市政工程有限公司	其他	其他有限责任公司	市政道路工程建筑
济南市市政工程建设集团有限公司	其他	其他有限责任公司	市政道路工程建筑
山东省邮电工程有限公司	其他	其他有限责任公司	架线及设备工程建筑
山东宏业发展集团有限公司	其他	私营有限责任公司	架线及设备工程建筑
山东鑫联通信科技有限公司	其他	私营有限责任公司	电气安装
山东省工业设备安装有限公司	地方	其他有限责任公司	其他建筑安装
中铁十四局集团电气化工程有限公司	中央	国有独资公司	架线及设备工程建筑
中铁十局集团电务工程有限公司	中央	其他有限责任公司	铁路工程建筑
山东亚特尔集团股份有限公司	地方	股份有限公司	管道和设备安装
山东福源设备安装有限公司	地方	其他有限责任公司	管道和设备安装
山东国舜建设集团有限公司	地方	其他有限责任公司	其他建筑安装
山东省深基建设工程总公司	地方	国有	住宅房屋建筑
济南岩土工程公司	其他	国有	其他土木工程建筑施工
山东正元建设工程有限责任公司	中央	其他有限责任公司	其他房屋建筑业
中铁济南工程技术有限公司	中央	其他有限责任公司	铁路工程建筑
山东省机械施工有限公司	地方	其他有限责任公司	场地准备活动
山东建科特种建筑工程技术中心	其他	国有	建筑幕墙装饰和装修
山东建勘集团有限公司	地方	国有独资公司	场地准备活动

13-7 续表 2 continued 2

企业名称 Name	隶属关系 Ownership	经济类 Economic Type	所属行业 Sector
山东昌舜岩土工程有限公司	其他	私营有限责任公司	场地准备活动
济南众联深基工程有限公司	其他	私营有限责任公司	其他房屋建筑业
济南振华岩土工程有限责任公司	其他	私营有限责任公司	提供施工设备服务
山东省亘基工程有限公司	其他	私营有限责任公司	其他房屋建筑业
山东航空港建设工程有限公司	其他	私营有限责任公司	其他土木工程建筑施工
山东省装饰集团有限公司	地方	国有独资公司	公共建筑装饰和装修
山东展鸿华商装饰工程有限公司	其他	私营有限责任公司	建筑幕墙装饰和装修
鸿鑫工程有限公司	其他	私营有限责任公司	公共建筑装饰和装修
中炬装饰工程集团有限公司	地方	其他有限责任公司	公共建筑装饰和装修
山东万得福装饰工程有限公司	其他	其他有限责任公司	公共建筑装饰和装修
永隆装饰工程有限公司	其他	私营有限责任公司	公共建筑装饰和装修
山东省建设建工集团装饰装璜有限公司	其他	其他有限责任公司	公共建筑装饰和装修
山东德铭工程建设有限公司	其他	私营有限责任公司	住宅装饰和装修
山东华森装饰工程有限公司	其他	私营有限责任公司	公共建筑装饰和装修
济南万泰建筑装饰工程有限公司	其他	私营股份有限公司	住宅装饰和装修
山东同大装饰有限公司	其他	其他有限责任公司	公共建筑装饰和装修
山东通海装饰工程有限公司	其他	私营有限责任公司	公共建筑装饰和装修
山东世纪装饰工程股份有限公司	其他	私营股份有限公司	住宅装饰和装修
济南宏铁建筑装饰工程有限公司	中央	其他有限责任公司	住宅装饰和装修
山东中大净化工程有限公司	其他	私营有限责任公司	其他建筑安装
风派特装饰工程有限公司	其他	私营有限责任公司	建筑幕墙装饰和装修
山东辉瑞净化工程有限公司	其他	私营有限责任公司	公共建筑装饰和装修
山东福缘来装饰有限公司	其他	私营有限责任公司	住宅装饰和装修
山东福思特建筑装饰有限公司	其他	私营有限责任公司	建筑幕墙装饰和装修
山东盛顺装饰有限公司	其他	私营有限责任公司	住宅装饰和装修
沃尔德项目管理有限公司	其他	其他有限责任公司	住宅装饰和装修
山东深装总装饰工程工业有限公司	其他	私营有限责任公司	公共建筑装饰和装修
山东鑫龙装饰工程有限公司	其他	私营有限责任公司	公共建筑装饰和装修
山东国宸装饰工程有限公司	地方	其他有限责任公司	公共建筑装饰和装修
山东欧瑞装饰有限公司	地方	其他有限责任公司	住宅装饰和装修
山东洁昕建筑装饰工程设计有限公司	其他	私营有限责任公司	公共建筑装饰和装修
山东省鲁美建材装饰有限公司	其他	私营有限责任公司	建筑幕墙装饰和装修
七彩建设发展有限公司	其他	私营有限责任公司	公共建筑装饰和装修
中直科创股份有限公司	其他	股份有限公司	建筑幕墙装饰和装修
万旭装饰工程有限公司	其他	私营有限责任公司	住宅装饰和装修
山东阿郎装饰工程股份有限公司	其他	私营股份有限公司	公共建筑装饰和装修
山东千业建设工程有限公司	其他	私营有限责任公司	建筑幕墙装饰和装修
山东万林建设工程有限公司	其他	私营有限责任公司	住宅装饰和装修
山东莱芜创艺装饰集团有限公司	地方	其他有限责任公司	住宅装饰和装修
山东英士力装饰工程有限公司	其他	私营有限责任公司	公共建筑装饰和装修
山东国创装饰工程有限公司	其他	私营有限责任公司	住宅装饰和装修
嘉林建设集团有限公司	其他	私营有限责任公司	建筑幕墙装饰和装修
山东津单幕墙有限公司	其他	私营有限责任公司	建筑幕墙装饰和装修
济南长兴安装工程公司	其他	其他有限责任公司	其他建筑安装
山东飞越钢结构工程有限公司	地方	其他有限责任公司	其他建筑安装
山东奥深智能工程有限公司	其他	私营有限责任公司	其他未列明建筑业
济南凯诚消防自控设备有限公司	其他	其他有限责任公司	电气安装

13-7 续表 3 continued 3

企业名称 Name	隶属关系 Ownership	经济类 Economic Type	所属行业 Sector
山东费尔消防技术工程有限公司	其他	私营有限责任公司	电气安装
山东涌泉安全科技有限公司	其他	私营有限责任公司	其他建筑安装
山东宏雁电子系统工程有限公司	其他	私营有限责任公司	电气安装
山东华森建筑消防项目管理有限公司	其他	私营有限责任公司	电气安装
山东坚瑞建设股份有限公司	其他	股份有限公司	其他未列明建筑业
山东润霖消防工程有限公司	其他	其他有限责任公司	管道和设备安装
济南消防工程有限公司	地方	其他有限责任公司	电气安装
山东泰景楼宇安全技术有限公司	其他	私营有限责任公司	其他未列明建筑业
山东宏岳消防工程有限公司	其他	私营有限责任公司	其他建筑安装
山东润诚机电工程有限公司	其他	其他有限责任公司	电气安装
济南信高工程技术有限公司	其他	私营有限责任公司	电气安装
山东天翼安全技术有限公司	其他	私营有限责任公司	电气安装
山东华尔泰建筑工程有限公司	其他	其他有限责任公司	电气安装
山东金岛消防安全工程有限公司	其他	私营有限责任公司	电气安装
山东华盛特克科技有限公司	其他	私营有限责任公司	电气安装
山东中安消防设施维修有限公司	其他	其他有限责任公司	其他未列明建筑业
山东三盛防水工程有限公司	其他	私营有限责任公司	环保工程施工
山东凯罗福环保节能科技有限公司	其他	私营有限责任公司	住宅装饰和装修
山东群雄建设工程有限公司	其他	其他有限责任公司	公共建筑装饰和装修
秦恒建设发展有限公司	其他	私营有限责任公司	节能工程施工
山东洪雨防水工程有限公司	其他	私营有限责任公司	其他未列明建筑业
山东志坚建筑工程有限公司	其他	私营有限责任公司	其他房屋建筑业
山东昶博建筑工程有限公司	其他	私营有限责任公司	其他房屋建筑业
济南长城空调公司	地方	股份合作	管道和设备安装
济南四建集团智能消防工程有限责任公司	其他	其他有限责任公司	其他建筑安装
中国铁路通信信号集团济南工程有限公司	中央	其他有限责任公司	架线及设备工程建筑
济南建设设备安装有限责任公司	地方	其他有限责任公司	管道和设备安装
山东科发建设工程有限公司	其他	其他有限责任公司	建筑幕墙装饰和装修
雪山集团有限公司	其他	私营有限责任公司	管道和设备安装
山东华埠特克智能机电工程有限公司	其他	私营有限责任公司	其他未列明建筑业
优士科技发展有限公司	其他	私营有限责任公司	电气安装
山东鲁光信息工程有限公司	其他	私营有限责任公司	电气安装
山东思达特信息科技有限公司	其他	私营有限责任公司	电气安装
中广核宏达环境科技有限责任公司	中央	其他有限责任公司	环保工程施工
山东太平洋环保股份有限公司	其他	私营有限责任公司	其他建筑安装
山东水发鲁润水务科技有限公司	其他	其他有限责任公司	环保工程施工
山东安泰智能工程有限公司	地方	其他有限责任公司	电气安装
山东天启智能工程有限公司	其他	私营有限责任公司	其他未列明建筑业
山东博安智能科技股份有限公司	其他	私营股份有限公司	电气安装
济南金宇公路产业发展有限公司	其他	其他有限责任公司	公路工程建筑
山东海威装饰工程有限公司	其他	私营有限责任公司	公共建筑装饰和装修
山东彩旺建设有限公司	其他	私营有限责任公司	电气安装
山东奥斯福市政工程有限公司	其他	私营有限责任公司	电气安装
山东清华康利城市照明研究设计院有限公司	其他	其他有限责任公司	电气安装
济南东元改建加固工程有限公司	其他	私营有限责任公司	其他房屋建筑业

主要统计指标解释

建筑业统计单位 指从事房屋、构筑物建造和设备安装活动的法人企业。建筑业法人企业应同时具备的条件是：①依法成立，有自己的名称、组织机构和场所，能够承担民事责任；②独立拥有和使用资产，承担负债，有权与其他单位签订合同；③独立核算盈亏，能够编制资产负债表。

建筑业总产值（即自行完成施工产值） 是以货币表现的建筑安装企业在一定时期内生产的建筑业产品的总和。建筑业总产值包括：

（1）建筑工程产值：指列入建筑工程预算内的各种工程价值。

（2）设备安装工程产值：指设备安装工程价值，不包括被安装设备本身价值。

（3）房屋、构筑物修理产值：指房屋、构筑物修理所完成的价值，但不包括被修理房屋、构筑物本身的价值和生产设备的修理价值。

（4）非标准设备制造产值：指加工制造没有定型的、非标准的生产设备的加工费和原材料价值，以及附属加工厂为本企业承建工程制作的非标准设备的价值。

建筑业增加值 指建筑业企业在报告期内以货币表现的建筑业生产经营活动的最终成果。目前建筑业增加值采用分配法（收入法）计算，即从收入的角度出发，根据生产要素在生产过程中应得的收入份额计算。具体计算公式为：

建筑业增加值＝本年提取的固定资产折旧＋应付工资＋应付福利费＋管理费用中的劳动待业保险金、税金＋工程结算税金及附加＋工程结算利润

房屋建筑施工面积 指在报告期内施工的全部房屋建筑面积，包括本期新开工的房屋面积、上期施工跨入本期继续施工的房屋面积、上期停缓建在本期恢复施工的房屋面积、本期竣工的房屋面积及本期施工后又停缓建的房屋面积。

房屋建筑竣工面积 指在报告期内房屋建筑按照设计要求全部完工，达到了住人和使用条件，经验收鉴定合格，正式移交使用单位的房屋建筑面积。

营业收入 指企业经营主要业务和其他业务所确认的收入总额。营业收入合计包括“主营业务收入”和“其他业务收入”。根据会计“利润表”中“营业收入”项目的本期总额数填报。

营业利润 指企业从事生产经营活动所取得的利润。执行2006年《企业会计准则》的企业，营业利润为营业收入减去营业成本、营业税金及附加、销售费用、管理费用、财务费用、资产减值损失，再加上公允价值变动收益和损益收益。未执行2006年《企业会计准则》的企业，营业利润为主营业务收入减去主营业务成本、主营业务税金及附加，加上其他业务利润后，再减支销售费用、管理费用、财务费用后的金额。

Explanatory Notes on Main Statistical Indicators

Statistical Unit in Construction refers to corporate enterprise engaged in the construction of buildings, structures and the installation of equipment. A corporate construction enterprise should meet the following requirements: ① being set up in line with relevant legal basis, having its full name, organization and location, and capable of taking civil liabilities; ② independently possessing and using its assets and assuming its liabilities, and entitled to sign contracts with other institutions; ③ making independent accounts of its profits and losses, and capable of compiling its own balance sheet.

Gross Output Value of Construction (i.e. complete construction output value independently) is the sum of construction products produced by construction and installation enterprises embodied with currency within a certain period. It includes:

(1) Output value of construction projects: the value of projects covered by the project budgets;

(2) Value of equipment installation projects: the value of the installation of equipment, (excluding the own value of the equipment to be installed);

(3) Output value of repair of buildings and structures: the value created through the repairs of buildings or structures. It does not include the value of buildings or structures being repaired and the value of the repair of production equipment;

(4) Output value of manufactured non-standard equipment: the value of non-standard production equipment including raw materials and manufacturing cost, made for the construction project. It also includes the output value of equipment manufactured by subsidiary workshops.

Value added of Construction refers to the final result of the activities of production and operation of enterprises of construction industry in monetary terms during the reporting period. Now, the construction value added is calculated in terms of distribution approach (income approach), namely calculation based on earned income of production factors in the production process from the perspective of the income. Specific calculation formula is:

Construction value added= depreciation of fixed assets extracted this year+ wages payable+ welfare payable+ unemployment insurance and taxes in the administration expense + project settlement tax and surcharge + project settlement profits

Floor Space of Buildings under Construction refers to floor space of buildings under construction during the reporting period, including newly started buildings, buildings started earlier and continued during the reporting period, and buildings suspended earlier but restarted during the reporting period, buildings completed during the reporting period, and buildings under construction and then suspended during the reporting period.

Floor Space of Buildings Completed refers to the floor space of buildings that are completed in the reporting period in accordance with the requirements of the design, up to the standard for living in and putting into use, and have been checked and accepted by concerned departments as qualified ones.

Operating Income refers to the total income of main business or other businesses of the enterprise confirmed. Total operating incomes include "main business income" and "other business income" which is filled in pursuant to total amount of "operating income" in the "profit statement" in the current period.

Operating Profit refers to the profit obtained by the enterprise after engaging in production and operation activities. As for enterprises subject to 2006 Accounting Standards for Business Enterprises, the operating profit is the result after the operating income minus operating cost, business tax and surcharge, selling expense, administration expense, financial expense and assets impairment loss and then plus income from fair value changes and income from profit and loss. As for enterprises do not subject to 2006 Accounting Standards for Business Enterprises, the operating profit is the amount after main business income minus main business cost and tax and extra charges of main business and then plus profit from other business and finally minus selling expense, administration expense and financial expense.

14

运输与邮电

TRANSPORTATION POST AND TELECOMMUNICATIONS

14-1 邮电业务量
Postal and Telecommunications Services

指　标	Indicator	单 位 Unit	2014 年	2015 年	2016 年	2017 年	2018 年	2019 年
国内分类业务量	**Domestic Classified Business Volume**							
固定电话数	Number of Fixed Telephone	万户 (10 000 subscribers)	176.90	165.30	155.90	153.10	135.27	148.82
年末市内电话	Urban Fixed Telephone Subscribers at Year-end	万户 (10 000 subscribers)	150.17	141.00	135.89	132.55	118.70	136.30
年末农村电话	Rural Telephone Subscribers at Year-end	万户 (10 000 subscribers)	26.73	24.30	19.07	19.23	16.47	12.20
年末住宅电话	Number of Fixed Telephone Subscribers at Year-end	万户 (10 000 subscribers)	102.61	86.40	71.79	79.54	67.64	25.56
年末移动电话用户	Number of Mobile Telephone Subscribers at Year-end	万户 (10 000 subscribers)	1177.87	1090.40	1087.71	971.10	1013.65	1122.86
4G 电话用户数	4G Mobile Phone Subscribers	万户 (10 000 subscribers)	74.30	306.60	442.10	623.50	725.01	888.81
宽带互联网接入用户数	Subscribers of Broad Band Internet	户 (subscriber)	2027279	2316600	2618800	2987500	3447000	3926200
每百人互联网用户数	Number of Internet User per 100 Population	户 / 百人 (subscriber/100 person)	32.61	37.02	41.38	46.81	53.05	49.63
邮电局所	Post & Telecommunication offices	处 (place)	216	204	204	207	207	252
国际及港澳分类业务量	**International.Hong kong and Macao Classified Business Volume**							
函　件	Letters	万件 (10 000 pieces)	115.40	19.49	16.10	27.67	51.95	45.75
包　件	Package	万件 (10 000 pieces)	0.92	0.84	1.24	1.35	0.76	0.60

14-2 交通运输业基本情况
Basic Conditions of Transportation

指　标	Indicator	2014 年	2015 年	2016 年	2017 年	2018 年	2019 年
铁路客运量(万人)	Railways Passenger Traffic(10 000 persons)	9507.8	10681.1	11923.7	13411.8	14547.7	15745.1
铁路客运周转量(亿人公里)	Railways Passenger Turnover (100 million passengers-km)	617.3	662.5	703.8	754.6	784.6	795.3
铁路货运量(万吨)	Railways Freight Traffic(10 000 tons)	16792.3	15793.8	16749.1	17865.2	18728.0	20869.8
铁路货运周转量(亿吨公里)	Railways Freight Turnover(100 million tonkm)	1238.1	1088.0	1153.0	1254.9	1288.4	1460.5
公路客运量(万人)	Highways Passenger Traffic(10 000 persons)	3729.0	3663.0	3212.0	3192.0	3149.0	3244.0
公路旅客周转量(亿人公里)	Highways Passenger Turnover (100 million passengers-km)	51.6	54.2	52.2	52.7	52.9	54.1
公路货运量(万吨)	Highways Freight Traffic(10 000 tons)	19359.0	20419.0	21212.0	24058.0	25571.0	34392.0
公路货物周转量(亿吨公里)	Highways Freight Turnover(100 million ton-km)	392.0	393.8	419.0	459.5	474.0	585.5
民航客运量(万人)	Civil Aviation Passenger Traffic (10 000 persons)	488.1	533.1	645.1	785.6	894.1	936.1
民航客运周转量(亿人公里)	Civil Aviation Passenger Turnover (100 million passengers-km)	195.3	227.7	272.9	334.3	368.5	376.5
民航货运量(万吨)	Civil Aviation Freight Turnover(10 000 tons)	3.9	4.2	5.1	5.0	5.6	6.7
公路通车里程(公里)	Length of Highways in Operation(km)						
公路通车里程	Length of Highways in Operation	12846	13104	12730.2	12856.8	12637.7	17770.9
#高速公路	Expressway	419	419	462.2	488.5	488.5	653.6
有铺装、简易铺装路面	Poved Roads	12602	12906	12603.9	12735.7	12579.4	17290.0
未铺装路面	UnPoved Roads	245	198	126.3	121.1	58.3	480.9
民用航空	Civil Aviation						
执行航线(条)	Perform Routes	103	152	125	150	182	198
通航城市(个)	Navigable Cities	53	55	64	82	96	120
起飞架次(架次)	Plane Flights	83551	86158	100152	115529	126828	129994
民用车辆(辆)	Civil Vehicles						
民用汽车	Civil Vehicles	1382459	1541045	1742313	1949707	2160748	2584278
私人汽车	Private Vehicles	1217636	1505308	1573761	1764574	1948815	2332421
载客汽车	Passenger Vehicles	1224763	1400588	1592737	1783848	1978951	2370437
#大型	Large	11966	11194	12206	13539	14002	15767
载货汽车	Trucks	134929	123801	134741	151141	166277	194957
#重型	Heavy	26303	24653	27303	31632	36720	41904
其它汽车	Others	22767	16656	14835	14718	15520	18884
摩托车	Motorcycle	174618	126540	73568	106168	133743	258382
挂车	Wheeler	7398	7497	8191	9102	9851	12538

注：1. 公路通车里程自 2006 年起调整统计口径，增加了村道公路统计。
2. 因省交通厅公路局统计口径变化，自 2012 年起，公路通车里程按路面类型分为有铺装路面、简易铺装路面和未铺装路面。
3. 铁路系统统计数据来自中国铁路济南局集团有限公司。
4. 自 2014 年起，交通部门执行新的公路运输量统计方案，调查范围较老口径有所缩小，2013 年及 2014 年数据均为新口径下交通部反馈数据。

Note: 1. The mileage in highway open to traffic was adjusted to be statistical caliber as of 2006, increasing statistics of village road highway.
2. Due to the change in statistical caliber of provincial communications department and highway administration bureau, the mileage in highway open to traffic was divided into dry pavement, easy pavement and unpaved road in light of pavement type as of 2012.
3. Statistical data of railway system comes from China Railway Jinan Group Co., Ltd.
4. Traffic departments started to execute new statistical project of highway transport volume with survey scope decreasing compared to old caliber as of 2014 and the data in 2014 and 2013 is the date reported by traffic departments based on new caliber.

14-3 规模以上交通运输、仓储和邮政业企业财务指标(2019 年)

Main Financial Indicators of Transport,Storage and Postal Services above Designated Size(2019)

单位：万元 (10 000 yuan)

指标	Indicator	交通运输、仓储和邮政业 Transport,Storage and Postal Services
单位数（个）	Number(unit)	323
年初存货	Inventory at Beginning of year	247006
流动资产合计	Total Liquid Assets	7933699
其中：应收账款	Receivable	1940661
其中：存货	Inventory	169034
固定资产原价	Original Value of Fixed Assets	24355409
本年折旧	Depreciation in the Year	980233
资产总计	Total Assets	43919826
负债合计	Total Liabilities	16706150
所有者权益合计	Total Creditors'Equity	27213676
营业收入	Business Revenue	11828713
营业成本	Business Cost	10562127
税金及附加	Taxes and Other Surcharges	26057
销售费用	Sales Expenses	161845
管理费用	Management Expenses	469834
研发费用	R&D expenses	3356
财务费用	Financial Expenses	218492
投资收益	Investment Interests	149539
其他收益	Other gains	172626
营业利润	Profits from Business	712549
营业外收入	Profits from Non–Business	41187
营业外支出	Expense from Non–Business	80653
利润总额	Total Profits	671678
所得税费用	Income Tax Expense	239397
应付职工薪酬(本年贷方累计发生额)	Total Wages Payable	2578456
应交增值税	Value–added Tax Payable	280187
从事服务业活动的从业人员平均人数(人)	Average of Empolyed (Person)	168831

14-4 分地区公路交通 (2019 年)
Road Transportation by Region(2019)

单位：公里 (km)

指　标	Indicator	济南市 Ji'nan	其中 of which		
			市 区 Urban	平阴县 Ping yin	商河县 Shang he
公路通车里程	Length of Highways in Operation	17770.9	14100.0	979.6	2691.3
#高速公路	Expressway	653.6	560.1	60.8	32.7
有铺装、简易铺装路面	Poved Roads	17290.0	13619.1	979.6	2691.3
未铺装路面	UnPoved Roads	480.9	480.9	0.0	0.0

主要统计指标解释

公路里程　指在一定时期内实际达到《公路工程技术标准JTJ01-88》规定的等级公路，并经公路主管部门正式验收交付使用的公路里程数。包括大中城市的郊区公路以及通过小城镇街道部分的公路里程和桥梁、渡口的长度，不包括大中城市的街道、厂矿、林区生产用道和农业生产用道的里程。两条或多条公路共同经由同一路段，只计算一次，不得重复计算里程长度。它是反映公路建设发展规模的重要指标，也是计算运输网密度等指标的基础资料。

民用航空航线里程　指民航运输定期班机飞行的航线长度的总和。航线长度按机场之间的距离计算，通常有两种计算方法：一是将每条航线长度相加称为重复计算航线里程；一是将两线或两条以上航线经过同一区段里程，只计算一次航线长度称为不重复计算航线里程。一般常用的是后者，它能确切反映民航运输网的规模，是表明民航事业为国民经济服务和方便人民生活程度的主要指标。

货（客）运量　指在一定时期内，各种运输工具实际运送的货物（旅客）数量。它是反映运输业为国民经济和人民生活服务的数量指标，也是制定和检查运输生产计划、研究运输发展规模和速度的重要指标。货运按吨计算，客运按人计算。货物不论运输距离长短、货物类别，均按实际重量统计。旅客不论行程远近或票价多少，均按一人一次客运量统计；半价票、小孩票也按一人统计。

货物（旅客）周转量　指在一定时期内，由各种运输工具运送的货物（旅客）数量与其相应运输距离的乘积之总和。它是反映运输业生产总成果的重要指标，也是编制和检查运输生产计划，计算运输效率、劳动生产率以及核算运输单位成本的主要基础资料。计算货物周转量通常按发出站与到达站之间的最短距离，也就是计费距离计算。计算公式为：

货物（旅客）周转量 = Σ（货物（旅客）运输量 × 运输距离）

移动电话用户　指在移动电话营业部门登记，通过移动电话交换机进入移动电话网、占有移动电话号码的电话用户。用户数量以实际办理登记手续进入邮电部门移动电话网的户数进行计算，一部或一台移动电话统计为一户。

电话用户　指接入国家公众固定电话网，并按固定电话业务进行经营管理的电话用户。1997 年以前，电话用户分为市内电话用户和农村电话用户。市内电话用户是指接入县城及县以上城市电话网上的电话用户；农村电话用户是指接入县邮电局农话台及县以下农村电话交换点，以县城为中心（除市话用户外）联通县、乡（镇）、行政村、村民小组的用户。从 1997 年起，电话用户数分组调整为以用户所在区域划分为“城市电话用户”和“乡村电话用户”，与过去的按市内电话和农村电话划分方法不同。而电话用户数、电话机部数统计方法不变。

Explanatory Notes on Main Statistical Indicators

Length of Highways refers to the length of highways which are built in conformity with the grades specified in the Technical Standard JTJ01–88 for Highway Engineering within a certain period of time, and have been formally checked and accepted by the departments of highways and put into use. The length of highways includes that of the suburb highways at large and medium sized cities, highways passing through streets at small cities and towns, and also the length of bridges and ferries. It does not include the length of streets in big and medium sized cities and highways built for the production purpose at factories, mines, forest areas and agricultural areas. If two or more highways go to the same section of the way, the length of the section is only calculated for once and no duplication is allowed. The length of highways is an important indicator to show the development of the highway construction and to provide essential information to calculate the transport network density.

Mileage of Civil Aviation Routes refers to the sum of the length of the route of scheduled civil aviation flight. The length of the route is calculated as the distance between airports. There are usually two calculation methods: First, repeated calculation of route mileage is deemed in case of adding the length of each route; Second, no repeated calculation of route mileage is deemed if the length of the route is only calculated once when no less than two routes pass the same zone. The second one is usually used, as it can precisely show the size of the civil aviation network and also is the major indicator of indicating the extent of civil aviation serving the national economy and the people.

Freight (Passenger) Traffic refers to the volume or freight (passenger) transported with various means in a certain period. It provides a quantitative measure to show how the transportation industry serves the national economy and people, and is also an important indicator for planning the transport industry and for studying the development scale and speed of the transport industry. Freight transport is calculated in tons and passenger traffic is calculated in the number of persons. Despite the type of freight and traveling distance, the freight transport is calculated in the actual weight of the goods. And despite the traveling distance and ticket price, the passenger traffic is calculated by the principle that one person can be counted only once in one travel. The passengers who travel with a half–price ticket or a child ticket is also calculated as one person.

Tonnage Mileage (Passenger turnover) refers to the sum of the products of the volume of transported cargos (passengers) multiplying by the transport distance. It is an important indicator to reflect the achievement of transportation industry, to prepare and examine the transport plan and to measure the efficiency, the labor productivity and the unit cost of transport. Normally, the shortest distance between the departure station and the destination station (i.e., the payable distance) is the basis to calculate the Tonnage mileage. The formula is as follows:

Tonnage mileage (passenger turnover) = Σ(freight (passenger) traffic* distance of transportation)

Wireless Subscribers refer to persons who have registered at the mobile phone business department and hence connected with the mobile telephone communication network through the mobile telephone switchboards and occupy mobile telephone numbers. The number of subscribers is calculated in line with the number of users actually handling the registration procedures and entering the mobile telephone network of the post and telecommunications departments. One mobile telephone is deemed as one household.

Telephone Subscribers refer to telephone subscribers entering the national public fixed telephone network and undergoing operating management based on fixed telephone services. Before 1997, telephone subscribers were divided into local telephone subscribers and rural telephone subscribers. Local telephone subscribers refer to telephone subscribers accessing to the urban telephone network of county and above; Rural telephone subscribers refer to telephone subscribers accessing to the agricultural telephone station of the county post and telecommunications office and the rural telephone exchange of those below country, and connecting with county, township (town), administrative village and group of villagers based on the county as the center (except for city telephone users). From 1997, grouping of telephone users is adjusted to "city telephone subscribers" and "rural telephone subscribers" in light of regions where subscribers are, which is different from partition method -- local call and rural call in the past. The statistical approaches for counting telephone subscribers and telephones numbers remain unchanged.

15

国内贸易

DOMESTIC TRADE

15-1 各时期分行业社会消费品零售
Total Retail Sales of Consumer Goods by Section in Each Period

单位：万元 (10 000 yuan)

年份 Year	社会消费品零售总额 Retail Sale of Consumer Goods						
	总计 Total	批发零售业 Wholesale and Retail Trades	住宿业 Hotels Services	餐饮业 Catering Services	制造业 Manufacture	其 他 Others	农民对非农业居民 Farmers to Non-agricultural Residents
1949	11426	7312		556	3514	–	44
1952	22248	16985		1223	3592	–	448
1957	34568	29279		1935	2381	3	970
1962	41436	35784		1655	2946	266	785
1965	40795	36470		1829	1856	287	353
1970	42993	39397		1537	1468	321	270
1975	60105	53239		2565	2914	1217	170
1978	81335	70661		2907	5120	2222	425
1979	96036	80703		4000	9060	823	1450
1980	119775	95121		4392	16489	1299	2474
"六五时期"							
1981	135236	103303		5388	21353	2157	3035
1982	152094	116241		8165	21398	2778	3512
1983	167948	127884		9225	23569	2953	4317
1984	200301	150233		11342	29563	4506	4657
1985	243080	181867		14823	32342	5535	8513
"七五时期"							
1986	294102	219730		17880	35565	5456	15471
1987	331504	240192		20305	45386	8963	16658
1988	425984	300090		30808	60463	12300	22323
1989	484392	343978		28634	71653	9729	30398
1990	528221	382047		25599	71505	10886	38184
"八五时期"							
1991	597989	424836		27443	78452	14186	53072
1992	711774	535080		37096	77951		61647
1993	985251	723914		56059	80101		125177
1994	1426472	1037687		86141	99621		203023
1995	1837618	1345321		133501	115105		243691

15-1 续表 continued

年份 Year	社会消费品零售总额 Retail Sale of Consumer Goods						
	总计 Total	批发零售业 Wholesale and Retail Trades	住宿业 Hotels Services	餐饮业 Catering Services	制造业 Manufacture	其 他 Others	农民对非农业居民 Farmers to Non-agricultural Residents
“九五时期”							
1996	2234590	1570947		176100	141201		346342
1997	2568584	1744014		216727	177219		430624
1998	2834024	1893486		255616	207595		477327
1999	3092091	2043078		305333	225132		518548
2000	3444527	2287545		377550	233128		546304
“十五时期”							
2001	3857141	2574216		485494	237545		559886
2002	4321225	2935804		613178	231947		540296
2003	5115396	4373831		741565	–		–
2004	6689452	5691288	57973	940191	–		–
2005	7726458	6575543	66490	1084425	–		–
“十一五时期”							
2006	8974064	7571831	78098	1324135	–		–
2007	10526639	8791908	86322	1648409	–		–
2008	12922856	10684195	96391	2142271	–		–
2009	15254265	12710608	105378	2438279	–		–
2010	17254574	14022650	150810	3081114	–		–
“十二五时期”							
2011	20231045	16338362	175067	3717616	–		–
2012	23235965	18740304	187466	4308195	–		–
2013	26338714	22006709	177160	4154845	–		–
2014	28640303	24120903	182090	4337310	–	–	–
2015	31410419	26484428	193710	4732280	–	–	–
“十三五时期”							
2016	34350723	28971634	210316	5168774	–	–	–
2017	37525226	31658152	228909	5638165	–	–	–
2018	40910775	34521369	248418	6140988	–	–	–
2019	44204092	37604716	275686	6323691			

注：1992 年至 2019 年社会消费品零售总额及分组数据根据第四次全国经济普查数据进行了修订。
Note: Total retail volume of social consumption and grouping data from 1992 to 2019 are revised according to the fourth national economic census.

15-2 限额以上批发零售业法人企业商品销售情况(2019年)

Total Purchase Sales and Inventory by Sector Above Designated Size(2019)

单位：万元 (10 000 yuan)

指　标	Indicator	商品销售总额 Total Sale Value		
		合计 Total	批发 Wholesalel	零售 Retail
总计	Total	65112629.1	51010068.0	14102561.1
一、批发业	Wholesalel Trade	52740620.2	50041882.5	2698737.7
农、林、牧、渔产品批发	Wholesale of Agriculture Forestry Animal Husbandry and Fishery	395087.2	378681.2	16406.0
食品、饮料及烟草制品批发	Wholesale of Food, Beverages and Tobaccos	3595117.3	3427458.4	167658.9
纺织、服装及家庭用品批发	Wholesale of Textiles, Garments and Daily Consumer Articles	2531321.6	2373610.6	157711.0
文化、体育用品及器材批发	Wholesale of Culture, Sports Appliances and Equipments	2339553.6	1600669.7	738883.9
医药及医疗器材批发	Wholesale of Medicines and Medical Appliances	6646379.7	6601162.0	45217.7
矿产品、建材及化工产品批发	Wholesale of Mineral Products, Building Materials and Chemical Products	29848533.1	28531180.3	1317352.8
机械设备、五金产品及电子产品批发	Wholesale of Machinery, Hardware and Electronic Equipment	6640813.2	6405159.2	235654.0
贸易经纪与代理	Trade Broker and Agency	148166.9	141078.3	7088.6
其他批发业	Other Wholesale not Classified Elsewhere	595647.6	582882.8	12764.8
内资企业	Domestic Funded Enterprises	49853726.2	47155306.3	2698419.9
国有企业	State-owned	63350.3	63350.3	
集体企业	Collective-owned			
股份合作企业	Cooperative Enterprises			
联营企业	Joint Ownership Enterprises			
有限责任公司	Limited Liability Corporations	26064679.3	24365338.0	1699341.3
股份有限公司	Share-holding Corporations Limited	3017264.6	2749516.7	267747.9
私营企业	Private Enterprises	20708432.0	19977101.3	731330.7
其他企业	Others			
港、澳、台商投资企业	Hong Kong,Macao and Taiwan Investment Enterprises	2515763.7	2515445.9	317.8

15-2 续表 continued

指 标	Indicator	商品销售总额 Total Sale Value 合计 Total	批发 Wholesalel	零售 Retail
外商投资企业	Foreign Funded Enterprises	371130.3	371130.3	
二、零售业	Retail Trade	12372008.9	968185.5	11403823.4
综合零售	Integrated Retail	2508095.4	156728.3	2351367.1
食品、饮料及烟草制品专门零售	Retail of Food, Beverages and Tobaccos	350628.0	48551.8	302076.2
纺织、服装及日用品专门零售	Special Retail of Textiles, Garments and Daily Consumer Articles	644222.9	117604.2	526618.7
文化、体育用品及器材专门零售	Retail of Culture, Sports Appliances and Equipments	435887.7	66704.4	369183.3
医药及医疗器材专门零售	Retail of Medicines and Medical Appliances	531333.7	30988.9	500344.8
汽车、摩托车、零配件和燃料及其他动力销售	Cars, Motorcycles, Spare Part and Fuel and Other Power Sales	5823728.2	361899.8	5461828.4
家用电器及电子产品专门零售	Special Retail of Household Electric Appliances and Electronic Products	1300485.8	56665.5	1243820.3
五金、家具及室内装饰材料专门零售	Special Retail of Hardware, Furniture and Decoration Materials	173505.5	15678.3	157827.2
货摊、无店铺及其他零售业	Non-shop and Other Retails	604121.7	113364.3	490757.4
内资企业	Domestic Funded Enterprises	11346193.7	967475.7	10378718.0
国有企业	State-owned	47703.3	11203.0	36500.3
集体企业	Collective-owned	20506.1		20506.1
股份合作企业	Cooperative Enterprises	13982.5	40.0	13942.5
联营企业	Joint Ownership Enterprises			
有限责任公司	Limited Liability Corporations	3849448.4	462666.1	3386782.3
股份有限公司	Share-holding Corporations Limited	1799516.3	54860.7	1744655.6
私营企业	Private Enterprises	5613916.4	438705.9	5175210.5
其他企业	Other Enterprises	1120.7		1120.7
港、澳、台商投资企业	Enterprises with Funds from Hong Kong, Macao and Taiwan	456832.9	654.9	456178.0
外商投资企业	Foreign Funded Enterprises	568982.3	54.9	568927.4

15-3 限额以上批发零售贸易企业资产实力 (2019 年)

Capital Power of Wholesales and Retail Sales Trade Above Designated Size(2019)

指标名称	Indicator	法人企业数(个) Number of Corporation Enterprises (unit)	流动资产合计 Total Working Capitals
总计	Total	2667	29252984.9
一、批发业	Wholesalel Trade	1804	22882429.6
农、林、牧、渔产品批发	Wholesale of Agriculture Forestry Animal Husbandry and Fishery	34	570731.8
食品、饮料及烟草制品批发	Wholesale of Food, Beverages and Tobaccos	122	1567684.6
纺织、服装及家庭用品批发	Wholesale of Textiles, Garments and Daily Consumer Articles	111	1360688.6
文化、体育用品及器材批发	Wholesale of Culture, Sports Appliances and Equipments	51	1186245.8
医药及医疗器材批发	Wholesale of Medicines and Medical Appliances	199	3844163.2
矿产品、建材及化工产品批发	Wholesale of Mineral Products, Building Materials and Chemical Products	868	11063412.2
机械设备、五金产品及电子产品批发	Wholesale of Machinery, Hardware and Electronic Equipment	390	3000974.2
贸易经纪与代理	Trade Broker and Agency	6	64269.2
其他批发业	Other Wholesale not Classified Elsewhere	23	224260.0
内资企业	Domestic Funded Enterprises	1792	21228901.5
国有企业	State-owned	7	47640.9
集体企业	Collective-owned		
股份合作企业	Cooperative Enterprises		
联营企业	Joint Ownership Enterprises		
有限责任公司	Limited Liability Corporations	358	10395844.2
股份有限公司	Share-holding Corporations Limited	19	4225535.5
私营企业	Private Enterprises	1408	6559880.9
其他企业	Others		
港、澳、台商投资企业	Hong Kong, Macao and Taiwan Investment Enterprises	6	1488582.1
外商投资企业	Foreign Funded Enterprises	6	164946.0

单位：万元 (10 000 yuan)

其中 of which 存货 Inventory	固定资产原价 Original Value of Fixed Assets	累计折旧 Depreciation	其中 of which 本年折旧 Depreciation in the Year	资产总计 Total Assets	负债合计 Total Liabilities	所有者权益合计 Total Creditors' Equity	其中 of which 实收资本 Paid-up Capital
3581334.5	2897618.7	1119825.4	157853.9	37437441.2	28514322.1	8918612.5	13902684.7
2584692.1	1785269.0	673822.8	84333.4	29170989.9	21937241.7	7233531.6	5203990.3
38033.4	30787.5	10354.7	1881.5	603963.0	548094.5	55868.5	34269.6
521397.2	299703.2	115774.5	22463.8	1941697.4	1291313.5	650167.2	509798.5
283104.5	95273.2	26527.7	5886.6	1594310.4	1398157.1	196153.3	93221.4
270394.0	277081.3	113088.4	11569.6	1732017.0	1099855.5	632161.5	150363.5
474985.7	262206.0	87555.3	19216.7	4380593.3	3568264.9	812328.4	518672.2
561551.6	674056.0	274987.8	6681.3	15375172.6	11083613.6	4291559.1	3486321.6
382271.0	124013.3	42041.9	15750.9	3228135.3	2725594.5	502540.8	347682.7
17308.6	393.9	315.2	47.0	64995.2	42552.4	22442.8	14600.0
35646.1	21754.6	3177.3	836.0	250105.7	179795.7	70310.0	49060.8
2168275.5	1674379.8	638613.5	72587.0	27328160.5	20421923.4	6906020.5	5008598.6
33563.3	22229.2	6249.4	619.4	69636.3	45824.5	23811.8	4438.3
1085927.9	1158308.6	454248.9	33387.8	14714499.4	12401202.0	2313297.4	1905655.1
18010.6	50749.3	28518.2	2507.4	4761562.1	1865819.9	2895742.2	1044646.7
1030773.7	443092.7	149597.0	36072.4	7782462.7	6109077.0	1673169.1	2053858.5
369912.3	105142.5	31366.1	11236.1	1659899.5	1411555.0	248344.5	147105.9
46504.3	5746.7	3843.2	510.3	182929.9	103763.3	79166.6	48285.8

15-3 续表 continued

指标名称	Indicator	法人企业数(个) Number of Corporation Enterprises (unit)	流动资产合计 Total Working Capitals
二、零售业	Retail Trade	863	6370555.3
综合零售	Integrated Retail	67	3023682.1
食品、饮料及烟草制品专门零售	Retail of Food, Beverages and Tobaccos	87	156904.2
纺织、服装及日用品专门零售	Special Retail of Textiles, Garments and Daily Consumer Articles	67	228933.1
文化、体育用品及器材专门零售	Retail of Culture, Sports Appliances and Equipments	51	193230.9
医药及医疗器材专门零售	Retail of Medicines and Medical Appliances	56	290031.3
汽车、摩托车、零配件和燃料及其他动力销售	Cars, Motorcycles, Spare Part and Fuel and Other Power Sales	341	1942350.1
家用电器及电子产品专门零售	Special Retail of Household Electric Appliances and Electronic Products	123	304009.4
五金、家具及室内装饰材料专门零售	Special Retail of Hardware, Furniture and Decoration Materials	30	51716.7
货摊、无店铺及其他零售业	Non-shop and Other Retails	41	179697.5
内资企业	Domestic Funded Enterprises	845	6158304.9
国有企业	State-owned	5	17221.7
集体企业	Collective-owned	8	6818.9
股份合作企业	Cooperative Enterprises	4	3629.1
联营企业	Joint Ownership Enterprises		
有限责任公司	Limited Liability Corporations	251	1612841.9
股份有限公司	Share-holding Corporations Limited	21	2880906.5
私营企业	Private Enterprises	555	1636652.6
其他企业	Other Enterprises	1	234.2
港、澳、台商投资企业	Enterprises with Funds from Hong Kong, Macao and Taiwan	8	87553.2
外商投资企业	Foreign Funded Enterprises	10	124697.2

其中 of which	固定资产原价 Original Value of Fixed Assets	累计折旧 Depreciation	其中 of which	资产总计 Total Assets	负债合计 Total Liabilities	所有者权益合计 Total Creditors' Equity	其中 of which
存货 Inventory			本年折旧 Depreciation in the Year				实收资本 Paid-up Capital
996642.4	1112349.7	446002.6	73520.5	8266451.3	6577080.4	1685080.9	8698694.4
132965.1	529422.2	225712.8	22712.7	3947947.0	3450458.4	497488.6	211771.1
41547.9	54012.7	21197.1	4561.0	199563.2	159275.6	40201.2	49269.7
85688.0	51962.1	10240.4	3285.4	353713.1	277642.1	74826.3	75860.3
76710.7	31498.4	9283.3	1027.7	232770.9	102533.8	130237.1	50768.6
73166.3	24365.1	14684.9	3812.5	360757.3	227438.8	132390.3	60640.5
492055.3	325079.4	139015.1	32043.4	2491672.5	1926193.6	565745.9	8086917.0
41736.2	15318.3	6964.6	1017.9	322531.0	241497.7	79032.8	48860.8
13620.5	43327.5	6101.7	2782.6	122039.0	79270.3	42768.7	41705.4
39152.4	37364.0	12802.7	2277.3	235457.3	112770.1	122390.0	72901.0
947017.7	954570.2	381809.7	61586.1	7725231.3	6290126.8	1430814.5	8484522.5
6667.4	10479.2	6224.7	443.3	21692.8	22687.1	-994.3	6297.5
1288.2	4035.0	1305.2	234.7	12063.7	1815.6	10248.1	604.3
2495.3	532.3	313.6	38.9	4368.8	4043.1	325.7	522.7
332690.3	353794.5	129331.4	24422.9	2087382.7	1597013.9	489215.5	1355571.0
115242.2	358534.5	153361.9	13122.3	3715260.7	3106507.6	608753.1	203892.6
488634.3	226264.0	91097.9	23241.0	1883334.8	1557897.2	322300.9	6917315.0
	930.7	175.0	83.0	1127.8	162.3	965.5	319.4
25000.6	51605.9	22418.5	4138.6	197843.3	117069.0	80774.3	47330.6
24624.1	106173.6	41774.4	7795.8	343376.7	169884.6	173492.1	166841.3

15-4 限额以上批发零售贸易企业损益及分配(2019年)
Profit Loss and Distribution of Wholesales and Retail Sales Trade Above Designated Size (2019)

指标名称	Indicator	法人企业数(个) Number of Corporation Enterprises (unit)	主营业务收入 Revenue from Principal Business	营业成本 Cost of Business
总计	Total	2667	57665077.8	54532091.1
一、批发业	Wholesalel Trade	1804	46939771.6	45074854.9
农、林、牧、渔产品批发	Wholesale of Agriculture Forestry Animal Husbandry and Fishery	34	370718.1	357938.7
食品、饮料及烟草制品批发	Wholesale of Food, Beverages and Tobaccos	122	3241982.9	2805576.4
纺织、服装及家庭用品批发	Wholesale of Textiles, Garments and Daily Consumer Articles	111	2231698.5	2139131.5
文化、体育用品及器材批发	Wholesale of Culture, Sports Appliances and Equipments	51	2228860.5	1913638.3
医药及医疗器材批发	Wholesale of Medicines and Medical Appliances	199	5916404.4	4981211.8
矿产品、建材及化工产品批发	Wholesale of Mineral Products, Building Materials and Chemical Products	868	26188154.0	26525198.8
机械设备、五金产品及电子产品批发	Wholesale of Machinery, Hardware and Electronic Equipment	390	6092293.3	5703775.5
贸易经纪与代理	Trade Broker and Agency	6	135503.1	130035.9
其他批发业	Other Wholesale not Classified Elsewhere	23	534156.8	518348.0
内资企业	Domestic Funded Enterprises	1792	44228189.9	42557573.4
国有企业	State-owned	7	61299.1	60117.5
集体企业	Collective-owned			
股份合作企业	Cooperative Enterprises			
联营企业	Joint Ownership Enterprises			
有限责任公司	Limited Liability Corporations	358	22664668.7	22120179.9
股份有限公司	Share-holding Corporations Limited	19	2945729.0	2845265.9
私营企业	Private Enterprises	1408	18556493.1	17532010.1
其他企业	Others			
港、澳、台商投资企业	Hong Kong,Macao and Taiwan Investment Enterprises	6	2383173.8	2208698.7
外商投资企业	Foreign Funded Enterprises	6	328407.9	308582.8

单位：万元 (10 000 yuan)

税金及附加 Taxes and Surcharges	销售费用 Cost of Sales	管理费用 Cost of Management	财务费用 Cost of Finance	营业利润 Profits from Business	利润总额 Total Profits	所得税费用 Income Tax Expense	应付职工薪酬（本年贷方累计发生额）Total Wages Payable	应交增值税 Value-added Tax Payable
560015.3	2037599.5	1071691.3	309361.5	815143.6	830334.3	153669.2	1118749.8	404318.1
501048.7	1135131.8	751331.0	207638.4	678598.7	685439.3	113141.6	668439.4	234017.3
295.6	5740.7	6936.5	21974.9	-2376.3	2013.1	342.2	27774.0	2155.0
110538.1	111638.1	131905.5	-3434.9	132850.9	139159.1	32287.1	95428.1	45744.6
3434.1	70456.7	29912.8	13098.7	66175.3	66726.3	3733.9	39394.5	15400.3
5096.6	104211.6	96025.9	-1495.3	135289.1	135026.9	5975.4	117687.3	5819.0
338192.3	342578.8	163134.4	50886.5	87029.8	88222.7	20738.8	134586.4	94862.8
34017.7	289683.9	213795.6	122906.4	165312.9	183915.3	36618.7	136319.7	29226.5
8950.6	197693.8	102400.0	664.2	92328.7	67366.7	12881.6	112325.7	37985.4
58.3	3987.1	924.2	604.8	143.3	695.5	31.5	1444.3	270.4
465.4	9141.1	6296.1	2433.1	1845.0	2313.7	532.4	3479.4	2553.3
499326.6	1044402.1	686894.0	211129.2	636795.5	643409.6	106807.4	631054.9	228673.3
110.7	2107.5	3094.6	1221.3	-3635.4	-1299.8	13.7	24736.0	175.1
470408.7	519894.0	325401.3	119401.5	464328.7	458411.7	62037.1	361905.5	150674.7
1812.6	38716.9	40247.9	21660.9	40301.2	41158.2	17544.0	26927.1	-48230.6
26994.6	483683.7	318150.2	68845.5	135801.0	145139.5	27212.6	217486.3	126054.1
1367.5	81929.2	59501.2	-4088.3	37605.8	37661.2	5490.0	33912.0	4203.3
354.6	8800.5	4935.8	597.5	4197.4	4368.5	844.2	3472.5	1140.7

15-4 续表 continued

指标名称	Indicator	法人企业数（个） Number of Corporation Enterprises (unit)	主营业务收入 Revenue from Principal Business	营业成本 Cost of Business
二、零售业	Retail Trade	863	10725306.2	9457236.2
综合零售	Integrated Retail	67	1988514.4	1728096.5
食品、饮料及烟草制品专门零售	Retail of Food, Beverages and Tobaccos	87	323388.8	246121.3
纺织、服装及日用品专门零售	Special Retail of Textiles, Garments and Daily Consumer Articles	67	641971.7	439524.2
文化、体育用品及器材专门零售	Retail of Culture, Sports Appliances and Equipments	51	401795.0	324193.6
医药及医疗器材专门零售	Retail of Medicines and Medical Appliances	56	491942.1	379970.0
汽车、摩托车、零配件和燃料及其他动力销售	Cars, Motorcycles, Spare Part and Fuel and Other Power Sales	341	5163709.7	4846611.4
家用电器及电子产品专门零售	Special Retail of Household Electric Appliances and Electronic Products	123	1066750.2	976423.1
五金、家具及室内装饰材料专门零售	Special Retail of Hardware, Furniture and Decoration Materials	30	156179.4	120279.6
货摊、无店铺及其他零售业	Non-shop and Other Retails	41	491054.9	396016.5
内资企业	Domestic Funded Enterprises	845	9737655.1	8650874.6
国有企业	State-owned	5	45100.4	35075.7
集体企业	Collective-owned	8	18105.9	16200.4
股份合作企业	Cooperative Enterprises	4	12316.6	10773.7
联营企业	Joint Ownership Enterprises			
有限责任公司	Limited Liability Corporations	251	3431796.0	3099907.4
股份有限公司	Share-holding Corporations Limited	21	1359486.5	1142276.4
私营企业	Private Enterprises	555	4869729.0	4346404.9
其他企业	Other Enterprises	1	1120.7	236.1
港、澳、台商投资企业	Enterprises with Funds from Hong Kong, Macao and Taiwan	8	477453.3	390414.9
外商投资企业	Foreign Funded Enterprises	10	510197.8	415946.7

税金及附加 Taxes and Surcharges	销售费用 Cost of Sales	管理费用 Cost of Management	财务费用 Cost of Finance	营业利润 Profits from Business	利润总额 Total Profits	所得税费用 Income Tax Expense	应付职工薪酬（本年贷方累计发生额） Total Wages Payable	应交增值税 Value-added Tax Payable
58966.6	902467.7	320360.3	101723.1	136544.9	144895.0	40527.6	450310.4	170300.8
13761.0	239009.2	68309.8	46639.7	37901.7	39949.4	9730.6	118871.9	27678.2
692.4	34165.0	12467.2	1550.7	12448.6	15513.0	3386.7	15437.3	6301.5
19915.7	126452.6	27186.1	4296.4	32256.1	31928.9	8866.4	28126.9	26474.2
4412.0	44921.0	14764.9	1228.6	14123.5	15420.3	2453.4	33677.9	4731.0
1946.1	88929.0	24411.5	336.2	8781.0	9318.5	2737.4	53472.0	6627.1
11256.0	212160.0	122405.7	43464.2	18091.7	19413.2	13676.8	141929.8	80637.9
2239.6	66971.4	22151.6	2140.6	-2441.2	-2296.2	249.5	23180.7	8332.0
985.2	13243.8	13995.9	1949.0	3776.7	3960.1	-994.0	8365.8	3203.7
3758.6	76615.7	14667.6	117.7	11606.8	11687.8	420.8	27248.1	6315.2
36946.0	806107.2	281252.7	97845.3	95230.6	103820.2	30478.7	417176.6	157863.5
184.8	5048.4	4470.5	137.1	603.6	841.8	24.0	4697.5	1344.3
36.5	742.8	1098.8	42.9	129.8	90.3	35.9	776.8	158.1
25.1	1281.7	209.7	16.4	17.6	25.5	15.5	524.1	146.6
13956.7	258615.4	97468.9	38679.1	16974.6	20312.7	13782.2	139041.5	55637.8
11346.8	180703.8	49977.6	40665.7	38877.2	40518.3	6973.4	99750.0	17781.4
11395.8	358977.3	128003.0	18303.9	38505.7	41909.5	9647.7	172248.2	82795.3
0.3	737.8	24.2	0.2	122.1	122.1		138.5	
20285.8	27767.6	7532.9	501.0	40366.8	39999.8	10251.1	12053.5	5113.5
1734.8	68592.9	31574.7	3376.8	947.5	1075.0	-202.2	21080.3	7323.8

15-5 限额以上餐饮业主要经济指标(2019 年)
Main Economic Indicators of Enterprises in Catering Trades Above Designated Size (2019)

指标名称	Indicator	法人企业数(个) Number of Corporation Enterprises (unit)	资产总计 Total Assests	负债合计 Total Liabilities	所有者权益 Creditors' Equity
总计	Total	284	552476.2	532510.0	19651.5
正餐服务	Dinner service	229	453149.9	451564.0	1403.5
快餐服务	Fast Food Service	40	71165.6	65880.1	5228.7
饮料及冷饮服务	Beverages and Cold Drinks Service				
餐饮配送及外卖送餐服务	Catering Distribution and Takeaway service	8	17823.3	5435.2	12378.1
其他餐饮业	Other Catering Services	7	10337.4	9630.7	641.2
内资企业	Domestic Funded Enterprises	282	526169.9	492826.6	32690.7
国有企业	State-owned	12	32937.8	33358.9	-421.1
集体企业	Collective-owned	1	1032.5	347.5	685.0
股份合作企业	Cooperative Enterprises	1	1176.7	287.3	889.4
联营企业	Joint Ownership Enterprises				
有限责任公司	Limited Liability Corporations	75	267040.6	247226.7	19742.0
股份有限公司	Share-holding Corporations Limited	4	3429.0	3860.7	-431.7
私营企业	Private Enterprises	189	220553.3	207745.5	12227.1
其他企业	Other Enterprises				
港、澳、台商投资企业	Enterprises with Funds from Hong Kong, Macao and Taiwan	2	26306.3	39683.4	-13039.2
外商投资企业	Foreign Funded Enterprises				

单位：万元 (10 000 yuan)

其中 of which 实收资本 Paid-up Capital	主营业务收入 Revenue from Principal Business	营业成本 Cost of Business	销售费用 Expenses on Business	管理费用 Expenses on Management	财务费用 Expenses on Finance	营业利润 Profits from Business	利润总额 Total Profits	应付职工薪酬（本年贷方累计发生额）Total Wages Payable
397459.4	429376.1	207077.6	140755.6	85948.0	10757.9	-12825.3	-10028.3	102401.8
377532.3	304744.0	134639.1	104997.7	76340.7	9619.7	-18889.8	-16482.2	77470.5
13484.5	83879.8	41032.2	32963.8	6187.7	1098.9	2920.8	3101.8	20582.9
5772.4	36323.3	28054.7	1997.3	3060.0	23.6	3245.6	3450.1	3044.2
670.2	4429.0	3351.6	796.8	359.6	15.7	-101.9	-98.0	1304.2
394976.0	394320.2	195962.1	121136.7	84238.6	9622.4	-14107.6	-11210.2	91199.8
6010.0	16499.1	4389.1	7886.1	7650.7	228.4	-3050.4	-2009.2	4690.3
300.0	1061.3	549.4	166.3	219.9	110.6	0.2	3.7	354.6
876.8	1252.4	375.3	385.3	503.8		-16.8	-8.7	406.1
40708.7	168588.9	92899.2	47574.9	33446.7	3986.9	-8236.2	-7040.8	37016.7
210.0	6312.8	2805.3	1676.5	1642.9	81.5	20.2	49.6	1249.5
346870.5	200605.7	94943.8	63447.6	40774.6	5215.0	-2824.6	-2204.8	47482.6
2483.4	35055.9	11115.5	19618.9	1709.4	1135.5	1282.3	1181.9	11202.0

15-6 限额以上住宿业主要经济指标(2019年)

Main Economic Indicators of Enterprises in Quartering Trades Above Designated Size(2019)

指标名称	Indicator	法人企业数(个) Number of Corporation Enterprises (unit)	资产总计 Total Assests	负债合计 Total Liabilities	所有者权益 Owners' Equity
总计	Total	153	751973.9	602831.0	147055.6
旅游饭店	Tourist Hotels	54	556152.2	379285.5	175993.7
一般旅馆	General Hotels	85	184960.3	204460.0	-20642.0
民宿服务	Home Lodging Services				
露营地服务	Campground Services				
其他住宿业	Other Accommodation Services	14	10861.4	19085.5	-8296.1
内资企业	Domestic Funded Enterprises	150	734914.2	579012.6	153814.3
国有企业	State-owned	14	222314.5	95795.7	125869.6
集体企业	Collective-owned	2	8685.4	8514.1	171.3
股份合作企业	Cooperative Enterprises	2	13364.3	11402.8	1961.5
联营企业	Joint Ownership Enterprises				
有限责任公司	Limited Liability Corporations	43	204895.1	206763.3	-3154.0
股份有限公司	Share-holding Corporations Ltd.	5	2371.4	1344.9	1026.5
私营企业	Private Enterprises	84	283283.5	255191.8	27939.4
其他企业	Other Enterprises				
港、澳、台商投资企业	Enterprises with Funds from Hong Kong, Macao and Taiwan	3	17059.7	23818.4	-6758.7
外商投资企业	Foreign Funded Enterprises				

单位：万元 (10 000 yuan)

其中 of which 实收资本 Paid-up Capital	主营业务收入 Revenue from Principal Business	营业成本 Cost of Business	销售费用 Expenses on Business	管理费用 Expenses on Management	财务费用 Expenses on Finance	营业利润 Profits from Business	利润总额 Total Profits	应付职工薪酬（本年贷方累计发生额）Total Wages Payable
112751.3	325135.5	98643.0	146763.5	83734.2	5609.3	-474.6	5575.4	90086.5
72543.0	196528.8	66949.2	81308.5	51408.6	3321.7	2262.7	9450.4	61017.4
37645.1	110901.9	26299.1	57192.9	28563.8	1751.1	-2448.6	-3601.9	25061.7
2563.2	17704.8	5394.7	8262.1	3761.8	536.5	-288.7	-273.1	4007.4
108165.7	317861.4	97652.6	143782.7	80515.3	5622.7	-232.1	5791.9	87656.1
39442.4	72756.2	22093.5	37357.1	23639.8	-1344.0	-2463.8	4795.1	25100.3
1883.4	3661.0	1030.8	2053.5	706.8	17.4	-133.6	-130.7	1449.1
1416.4	4902.6	2379.1	1300.7	1243.6	10.9	-53.6	-37.7	964.0
29089.2	152534.5	38581.5	73769.7	34208.2	3223.5	347.1	-1004.3	45453.2
761.0	2870.2	622.2	1864.8	432.2	35.7	-150.8	-158.0	819.9
35573.3	81136.9	32945.5	27436.9	20284.7	3679.2	2222.6	2327.5	13869.6
4585.6	7274.1	990.4	2980.8	3218.9	-13.4	-242.5	-216.5	2430.4

15-7 限额以上住宿业和餐饮业法人企业经营情况(2019年)
Main Economic Indicators of Enterprises in Quartering Trades and Cataring Trades Above Designated Size(2019)

指标名称	Indicator	法人企业数(个) Number of Corporation Enterprises (unit)	从业人员期末人数(人) Engaged Persons at Year-end (person)	营业额(万元) Business Revenue (10 000yuan)
总计	Total	437	37111	795936.0
一、住宿业	Hotels	153	15392	342571.3
旅游饭店	Tourist Hotels	54	9067	209092.2
一般旅馆	General Hotels	85	5526	115025.3
民宿服务	Home Lodging Services			
露营地服务	Campground Services			
其他住宿业	Other Accommodation Services	14	799	18453.8
内资企业	Domestic Funded Enterprises	150	15012	334886.4
国有企业	State-owned	14	3502	76691.3
集体企业	Collective-owned	2	241	3916.2
股份合作企业	Cooperative Enterprises	2	221	5072.4
联营企业	Joint Ownership Enterprises			
有限责任公司	Limited Liability Corporations	43	7933	160873.5
股份有限公司	Share-holding Corporations Ltd.	5	159	2942.3
私营企业	Private Enterprises	84	2956	85390.7
其他企业	Other Enterprises			
港、澳、台商投资企业	Enterprises with Funds from Hong Kong, Macao and Taiwan	3	380	7684.9
外商投资企业	Foreign Funded Enterprises			
二、餐饮业	Catering Services	284	21719	453364.7
正餐服务	Dinner Service	229	15815	315274.1
快餐服务	Fast Food Service	40	4940	93139.4
饮料及冷饮服务	Beverages and Cold Drinks Service			
餐饮配送及外卖送餐服务	Catering Distribution and Takeaway Service	8	676	40638.4
其他餐饮业	Other Catering Services	7	288	4312.8
内资企业	Domestic Funded Enterprises	282	18549	416202.5
国有企业	State-owned	12	1354	15966.2
集体企业	Collective-owned	1	85	1128.0
股份合作企业	Cooperative Enterprises	1	85	1325.6
联营企业	Joint Ownership Enterprises			
有限责任公司	Limited Liability Corporations	75	6929	180493.5
股份有限公司	Share-holding Corporations Ltd.	4	308	6589.0
私营企业	Private Enterprises	189	9788	210700.2
其他企业	Other Enterprises			
港、澳、台商投资企业	Enterprises with Funds from Hong Kong, Macao and Taiwan	2	3170	37162.2
外商投资企业	Foreign Funded Enterprises			

其中 of which				客房数（间）Number of Room (room)	床位数（个）Number of Beds (bed)	餐位数（位）Number of Dining-seats (seat)	年末餐饮营业面积（平方米）Business Area of Catering Services at Year-end (sq.m)
客房收入 From Hotel Rooms	餐费收入 From Meals	商品销售收入 Revenue from Commodities	其他收入 Other Revenue				
241601.0	474458.2	16763.8	63113.0	41404	63408	170034	1180645.0
177688.7	107756.6	7454.2	49671.8	31050	45597	37231	514491.0
85326.5	83373.2	5888.8	34503.7	9278	15017	23388	257748.0
80264.6	18612.0	1485.0	14663.7	20098	28108	12554	217227.0
12097.6	5771.4	80.4	504.4	1674	2472	1289	39516.0
174006.8	105793.2	7454.2	47632.2	30452	44617	36251	510391.0
28752.9	36261.9	3698.0	7978.5	2492	4097	7994	67134.0
1627.6	2250.6		38.0	392	718	2100	7707.0
1647.1	3195.8	5.5	224.0	297	570	800	3200.0
86479.2	45086.1	2823.6	26484.6	14906	22665	18655	266092.0
2583.5	199.0	20.3	139.5	664	1088	216	9176.0
52916.5	18799.8	906.8	12767.6	11701	15479	6486	157082.0
3681.9	1963.4		2039.6	598	980	980	4100.0
63912.3	366701.6	9309.6	13441.2	10354	17811	132803	666154.0
63912.3	234291.6	4545.6	12524.6	10354	17811	111025	589628.0
	90591.2	2353.8	194.4			20305	60761.0
	37530.0	2387.2	721.2				9600.0
	4288.8	23.0	1.0			1473	6165.0
63912.3	329539.4	9309.6	13441.2	10354	17811	125896	638222.0
7327.3	8330.8	88.9	219.2	1451	2698	6244	48415.0
361.2	766.8			118	240	500	7000.0
750.4	558.5	12.8	3.9	76	140	380	1000.0
20153.7	147051.6	4554.9	8733.3	3085	5227	55632	266307.0
1276.7	5228.1		84.2	245	320	1560	7700.0
34043.0	167603.6	4653.0	4400.6	5379	9186	61580	307800.0
	37162.2					6907	27932.0

15-8 商品交易市场分类情况(2019年)
Free Markets in Urban and Rural Areas(2019)

单位：个 (unit)

指标	Indicator	合计 Total	其中 of which 城市 Urban	农村 Rural
商品交易市场个数总计(个)	Total Number of Commodity Transaction Market	425	251	174
消费品市场	Consumer Products Markets	356	203	153
消费品综合市场	Consumer Products Comprehensive Markets	34	12	22
农副产品市场	Farmer Produces Markets	207	82	125
农副产品综合市场	Farmer Produces Comprehensive Markets	165	66	99
农副产品专业市场	Farmer Produces Special Markets	52	26	26
工业消费品市场	Industrial Consumer Products Markets	111	106	5
工业消费品综合市场	Industrial Consumer Products Comprehensive Markets	84	81	3
工业消费品专业市场	Industrial Consumer Products Special Markets	27	25	2
其他	Others	4	3	1
生产资料市场	Means of Production Markets	69	48	21
生产资料综合市场	Means of Production Comprehensive Markets	10	3	7
工业生产资料市场	Industrial Production Markets	40	32	8
农业生产资料市场	Agricultural Production Markets	10	4	6
农业生产资料综合市场	Agricultural Production Comprehensive Markets	6	2	4
农业生产资料专业市场	Agricultural Production Special Markets	4	2	2
其他	Others	9	9	

15-9 销售过亿元的商品交易市场一览表（2019 年）

Summary of Consumer Goods Markets with Annual Transaction Value Above 100 Million Rmb Yuan(2019)

市场名称 Name	市场类别 Category	年末营业面积（平方米） Operating Area at Year-End (sq.m)	市场总摊位（个） Number of ooths (unit)	年成交额（万元） Annual Turnover (10 000 yuan)
济南海鲜大市场	水产品市场	30000	1200	390000
济南市新世界商城	工业消费品综合市场	27850	1067	88270
济南西市场小商品批发市场	工业消费品综合市场	26000	620	11280
济南博茗茶叶市场	茶叶市场	82000	680	185300
山东匡山汽车大世界	汽车市场	130000	71	267510
山东匡山农产品综合交易市场	蔬菜市场	21000	793	233246
山东匡山钢材市场	金属材料市场	10000	60	22000
山东老屯汽车配件城	机动车零配件市场	35000	489	26750
山东老屯茶城	茶叶市场	8000	120	12020
槐荫区红旗钢材市场	金属材料市场	35000	112	77920
山东齐鲁鞋城	鞋帽市场	19176	768	102100
济南众鑫鞋城	鞋帽市场	38765	698	90354
济南市堤口路果品批发市场	干鲜果品市场	110000	220	107784
济南中恒商场	工业消费品综合市场	71665	2195	52767
济南红星美凯龙世博家居生活广场	家具市场	97741	497	185900
济南黄台家居广场	家具市场	15000	200	20000
山东东亚金星家居	家具市场	69300	530	36000
济南泺口服装批发市场	服装市场	200000	2770	207688
山东济南重汽配件城	机动车零配件市场	61938	435	220000
七里堡蔬菜综合批发市场	农产品综合市场	150000	1800	356200
山东济南维尔康肉类水产综合批发市场	水产品市场	200000	1000	2275045
济南金田义乌小商品交易市场	小商品市场	45000	1500	115490
济南市章丘区刁镇蔬菜批发市场	蔬菜市场	40600	600	159380
济南曲堤蔬菜销售市场	蔬菜市场	23310	105	28015
商河县小商品批发城	工业消费品综合市场	19000	300	20935
商河县富东农贸综合市场	农产品综合市场	27000	525	24914

主要统计指标解释

社会消费品零售总额 指企业（单位、个体户）通过交易直接售给个人、社会集团非生产、非经营用的实物商品金额，以及提供餐饮服务所取得的收入金额。个人包括城乡居民和入境人员，社会集团包括机关、社会团体、部队、学校、企事业单位、居委会或村委会等。

商品销售额 指对本单位以外的单位和个人出售的商品金额（包括售给本单位消费用的商品，含增值税），在批发和零售业中，本指标反映在国内市场上销售商品以及出口商品的总价。

商品销售包括：（1）售给个人和社会集团消费用的商品；（2）售给农业、工业、建筑业、服务业等国民经济各行业用于生产、经营用的商品，包括售予批发和零售业作为转卖或加工后转卖的商品；（3）对国（境）外直接出口的商品。

商品销售不包括：（1）未通过买卖行为付出的商品，如因机构变动移交给其他企业单位的商品、借出的商品、归还受其他单位委托代保管的商品、付出的加工原料和赠送给其他单位的样品等;（2)促销返券所销售的、不计入营业收入的商品;（3）经本单位介绍，由买卖双方直接结算，本单位只收取手续费的业务；（4）未发生所有权转移的商品预付卡销售，如加油卡；（5）汽车维修、电话卡销售等服务性经济活动；（6）购货退回的商品；（7）商品损耗和损失；（8）出售本单位自用的废旧物资；（9）期货交易商品；（10）自来水供应企业、电力企业、天然气供应企业提供的水、电、气。

批发额 指售给国民经济各行业用于生产、经营用的商品金额。

商品批发包括：（1）售给农业、工业、建筑业等行业用于生产的各种机器设备、工具、原料、材料、燃料、建筑材料，售给农民的农业生产资料，售给交通运输、仓储和邮政业用于业务活动的设备、车辆和燃料等；（2）售给信息传输、软件和信息技术服务，科学研究和技术服务业，水利、环境和公共设施管理业等行业用于生产经营、勘察设计、科研试验等业务经营使用的商品，售给批发和零售业、住宿和餐饮业使用的各种设备、工具、原材料、燃料、仓储运输用的商品；（3）售给居民服务、修理和其他服务业各种营业用品，如售给理发业的理发工具、毛巾等，日用品修理业的设备、工具、材料、零配件等，售给民政部门救灾用的商品等；（4）售给批发和零售业作为转卖用的商品；售给餐饮业用于烹饪、调制加工后出售的商品和转卖的商品；售给服务业转卖的商品；（5）出口的商品。

零售额 指售给个人用于生活消费和社会集团用于公共消费的商品金额。

商品零售包括：（1）售给城乡居民和入境外国人、华侨、港澳台同胞的各类生活消费品；（2）售给行政事业单位、社会团体、军队和武警等机构的商品，以及以零售方式售给各类企业的商品。具体包括：用于非生产和社会交往的办公用品，如通讯设备、计算器具和设备、电讯网络设备、文印设备、音像视听器材和设备、纸张、本册、文具及装订文印材料、家具、日用电器、针纺织品、清洁卫生用品、文体用品、奖品、纪念品、礼品等；供内部人员乘坐的交通工具和燃料；用于办公设施修缮的各类配件、材料、工具等；用于取暖和防暑降温的设备、燃料、材料及食品等；专用于教学的用品和设备；非专用的劳动保护用品；不对外营业的内部食堂用的餐具、炊具、设备、清洁卫生工具和食品、燃料等；军队、武警用于其人员生活的衣着品和个人用品；其他各类非生产性设备和用品。

商品零售不包括：（1）售给城乡居民已确知是用于生产、经营的商品；（2）售给各类农业生产者的生产资料类商品，如农机、农药化肥、农膜、种子饲料等商品；（3）售给企业单位生产用具及生产上专用的劳动保护用品；（4）专用于科研的用品和设备；（5）售给医疗机构的中、西药品、中药材和医疗设备器材；（6）以投资为目的的商品，如黄金、收藏品等。

住宿餐饮业营业额 指住宿和餐饮业单位在经营活动中，因提供服务或销售商品等取得的全部收入（含增值税），收入主要来源于提供客房、餐费服务、商品销售和其他服务，如商务服务。不包括多产业法人企业附营的其他行业产业活动单位的餐费收入、商品销售收入等各项收入。

Explanatory Notes on Main Statistical Indicators

Total Retail Sales of Consumer Goods refer to the amount obtained by enterprises (units, self–employed individuals) through the direct sales of non–production & non–business physical commodity to individuals, social institutions, and the revenue from providing catering services. Individuals include rural and urban households, population from abroad, social institutions include government agencies, social organizations, military units, schools, institutions. neighborhood or village committees.

Total Sales of Commodities refers to value of commodities sold by the establishments to other establishments and individuals (including commodities sold to their own establishments for consumption, including VAT). This indicator is used to show the total value of sales of commodities at domestic markets and export.

The commodities includes: (1) commodities sold to urban and rural residents and social groups for their consumption; (2) commodities sold to establishments in agriculture, industry, construction, service and various sectors of national economy for their production and operation, including commodities sold to wholesale and retail establishments for re–selling with or without further processing; (3) commodities for directing export to other countries.

Commodities exclude: (1) Commodities given not based on purchase and sale activities, such as commodities handed over to other enterprises due to the change in the institution, commodities lent, commodities which are kept by other unit based on entrustment returned, raw materials for processing given and samples given away to other units; (2) Commodities sold based on promotion coupons and not included into operating income; (3) Businesses introduced by the unit based on direct settlement by the buyer and the seller for which the unit only charges for the service charges; (4) Sales of the prepaid card of commodities without transfer of ownership (such as oil filling card); (5) Service economic activities such as vehicle maintenance and repair and sales of phone card; (6) Commodities returned; (7) Commodity loss and damage; (8) Sale of self–used waste and old materials of the unit; (9) Futures trading commodity; (10) Water, electricity and gas provided by the tap water supply enterprise, the power enterprise and the natural gas supply enterprise.

Wholesale Amount refers to the amount of commodities sold to all industries of national economy for production and operation.

The wholesale includes: (1) Various machines and equipment, tools, raw materials, materials, fuel and building materials sold to agriculture, industry and construction industry, etc. for production as well as equipment, vehicles and fuel sold to transportation, warehousing and mail business for business activities; (2) Commodities sold to information transmission, software and information technology services, scientific research and technological services, water conservancy, environment and public facilities management for production, operation, survey and design, scientific research and test, various equipment, tools, raw materials and fuel sold to the wholesale and retail and accommodation and catering industries for use as well as commodities for warehousing and transportation; (3) Various operating supplies sold to neighborhood services, repair and other service industries, such as barber tools and towels sold to the hairdressing industry; equipment, tools, materials and spare and accessory parts for the commodity repair industry and commodities sold to the civil administration department for relieving the victims of a disaster; (4) Commodities sold to wholesale and retail industries for reselling; commodities sold to the catering industry for cooking, selling after processing and reselling; commodities sold to the service industry for reselling; (5) Exported commodities.

Retail Sales refer to the amount of commodities sold to individuals for living consumption and social groups for public consumption.

Commodity retail includes: (1) Various consumer goods sold to urban and rural residents, inbound foreigners, overseas Chinese and compatriots from Hong Kong, Macao and Taiwan; (2) Commodities sold to such institutions as administrative institution, social organization, army and armed police as well as commodities sold to various enterprises in the form of retails. Specifically include: Office supplies not for production and social interaction, such as communication equipment, calculation appliances and equipment, telecommunication network equipment, printing equipment, audio–visual devices and equipment, paper, books, stationery, binding and printing materials, furniture, household electrical appliance, knitwear and textile, sanitary articles, stationery and sporting goods, prizes, souvenirs and presents; communication media for internal personnel and fuel; various accessories, materials and tools for repair of office facilities; equipment, fuel, materials and food for heating and heatstroke prevention; supplies and equipment for teaching; non–special labor protection appliances; tableware, cooking utensils, equipment, cleaning and sanitation tools, food and fuel for internal canteen only; clothing and personal belongings for personnel from the army and armed police living; all other kinds of nonproductive equipment and supplies.

Commodity retail excludes: (1) Commodities sold to urban and rural residents, having been confirmed to be used for production and operation; (2) Means of production (such as agricultural machinery, pesticide and fertilizer, agricultural film and seed feed) sold to various agricultural producers; (3) Production equipment sold to enterprises and special labor protection articles for production; (4) Supplies and equipment for scientific research; (5) Traditional Chinese and Western medicines, traditional Chinese medicinal materials, and medical equipment and supply sold to medical establishments; (6) Commodities for investment, such as gold and collection.

Sales Revenue of Accommodation and Catering industry refers to the total revenue (included VAT) received by accommodation and catering industries from services provided and goods sold, where the main sources are: guest rooms provided, catering services, goods sold and other services such as business services, other than catering income, goods sold income or income from other activities of other industry activity units additive by multi–industry corporate enterprises.

16

对外贸易与国际旅游

FOREIGN TRADE AND INTERNATIONAL TOURISM

16-1 海关进出口商品总额
Total Value of Imports and Exports by Category of Commodities

单位：万美元 (10 000 USD)

指 标	Indicator	2019 年进出口总额 Total Value of Imports and Exports in 2019	其中 of which 出 口 Export	其中 of which 进 口 Import	2018 年进出口总额 Total Value of Imports and Exports in 2018	其中 of which 出 口 Export	其中 of which 进 口 Import
总 额	**Total**	1630123	935059	695064	1318209	855090	463119
按贸易方式分	**By Trade**						
一般贸易	General Trade	1457574	849750	607824	1163296	740340	422956
援助物资	Aid Material	530	530	0	–	–	–
捐赠物资	Donation Material				–	–	–
补偿贸易	Compensation Trade				–	–	–
来料加工装配贸易	Processing and Assembling Trade with Sent Materials	2324	1566	758	2750	1770	980
进料加工贸易	Processing Trade with Imported Materials	54384	42618	11767	63425	48804	14622
对外承包工程出口货物	Export of Contracted Projects	10755	10755	0	50279	50279	0
投资设备	Investment Goods	252	0	252	603	–	603
出料加工贸易	Export Processing Trade				–	–	–
海关特殊监管区域进口设备	**Import of Equipment in Special Customs Supervision Area**	0	0	0	95	–	95
海关特殊监管区域物流货物	**Logistics Freight of Equipment in Special Customs Supervision Area**	43517	10626	32892	8852	2473	6379
易货贸易	Barter Trade				–	–	–
保税监管场所进出境货物	**Bonded Supervision Entry and Exit Goods**	49387	15078	34309	26940	10030	16910
来料加工装配进口设备	Imported Equipment for Processing Incoming Materials					–	–
租赁贸易	Leasing Trade	2862	0	2862	–	–	–
其他贸易	Other Trade	8538	4136	4402	838	265	573
按运输方式分	**By Ways of Transport**						
水路运输	Waterway Transport	1117942	774128	343814	932819	698290	234529
铁路运输	Railway Transport	22864	16055	6809	15897	10611	5285
公路运输	Road Transport	286356	47033	239323	187772	44792	142980
航空运输	Air Transport	192414	94118	98296	181597	101326	80271
邮件运输	Mail Transport	7504	3586	3918	47	10	37
其他运输	Others	3044	139	2904	77	61	16
按企业性质分	**By Natural of Enterprises**						
国有企业	State-owned Enterprises	356339	56857	299483	269741	61894	207847
集体企业	Collective-owned Enterprises	72921	21843	51078	22820	21906	913
外商投资企业	Foreign Funded Enterprises	327203	248186	79017	306258	218474	87785
中外合资	Joint-venture Enterprises	114539	74860	39679	106127	75603	30524
中外合作	Cooperation Enterprises	1203	1202	2	597	551	46
外商独资	Wholly Foreign-owned Enterprises	211460	172124	39336	199535	142320	57214
其 他	Others	7606	3539	4067	719389	552815	166574

16-2 主要国别(地区)海关进出口商品总额
Total Value of Imports and Exports of Main Countries or Territories by Categoty of Commodities

单位：万美元 (10 000 USD)

国别(地区)	Country (region)	2019年进出口总值 Total Value of Imports and Exports in 2019	其中 of which		2018年进出口总值 Total Value of Imports and Exports in 2018	其中 of which	
			出口 Export	进口 Import		出口 Export	进口 Import
总　额	Total	1630123	935059	695064	1318209	855090	463119
亚　洲	Asia	766032	432213	333818	587966	379039	208927
香 港	Hong kong	14771	14614	158	12382	11306	1076
印 度	India	54548	40061	14486	39895	35204	4692
印度尼西亚	Indonesia	29840	24735	5105	66731	59207	7525
日 本	Japan	80069	49571	30498	61049	44098	16950
马来西亚	Malaysia	117718	23333	94385	66735	20138	46597
巴基斯坦	Pakistan	13441	13417	24	8517	8396	121
菲律宾	Philippines	49009	41799	7209	37277	32594	4683
卡塔尔	Katar	2398	2078	320	1905	1143	762
沙特阿拉伯	Saudi Arabia	15022	8522	6500	11458	5309	6150
新加坡	Singapore	20787	15405	5382	31746	22805	8942
韩 国	Repulic of Korea	46904	33242	13662	38631	27410	11221
泰 国	Thailand	80849	13367	67482	74476	13062	61414
土耳其	Kurtey	8388	8161	226	7832	7680	151
阿拉伯联合酋长国	The United Arab Emirates	15480	13071	2409	10489	8095	2394
越 南	Vietnam	38424	34352	4072	19388	17754	1634
台湾省	Taiwan	40203	13324	26879	18681	10804	7877
非　洲	Africa	126353	123112	3241	117829	112174	5655
埃 及	Egypt	5845	5828	17	4581	4572	9
南 非	South Africa	9028	7908	1120	12492	8856	3636
尼日利亚	Nigeria	25614	25614	0	17761	17760	1

16–2 续表 continued

国别（地区）	Country (region)	2019 年进出口总值 Total Value of Imports and Exports in 2019	其中 of which 出口 Export	进口 Import	2018 年进出口总值 Total Value of Imports and Exports in 2018	其中 of which 出口 Export	进口 Import
欧　洲	**Europe**	274920	172065	102854	253350	140935	112415
比利时	Belgium	6670	5466	1204	5859	4663	1196
英　国	United Kingdom	19055	14832	4223	19406	11647	7759
德　国	Germany	68161	28037	40123	80690	24293	56398
法　国	France	17360	10480	6881	14796	10039	4757
意大利	Italy	17635	13038	4597	17212	13190	4022
荷　兰	Netherlands	16465	12737	3728	8592	6479	2113
西班牙	Spain	12876	10171	2706	9941	8434	1508
芬　兰	Finland	2900	2137	762	1622	1323	299
瑞　典	Sweden	10612	3006	7606	8246	2917	5329
瑞　士	Switzerland	7199	844	6355	5701	724	4976
俄罗斯	Russia	32780	29631	3149	26015	22227	3788
拉丁美洲	**Latin America**	141893	71717	70176	104765	63436	41329
阿根廷	Argentina	11334	4523	6811	6846	4226	2620
巴　西	Brazil	57719	15352	42367	32383	13720	18662
智　利	Chile	17035	6794	10241	19018	6376	12641
墨西哥	Mexico	14820	14296	524	13212	12872	340
北美洲	**North America**	184269	114435	69834	189906	140622	49284
加拿大	United States	43451	24333	19119	32309	22802	9508
美　国	Canada	139115	90079	49036	156999	117816	39183
大洋洲	**Oceanic**	132740	21517	111223	64361	18883	45478
澳大利亚	Australia	120155	15213	104943	52399	13780	38619
新西兰	New Zealand	9765	3488	6277	9231	2375	6856

16-3 海关进出口商品分类金额
Value of Imports and Exports by Category of Commodities

单位：万美元 (10 000 USD)

商品类别	Indicator	2019年		2018年	
		出口 Export	进口 Import	出口 Export	进口 Import
总额	Total	935059	695064	855090	463119
活动物；动物产品	Live Animals & Animal Products	348	39314	489	22849
活动物	Live Animals			0	0
肉及食用杂碎	Meat and Edible Met Offal		22504	0	9582
鱼、甲壳动物、软体动物及其他水生无脊椎动物	Fish,Crustacean,Mollusc and Other Aquatic Invertebrates	58	11809	80	9241
乳品；蛋品；天然蜂蜜；其他食用动物产品	Milk,Eggs,Natural Honey and Other Edible Animal Products	49	5001	55	4023
其他动物产品	Other Animal Products	241		354	4
植物产品	Plant Products	59523	11482	4401	4075
活树及其他活植物；鳞茎、根及类似品；插花及装饰用簇叶	Plant,Root,Flower Arrangement	9	69	3	55
食用蔬菜、根及块茎	Vegetable,Root and Tuber	33551	50	1725	58
食用水果及坚果；柑桔属水果或甜瓜的果皮	Fruit and Nut	14676	156	1732	439
咖啡、茶、马黛茶及调味香料	Coffee,Tea and Aromatic Flavouring	11175	987	766	98
谷物	Cereal		6467	2	0
制粉工业产品；麦芽；淀粉、菊粉；面筋	Powder Industrial Products,Starch ,Malt	2	19	15	174
含油子仁及果实；杂项子仁及果实；工业用或药用植物；	Industrial or Medical Plants		3693	90	3230
稻草、秸秆及饲料	Straw and Fodder	63		0	0
虫胶；树胶、树脂及其他植物液、汁	Gum,Resin and Other Juice from Plants	39	12	69	13
编结用植物材料；其他植物产品	Plant Material for Weaving	7	29	0	9
动、植物油、脂及其分解产品；精制的食用油脂；动、植物蜡	Animal and Vegetable Oils; Fats and Wax; Edible Oils and Fats	181	659	34	2749
动、植物油、脂及其分解产品；精制的食用油脂；动、植物蜡	Animal and Vegetable Oils; Fats and Wax;Edible Oils and Fats	181	659	34	2749
食品；饮料、酒及醋；烟草、烟草及烟草用品的制品	Food; Beverages; Liquor and Vinegar;Tobacco and Tobacco Substitutes	15701	7703	1953	4193
肉、鱼、甲壳动物、软体动物及其他水生无脊椎动物的制品	Meat,Fish Crustaceans,Mollusks and Other Aquatic Invertebrates		3	1	1
糖及糖食	Sugar and Sugar Products	104	113	105	37
可可及可可制品	Cocoa and Cocoa Products		77	0	6
谷物、粮食粉、淀粉或乳的制品；糕饼点心	Grain,Flour,Starch and Milk Products,Cakes	3356	9	99	19
蔬菜、水果、坚果或植物其他部分的制品	Vegetables,Fruits,Nuts Products	10126	1879	935	75
杂项食品	Miscellaneous Food	1722	2282	448	1354
饮料、酒及醋	Drink,Wine and Vinegar	44	3104	13	2273
食品工业的残渣及废料；配制的动物饲料	Food Industrial Waste,Animal Feed	349	236	352	428
烟草、烟草及烟草代用品的制品	Tobaccoa and Tobaccoa Products			0	0
矿产品	Minerals	338	166657	221	72805
盐；硫磺；泥土及石料；石膏料、石灰及水泥	Salt,Asaulfer,Stone,Cement	310	2307	96	624
矿砂、矿渣及矿灰	Ore,Slag,Ash	1	147516	1	59419
矿物燃料、矿物油及其蒸馏产品；沥青物质；矿物蜡	Fossil Fuels,Mineral Oil,Asphalt,Mineral Wax	27	16833	124	12762

16-3 续表 1 continued 1

商品类别	Indicator	2019年 出口 Export	2019年 进口 Import	2018年 出口 Export	2018年 进口 Import
化学工业及其相关工业的产品	Chemicals and Related Products	108608	7745	109403	7364
无机化学品；贵金属、稀土金属、放射性元素及其同位素的	Inorganic Chemical,Precious Metals,Radioactive Elements	3743	418	3508	398
有机及无机化合物	Organic and Inorganic Compounds				
有机化学品	Organic Chemicals	50485	2039	40449	2109
药 品	Drugs	21836	1242	24257	951
肥 料	Fertilizer	1465	40	3102	0
鞣料浸膏及染料浸膏；鞣酸及其衍生物；染料、颜料	Dye,Ink,Graphite	13787	632	17410	653
精油及香膏；芳香料制品及化妆盥洗品	Essential Ois and Ointments,Cosmetic	177	201	260	462
肥皂、有机表面活性剂、洗涤剂、润滑剂、人造蜡、调制蜡、光洁剂、蜡烛及类似品、塑料用膏、"牙科用蜡"及牙料用熟石膏制剂	Soap,Surfactant,Detergents,Lubrifiants,Cire Artificielle Candles,Plaster	833	318	986	279
蛋白类物质；改性淀粉；胶；酶	Protein,Starch,Glue,Enzymes	1344	86	1064	42
炸药；烟火制品；火柴；引火合金；易燃材料制品	Explosives,Matches,Flammable Materials	0		0	
照相及电影用品	Photographic and Film Supplies	11	3	18	1
杂项化学产品	Miscellaneous Chemical Products	14926	2766	18347	2470
塑料及其制品；橡胶及其制品	Plastics and Related Products;Rubber and Related Products	32576	21358	27305	21175
塑料及其制品	Plastics and Related Products	27317	18314	24310	19635
橡胶及其制品	Rubber and Related Products	5259	3044	2995	1540
生皮、皮革、毛皮及其制品；鞍具及挽具；旅行用品、手提包及类似容器、动物肠线（蚕胶丝除外）制品	Leather,fur Products,Saddle and Harness,Travel Acessories	4531	96	3969	32
生皮（毛皮除外）及皮革	Leather,Fur	15	30	4	4
皮革制品；鞍具及挽具；旅行用品、手提包及类似容器；动物肠线（蚕胶丝除外）制品	Fur Products,Saddle and Harness,Travel Acessories Animal Intestine Products	3199	65	2803	27
毛皮、人造毛皮及其制品	Leather,Artificial Fur and Its Products	1316	0	1163	1
木及木制品；木炭；软木及软木制品；稻草、秸秆、针茅或其他编结材料制品；蓝筐及柳条编结品	Wood and Wooden Products; Cork and Cork Products Straw and Other Woven Product	8319	1968	11084	3446
木及木制品；木炭	Wood and Wooden Products;	6466	1968	9346	3446
软木及软木制品	Cork and Cork Products	13		14	0
稻草、秸秆、针茅或其他编结材料制品；蓝筐及柳条编结品	Straw and Other Woven Product	1840	1	1724	0
木浆及其他纤维状纤维素浆；回收（废碎）纸或纸板；纸、纸板及其制品	Paper Pulp and Cellulose Pulp; Paper and Waste Paper; Paperboard and Related Products	4626	37442	3101	33005
木浆及其他纤维状纤维素浆；回收（废碎）纸或纸板	Paper Pulp and Other Cellulose Pulp; Recycling and Waste Paper or Paperboard	21	34277	17	29174
纸及纸板；纸浆、纸或纸板制品	Paper and Paperboard; Paper Pulp, Paper and Paper Products	4439	3095	2929	3804
书籍、报纸、印刷图画及其他印刷品；手稿、打字稿及设计图纸	Books,Newspapers,Print Paintings and other Products; Manuscripts, Typoscript and Design Drawings	166	70	154	27

16-3 续表 2 continued 2

商 品 类 别	Indicator	2019 年		2018 年	
		出 口 Export	进 口 Import	出 口 Export	进 口 Import
纺织原料及纺织制品	Textile Materials and Products	51026	2948	43444	3701
蚕 丝	Silk	0		13	0
羊毛、动物细毛或粗毛；马毛纱线及其机织物	Wool and Other Textile Materials	156	18	195	26
棉 花	Cotton	1039	1340	1016	1994
其他植物纺织纤维；纸纱线及其机织物	Other Vegetable Textile Fibers and Its Products	33	4	174	3
化学纤维长丝	Chemical Fiber Filament	3460	289	2170	249
化学纤维短纤	Chemical Fiber Staple	6856	465	4292	462
絮胎、毡呢及无纺织物；特种纱线；线、绳、索、缆及其制品	Wadding,Nonwoven Fabrics,Wire and Other Related Products	5911	215	5642	284
地毯及纺织材料的其他铺地制品	Carpet and Other Floor Covering Products	3404	21	2040	16
特种机织物；簇绒织物；花边；装饰毯；装饰带；刺绣品	Textile,Lace,Tapestry,Embroidery	454	102	640	161
浸渍、涂布、包覆或层压的纺织物；工业用纺织制品	Textile and Other Industrial Textile	1327	57	1244	21
针织物或钩编织物	Knitted Fabric	181	143	258	202
针织或钩编的服装及衣着附件	Accessory of Knitted Fabric	9610	124	10853	23
非针织或非钩编的服装及衣着附件	Accessory of Unknitted Fabric	9104	40	8149	42
其他纺织制成品；成套物品；旧衣着及旧纺织品；碎织物	Other Knitted Fabric,Pieces of Fabric	9490	130	6761	218
鞋、帽、伞、杖、鞭及其零件；已加工的羽毛及其制品；人造花；人发制品	Footwear; Headgear; Umbrellas; Canes;Whips;Feather and Wigs and Related Products	3844	32	3986	45
鞋靴、护腿和类似品及其零件	Shoes and Other Related Products	839	32	1293	42
帽类及其零件	Hats and Other Related Products	808	2	423	3
雨伞、阳伞、手杖、鞭子、马鞭及其零件	Umbrellas,Cane,Whip and Other Related Products	54	0	22	0
已加工羽毛、羽绒及其制品；人造花；人发制品	Feather and Wigs and Related Products	2143	0	2248	0
石料、石膏、水泥、石棉、云母及类似材料的制品；陶瓷产品；玻璃及其制品	Gypsum; Cement; Asbestos; Mica; Ceramic Glass and Its Products	25829	1153	24528	1760
石料、石膏、水泥、石棉、云母及类似材料的制品	Gypsum, Cement, Asbestos, Mica	7862	168	7740	194
陶瓷产品	Ceramic Products	3348	101	4016	655
玻璃及其制品	Glass and Its Products	14619	884	12772	911
天然或养殖珍珠、宝石或半宝石、贵金属、包贵金属及其制品；仿手饰；硬币	Pearls and Precious Stones;Precious Metal and Related Products; Artificial Jewelry	357	196	752	255
天然或养殖珍珠、宝石或半宝石、贵金属、包贵金属及其制品；仿手饰；硬币	Pearls and Precious Stones;Precious Metal and Related Products;Artificial Jewelry	357	196	752	255
贱金属及其制品	Base Metals and Related Products	123862	9866	116488	10044
钢 铁	Steel	29668	2306	13223	533
钢铁制品	Steel Products	75662	2400	84709	2815
铜及其制品	Coper and Related Products	2042	2099	3980	3981
镍及其制品	Nickel and Related Products	8	37	18	23

16-3 续表 3 continued 3

商 品 类 别	Indicator	2019 年		2018 年	
		出 口 Export	进 口 Import	出 口 Export	进 口 Import
铝及其制品	Aluminum and Related Products	12621	1946	11770	1714
铅及其制品	Plumbum and Related Products	2	5	2	3
锌及其制品	Zinc and Related Products	37	343	34	30
锡及其制品	Stannum and Related Products		0	0	0
其他贱金属、金属陶瓷及其制品	Other Base Metals,Metal Ceramic and Related Products	67	222	42	239
贱金属工具、器具、利口器、餐匙、餐叉及其零件	Base Metals Equipment,Tableware and Its Part	2423	325	1612	387
贱金属杂项制品	Base Metals Miscellaneous Products	1332	184	1099	320
机器、机械器具、电气设备及其零件;录音机及放声机、电视图像、声音的录制和重放设备及其零件、附件	**Machinery; Electric Equipment;TV Sets and Audio**	**267071**	**331497**	**309148**	**227510**
核反应堆、锅炉、机器、机械器具及其零件	Nuclear Reator,Boiler ,Machinery and Other Parts	195412	213531	236524	155376
电机、电气设备及其零件;录音机及放声机、电视图像、声音的录制和重放设备及其零件、附件	Electric Equipment and Its Part TV Sets and Audio and Its Part	71658	117966	72624	72134
车辆、航空器、船舶及有关运输设备	**Locomotives; Vehicles; Aircraft; Ship and Related Transportation Equipment**	**195151**	**11108**	**168611**	**12110**
铁道及电车道机车、车辆及其零件;铁道及电车道轨道固定装置及其零件、附件;各种机械(包括电动机械)交通信号设备	Railway and Vehicles and Its Part Machinery and Transportation Equipment	2092	473	4468	515
车辆及其零件、附件,但铁道及电车道车辆除外	Vehicles and Its Part	189357	1879	161708	8427
航空器、航空器及其零件	Aircraftand Its Part	2594	8670	1940	3123
船舶及浮动结构体	Ship and Floating Structures	1107	86	495	44
光学、照相、电影、计量、检验、医疗或外科用仪器及设备、精密仪器及设备;钟表;乐器;上述物品的零件、附件	**Photographic,Measuring and Medical Instruments and Equipment Presion Instrument and Machinery**	**11669**	**39012**	**11762**	**35451**
光学、照相、计量、检验、医疗或外科用仪器及设备、精密仪器及设备;上述物品的零件、附件	Photographic,Measuring and Medical Instruments and Equipment Presion Instrument and Machinery	10754	38964	10927	35253
钟表及其零件	Clock Equipment	76	48	35	49
乐器及其零件、附件	Musical Instruments Equipment	839	1	800	149
武器、弹药及其零件、附件	**Weapons and Ammunition; Related Parts and Accessories**	**0**		**84**	**0**
武器、弹药及其零件、附件	Weapons and Ammunition; Related Parts and Accessories			84	0
杂项制品	**Miscellaneous Products**	**17907**	**748**	**14290**	**543**
家具;寝具、褥垫、弹簧床垫、软坐垫及类似的填充制品	Furniture,Bedding,Mattess and other Lighting Equipment, Luminous Sign and Portakabin	10938	645	8603	439
		5424		0	0
玩具、游戏品、运动用品及其零件、附件	Toy,Game,Sports Products	1546	57	4093	46
杂项制品	Miscellaneous Products		46	1593	58
艺术品、收藏品及古物	**Works of Art, Collectibles and Antiques**	**33**	**1**	**19**	**1**
特殊交易品及未分类商品	**Special Transactions Goods and Products Not Otherwise Classified**	**3560**	**4075**	**18**	**6**

16-4 按企业性质分海关进出口商品总额 (2019 年)

Import and Export Value of Commodities by Ownership(2019)

单位：万美元 (10 000 USD)

指 标	Indicator	合 计 Total	国有企业 State-owned Enterprises	外商投资企业 Foreign Funded Nterprises				集体企业 Collective-owned Enterprises	其 他 Others
				小 计 Total	中外合作 Cooperation Enterprises	中外合资 Jointv-enture Enterprises	外商独资 Wholly Foreign-owned		
进口商品总额	Total Value of Imports	695064	299483	79017	2	39679	39336	51078	4067
一般贸易	General Trade	607824	296899	49764	2	12653	37109	50986	
来料加工装配贸易	Processing and Assembling Trade with Sent Materials	758		215		146	69	5	
进料加工贸易	Processing Trade with Imported Materials	11767	2307	3178		1475	1703		
租赁贸易	Leasing Trate	2862		2862		2862			
海关特殊监管区域进口设备	Import of Equipment in Special Customs Supervision Area	0.15		0.15			0.15		
海关特殊监管区域物流货物	Logistics Freight of Equipment in Special Customs Supervision Area	32892	35	146		11	135	87	
投资设备	Investment Goods	252		252			252		
保税监管场所进出境货物	Bonded Supervision Entry and Exit Goods	34309	161	22444		22444			
国际无偿援助和捐赠物资	International Aid and Material Donations								
其他贸易	Others	4402	81	155		88	68	0.20	4067
出口商品总值	Total Value of Exports	935059	56857	248186	1202	74860	172124	21843	3539
一般贸易	General Trade	849750	39904	215131	1202	52675	161255	21232	
国际无偿援助和捐赠物资	International Aid and Material Donations	530	334					196	
来料加工装配贸易	Processing and Assembling Trade with Sent Materials	1566		499		327	173		
进料加工贸易	Processing Trade with Imported Materials	42618	7608	14503		6735	7768	160	
对外承包工程出口货物	Export of Contracted projects	10755	7461					255	
保税监管场所进出境货物	Bonded Supervision Entry and Exit Goods	15078	15076			15076			
海关特殊监管区域物流货物	Logistics Freight of Equipment in Special Customs Supervision Area	10626	1313	2815		1	2814		
其他贸易	Others	4136	237	161		47	114	0.07	3539

16-5 历年海关进出口总额
Total Imports and Exports by Category(Customs Statistics)

单位：万美元（10 000 USD）

年份 Year	进出口总额 Total Value of Imports and Exports	进口总额 Total Value of Imports	出口总额 Total Value of Exports
1993	27446	21371	6075
1994	41746	23579	18167
1995	66587	29812	36775
1996	91347	48193	43154
1997	104230	52862	51368
1998	79943	45096	34847
1999	96125	60199	35926
2000	143935	86827	57108
2001	150143	90746	59397
2002	149264	79755	69509
2003	201554	117980	83545
2004	304678	167373	137305
2005	376213	198370	177843
2006	438930	194981	243949
2007	621804	278277	343527
2008	802699	342979	459720
2009	565704	260998	304706
2010	743776	338888	404888
2011	1041422	436966	604456
2012	913286	341844	571442
2013	957442	409126	548316
2014	1048867	442950	605917
2015	911424	311763	599661
2016	1086259	352229	734030
2017	1130449	379887	750562
2018	1318209	463119	855090
2019	1630123	695064	935059

16-6 利用外资情况
Utilization of Foreign Capital

指　标	Indicator	2014 年	2015 年	2016 年	2017 年	2018 年	2019 年
新批外商投资企业个数（个）	Newly established Foreign Investment Enterprises(unit)	78	104	104	110	239	228
外商直接投资	Foreign Direct Investments	78	104	104	110	239	228
合同外资金额（万美元）	Total Amount of Contracted Foreign Capita(10 000 USD)	187974	303100	179479	218692	556119	683441
外商直接投资	Foreign Direct Investments	187974	303100	179479	218692	556119	683441
实际使用外资（万美元）	Total Amount of Foreign Capital Actually Utilized(10 000 USD)	143497	157851	171625	187623	272847	224249
外商直接投资	Foreign Direct Investments	143497	157851	171625	187623	272847	224249

16-7 对外经济技术合作
Technological Cooperation with Foreign Countries or Territories

指　标	Indicator	单 位 Unit	2014 年	2015 年	2016 年	2017 年	2018 年	2019 年
对外承包和劳务合作合同金额	Foreign Contracted Projects and Service Contrate	万美元 (10 000 USD)	519758	530383	539589	539598	565706	573114
对外承包	Contracted Projects with Foreign Countries or Regions	万美元 (10 000 USD)	519758	530383	539589	539598	565706	573114
对外承包和劳务合作营业额	Foreign Contracted Projects and Service Contrate	万美元 (10 000 USD)	215461	308737	350099	373739	408427	408820
对外承包	Contracted Projects with Foreign Countries or Regions	万美元 (10 000 USD)	215461	308737	350099	373739	408427	408820
外派劳务人数	Number of Persons Sent out	人 (person)	6833	6886	6976	7037	6586	8047
境外投资企业数	Number of Overseas Investment Enterprises	个 (unit)	48	50	55	42	50	79
中方实际投资额	China Actual Investment	万美元 (10 000 USD)	60174	70052	70175	83760	102434	110798

注："中方实际投资额"，2016 年以前为"中方协议投资额"口径。
Note: "China's actual investment" was the caliber of "agreed investment amount of China" before 2016.

16-8 出口1000万美元以上企业一览(2019年)

Summary of Enterprises with Annual Exports Value Above 10 Million Dollar(2019)

单位名称 Name of Enterprises	单位名称 Name of Enterprises
中国重汽集团国际有限公司	莱芜泰丰食品有限公司
山东一达通企业服务有限公司	山东省万兴食品有限公司
山东浪潮进出口有限公司	莱芜泰禾生化有限公司
济南玫德铸造有限公司	莱芜钢铁集团银山型钢有限公司
山东太古飞机工程有限公司	山东莱芜金雷风电科技股份有限公司
山东齐鲁医药进出口有限公司	莱芜万兴果菜食品加工有限公司
济南裕兴化工有限责任公司	莱芜市晔霖农产品进出口有限公司
山东临沃重机有限公司	山东钢铁股份有限公司莱芜分公司
山东伊莱特重工有限公司	山东泰山钢铁集团有限公司
济南邦德数控设备有限公司	莱芜英拓进出口有限公司
济南金麒麟刹车系统有限公司	莱芜永保电子有限公司
济南澳海炭素有限公司	山东汇金股份有限公司
山东齐发药业有限公司	山东慧通轮胎有限公司
济南迈克管道科技股份有限公司	莱芜市万鑫经贸有限公司
山东中农联合生物科技有限公司	莱芜长荣食品有限公司
齐鲁安替制药有限公司	莱芜市诚信食品有限公司
山东电力设备有限公司	山东月笙果蔬有限公司
济南圣泉集团股份有限公司	山东冠世针织有限公司
济南万方炭素进出口有限公司	济南邦和工贸有限公司
济南鲁东耐火材料有限公司	山东信敏惠供应链管理有限公司
济南大自然化学有限公司	济南瑞泰克制冷设备有限公司
济南绿霸化学品有限责任公司	济南东烨国际贸易有限公司
济南金威刻科技发展有限公司	章丘东铁铸锻有限公司
济南四海永联汽车销售有限公司	山东电力建设第一工程公司
济南轻骑标致摩托车有限公司	济南创凯科技有限公司
费斯托气动有限公司	山东商龙经贸有限公司
华熙生物科技股份有限公司	齐鲁天和惠世制药有限公司
山东希诺金属材料有限公司	济南星辉数控机械科技有限公司
山东齐鲁医药进出口有限公司	福士汽车零部件(济南)有限公司
山东省冶金设计院股份有限公司	济南中外运保税仓储物流有限公司
迈大食品(山东)有限公司	山东力诺光伏高科技有限公司

16-8 续表 continued

单位名称 Name of Enterprises	单位名称 Name of Enterprises
山东信久进出口有限公司	山东三禾农业开发有限公司
济南弘正科技有限公司	济南尼克焊接技术有限公司
卧龙电气章丘海尔电机有限公司	山东凯莱（国际）贸易有限公司
山东润科国际贸易有限公司	山东中天重工有限公司
九阳股份有限公司	山东镭鸣数控激光装备有限公司
山东冠世时装加工有限公司	瀚瑞森（中国）汽车悬挂系统有限公司
济南鸿天国际贸易有限公司	济南东进皮草有限公司
济南西门子变压器有限公司	济南文耀贸易有限公司
济南森峰科技有限公司	济南汉锦源电子有限公司
济南二机床集团有限公司	济南九鼎中泰国际贸易有限公司
山东大鲁阁织染工业有限公司	济南圣泉唐和唐生物科技有限公司
济南台有玻璃制品有限公司	山东天下鲁商商务有限公司
济南力诺玻璃制品有限公司	济南浩丰进出口有限公司
山东省永信非织造材料有限公司	贝斯济钢（山东）钢板有限公司
济南沃德汽车零部件有限公司	山东凯信达工贸有限公司
山东科兴生物制品有限公司	山东百利通亚陶科技有限公司
山东圣泉化工股份有限公司	济南特亚国际贸易有限公司
济南诚信通铝业有限公司	济南海航国际贸易有限公司
济南实达紧固件有限公司	山东科赛怡锐化工有限公司
中铁十四局集团有限公司	济南博意达商贸有限公司
济南迅吉安保税物流有限公司	山东鲁电国际贸易有限公司
山东华民钢球股份有限公司	浪潮软件集团有限公司
山东立达进出口公司	山东盈健国际贸易有限公司
浪潮集团有限公司	济南市冶金科学研究所
济南轻骑对外贸易有限责任公司	中国电建集团山东电力建设有限公司
斯凯孚（济南）轴承与精密技术产品有限公司	兰剑智能科技股份有限公司
济南锅炉集团有限公司	山东威明汽车产品有限公司
济南华辰实业有限责任公司	济南银丰化工有限公司
山东华辰国际集团有限公司	齐鲁制药有限公司
济南轻骑铃木摩托车有限公司	济南轨道交通装备有限责任公司
济南乐邦贸易有限公司	章丘美华进出口贸易有限公司
济南宏创博展汽车销售有限公司	济南嘉亚经贸发展有限公司

16-9 旅游住宿单位接待入境游客
Received Inbound Tourists by Hotels

指 标	Indicator	2014年	2015年	2016年	2017年	2018年	2019年
入境游客人数（人次）	Number of Inbound Tourists (person-time)	314536	332942	351526	375469	398721	456585
外国人	Foreigners	194567	205477	216899	232260	247086	285071
# 日 本	Japan	22336	22154	21972	21967	23123	28653
菲律宾	Philippines	2237	2215	2357	2622	2901	3500
新加坡	Singapore	13840	14837	15586	16588	17503	18092
韩 国	Republic of Korea	33839	34238	36137	34695	37432	41390
加拿大	Canada	5361	5697	5558	6445	6970	7859
英 国	United Kingdom	9164	9693	10286	10918	11602	12910
德 国	Germany	13722	14688	15608	16543	17706	19384
法 国	France	6207	6694	7041	7532	8000	8893
意大利	Italy	3825	4086	4330	5190	5524	6069
瑞 士	Switzerland	931	986	1051	1119	1216	1348
澳大利亚	Australia	8411	8934	9456	10089	10762	12422
新西兰	New Zealand	1519	1625	1825	1958	2078	2113
美 国	United States	19844	21396	23187	24797	26325	29556
港澳和台湾同胞	Compatriots from Hong Kong Macao and Taiwan	119969	127465	134627	143209	151635	171514
# 台湾同胞	Compatriots from Taiwan	57586	61726	65050	68839	72667	87086
入境游客人天数（人天）	Number of Days on Inbound Tourists (person-day)	739926	786451	829300	878238	1086701	1276852
外国人	Foreigners	443823	460937	483753	513621	683730	806837
港澳和台湾同胞	Compatriots from Hong Kong and Macao	296061	325514	345547	364617	402971	959122
# 台湾同胞	Compatriots from Taiwan	138269	172776	178839	187351	265047	317730
旅游外汇收入（亿美元）	Foreign Exchange Income of Tourism (100 million USD)	1.71	1.84	1.96	2.08	2.23	2.75
# 商品性收入	Commecial Income	0.58	0.53	0.51	0.54	0.6	0.7
附：平均每天来济国际旅游人数（人次）	Number of Tourists Per Day (person-time)	862	912	963	1029	1092	1251
星级宾馆客房出租率(%)	Star Hotel Room Rate(%)	62.55	61.0	64.5	64.56	63.4	62.0

注：2018 年起接待入境游客包含了过夜游客和一日游游客。
Notes: Starting in 2018, inbound tourists include overnight vsitors and day-trippers.

16-10 济南与国外结成友好城市一览表(2019年末)
Foreign Friendly Cities of Jinan(End of 2019)

国别	Country	城市	City	缔结日期 Day
日本	Japan	和歌山市(和歌山县首府)	Wakayama	1983.01.14
英国	United Kingdom	考文垂市(英国汽车工业故乡，制造业中心之一)	Coventry	1983.10.03
日本	Japan	山口市(山口县首府)	Yamaguchi	1985.09.20
美国	United States	萨克拉门托市(加利福尼亚州首府)	Sacramento	1985.05.29
加拿大	Canada	里贾纳市(萨斯喀彻温省省会)	Regina	1987.08.10
巴布亚新几内亚	Papua New Guinea	莫尔斯比港(巴布亚新几内亚首都)	Port Moresby	1988.09.28
韩国	Republic of Korea	水原市(京畿道首府)	Suwon	1993.10.27
俄罗斯	Russia	下诺夫哥罗德市(下诺夫哥罗德州首府)	Nizhny novgorod	1994.09.25
芬兰	Finland	万达市(欧洲机场城市、芬兰第四大城市)	Vantaa	2001.08.27
法国	France	雷恩市(布列塔尼大区首府)	Renne	2002.07.17
澳大利亚	Australia	郡德勒普市(西澳洲新兴教育科技中心)	Draper	2004.09.04
德国	Germany	奥格斯堡市(施瓦本地区首府)	Augsburg	2004.10.10
乌克兰	Ukraine	哈尔科夫市(哈尔科夫州首府)	Kharkov	2007.05.23
以色列	Israel	卡法萨巴市(沙龙地区中心城市)	Kafassaba	2009.05.11
白俄罗斯	Belorussia	维捷布斯克市(维捷布斯克州首府)	Vitebsk	2009.09.20
佛得角	Cape Verde	普拉亚市(佛得角首都)	Praia	2009.09.22
巴西	Brazil	波多韦柳市(朗多尼亚州首府)	Bothoweri	2011.10.13
土耳其	Turkey	马尔马里斯市(地中海沿岸港口城市和旅游胜地)	Marmaris	2011.10.21
白俄罗斯	The Republic of Belarus	明斯克市苏维埃区(白俄罗斯首都明斯克市历史最悠久的区之一)	Savetski (Soviet) District , Minsk	2012.08.03
印度尼西亚	Indonesia	徐图利祖市(东爪哇省泗水市机场城市、新兴经济城市)	Xu Tzu Chi City	2012.09.21
保加利亚	Bulgaria	卡赞勒格市(保加利亚玫瑰精油生产中心)	Kazanlak	2013.08.29
墨西哥	Mexico	萨博潘市(哈利斯科州经济首府)	Saab Pan	2014.05.20
格鲁吉亚	Georgia	库塔伊西市(格鲁吉亚西部历史名城和第二大工业城市)	Kutaisi	2016.05.26
意大利	Italy	奇维塔韦基亚市(欧洲第三大客运港)	Civitavecchia	2016.06.20
印度	India	那格浦尔市(印度地理中心城市、马哈拉施特拉邦第二首府)	Nagpur	2017.12.08
埃塞俄比亚	Ethiopia	阿尔巴门奇市(埃塞俄比亚西南部重要城镇，格穆戈法州首府)	Arba Minch	2018.09.06
斯洛文尼亚	Slovenia	马里博尔(斯洛文尼亚第二大城市、重要的工业中心)	Maribor	2019.09.26

16-11 济南市与各友好城市交流
Basic Statistics of Transmission Between Foreign Friendly Cities and Jinan

单位：批数、人次 (batch.person-time)

指标	Indicator	2013年	2014年	2015年	2016年	2017年	2018年	2019年
因公出访交流考察	Business Trip							
批数	Batch	257	430	583	780	747	781	718
人次	Number	866	994	1444	1907	1906	2107	1798
接待来访团组	Receive Visitors							
批数	Batch	140	128	123	204	207	206	–
人次	Number	1786	1296	1107	1352	1829	1730	–

注：本表指标为“–”的，部门相关统计制度中已经不再进行统计。
Notes: The indicator “–” in this table means statistics are no longer in the relevant statistical system of the department.

主要统计指标解释

海关进出口商品总额　指实际进出我国国境的货物总金额。包括对外贸易实际进出口货物，来料加工装配进出口货物，国家间、联合国及国际组织无偿援助物资和赠送品，华侨、港澳台同胞和外籍华人捐赠品，租赁期满归承租人所有的租赁货物，进料加工进出口货物，边境地方贸易及边境地区小额贸易进出口货物（边民互市贸易除外），中外合资企业、中外合作经营企业、外商独资经营企业进出口货物和公用物品，到、离岸价格在规定限额以上的进出口货样和广告品（无商业价值、无使用价值和免费提供出口的除外），从保税仓库提取在中国境内销售的进口货物，以及其他进出口货物。进出口总额用以观察一个国家在对外贸易方面的总规模。我国规定出口货物按离岸价格统计，进口货物按到岸价格统计。

利用外资　指我国各级政府、部门、企业和其他经济组织通过对外借款、吸收外商直接投资以及用其他方式筹措的境外现汇、设备、技术等。

外商直接投资　指外国企业和经济组织或个人（包括华侨、港澳台胞以及我国在境外注册的企业）按我国有关政策、法规，用现汇、实物、技术等在我国境内开办外商独资企业、与我国境内的企业或经济组织共同举办中外合资经营企业、合作经营企业或合作开发资源的投资（包括外商投资收益的再投资）。即“外方投资者的投资股本”和总投资与注册资本差额部分的“外方股东对企业的直接贷款”。

对外承包工程　指各对外承包公司以招标议标承包方式承揽的下列业务：（1）承包国外工程建设项目，（2）承包我国对外经援项目，（3）承包我国驻外机构的工程建设项目，（4）承包我国境内利用外资进行建设的工程项目，（5）与外国承包公司合营或联合承包工程项目时我国公司分包部分，（6）对外承包兼营的房屋开发业务。对外承包工程的营业额是以货币表现的本期内完成的对外承包工程的工作量，包括以前年度签订的合同和本年度新签订的合同在报告期内完成的工作量。

对外劳务合作　指以收取工资的形式向业主或承包商提供技术和劳动服务的活动。我国对外承包公司在境外开办的合营企业，中国公司同时又提供劳务的，其劳务部分也纳入劳务合作统计。劳务合作营业额按报告期内向雇主提交的结算数（包括工资、加班费和奖金等）统计。

入境游客　指报告期内来中国（大陆）观光、度假、探亲访友、就医疗养、购物、参加会议或从事经济、文化、体育、宗教活动的外国人、港澳台同胞等游客（即入境旅游人数）。

外国人　指属外国国籍的人，加入外国国籍的中国血统华人也计入外国人。

旅游外汇收入　入境游客在中国（大陆）境内旅行、游览过程中用于交通、参观游览、住宿、餐饮、购物、娱乐等全部花费。

Explanatory Notes on Main Statistical Indicators

Total Value of Customs Export-import Commodities refers to the total value of cargoes actually importing from and exported to China. It includes cargoes actually imported and exported in the foreign trade; cargoes imported and exported of processing and assembly of supplied materials; free aid and gift between countries, from The United Nations and international organizations; donation of overseas Chinese, Hong Kong, Macao and Taiwan compatriots and Chinese of foreign nationality; lease cargoes belonging to the tenant when the lease term expires; cargoes imported and exported of processing with imported materials; cargoes imported and exported of local border trade and small trade in border areas (except for fair among the inhabitants of border areas); cargoes imported and exported and public objects of Sino-foreign joint venture, Chinese-foreign co-operative enterprise and wholly foreign-owned enterprises; sample goods and advertising samples imported and exported based on cost insurance and freight and FOB above the specified limit (except for export without commercial value or use value and freely provided); import goods extracted from bonded warehouse which are sold in China and other cargoes imported and exported. Total export-import volume is used to observe the total scale of a country in the aspect of foreign trade. China specifies exported goods are subject to statistics as per FOB and import goods are subject to statistics pursuant to cost insurance and freight.

Utilization of Foreign Capital refers to remittance, equipment and technology financed from abroad, by foreign loans, attracting foreign direct investment and other forms undertaken by the Chinese governments at all levels, by various departments, enterprises and other economic organizations.

Foreign Direct Investment refers to investments by exclusively foreign-owned enterprises established by foreign enterprise and economic organization or individual (including overseas Chinese, Hong Kong, Macao and Taiwan compatriots and China's enterprise registered abroad) in China according to related policies and regulations of China based on spot exchange, material object and technology, joint venture with Chinese and foreign investment, cooperative enterprise or cooperative development resources jointly organized by enterprises or economic organizations in China, (including reinvestment of foreign direct investment income), namely "direct loan from foreign shareholders to enterprises" of the balance between "investment capital of foreign investors" and total investment as well as registered capital.

Contract Foreign Projects refer to the following business undertaken by all foreign contract companies based on the method of contract through bidding negotiation: (1) Contracting foreign construction projects, (2) Contracting China's foreign economic assistance projects, (3) Contracting construction projects of China's institution functioning abroad, (4) Contracting projects constructed based on foreign capital in China, (5) Subcontracting part of China's company at the time of joint operation with foreign contracting company or united contracting of the project, and (6) Contracting the housing development business operated concurrently. Turnover of contract foreign projects is the workload of contract foreign projects completed in the current period embodied with currency, including workload of the contract signed in previous year and the contract newly signed in this year which is completed in the reporting period.

Foreign Labor Cooperation refers to the activities of providing technology and labor services for owners or contractors in the forms of receiving salaries and wages. China's foreign contract companies refer to cooperative enterprises established outside the border with labor service provided by Chinese company at the same time whose labor service is included into labor service cooperation statistics as well. The business volume of labor service cooperation shall be counted in accordance with the settlement amount (wages and salaries, overtime pay, bonuses and other remuneration) submitted to the employers during the reporting period.

Entry Visitors refer to foreigners and compatriots from Hong Kong, Macao and Taiwan coming to China (Chinese Mainland) for sightseeing, vacation, visiting relatives and friends, medical treatment, shopping, attending the meeting or engaging in economic, cultural, sports and religious activities in the reporting period (namely the number of inbound travelers). The entry visitors of year 2018 including tourists staying overnight and one-day tour tourists.

Foreigners refer to persons with foreign nationality and ethnic Chinese with Chinese descent and foreign nationality is also included into foreigners.

Income from Tourism Foreign Exchange refers to total cost spent by entry visitors on transportation, sightseeing, accommodation, catering, shopping and entertainment, etc. in the process of travelling and sightseeing in China (Chinese Mainland).

17

科　技

SCIENCE AND TECHNOLOGY

17-1 科技综合情况
Basic Statistics on Science and Technology

指　标	Indicator	单位 Unit	2011 年	2012 年	2013 年	2014 年	2015 年	2016 年	2017 年	2018 年
R&D 活动单位	R&D Activity Units	个 (Unit)	401	446	573	660	803	890	964	821
R&D 活动全时人员	Full-time R&D Personnel	人年 (man-years)	37048	37824	41643	46796	51297	52395	57506	59995
R&D 活动经费内部支出	Internal Expenditure on R&D	万元 (10 000 yuan)	955341	989528	1111522	1205441.6	1330543.8	1567365	1851538.7	2085980.1
# 基础研究	Basic Research	万元 (10 000 yuan)	53609	72717	77918	81092.8	106229	128504.7	152909.2	144105.1
# 应用研究	Applied Research	万元 (10 000 yuan)	126146	135575	127176	142847.5	136507.2	151841.2	208526.4	246533.3
# 试验发展	Experimental Development	万元 (10 000 yuan)	775586	781236	906428	981501.4	1087807.6	1287019.1	1490103.1	1695281.7
# 日常性支出	Daily Expenditure	万元 (10 000 yuan)	852242	859567	967345	1068380.6	1161517.8	1376837.7	1636821.4	1843653.3
人员劳务费	Staff Service Fee	万元 (10 000 yuan)	266312	277486	320273	376372.8	470989.9	522676.7	616187.2	763134.5
# 资产性支出	Capital Expenditure	万元 (10 000 yuan)	103101	129961	144177	137061	169026	190527.3	214717.4	242326.8
仪器设备	Instrument and Equipment	万元 (10 000 yuan)	96654	123932	135607	126101.9	160989.5	185967.8	188836.8	236760.3
R&D 活动经费外部支出	External Expenditure on R&D	万元 (10 000 yuan)	40140	38990	46679	57993	42612	62140.8	70569.2	79731.3
科技成果情况	Scientific Achievements									
专利申请数	Patent Applications	件 (pieces)	6301	8699	10221	12196	14178	15490	19645	
# 发明专利申请数	Inventions	件 (pieces)	2678	3903	4755	6234	8454	9138	12027	
拥有发明专利数	Number of Invention Patents	件 (pieces)	5624	4973	6087	7712	10007	13808	20059	
科技项目（课题）情况	Scientific Projects									
项目（课题）数	Number of Projects	项 (item)	11174	15899	17683	18811	21177	22570	27666	
项目参加人员折合全时当年	Number of Participants	人年 (man-years)	35518	36702	39557	43828.2	46715	44188	46457.1	

注：1. 2018 年数据为行政区划调整前口径，以下各表同。
　　2. "科技成果情况" 2018 年相关数据，山东省统计局未反馈。

Note: 1. Data used in 2018 is the statistical scale before the adjustment of administrative division (the same below).
　　2. "Scientific Achievements" in 2018 have been not reflected by Shandong Provincial Bureau of Statistics.

17-2 科技投入情况(2018 年)
Basic Statistics on Scientific and Technological Funds(2018)

指 标	Indicator	单位 Unit	合计 Total	科研机构 Research Institutions	高等院校 Colleges and Universities	规模以上工业企业 Industrial Enterprises Above Designated Size	其他 Others
有 R&D 活动单位数	Number of Enterprises with R&D Activities	个 (unit)	821	67	62	561	131
R&D 人员	R&D Personnel	人 (Person)	87872	6137	18199	47923	15613
# 研究人员	Research Personnel	人 (Person)	49111	4931	15914	20730	7536
R&D 人员折合全时人员	Full-time Equivalent of R&D Personnel	人年 (man-years)	53835	5678	8083	30570	9504
基础研究	Basic Research	人年 (man-years)	6928	1899	3681.4	52	1296
应用研究	Applied Research	人年 (man-years)	8161	2328	4109.6	265	1459
试验发展	Experimental Development	人年 (man-years)	38748	1451	292	30254	6751
R&D 经费内部支出	Internal Expenditure on R&D	万元 (10 000 yuan)	2085980	141236	214526	1312225	417993
基础研究	Basic Research	万元 (10 000 yuan)	144105	30531	88552	1109	23913
应用研究	Applied Research	万元 (10 000 yuan)	246533	58618	117838	9484	60594
试验发展	Experimental Development	万元 (10 000 yuan)	1695282	52087	8136	1301633	333427
日常性支出	Routine Expenses	万元 (10 000 yuan)	1843653	117461	191579	1151760	382854
# 人员劳务费	Labor Cost	万元 (10 000 yuan)	763135	70168	35951	522210	134806
资产性支出	Assets Expenditure	万元 (10 000yuan)	242327	23775	22947	160466	35140
# 仪器和设备	Instrument and Equipment	万元 (10 000 yuan)	236760	22723	20545	158732	34762

17-3 规模以上工业企业科技活动情况 (2018 年)

Main Indicators of Industrial Enterprises Above Designated Size(2018)

单位：个 (unit)

指标	Indicator	企业数 Number of Industial Enterprises	# 有 R&D 活动的单位数 Number of Units with Research and Development Activities	企业办科技机构数 Number of Technology Institutions Run By Enterprises
总计	Total	1890	561	288
按登记注册类型分	by Status of Registration			
内资企业	Domestic Funded Enterprises	1766	513	262
国有企业	State-owned Enterprises	13	1	
集体企业	Collective-owned Enterprises	9	1	
股份合作企业	Cooperative Enterprises	5	1	1
有限责任公司	Private Limited Liability Corporations	546	185	114
国有独资公司	State Sole Funded Corporations	31	19	23
其他有限责任公司	Other Limited Liability Corporations	515	166	91
股份有限公司	Share-holding Corporations Ltd.	81	54	37
私营企业	Private Enterprises	1112	271	110
私营独资企业	Private-funded Enterprises	53	1	
私营合伙企业	Private Partnership Enterprises	1	1	1
私营有限责任公司	Private Limited Liability Corporations	1005	246	83
私营股份有限公司	Private Share-holding Corporations Ltd.	53	23	26
港、澳、台商投资企业	Enterprises with Funds from Hong Kong,Macao and Taiwan	40	13	7
合资经营企业（港或澳、台资）	Joint-venture Enterprises	18	6	4
合作经营企业（港或澳、台资）	Cooperative Enterprises	1	1	
港、澳、台商独资经营企业	Enterprises with Sole Investment	19	5	2
港、澳、台商投资股份有限公司	Share-holding Corporations Ltd.	1		1
其他港澳台投资企业	Other Enterprises	1	1	
外商投资企业	Foreign Funded Enterprises	84	35	19
中外合资经营企业	Joint-venture Enterprises	39	19	7
中外合作经营企业	Cooperation Enterprises	3	1	
外资企业	Enterprises with Sole Fund	40	14	7
外商投资股份有限公司	Share-holding CorporationsLtd.with Foreign Investment	2	1	5
按工业行业大类分	by Sector			
煤炭开采和洗选业	Mining and Washing of Coal	1	1	
石油和天然气开采业	Extraction of Petroleum and Natural Gas	3		
黑色金属矿采选业	Mining and Processing of Ferrous Metal Ores			
非金属矿采选业	Mining and Processing of Nonmetal Ores	8	2	2
农副食品加工业	Processing of Food from Agricultural Products	57	10	8
食品制造业	Manufacture of Foods	66	19	11

17-3 续表 continued

指标	Indicator	企业数 Number of Industial Enterprises	# 有 R&D 活动的单位数 Number of Units with Research and Development Activities	企业办科技机构数 Number of Technology Institutions Run By Enterprises
酒、饮料和精制茶制造业	Manufacture of Wine, Drinks and Refined Tea	21	6	3
烟草制品业	Manufacture of Tobacco	1		
纺织业	Manufacture of Textile	40	5	
纺织服装、服饰业	Manufacture of Textile Wearing Apparel and Finery	30	2	1
皮革、毛皮、羽毛及其制品和制鞋业	Manufacture of Leather, Fur,Feather &Its Products and Footwear	7	1	1
木材加工和木、竹、藤、棕、草制品业	Processing of Timbers,Manufacture of Wood,Bamboo, Rattan,Palm,and Straw Products	11		
家具制造业	Manufacture of Furniture	12	2	
造纸和纸制品业	Manufacture of Paper and Paper Products	27	2	
印刷和记录媒介复制业	Printing, Reproduction of Recording Media	50	9	4
文教、工美、体育和娱乐用品制造业	Manufacture of Culture,Education,Arts and crafts,Sport and Entertainment Goods	28	6	1
石油加工、炼焦和核燃料加工业	Processing of Petroleum, Coking and Nucleus Fuel	10	1	1
化学原料和化学制品制造业	Manufacture of Chemical Raw Material and Chemical Products	103	36	19
医药制造业	Manufacture of Medicines	60	34	31
化学纤维制造业	Manufacture of Chemical Fiber	5	2	
橡胶和塑料制品业	Manufacture of Rubber and Plastic	63	13	8
非金属矿物制品业	Manufacture of Non-metallic Mineral Products	186	31	21
黑色金属冶炼和压延加工业	Manufacture and Processing of Ferrous Metals	13	4	1
有色金属冶炼和压延加工业	Manufacture & Processing of Non-ferrous Metals	17	2	
金属制品业	Manufacture of Metal Products	235	36	19
通用设备制造业	Manufacture of General Purpose Machinery	269	95	36
专用设备制造业	Manufacture of Special Purpose Machinery	169	77	27
汽车制造业	Manufacture of Automotive	109	26	10
铁路、船舶、航空航天和其他运输设备制造业	Manufacture of Railroad,Marine, Aerospace and Other Transportation Equipment	32	8	2
电气机械和器材制造业	Manufacture of Electrical Machinery & Equipment	95	48	26
计算机、通信和其他电子设备制造业	Manufacture of Computer,Communications and Other Electronic Equipment	48	32	24
仪器仪表制造业	Manufacture of Measuring Instrument	64	38	27
其他制造业	Other Manufacture	1	1	
废弃资源综合利用业	Comprehensive Utilization of Waste	2		
金属制品、机械和设备修理业	Metal Products, Machinery and Equipment Repair Industry	3	2	4
电力、热力生产和供应业	Production and Supply of Electric Power and Heat Power	21	5	
燃气生产和供应业	Production and Supply of Gas	14		
水的生产和供应业	Production and Supply of Water	9	5	1

17-4 规模以上工业企业技术改造及引进吸收（2018 年）
Innovation and Resorb of Industrial Enterprises Above Designated Size（2018）

单位：万元 (10 000 yuan)

指标	Indicator	技术改造经费支出 Technical Reform Expenditure	引进国外技术经费支出 Acquisition of Foreign Technology Expenditure	引进技术的消化吸收经费支出 Expenditure for Assimilation Technology	购买国内技术经费支出 Expenditure for Purchase Domestic Technology
总计	Total	484134	4681	142	13016
按登记注册类型分	by Status of Registration				
国有企业	State-owned Enterprises				
集体企业	Collective-owned Enterprises				
股份合作企业	Cooperative Enterprises				
有限责任公司	Private Limited Liability Corporations	378530	1052	127	10659
国有独资公司	State Sole funded Corporations	115700	106	77	120
其他有限责任公司	Other Limited Liability Corporations	262830	945	50	10539
股份有限公司	Share-holding Corporations Ltd.	52159	406	15	449
私营企业	Private Enterprises	39266			274
私营独资企业	Private-funded Enterprises				
私营合伙企业	Private Partnership Enterprises				
私营有限责任公司	Private Limited Liability Corporations	11381			274
私营股份有限公司	Private Share-holding Corporations Ltd.	27885			
其他企业	Other Enterprises				
合资经营企业（港或澳、台资）	Joint-venture Enterprises	916			
合作经营企业（港或澳、台资）	Cooperative Enterprises	380			
港、澳、台商独资经营企业	Enterprises with Sole Investment				
港、澳、台商投资股份有限公司	Share-holding Corporations Ltd.	769			
其他港澳台投资企业	Other Enterprises				
中外合资经营企业	Joint-venture Enterprises	9434	3224		1634
中外合作经营企业	Cooperation Enterprises				
外资企业	Enterprises with Sole Fund	683			
外商投资股份有限公司	Share-holding Corporations Ltd. with Foreign Investment	1998			
按工业行业大类分	by Sector				
煤炭开采和洗选业	Mining and Washing of Coal				
石油和天然气开采业	Extraction of Petroleum and Natural Gas				
黑色金属矿采选业	Mining of Ferrous Metal Ores				
非金属矿采选业	Mining and Processing of Nonmetal Ores				
农副食品加工业	Processing of Food from Agricultural Products	72			60
食品制造业	Manufacture of Foods	414			21
酒、饮料和精制茶制造业	Manufacture of Wine, Drinks and Refined Tea	1131			
烟草制品业	Manufacture of Tobacco				
纺织业	Manufacture of Textile	823			
纺织服装、服饰业	Manufacture of Textile Wearing Apparel and Finery				

17-4 续表 continued

指标	Indicator	技术改造经费支出 Technical Reform Expenditure	引进国外技术经费支出 Acquisition of Foreign Technology Expenditure	引进技术的消化吸收经费支出 Expenditure for Assimilation Technology	购买国内技术经费支出 Expenditure for Purchase Domestic Technology
皮革、毛皮、羽毛及其制品和制鞋业	Manufacture of Leather, Fur, Feather & Its Products and Footwear				
木材加工和木、竹、藤、棕、草制品业	Processing of Timbers, Manufacture of Wood, Bamboo, Rattan, Palm, and Straw Products				
家具制造业	Manufacture of Furniture				
造纸和纸制品业	Manufacture of Paper and Paper Products				
印刷和记录媒介复制业	Printing, Reproduction of Recording Media	550			
文教、工美、体育和娱乐用品制造业	Manufacture of Culture, Education,Arts and crafts, Sport and Entertainment Goods	68			
石油加工、炼焦和核燃料加工业	Processing of Petroleum, Coking and Nucleus Fuel	49615			350
化学原料和化学制品制造业	Manufacture of Chemical Raw Material and Chemical Products	30734	288		152
医药制造业	Manufacture of Medicines	80733	823		9985
化学纤维制造业	Manufacture of Chemical Fiber				
橡胶和塑料制品业	Manufacture of Rubber and Plastic	113			
非金属矿物制品业	Manufacture of Non-metallic Mineral Products	3473			
黑色金属冶炼和压延加工业	Manufacture and Processing of Ferrous Metals				
有色金属冶炼和压延加工业	Manufacture & Processing of Non-ferrous Metals	270			
金属制品业	Manufacture of Metal Products	23585			29
通用设备制造业	Manufacture of General Purpose Machinery	14949	138	92	129
专用设备制造业	Manufacture of Special Purpose Machinery	10114			241
汽车制造业	Manufacture of Automotive	108508			70
铁路、船舶、航空航天和其他运输设备制造业	Manufacture of Railroad,Marine,Aerospace and Other Transportation Equipment		3224		
电气机械和器材制造业	Manufacture of Electrical Machinery & Equipment	3084	208	50	1943
计算机、通信和其他电子设备制造业	Manufacture of Computer, Communications and Other Electronic Equipment	152188			10
仪器仪表制造业	Manufacture of Measuring Instrument	967			26
其他制造业	Other Manufacture				
废弃资源综合利用业	Comprehensive Utilization of Waste				
金属制品、机械和设备修理业	Metal Products, Machinery and Equipment Repair Industry	842			
电力、热力生产和供应业	Production and Supply of Electric Power and Heat Power	1902			
燃气生产和供应业	Production and Supply of Gas				
水的生产和供应业	Production and Supply of Water				

17-5 规模以上工业企业技术资源 (2018 年)

Technical Resources of Industrial Enterprises Above Desitnated Size (2018)

指 标	Indicator	R&D 经费内部支出合计 (万元) Internal Expenditure on R&D (10 000 yuan)	新产品销售收入 (万元) Output Value of New Products (10 000 yuan)	研究与试验发展 (R&D) 人员 (人) R&D Sonnel (Person)	R&D 人员折合全时当量 (人年) R&D Rsonnel Equivalent in Full Time (man-years)
总计	Total	1312225	1693549	47923	30570
按登记注册类型分	by Status of Registration				
国有企业	State-owned Enterprises	113		14	11
集体企业	Collective-owned Enterprises	1251	2838	100	95
股份合作企业	Cooperative Enterprises	1036	6027	55	52
有限责任公司	Private Limited Liability Corporations	980341	13079645	33357	21610
国有独资公司	State Sole Funded Corporations	233202	4226979	7707	5227
其他有限责任公司	Other Limited Liability Corporations	747139	8852666	25650	16383
股份有限公司	Share-holding Corporations Ltd.	99011	1533178	4413	2620
私营企业	Private Enterprises	171495	179375	7388	4578
私营独资企业	Private-funded Enterprises	302.6	0	21	0
私营合伙企业	Private Partnership Enterprises	1746	0	36	24
私营有限责任公司	Private Limited Liability Corporations	122047	1159707	5997	3735
私营股份有限公司	Private Share-holding Corporations Ltd.	47400	633970	1334	818
其他企业	Other Enterprises		0	0	0
合资经营企业(港或澳、台资)	Joint-venture Enterprises	9146	69750	619	421
合作经营企业(港或澳、台资)	Cooperative Enterprises	400	0	21	17
港、澳、台商独资经营企业	Enterprises with Sole Investment	6556	33054	175	80
港、澳、台商投资股份有限公司	Share-holding Corporations Ltd.			0	0
其他港澳台投资企业	Other Enterprises	165	100	11	9
中外合资经营企业	Joint-venture Enterprises	20538	246870	726	441
中外合作经营企业	Cooperation Enterprises	794	365	23	18
外资企业	Enterprises with Sole Fund	16573	146170	858	589
外商投资股份有限公司	Share-holding Corporations Ltd. with Foreign Investment	4808	18875	163	29
按工业行业大类分	by Sector				
煤炭开采和洗选业	Mining and Washing of Coal	3343		370	247
石油和天然气开采业	Extraction of Petroleum and Natural Gas				
黑色金属矿采选业	Mining of Ferrous Metal Ores				
非金属矿采选业	Mining and Processing of Nonmetal Ores	1996	3010	8	7
农副食品加工业	Processing of Food from Agricultural Products	6323	63432	194	81
食品制造业	Manufacture of Foods	11622	66687	691	486
酒、饮料和精制茶制造业	Manufacture of Wine, Drinks and Refined Tea	2536	17613	127	88
烟草制品业	Manufacture of Tobacco				
纺织业	Manufacture of Textile	5778	101211	336	199

17-5 续表 continued

指 标	Indicator	R&D 经费内部支出合计（万元）Internal Expenditure on R&D (10 000 yuan)	新产品销售收入（万元）Output Value of New Products (10 000 yuan)	研究与试验发展 (R&D) 人员（人）R&D Sonnel (Person)	R&D 人员折合全时当量（人年）R&D Rsonnel Equivalent in Full Time (man-years)
纺织服装、服饰业	Manufacture of Textile Wearing Apparel and Finery	1067	766	139	64
皮革、毛皮、羽毛及其制品和制鞋业	Manufacture of Leather, Fur, Feather & Its Products and Footwear	499	9046	30	28
木材加工和木、竹、藤、棕、草制品业	Processing of Timbers, Manufacture of Wood, Bamboo, Rattan, Palm, and Straw Products				
家具制造业	Manufacture of Furniture	514	436	26	4
造纸和纸制品业	Manufacture of Paper and Paper Products	1336	25289	60	42
印刷和记录媒介复制业	Printing, Reproduction of Recording Media	10690	125647	358	289
文教、工美、体育和娱乐用品制造业	Manufacture of Culture, Education,Arts and crafts， Sport and Entertainment Goods	1753	29643	128	88
石油加工、炼焦和核燃料加工业	Processing of Petroleum, Coking and Nucleus Fuel	2587	335674	199	97
化学原料和化学制品制造业	Manufacture of Chemical Raw Material and Chemical Products	90875	1034759	1843	1067
医药制造业	Manufacture of Medicines	177593	1502871	4187	3223
化学纤维制造业	Manufacture of Chemical Fiber	3035	5330	21	8
橡胶和塑料制品业	Manufacture of Rubber and Plastic	6373	20392	220	139
非金属矿物制品业	Manufacture of Non-metallic Mineral Products	36945	595156	1597	840
黑色金属冶炼和压延加工业	Manufacture and Processing of Ferrous Metals	27742	8553	70	17
有色金属冶炼和压延加工业	Manufacture & Processing of Non-ferrous Metals	1685		106	95
金属制品业	Manufacture of Metal Products	44176	497746	1793	981
通用设备制造业	Manufacture of General Purpose Machinery	92278	736898	4968	3233
专用设备制造业	Manufacture of Special Purpose Machinery	51591	505812	2354	1350
汽车制造业	Manufacture of Automotive	193338	3877570	5532	3652
铁路、船舶、航空航天和其他运输设备制造业	Manufacture of Railroad,Marine,Aerospace and Other Transportation Equipment	20535	338602	479	234
电气机械和器材制造业	Manufacture of Electrical Machinery & Equipment	88066	1400817	2971	1868
计算机、通信和其他电子设备制造业	Manufacture of Computer, Communications and Other Electronic Equipment	382473	5401839	16404	10351
仪器仪表制造业	Manufacture of Measuring Instrument	31182	156498	1989	1343
其他制造业	Other Manufacture	20	1431	3	1
废弃资源综合利用业	Comprehensive Utilization of Waste				
金属制品、机械和设备修理业	Metal Products, Machinery and Equipment Repair Industry	5926	36275	433	314
电力、热力生产和供应业	Production and Supply of Electric Power and Heat Power	6301	31550	193	77
燃气生产和供应业	Production and Supply of Gas				
水的生产和供应业	Production and Supply of Water	2049		94	57

17-6 规模以上工业企业科技活动项目(2018年)
Technology Project Activities of Industrial Enterprises Above Designated Size(2018)

指 标	Indicator	R&D经费内部支出合计(万元) Internal Expenditure on R&D (10 000 yuan)	新产品开发项目数(项) Number of on New Products Development (unit)	新产品开发经费支出(万元) Expenditure on New Products Development (10 000 yuan)
总计	Total	1312225	4633	1183216
按登记注册类型分	by Status of Registration			
国有企业	State-owned Enterprises	113	3	113
集体企业	Collective-owned Enterprises	1251	1	96
股份合作企业	Cooperative Enterprises	1036	7	1036
有限责任公司	Private Limited Liability Corporations	980341	2340	880304
国有独资公司	State Sole Funded Corporations	233202	598	214637
其他有限责任公司	Other Limited Liability Corporations	747139	1742	665666
股份有限公司	Share-holding Corporations Ltd.	99011	516	83067
私营企业	Private Enterprises	171495	1406	158155
私营独资企业	Private-funded Enterprises	303	1	303
私营合伙企业	Private Partnership Enterprises	1746		
私营有限责任公司	Private Limited Liability Corporations	122047	1185	111622
私营股份有限公司	Private Share-holding Corporations Ltd.	47400	220	46230
其他企业	Other Enterprises			
合资经营企业(港或澳、台资)	Joint-venture Enterprises	9146	71	17992
合作经营企业(港或澳、台资)	Cooperative Enterprises	400	2	413
港、澳、台商独资经营企业	Enterprises with Sole Investment	6556	34	6877
港、澳、台商投资股份有限公司	Share-holding Corporations Ltd.			
其他港澳台投资企业	Other Enterprises	165	2	495
中外合资经营企业	Joint-venture Enterprises	20538	130	20163
中外合作经营企业	Cooperation Enterprises	794	6	520
外资企业	Enterprises with Sole Fund	16573	86	9195
外商投资股份有限公司	Share-holding Corporations Ltd. with Foreign Investment	4808	29	1996
按工业行业大类分	by Sector			
煤炭开采和洗选业	Mining and Washing of Coal	3343		
石油和天然气开采业	Extraction of Petroleum and Natural Gas			
黑色金属矿采选业	Mining of Ferrous Metal Ores			
非金属矿采选业	Mining and Processing of Nonmetal Ores	1996	2	1996
农副食品加工业	Processing of Food from Agricultural Products	6323	37	6780
食品制造业	Manufacture of Foods	11622	101	11584
酒、饮料和精制茶制造业	Manufacture of Wine, Drinks and Refined Tea	2536	15	1587

17-6 续表 continued

指 标	Indicator	R&D 经费内部支出合计（万元）Internal Expenditure on R&D (10 000 yuan)	新产品开发项目数（项）Number of on New Products Development (unit)	新产品开发经费支出（万元）Expenditure on New Products Development (10 000 yuan)
烟草制品业	Manufacture of Tobacco		5	515
纺织业	Manufacture of Textile	5778	33	5605
纺织服装、服饰业	Manufacture of Textile Wearing Apparel and Finery	1067	12	1067
皮革、毛皮、羽毛及其制品和制鞋业	Manufacture of Leather, Fur, Feather & Its Products and ootwear	499	7	419
木材加工和木、竹、藤、棕、草制品业	Processing of Timbers,Manufacture of Wood, Bamboo, Rattan, Palm, and Straw Products			
家具制造业	Manufacture of Furniture	514	5	514
造纸和纸制品业	Manufacture of Paper and Paper Products	1336	17	1937
印刷和记录媒介复制业	Printing, Reproduction of Recording Media	10690	39	8018
文教、工美、体育和娱乐用品制造业	Manufacture of Culture, Education,Arts and Crafts, Sport and Entertainment Goods	1753	27	1680
石油加工、炼焦和核燃料加工业	Processing of Petroleum, Coking and Nucleus Fuel	2587	10	2727
化学原料和化学制品制造业	Manufacture of Chemical Raw Material and Chemical Products	90875	291	73531
医药制造业	Manufacture of Medicines	177593	680	163198
化学纤维制造业	Manufacture of Chemical Fiber	3035	12	3928
橡胶和塑料制品业	Manufacture of Rubber and Plastic	6373	65	5844
非金属矿物制品业	Manufacture of Non-metallic Mineral Products	36945	154	25209
黑色金属冶炼和压延加工业	Manufacture and Processing of Ferrous Metals	27742	6	777
有色金属冶炼和压延加工业	Manufacture & Processing of Non-ferrous Metals	1685	13	1719
金属制品业	Manufacture of Metal Products	44176	203	38058
通用设备制造业	Manufacture of General Purpose Machinery	92278	742	75671
专用设备制造业	Manufacture of Special Purpose Machinery	51591	409	43596
汽车制造业	Manufacture of Automotive	193338	391	186867
铁路、船舶、航空航天和其他运输设备制造业	Manufacture of Railroad,Marine,Aerospace and Other Ransportation Quipment	20535	97	19631
电气机械和器材制造业	Manufacture of Electrical Machinery & Equipment	88066	453	84284
计算机、通信和其他电子设备制造业	Manufacture of Computer, Communications and Other Electronic Equipment	382473	426	378321
仪器仪表制造业	Manufacture of Measuring Instrument	31182	324	31399
其他制造业	Other Manufacture	20	3	146
废弃资源综合利用业	Comprehensive Utilization of Waste			
金属制品、机械和设备修理业	Metal Products, Machinery and Equipment Repair Industry	5926	41	5729
电力、热力生产和供应业	Production and Supply of Electric Power and Heat Power	6301	13	883
燃气生产和供应业	Production and Supply of Gas			
水的生产和供应业	Production and Supply of Water	2049		

17-7 规模以上工业企业 R&D 经费情况 (2018 年)

R&D Funds of Industrial Enterprises Above Designated Size(2018)

指 标	Indicator	合计 Total	按支出用途分组 By Object of Expenditure	
			经常费支出 Daily Expenditure	资产性支出 Capital Expenditure
总计	Total	1312225	1151760	160466
按登记注册类型分	by Status of Registration			
国有企业	State-owned Enterprises	113	113	
集体企业	Collective-owned Enterprises	1251	1251	
股份合作企业	Cooperative Enterprises	1036	1009	27
有限责任公司	Private Limited Liability Corporations	980341	840169	140173
国有独资公司	State Sole Funded Corporations	233202	193261	39941
其他有限责任公司	Other Limited Liability Corporations	747139	646907	100232
股份有限公司	Share-holding Corporations Ltd.	99011	94772	4239
私营企业	Private Enterprises	171495	158787	12708
私营独资企业	Private-funded Enterprises	303	303	
私营合伙企业	Private Partnership Enterprises	1746	1746	
私营有限责任公司	Private Limited Liability Corporations	122047	114496	7550
私营股份有限公司	Private Share-holding Corporations Ltd.	47400	42242	5157
其他企业	Other Enterprises			
合资经营企业(港或澳、台资)	Joint-venture Enterprises	9146	8036	1110
合作经营企业(港或澳、台资)	Cooperative Enterprises	400	380	20
港、澳、台商独资经营企业	Enterprises with Sole Investment	6556	6489	68
港、澳、台商投资股份有限公司	Share-holding Corporations Ltd.			
其他港澳台投资企业	Other Enterprises	165	165	
中外合资经营企业	Joint-venture Enterprises	20538	19040	1498
中外合作经营企业	Cooperation Enterprises	794	794	
外资企业	Enterprises with Sole Fund	16573	16174	399
外商投资股份有限公司	Share-holding Corporations Ltd. with Foreign Investment	4808	4583	225
按工业行业大类分	by Sector			
煤炭开采和洗选业	Mining and Washing of Coal	3343	3343	
石油和天然气开采业	Extraction of Petroleum and Natural Gas			
黑色金属矿采选业	Mining of Ferrous Metal Ores			
非金属矿采选业	Mining and Processing of Nonmetal Ores	1996	1371	625
农副食品加工业	Processing of Food from Agricultural Products	6323	5939	384
食品制造业	Manufacture of Foods	11622	11221	401
酒、饮料和精制茶制造业	Manufacture of Wine, Drinks and Refined Tea	2536	2386	150

单位：万元 (10 000 yuan)

R&D 经费内部支出 Internal Expenditure on R&D				R&D 经费外部支出 External Expenditure on R&D
按资金来源分组 By Capital Source				
政府资金 Government Appropriation Funds	企业资金 Self-raised Funds by Enterprises	境外资金 Foreign funds	其他资金 Other Funds	
44756	1248059	887	18523	52827
	71		42	
	1251			
40	996			
32597	929473	258	18013	43805
4838	228364			19742
27759	701110	258	18013	24064
4452	94453	69	37	2328
7134	163683	247	431	5609
	303			
	1746			
6355	115062	199	431	4847
779	46573	48		762
148	8998			234
	400			
	6556			
	165			
285	19940	314		277
	794			
	16573			575
100	4708			
	3343			
	1996			
40	6267	16		24
1765	9799		58	264
	2536			161

17-7 续表 continued

指 标	Indicator	合计 Total	按支出用途分组 By Object of Expenditure	
			经常费支出 Daily Expenditure	资产性支出 Capital Expenditure
烟草制品业	Manufacture of Tobacco			
纺织业	Manufacture of Textile	5778	4945	833
纺织服装、服饰业	Manufacture of Textile Wearing Apparel and Finery	1067	1048	19
皮革、毛皮、羽毛及其制品和制鞋业	Manufacture of Leather, Fur, Feather & Its Products and Footwear	499	484	14
木材加工和木、竹、藤、棕、草制品业	Processing of Timbers, Manufacture of Wood,Bamboo, Rattan, Palm, and Straw Products			
家具制造业	Manufacture of Furniture	514	514	
造纸和纸制品业	Manufacture of Paper and Paper Products	1336	1336	
印刷和记录媒介复制业	Printing, Reproduction of Recording Media	10690	6832	3858
文教、工美、体育和娱乐用品制造业	Manufacture of Culture, Education,Arts and crafts, Sport and Entertainment Goods	1753	1753	
石油加工、炼焦和核燃料加工业	Processing of Petroleum, Coking and Nucleus Fuel	2587	2587	
化学原料和化学制品制造业	Manufacture of Chemical Raw Material and Chemical Products	90875	79287	11589
医药制造业	Manufacture of Medicines	177593	156822	20771
化学纤维制造业	Manufacture of Chemical Fiber	3035	3035	
橡胶和塑料制品业	Manufacture of Rubber and Plastic	6373	5856	516
非金属矿物制品业	Manufacture of Non-metallic Mineral Products	36945	35741	1204
黑色金属冶炼和压延加工业	Manufacture and Processing of Ferrous Metals	27742	16742	11000
有色金属冶炼和压延加工业	Manufacture & Processing of Non-ferrous Metals	1685	1485	200
金属制品业	Manufacture of Metal Products	44176	42729	1447
通用设备制造业	Manufacture of General Purpose Machinery	92278	88293	3985
专用设备制造业	Manufacture of Special Purpose Machinery	51591	48499	3092
汽车制造业	Manufacture of Automotive	193338	152630	40708
铁路、船舶、航空航天和其他运输设备制造业	Manufacture of Railroad,Marine,Aerospace and Other Transportation Equipment	20535	20512	23
电气机械和器材制造业	Manufacture of Electrical Machinery & Equipment	88066	85438	2627
计算机、通信和其他电子设备制造业	Manufacture of Computer, Communications and Other Electronic Equipment	382473	329779	52694
仪器仪表制造业	Manufacture of Measuring Instrument	31182	30265	917
其他制造业	Other Manufacture	20	19	1
废弃资源综合利用业	Comprehensive Utilization of Waste			
金属制品、机械和设备修理业	Metal Products, Machinery and Equipment Repair Industry	5926	4263	1663
电力、热力生产和供应业	Production and Supply of Electric Power and Heat Power	6301	4998	1303
燃气生产和供应业	Production and Supply of Gas			
水的生产和供应业	Production and Supply of Water	2049	1608	441

R&D 经费内部支出 Internal Expenditure on R&D				R&D 经费外部支出 External Expenditure on R&D
按资金来源分组 By Capital Source				
政府资金 Government Appropriation Funds	企业资金 Self-raised Funds by Enterprises	境外资金 Foreign funds	其他资金 Other Funds	
	5778			
	1067			
	499			
	514			
	1336			
15	10672		3	20
255	1498			
	2587			348
14576	76279		20	2139
8950	168588	18	37	10847
	3035			
135	6237			25
312	36516	117		1640
	20042		7700	24
	1685			
424	43693		58	32
5856	85521	183	719	2186
2670	48895		26	2338
713	192444	181		15527
46	20356	133		228
580	87419	67		5388
7147	365250	173	9903	9217
1122	30061			1128
20				
130	5796			
	6301			1062
	2049			230

17-8 规模以上工业企业办科技机构情况(2018 年)

Science and Technology Institutions of Industrial Enterprises Above Designated Size (2018)

指 标	Indicator	机构数(个) Number (unit)	机构人员(人) Research Personnel (Person)			机构经费支出(万元) Agency Expenditure (10 000 yuan)	仪器和设备原价(万元) Original Price of Equipment (10 000 yuan)
			合计 Total	博士毕业 Doctor	硕士毕业 Master		
总计	Total	288	28953	400	6351	827997	861338
按登记注册类型分	by Status of Registration						
国有企业	State-owned Enterprises						
集体企业	Collective-owned Enterprises						
股份合作企业	Cooperative Enterprises	1	68		7	1039	1392
有限责任公司	Private Limited Liability Corporations	114	22339	292	5579	669481	695458
国有独资公司	State Sole funded Corporations	23	3541	19	733	128061	105587
其他有限责任公司	Other Limited Liability Corporations	91	18798	273	4846	541420	589871
股份有限公司	Share-holding Corporations Ltd.	37	1884	37	277	33116	57487
私营企业	Private Enterprises	110	3078	61	408	95061	64303
私营独资企业	Private-funded Enterprises						
私营合伙企业	Private Partnership Enterprises	1	43	2	2	689	1152
私营有限责任公司	Private Limited Liability Corporations	83	2119	37	270	53578	40782
私营股份有限公司	Private Share-holding Corporations Ltd.	26	916	22	136	40794	22369
其他企业	Other Enterprises						
合资经营企业(港或澳、台资)	Joint-venture Enterprises	4	497		18	5172	5319
合作经营企业(港或澳、台资)	Cooperative Enterprises						
港、澳、台商独资经营企业	Enterprises with Sole Investment	2	92			2672	1902
港、澳、台商投资股份有限公司	Share-holding Corporations Ltd.	1	35		3	42	800
其他港澳台投资企业	Other Enterprises						
中外合资经营企业	Joint-venture Enterprises	7	410		18	9153	19151
中外合作经营企业	Cooperation Enterprises						
外资企业	Enterprises with Sole Fund	7	452	6	35	7363	15450
外商投资股份有限公司	Share-holding Corporations Ltd. with Foreign Investment	5	98	4	6	4898	78
按工业行业大类分	by Sector						
煤炭开采和洗选业	Mining and Washing of Coal						
石油和天然气开采业	Extraction of Petroleum and Natural Gas						
非金属矿采选业	Mining and Processing of Nonmetal Ores	2	8			1371	625
农副食品加工业	Processing of Food from Agricultural Products	8	232	19	105	5019	1980
食品制造业	Manufacture of Foods	11	551	4	22	7464	14364
酒、饮料和精制茶制造业	Manufacture of Wine, Drinks and Refined Tea	3	125	2	5	1785	1528

17-8 续表 continued

指 标	Indicator	机构数（个）Number (unit)	机构人员（人）Research Personnel (Person) 合计 Total	博士毕业 Doctor	硕士毕业 Master	机构经费支出（万元）Agency Expenditure (10 000 yuan)	仪器和设备原价（万元）Original Price of Equipment (10 000 yuan)
烟草制品业	Manufacture of Tobacco						
纺织业	Manufacture of Textile						
纺织服装、服饰业	Manufacture of Textile Wearing Apparel and Finery	1	1		1	327	139
皮革、毛皮、羽毛及其制品和制鞋业	Manufacture of Leather, Fur, Feather& Its Products and Footwear	1	27			514	781
木材加工和木、竹、藤、棕、草制品业	Processing of Timbers, Manufacture of Wood, Bamboo, Rattan, Palm, and Straw Products						
家具制造业	Manufacture of Furniture						
造纸和纸制品业	Manufacture of Paper and Paper Products						
印刷和记录媒介复制业	Printing, Reproduction of Recording Media	4	249		3	6038	22023
文教、工美、体育和娱乐用品制造业	Manufacture of Culture, Education, Arts and Crafts, Sport and Entertainment Goods	1	18			325	269
石油加工、炼焦和核燃料加工业	Processing of Petroleum, Coking and Nucleus Fuel	1	14		1	855	72
化学原料和化学制品制造业	Manufacture of Chemical Raw Material and Chemical Products	19	1166	36	180	69186	31143
医药制造业	Manufacture of Medicines	31	2703	99	862	166570	114801
化学纤维制造业	Manufacture of Chemical Fiber						
橡胶和塑料制品业	Manufacture of Rubber and Plastic	8	109	3	5	2592	1871
非金属矿物制品业	Manufacture of Non-metallic Mineral Products	21	597	3	39	17836	18798
黑色金属冶炼和压延加工业	Manufacture and Processing of Ferrous Metals	1	26	5	3	320	350
有色金属冶炼和压延加工业	Manufacture & Processing of Non-ferrous Metals						
金属制品业	Manufacture of Metal Products	19	399	4	36	9695	4657
通用设备制造业	Manufacture of General Purpose Machinery	36	2416	20	314	47441	36943
专用设备制造业	Manufacture of Special Purpose Machinery	27	853	11	87	21144	18405
汽车制造业	Manufacture of Automotive	10	2021	19	407	84419	66428
铁路、船舶、航空航天和其他运输设备制造业	Manufacture of Railroad,Marine, Aerospace and Other Transportation Equipment	2	222		4	3583	4625
电气机械和器材制造业	Manufacture of Electrical Machinery & Equipment	26	1121	29	230	36021	72125
计算机、通信和其他电子设备制造业	Manufacture of Computer, Communications and Other Electronic Equipment	24	14388	138	3891	322529	432749
仪器仪表制造业	Manufacture of Measuring Instrument	27	1236	8	133	17910	10226
其他制造业	Other Manufacture						
废弃资源综合利用业	Comprehensive Utilization of Waste						
金属制品、机械和设备修理业	Metal Products, Machinery and Equipment Repair Industry	4	458		20	5039	6153
电力、热力生产和供应业	Production and Supply of Electric Power and Heat Power						
燃气生产和供应业	Production and Supply of Gas						
水的生产和供应业	Production and Supply of Water	1	13		3	13	285

17-9 规模以上工业企业自主知识产权及相关情况（2018年）

Independent Intellectual Property Rights of Industrial Enterprises Above Designated Size(2018)

指　标	Indicator	专利申请数（件）Patent Applications (piece)	#发明专利（件）Inventions (piece)
总计	Total	12596	7913
按登记注册类型分	by Status of Registration		
国有企业	State-owned Enterprises		
集体企业	Collective-owned Enterprises	3	
股份合作企业	Cooperative Enterprises	11	1
有限责任公司	Private Limited Liability Corporations	9374	6943
国有独资公司	State Sole Funded Corporations	716	241
其他有限责任公司	Other Limited Liability Corporations	8658	6702
股份有限公司	Share-holding Corporations Ltd.	1525	363
私营企业	Private Enterprises	1327	428
私营独资企业	Private-funded Enterprises		
私营合伙企业	Private Partnership Enterprises		
私营有限责任公司	Private Limited Liability Corporations	1181	350
私营股份有限公司	Private Share-holding Corporations Ltd.	146	78
其他企业	Other Enterprises		
合资经营企业（港或澳、台资）	Joint-venture Enterprises	206	166
合作经营企业（港或澳、台资）	Cooperative Enterprises		
港、澳、台商独资经营企业	Enterprises with Sole Investment	2	
港、澳、台商投资股份有限公司	Share-holding Corporations Ltd.		
其他港澳台投资企业	Other Enterprises		
中外合资经营企业	Joint-venture Enterprises	85	6
中外合作经营企业	Cooperation Enterprises	7	2
外资企业	Enterprises with Sole Fund	46	
外商投资股份有限公司	Share-holding Corporations Ltd. with Foreign Investment	10	4
按工业行业大类分	by Sector		
煤炭开采和洗选业	Mining and Washing of Coal	5	3
石油和天然气开采业	Extraction of Petroleum and Natural Gas		
黑色金属矿采选业	Mining of Ferrous Metal Ores		
非金属矿采选业	Mining and Processing of Nonmetal Ores		
农副食品加工业	Processing of Food from Agricultural Products	20	13
食品制造业	Manufacture of Foods	71	27
酒、饮料和精制茶制造业	Manufacture of Wine, Drinks and Refined Tea	5	1

有效发明专利数（件） Effective Invention Patent(piece)	拥有注册商标数（件） Registered Trademarks (piece)	# 境外注册（件） Overseas Registered (piece)	形成国家或行业标准数（项） Industry or National Standards(unit)
7797	7295	2540	390
6	2		
9			
1	4		3
4064	4733	2249	229
539	2389	1819	51
3525	2344	430	178
1124	907	156	22
2268	1146	66	99
99			
1551	902	48	50
618	244	18	49
60	289		5
3	3		
	2		
148	151	60	31
20			
82	42	7	
12	16	2	1
6			
	2		
93	39		1
132	72	2	2
5	70		

17-9 续表 continued

指　标	Indicator	专利申请数（件）Patent Applications (piece)	# 发明专利（件）Inventions (piece)
烟草制品业	Manufacture of Tobacco		
纺织业	Manufacture of Textile	110	63
纺织服装、服饰业	Manufacture of Textile Wearing Apparel andFinery		
皮革、毛皮、羽毛及其制品和制鞋业	Manufacture of Leather, Fur, Feather & Its Products and Footwear	4	4
木材加工和木、竹、藤、棕、草制品业	Processing of Timbers, Manufacture of Wood, Bamboo, Rattan, Palm, and Straw Products		
家具制造业	Manufacture of Furniture	13	13
造纸和纸制品业	Manufacture of Paper and Paper Products	3	2
印刷和记录媒介复制业	Printing, Reproduction of Recording Media	50	6
文教、工美、体育和娱乐用品制造业	Manufacture of Culture, Education, Arts and crafts, Sport and Entertainment Goods	61	26
石油加工、炼焦和核燃料加工业	Processing of Petroleum, Coking and Nucleus Fuel	16	2
化学原料和化学制品制造业	Manufacture of Chemical Raw Material and Chemical Products	228	136
医药制造业	Manufacture of Medicines	186	132
化学纤维制造业	Manufacture of Chemical Fiber	11	
橡胶和塑料制品业	Manufacture of Rubber and Plastic	47	8
非金属矿物制品业	Manufacture of Non-metallic Mineral Products	197	80
黑色金属冶炼和压延加工业	Manufacture and Processing of Ferrous Metals	15	9
有色金属冶炼和压延加工业	Manufacture & Processing of Non-ferrous Metals		
金属制品业	Manufacture of Metal Products	159	40
通用设备制造业	Manufacture of General Purpose Machinery	635	142
专用设备制造业	Manufacture of Special Purpose Machinery	451	161
汽车制造业	Manufacture of Automotive	486	129
铁路、船舶、航空航天和其他运输设备制造业	Manufacture of Railroad,Marine,Aerospace and Other Transportation Equipment	132	88
电气机械和器材制造业	Manufacture of Electrical Machinery & Equipment	1455	346
计算机、通信和其他电子设备制造业	Manufacture of Computer, Communications and Other Electronic Equipment	7803	6385
仪器仪表制造业	Manufacture of Measuring Instrument	364	77
其他制造业	Other Manufacture	1	
废弃资源综合利用业	Comprehensive Utilization of Waste		
金属制品、机械和设备修理业	Metal Products, Machinery and Equipment Repair Industry	16	8
电力、热力生产和供应业	Production and Supply of Electric Power and Heat Power	42	9
燃气生产和供应业	Production and Supply of Gas		
水的生产和供应业	Production and Supply of Water	10	3

有效发明专利数（件）Effective Invention Patent(piece)	拥有注册商标数（件）Registered Trademarks (piece)	# 境外注册（件）Overseas Registered (piece)	形成国家或行业标准数（项）Industry or National Standards(unit)
1			3
19	19	15	6
3	4		
	7		1
	1		
64	20	2	
115	55		
18	4	1	
930	729	23	110
685	1862	65	26
4	3		
30	19	2	3
442	61	7	15
28	23		1
	1		
202	215	98	22
792	474	175	43
575	202	12	17
461	2367	1787	12
531	5		4
1075	272	74	64
1098	640	269	20
406	127	8	36
39	1		4
39	1		
4			

17-10 行政区划调整前原莱芜市规模以上工业企业主要指标情况(2018年)
Science and Technology Activities Main Indicators of Industrial Enterprises Above Designated Size of Laiwu Before the Administrative Division Adjustment(2018)

指 标	Indicator	单位	2018年
企业数	Number of Industial Enterprises	个(unit)	551
#有R&D活动的单位数	Number of Units with Research and Development Activities	个(unit)	113
技术改造经费支出	Technical Reform Expenditure	万元(10 000 yuan)	112216.2
引进国外技术经费支出	Acquisition of Foreign Technology Expenditure	万元(10 000 yuan)	284.5
引进技术的消化吸收经费支出	Expenditure for Assimilation Technology	万元(10 000 yuan)	
购买国内技术经费支出	Expenditurefor Purchase Domestic Technology	万元(10 000 yuan)	1712.0
新产品销售收入	Output Value of New Products	万元(10 000 yuan)	3263959.1
研究与试验发展(R&D)人员	R&D Sonnel	人(Person)	8363
R&D人员折合全时当量	R&D Rsonnel Equivalent in Full Time	人年(man-years)	4893
新产品开发项目数	Number of on New Products Development	项(unit)	725
新产品开发经费支出	Expenditure on New Products Development	万元(10 000 yuan)	186762.9
R&D经费内部支出合计	Internal Expenditure on R&D	万元(10 000 yuan)	267069.5
#经常费支出	Daily Expenditure	万元(10 000 yuan)	247448.6
#资产性支出	Capital Expenditure	万元(10 000 yuan)	19620.9
政府资金	GovernmentAppropriation Funds	万元(10 000 yuan)	2285.9
企业资金	Self-raised Funds by Enterprises	万元(10 000 yuan)	263865.0
境外资金	Foreign Funds	万元(10 000 yuan)	234.3
其他资金	Other Funds	万元(10 000 yuan)	684.3
R&D经费外部支出	External Expenditure on R&D	万元(10 000 yuan)	4652.8
机构数	Number Scientific Research Institutions	个(unit)	45
机构人员合计	Research Personnel	人(Person)	1871
#博士毕业	Doctor	人(Person)	55
#硕士毕业	Master	人(Person)	308
机构经费支出	Agency Expenditure	万元(10 000 yuan)	146076.9
仪器和设备原价	Original Price of Equipment	万元(10 000 yuan)	57645.4
专利申请数	Patent Applications	件(piece)	1066
#发明专利	Inventions	件(piece)	384
有效发明专利数	Effective Invention Patent	件(piece)	1405
拥有注册商标数	Registered Trademarks	件(piece)	259
#境外注册	Overseas Registered	件(piece)	50
形成国家或行业标准数	Industry or National Standards	项(unit)	15

主要统计指标解释

科技活动 是指在自然科学、农业科学、医药科学、工程与技术科学、人文与社会科学领域（简称科学技术领域）中，与科技知识的产生、发展、传播和应用密切相关的有组织的活动。在企（事）业中只有列入单位工作计划的科技活动才予以统计，而独立发明人等在企（事）业外或计划外进行的科技活动不在统计范围之内。科研活动可分为研究与试验发展（简称R&D，包括基础研究、应用研究和试验发展）、研究与试验发展（R&D）成果应用及相关的科技服务三类活动。

基础研究 是指为了获得关于现象和可观察事实的基本原理的新知识（揭示客观事物的本质、运动规律，获得新发现、新学说）而进行的实验性或理论性研究。基础研究属于科学研究范畴。从研究目的看，基础研究不以任何专门或特定的应用或使用为目的，它只是通过试验分析或理论性研究对事物的特性、结构和各种关系进行分析，加深对客观事物的认识，解释现象的本质，揭示物质运动的规律或提出和验证各种设想、理论和定律。从研究结果看，基础研究的结果具有一般的或普遍的正确性，通常表现为一般的原则、理论和规律，其成果以科学论文和科学著作为主要形式。

应用研究 是指为获得新知识而进行的创造性研究，主要针对某一特定的目的或目标。应用研究也属于科学研究范畴。从研究目的看，应用研究是探索基础研究成果的可能用途，或是为达到预定的目标探索应采取的新方法（原理性）或新途径，为解决实际问题提供科学依据。从研究结果看，应用研究的成果一般只影响科学技术的某些领域和有限范围，并具有专门的性质，针对具体的领域、问题或情况，其成果形式以科学论文、专著、原理性模型或发明专利等为主。

试验发展 是指利用从基础研究、应用研究和实际经验所获得的现有知识，为产生新的产品、材料和装置，建立新的工艺、系统和服务，以及对已产生和建立的上述各项做实质性的改进而进行的系统性工作。在社会科学领域，试验发展是指通过把基础研究、应用研究获得的知识转变成可以实施的计划（包括为检验和评估实施示范项目）的过程。

专利申请数 指企业在报告期内向国内外知识产权行政部门提出专利申请并被受理的件数。

专利申请数中发明专利 指企业在报告期内向国内外知识产权行政部门提出发明专利申请并被受理的件数。

新产品产值 指报告期企业生产的新产品的产值。新产品是指采用新技术原理、新设计构思研制、生产的全新产品，或在结构、材质、工艺等某一方面比原有产品有明显改进，从而显著提高了产品性能或扩大了使用功能的产品。新产品产值、新产品销售收入既包括经政府有关部门认定并在有效期内的新产品，也包括企业自行研制开发，未经政府有关部门认定，从投产之日起一年之内的新产品。

拥有注册商标 指企业在报告期末拥有的注册商标件数。包括在境内和境外注册的商标件数，一件商标在境内外同时注册时只统计一件。

技术改造经费支出 指企业在报告期进行技术改造而发生的费用支出。技术改造指企业在坚持科技进步的前提下，将科技成果应用于生产的各个领域（产品、设备、工艺等），用先进工艺、设备代替落后工艺、设备，实现以内涵为主的扩大再生产，从而提高产品质量、促进产品更新换代、节约能源、降低消耗，全面提高综合经济效益。

Explanatory Notes on Main Statistical Indicators

Scientific and Technological Activities refer to organized activities closely related to generation, development, dissemination and application of knowledge of science and technology in natural science, agricultural science, pharmaceutical science, engineering and technical science, humanities and social sciences field (called as science and technology field for short). Only scientific and technological activities listed into the work plan of the enterprise (institution) will be included, while scientific and technological activities by independent inventors outside the enterprise (institution) or the plan are out of the statistics scope. Scientific research activities can be divided into three categories -- research and experimental development (called as R&D for short, including fundamental research, application research and experimental development), application of results of research and experimental development (R&D) and related science and technology services.

Fundamental Research refers to empirical or theoretical research aiming at obtaining new knowledge on the fundamental principles of phenomena of observable facts to reveal the nature and law of movement of objects and to acquire new discoveries or new theories. Fundamental research falls into scientific research. From the perspective of research purpose, fundamental research takes no specific or designated application as the aim of the research which only involves analysis on features, structures and various relationships of things by experimental analysis or theoretical research to deepen the understanding of objective things, explain the nature of the phenomenon and reveal the laws of the motion of matter or put forward and verify various assumptions, theories and laws. From the perspective of research result, the result of fundamental research is of general or universal correctness, usually presented as general principle, theory and law. Results of fundamental research are mainly released or disseminated in the form of scientific papers or monographs.

Applied Research refers to creative research aiming at obtaining new knowledge on a specific objective or target. Applied research also falls into scientific research. From the perspective of research purpose, purpose of the applied research is to identify the possible use of results from basic research, or to explore new (fundamental) methods or new approaches as well as provide scientific basis for solving practical problems. From the perspective of research result, achievements of application research only influence some fields and limited scope of science and technology generally and are of a specialized nature and expressed in the form of scientific papers, monographs, fundamental models or invention patents on the basis of specific field, problem or situation.

Experiments and Development refer to systematic activities aiming at using the knowledge from fundamental and applied researches or from practical experience to develop new products, materials and equipment, to establish new production process, systems and services, or to make substantial improvement on the existing products, process or services. In social sciences, experiment and development activities refer to the process of converting the knowledge from or applied researches into feasible programs (including conduct of demonstration projects for assessment and evaluation).

Quantity of Patents Applied refers to the quantity of patents accepted with application for a patent filed by the enterprise to intellectual property administrative departments at the home and abroad in the reporting period.

Quantity of Invention Patent in the Patents Applied refers to the quantity of patents for invention accepted with application for an invention patent filed by the enterprise to intellectual property administrative departments at the home and abroad in the reporting period.

Output Value of New Products refers to output value of new products produced by enterprises in the reporting period. New products refer to new products developed or produced by new know-why and design concept and products with properties of products obviously improved or use function expanded due to the obvious improvement in structure, texture or technology in comparison to those of original products. Output value of new products and sales revenue from new products include new products approved by relevant government departments whose valid term fails to expire and new products developed independently by the enterprise and not approved by relevant government departments which exist for less than one year as of the date of going into operation.

Possession of Registered Trademark refers to the quantity of registered trademarks owned by the enterprise at the end of the reporting period, including quantity of trademark registered at home and abroad. Statistics of a trademark are only conducted once at the moment of being registered at the home and abroad at the same time.

Expenditure on Technological Transformation refers to the expenditure incurred by technological transformation by the enterprise in the reporting period. Technological transformation refers to the enterprise applying scientific and technological achievements to all fields of production (product, equipment and technology, etc.) and replacing backward technology and equipment with advance technology and equipment to realize intention-based expanded reproduction, thus to improve product quality, promote product upgrading, save energy, lower consumption and comprehensively enhance composite economic results in the premise of insisting on scientific and technological progress.

18

教育与文化

EDUCATION AND CULTURE

18-1 教育事业基本情况
Basic Statistics on Education

指　　标	Indicator	1952年	1957年	1962年	1965年	1970年
学校数（所）	Number of Schools(nuit)	2679	3106	3731	4318	5359
#驻济高等学校	Higher Education in Ji'nan	5	4	12	8	2
中等教育	Secondary Education	37	67	112	410	1204
#中等职业学校	Vocational Secondary Education	16	16	15	15	17
普通中学	Regular Junior Secondary Schools	21	51	93	159	1024
小 学	Primary Schools	2636	3034	3606	3899	4152
专任教师（人）	Full-time Teachers(person)	8555	13452	19606	26760	32508
#驻济高等学校	Higher Education in Ji'nan	671	1325	2598	2451	922
中等教育	Secondary Education	1108	2569	3418	5321	9607
#中等职业学校	Vocational Secondary Education	311	787	765	685	914
普通中学	Regular Junior Secondary Schools	797	1782	2629	3502	8445
小 学	Primary Schools	6773	9550	13571	18971	21954
在校学生（万人）	Total Enrollment(10 000 persons)	26.87	31.95	49.82	68.27	80.20
#驻济高等学校	Higher Education in Ji'nan	0.43	0.82	1.65	1.40	0.30
中等教育	Secondary Education	2.73	5.14	5.80	10.43	18.97
#中等职业学校	Vocational Secondary Education	0.69	0.93	0.51	0.65	0.12
普通中学	Regular Junior Secondary Schools	2.04	4.21	5.22	7.50	17.81
小 学	Primary Schools	23.70	25.98	42.35	56.42	60.91
各类学校毕业生数（万人）	Graduates(10 000 persons)	4.38	8.58	10.60	10.45	12.09
#驻济高等学校	Higher Education in Ji'nan	0.14	0.11	0.31	0.43	—
中等教育	Secondary Education	0.60	1.14	1.72	1.90	1.02
#中等职业学校	Vocational Secondary Education	0.13	0.14	0.32	0.03	—
普通中学	Regular Junior Secondary Schools	0.46	1.00	1.40	1.80	0.38
每一教师负担学生数（人）	Each Teacher Burden Number of Students(person)	31.41	23.75	25.41	23.27	24.67
#驻济高等学校	Higher Education in Ji'nan	6.41	6.19	6.35	5.71	3.25
中等教育	Secondary Education	24.64	20.01	16.97	19.60	19.75
#中等职业学校	Vocational Secondary Education	22.33	11.84	6.64	9.51	1.36
普通中学	Regular Junior Secondary Schools	25.63	23.64	19.84	21.41	21.09
小 学	Primary Schools	34.99	27.20	31.21	29.74	27.74
平均每万人口在校学生（人）	Number of Enrollment Per 10000 Population(person)	843	922	1418	1829	1968
#大学生	Undergraduate	14	24	47	38	7
中专生	Secondary Students	22	27	14	17	3
中学生	Middle School Students	64	122	150	256	463
小学生	Elementary School Students	743	750	1206	1513	1494

注：1. 驻济高等学校在校生含普通专本科、成人本专科、研究生在校生。
2. 驻济高等学校毕业生为普通本专科毕业生。

1975年	1980年	1985年	1990年	1995年	2000年	2005年	2010年	2015年	2017年	2018年	2019年
5412	5066	4511	3924	3360	1725	1251	1025	946	953	930	1110
4	11	16	16	16	16	59	66	72	69	51	52
922	759	593	529	440	423	348	302	280	293	304	375
21	30	40	39	41	40	91	73	41	35	34	40
783	710	491	417	312	297	247	209	214	238	251	312
4485	4295	3899	3368	2890	1273	832	645	582	580	575	683
42432	49608	46806	55978	58779	62869	77334	83106	88487	95704	101305	118342
2468	3744	4614	7245	7500	8269	24341	29526	31693	33282	37539	40627
15274	19062	17530	21618	23946	26817	27435	28370	30589	32892	33161	41112
985	1338	2367	2890	2941	2916	4738	4511	4068	3978	3711	4058
13571	17294	13572	16065	17621	20585	21915	21943	23643	25676	26588	34177
24654	26775	24579	26922	27417	27417	25201	24801	25795	29109	30605	36067
90.28	83.56	78.38	79.48	91.69	95.79	129.28	144.60	153.71	163.59	168.97	182.68
0.61	1.58	3.02	3.73	5.66	9.30	48.71	64.25	71.40	79.21	79.63	76.20
25.43	20.24	25.34	28.08	36.64	44.99	42.50	41.76	40.77	39.62	42.68	52.24
0.58	0.31	1.92	2.51	4.79	5.75	9.88	8.10	5.93	5.52	5.16	5.68
23.86	19.63	21.49	22.45	27.15	33.82	30.91	30.18	30.16	30.56	31.18	39.35
64.22	61.47	49.98	47.57	49.23	41.40	37.88	38.40	41.44	44.66	46.66	54.14
22.66	18.07	17.31	17.12	20.88	23.65	33.58	38.10	39.83	47.24	50.65	55.99
0.20	0.03	0.45	1.03	1.68	1.55	13.49	17.57	19.48	27.37	26.29	17.07
11.83	8.41	7.36	8.24	10.39	10.80	14.03	13.55	14.22	12.73	12.28	16.47
0.20	0.46	0.52	0.62	1.16	1.84	3.29	3.13	2.75	1.68	2.43	2.05
11.58	7.89	6.39	6.66	7.78	8.16	10.40	9.20	10.23	10.03	9.65	12.30
21.28	16.84	16.75	14.20	15.60	15.24	16.72	17.40	17.37	17.09	16.68	15.44
2.47	4.22	6.55	5.15	7.54	11.25	20.01	21.76	22.53	23.79	21.21	18.76
16.65	10.62	14.46	12.99	15.30	16.78	15.49	14.72	13.33	12.04	12.87	12.71
5.95	2.29	8.12	8.69	16.30	18.84	20.86	17.96	14.58	13.80	13.90	14.00
17.58	11.35	15.83	13.98	15.41	16.43	14.10	13.75	12.76	11.89	11.73	11.51
26.05	22.96	20.33	17.67	18.20	15.10	15.03	15.48	16.07	15.35	15.25	15.01
2062	1822	1605	1518	1691	1702	2177	2395	2465	2563	2600	2505
14	34	62	71	104	165	820	1064	1145	1241	1226	1040
13	7	39	48	88	102	195	192	170	142	177	178
566	429	473	473	553	601	521	500	484	479	480	542
1466	1339	1024	908	908	736	638	636	664	700	718	745

Note: 1. Students under high education in Jinan include regular college students, regular junior college students, adult college students, adult junior students and postgraduate students.

2. Graduates under high education in Jinan are those of regular college and jounior college programme.

18-2 普通高等院校一览(2019年)

Basic Statistics on Institutions of Higher Education(2019)

单位：人 (person)

指 标	普通本专科在校学生数 Total Enrollment	普通本专科毕业生数 Graduates	普通本专科招生数 New Enrollment	教职工人 Teachers and Staff	# 专任教师 Full-time Teachers		
					合 计 Total	# 正高级 Senior	# 副高级 Sub-Senior
总 计	671276	170709	209093	53452	39401	5436	12276
综合性大学							
山东大学	41037	9642	10089	7231	4530	1501	1727
济南大学	34783	7851	8497	2851	2145	333	781
山东青年政治学院	13647	3807	4599	864	632	44	168
山东女子学院	14949	2265	5158	752	525	45	174
理工院校							
山东建筑大学	25513	5550	5865	2145	1726	252	666
山东科技大学	36130	8091	8557	3157	2147	310	646
齐鲁工业大学	28525	6461	7131	2640	2058	274	737
山东交通学院	25203	6497	6341	1752	1519	98	395
山东电力高等专科学校	2638	732	1258	313	150	32	35
医药院校							
山东第一医科大学	22111	5610	5412	2065	1526	257	585
山东中医药大学	18801	4063	4598	1411	1182	281	384
山东医学高等专科学校	25566	6513	9978	1127	901	63	200
济南护理职业学院	5368	2059	2014	415	248	28	92
师范院校							
山东师范大学	30915	7492	7271	2590	2010	371	568
齐鲁师范学院	15320	3318	5833	875	702	86	192
济南幼儿师范专科学校	5309	1340	2651	519	260		71
财经院校							
山东财经大学	29814	7059	6841	2430	1957	292	726
山东财经大学燕山学院	7110	1982	2048	450	397	48	152
政法院校							
山东警察学院	4941	860	1297	582	266	20	120
山东司法警官职业学院	6134	2182	2528	237	136	2	39
山东政法学院	11602	3516	2663	950	696	59	165
体育院校							
山东体育学院	8453	1926	2125	705	567	49	199
艺术院校							
山东艺术学院	9923	2449	2414	1075	916	87	259
山东工艺美术学院	7193	1543	1832	733	537	67	168
职业技术学院							
山东协和学院	22899	5019	9130	1253	981	70	295
山东商业职业技术学院	14564	4741	5321	1023	749	40	202
山东劳动职业技术学院	11463	3737	4403	744	601	32	158
山东职业学院	15186	5168	5325	847	642	30	170
山东圣翰财贸职业学院	9105	2590	4574	732	408	13	85
山东艺术设计职业学院	2939	724	1466	290	238	34	22
山东英才学院	21701	5231	7757	1604	1138	114	407
山东旅游职业学院	8614	2316	3600	514	423	14	77
济南工程职业技术学院	11393	3795	4543	664	531	16	144
山东电子职业技术学院	9381	2895	3553	576	448	10	114
济南职业学院	12926	4389	5006	885	669	37	122
山东现代学院	16460	4813	5896	996	796	86	213
山东工程职业技术大学	10439	2658	7036	699	496	89	162
山东城市建设职业学院	12239	4192	4871	675	561	10	182
山东管理学院	11705	2665	2933	692	565	46	105
齐鲁理工学院	16441	3571	5156	1316	836	124	207
山东农业工程学院	12628	3304	3265	704	541	37	126
山东特殊教育职业学院	1194	287	597	187	131	2	18
山东传媒职业学院	8584	2304	3663	461	389	15	73
莱芜职业技术学院	10430	3502	3998	721	525	18	145

18-3 中等专业学校一览 (2019 年)
Basic Statistics on Specialized Secondary Schools(2019)

单位：人 (person)

指 标	在校学生数 Total Enrollment	毕业生数 Graduates	招生数 New Enrollment	教职工人 Teachers and Staff	# 专任教师 Full-time Teachers		
					合 计 Total	# 副高级 Sub-Senior	# 中级 Middle
总计	10567	3845	3468	1291	905	253	467
工科学校							
济南信息工程学校	2780	903	991	188	139	42	90
济南电子机械工程学校	1692	656	602	194	154	46	79
济南铁路学校	216	147	40	50	50	20	25
山东冶金中等专业学校	820	414	239	151	69	31	27
财经学校							
山东省济南商贸学校	1430	811	474	252	184	52	93
体育学校							
济南市体育运动学校	761	293	310	119	46	11	16
山东体育学院附属中学	1372	231	386				
艺术学校							
山东省文化艺术学校	723	144	176	139	93	11	55
山东工艺美术学院附属中等美术学校	138	50	49	21	19	5	4
济南艺术学校	635	196	201	177	151	35	78

18-4 分县区儿童学前教育基本情况 (2019 年)
Student Enrollment in Pre-school Education(2019)

单位：人 (person)

指 标	Indicator	幼儿园数 (所) Number of Kindergartens (unit)	在园人数 Enrolment	入园人数 Entrants	教职工数 Teachers and Staff	# 专任教师 Full Time Teachers
全市	total	2147	319800	120164	41329	23234
历下区	Li xia	112	31187	10502	4594	2447
市中区	Shi zhong	190	32262	12471	5216	2777
槐荫区	Huai yin	143	30478	11979	4411	2246
天桥区	Tian qiao	148	27423	8331	4193	2038
历城区	Li cheng	204	38909	19442	5519	2972
长清区	Chang qing	140	15912	5023	1646	1096
章丘区	Zhang qiu	210	27932	11183	3244	1873
济阳区	Ji yang	148	16150	5988	1447	755
莱芜区	Lai wu	298	28792	9858	2963	2102
钢城区	Gang cheng	79	10889	3698	1150	801
济南高新区	Ji'nan Gao xin	98	17080	6463	2554	1373
莱芜高新区	Lai wu Gao xin	48	7143	3139	688	460
南部山区	Nan shan	57	6368	2290	737	399
平阴县	Ping yin	55	9690	2998	948	681
商河县	Shang he	217	19585	6799	2019	1214

18-5 文化事业机构和人员
Number of Institutions and Persons in Culture

指　标	Indicator	2014 年	2015 年	2016 年	2017 年	2018 年	2019 年
机构数（个）	Number(unit)						
电影业	Movies	30	38	44	52	54	65
艺术业	Arts	27	27	27	27	27	25
文物业	Cultural Relics	40	42	48	48	48	67
图书馆业	Libraries	12	12	12	12	12	14
群众文化业	Mass Culture	153	152	155	153	153	175
艺术教育业	Art Education	1	1	1	1	1	1
文艺科研业	Culture Research	1	1	1	1	1	1
从业人员数（人）	Personnel(person)						
电影业	Movies	637	705	913	936	1380	1075
艺术业	Arts	1608	1569	1557	1569	1537	1475
文物业	Cultural Relics	1083	1119	1173	1158	1068	1365
图书馆业	Libraries	447	431	447	462	472	507
群众文化业	Mass Culture	908	699	710	719	695	745
艺术教育业	Art Education	112	123	164	167	170	175
文艺科研业	Culture Research	46	49	51	49	47	47

注：电影业机构、从业人员数据为城市电影院线数据，不含农村。
Notes: The data of the film industry institutions and employees are urban cinema line data, excluding rural areas.

主要统计指标解释

普通高等学校　指按照国家规定的设置标准和审批程序批准举办，通过国家统一招生考试，招收高中毕业生为主要培养对象，实施高等教育的全日制大学、独立设置的学院和高等专科学校、短期职业大学。

文化事业机构　指从事专业文化工作和为专业文化工作服务的独立建制的单位。不包括这些单位另外举办独立核算的其他机构和各部门的业余文化组织。

Explanatory Notes on Main Statistical Indicators

Regular Institutions of Higher Education refer to educational establishments that set up according to the government evaluation and approval procedures, enrolling graduates from senior secondary schools and providing higher education courses and training for senior professionals. They include full time universities, colleges and high professional schools which set up independently as well as short-term vocational colleges.

Cultural Institutions refer to units which have their own organizational system, work on professional culture work and serve the professional culture work, excluding other institutions for independent accounting established by such units separately and amateur cultural organizations of all departments.

19

体育与卫生

SPORTS AND PUBLIC HEALTH

19-1 体育事业
Statistics of Sports Instituons

指　　标	Indicator	2014 年	2015 年	2016 年	2017 年	2018 年	2019 年
体育部门职工人数（人）	Number of Persons of Physical System(person)	671	656	724	720	591	672
#业余体育学校	Spare-time Sports School	166	219	221	9	423	402
总计中：教练员	Referees	241	232	151	231	191	183
等级裁判员（人）	Number of Referees in Grades(person)						
一级裁判员	First Grade Referees				7		
二级裁判员	Second Grade Referees	184	246	122	153	268	344
三级裁判员	Third Grade Referees				55		
二级运动员发展人数（人）	Number of Second Grade Sportsmen(person)	376	359	401	465	279	534
少年儿童业余体校在校学生（人）	Enrollment Spare-time Sports School(person)	898	973	1036	845	1140	1286
业余体校（所）	Spare-time Sports School(unit)	3	3	5	7	5	10
运动员获奖牌数（枚）	Number of Medals Wonby Athletes(unit)	594.5	585	1110	1188.5	1186	1353
#世界级 金 牌	World Gold Medals	6	5	12	1	3	13
银 牌	Silver Medals	4	3	4	2	1	7
铜 牌	Copper Medal	6		4	1	2	8
#洲 际 金 牌	Intercontinental Gold Medals	5	5	7	3	3	10
银 牌	Silver Medals	1	1	4	3	2	11
铜 牌	Copper Medal		2	4		1	7
#全 国 金 牌	Country Gold Medals	75	48	43	85	50	100
银 牌	Silver Medals	32	23	29	61	36	91
铜 牌	Copper Medal	43	29	16	100	41	132
#全 省 金 牌	Province Gold Medals	201.5	215	402	395.5	430	442
银 牌	Silver Medals	93.5	119	292	273	319	248
铜 牌	Copper Medal	127.5	135	293	264	288	284
体育设施（个）	Sports Facility(unit)						
体育场	Stadium	12	12	12	6	12	14
体育馆	Gymnasium	9	9	9	17	9	10
游泳馆	Natatorium	5	5	5	11	5	9
室内外游泳池	Indoor Swimming Pool	2	2	2	5	4	10
有固定看台的灯光球场	Light Count With Fixed Stand	2	2	2	7	2	5

注：1. 等级裁判员为当年新评定的人数。
2. 2017 年体育设施统计口径为市、区县体育部门主管的设施数量。
3. 2017 年业余体育学校统计口径只指学位，不包括业训网点。

Note: 1.The number of referees is the number of new assessments in the current year.
2.The number of sports facilities in 2017 is the number of facilities in charge of the sports department of the city, district and county.
3.In 2017, the statistical caliber of amateur sports schools only refers to degree, excluding amateur training outlets.

19-2 各时期卫生事业情况
Statistics of Health Institutions in Major Years

年份 Year	卫生机构（个） Number of Health Institutions(unit)		卫生工作人员（人） Medical Technical Personnel(person)		卫生机构床位（张） Number of Health Institutions Beds(set)	
	小计 Total	#医院及卫生院 Hospitals and Township Hospitals	小计 Total	#卫生技术人员 Medical Technical Personnel	小计 Total	#医院及卫生院 Hospitals and Township Hospitals
1952	208	22	6277	4778	3160	1906
1957	708	45	10740	7991	5972	3401
1962	1191	98	13705	9648	7917	5662
1965	1144	114	18885	14881	9035	6438
1970	682	130	13273	10341	7878	6462
1975	934	137	20021	14956	9066	8050
1978	1017	148	24949	19198	11496	9856
1979	1078	152	26385	20110	11902	10781
1980	1091	151	27843	21295	12301	11052
"六五"时期						
1981	1188	152	29597	22559	12428	11436
1982	1159	151	30636	22814	12379	11383
1983	1177	156	31924	23948	12966	11674
1984	1160	157	32967	24502	13728	12960
1985	1175	165	34232	26185	14356	13791
"七五"时期						
1986	1184	167	35803	27360	14757	14165
1987	1137	166	37129	28159	15457	14721
1988	1103	171	38384	29167	16165	15580
1989	1137	180	39926	29878	16698	16176
1990	1300	178	41444	31130	18214	17216
"八五"时期						
1991	1233	177	40957	30815	18439	17538
1992	1331	180	41996	31541	18818	18178
1993	1285	193	43274	32871	20243	19320
1994	1228	213	43630	33007	20001	19064
1995	1185	216	43648	32848	20747	19534

19-2 续表 continued

年份 Year	卫生机构(个) Number of Health Institutions(unit)		卫生工作人员(人) Medical Technical Personnel(person)		卫生机构床位(张) Number of Health Institutions Beds(set)	
	小 计 Total	# 医院及卫生院 Hospitals and Township Hospitals	小 计 Total	# 卫生技术人员 Medical Technical Personnel	小 计 Total	# 医院及卫生院 Hospitals and Township Hospitals
"九五"时期						
1996	1674	214	45765	35219	20428	19716
1997	1567	220	44664	34188	21422	20706
1998	1574	227	45110	34596	21965	21130
1999	1570	226	45121	34000	21735	21086
2000	1414	231	45166	35669	21698	20830
"十五"时期						
2001	1414	231	45296	35790	21906	21033
2002	1708	243	39386	31945	21576	21042
2003	1868	246	41925	33803	22674	22262
2004	1917	243	41625	33998	24044	22588
2005	2138	246	41499	34129	24695	23524
"十一五"时期						
2006	2285	240	43023	35124	27695	26101
2007	2265	243	42513	34579	26055	25328
2008	5092	286	44416	36143	28939	27555
2009	5163	281	46311	37648	30920	28749
2010	5086	277	54711	39366	31947	29844
"十二五"时期						
2011	5159	262	58590	42116	34920	31545
2012	5239	243	60426	44331	38834	35194
2013	5368	255	76955	57700	45465	41287
2014	5784	265	84515	63604	48280	44058
2015	5947	269	89117	71778	49311	45195
"十三五"时期						
2016	6188	270	92060	76447	52191	47524
2017	5770	289	97663	76273	54855	50142
2018	6030	293	104347	82834	57460	51207
2019	7487	351	122370	97532	66623	59697

注：2015 年及 2016 年的卫生技术人员为注册卫生技术人员，其他年份为在岗卫生技术人员。
Notes: Health technicians in 2015 and 2016 are registered health technicians, and other years are on-the-job health technicians.

19-3 卫生事业机构及床位
Number of Health Institutions and Beds

指　标	Indicator	2014 年	2015 年	2016 年	2017 年	2018 年	2019 年
各类卫生机构数（个）	Number of Health Institutions (unit)	5784	5947	6188	5770	6030	7487
医院	Hospital	207	213	217	238	246	289
社区卫生服务中心（站）	Health Service Center for Community	268	275	286	283	314	352
卫生院	Health Centers	58	56	53	51	47	62
门诊部	Outpatient Department	66	72	89	115	135	156
急救中心（站）	First-Aid Center	2	2	2	1	1	1
采血供应机构	Pick and Supply Blood Institution	4	4	4	2	2	3
妇幼保健院（所、站）	Women and Children Care Agencies	12	12	12	12	12	15
专科疾病防治院（所、站）	Specialized Disease Prevention & Treatment Institution	10	10	10	10	11	13
疾病预防控制中心（防疫站）	Center for Disease Control and Prevention	12	12	12	12	12	15
医学科学研究机构	Medical Science Research Institutes	2	2	2	2	2	2
其他卫生机构	Other Medical Institutions	15	17	18	27	29	39
各类卫生机构病床数（张）	Number of Health Institutions Beds(set)	48280	49311	52191	54855	57460	66623
医院	Hospital	40874	42204	44526	47575	48843	56315
社区卫生服务中心（站）	Health Service Center for Community	2857	2792	2946	3195	3361	3791
卫生院	Health Centers	3184	2991	2998	2567	2364	3382
门诊部	Outpatient Department	133	127	112	46	65	33
妇幼保健院（所、站）	Women and Children Care Agencies	777	834	1243	1126	1158	1444
专科疾病防治院（所、站）	Specialized Disease Prevention	455	360	366	346	1669	1658
千人拥有量（张、人）	Number Per 1000 Population(set.person)						
平均每千人拥有病床	Number Of Beds Per 1000 Population	6.83	6.91	7.22	7.49	7.70	7.48
每千人拥有卫生技术人员	Number Of Medical Technical Personnel Per 1000 Population	9.00	10.06	10.57	10.42	11.10	10.95
每千人拥有医生	Number Of Doctors Per 1000 Population	3.50	4.60	4.75	3.97	4.31	4.30
每千人拥有护士	Number Of Nurses Per 1000 Population	3.89	5.32	5.82	4.62	5.03	4.91

19-4 分地区卫生事业机构及床位(2019年)
Number of Health Institutions and Beds by District(2019)

指　标	Indicator	全市 Total	市区 Urban	平阴县 Ping yin	商河县 Shang he
各类卫生机构数(个)	**Number of Institutions(unit)**	7487	6749	253	485
医院	Hospital	289	280	4	5
疗养院	Health Service Center for Community				
社区卫生服务中心(站)	Health Centers	352	337	6	9
卫生院	Outpatient Department	62	45	6	11
门诊部	Outpatient Department	156	149	2	5
诊所、卫生所、医务室	Infirmaries and Clinics	2781	2630	62	89
急救中心(站)	First-Aid Center	1	1		
采血供应机构	Pick and Supply Blood Institution	3	3		
妇幼保健院(所、站)	Women and Children Care Agencies	15	13	1	1
专科疾病防治院(所、站)	Specialized Disease Prevention &Treatment Institution	13	11	2	
疾病预防控制中心(防疫站)	Center for Disease Control and Prevention	15	13	1	1
卫生监督所	Medical Supervision Institution	15	13	1	1
医学科学研究机构	Medical Science Research Institutes	2	2		
其他卫生构	Other Medical Institutions	39	39		
各类卫生机构病床数(张)	**Number of Institutions Beds(set)**	66623	61699	2490	2434
医院	Hospital	56315	52627	1786	1902
疗养院	Sanatorium				
社区卫生服务中心(站)	Health Service Center for Community	3791	3739		52
卫生院	Health Centers	3382	2344	558	480
门诊部	Outpatient Department	33	33		
妇幼保健院(所、站)	Women and Children Care Agencies	1444	1438	6	
专科疾病防治院(所、站)	Specialized Disease Prevention&Treatment Institution	1658	1518	140	
千人拥有量(张、人)	**Number Per 1000 Population(set.person)**				
平均每千人拥有病床	Number Of Beds Per 1000 Population	7.48	774	6.91	4.19
每千人拥有卫生技术人员	Number Of Medical Technical Personnel Per 1000 Population	10.95	11.61	6.35	4.76
每千人拥有医生	Number Of Doctors Per 1000 Population	4.30	4.54	2.34	2.11
每千人拥有护士	Number Of Nurses Per 1000 Population	4.91	5.22	2.96	1.84

19-5 医疗机构年收入与支出（2019 年）
Revenue and Expenditure in Health Insititutions(2019)

单位：万元 (10 000 yuan)

机构分类	Institutions	总支出 Total Expenditure 合计 Total	财政补助收入 Financial Subsidy Income	上级补助收入 Grant From Higher Authority	业务收入／事业收入 Business Income
合计	Total	5410919.8	593855.6	23542.3	4579537.6
医院	Hospital	4583655.1	328219.2	5447.7	4140917.2
社区卫生服务中心（站）	Health Service Center for Community	184324.5	59099.4	3960.9	117257.6
卫生院	Health Centers	101618.4	52194.1	874.0	47532.7
门诊部	Outpatient Department	19344.8	0.0	0.0	11800.2
诊所、卫生所、医务室	Infirmaries and Clinics	48920.8	0.0	0.0	39780.3
急救中心（站）	First-Aid Center	2375.2	2288.2	1.0	81.0
妇幼保健院（所、站）	Women and Children Care Agencies	175182.4	22961.2	534.9	141689.0
专科疾病防治院（所、站）	Specialized Disease Revention& Treatment Institution	51175.1	11258.5	344.4	39143.5

19-5 续表 continued

机构分类	Institutions	总支出 Total Expenditure 合计 Total	财政专项支出 Financial Expenditure	业务支出／事业支出 Business Expenditure	总支出中：人员支出 Staff Expenditure
合计	Total	5115516.7	300597.0	4250704.6	1723655.1
医院	Hospital	4339708.2	196099.0	3671273.8	1416691.9
社区卫生服务中心（站）	Health Service Center for Community	179605.2	0.0	164257.7	66688.7
卫生院	Health Centers	104040.1	0.0	97657.7	47933.1
门诊部	Outpatient Department	11997.7	0.0	0.0	6411.2
诊所、卫生所、医务室	Infirmaries and Clinics	38151.1	0.0	0.0	21408.1
急救中心（站）	First-Aid Center	2374.5	388.0	1986.5	1448.1
妇幼保健院（所、站）	Women and Children Care Agencies	161266.7	11680.5	137644.1	71551.7
专科疾病防治院（所、站）	Specialized Disease Revention& Treatment Institution	51166.6	4539.4	41403.8	22484.4

注：门诊部及诊所、卫生所、医务室不填报财政补助收入、上级补助收入、财政专项支出、业务支出／事业支出四项指标。

Notes: Outpatient department and clinic. Health clinic. The medical office does not report four indicators: financial subsidy income,superior subsidy income, fiscal special expenditure, business expenditure/business expenditure.

19-6 医院、卫生院工作情况
Basic Statistics on Hospitals and Health Institutions in Rural Areas

指　标	Indicator	2014年	2015年	2016年	2017年	2018年	2019年
医院	Hospital						
单位数（个）	Unit Number(unit)	207	213	217	238	246	289
诊疗人次数（万人次）	Visits (10 000 person-times)	2594	2716	2865	3157	3309	3922
#门诊人次数	OutPatients	2352	2446	2570	2779	2960	3449
急诊人次数	Emergency Patients	126	150	165	207	228	300
健康检查人数（万人次）	Check-up(10 000 person-times)	132	131	154	166	201	260
入院人数（万人）	Inpatients(10 000 person)	106.3	112.5	127.9	140.4	150.0	182.2
出院人数（万人）	Discharged(10 000 person)	106.1	112.1	127.3	139.7	149.4	181.5
平均开放病床数（张）	Average Bed Opened(set)	37218	39632	41402	44400	45132	52359
病床使用率(%)	Utilization Rate of Beds(%)	84.14	82.37	86.12	87.52	87.28	87.27
病床周转次数（次）	Turnover of Beds(time)	28.52	28.30	30.70	31.50	33.10	34.70
出院者平均住院日（日）	Average Stay Days in Hospital(day)	10.74	10.60	10.10	9.90	9.40	9.20
卫生院	Health Centers						
单位数（个）	Unit Number(unit)	58	56	53	51	47	62
诊疗人次数（万人次）	Visits (10 000 person-times)	280.5	211.7	233.4	208.1	195.2	301.9
#门诊人次数	OutPatients	271.4	205.7	224.6	197.6	190.3	292.1
急诊人次数	Emergency Patients	4.6	3.0	3.4	6.5	3.3	3.6
健康检查人数（万人次）	Check-up(10 000 person-times)	30.3	23.9	23.0	20.2	20.4	35.8
入院人数（万人）	Inpatients(10 000 person)	6.4	4.7	6.6	5.3	4.4	7.2
出院人数（万人）	Discharged(10 000 person)	6.4	4.7	6.5	5.3	4.4	7.2
平均开放病床数（张）	Average Bed Opened(set)	3062	2930	2907	2479	2277	3187
病床使用率(%)	Utilization Rate of Beds(%)	46.60	38.62	54.54	52.00	54.85	58.03
病床周转次数（次）	Turnover of Beds(time)	20.87	15.90	22.40	21.40	19.40	22.70
出院者平均住院日（日）	Average Stay Days in Hospital(day)	8.33	8.20	8.40	8.30	9.70	7.80

19-7 分地区卫生技术人员分类情况（2019年）
Medical Technical Personnel by Region(2019)

单位：人 (person)

指 标	Indicator	全市 Total	市区 Urban	平阴县 Ping yin	商河县 Shang he
各类卫生机构工作人员合计	Medical Technical Personnel	122370	115277	3031	4062
#卫生技术人员小计	Medical Technical Personnel	97532	92479	2287	2766
医 生	Licensed Doctors	38267	36202	842	1223
注册护士	Registered Nurse	43723	41592	1065	1066
其 他	Others	15542	14685	380	477

主要统计指标解释

等级裁判员人数 指经考核正式批准授予等级裁判员称号的人数。裁判员等级分为国际裁判、国家级裁判、一级裁判、二级裁判、三级裁判。

体育场 指有400米跑道（中心含足球场），有固定道牙，跑道6条以上，并有固定看台的室外田径场地。体育场按看台容纳观众人数分为：甲级25000人以上，乙级15000-25000人，丙级5000-15000人，丁级5000人以下。

体育馆 指有固定看台，可供篮球、排球、羽毛球、乒乓球、体操等项目训练比赛活动用的室内运动场地。体育馆按看台容纳观众人数分为：甲级6000人以上，乙级4000-6000人，丙级2000-4000人，丁级2000人以下。

医院 包括综合医院、中医医院、中西医结合医院、民族医医院、各类专科医院和护理院，不包括专科疾病防治院、妇幼保健院和疗养院，包括医学院校附属医院。

卫生技术人员 包括执业医师、执业助理医师、注册护士、药师（士）、检验及影像技师（士）、卫生监督员和见习医（药、护、技）师（士）等卫生专业人员。

医生 指取得医师执业证书且实际从事临床工作的人。

卫生机构 指从卫生（卫生健康）行政部门取得《医疗机构执业许可证》、《中医诊所备案证》、《计划生育技术服务许可证》或从民政、工商行政、机构编制管理部门取得法人单位登记证书，为社会提供医疗服务、公共卫生服务或从事医学科研和学在职培训等工作的单位。

Explanatory Notes on Main Statistical Indicators

Number of Grade Referees refers to the number of referees formally approved upon evaluation to be granted with the title of grade referee. Referees are divided into international referee, national referee, Level I referee, Level II referee and Level III referee.

Stadium refers to outdoor athletic field with 400m track (football field in the center), fixed kerbs, more than 6 tracks and fixed stands. Stadiums can be divided as follows as per the quantity of spectators contained by the standard: Class A stadium for above 25,000 persons, Class B stadium for 15,000–25,000 persons, Class C stadium for 5,000–15,000 persons and Class D stadium for less than 5,000 persons.

Gymnasium refers to indoor sports ground with fixed stands which can be used for training and competition of basketball, volleyball, badminton, table tennis and gymnastics. Gymnasium can be divided as follows as per the quantity of spectators contained by the standard: Class A gymnasium for above 6,000 persons, Class B gymnasium for 4,000–6,000 persons, Class C gymnasium for 2,000–4,000 persons and Class D gymnasium for less than 2,000 persons.

Hospital includes general hospital, traditional Chinese medicine hospital, hospital of traditional Chinese and Western medicine, ethnic medical hospital, various specialized hospital and nursing home and affiliated hospital of medical college other than specialized disease prevention and maternity and child care center and nursing home.

Medical Technical Personnel refers to health professionals such as medical practitioner, assistant medical practitioner, registered nurse, pharmacist, senior pharmacist (assistant pharmacist), inspection and imaging technician (assistant technician), health supervisor and medical intern (trainee medical assistant), pharmacy intern (probationary pharmacist), trainee nurse (practice nurse) or medical trainee (apprentice technician).

Doctors refer to persons getting the medical practitioner certificate and actually engaging in clinical work.

Health Care Institution refers to units getting Practicing License of Medical Institution, Registration Certificate of TCM Clinic and Family Planning Technical Service License from the administrative department of health (hygiene and health) or getting the registration certificate of legal entity from civil affairs, industrial and commercial administration, institutional establishment management departments, providing the society with medical service and public health service or engaging in medical scientific research and studying on–the–job training.

20

民政、司法和其他

SOCIAL WELFARE CIVIL ADMINISTRATION AND OTHERS

20-1 社会治安主要指标
Main Indicators of Social Offense

指　标	Indicator	2014 年	2015 年	2016 年	2017 年	2018 年	2019 年
刑事案件（件）	Criminal Cases(case)						
当年全部立案数	Put on Record	45118	35047	21142	19648	18594	25382
破获当年刑事案件数	Cracked the Number of Criminal Cases	26939	20806	7610	8571	7103	9259
治安案件（件）	Public Security Cases(case)						
受理数	Cases Accepted	91877	86217	71868	66375	75393	79355
查处数	Cases Punished	87656	81754	68439	63734	73700	72593
城市交通事故	Traffic Accidents						
交通事故（起）	Number of Traffic Accidents(case)	2948	2946	2944	3075	3071	3334
伤亡人数（人）	Number of Injuries and Deaths(person)	3708	3885	3573	3219	3618	3925
#死亡人数（人）	Number of Deathsa(person)	440	439	403	421	419	472
损失折款（万元）	Direct Losses(10 000 yuan)	737	840	875.2	1020.3	947.4	905.48
火灾事故	Fires						
火灾起数（起）	Number of Fire Accidents(case)	2848	2609	1825	1752	1539	4577
伤亡人数（人）	Number of Injuries and Deaths(person)	7	12	15	11	12	12
#死亡人数（人）	Number of Deaths(person)	6	12	13	10	10	10
损失折款（万元）	Direct Losses(10 000 yuan)	1104	1571	1903	599	827	1529

注："破获当年刑事案件数" 2015 年以前为当年全部破案数口径。
Note:"The number of uncovering criminal cases in the year"was the total quantity before 2015.

20-2 分地区社会治安主要指标(2019 年)
Main Indicators of Social Offense by District(2019)

指 标	Indicator	全市 Total	其中 of which		
			市区 Urban	平阴县 Ping yin	商河县 Shang he
刑事案件(件)	Criminal Cases(case)				
当年全部立案数	Put on Record	25382	24272	582	528
破获当年刑事案件数	Cracked the Number of Criminal Cases	9259	8668	373	218
治安案件(件)	Public Security Cases(case)				
受理数	Cases Accepted	79355	74447	3597	1311
查处数	Cases Punished	72593	68381	3597	615
城市交通事故	Traffic Accidents				
交通事故(起)	Number of Traffic Accidents(case)	3334	3253	46	35
伤亡人数(人)	Number of Injuries and Deaths(person)	3925	3832	62	31
#死亡人数(人)	Number of Deathsa(person)	472	435	28	9
损失折款(万元)	Direct Losses(10 000 yuan)	905	893	7	5
火灾事故	Fires				
火灾起数(起)	Number of Fire Accidents(case)	4577	4103	127	347
伤亡人数(人)	Number of Injuries and Deaths(person)	12	12		
#死亡人数(人)	Number of Deaths(person)	10	10		
损失折款(万元)	Direct Losses(10 000 yuan)	1529	1395	36	68

20-3 社会保障和救济
Basic Statistics on Social Security and Receiving Relief Flinds

指　标	Indicator	2014 年	2015 年	2016 年	2017 年	2018 年	2019 年
优抚情况（人）	Veteran Benefit and Placement(person)						
享受定期抚恤金人数	Number of Receiving Periodic Pensions	1169	939	907	831	784	914
在乡复员军人	Demobilized Soldiers in Countryside	3708	2725	2319	1892	1486	1727
参战退役人员	Veterans	4524	4454	4741	4705	4630	5636
社会救济情况（人）	Social Relief(person)						
城镇居民最低生活保障人数	Number of Urban Residents for Minimum Livelihood Guarantee	24925	22303	19742	16742	13364	15491
农村居民最低生活保障人数	Number of Rural residents for Minimum Livelihood Guarantee	80535	81215	80147	77121	64271	73305
民政经费（万元）	Civil Affairs Expenditures(10 000 yuan)						
退役安置费	Decommissioning Costs	71530	89415	96164	134557	12656	13538
城市居民最低生活保障费	Urban Residents for Minimum Livelihood Guarantee	12882	8585	11573	10966	9563	9657
农村最低生活保障费	Rural residents for Minimum Livelihood Guarantee	16376	13343	24938	26929	26439	26039
其它社会救助费	Other Social Assistance Expenses	7397	11446	6614	5757	3088	1158
社会福利费	Social Welfare Funds	28987	33569	35898	32194	47654	60731
自然灾害生活救助费	Natural Disaster Assistance Expenses	570	1646	654	259	–	–
医疗救助费	Medical Assistance Expenses	6788	4581	7245	8396	131	–
社会保障及扶贫（个、元）	Social Security and Poverty Alleviation(unit.yuan)						
建立社会保障服务网络的乡镇数	Number of Towns With Social Security Service Network	53	48	39	29	29	40
城市市区居民最低生活保障金标准	Minimum Living Standards for Urban Residents	550	550	580	596	616	685

注：本表指标为“–”的，部门相关统计制度中已经不再进行统计。
Notes: The indicator “–” in this table means statistics are no longer in the relevant statistical system of the department.

20-4 分地区社会保障和救济(2019年)
Basic Statistics on Social Security and Receiving Relief Flinds by Region(2019)

指标	Indicator	济南市(汇总) Total	济南市(市本级) Urban	历下区 Li xia	市中区 Shi zhong	槐荫区 Huai yin
优抚情况(人)	Veteran Benefit and Placement(person)					
享受定期抚恤金人数	Number of Receiving Periodic Pensions	914		41	64	31
在乡复员军人	Demobilized Soldiers in Countryside	1727		25	48	31
参战退役人员	Veterans	5636		70	203	139
社会救济情况(人)	Social Relief(person)					
城镇居民最低生活保障人数	Number of Urban Residents for Minimum Livelihood Guarantee	15491		1761	2081	1345
农村居民最低生活保障人数	Number of Rural residents for Minimum Livelihood Guarantee	73305			1180	328
民政经费(万元)	Civil Affairs Expenditures(10 000 yuan)					
退役安置费	Decommissioning Costs	13537.7	1749.7	463.9	764.6	599.5
城市居民最低生活保障费	Urban Residents for Minimum Livelihood Guarantee	9659.9		1185.5	1386.7	842.2
农村最低生活保障费	Rural residents for Minimum Livelihood Guarantee	26038.5			502.2	150.0
其它社会救助费	Other Social Assistance Expenses	1158.1			175.8	244.2
社会福利费	Social Welfare Funds	60731.2	18333.2	4538.3	2221.8	1676.7
社会保障及扶贫(个、元)	Social Security and Povert Alleviation(unit.yuan)					
建立社会保障服务网络的乡镇数	Number of Towns With Social Security Service Network	40				
城市市区居民最低生活保障金标准	Minimum Living Standards for Urban Residents	685.0		685.0	685.0	685.0

天桥区 Tian qiao	历城区 Li cheng	长清区 Chang qing	章丘区 Zhang qiu	济阳区 Ji yang	莱芜区 Lai wu	钢城区 Gang cheng	济南高新区 Ji'nan Gao xin	莱芜高新区 Lai wu Gao xin	济南先行区 JN Pioneer Area	南部山区 Nan shan	平阴县 Ping yin	商河县 Shang he
28	70	102	135	49	136	32	25	7	26	32	55	81
38	213	101	265	171	240	63	74	25	116	142	84	91
212	327	787	895	397	732	228	193	76	284	196	297	600
3701	461	453	911	133	3373	674	18				163	417
1101	5761	9585	17440	8963	7930	2633	768				4172	13444
612.4	889.2	645.0	1069.9	4432.6	745.6	8.4	398.9				625.1	457.7
2478.0	322.5	248.5	628.6	75.9	1831.9	310.2	13.7				107.3	225.9
472.0	2370.9	3500.9	6675.1	3204.1	2344.7	683.4	338.2				1444.3	4352.7
			486.0	13.9			238.2					
2822.3	3229.3	3395.5	6821.1	2977.7	4082.0	1368.5	2339.1				2763.6	4162.1
		3	3	4	11	2					6	11
685.0	685.0	685.0	685.0	685.0	685.0	685.0	685.0				685.0	685.0

20-5 律师、公证、司法基本情况 (2019 年)
Basic Statistics on Law, Notarizations and Mendiation(2019)

指 标	Indicator	单 位 Unit	全 市 Total	市 区 Urban	平阴县 Ping yin	商河县 Shang he
律师工作	Lawyers					
律师事务所	Number of Law Offices	个 (unit)	433	425	6	2
执业律师	Number of Lawyers	人 (person)	6445	6401	31	13
担任常年法律顾问	Permanent Legal Advisor	家 (unit)	7137	7020	85	32
民事诉讼代理	Civil Agent	件 (case)	58245	57202	709	334
刑事诉讼辩护及代理	Criminal Defense and Agent	件 (case)	7853	7372	306	175
行政诉讼代理	Administrative Agent	件 (case)	3260	3247	3	10
非诉讼法律事务	Non-litigation Legal Matters	件 (case)	16151	16125	14	12
公证工作	Notarization					
公证处	Number of Notary Offices	个 (unit)	16	14	1	1
公证处人员	Personnel of Notary Offices	人 (person)	419	402	10	7
#公证员	Notaries	人 (person)	140	134	4	2
办理公证总数	Number of Notarized Affair	件 (case)	158040	153288	1740	3012
#国内民事公证	Domestic Civil Notarization	件 (case)	46858	45003	1335	520
国内经济公证	Domestic Commerce Notarization	件 (case)	87901	85004	405	2492
涉外公证	Foreign-related Notarization	件 (case)	23281	23281	0	0
办理经济公证涉及金额	Money of Commerce Notarization	亿元 (100 million yuan)	12.80	12.74	0.02	0.04
基层司法行政工作	Basic Judicical Administration					
人民调解委员会	People's Mediation Committee	个 (unit)	6559	5216	366	977
人民调解员	People's Mediators	人 (person)	23776	19280	1390	3106
调解纠纷总数	Number of Mediation Disputes	件 (case)	28577	21956	1003	5618
#调解成功	Success Mediation	件 (case)	27952	21401	976	5575
法律服务所	Legal Service Office	个 (unit)	151	139	9	3
基层法律工作者	Grassroots Legal Workers	人 (person)	966	914	39	13
担任法律顾问	Legal Advisor	家 (unit)	2340	2176	91	73
民事诉讼代理	Civil Agent	件 (case)	7593	6844	367	382
非诉讼代理	Non-litigation Agent	件 (case)	2597	2451	78	68
法律援助工作	Legal Aid					
法律援助机构	Legal Aid Institution	个 (unit)	13	11	1	1
执业人员	Practitioners	人 (person)	107	94	3	10
办理法律援助案件	Legal Aid Cases	件 (case)	14573	13072	744	757

主要统计指标解释

律师 指受聘参加法律顾问处工作，担任法律顾问、刑(民)事代理人、刑事辩护人，办理非诉讼事件、解答法律询问，代写法律事务文书等主要从事律师业务的专职法律工作者和兼职律师。

公证人员 指在国家公证机关依法办理公证事务的司法人员，包括公证员、助理公证员和在公证处工作的其他人员。

调解人员 指在人民调解委员会担负调解民间一般民事纠纷和轻微违法行为引起纠纷的工作人员，包括调解委员会的委员和调解小组的调解员。

立案 指检察机关对犯罪线索进行初步调查后，认为存在职务犯罪事实并需要追究刑事责任时，依法决定作为刑事案件进行侦查的诉讼活动，是追究犯罪的开始。

Explanatory Notes on Main Statistical Indicators

Lawyers refer to full-time legal workers and part-time lawyers hired to work in the legal advisory office, serving as legal adviser, criminal (civil) agent and criminal advocate and mainly engaging in law practice (such as handling non-contentious matter, answering legal questions and ghostwriting legal papers).

Notary Personnel refers to judicial personnel legally handling notarial affairs at the state notary organ, including notary, assistant notary and other personnel working in the notary office.

Mediation Personnel refers to staff taking charge of mediating ordinary civil disputes among the people and disputes arising from minor infraction at the people's mediation committee, including the member of the mediation committee and the mediator of the mediation team.

Case Filing refers to the litigious activity involving investigation of criminal case according to law when existence of duty-related crimes is deemed and it is necessary to investigate the criminal responsibility after preliminary investigation of crime clues by the investigating and prosecuting apparatus. It is the start of the investigation of crime.

附 录

APPENDIX

附录一 山东省十六城市主要经济指标（2019年）
Main Statistical Indicators of 16 Cities in Shandong(2019)

城市名称	Region	地区生产总值 Gross Domestic Product	第一产业 Primary Industry	第二产业 Secondary Industry	第三产业 Tertiary Industry	固定资产投资比上年增长(%) Growth Rate Investment in Fixed Assets (%)	房地产开发投资额 Estate Development Investment	一般公共预算收入 General Pubilic Budget Revenue	一般公共预算支出 General Pubilic Budget Expenditure	金融机构本外币存款余额 The Balance of RMB and Foreign Currencies Deposits in Financial Institutions
全省	Total	71067.5	5116.4	28310.9	37640.2	−8.4	8614.9	6526.6	10736.8	104738.9
济南市	Ji'nan	9443.4	343.1	3265.2	5835.1	12.6	1576.9	874.2	1197.3	18646.1
青岛市	Qingdao	11741.3	410.0	4182.8	7148.6	21.6	1803.8	1241.7	1576.6	17876.3
淄博市	Zibo	3642.4	149.3	1817.8	1675.3	−44.6	313.3	368.7	499.4	5023.4
枣庄市	Zaozhuang	1693.9	158.9	737.0	798.1	−15.8	257.5	147.3	267.1	2197.6
东营市	Dongying	2916.2	145.7	1675.1	1095.4	−32.6	185.4	245.1	306.2	3865.7
烟台市	Yantai	7653.5	550.4	3185.5	3917.6	5.0	661.9	595.4	774.5	9115.8
潍坊市	Weifang	5688.5	517.4	2291.0	2880.0	−23.2	762.6	5 71.1	777.9	8750.6
济宁市	Jining	4370.2	503.8	1760.0	2106.3	−3.6	457.1	405.0	667.3	5927.2
泰安市	Taian	2663.6	288.7	1036.2	1338.7	−23.3	205.9	224.7	414.5	4132.7
威海市	Weiha	2963.7	288.6	1196.3	1478.8	−15.0	383.2	249.9	343.2	4251.0
日照市	Rizhao	1949.4	167.8	831.9	949.7	−16.5	192.1	170.4	267.4	2727.2
临沂市	Linyi	4600.3	409.5	1742.5	2448.3	−23.5	595.5	330.0	710.9	7083.3
德州市	Dezhou	3022.3	311.9	1263.7	1446.7	−13.6	353.6	206.3	437.4	3801.1
聊城市	Liaocheng	2259.8	317.6	806.9	1135.3	−41.2	360.0	196.6	427.1	3881.9
滨州市	Binzhou	2457.2	230.2	1041.0	1186.0	−23.5	192.7	243.0	378.1	2958.0
菏泽市	Heze	3410.0	323.6	1453.7	1632.7	8.1	313.3	221.9	618.7	4340.2
济南位次	Position	2	6	2	2	2	2	2	2	1

注：本表内其他城市数据根据内部资料整理，不做正式发布，仅供参考。各项指标最终数据，敬请关注各城市官方发布机构。

Note: The data regarding other cities in this table is sorted out according to internal data which is for reference only instead of being released officially. As for final data regarding various indicators, refer to official release mechanism in each city.

单位：亿元 (100 million yuan)

# 住户存款 House-–hold Deposits	金融机构本外币贷款余额 The Balance of RMB and Foreign Currencies Loans in Financial Institutions	社会消费品零售总额比上年增长 (%) Growth Rate Total Retail Sales of Consumer Goods(%)	货物进出口总额 Total Import & Export	# 出口总额 Total Export	实际使用外资（亿美元） Actual Use of Foreign Capital (100 million USD)	城镇居民人均可支配收入（元） Per Capita Disposable Income of Urban Households (yuan)	城镇居民人均消费支出（元） Per Capita Consumption Expenditure of Urban Households (yuan)	农村居民人均可支配收入（元） Per Capita Disposable Income of Rural Households (yuan)	农村居民人均消费支出（元） Per Capita Consumption Expenditure of Rural Households (yuan)	居民消费价格指数 (%) Consumer Price Indices (%)
55580.6	86325.6	6.4	20420.9	11130.4	146.9	42329	26731	17775	12309	103.2
6497.0	18768.7	8.1	1103.3	622.5	22.4	51913	33439	19454	12300	103.3
6876.6	18209.9	8.1	5925.6	3411.9	58.4	54484	35266	22573	14899	103.3
3111.5	3593.9	6.2	883.1	419.0	2.3	45237	28939	19916	14452	103.0
1464.0	1557.8	4.9	146.7	139.4	1.4	34030	19791	16747	10930	102.9
1842.0	3252.2	2.2	1629.1	342.8	2.4	51128	30730	19013	14344	102.9
5099.7	5813.3	7.4	2906.8	1733.7	19.4	47977	31259	21218	15125	103.0
5320.3	6538.8	5.6	1788.1	1131.9	7.0	41664	26103	20369	13231	102.6
3804.8	4080.9	2.2	461.8	285.2	4.5	37139	22218	17644	11373	103.4
2676.0	2698.6	3.7	172.2	134.5	4.6	37695	22500	18621	12020	102.4
2510.1	2884.0	9.3	1402.1	921.4	12.2	49044	31767	22171	13722	102.5
1562.3	2545.1	8.0	1052.6	406.6	1.9	35732	21993	17312	9271	102.4
4477.6	5920.2	3.5	836.7	681.3	3.9	37912	18495	14979	9557	102.9
2606.3	2216.2	7.0	345.4	204.0	1.6	28536	17523	16028	12783	103.3
2684.4	2645.4	6.0	409.1	207.4	0.7	29215	17204	14816	10811	102.9
1707.2	2682.7	6.8	873.0	311.6	2.2	37378	24384	17480	11961	102.3
3336.5	2626.0	9.2	485.3	177.0	1.9	28327	18179	14176	11274	102.4
2	1	3	6	6	2	2	2	6	8	2

附录二 十五副省市主要经济指标（2019 年）
Main Statistical Indicators of 15 Vice-provincial Cities(2019)

城市名称	Region	地区生产总值 Gross Dmoestic Product	第一产业 Primary Industry	第二产业 Secondary Industry	第三产业 Tertiary Industry	固定资产投资比上年增长(%) Growth Rate Investment in Fixed Assets (%)	房地产开发投资比上年增长(%) Growth Rate Estate Development Investment (%)	一般公共预算收入 General Pubilic Budget Revenue	一般公共预算支出 General Pubilic Budget Expenditure	金融机构本外币存款余额 The Balance of RMB and Foreign Currencies Deposits in Financial Institutions
济南	Ji'nan	9443.4	343.1	3265.2	5835.1	12.6	9.7	874.2	1197.3	18646.1
沈阳	Shenyang	6470.3	284.0	2178.6	4007.6	13.2	17.9	730.3	1048.2	18869.5
大连	Dalian	7001.7	458.5	2799.8	3743.3	–19.8	3.3	692.8	1016.3	14633.6
长春	Changchun	5904.1	348.1	2495.4	3060.6	–19.0	12.6	420.0	896.0	12681.9
哈尔滨	Harbin	5249.4	569.5	1127.3	3552.6	7.3	6.1	370.9	1101.1	12353.1
南京	Nanjing	14030.2	289.8	5040.9	8699.5	8.0	6.2	1580.0	1658.6	35536.1
杭州	Hangzhou	15373.0	326.0	4875.0	10172.0	11.6	10.7	1966.0	1953.0	45287.0
宁波	Ningbo	11985.1	322.3	5782.9	5879.9	8.1	7.3	1468.5	1767.9	20857.8
厦门	Xiamen	5995.0	26.5	2494.0	3474.6	9.0	1.7	768.3	914.7	11609.6
青岛	Qingdao	11741.3	410.0	4182.8	7148.6	21.6	21.5	1241.7	1576.6	17876.3
武汉	Wuhan	16223.2	379.0	5988.9	9855.3	9.8	6.7	1564.1	2237.1	28658.9
广州	Guangzhou	23628.6	251.4	6454.0	16923.2	16.5	14.8	1697.2	2865.1	59131.2
深圳	Shenzhen	26927.1	25.2	10495.8	16406.1	18.8	15.9	3773.2	4551.0	83942.5
成都	Chengdu	17012.7	612.2	5244.6	11155.9	10.0	14.9	1483.0	2006.8	39828.0
西安	Xi'an	9321.2	279.1	3167.4	5874.6	1.1	–2.1	702.6	1250.4	23340.8
济南位次	Position	9	7	9	10	5	8	9	10	10

注：1. 为便于排序，济南、厦门实际使用外资数据根据人民币口径和年均汇率推算。
2. 本表内其他城市数据根据内部资料整理，不做正式发布，仅供参考。各项指标最终数据，敬请关注各城市官方发布机构。

Note: 1. To facilitate ranking, the data regarding foreign investment actually used by Xiamen is calculated as per RMB caliber and average annual rate.
2.The data regarding other cities in this table is sorted out according to internal data which is for reference only instead of being released officially. As for final data regarding various indicators, refer to official release mechanism in each city.

单位：亿元 (100 million yuan)

金融机构本外币贷款余额 The Balance of RMB and Foreign Currencies Loans in Financial Institutions	社会消费品零售总额 Total Retail Sales of Consumer Goods	货物进出口总额 Total Import & Export	# 出口总额 Total Export	实际使用外资（亿美元） Actual Use of Foreign Capital (USD 100 million)	城镇居民人均可支配收入（元） Per Capita Disposable Income of Urban Households (yuan)	农村居民人均可支配收入（元） Per Capita Disposable Income of Rural Households (yuan)	居民消费价格指数 (%) Consumer Price Indices (%)
18768.7	5162.2	1103.3	622.5	22.4	51913	19454	103.3
16811.9	4479.6	1072.8	315.9	16.5	46786	18124	102.4
12526.3	3948.7	4352.8	1914.8	8.7	46468	19974	102.4
13096.4		995.8	148.6	3.3	37844	15455	102.9
12181.8		251.5	119.8	3.4	40007	18238	102.6
33585.9	6135.7	4828.2	3006.9	40.0	64372	27636	103.1
42245.0	6215.0	5597.0	3613.0	61.3	66068	36255	103.1
22187.2	4473.7	9170.3	5969.6	23.6	64886	36632	103.0
11800.9	1731.9	6412.9	3528.7	19.2	59018	24802	103.0
18209.9	5234.2	5925.6	3411.9	58.4	54484	22573	103.3
32114.3	7449.6	2440.2	1362.3		51706	24716	103.2
47103.3		9995.8	5258.0	71.4	65052	28868	103.0
59461.4	6582.9	29773.9	16709.0	78.1	62522		103.4
36464.0	7478.4	5822.7	3309.8	80.4	45878	24357	102.8
22436.7		3243.1	1730.2	70.6	41850	14588	102.7
9	7	12	12	9	8	10	2

附录三 二十六省会城市主要经济指标（2019年）
Main Statistical Indicators of 26 Provincial Capitals (2019)

城市名称	Region	地区生产总值 Gross Dmoestic Product	第一产业 Primary Industry	第二产业 Secondary Industry	第三产业 Tertiary Industry	固定资产投资比上年增长(%) Growth Rate Investment in Fixed Assets (%)	房地产开发投资比上年增长(%) Growth Rate Estate Development Investment (%)	一般公共预算收入 General Public Budget Revenue	一般公共预算支出 General Public Budget Expenditure	金融机构本外币存款余额 The Balance of RMB and Foreign Currencies Deposits in Financial Institutions
济南	Ji'nan	9443.4	343.1	3265.2	5835.1	12.6	9.7	874.2	1197.3	18646.1
石家庄	Shijiazhuang	5809.9	449.5	1831.7	3528.7	6.2	−14.2	569.1	1053.4	15051.7
太原	Taiyuan	4028.5	42.5	1518.6	2467.4	10.2	31.3	386.6	610.6	13117.2
呼和浩特	Hohehot	2791.5	114.2	823.8	1853.4	5.2	0.6	203.1	421.7	5918.9
沈阳	Shenyang	6470.3	284.0	2178.6	4007.6	13.2	17.9	730.3	1048.2	18869.5
长春	Changchun	5904.1	348.1	2495.4	3060.6	−19.0	12.6	420.0	896.0	12681.9
哈尔滨	Harbin	5249.4	569.5	1127.3	3552.6	7.3	6.1	370.9	1101.1	12353.1
南京	Nanjing	14030.2	289.8	5040.9	8699.5	8.0	6.2	1580.0	1658.6	35536.1
杭州	Hangzhou	15373.0	326.0	4875.0	10172.0	11.6	10.7	1966.0	1953.0	45287.0
合肥	Hefei	9409.4	291.9	3415.3	5702.2	9.0	1.9	746.0	1122.7	16417.3
福州	Fuzhou	9392.3	526.5	3831.0	5034.8	9.0	25.9	668.1	952.2	1547.9
南昌	Nanchang	5596.2	212.9	2653.8	2729.5	10.2	2.5	476.1	834.1	12096.8
郑州	Zhengzhou	11589.7	140.9	4617.0	6831.8	2.8	2.8	1222.5	1910.6	24461.2
武汉	Wuhan	16223.2	379.0	5988.9	9855.3	9.8	6.7	1564.1	2237.1	28658.9
长沙	Changsha	11574.2	359.7	4439.3	6775.2	10.1	11.2	950.2	1456.5	21048.5
广州	Guangzhou	23628.6	251.4	6454.0	16923.2	16.5	14.8	1697.2	2865.1	59131.2
南宁	Nanning	4506.6	507.3	1045.0	2954.3	9.9	32.1	370.9	787.7	10718.3
海口	Haikou	1671.9	71.2	276.0	1324.8	−15.4	−21.1	185.3	265.2	4949.4
成都	Chengdu	17012.7	612.2	5244.6	11155.9	10.0	14.9	1483.0	2006.8	39828.0
贵阳	Guiyang	4039.6	161.3	1496.7	2381.6	1.5	−3.9	417.3	718.7	11979.5
昆明	Kunming	6475.9	270.3	2078.8	4126.8	2.8	13.9	630.0	820.9	
西安	Xi'an	9321.2	279.1	3167.4	5874.6	1.1	−2.1	702.6	1250.4	23340.8
兰州	Lanzhou	2837.4	51.7	945.4	1840.3	−4.7	−4.5	233.2	460.4	8814.3
西宁	Xining					2.6	−0.4	101.8	328.0	
银川	Yinchuan					−6.2	−6.7	154.7	346.6	4027.4
乌鲁木齐	Urumqi	3413.3	27.7	906.1	2479.4	2.0	−16.8	472.5	620.3	8927.5
济南位次	Position	8	9	10	9	3	11	8	9	10

注：1. 为便于排序，贵阳、昆明进出口总额、出口总额数据根据美元口径和年均汇率推算；福州实际使用外资数据根据人民币口径和年均汇率推算。
2. 本表内其他城市数据根据内部资料整理，不做正式发布，仅供参考。各项指标最终数据，敬请关注各城市官方发布机构。

Note: 1.To facilitate ranking, total export-import volume and total export of Guiyang and Kunming are calculated pursuant to USD caliber and average annual exchange rate; The data regarding foreign investment actually used by Fuzhou is calculated in terms of RMB caliber and average annual exchange rate.
2.The data regarding other cities in this table is sorted out according to internal data which is for reference only instead of being released officially. As for final data regarding various indicators, refer to official release mechanism in each city.

单位：亿元 (100 million yuan)

金融机构本外币贷款余额 The Balance of RMB and Foreign Currencies Loans in Financial Institutions	社会消费品零售总额 Total Retail Sales of Consumer Goods	货物进出口总额 Total Import & Export	# 出口总额 Total Export	实际使用外资（亿美元）Actual Use of Foreign Capital (USD 100 million)	城镇居民人均可支配收入（元）Per Capita Disposable Income of Urban Households (yuan)	农村居民人均可支配收入（元）Per Capita Disposable Income of Rural Households (yuan)	居民消费价格指数(%) Consumer Price Indices (%)
18768.7	**5162.2**	**1103.3**	**622.5**	**22.4**	**51913**	**19454**	**103.3**
11406.7	3545.4	1178.8	655.1	16.2	38550	15853	102.7
14063.1	1952.8	1119.6	651.7	1.0	36362	18377	102.7
8599.4	1646.5	116.7	63.5	–	49397	18974	102.6
16811.9	4479.6	1072.8	315.9	16.5	46786	18124	102.4
13096.4		995.8	148.6	3.3	37844	15455	102.9
12181.8		251.5	119.8	3.4	40007	18238	102.6
33585.9	6135.7	4828.2	3006.9	41.0	64372	27636	103.1
42245.0	6215.0	5597.0	3613.0	61.3	66068	36255	103.1
15854.8	3234.5	2221.2	1392.5	33.9	45404	22462	102.9
2000.5	5120.3	2525.8	1802.0	9.4	47920	21320	102.5
14047.3	2369.3	1061.8	645.8	37.7	44136	19498	102.8
26476.8	4671.5	4129.9	2678.3	44.1	42087	23536	103.1
32114.3	7449.6	2440.2	1362.3		51706	24776	103.2
21248.7	5247.0	2002.0	1396.4	63.7	55211	32329	102.9
47103.3		9995.8	5258.0	71.4	65052	28868	103.0
13964.4	2307.4	747.8	363.9	3.1	37675	15047	103.4
6220.5	785.6	331.4	86.3	6.7	38977	16116	103.3
36464.0	7478.4	5822.7	3309.8	80.4	45878	24357	102.8
14141.3	1380.4	231.1	210.0	17.8	38240	17275	101.6
	3056.6	867.7	248.6	6.5	46289	16356	102.3
22436.7		3243.1	1730.2	70.6	41850	14588	102.7
11269.2	1454.9	119.4	71.8		38095	13605	102.2
	592.6	26.4	14.6		34846	12577	102.5
5359.5		157.6	104.4	2.0	38217	15282	102.2
7817.8	1389.2	512.6	334.4	0.1	42667	21448	102.0
9	6	13	14	10	5	12	2

附录四

中华人民共和国统计法

Statistical Law of The People's Republic of China

（1983 年 12 月 8 日第六届全国人民代表大会常务委员会第三次会议通过 根据 1996 年 5 月 15 日第八届全国人民代表大会常务委员会第十九次会议《关于修改〈中华人民共和国统计法〉的决定》修正 2009 年 6 月 27 日第十一届全国人民代表大会常务委员会第九次会议修订）

第一章 总 则

第一条 为了科学、有效地组织统计工作，保障统计资料的真实性、准确性、完整性和及时性，发挥统计在了解国情国力、服务经济社会发展中的重要作用，促进社会主义现代化建设事业发展，制定本法。

第二条 本法适用于各级人民政府、县级以上人民政府统计机构和有关部门组织实施的统计活动。

统计的基本任务是对经济社会发展情况进行统计调查、统计分析，提供统计资料和统计咨询意见，实行统计监督。

第三条 国家建立集中统一的统计系统，实行统一领导、分级负责的统计管理体制。

第四条 国务院和地方各级人民政府、各有关部门应当加强对统计工作的组织领导，为统计工作提供必要的保障。

第五条 国家加强统计科学研究，健全科学的统计指标体系，不断改进统计调查方法，提高统计的科学性。

国家有计划地加强统计信息化建设，推进统计信息搜集、处理、传输、共享、存储技术和统计数据库体系的现代化。

第六条 统计机构和统计人员依照本法规定独立行使统计调查、统计报告、统计监督的职权，不受侵犯。

地方各级人民政府、政府统计机构和有关部门以及各单位的负责人，不得自行修改统计机构和统计人员依法搜集、整理的统计资料，不得以任何方式要求统计机构、统计人员及其他机构、人员伪造、篡改统计资料，不得对依法履行职责或者拒绝、抵制统计违法行为的统计人员打击报复。

第七条 国家机关、企业事业单位和其他组织以及个体工商户和个人等统计调查对象，必须依照本法和国家有关规定，真实、准确、完整、及时地提供统计调查所需的资料，不得提供不真实或者不完整的统计资料，不得迟报、拒报统计资料。

第八条 统计工作应当接受社会公众的监督。任何单位和个人有权检举统计中弄虚作假等违法行为。对检举有功的单位和个人应当给予表彰和奖励。

第九条 统计机构和统计人员对在统计工作中知悉的国家秘密、商业秘密和个人信息，应当予以保密。

第十条 任何单位和个人不得利用虚假统计资料骗取荣誉称号、物质利益或者职务晋升。

第二章 统计调查管理

第十一条 统计调查项目包括国家统计调查项目、部门统计调查项目和地方统计调查项目。

国家统计调查项目是指全国性基本情况的统计调查项目。部门统计调查项目是指国务院有关部门的专业性统计调查项目。地方统计调查项目是指县级以上地方人民政府及其部门的地方性统计调查项目。

国家统计调查项目、部门统计调查项目、地方统计调查项目应当明确分工，互相衔接，不得重复。

第十二条 国家统计调查项目由国家统计局制定，或者由国家统计局和国务院有关部门共同制定，报国务院备案；重大的国家统计调查项目报国务院审批。

部门统计调查项目由国务院有关部门制定。统计调查对象属于本部门管辖系统的，报国家统计局备案；统计调查对象超出本部门管辖系统的，报国家统计局审批。

地方统计调查项目由县级以上地方人民政府统计机构和有关部门分别制定或者共同制定。其中，由省级人民政府统计机构单独制定或者和有关部门共同制定的，报国家统计局审批；由省级以下人民政府统计机构单独制定或者和有关部门共同制定的，报省级人民政府统计机构审批；由县级以上地方人民政府有关部门制定的，报本级人民政府统计机构审批。

第十三条 统计调查项目的审批机关应当对调查项目的必要性、可行性、科学性进行审查，对符合法定条件的，作出予以批准的书面决定，并公布；对不符合法定条件的，作出不予批准的书面决定，并说明理由。

第十四条 制定统计调查项目，应当同时制定该项目的统计调查制度，并依照本法第十二条的规定一并报经审批或者备案。

统计调查制度应当对调查目的、调查内容、调查方法、调查对象、调查组织方式、调查表式、统计资料的报送和公布等作出规定。

统计调查应当按照统计调查制度组织实施。变更统计调查制度的内容，应当报经原审批机关批准或者原备案机关备案。

第十五条 统计调查表应当标明表号、制定机关、批准或者备案文号、有效期限等标志。

对未标明前款规定的标志或者超过有效期限的统计调查表，统计调查对象有权拒绝填报；县级以上人民政府统计机构应当依法责令停止有关统计调查活动。

第十六条 搜集、整理统计资料，应当以周期性普查为基础，以经常性抽样调查为主体，综合运用全面调查、重点调查等方法，并充分利用行政记录等资料。

重大国情国力普查由国务院统一领导，国务院和地方人民政府组织统计机构和有关部门共同实施。

第十七条 国家制定统一的统计标准，保障统计调查采用的指标涵义、计算方法、分类目录、调查表式和统计编码等的标准化。

国家统计标准由国家统计局制定，或者由国家统计局和国务院标准化主管部门共同制定。

国务院有关部门可以制定补充性的部门统计标准，报国家统计局审批。部门统计标准不得与国家统计标准相抵触。

第十八条 县级以上人民政府统计机构根据统计任务的需要，可以在统计调查对象中推广使用计算机网络报送统计资料。

第十九条 县级以上人民政府应当将统计工作所需经费列入财政预算。

重大国情国力普查所需经费，由国务院和地方人民政府共同负担，列入相应年度的财政预算，按时拨付，确保到位。

第三章 统计资料的管理和公布

第二十条 县级以上人民政府统计机构和有关部门以及乡、镇人民政府，应当按照国家有关规定建立统计资料的保存、管理制度，建立健全统计信息共享机制。

第二十一条 国家机关、企业事业单位和其他组织等统计调查对象，应当按照国家有关规定设置原始记录、统计台账，建立健全统计资料的审核、签署、交接、归档等管理制度。

统计资料的审核、签署人员应当对其审核、签署的统计资料的真实性、准确性和完整性负责。

第二十二条 县级以上人民政府有关部门应当及时向本级人民政府统计机构提供统计所需的行政记录资料和国民经济核算所需的财务资料、财政资料及其他资料，并按照统计调查制度的规定及时向本级人民政府统计机构报送其组织实施统计调查取得的有关资料。

县级以上人民政府统计机构应当及时向本级人民政府有关部门提供有关统计资料。

第二十三条 县级以上人民政府统计机构按照国家有关规定，定期公布统计资料。

国家统计数据以国家统计局公布的数据为准。

第二十四条 县级以上人民政府有关部门统计调查取得的统计资料，由本部门按照国家有关规定公布。

第二十五条 统计调查中获得的能够识别或者推断单个统计调查对象身份的资料，任何单位和个人不得对外提供、泄露，不得用于统计以外的目的。

第二十六条 县级以上人民政府统计机构和有关部门统计调查取得的统计资料，除依法应当保密的外，应当及时公开，供社会公众查询。

第四章 统计机构和统计人员

第二十七条 国务院设立国家统计局，依法组织领导和协调全国的统计工作。

国家统计局根据工作需要设立的派出调查机构，承担国家统计局布置的统计调查等任务。

县级以上地方人民政府设立独立的统计机构，乡、镇人民政府设置统计工作岗位，配备专职或者兼职统计人员，依法管理、开展统计工作，实施统计调查。

第二十八条 县级以上人民政府有关部门根据统计任务的需要设立统计机构，或者在有关机构中设置统计人员，并指定统计负责人，依法组织、管理本部门职责范围内的统计工作，实施统计调查，在统计业务上受本级人民政府统计机构的指导。

第二十九条 统计机构、统计人员应当依法履行职责，如实搜集、报送统计资料，不得伪造、篡改统计资料，不得以任何方式要求任何单位和个人提供不真实的统计资料，不得有其他违反本法规定的行为。

统计人员应当坚持实事求是，恪守职业道德，对其负责搜集、审核、录入的统计资料与统计调查对象报送的统计资料的一致性负责。

第三十条 统计人员进行统计调查时，有权就与统计有关的问题询问有关人员，要求其如实提供有关情况、资料并改正不真实、不准确的资料。

统计人员进行统计调查时，应当出示县级以上人民政府统计机构或者有关部门颁发的工作证件；未出示的，统计调查对象有权拒绝调查。

第三十一条 国家实行统计专业技术职务资格考试、评聘制度，提高统计人员的专业素质，保障统计队伍的稳定性。

统计人员应当具备与其从事的统计工作相适应的专业知识和业务能力。

县级以上人民政府统计机构和有关部门应当加强对统计人员的专业培训和职业道德教育。

第五章 监督检查

第三十二条 县级以上人民政府及其监察机关对下级人民政府、本级人民政府统计机构和有关部门执行本法的情况，实施监督。

第三十三条 国家统计局组织管理全国统计工作的监督检查，查处重大统计违法行为。

县级以上地方人民政府统计机构依法查处本行政区域内发生的统计违法行为。但是，国家统计局派出的调查机构组织实施的统计调查活动中发生的统计违法行为，由组织实施该项统计调查的调查机构负责查处。

法律、行政法规对有关部门查处统计违法行为另有规定的，从其规定。

第三十四条 县级以上人民政府有关部门应当积极协助本级人民政府统计机构查处统计违法行为，及时向本级人民政府统计机构移送有关统计违法案件材料。

第三十五条 县级以上人民政府统计机构在调查统计违法行为或者核查统计数据时，有权采取下列措施：

（一）发出统计检查查询书，向检查对象查询有关事项；

（二）要求检查对象提供有关原始记录和凭证、统计台账、统计调查表、会计资料及其他相关证明和资料；

（三）就与检查有关的事项询问有关人员；

（四）进入检查对象的业务场所和统计数据处理信息系统进行检查、核对；

（五）经本机构负责人批准，登记保存检查对象的有关原始记录和凭证、统计台账、统计调查表、会计资料及其他相关证明和资料；

（六）对与检查事项有关的情况和资料进行记录、录音、录像、照相和复制。

县级以上人民政府统计机构进行监督检查时，监督检查人员不得少于二人，并应当出示执法证件；未出示的，有关单位和个人有权拒绝检查。

第三十六条 县级以上人民政府统计机构履行监督检查职责时，有关单位和个人应当如实反映情况，提供相关证明和资料，不得拒绝、阻碍检查，不得转移、隐匿、篡改、毁弃原始记录和凭证、统计台账、统计调查表、会计资料及其他相关证明和资料。

第六章 法律责任

第三十七条 地方人民政府、政府统计机构或者有关部门、单位的负责人有下列行为之一的，由任免机关或者监察机关依法给予处分，并由县级以上人民政府统计机构予以通报：

（一）自行修改统计资料、编造虚假统计数据的；

（二）要求统计机构、统计人员或者其他机构、人员伪造、篡改统计资料的；

（三）对依法履行职责或者拒绝、抵制统计违法行为的统计人员打击报复的；

（四）对本地方、本部门、本单位发生的严重统计违法行为失察的。

第三十八条 县级以上人民政府统计机构或者有关部门在组织实施统计调查活动中有下列行为之一的，由本级人民政府、上级人民政府统计机构或者本级人民政府统计机构责令改正，予以通报；对直接负责的主管人员和其他直接责任人员，由任免机关或者监察机关依法给予处分：

（一）未经批准擅自组织实施统计调查的；

（二）未经批准擅自变更统计调查制度的内容的；

（三）伪造、篡改统计资料的；

（四）要求统计调查对象或者其他机构、人员提供不真实的统计资料的；

（五）未按照统计调查制度的规定报送有关资料的。

统计人员有前款第三项至第五项所列行为之一的，责令改正，依法给予处分。

第三十九条 县级以上人民政府统计机构或者有关部门有下列行为之一的，对直接负责的主管人员和其他直接责任人员由任免机关或者监察机关依法给予处分：

（一）违法公布统计资料的；

（二）泄露统计调查对象的商业秘密、个人信息或者提供、泄露在统计调查中获得的能够识别或者推断单个统计调查对象身份的资料的；

（三）违反国家有关规定，造成统计资料毁损、灭失的。

统计人员有前款所列行为之一的，依法给予处分。

第四十条 统计机构、统计人员泄露国家秘密的，依法追究法律责任。

第四十一条 作为统计调查对象的国家机关、企业事业单位或者其他组织有下列行为之一的，由县级以上人民政府统计机构责令改正，给予警告，可以予以通报；其直接负责的主管人员和其他直接责任人员属于国家工作人员的，由任免机关或者监察机关依法给予处分：

（一）拒绝提供统计资料或者经催报后仍未按时提供统计资料的；

（二）提供不真实或者不完整的统计资料的；

（三）拒绝答复或者不如实答复统计检查查询书的；

（四）拒绝、阻碍统计调查、统计检查的；

（五）转移、隐匿、篡改、毁弃或者拒绝提供原始记录和凭证、统计台账、统计调查表及其他相关证明和资料的。

企业事业单位或者其他组织有前款所列行为之一的，可以并处五万元以下的罚款；情节严重的，并处五万元以上二十万元以下的罚款。

个体工商户有本条第一款所列行为之一的，由县级以上人民政府统计机构责令改正，给予警告，可以并处一万元以下的罚款。

第四十二条 作为统计调查对象的国家机关、企业事业单位或者其他组织迟报统计资料，或者未按照国家有关规定设置原始记录、统计台账的，由县级以上人民政府统计机构责令改正，给予警告。

企业事业单位或者其他组织有前款所列行为之一的，可以并处一万元以下的罚款。

个体工商户迟报统计资料的，由县级以上人民政府统计机构责令改正，给予警告，可以并处一千元以下的罚款。

第四十三条 县级以上人民政府统计机构查处统计违法行为时，认为对有关国家工作人员依法应当给予处分的，应当提出给予处分的建议；该国家工作人员的任免机关或者监察机关应当依法及时作出决定，并将结果书面通知县级以上人民政府统计机构。

第四十四条 作为统计调查对象的个人在重大国情国力普查活动中拒绝、阻碍统计调查，或者提供不真实或者不完整的普查资料的，由县级以上人民政府统计机构责令改正，予以批评教育。

第四十五条 违反本法规定，利用虚假统计资料骗取荣誉称号、物质利益或者职务晋升的，除对其编造虚假统计资料或者要求他人编造虚假统计资料的行为依法追究法律责任外，由作出有关决定的单位或者其上级单位、监察机关取消其荣誉称号，追缴获得的物质利益，撤销晋升的职务。

第四十六条 当事人对县级以上人民政府统计机构作出的行政处罚决定不服的，可以依法申请行政复议或者提起行政诉讼。其中，对国家统计局在省、自治区、直辖市派出的调查机构作出的行政处罚决定不服的，向国家统计局申请行政复议；对国家统计局派出的其他调查机构作出的行政处罚决定不服的，向国家统计局在该派出机构所在的省、自治区、直辖市派出的调查机构申请行政复议。

第四十七条 违反本法规定，构成犯罪的，依法追究刑事责任。

第七章 附 则

第四十八条 本法所称县级以上人民政府统计机构，是指国家统计局及其派出的调查机构、县级以上地方人民政府统计机构。

第四十九条 民间统计调查活动的管理办法，由国务院制定。

中华人民共和国境外的组织、个人需要在中华人民共和国境内进行统计调查活动的，应当按照国务院的规定报请审批。

利用统计调查危害国家安全、损害社会公共利益或者进行欺诈活动的，依法追究法律责任。

第五十条 本法自 2010 年 1 月 1 日起施行。

附录五

中华人民共和国统计法实施条例

Regulations for the Implementation of the Statistics Law of the People's Republic of China

中华人民共和国国务院令

第 681 号

《中华人民共和国统计法实施条例》已经 2017 年 4 月 12 日国务院第 168 次常务会议通过，现予公布，自 2017 年 8 月 1 日起施行。

总理　李克强

2017 年 5 月 28 日

中华人民共和国统计法实施条例

第一章　总　则

第一条　根据《中华人民共和国统计法》（以下简称统计法），制定本条例。

第二条　统计资料能够通过行政记录取得的，不得组织实施调查。通过抽样调查、重点调查能够满足统计需要的，不得组织实施全面调查。

第三条　县级以上人民政府统计机构和有关部门应当加强统计规律研究，健全新兴产业等统计，完善经济、社会、科技、资源和环境统计，推进互联网、大数据、云计算等现代信息技术在统计工作中的应用，满足经济社会发展需要。

第四条　地方人民政府、县级以上人民政府统计机构和有关部门应当根据国家有关规定，明确本单位防范和惩治统计造假、弄虚作假的责任主体，严格执行统计法和本条例的规定。

地方人民政府、县级以上人民政府统计机构和有关部门及其负责人应当保障统计活动依法进行，不得侵犯统计机构、统计人员独立行使统计调查、统计报告、统计监督职权，不得非法干预统计调查对象提供统计资料，不得统计造假、弄虚作假。

统计调查对象应当依照统计法和国家有关规定，真实、准确、完整、及时地提供统计资料，拒绝、抵制弄虚作假等违法行为。

第五条　县级以上人民政府统计机构和有关部门不得组织实施营利性统计调查。

国家有计划地推进县级以上人民政府统计机构和有关部门通过向社会购买服务组织实施统计调查和资料开发。

第二章　统计调查项目

第六条　部门统计调查项目、地方统计调查项目的主要内容不得与国家统计调查项目的内容重复、矛盾。

第七条　统计调查项目的制定机关（以下简称制定机关）应当就项目的必要性、可行性、科学性进行论证，征求有关地方、部门、统计调查对象和专家的意见，并由制定机关按照会议制度集体讨论决定。

重要统计调查项目应当进行试点。

第八条　制定机关申请审批统计调查项目，应当以公文形式向审批机关提交统计调查项目审批申请表、项目的统计调查制度和工作经费来源说明。

申请材料不齐全或者不符合法定形式的，审批机关应当一次性告知需要补正的全部内容，制定机关应当按照审批机关的要求予以补正。

申请材料齐全、符合法定形式的，审批机关应当受理。

第九条　统计调查项目符合下列条件的，审批机关应当作出予以批准的书面决定：

（一）具有法定依据或者确为公共管理和服务所必需；

（二）与已批准或者备案的统计调查项目的主要内容不重复、不矛盾；

（三）主要统计指标无法通过行政记录或者已有统计调查资料加工整理取得；

（四）统计调查制度符合统计法律法规规定，科学、合理、

可行;

（五）采用的统计标准符合国家有关规定;

（六）制定机关具备项目执行能力。

不符合前款规定条件的，审批机关应当向制定机关提出修改意见；修改后仍不符合前款规定条件的，审批机关应当作出不予批准的书面决定并说明理由。

第十条 统计调查项目涉及其他部门职责的，审批机关应当在作出审批决定前，征求相关部门的意见。

第十一条 审批机关应当自受理统计调查项目审批申请之日起20日内作出决定。20日内不能作出决定的，经审批机关负责人批准可以延长10日，并应当将延长审批期限的理由告知制定机关。

制定机关修改统计调查项目的时间，不计算在审批期限内。

第十二条 制定机关申请备案统计调查项目，应当以公文形式向备案机关提交统计调查项目备案申请表和项目的统计调查制度。

统计调查项目的调查对象属于制定机关管辖系统，且主要内容与已批准、备案的统计调查项目不重复、不矛盾的，备案机关应当依法给予备案文号。

第十三条 统计调查项目经批准或者备案的，审批机关或者备案机关应当及时公布统计调查项目及其统计调查制度的主要内容。涉及国家秘密的统计调查项目除外。

第十四条 统计调查项目有下列情形之一的，审批机关或者备案机关应当简化审批或者备案程序，缩短期限:

（一）发生突发事件需要迅速实施统计调查;

（二）统计调查制度内容未作变动，统计调查项目有效期届满需要延长期限。

第十五条 统计法第十七条第二款规定的国家统计标准是强制执行标准。各级人民政府、县级以上人民政府统计机构和有关部门组织实施的统计调查活动，应当执行国家统计标准。

制定国家统计标准，应当征求国务院有关部门的意见。

第三章 统计调查的组织实施

第十六条 统计机构、统计人员组织实施统计调查，应当就统计调查对象的法定填报义务、主要指标涵义和有关填报要求等，向统计调查对象作出说明。

第十七条 国家机关、企业事业单位或者其他组织等统计调查对象提供统计资料，应当由填报人员和单位负责人签字，并加盖公章。个人作为统计调查对象提供统计资料，应当由本人签字。统计调查制度规定不需要签字、加盖公章的除外。

统计调查对象使用网络提供统计资料的，按照国家有关规定执行。

第十八条 县级以上人民政府统计机构、有关部门推广使用网络报送统计资料，应当采取有效的网络安全保障措施。

第十九条 县级以上人民政府统计机构、有关部门和乡、镇统计人员，应当对统计调查对象提供的统计资料进行审核。统计资料不完整或者存在明显错误的，应当由统计调查对象依法予以补充或者改正。

第二十条 国家统计局应当建立健全统计数据质量监控和评估制度，加强对各省、自治区、直辖市重要统计数据的监控和评估。

第四章 统计资料的管理和公布

第二十一条 县级以上人民政府统计机构、有关部门和乡、镇人民政府应当妥善保管统计调查中取得的统计资料。

国家建立统计资料灾难备份系统。

第二十二条 统计调查中取得的统计调查对象的原始资料，应当至少保存2年。

汇总性统计资料应当至少保存10年，重要的汇总性统计资料应当永久保存。法律法规另有规定的，从其规定。

第二十三条 统计调查对象按照国家有关规定设置的原始记录和统计台账，应当至少保存2年。

第二十四条 国家统计局统计调查取得的全国性统计数据和分省、自治区、直辖市统计数据，由国家统计局公布或者由国家统计局授权其派出的调查机构或者省级人民政府统计机构公布。

第二十五条 国务院有关部门统计调查取得的统计数据，由国务院有关部门按照国家有关规定和已批准或者备案的统计调查制度公布。

县级以上地方人民政府有关部门公布其统计调查取得的统计数据，比照前款规定执行。

第二十六条 已公布的统计数据按照国家有关规定需要进行修订的，县级以上人民政府统计机构和有关部门应当及时公布修订后的数据，并就修订依据和情况作出说明。

第二十七条 县级以上人民政府统计机构和有关部门应当及时公布主要统计指标涵义、调查范围、调查方法、计算方法、抽样调查样本量等信息，对统计数据进行解释说明。

第二十八条 公布统计资料应当按照国家有关规定进行。公布前，任何单位和个人不得违反国家有关规定对外提供，不得利用尚未公布的统计资料谋取不正当利益。

第二十九条 统计法第二十五条规定的能够识别或者推断单个统计调查对象身份的资料包括:

（一）直接标明单个统计调查对象身份的资料;

（二）虽未直接标明单个统计调查对象身份，但是通过已标明的地址、编码等相关信息可以识别或者推断单个统计调查对象身份的资料;

（三）可以推断单个统计调查对象身份的汇总资料。

第三十条 统计调查中获得的能够识别或者推断单个统计调查对象身份的资料应当依法严格管理，除作为统计执法依据外，不得直接作为对统计调查对象实施行政许可、行政处罚等具体行政行为的依据，不得用于完成统计任务以外的目的。

第三十一条 国家建立健全统计信息共享机制，实现县级以上人民政府统计机构和有关部门统计调查取得的资料共享。制定机关共同制定的统计调查项目，可以共同使用获取的统计资料。

统计调查制度应当对统计信息共享的内容、方式、时限、渠道和责任等作出规定。

第五章　统计机构和统计人员

第三十二条　县级以上地方人民政府统计机构受本级人民政府和上级人民政府统计机构的双重领导，在统计业务上以上级人民政府统计机构的领导为主。

乡、镇人民政府应当设置统计工作岗位，配备专职或者兼职统计人员，履行统计职责，在统计业务上受上级人民政府统计机构领导。乡、镇统计人员的调动，应当征得县级人民政府统计机构的同意。

县级以上人民政府有关部门在统计业务上受本级人民政府统计机构指导。

第三十三条　县级以上人民政府统计机构和有关部门应当完成国家统计调查任务，执行国家统计调查项目的统计调查制度，组织实施本地方、本部门的统计调查活动。

第三十四条　国家机关、企业事业单位和其他组织应当加强统计基础工作，为履行法定的统计资料报送义务提供组织、人员和工作条件保障。

第三十五条　对在统计工作中做出突出贡献、取得显著成绩的单位和个人，按照国家有关规定给予表彰和奖励。

第六章　监督检查

第三十六条　县级以上人民政府统计机构从事统计执法工作的人员，应当具备必要的法律知识和统计业务知识，参加统计执法培训，并取得由国家统计局统一印制的统计执法证。

第三十七条　任何单位和个人不得拒绝、阻碍对统计工作的监督检查和对统计违法行为的查处工作，不得包庇、纵容统计违法行为。

第三十八条　任何单位和个人有权向县级以上人民政府统计机构举报统计违法行为。

县级以上人民政府统计机构应当公布举报统计违法行为的方式和途径，依法受理、核实、处理举报，并为举报人保密。

第三十九条　县级以上人民政府统计机构负责查处统计违法行为；法律、行政法规对有关部门查处统计违法行为另有规定的，从其规定。

第七章　法律责任

第四十条　下列情形属于统计法第三十七条第四项规定的对严重统计违法行为失察，对地方人民政府、政府统计机构或者有关部门、单位的负责人，由任免机关或者监察机关依法给予处分，并由县级以上人民政府统计机构予以通报：

（一）本地方、本部门、本单位大面积发生或者连续发生统计造假、弄虚作假；

（二）本地方、本部门、本单位统计数据严重失实，应当发现而未发现；

（三）发现本地方、本部门、本单位统计数据严重失实不予纠正。

第四十一条　县级以上人民政府统计机构或者有关部门组织实施营利性统计调查的，由本级人民政府、上级人民政府统计机构或者本级人民政府统计机构责令改正，予以通报；有违法所得的，没收违法所得。

第四十二条　地方各级人民政府、县级以上人民政府统计机构或者有关部门及其负责人，侵犯统计机构、统计人员独立行使统计调查、统计报告、统计监督职权，或者采用下发文件、会议布置以及其他方式授意、指使、强令统计调查对象或者其他单位、人员编造虚假统计资料的，由上级人民政府、本级人民政府、上级人民政府统计机构或者本级人民政府统计机构责令改正，予以通报。

第四十三条　县级以上人民政府统计机构或者有关部门在组织实施统计调查活动中有下列行为之一的，由本级人民政府、上级人民政府统计机构或者本级人民政府统计机构责令改正，予以通报：

（一）违法制定、审批或者备案统计调查项目；

（二）未按照规定公布经批准或者备案的统计调查项目及其统计调查制度的主要内容；

（三）未执行国家统计标准；

（四）未执行统计调查制度；

（五）自行修改单个统计调查对象的统计资料。

乡、镇统计人员有前款第三项至第五项所列行为的，责令改正，依法给予处分。

第四十四条　县级以上人民政府统计机构或者有关部门违反本条例第二十四条、第二十五条规定公布统计数据的，由本级人民政府、上级人民政府统计机构或者本级人民政府统计机构责令改正，予以通报。

第四十五条　违反国家有关规定对外提供尚未公布的统计资料或者利用尚未公布的统计资料谋取不正当利益的，由任免机关或者监察机关依法给予处分，并由县级以上人民政府统计机构予以通报。

第四十六条　统计机构及其工作人员有下列行为之一的，由本级人民政府或者上级人民政府统计机构责令改正，予以通报：

（一）拒绝、阻碍对统计工作的监督检查和对统计违法行为的查处工作；

（二）包庇、纵容统计违法行为；

（三）向有统计违法行为的单位或者个人通风报信，帮助其逃避查处；

（四）未依法受理、核实、处理对统计违法行为的举报；

（五）泄露对统计违法行为的举报情况。

第四十七条　地方各级人民政府、县级以上人民政府有关部门拒绝、阻碍统计监督检查或者转移、隐匿、篡改、毁弃原始记录和凭证、统计台账、统计调查表及其他相关证明和资料的，由上级人民政府、上级人民政府统计机构或者本级人民政府统计机构责令改正，予以通报。

第四十八条 地方各级人民政府、县级以上人民政府统计机构和有关部门有本条例第四十一条至第四十七条所列违法行为之一的，对直接负责的主管人员和其他直接责任人员，由任免机关或者监察机关依法给予处分。

第四十九条 乡、镇人民政府有统计法第三十八条第一款、第三十九条第一款所列行为之一的，依照统计法第三十八条、第三十九条的规定追究法律责任。

第五十条 下列情形属于统计法第四十一条第二款规定的情节严重行为：

（一）使用暴力或者威胁方法拒绝、阻碍统计调查、统计监督检查；

（二）拒绝、阻碍统计调查、统计监督检查，严重影响相关工作正常开展；

（三）提供不真实、不完整的统计资料，造成严重后果或者恶劣影响；

（四）有统计法第四十一条第一款所列违法行为之一，1年内被责令改正3次以上。

第五十一条 统计违法行为涉嫌犯罪的，县级以上人民政府统计机构应当将案件移送司法机关处理。

第八章 附 则

第五十二条 中华人民共和国境外的组织、个人需要在中华人民共和国境内进行统计调查活动的，应当委托中华人民共和国境内具有涉外统计调查资格的机构进行。涉外统计调查资格应当依法报经批准。统计调查范围限于省、自治区、直辖市行政区域内的，由省级人民政府统计机构审批；统计调查范围跨省、自治区、直辖市行政区域的，由国家统计局审批。

涉外社会调查项目应当依法报经批准。统计调查范围限于省、自治区、直辖市行政区域内的，由省级人民政府统计机构审批；统计调查范围跨省、自治区、直辖市行政区域的，由国家统计局审批。

第五十三条 国家统计局或者省级人民政府统计机构对涉外统计违法行为进行调查，有权采取统计法第三十五条规定的措施。

第五十四条 对违法从事涉外统计调查活动的单位、个人，由国家统计局或者省级人民政府统计机构责令改正或者责令停止调查，有违法所得的，没收违法所得；违法所得50万元以上的，并处违法所得1倍以上3倍以下的罚款；违法所得不足50万元或者没有违法所得的，处200万元以下的罚款；情节严重的，暂停或者取消涉外统计调查资格，撤销涉外社会调查项目批准决定；构成犯罪的，依法追究刑事责任。

第五十五条 本条例自2017年8月1日起施行。1987年1月19日国务院批准、1987年2月15日国家统计局公布，2000年6月2日国务院批准修订、2000年6月15日国家统计局公布，2005年12月16日国务院修订的《中华人民共和国统计法实施细则》同时废止。

附录六

统计违法违纪行为处分规定

Statistics Regulation Violations of Law

中华人民共和国监察部
中华人民共和国人力资源和社会保障部　令
国家统计局

第 18 号

《统计违法违纪行为处分规定》已经监察部2009年2月9日第一次部长办公会议、人力资源社会保障部2008年12月30日第十六次部务会议、国家统计局2008年11月6日第十八次局务会议审议通过。现予公布，自2009年5月1日起施行。

监察部部长　马　馼
人力资源社会保障部部长　尹蔚民
国家统计局局长　马建堂
二〇〇九年三月二十五日

统计违法违纪行为处分规定

第一条　为了加强统计工作，提高统计数据的准确性和及时性，惩处和预防统计违法违纪行为，促进统计法律法规的贯彻实施，根据《中华人民共和国统计法》、《中华人民共和国行政监察法》、《中华人民共和国公务员法》、《行政机关公务员处分条例》及其他有关法律、行政法规，制定本规定。

第二条　有统计违法违纪行为的单位中负有责任的领导人员和直接责任人员，以及有统计违法违纪行为的个人，应当承担纪律责任。属于下列人员的（以下统称有关责任人员），由任免机关或者监察机关按照管理权限依法给予处分：

（一）行政机关公务员；

（二）法律、法规授权的具有公共事务管理职能的事业单位中经批准参照《中华人民共和国公务员法》管理的工作人员；

（三）行政机关依法委托的组织中除工勤人员以外的工作人员；

（四）企业、事业单位、社会团体中由行政机关任命的人员。

法律、行政法规、国务院决定和国务院监察机关、国务院人力资源社会保障部门制定的处分规章对统计违法违纪行为的处分另有规定的，从其规定。

第三条　地方、部门以及企业、事业单位、社会团体的领导人员有下列行为之一的，给予记过或者记大过处分；情节较重的，给予降级或者撤职处分；情节严重的，给予开除处分：

（一）自行修改统计资料、编造虚假数据的；

（二）强令、授意本地区、本部门、本单位统计机构、统计人员或者其他有关机构、人员拒报、虚报、瞒报或者篡改统计资料、编造虚假数据的；

（三）对拒绝、抵制篡改统计资料或者对拒绝、抵制编造虚假数据的人员进行打击报复的；

（四）对揭发、检举统计违法违纪行为的人员进行打击报复的。

有前款第（三）项、第（四）项规定行为的，应当从重处分。

第四条　地方、部门以及企业、事业单位、社会团体的领导人员，对本地区、本部门、本单位严重失实的统计数据，应当发现而未发现或者发现后不予纠正，造成不良后果的，给予警告或者记过处分；造成严重后果的，给予记大过或者降级处分；造成特别严重后果的，给予撤职或者开除处分。

第五条　各级人民政府统计机构、有关部门及其工作人员在实施统计调查活动中，有下列行为之一的，对有关责任人员，给予记过或者记大过处分；情节较重的，给予降级或者撤职处分；情节严重的，给予开除处分：

（一）强令、授意统计调查对象虚报、瞒报或者伪造、篡改统计资料的；

（二）参与篡改统计资料、编造虚假数据的。

第六条 各级人民政府统计机构、有关部门及其工作人员在实施统计调查活动中，有下列行为之一的，对有关责任人员，给予警告、记过或者记大过处分；情节较重的，给予降级处分；情节严重的，给予撤职处分：

（一）故意拖延或者拒报统计资料的；

（二）明知统计数据不实，不履行职责调查核实，造成不良后果的。

第七条 统计调查对象中的单位有下列行为之一，情节较重的，对有关责任人员，给予警告、记过或者记大过处分；情节严重的，给予降级或者撤职处分；情节特别严重的，给予开除处分：

（一）虚报、瞒报统计资料的；

（二）伪造、篡改统计资料的；

（三）拒报或者屡次迟报统计资料的；

（四）拒绝提供情况、提供虚假情况或者转移、隐匿、毁弃原始统计记录、统计台账、统计报表以及与统计有关的其他资料的。

第八条 违反国家规定的权限和程序公布统计资料，造成不良后果的，对有关责任人员，给予警告或者记过处分；情节较重的，给予记大过或者降级处分；情节严重的，给予撤职处分。

第九条 有下列行为之一，造成不良后果的，对有关责任人员，给予警告、记过或者记大过处分；情节较重的，给予降级或者撤职处分；情节严重的，给予开除处分：

（一）泄露属于国家秘密的统计资料的；

（二）未经本人同意，泄露统计调查对象个人、家庭资料的；

（三）泄露统计调查中知悉的统计调查对象商业秘密的。

第十条 包庇、纵容统计违法违纪行为的，对有关责任人员，给予记过或者记大过处分；情节较重的，给予降级或者撤职处分；情节严重的，给予开除处分。

第十一条 受到处分的人员对处分决定不服的，依照《中华人民共和国行政监察法》、《中华人民共和国公务员法》、《行政机关公务员处分条例》等有关规定，可以申请复核或者申诉。

第十二条 任免机关、监察机关和人民政府统计机构建立案件移送制度。

任免机关、监察机关查处统计违法违纪案件，认为应当由人民政府统计机构给予行政处罚的，应当将有关案件材料移送人民政府统计机构。人民政府统计机构应当依法及时查处，并将处理结果书面告知任免机关、监察机关。

人民政府统计机构查处统计行政违法案件，认为应当由任免机关或者监察机关给予处分的，应当及时将有关案件材料移送任免机关或者监察机关。任免机关或者监察机关应当依法及时查处，并将处理结果书面告知人民政府统计机构。

第十三条 有统计违法违纪行为，应当给予党纪处分的，移送党的纪律检查机关处理。涉嫌犯罪的，移送司法机关依法追究刑事责任。

第十四条 本规定由监察部、人力资源社会保障部、国家统计局负责解释。

第十五条 本规定自 2009 年 5 月 1 日起施行。

附录七

济南市统计局二〇一九年统计工作大事记

Chronicle of Events of Jinan Statistical Undertaking

1月1日，第四次全国经济普查入户登记工作全面启动。副省长、省第四次经济普查领导小组组长王书坚到济南市市中区四里村街道办事处，检查指导经济普查现场登记工作，慰问一线普查人员。省统计局局长郭训成，济南市副市长王京文，市统计局局长苑子建参加活动。

1月9日，济南市统计局、市发改委、市经济和信息化委、市城乡建设委、市商务局联合召开2019年“四上”单位上规入库工作会议。会议通报2018年全市“四上”单位上规入库增减变动情况，安排部署2019年“四上”单位上规入库工作；济南市统计局党组成员、副局长谈友军出席会议并讲话。

1月18日，山东省统计局服务业处四级调研员倪华桥一行三人到济南对物业管理、居民服务业和商务服务业开展调研，对部分企业进行普查表试填工作。

1月23日，济南市统计局赴平阴县东阿镇西南坝村开展帮扶活动。党组书记、局长苑子建带领一行20人参加了此次活动。参加帮扶人员分别走到贫困户家中，了解困难群众生活情况，倾听群众的困难和诉求，并送去慰问物资。苑子建局长在贫困户家中，细心询问冬季的采暖情况，通过拉家常的方式鼓励困难户建立信心，体现了党和政府的关怀和帮助困难群众脱贫致富的决心。

1月24日，济南市统计局党组书记、局长苑子建一行到南辛庄街道开展走访调研，并看望慰问辖区3户困难党员群众，为他们送去春节祝福和慰问品，并致以诚挚的新春祝福。槐荫区委书记国承彦，区委副书记、区长朱玉明亲切会见苑子建一行。

1月27日，根据市统一安排，济南局承担市人代会现场统计咨询服务工作，负责数据查询、为人大代表解答有关统计方面的问题，圆满完成济南人代会统计信息咨询服务工作。

1月30日，济南市统计局区划调整筹备组组长苑子建一行，在筹备组副组长张兴利、筹备组成员沈桂欣的陪同下，先后到4个直属分局，看望慰问干部职工并进行实地调研。

2月1日，市统计局在龙奥大厦G1114召开支部书记述职评议工作会议，局所属5个党支部书记进行现场述职。全体机关党委委员、各支部书记、党员及群团代表参加会议。局机关党委书记崔瑞宁对各支部的述职情况进行点评并对下年的工作提出要求。

2月1日，为营造喜庆祥和的节日气氛，弘扬优秀传统文化，市统计局举办了一场“写春联 剪纸 送福”迎新春活动，现场气氛热烈，互动踊跃，活动持续了一个下午，依然意兴未尽，生动体现了统计干部职工的良好精神风貌。本次活动特邀市统计局退休老干部老党员张思勇参加活动。

2月1日，济南市统计局研究制定《济南市十强产业及十大千亿产业监测通报制度实施方案的责任分工和实施办法》，市政府办公厅文件正式印发（济政办字〔2019〕5号）。

2月21日，国家统计局人口和就业司专项处处长于弘文、普查处调研员曹燕一行到济南我市调研。山东省统计局城镇化和人口就业处处长孙明清、济南市统计局副局长崔瑞宁、历下区副区长张涛等陪同调研。

2月26日，为积极响应无偿献血活动倡议，展现文明单位风采，市统计局10名党员干部自愿参加无偿献血活动。

2月26日，济南市统计局、济南市科技局联合召开2019年全市科技统计工作电视电话会议，对全市2018年度科技统计工作进行部署，并对企业R&D经费投入统计填报和高新技术产业产值业务进行培训，对加计扣除税收政策进行了解读。各区县科技、统计部门工作人员和重点企业有关人员共约1000余人分别在主会场和各分会场同步参加会议。市统计局党组书记、局长苑子建参加会议并讲话。

2月27日，济南市统计局召开专题会议部署十强产业及十大千亿产业统计监测工作。市统计局局长苑子建、市社会经济调查局局长唐军出席会议并做出指示，各相关专业处室负责人参加会议。

3月4日，济南市经普办召开全市经普工作会议，市统计局局长、市第四次经济普查领导小组办公室主任苑子建出席会议并讲话，市统计局副局长、市第四次经济普查领导小组办公室常务副主任谈友军主持会议。

3月5日，为纪念“三八”国际妇女劳动节109周年，济南市统计局女职工参加市直机关工委举办庆“三八”趣味健步走活动。

3月8日，济南市人大代表对济南市统计局建议答复事宜当面致谢。陈元德代表就新经济考核工作进行座谈。市统计局党组成员、副局长吕历源，综合处、核算处、能源处负责人参加座谈。

3月8日，济南市统计局组织机关及所属事业单位女干部职工参观山东省博物馆，重读历史责任和时代担当，共同庆祝“三八”国际妇女节。

3月18日，济南市统计局组织全市统计系统副处级以上干部收看“山东统计大讲堂”直播视频。

3月18日，济南市统计局组织局机关及局属事业单位副处以上干部收看全国统计部门全面从严治党视频会议，并邀请市纪委派驻六组的人员参加。

3月19日，为加强党风廉政教育，济南市统计局组织全体在职人员集中观看三部专题警示教育片。

3月20日，济南市统计局副局长吕历源一行，赴平阴县调研指导四经普登记入户工作。

3月21日，市政府办公厅对2018年度政务信息报送、政务公开及政府网站信息内容建设工作情况进行通报。济南市统计局和济南市统计局办公室分别获得政府网站信息内容建设工作成绩突出单位、政务信息工作成绩突出单位。

3月25日，济南市统计局副局长李士营一行赴市中区巡检四经普登记工作。

3月26日，济南市统计局组织开展“合法权益我知晓——女职工权益保护知识答卷”活动。全局女职工积极参加活动，认真学习女职工权益保护相关法律法规，并填交答卷。

3月26日，济南市统计局副局长李士营一行赴长清区巡检四经普登记工作。巡检组前往普查一线，深入企业，实地进行普查巡检工作。

3月26日， 济南市统计局副局长张谨国一行，赴天桥区和济阳区进行经济普查调研指导工作，

3月27日，济南市统计局党组书记、局长苑子建听取下派干部汇报挂职以来思想和工作情况。苑子建听取汇报后，对下派挂职以来所做的工作给予充分肯定，提出3项具体要求。

3月，济南市统计局帮扶的平阴县东阿镇西南坝村为进一步壮大集体经济，完成10余亩3600株的木瓜苗木种植。

4月8日，济南市统计局建立“四新”统计监测制度（试行），为全面、准确、及时反映济南市新技术、新产业、新业态、新商业模式等新经济取得的进展和成效，为政府加强管理和宏观调控提供更好的统计服务。

4月10日，济南电台《新闻时间》和《公共之声》同步系列报道市统计局驻村第一书记朱效霞工作事迹——《朱效霞：第一书记驻村记》。

4月12日，济南市统计局组织新任处科级干部进行集体谈话。市统计局党组副书记、市社会经济调查局局长唐军主持会议并宣布新任处科级干部和原莱芜市统计局干部职级晋升意见。党组书记、局长苑子建出席会议并讲话。市统计局分管领导、各处室负责人、新任处科级干部等参加会议。

4月12日，济南市统计局党组书记、局长苑子建听取驻村帮扶专题汇报，驻颜庄镇中当峪村第一书记朱效霞详细介绍一年多驻村工作开展情况、取得的成效及工作打算。

4月22日，省统计局能源处处长孙明清一行3人在济南市对2018年全年能源消耗数据进行核查。

4月26日，济南市统计系统的16名爱心妈妈到济南市儿童福利院，参加由市妇联、市民政局和济南日报报业集团联合开展的“爱心妈妈拥抱福娃”活动，把爱心和温暖送给福利院的孩子们，与孩子们一起度过了一段温馨而难忘的时光。

4月28日，在全市机关党的工作暨深入开展“坚持以人民为中心的发展思想”教育活动动员部署会议上，市委市直机关工委发文对2018年度市直机关党建工作情况进行表扬通报，市统计局机关第二党支部作为全市185个入选基层党支部之一，被评为市直机关“过硬党支部”。

4月29日，济南市召开庆祝“五一”国际劳动节暨2018年度经济社会发展综合考核表彰大会。济南市统计局被市委、市政府评为2018年度经济社会发展综合考核先进单位、2018年度经济社会发展综合考核泉城创新奖；被市委办公厅、市政府办公厅评为双招双引信息服务类一等奖。

4月29日，济南市人民政府新闻办公室举办新闻发布会，通报一季度全市经济社会运行情况。

4月29日，为纪念“五四”运动100周年，进一步继承和发扬“五四”运动的优良传统，增强中青年干部的凝聚力和团队意识，济南局青年志愿者在山东省山青世界青少年活动中心开展户外拓展训练活动。

5月5日上午，市统计局团支部组织召开学习习总书记“五四”讲话精神座谈会，局35岁以下青年干部参加会议。

5月7日，济南市局召开全市贸易统计工作会议，有关区县统计局分管贸易统计的局长参加会议，副局长张谨国出席会议并讲话。

5月8日，济南市统计局印发《济南市部门统计工作规范化管理办法》的通知（济统字〔2019〕11号），办法分总则、部门统计机构和统计人员、部门统计调查项目、组织实施、部门统计资料、部门统计信息化、检查与管理、附则等八章共三十六条。

5月8日，济南市局召开“坚持以人民为中心的发展思想”教育活动暨“扬起龙头、干在实处、走在前列”大竞赛大比武动员大会，济南市统计局党组副书记、市社会经济调查中心主任唐军主持会议并传达市委、市政府有关通知精神，济南市统计局党组书记、局长苑子建出席会议并作动员讲话。

5月9日，济南市局召开第四次经济普查数据审核培训会议。济南市统计局党组书记、局长，市第四次经济普查领导小组办公室主任苑子建出席会议并讲话，市统计局领导班子成员出席会议。

5月10日，济南市统计局组织党组理论学习中心组第二次集体学习，党组书记、局长苑子建主持学习研讨，全体中心组成员参加学习讨论，市纪委派驻第六纪检监察组朱文君到会指导，其他市管干部及办公室、组织人事处、机关党委等主要负责人列席会议。

5月12日，济南市统计系统党务干部培训班在中山大学珠海校区举办，为加强组织管理，培训期间成立市统计系统党务培训班临时党支部，下设6个党小组。

5月15日，国家统计局贸易外经司外经处处长刘晓燕一行到济南，对部分进出口企业加工贸易创新情况进行专题调研。

5月16日，济南市统计局组织开展经典诵读活动，市统计局党组副书记、市社会经济调查中心唐军，以及全市统计系统党务干部参加此次活动。

5月22日，省统计局服务业处副处长杨志刚、四级调研员倪化桥等在济南市对四经普服务业单位登记情况进行调研。

5月25日，济南市召开全市第四次经济普查工作推进会。济南市副市长孙斌出席会议并讲话，市统计局局长、市第四次经济普查领导小组办公室主任苑子建通报全市经济普查工作情况，市政府副秘书长张蓉主持会议。

5月15日—25日，济南市局在北京牵头组织中国营商环境评价测评工作。

5月30日，济南市局机关党委组织部分党员干部观看法制

教育影片《特别追踪》。

5月30日上午，济南市局组织干部职工开展“精准扶贫慈心一日捐”活动。

6月5日，济南市局举办“我们的节日·端午节”包粽子活动。

6月5日，济南市统计局局长、市第四次经济普查领导小组办公室主任苑子建赴平阴县指导检查数据审核验收工作。

6月5日，济南市统计局党组成员、市管正处级领导干部张兴利和市农业农村局副局长赵建民带队到历城区、章丘区对现代农业生产情况进行调研。

6月6日，济南市局组织召开专题会议，协调莱芜区、莱芜高新区统计事权划转工作。

6月10日，济南市局召开“不忘初心、牢记使命”主题教育工作会议，济南市统计局党组书记、局长苑子建在会上作动员讲话，党组副书记、市社会经济调查中心主任唐军主持会议。市委第一巡回指导组组长岳绍红出席会议并讲话，市委第一巡回指导组全体成员到会指导。济南市局全体副处级以上干部参加会议。

6月12日，郑州济南统计局副局长赵广程一行3人，在济南考察交流“四新”统计等工作情况。

6月13日，济南市局召开全市统计局长会议。济南市局党组书记、局长苑子建作工作报告。济南市局党组副书记、市社会经济调查中心主任唐军主持会议。

6月13日，济南市局召开2019年全市统计系统党风廉政建设暨行风建设工作会议。

6月14日，济南市统计局党组副书记、市社会经济调查中心主任唐军一行到历城区山大路街道洪北社区开展“双报到”对接活动。

6月14日，济南市统计局党组成员、正处级领导干部张兴利带领农村统计处一行，到莱芜区、钢城区深入农业园区和涉农企业开展现代农业调研。

6月19日，全国第四次经济普查事后质量检查组到商河县检查指导济南市经济普查工作。济南市副市长孙斌出席首日见面会，省统计局二级巡视员王志珍，济南市统计局局长、市第四次经济普查领导小组办公室主任苑子建出席会议。

6月24日下午，济南市局召开“不忘初心、牢记使命”主题教育推进工作会议。全局副处级以上干部参加会议。

6月27日上午，济南市局“不忘初心、牢记使命”主题教育读书班举办开班式并组织党组理论学习中心组（扩大）集体学习。全局副处级以上干部参加会议，市委第一巡回指导组副组长尹希芳到会指导，党组书记、局长苑子建出席会议并讲话，党组副书记、市社会经济调查中心主任唐军主持会议并就有关问题提出具体要求。

7月1日，全市市直机关庆祝中国共产党成立98周年暨表彰大会召开，市统计局何宇晖被授予“济南市市直机关优秀共产党员”称号、李咏梅被授予“济南市市直机关优秀党务工作者”称号，局机关第二党支部被授予“先进基层党组织”称号。

7月1日，为深入学习贯彻《中国共产党党员教育管理工作条例》，结合开展“不忘初心、牢记使命”主题教育，根据市委组织部通知要求，济南市统计局组织全体在职党员集中收看由省委组织部举办的“灯塔大课堂”第一课。

7月5日，济南市局举办“不忘初心、牢记使命”先进典型教育，组织副处级以上干部收看张保国、郭永怀先进事迹报告会。

7月8日，济南市统计局党组副书记、市社会经济调查中心主任唐军一行5人到莱芜区统计局开展专题调研。

7月9日，济南市统计局党组副书记、市社会经济调查中心主任唐军一行4人到槐荫区匡山街道匡山村开展领导干部“一对一”帮包服务民营企业活动并参加对接会。

7月9日，济南市局主题教育专题调研第六组组长张兴利带领有关处室人员到历城区开展专题调研。

7月10日，济南市局副局长李士营带领第五调研组一行5人，赴槐荫区就上半年经济运行情况，基层对统计工作的意见和建议以及“四上”企业统计台账使用情况进行走访调研。

7月11日，济南市统计局党组成员、副局长张谨国带领市统计局“不忘初心、牢记使命”主题教育专题调研第三组，到历下区走访调研。

7月11日，济南市统计局党组成员、主题教育专题调研第九组组长周光萍带领调研组到济阳区开展调研。

7月11日，济南市统计局党组成员、主题教育专题调研第十组组长张秀玲带领局贸易处、工业处、普查处、服务业处相关人员到平阴县开展专题调研活动。

7月12日，济南市统计局班子成员李登杰带领第八调研组成员，深入章丘区开展集中调研活动。

7月16日，济南市统计局“不忘初心、牢记使命”主题教育第七调研组一行4人由局党组成员、正处级领导干部沈桂欣带队赴长清区开展专题调研。

7月16日，济南市统计局副局级领导干部吕历源带领第十三调研组一行5人，赴钢城区进行专题调研。

7月17日，济南市统计局党组书记、局长苑子建带领机关党委和机关第一党支部20余名党员组成服务队，深入历城区山大路街道洪北社区开展党组织、党员“双报到”工作。

7月22日，济南市统计局党组成员、副局长张谨国同志赴“一对一”帮包的山东新华能源物资有限公司和山东昌隆建设咨询股份有限公司进行现场对接和工作调研。

7月23日，济南市统计局组织“不忘初心、牢记使命”主题教育第二次专题学习研讨暨第六次党组理论学习中心组集体学习。

7月23日，济南市人民政府新闻办公室举办新闻发布会，通报上半年全市经济社会运行情况。市统计局党组副书记、市社会经济调查中心主任、新闻发言人唐军出席新闻发布会，并就上半年全市经济运行情况、当前济南市就业形势、下一阶段济南经济运行走势等问题现场回答新闻记者的提问。

7月24日，济南市局副局长谈友军一行4人到莱芜区开展调研活动。

7月25日，济南市统计局党组书记、局长苑子建带领80余名干部职工赴济南市人民检察院预防职务犯罪警示教育基地参观学习。

7月26日，济南市统计局党组书记、局长苑子建带队到先行区开展“不忘初心、牢记使命”主题教育专题调研。

7月30日，上海市统计局人口和就业统计处副处长樊佳佳一行4人，到济南市局调研第七次人口普查工作，省统计局人口处高级统计师张强陪同调研。

7月31日，济南市统计局党组召开“不忘初心、牢记使命”主题教育调研成果交流会。市委第一巡回指导组组长岳绍红、市纪委派驻第六纪检监察组副处级领导干部朱文君到会指导。市统计局党组书记、局长苑子建主持会议并带头发言，局党组成员围绕调研情况分别作交流发言。

8月1日，按照《济南新旧动能转换先行区管委会代管区域划转工作方案》（以下简称先行区）要求，济南市局组织召开天桥区、济阳区、先行区统计事权划转工作会议。

8月8日，济南市统计局党组书记、局长苑子建结合学习思考、调查研究和问题检视情况，结合统计工作和统计队伍建设实际，为全局党员讲了一堂“不忘初心、牢记使命，努力锻造一支忠诚干净担当的统计干部队伍”的主题教育专题党课。

8月8日，济南市统计局党组成员、正处级领导干部张兴利为三支部全体党员干部上“不忘初心、牢记使命”主题教育专题党课。

8月9日，为贯彻落实全市重点耗能企业煤炭消费情况核查工作视频会议精神，济南市局组织召开重点耗能企业数据核查业务培训会，济南市局局长苑子建出席会议并讲话。

8月13日，国家服务业司副司长王群英一行3人到济南市调研服务业统计情况。省统计局服务业处处长刘福军，济南市局副局长张谨国，天桥区副区长韩利师陪同调研。

8月15日，按照全市统一部署，济南市统计局党组成员、副局长李士营一行5人，到莱芜区对重点耗能企业煤炭消费情况和工业月报数据进行核查。

8月16日，济南市市委“不忘初心、牢记使命”主题教育第一巡回指导组副组长尹希芳一行到济南市局指导检查主题教育档案整理工作。

8月16日，根据《关于对全市重点耗能企业煤炭消费情况进行核查的通知》要求，济南市统计局、发展改革委、工业和信息化局及生态环境局四部门共计35人组成7个专项核查组，对全市72家重点耗能企业进行了现场核查。

8月19日，济南市统计局党组成员、副局长孙夕良为综合处、能源处和农村处全体党员干部讲了一堂“不忘初心、牢记使命”专题党课。

8月21日，济南市局在市委党校莱芜校区召开党组对照党章党规找差距专题会议。

8月21日，济南市统计局党组理论学习中心组（扩大）读书会集中观看《党的十八大以来我省党员干部违纪违法典型案件警示录》，影片通过违纪违法当事人的深刻忏悔，警示教育广大党员领导干部要坚定理想信念，增强党纪和党性意识，自觉遵守党的规章制度，做一名忠诚、干净、担当的好干部。

8月22日，济南市统计局党组理论学习中心组（扩大）读书暨统计业务培训班全体学员赴莱芜战役纪念馆开展现场教学，接受党性教育。

8月23日，济南市统计局党组组织主题教育第五次专题学习研讨暨党组中心组（扩大）第九次集体学习会。

8月27日，济南市统计局党组召开“不忘初心、牢记使命”专题民主生活会。

8月28日，济南市统计局党组书记、局长苑子建带领70余名干部职工参观“不忘初心 奋发图强——新中国工业档案文献展暨济南市工业和信息化成果展”。

8月28日，郑州市统计局副局长张庆华一行5人，到济南考察交流农业统计工作情况。

8月29日，泰安市统计局副局长刘林一行7人到济南市考察交流四经普等工作情况。济南市统计局党组成员，副局长谈友军参加座谈。

8月30日上午，省统计局服务业处处长刘福军一行2人，在济南市调研服务业企业。济南市局副局长李士营、市中区政府党组成员张立光陪同调研。

9月4日，济南市统计局党组书记、局长苑子建深入到民营企业送政策，了解企业经营状况和制约企业发展的困难，听取民营企业对市委、市政府的意见建议。

9月4日，山东省统计局副局长周尊考、数据管理中心领导一行到市统计局调研统计大数据建设试点工作，副局长张谨国参加座谈，计算中心汇报统计大数据平台建设的工作情况。

9月4日，济南市局张兴利带领工业统计处有关人员赴长清区进行专题调研。

9月10日，中秋来临之际，济南市局组织“我们的节日中秋”暨“和谐社区，情满中秋”月饼DIY活动，党员志愿服务队赴洪北社区给社区居民送上美好的节日祝福，和社区居民一起制作月饼，喜迎中秋佳节。

9月10日，山东省统计局局长郭训成一行在济南市开展2018年重点能耗企业煤炭消费情况核查工作。济南市委常委、副市长郑德雁主持座谈会，市统计局党组书记、局长苑子建就济南市开展2018年重点能耗企业煤炭消费核查情况进行详细的汇报。

9月11日，济南市局张兴利带领工业统计处有关人员赴莱芜区莱芜钢铁集团莱芜矿业有限公司和莱芜高新区莱芜圆泰新能源有限责任公司、山东美貌制药有限公司进行专题调研。

9月16日，济南市统计局党组书记、局长苑子建带队参加济南人民广播电台《作风监督热线》节目，向听众介绍统计工作，并接听解答听众提问。局、队相关处室参加节目。

9月17日，济南市委市直机关工委副书记解胜利、党建督察室陈元旺等一行到济南市统计局就机关党的政治建设、落实党建工作责任制、基层组织建设、党员教育管理、落实机关党建重点任务等情况进行督导调研，局党组书记、局长苑子建汇报了市统计党建工作情况，机关党委专职副书记和党务工作者、各支部书记和部分党员代表参加工作汇报会。

9月20日，由济南市统计局、国家统计局济南调查队和莱芜区人民政府联合举办的第十届“中国统计开放日”活动在莱芜区文化广场举行。

9月24日，济南市统计局党组书记、局长苑子建一行走访慰问济南市局两位离休老干部。

9月26日，济南市局举办“朗读者：我爱你中国——济南统计人的心声”主题汇演活动，喜迎新中国成立70周年。党组书记、局长苑子建致开幕词。市纪委派驻第六纪检监察组组长郭尚兰莅临现场进行指导。

10月9日，为强力推进济南市“上规入库”工作，济南市政府成立市委常委、副市长郑德雁任组长，杨永斌副秘书长、市统计局苑子建局长任副组长，市发改委、市工信局、市财政局、市商务局、市住建局、市行政审批服务局、市税务局、市统计局等8个部门分管领导任成员的“上规入库”工作专班。工作专班办公室设在市统计局。

10月14日，济南市统计局党组成员张兴利按照市局“一套表”调查单位核查工作安排，带领相关处室有关人员赴莱芜区牛泉镇、寨里镇、和庄镇对88家“一套表”调查单位进行现场核查。

10月15日，济南市统计局党组副书记、市社会经济调查中心主任唐军等一行6人赴钢城区颜庄镇中当峪村与钢城区统计局共同开展“走进扶贫村、共度扶贫日”主题党日活动。

10月15日，济南市统计局党组副书记、市社会经济调查中心主任唐军带队对钢城区统计局党建和行风建设工作进行调研督导。

10月22日，济南市局蓝色春风志愿服务队到济南市历城区洪北社区开展《统计法》普法宣传活动。

10月23日，济南市统计局、发展改革委、工业和信息化局、商务局、住建局五部门联合组织召开全市上规入库工作培训会议，会议传达《济南市上规入库工作方案》，就如何做好2019年年度及2020年月度“四上”单位上规入库工作进行了业务知识培训，分部门召开上规入库工作座谈研讨会。

10月24日，济南市局组织召开全市统计系统办公室工作培训会，市统计局党组副书记、市社会经济调查中心主任唐军出席会议并讲话，各区县办公室主任、政务公开、财务人员及市局各处室相关负责人参加会议。

10月24日，济南市统计局党组成员、副局长孙夕良带领农村统计处数据核查一组赴历城区和章丘区开展农业统计数据核查工作。

10月28日，济南市人民政府新闻办公室举办新闻发布会，通报前三季度全市经济社会运行情况。济南市统计局党组副书记、市社会经济调查中心主任、新闻发言人唐军出席新闻发布会，并就前三季度全市经济运行情况、今后房地产市场及房价走势、全年经济走势等问题现场回答新闻记者的提问。

10月30日，《济南日报》头版刊登济南市统计局党组书记、局长苑子建《关于做好“上规入库”(小升规)提高统计数据质量》的“上规入库”工作专访。

10月31日，《济南日报》《济南时报》、爱济南新闻客户端等新闻媒体刊登济南市发展改革委、工业和信息化局、住房和城乡建设局、商务局、统计局等五部门《致全市统计调查单位“上规入库”对象的一封信》。

11月1日，省统计局一级巡视员刘银田一行，在济南市视察1%人口抽样调查入户现场登记工作。济南市副市长孙斌，市统计局局长苑子建陪同。

11月5日—8日，济南市统计局党组书记、局长苑子建带队先后巡检济南高新区、历下区、历城区、市中区、槐荫区、天桥区等重点区县的“上规入库”工作。

11月12日，济南市局在中国政法大学举办济南市统计执法骨干培训班，进一步提升统计执法骨干综合能力。

11月14日，济南市统计局党组成员、正处级领导干部张兴利带领工业处一行3人，到天桥区、槐荫区调研当前工业经济形势，并到“遍访民企”服务企业对接座谈。

11月15日，济南市政府召开“上规入库”纳统工作推进会议，会议通报全市“上规入库”工作最新的进展情况，安排部署全市下一步“上规入库”纳统工作。

11月16日，在济南市全市党的建设工作推进会议上，山东省委省直机关工委、济南市委组织部、济南市委市直机关工委、济南市教育工委、济南市国资委党委等五部门联合印发《机关企事业单位党组织、在职党员“双报到”经验做法、典型案例汇编》，济南市局“双报到”工作入选典型案例。

11月18日，济南市局张兴利带领工业统计处有关人员赴平阴县、历城区对4家纳新企业进行现场核查，切实把好新增规模企业的进入关口。

11月20日，济南市统计局张兴利、市工业和信息化局副局长吕春明带领济南市统计局工业处、市工业和信息化局运行监测协调处到齐鲁制药进行联合调研。

11月21日，省统计局设管处处长刘东华一行2人到济南市章丘区、历城区对城乡划分质量情况进行调研。

11月27日，济南市局张兴利带领工业统计处有关人员到济阳区、商河县开展调研工作，并对新纳统单位进行现场核查。

11月28日，济南市局组织副处级以上干部集体观看《叩问初心》警示教育片。

11月28日，济南市统计局党组成员、副局长孙夕良带领农村处相关人员，到平阴县调研农村改厕工作开展情况。

12月2日—3日，济南市局召开人口就业暨社会科技2019年统计年报和2020年统计定报培训会议。党组成员、副局长卜繁钢参加会议并讲话。

12月3日—4日，济南市统计局党组成员、副局长孙夕良带领农村处相关人员赴商河县开展厕改工作专题调研。

12月7日，济南市局、天桥区委区政府联合举办《统计法》宣传日活动，党组书记、局长苑子建参加活动并讲话。

12月9日—10日，济南市统计局党组成员、副局长孙夕良带领农村处相关人员到莱芜区开展农村厕改推进情况专题调研。

12月10日，国家统计局服务业司处长张双喜、省统计局副局长陈汉臻、刘福军处长一行到济南调研服务业单位上规入库纳统工作，济南市统计局党组书记、局长苑子建参加座谈并汇报情况。

12 月 13 日，济南市局组织学习贯彻党的十九届四中全会精神宣讲会，邀请市直机关学习贯彻党的十九届四中全会精神宣讲团成员、市委党校公共管理教研部副教授吴春为全局全体党员宣讲十九届四中全会精神。党组书记、局长苑子建主持会议并讲话。

12 月 30 日，济南市局参加济南市电视问政工作领导小组办公室《作风监督面对面》节目录制。

12 月 30 日—31 日，济南市局举办处级领导干部党的十九届四中全会精神专题学习班。

12 月 31 日，省统计局局长郭训成一行济南圣泉集团股份有限公司调研座谈，济南市委常委、副市长郑德雁、济南市统计局局长苑子建陪同调研。

12 月下旬，济南市平阴县委挂职副书记孟克非到济南市局对脱贫攻坚方面所做的工作表示感谢，并对济南市局派驻平阴县东阿镇西南坝村第一书记潘鲁军两年来的工作给予充分肯定。

中国统计出版社有限公司最新图书简目

(仅供参考,以实际出版为准)

统计资料

中国统计年鉴　中国统计摘要　中国第三产业统计年鉴
中国第三次全国农业普查综合资料　国际统计年鉴　金砖国家联合统计手册
中国-东盟国家统计手册　中国农村统计年鉴　中国县域统计年鉴
中国农产品价格调查年鉴　中国城市统计年鉴　中国价格统计年鉴
中国贸易外经统计年鉴　中国零售和餐饮连锁企业统计年鉴　中国商品交易市场统计年鉴
大中型批发零售和住宿餐饮企业统计年鉴　中国住户调查年鉴　中国工业统计年鉴
中国环境统计年鉴　中国能源统计年鉴　中国建筑业统计年鉴
中国房地产统计年鉴　投资领域统计年鉴　中国对外直接投资统计公报
中国人口和就业统计年鉴　中国劳动统计年鉴　中国社会统计年鉴
中国科技统计年鉴　中国高技术产业统计年鉴　全国企业创新调查年鉴
中国文化及相关产业统计年鉴　2018年时间利用调查资料　中国妇女儿童状况统计资料
中国基本单位统计年鉴　中国教育统计年鉴　中国教育经费统计年鉴
中国民族统计年鉴　中国残疾人事业统计年鉴　长江经济带发展统计年鉴

省级综合统计年鉴系列

北京 天津 河北 山西 内蒙古 辽宁 吉林 黑龙江 上海 江苏 浙江 安徽 福建 江西 山东 河南 湖北 湖南
广东 广西 海南 重庆 四川 贵州 云南 西藏 陕西 甘肃 青海 宁夏 新疆 新疆生产建设兵团

市(县)级综合统计年鉴系列

滨海新区 石家庄 唐山 邯郸 保定 沧州 邢台 廊坊 承德 衡水 秦皇岛 张家口 太原 大同 阳泉 长治 晋城
朔州 晋中 运城 忻州 临汾 吕梁 呼和浩特 鄂尔多斯 包头 沈阳 大连 长春 延吉 四平 白山 通化 哈尔滨
齐齐哈尔 黑龙江垦区 上海浦东新区 南京 无锡 徐州 常州 苏州 南通 连云港 淮安 盐城 扬州 镇江 泰州
宿迁 江阴 丹阳 海门 张家港 杭州 宁波 温州 嘉兴 湖州 绍兴 金华 衢州 舟山 台州 丽水 合肥 安庆 福州
厦门 宁德 漳州 龙岩 莆田 泉州 三明 南平 南昌 九江 上饶 新余 抚州 赣州 景德镇 济南 青岛 枣庄
潍坊 聊城 郑州 洛阳 平顶山 三门峡 南阳 商丘 信阳 济源 汝州 武汉 十堰 荆州 宜昌 荆门 咸宁 黄冈
长沙 鹰潭 广州 深圳 惠州 东莞 汕尾 湛江 肇庆 南宁 柳州 桂林 贵港 梧州 来宾 河池 防城港 海口 三亚
儋州 成都 内江 贵阳 黔南 毕节 昆明 文山 德宏 西安 延安 安康 铜川 汉中 商洛 银川 兰州 庆阳 乌鲁木齐
昌吉 阿勒泰 兵团一师、二师、三师、四师、六师、七师、八师、十师、十三师、十四师

调查年鉴系列

天津 内蒙古 上海 河南 湖北 湖南 广东 广西 重庆 四川 云南 甘肃 宁夏 南宁 贵港 昆明

统计方法应用/实用手册

Python数据分析基础（第二版）　非参数统计（第五版）　现代金融投资统计分析（第四版）
国民经济核算初级教程（第二版）　国民经济核算教程（第五版）　概率统计基础
全国统计专业技术资格考试系列考试用书：统计业务知识（第四版修订版）　统计业务知识学习指导与习题
全国统计专业技术资格考试系列考试用书：统计相关知识（第四版）　统计相关知识学习指导与习题

统计通俗读物/统计科普图书

领导干部统计知识问答　统计公文写作及会议办理实用手册　大数据在统计工作中的应用案例汇编
中国国民经济核算知识问答（修订版）　地区生产总值核算国际比较研究　新中国统计制度方法的发展与改革

重点图书

中国农业统计资料1949-2019　第四次全国经济普查地图集　中国经济普查年鉴2018
新编英汉汉英统计大词典　中国国民经济核算体系2016　国民经济行业分类注释
挑大学选专业2020—考研择校指南　挑大学选专业2020—高考志愿填报指南　中华医学统计百科全书